The Letters of
Muriel Spark

The Letters of Muriel Spark

Volume I: 1944–1963

Edited by Dan Gunn

virago

VIRAGO

First published in Great Britain in 2025 by Virago Press

1 3 5 7 9 10 8 6 4 2

A CIP catalogue record for this book
is available from the British Library.

ISBN 978-0-349-01434-0

Typeset in Perpetua by M Rules
Printed and bound in Great Britain by
Clays Ltd, Elcograf S.p.A.

Papers used by Virago are from well-managed forests
and other responsible sources.

Virago Press
An imprint of
Little, Brown Book Group
Carmelite House
50 Victoria Embankment
London EC4Y 0DZ

The authorised representative
in the EEA is
Hachette Ireland
8 Castlecourt Centre
Dublin 15, D15 XTP3, Ireland
(email: info@hbgi.ie)

An Hachette UK Company
www.hachette.co.uk

www.virago.co.uk

To Penelope and to Kristina

Contents

Introduction

In 1944, when this first volume of her letters begins, Muriel Spark was a writer unknown to any but a few close friends, and even ten years later she was still known only to a small circle of readers, mostly as a poet. Yet by the time the volume ends, in December 1963, she had become the internationally renowned bestselling author of seven successful, critically acclaimed novels. On 1 January 1962, *Good Housekeeping* published a flattering article on her, with portraits by the society photographer Mark Gerson, whose title was only a slight exaggeration: 'Fame in Four Years'.[1] What would go on to become her most celebrated and commercially successful novel, *The Prime of Miss Jean Brodie* (published 1961), raised her reputation dramatically in the United Kingdom, and even more so in the United States when it was published in a single issue of the *New Yorker*. Neither Spark herself nor her publishers realised just how rich and long a life this novel would enjoy, with its many adaptations, for screen, television, and stage, but the ground was firmly laid for literary celebrity. Critics and novelists of the highest calibre were drawn to her work and were vocal in praise of its unpredictability and inventiveness; and this enthusiasm has scarcely ebbed since, leaving her to this day as one of the most appreciated writers of the second half of the twentieth century. Even at the height of her fame as a novelist, she did continue to consider herself a poet: on her tombstone in the graveyard where she is buried in Tuscany is inscribed the word 'POETA'. But it is in the novels that she wrote during the years presented here that her reputation was established, through a combination of inspiration, desperation, and sheer hard work.

Although later in her career she would claim that novels came to her unbidden and required almost no editing, Spark's letters reveal that while she was drafting her first venture in the novel genre and trying out possible titles, settling finally on *The Comforters* (1957), she experienced hesitation, loss of confidence, depression, and writer's block. She followed this distinctly autobiographical debut, in which she recast her recent experience of psychological collapse, with a fantastical desert-island tale, *Robinson* (1958); hard on its heels came her novel about old age, *Memento Mori* (1959); then a tale of diabolic possession and manipulation, *The Ballad of Peckham Rye*, and a novel rooted in her life in London bedsits during the post-war years, *The Bachelors* (both 1960); the creation of her most famous character followed, the eponymous Jean Brodie, based loosely on one of her childhood schoolteachers; then her reworking of her time in London during the closing years of World War II, *The Girls of Slender Means* (1963). Each novel is quite distinct: recognisably part of the Spark oeuvre yet unlike its predecessor and, for her growing public at the time of publication, always surprising. Spark became a novelist relatively late in life, publishing *The Comforters* when she was already thirty-nine years old. But before this, throughout the second half of the 1940s and into the mid-1950s, she was working furiously – not only from her passion for the written word but also in the hope of making money with which to support herself and her family. She wrote short stories, biographies, introductions, reviews, summaries of business articles, pieces for commercial magazines, and she prepared several editions of the work of writers she admired. She was a pen – and, more occasionally, a typewriter – for hire, and her output was formidable.

Though in *The Comforters* Spark comments on novel-writing and the impulse to invent stories – in a 'meta' manner that comes later to be known as 'postmodern' – in her letters she is usually too keen to communicate her message to be reflexive about what letter-writing means to her. But her view of the role and importance of letters is offered in the introduction she wrote to *Letters of John Henry Newman*, a volume she edited in 1957 with her former lover and chief cor-respondent of the 1950s, Derek Stanford. There, she states: 'That Newman's life should be represented by his letters is in accordance with his own mind.'[2] She continues: 'On the subject of biography, he informed a correspondent in 1866, "My own notion of writing a life is the notion of Hurrell Froude – viz. to do it by letters, and to bring in as little letterpress of one's own as possible . . . It is far more real, and therefore interesting, than any other way."' Newman was hugely important to Spark: his work a major stimulus for her conversion to Catholicism, which in turn opened the way, she often claimed, to her becoming a novelist. She makes it clear that Newman's letters are the key to understanding his life and thought: 'And a few years earlier he had pointed out in a letter to his sister, "Contemporary letters are facts, and as such they reveal the true life of a man."' She concludes: 'So far as the style is the man, his letters stand for one special aspect of Newman, that of his personal relationships. This, in a man who approached everything with a personal involvement, is an important aspect.'

Even when dealing with the business side of her career, Spark's letters convey just this sense of 'personal involvement' – at times to an almost perilous pitch, as the fluctuations of affection and repul-sion to which she was susceptible are translated onto the page. For one who sought the solitude and peace that her poetry and fiction demanded, but who also craved company and was anything but a hermit, letters were an ideal medium. They allowed her to feel connected while leaving space and time for what she considered from early in her life to be her poetic vocation. She was certainly aware that they could reveal aspects of her life and character of which, later, she might not be proud. Yet her conviction was clear: that all her papers, including her letters, should be made available, when appropriate, to scholars of her work as well as to the larger public. In 1970, an American academic asked for her view on Max Brod's failure to carry out Franz Kafka's instructions to burn his unpublished work, and her response indicates her view on her lit-erary legacy: 'The answer to your question is that I would not want any of my papers found after my death to be burnt however badly they reflected on my professional or personal reputation.'[3] In the event, because her relations with her several biographers turned tumultuous, she never in fact permitted extensive quotation of her letters, but her intention was clearly established by the care with which she built her personal archive. To the enquirer about Kafka's instructions, she continued: 'I would always have faith that papers relating to any strange-seeming story emerging from the papers littered around me at my death would turn up sooner or later.' After Derek Stanford sold the letters she had sent him, in the early 1960s, and wrote the first biography of her, Spark's tendency to collect her papers (which included carbon copies of the letters she sent as well as copies of her faxes) turned into a compulsion to hoard. Her archive, now in the National Library of Scotland, came to include almost every document that passed through her hands; the quantity of box-files and folders is astonishing.

The life on which Spark reports in her letters during the years covered by the present volume was not simple, nor was it without conflict and hardship. Having emigrated to Southern Rhodesia in 1937 to marry a man she barely knew, Sydney Oswald Spark, and having given birth to their son one year later, she returned to England from South Africa in 1944 on a troop ship, running the gauntlet of German U-boats. She left behind her son Samuel (later known as Robin), having divorced her husband, whom she judged dangerous and who would spend much of the remainder of his life in psychiatric institutions. When Sydney Spark arrived in England with Robin immediately after the war, she had to militate for custody of the child, her ex-husband being patently unable to look after him yet determined to hold on to him and the child allowance that went with him. Spark opened the door to later discord when she deposited Robin with her parents in Edinburgh while she attempted to make a living in London. In the following years, she passed from a lover who was married and jealous (the poet and editor Howard Sergeant) to a hypochondriac unmarried one (the essayist and biographer Derek Stanford), both of whom she came to feel were inhibiting her talent rather than allowing it to flourish. When she tried to modernise the Poetry Society, of which she became Secretary in 1947, she was rudely ousted from her job there. In the early 1950s, she was so poor she could barely afford to eat, and took to consuming Dexedrine as an appetite-suppressant – an amphetamine that contributed to a mental breakdown in 1953, accompanied by paranoid delusions. Later, in 1962, she lost the one family member, her father, with whom she enjoyed harmonious loving relations. She was condescended to by men in positions of power throughout the period, she was preyed upon, and once she was almost raped. She was obliged to move house repeatedly – move bedsits, more precisely – and feared the taxman at the door.

These were the often distressing experiences which she funnelled into her writing, including the writing of and in her letters. Addressing the poet laureate John Masefield, on whom she intended to write a book, Spark faced the challenge head-on: 'We have to address a disintegrated world', she wrote to him.[4] The depth of experience and feeling that went into that judgement is attested to in most of Spark's letters from the 1950s. She continued: 'The world we draw our inspiration from is disintegrated. When we write a poem we are trying, in a manner, to write several poems at once and to speak on different levels and to make divided things whole.' If her attempts to achieve harmony in her private and family life met with no great success, the same cannot be said of her attempts, through her fiction, 'to speak on different levels' and thereby 'to make divided things whole'. At the end of her first visit to Masefield's home, on a freezing December day in 1950, the elderly poet told her something that would console her in her hardships and become virtually a mantra: '"All experience is good for an artist."'[5] Letters – which exist between the life, with its travails, and the work, with its triumphs – performed their own special magic, allowing experience to be converted into words, while connecting their author to those responsive readers to whom she could express her joys, her frustrations, and her ambitions.

The shift from poet to prose-writer and novelist was rehearsed in detail in the letters as Spark discovered, and then exercised, her aptitude for narrative. The discovery was given a boost when her story 'The Seraph and the Zambesi' won the *Observer* short story competition in 1951. But she had already invested time and critical energy in exploring the possibilities of narrative – in verse. In the year she won the prize, she stated, in explication of her long poem 'The Fanfarlo', that 'it is consciously intended, on one level as a plain narrative, using the border ballad style as the most natural one for me, and as a convenient one for narrative'.[6] To Masefield, when proposing her book on him, she wrote: 'I should, of course, devote considerable attention to you as a narrative poet, tracing the course of the English narrative poem to the present time, and showing its complex development in your work.'[7] Even if early intuitions should not be turned into announcements of later tendencies, it is hard not to hear (especially if one elides the word 'poetry') a harbinger of the programme Spark would establish in her novels: 'On the question of your narrative poetry, I feel that your innovations here, represent your primary contribution to English literature; and that their strength lies partly in the Chaucerian objectivity of your statement.' Spark's 'objectivity' implies a narrator's willingness to present the evidence without issuing judgement, to maintain distance from characters and their vicissitudes, to allow the workings to become evidence of a force free of human agency. Spark's hallmark 'objectivity' as a novelist may have its roots in a rather different tradition from the Chaucerian – for her, the Old Testament and the Scottish Border Ballads were primordial. But the characteristic novelistic voice is already audible as she continues: 'Many narrative poems in our language have failed, I think, because of a subjective attitude on the part of the poet – a moralising attitude, with the effect of sentimentality, which is absent in your works.' It is in a heightened sense of observation that the shift from poet to novelist may be most obvious: eye and ear becoming attuned to rhythms and rhymes other than the poetic, to patterns of behaviour, plot, speech, setting. On an overnight train from London to Edinburgh, Spark studies 'my Gothic travelling companion' and issues a lively and humorous account of her.[8] To an editor at the *Observer*, while planning to visit and report on the Edinburgh International Festival, she writes: 'Some of these aspects of Festival-time, I would like to present in the form of reported conversations. I very much enjoy telling a story by using exaggerated dialogue.'[9] From her retreat in the grounds of the nunnery at Allington Castle, Kent, following her mental breakdown, she dispatched letter after letter in which the inhabitants of the monastery come alive as *characters* — personages sketched with their quirks and tics who would not be out of place in her early novels (and who indeed served as models for certain of them). The success and self-confidence of Spark the novelist never quite submerged the poet's longings; instead, the shift came to be viewed as less of a conversion and more of a fall: 'I was a poet once', she puts it to fellow-poet Ned O'Gorman, 'but am cast out from Paradise to labour at novels. That is why I am not really a novelist either, but a creature half here half there, composing figments.'[10]

Letters were sent not only to tell stories but also to *accompany* stories, poems, later novels — and to elicit reactions. To Alan Maclean, the generous editor who in 1955 sensed her promise and took her on at the publishing house Macmillan, she openly expressed her doubts about *The Comforters*. She had turned the delusions from which she suffered during her breakdown into voices that her protagonist hears, but she remained unconvinced: 'About the novel: I am not sure that the incidence of "voices" hasn't been overdone in the first part of the book. The voices are essential to the story, but only as a contributory factor.'[11] So she sought advice: 'If you as a reader get the impression that the voices are going to constitute the main theme, this may indicate some over-balance which it will be easier to adjust when I have drafted the remaining chapters. I am glad to have your reaction, and happy to know that on the whole you like what I have written.' On the day she wrote to Maclean she also wrote to Stanford, with the first sentence of what was to become one of her most significant stories, 'The Portobello Road': 'I haven't thought of the theme of my story, but already I have the feeling of it.'[12] She delivered the first sentence, and then: 'Write to me quickly & say what you think of this opening.' A more confident attitude was developing, certainly, but it required nourishment; it was presumably with a touch of irony that she cited her story's chief source of inspiration – 'For the actual writing none but the Holy Ghost can help me.'[13]

To someone she never met but with whom, through letters, she found an affinity, she explained what would be an abiding relation to her fictional characters: 'To me, a character one really hates is likely to be the most interesting creatively, and one comes to hate such a character with a kind of savage love.'[14] She trusted her correspondent, the dramatist John Van Druten, to comprehend her idiosyncratic notion of character-development: 'I believe it is a danger – and bad art – when an author hates, and thinks himself justified, righteous.' That word 'justified' was to prove crucial for her fiction, where her protagonists often act as if they were predestined to be among God's elect, *justified* in the Calvinist sense (which Sandy Stranger identifies in her schoolteacher Jean Brodie). 'Perhaps the answer is, to make one's fierce prejudices an obvious idiosyncrasy on the narrator's part? I speak, of course, as one trying to master the practical problems of fiction – and perhaps within the limits of satire.' She concludes her thought in a characteristic manner, by appeal to a higher realm: 'As you say, the greatest art sees human nature dispassionately.' And to Van Druten, later in 1957, she canvases her 'idea going round my mind for a new novel called MEMENTO MORI', explaining: 'I wish to experiment with the time-factor, or rather partly to ignore it, so that a character who may have died at one stage in the story is repre-sented, say two weeks later, as carrying on his normal life; and yet, the character would not be a ghost.'[15] The lynchpin not only of this novel but of Spark's enduring fascination with tenses and their related temporalities, her developing fondness for leaps-forward in time, was being worked out here: 'My main problem is, whether I should make clear to the reader what I am doing, or simply let the irrationality be an accepted thing. I think the irrational is acceptable if it is consistent.' The elliptical style for which she would become famous was being tested too – 'I hate to ram home my ideas with explanations.'

As she grew in confidence, Spark's reliance for inspiration (ironic or not) on the Holy Ghost diminished, and her reliance on Derek Stanford, her chief correspondent, for anything at all gradually vanished. When at the end of 1962 she submitted *The Girls of Slender*

Means to Robert Yeatman, her new editor at Macmillan, the letter accompanying it was confidently self-ironising: 'The novel reads like something written by an octopus in a space-ship with a pen in every hand, being serenaded by Siamese twins.'[16] And when Yeatman had the temerity to question her grammar, she scolded him: 'It is grammatically O.K. It's exactly what I intend, and the style is my own.'[17] She rolled out her credentials: 'I won hands down with the English department at school and have some bound prizes to show for it, Scott's novels and so on. Naturally I'm not going to climb down at my age.'

Considering the *bonne vivante* and grande dame of literature that she would become, and in view of the scathing critiques of religious practice contained in her novels, it may be hard to recollect that during the period covered here Spark converted not just once but twice – to Anglicanism and then to Catholicism – and that she even considered becoming a nun. Her letters reveal the depth of her fascination and involvement with Catholicism and Catholic theology, even if they also reveal that her most intensely devotional period was bound up with the breakdown that was gathering at the time. No letter emerges from the eye of the psychological storm, but the several leading up to it reveal an alarmingly lucid and insistent writer using ever bolder analogies as she relinquished control over her daily life and reason. When she visited Edinburgh to report on the Festival in 1953, she wrote of losing her grip: 'The "here and now" as it is lived by most intelligent people bewilders me.'[18] The loss was the more worrying when it combined with her theological obsessions:

> *I can't grasp what is actually happening in the present tense.* I can't
> follow the evidence of things which come to pass. When I come
> back I'll tell you what I have come to think is the meaning of
> 'Life Everlasting' and 'World Without End' – for the pres-
> ent, I'll only say that I think the meaning lies within temporal
> experience, and that anyone who slips unawares into the habit
> of directing their intelligence towards Life Everlasting, finds
> it awfully difficult to keep up with the normal intelligence of
> well-informed people.

In a letter to Stanford one month later, a letter retained here partly for its symptomatic significance, it is the pagan gods – Prometheus in particular – rather than the Christian one who seem to have induced a sort of logorrhoea that threatens to render the letter interminable . . .[19]

And as she emerged from her crisis, letters played a crucial role too. Spark believed T. S. Eliot to have been communicating with her in code, in anagrams, and sometimes in Greek. Stanford wrote to Eliot about this and received a letter back that gave written (and humorous) confirmation that this was not the case. After reading Eliot's letter, 'Now', Spark wrote, 'I feel released from a very real bondage & can make use of the experience.'[20] And this was indeed what she promptly went on to do, converting the written 'codes' into the 'voices' of *The Comforters*, her first novel. 'I'm sure I am getting better', she wrote, one year later.[21] 'The process of recovery isn't perceptible from day to day – and this is the most difficult part. It calls for something like faith.' The 'something like' is the leap, surely – the wager – that took her headlong into fiction. 'Also,' she continued, 'I'm beginning to take an *objective* interest in my state of mind. I feel the experience of a breakdown really can be *used* profitably; certainly it widens one's capacity for sympathy.' It is precisely this capacity to combine sympathy for human foibles and folly with a ruthless objectivity that Spark came to exercise in her fiction. 'This can be a glorious experience, or a horrifying one, according as one is, or isn't, able to reflect upon it.' The reflection was about to happen in her first novel, assisted of course by what she could express in her letters.

Spark did indeed 'get better'; and even if it is correct to suggest that her faith was channelled into novels critical of religious orthodoxy, this faith did not disappear. As early as 1949, she asked Stanford, 'Have you ever wanted to become a Catholic?'[22] 'I would,' she wrote, 'if I could find Faith.' She deploys her characteristic ironies in what follows: 'I shall set out on a pilgrimage, I think, turning over small stones and leaves, climbing rare mountains in Tibet and making odd enquiries in public libraries, searching for Faith.' But irony was feeble when set against the determination and desperation (when the two were practically indistinguishable) with which she did in fact pursue her 'pilgrimage'. Only at the height of her period of religious fervour – or of psychic distress – did she lose her sense of irony and wit. Readers will form their own opinion of what was cause and what effect, when she renounced sex with her lover Stanford in favour of religion. Was celibacy a way of achieving a break from a man whose attractions were already waning and whose neediness was becoming burdensome? Or did the renunciation amount to an excruciating deprivation, as she herself protested? She will later tell Stanford that 'As lovers we were all right on the sexual side', adding, 'but hopeless on the intercommunication side of lovers' minds.'[23] Later, distancing herself still further from him, she will claim that 'all right' was overstating it, and that Stanford was, if not homosexual, then certainly bisexual.[24]

To intimate that her celibacy may have been an escape route is not to doubt Spark's ongoing commitment to Catholicism. Yet, while she may not have been as savage in her assaults on religion and its conventions as her near-contemporaries Samuel Beckett and Thomas Bernhard, a novel such as *The Abbess of Crewe* insinuates that the 'pilgrimage' was also that of a novelist in search of a subject to satirise. Of a woman she met at Aylesford Priory, to which she retreated after her breakdown, she writes: 'This gem of a lady is, by the way, much troubled because Catholics won't say yea or nay to the proposition that dogs have souls & go to heaven.'[25] Even as she contemplated the life of a nun, she was critiquing 'the average intelligent Catholic' for whom 'the limitations of human nature take a form which I feel it a need to avoid participation with, and a duty to oppose by pursuing the revealed facts of experience without fear or guilt'.[26] By 1958, four years after her confirmation as a Roman Catholic, she could write: 'And it is true that the "God-inspired" are the most irresponsible of people.'[27] In one of her last letters to Stanford, she strikes an assuredly Beckettian note as she teases him for his hypochondriac tendencies and quibbles over doctrine. Stanford was about to have gallstones removed. 'It is a moot point', she writes, 'whether such stones & appendices & suchlike are counted as part of one's natural body at the Resurrection.'[28] She administers her merciless mocking advice: 'So hang on to your stones, in case. Also warn them against removing any other fittings whilst the mood is on them.' The barb of 'fittings' must surely have hurt (if not as much as his gallstones).

If Spark's letters offer direct insight into her religious impulses, they offer it only indirectly into the object of her mockery, the single most important correspondent in her letter-writing life and surely her most significant love-interest, about whom she is at first enthusiastic, then ironic, and finally vitriolic. When, in the late 1980s, she comes to write her autobiography, *Curriculum Vitae*, she shrinks Derek Stanford in stature, but in doing so she seriously underrates his importance to her in the 1950s and the quantity and quality of the letters she sent him. She estimates that those sold to the Harry Ransom Center at the University of Texas at Austin were 'about seventy in number' when in fact they were 179 (with twenty or more in other archives).[29] She claims: 'These letters are fluent, affectionate, sexless. They deal mainly with publishers and payments for work, literature and religion.' Readers may demur at 'sexless' as the erotic dimension is certainly not negligible; and a dismissal of letters because they deal with literature and religion is hardly dismissive at all, given that almost nothing was more important to Spark during the 1950s. What is made clear by the correspondence is that he was unable to commit to her, a fact signalled by the very abundance of letters they exchanged; Stanford continued, well into his forties, to maintain as his official residence his parents' house in the London suburb of Hounslow. Yet there may have been something in his very unavailability that contributed to Stanford's attractive-ness, his remoteness corresponding to some fundamental existential solitude that she herself had always felt and that she found echoed in her reading of Kierkegaard.[30] Near the start of their affair, she addressed to him a conventionally romantic sentiment: 'I can't begin my day's work until I tell you how greatly I love you.'[31] Then, eight days later, in a far less traditional vein: 'You are the first man I have ever known closely who has recognised the essential isolation of human nature; men usually do not like to see a woman as an island and attempt to land and set their flag upon it.'[32] She sets out her singularity as she continues: 'I suppose most women want this, but in my experience I have always had to leave off tilling the ground or bringing in the harvest in order to build up defences.' The play upon Donne's famous notion is one she assumes he will appreciate: 'Whereas you, my darling, come to give me a hand with the fortifications and bring me lovely, exotic herbs to plant as well; and you are my most welcome guest.'

That Spark felt hemmed in not just by an existential solitude but also by an environment dominated by men was surely another factor contributing to her appreciation of Stanford, who could be self-involved and self-pitying, but was no bully, rapist, or fool. When compared to the members of the Poetry Society who hoped to seduce her or to Rayner Heppenstall of the BBC who attempted to rape her, he must have appeared reassuring, as did the many gay men she cultivated, most important of whom was her American literary agent Ivan von Auw who was increasingly responsible for her work from the late 1950s onwards, at Harold Ober Associates, and whom she describes as 'the only man I've ever had to do with who hasn't tried to push me around'.[33] When it came to her avowed wish to be married to Stanford, she found herself in a curious position – dominant intellectually and artistically, yet wishing to play a damsel's role: 'I am only a wee thing', she wrote to him, 'but I'm a woman, in case you've forgot. Therefore, consider yourself, my snooty-pie, as not yet accepted.'[34] She who scoffed at rituals expected – or did she? – that he act the courtly suitor: 'On principle, you would have to propose to me *three times* before you were accepted, if at all. It is my due, as a bonny girl, and I deserve no less.' As she continues, it is almost as if she were placing herself not within the unchivalrous Stanford's realm of possibilities, but in one of the Border Ballads she so loved, or in a novel by Walter Scott she read as a youngster; by writing in these terms – and she employs a rare Scots inflection, with her 'wee' and her 'bonny' – she may have been ensuring that it could not happen at all, because these were not terms Stanford could possibly offer: 'Furthermore, each proposal is to be framed in different phraseology, & a lot depends on the same. Also on deportment & general demeanour.' She concludes her long letter

with a doubtless accurate and probably annihilating further observation – 'Even then . . . . . . but you are quaking already & I am your
garrulous' – before signing off, as she very occasionally does, with
the more biblical of her names, the middle one, 'Sarah'.

The preponderance of bullish bullying men may also offer a context in which to read Spark's infrequent but nonetheless trenchant
statements on politics, such as when she addresses issues of racism
in Africa or Fascism in the United Kingdom.[35] And while she never
explicitly made gender a political issue or claimed to be a feminist,
she clearly felt an almost constant need to be defending her ground
as a woman – not least when she was running the Poetry Society
with its membership of mostly ageing, demanding men. Having
come to believe that attack was often the best means of defence,
soon after a dramatic blow-up with her publisher Macmillan, she
wrote to the novelist Paul Scott, who was then her UK literary
agent: 'much of my own difficulty with Macm. has been outside
the normal publisher-author field – it has been a psychologically
male-female thing as well. When a woman, more especially a fluffy
woman, starts laying down the law (even tho', as author, perfectly
entitled to do so), *any* male of the species gives an automatic growl,
followed frequently by a gurk.'[36] The gender issue typically merged
with the economic one, and though never couching her demands
and complaints explicitly in class terms, she did sometimes feel
compelled to foreground her underprivilege, aware as she was that
she needed to support not just herself, but her incapacitated ex-
husband, her elderly parents, and her son as well. To the chief editor
at Macmillan, Rache Lovat Dickson, she wrote: 'I am sometimes
given to think that you are accustomed to deal with writers who are
less deeply involved in their work than I am; without any disrespect
to them, I see they are doing other things with their time, they are
civil servants and housewives or have private means or teach in universities'.[37] Never having been able, for financial reasons and being
the girl-child, to attend university, Spark refused to be intellectually
patronised or trivialised: 'I know of no other writer on your list but
myself who has had the opportunity to build an intelligent career in

the world, or to get married, and who has consciously and deliberately set these safeties aside and endured poverty, and taken the risk
of failure, in order to write well.' She concludes: 'It is not a spare-
time hobby I am engaged in, but something for which I have had to
sacrifice pleasures, and continually have to give up pleasures to do,
and no matter how successful I become I shall always have to make
these sacrifices.' The conviction that her publishers and agents were
not doing enough to promote her interests became almost constitu-
tional, and led to recurrent dreams of greener pastures elsewhere.
When informed at one point that she was Macmillan's highest-paid
author, she remained dissatisfied, writing to Alan Maclean in one
of her periodic blasts: 'I am tired of people telling me how well
Macmillan have done for me, when in fact Macmillan have done
badly for me and I have done well for them.'[38] Even after recovery
from her breakdown, with its paranoid episodes, she remained susceptible to slights: she was prone to feeling neglected, to worries
about insufficient print-runs of her novels, to suspicions that her
publishers were not taking her vocation as seriously as she took it
herself. Not until old age – and perhaps not even then – did she feel
secure in her finances or in the esteem of others; it was the role of
her representatives to mitigate that insecurity. It is indeed remarkable that she managed to stay on such friendly terms with virtually
all her editors and agents: despite her recriminations and occasional
verbal assaults, it was her charisma and charm that carried the day.

And if she could be demanding, Spark could also be selfless and
generous, not least in her support of artistic endeavours. She encouraged, among others, the unknown Irish author Paul Allen;
the admired but commercially unsuccessful experimental novelist
Christine Brooke-Rose; the not-yet-renowned novelist Paul Scott;
the novice novelist Shirley Hazzard; the hugely successful John
Updike – and many more. The generosity she displayed towards
fellow writers extended to aspects of her relations with her family,
too, even if in the present selection of her letters this will not be
immediately evident. The letters to her mother, and later to her
son, are rarely fascinating, but were almost always accompanied

by a cheque, even when she had barely the money to feed herself. Spark may have had little of the traditional 'maternal instinct', but through efforts of organisation and labour she strove to compensate for this, and for the adverse circumstances impacting her relationship with her son – only to be regularly thwarted by her ex-husband who was agitating and obstructing in the background. The frequent letters to family members maintained connection while serving the even more important role of maintaining distance. Yet, however frequently sent, they could only do so much, especially when the telephone became more readily available as a means of communication. Recounting to Shirley Hazzard a row she has just had on the phone with her mother and son, Spark draws some harsh conclusions about them, before drawing some crucial conclusions about herself: 'all lead to another escape to N. York'.[39] Having 'escaped' her hometown and family members at the age of nineteen, Spark chose never to live there, or with them, again. When London ceased to be distant enough, New York became enticing, for a period – before Italy provided a more permanently sustaining elsewhere.

And before these migrations, when her finances improved to the point that she could afford to take holidays, Spark did so with relish, usually taking her work with her, as when she first visited Austria in 1959. Her journey to 'The Holy Land' in 1961 proved challenging, for, although she attended the Adolf Eichmann trial for the *Observer*, she found the experience so distressing that she was unable to write about it – a rare exception to her usual professionalism. But she did write long and enthusiastic letters conveying her impressions of the sights she saw and the people she met in Israel and Jordan; and here too she was working, as she sought out locations for her novel in progress, *The Mandelbaum Gate*. As her fame grew, she began to imagine yet more escape routes, and no sooner had she moved into new rooms in her landlady's house in London than she was thinking of crossing the Atlantic to America. The reason New York did not become a permanent home may also be linked to the question of distance: it offered that geographically, but not historically. In order to find what she lacked there – the possibility of living *sub specie aeternitatis* that *guaranteed* distance, which linked to what she said to Van Druten about how 'the greatest art sees human nature dispassionately' – it was to Rome, the hub of her faith, that she had to turn. She relocated to 'Roma Aeterna' in the knowledge that, when on any given day the eternal was not offering itself, eloquent strata of ancient history were there to fill the gap. As she explained in an essay on the city written in 1983, sixteen years after she moved there: 'what attracted me most was the immediate touch of antiquity on everyday life'.[40] Already her departure from New York is being anticipated, in a letter from 1963: 'I can always count on friends in Rome, as they keep on writing to urge me Romewards.'[41]

One further complexity relating to distances became evident even before Spark became famous, in the vexed relation between her private and her public lives. When in 1948 the prolific author and family-planning pioneer Marie Stopes sought to besmirch Spark's reputation at the Poetry Society by raking up scandal, Spark riposted: 'I shall give you no information about myself.' And she mounted her own attack – 'I must say that your attitude fills me with contempt, as it would all right-thinking people.'[42] Yet she did learn to court attention, giving interviews to journals, radio, and television; she adapted her work for screen and stage, coping with the public attention these media required; she welcomed the honours and prizes that accompanied celebrity; and she did this while longing to retreat into the quiet required for her writing. The balance was a hard one to find, and the avoidance of excessive publicity would be a further reason for the retreat to Italy, when her fame reached its apogee. But if it was hard for her, it was even harder for those whose job it was to promote her and who were required to cater to her ambivalence about fame. She wished her publishers to maximise sales, and was aware that this would require self-exposure – yet she felt her life invaded, usurped by what she called the 'personal probings of reporters and interviewers'.[43] The disquiet that assailed her when she found herself in the spotlight was heightened to fever pitch when she learned, in 1963, that Stanford was set to publish a book about her work *and* her life. She declared in a letter of denunciation to the Editor of the *Times Literary Supplement*, with modesty barely masking defensiveness: 'I wish it to be known that if Mr. Stanford had applied to me, I would have advised against this undertaking, on the grounds that my work is only begun, it is not yet ready to be assessed.'[44] The brutal demotion of the seven novels she had written may speak to her disaffection with Stanford, but also, surely, to her dread that biography was turning into necrology: 'I have not yet covered anything like the novels that I have in mind to do if I am spared. And I think it a pity to dignify, as it were, a small group of minor sketches by subjecting them to a whole work of criticism.'

Perhaps it is within this perspective of necessary distances that one of the letters' more touching recurrent themes can best be understood: Spark's love of animals. Animals could be quiet, undemanding, graceful, companionable yet ferociously independent – cats especially, and one cat above all. In 1957, Spark published an essay that begins: 'If I were not a Christian I would worship the Cat. The ancient Egyptians did so with much success.'[45] Entitled 'Ailourophilia', this essay was inspired by her cat Bluebell, who features in the letters and even contributes to them – 'Bluebell has walked over this page with her sooty paws.'[46] Spark devotes barely two lines to the death of her father, but on the death of Bluebell she writes pages, not to one but to two correspondents.[47] After recounting (to her good friend Dina Barnsley) the discovery of an infection from which Bluebell was suffering, with no explanation of how her correspondent should take this introjected statement, she adds: 'Simultaneously I read in the paper about a mother who neglected her baby & gave it away to a neighbour, but fed the cat on the best – said she preferred cats.' And, tellingly for the relation of her letter-writing to her fiction-writing, after an account (to Dina Barnsley again) of the euthanasia of Bluebell that bewilderingly blends compassionate closeness with dispassionate distance, she concludes: 'Please keep this letter as I may want to refer to it some time for a story.'

It is not only the relation between Spark the letter-writer and Spark the writer of fiction that is evident in this letter, but also the relation between the letter-writer and the critic – including the inner self-critic. The role of critic was foundational for Spark, who continued to write reviews throughout her life, and who was talented enough to find, and wise enough to cultivate, supporters among literary critics of the quality of Frank Kermode and, later, Gabriel Josipovici. When she wrote to the taxman in 1952 she was not being merely strategic in saying 'I am not a short story writer. I am a critic and biographer.'[48] Given how increasingly elliptical her novels became, and how deflationary of anything approaching academic pomposity, it may be easy to overlook just how fine a critic she was: acute, learned, intuitive, cogent, able to see potential as well as achievement. She read broadly and commented in her letters on what she was reading: Joyce Cary; Arthur Hugh Clough; Wilkie Collins; Graham Greene; Ian Hamilton Finlay; Andrew Marvell; Frank O'Connor; Katherine Anne Porter; T. F. Powys; Marcel Proust; I. A. Richards; Arthur Rimbaud; Allen Tate; Alfred, Lord Tennyson; Paul Verlaine; Evelyn Waugh; Nathanael West; William Wordsworth . . . The duty of the trained critic was to 'penetrate' and at the same time 'reveal' what in her introduction to her 1954 edition of *The Brontë Letters* she calls 'the operation of the creative mind, interpreting the spirit which motivated it'.[49] That there might exist an antagonism between *penetration* and *revelation* she was aware, but the possibilities offered by the combination of plunder and reverence only gained in potency as her creative drive shed its inhibitions. When John Van Druten told her of his new play, she instantly rethought it in terms of her own fiction: 'I am greatly attracted by the idea of your probably arranging the scenes in a different sequence from that in which they were written. The poetic-logical order of things is not always compatible with their chronological order, it seems to me.'[50] It is perhaps unsurprising that she came close to sighting her ideal in a critic who was a poet – and not just any poet. 'Auden's criticism has one peculiarity which reveals the poet', she writes: 'his tendency to illustrate his points with apparently irrelevant quotations; so that you have to penetrate his personal mystique, almost, in order to really get his point.'[51]

Spark's *inner* critic had one eye forever focused on the deeply ingrained sense of stylistic decorum that was drummed into her by her Edinburgh education, then refined by her secretarial training and her work during World War II with the counter-intelligence service.

But in her letters this decorum disappears on occasion, delightfully, as the inner critic lets her hair down. Although she resisted employment of the demotic or brogue in her fiction, she could turn it on when she chose: 'We had a lot of ladies to tea the other day', she writes from Edinburgh.[52] 'The old housekeeper said, "Weel, Mrs Camberg, when I got yon' letter from yon' lawyer I said to mysel' 'Weel, the deil's aye guid tae his ain.'"' On the publication of *The Ballad of Peckham Rye* she addresses her publisher in Cockney imitation of how 'ME AND MY PALS UP PECKHAM' might threaten revenge.[53] She invents a plethora of names of questionable taste with which to address Stanford, she throws in doggerel, she adds (untranscribable) doodles. A rare obscenity adorns a postcard sent (in a prophylactic envelope) from the Lake District where she revisited the field 'where Wordsworth fucked Dora', and later 'where W. f'd the leech gatherer'.[54] With Shirley Hazzard more than with anyone, the language deviates from the Queen's English, as the two assume an American accent – 'Lemme know how you like Maurice' – or add the suffix '-ers' to practically any word, not least the proper name, as in this same letter from 1963 which opens 'Dearest Shirlers'.[55]

In an essay entitled 'What Images Return', written in 1962, Spark writes about her childhood in Edinburgh. She outlines how her fondness for one particular term was formed during her early years there – 'my whole education, in and out of school, seemed even then to pivot around this word' – and explains that 'It is my own instinct to associate the word, as the core of a thought-pattern, with Edinburgh particularly.' The word is 'nevertheless'. She admits that 'I believe myself to be fairly indoctrinated by the habit of thought which calls for this word.'[56] But she is adamant that it was a happy indoctrination: 'I find that much of my literary composition is based on the nevertheless idea.' And, she adds, not only her literary life has been influenced by this word: 'I act upon it. It was on the nevertheless principle that I turned Catholic.'

In the period represented by the present volume, Spark went through impoverishment, betrayal, discrimination, assault, hunger, paranoid delusions, romantic disappointment, harassment from an erratic ex-husband, the death of a beloved father; *nevertheless*, she produced seven novels, an array of poems, essays, biographies, and critical introductions, as well as 1,500 letters – doubtless more, given some have been lost. Circumstances were stacked against her; *nevertheless*, she transformed herself from a little-known poet into a hugely successful and critically acclaimed novelist; and she did so by a constancy of purpose that counterbalanced the deep-seated ambivalences that often drew her into conflict with the world around her. She opens her introduction to *The Brontë Letters*: 'The letters of famous people can be placed into two categories: there is the type of letter which becomes itself a valuable contribution to literature through its wit, style or wisdom; another kind is that whose main importance lies in the provision of a background to its author's life.'[57] It is to the latter category that she assigns the Brontë letters, which, she says, 'is not to imply that the correspondence of this remarkable family is devoid of grace, humour and perspicacity, for it contains all these attributes'. Spark was not to know, in 1954, when writing this introduction to the Brontës' letters, that one day readers would be invited to consider if her own letters constitute 'a valuable contribution to literature' or simply 'the provision of a background'. But her conclusion offers an aspirational possibility: 'Especially in the correspondence of great writers and poets, these two factors are very often combined.'

1. Unsigned article in *Good Housekeeping* (vol. 81, no. 1, 1 January 1962).
2. *Letters of John Henry Newman*, ed. Muriel Spark and Derek Stanford (Peter Owen Ltd, 1957), p. 150.
3. Letter to Dorothy Hite Claybourne, 18 December 1970 (NLS).
4. Letter to John Masefield, 28 November 1950.
5. Letter to John Masefield, 26 May 1951.
6. Letter to Howard Sergeant, 12 June 1951.
7. Letter to John Masefield, 28 November 1950.
8. Letter to Derek Stanford, 27 February 1952.
9. Letter to John Davy, 25 July 1953.
10. Letter to Ned O'Gorman, 21 March 1962.
11. Letter to Alan Maclean, 1 July 1955.
12. Letter to Derek Stanford, 1 July 1955.
13. Letter to Derek Stanford, 4 July 1955.

14. Letter to John Van Druten, 17 July 1957.
15. Letter to John Van Druten, 5 September 1957.
16. Letter to Robert Yeatman, 30 December 1962.
17. Letter to Robert Yeatman, 2 March 1963.
18. Letter to Derek Stanford, 27 August 1953.
19. See letter to Derek Stanford, 27 September 1953.
20. Letter to Derek Stanford, 26 March 1954.
21. Letter to Frank Sheed, 23 March 1955.
22. Letter to Derek Stanford, 6 February 1949.
23. Letter to Derek Stanford, 6 June 1953.
24. Muriel Spark, *Curriculum Vitae* (henceforth, in the notes, *CV*; Constable, 1992), p. 187.
25. Letter to Derek Stanford, 3 November 1954.
26. Letter to Derek Stanford, 31 May 1954.
27. Letter to Derek Stanford, 12 June 1958 (HRC).
28. Letter to Derek Stanford, 2 March 1959.
29. *CV*, p. 187.
30. See Muriel Spark, 'Kierkegaard', in *The Golden Fleece*, ed. Penelope Jardine (henceforth, in the notes, *TGF*; Carcanet, 2014), p. 201; and Cairns Craig, *Muriel Spark, Existentialism and the Art of Death* (Edinburgh University Press, 2020), ch. 3 and *passim*.
31. Letter to Derek Stanford, 11 July 1949.
32. Letter to Derek Stanford, circa 19 July 1949.
33. Letter to Shirley Hazzard, 6 February 1963.
34. Letter to Derek Stanford, 9 November 1952.
35. See letters to: Father Brocard Sewell, circa 24 March 1958; the Editor of *Public Opinion*, mid-November 1950; Clifford Rhodes, Editor of the *Church of England Newspaper*, 4 July 1953.
36. Letter to Paul Scott, 17 October 1961.
37. Letter to Rache Lovat Dickson, 13 November 1961.
38. Letter to Alan Maclean, 13 November 1960.
39. Letter to Shirley Hazzard, 29 June 1963.
40. 'Living in Rome', in *TGF*, p. 80.
41. Letter to Shirley Hazzard, 23 June 1963.
42. Letter to Marie Stopes, 29 May 1948.
43. Letter to the Editor, *Time and Tide*, early November 1961.
44. Letter to the Editor, *Times Literary Supplement*, circa 30 September 1963.
45. 'Ailourophilia', in *TGF*, p. 166.
46. Letter to Derek Stanford, 9 December 1954.
47. Letters to: Dina Barnsley, 14 August 1958; Derek Stanford, 23 September 1958.
48. Letter to H. M. Inspector of Taxes, 18 May 1952.
49. Reprinted as 'Letters of the Brontës', in *The Essence of the Brontës: A Compilation with Essays* (Carcanet, 2014), p. 27.

50. Letter to John Van Druten, 23 September 1957.

51. Letter to Derek Stanford, 3 November 1954.

52. Letter to Derek Stanford, 7 September 1957.

53. Letter to Alan Maclean, circa May 1959.

54. Postcard to Derek Stanford, circa 25 August 1950.

55. Letter to Shirley Hazzard, 9 March 1963. On the use of the suffix 'er(s)', see the entries 'HARRY, as a meaningless prefix' and 'OXFORD -ER(S)' in Eric Partridge, *A Dictionary of Slang and Unconventional English*, ed. Paul Beale (8th edition, Routledge & Kegan Paul, 1985), pp. 1382, 1390.

56. *TGF*, pp. 64, 65.

57. *The Essence of the Brontës*, p. 27.

Editorial Principles

An editor who has the temerity to commit the word 'principles' to paper is liable to be assailed by doubts, for whenever a principle is adopted, an exception will appear. Nevertheless, I wish to explain what has guided my choices in preparing Muriel Spark's letters for publication, drawing comfort from something Spark wrote to her former lover and confidant of the 1950s, Derek Stanford, when responding to a positive review of her edition of the letters of the Brontë sisters: 'The feeling that a job of editing can be a creative work is very important – but hardly any critics bother to weigh up the selective part of the editing of popular selections.'[1]

There are several overlapping stages that go into the making of an edition such as the present one: collection, transcription, selection, annotation, presentation. Each stage seems to require, and at the same time vitiate, the notion of principles.

Collection

When Stanford sold Spark's letters to him and they were then sold on to the Harry Ransom Center at the University of Texas at Austin, he committed what Spark considered a supreme act of betrayal – but he did posterity an enormous favour. These letters constitute a rich trove, and formed an excellent basis, given the efficiency and graciousness with which the Harry Ransom Center archivists responded, for the corpus I have been working to establish. Despite the spanners that Covid and lockdowns threw in the works, this corpus now comprises approximately 4,000 letters, with roughly twice that number of letters addressed *to* Spark. The letters exist in approximately twenty university and public archives, central among which is the National Library of Scotland (NLS) which holds incomparably the biggest Spark archive. Because it consists principally of Spark's own archives, the NLS has mostly those letters of which she made a carbon copy (while in the first fifteen years covered by the present volume, paper and carbon paper were scarce and a typewriter even scarcer). In addition to the public archives, private archives have proved invaluable. No owner has shown reluctance in sharing Spark letters – rather the contrary, efforts have been made to make me feel welcome and to answer my (often obsessively detailed) questions. That more Spark letters do exist is certain. My hope is that if the publication of this volume elicits any that are not already part of the corpus, then outstanding ones can be made available in an appendix to Volume II of the present edition.

It would be misleading of me to imply that the process of collection has been merely straightforward and satisfying. Chief among frustrations was discovery of what refused to be discovered – what in editorial parlance goes by the name of 'lacunae'. Readers will find only one reference – it is all I have unearthed – to what may, just possibly, be a partial explanation for why there are no letters from Spark (who was at first Muriel Camberg) from before or during the early years of World War II; in a letter to her childhood friend Frances Cowell, she writes, 'Somewhere or other I dumped some juvenilia before going to Africa.'[2] It is unimaginable to me that, when she emigrated to Southern Rhodesia in 1937 to marry Sydney Oswald Spark, she did not write regularly to her parents and friends. However unhappy she was in Africa – or precisely because she was so unhappy – she surely did write home. Yet not a single example of such letters has been traced, despite the indefatigable detective work of Spark's biographer Martin Stannard, and despite my own attempts to coax such letters into being. Did her parents throw them out or lose them? Did her son later dispose of them? Neither explanation seems plausible, and even something she says in a letter from 1987 offers only a partial explanation, given that by 'my correspondence' she will be referring principally to letters received rather than sent: 'Penny is busy cataloguing my correspondence which goes back to about 1949,' she writes (referring to her companion and helper Penelope Jardine). She continues: 'I destroyed everything before that, never dreaming it would be of the slightest interest to anybody.'[3] And then, why have I found only a small handful of letters written between July 1955 and January 1956? I do not have an answer to this question, and Spark herself does not allude to the apparent dearth.

Other collections of letters that have not been discovered, and which at this point it may be safe to assume have been lost or destroyed, include the letters to Spark's great friend and loyal supporter Colin Methven. And they include letters to Spark's sometime lover and literary collaborator Howard Sergeant, letters which exist in no archive and which Sergeant's heirs do not possess either. This last lacuna is particularly frustrating when the other side of the correspondence, Sergeant's voluminous outpouring, is available in the NLS, and when Sergeant remarks: 'I have just been re-reading your letters. How moving and how lovely they are! It makes me wonder how we could ever part.'[4] (Part, they decisively did; vanish, the letters just as decisively did.)

Transcription

After decades of wrestling with the indescribably erratic hand of Samuel Beckett, I have found the transcription of Spark's letters to be almost relaxing. Not only did she have an impeccably clear hand, even when in distress, but her secretarial training meant that she was very comfortable in her use of the typewriter – when she had a typewriter, that is, which was rarely the case during the first fifteen years that the present volume covers. In the very rare instances where there is doubt over a transcription, the reader will find [?] following the questionable word.

When transcribing Spark's letters, I followed exactly what she herself wrote, correcting nothing. I was relieved to find how few instances of '[sic]' were required – a testament to how punctilious a letter-writer Spark was, whether typing or writing longhand.

Selection

Several choices face any editor of a selection of an author's letters, choices in some respects different from those facing an editor charged, usually decades or centuries after that author's death, with compiling a *collected* letters. One choice is primordial, dictated as it is by the limits of space entailed by one, two (as here), or even more numerous volumes. Should one publish sections of letters, introduced by '[. . .]', omitting the dull or trivial passages? Or should one publish only complete letters? The alternatives are clear; the reasons determining any final choice are likely to be complex.

For two reasons I have decided to publish, in the body of the text, only complete letters. The first is that I believe that, for serious letter-writers such as Spark, a letter has its own integrity: it has form, rhythm, a beginning, a middle, an end. By filleting a letter and presenting it as if it were the whole thing, the editor risks presenting the letter as principally the purveyor of information. (That not every editor agrees with me is evinced by many excellent recent editions, such as the selected letters of Iris Murdoch or Seamus Heaney.) The second reason is because, in the back of my mind, I have had, from early in the editorial project, the following dictum of Spark herself: 'I would not like to suppress the passage in Rose Macaulay's letter, as the suppression of letters and parts of letters is a kind of falsehood and a great nuisance to impartial scholars.'[5] Spark was fiercely against censorship, and the filleting of letters can – even if this is not the intention – come to *appear* like censorship. Nobody from among Spark's correspondents or their heirs, nobody from the Spark Estate or the agency which represents it, has exerted the slightest pressure upon me in my selection of letters, nor has anyone sought to excise passages or letters from the current edition.

I have sought, in making my selection, to present the range of Spark's letters: their variety in length, tone, intensity, directness and indirectness, register, formality, oddity. I have chosen letters that seem to me representative of larger patterns of affect and practice, such as when she falls out with her editors at Macmillan in 1961 and writes a series of vitriolic letters to them – only to continue with the

Macmillan team shortly after on friendly terms. I have chosen letters that illustrate the number and diversity of her interlocutors, ranging from her mother to the son of a prime minister, from a priest to a newspaper baron, from a lover to one judged an enemy (and a lover who turns *into* an enemy). I have chosen letters that seem to me symptomatic: of tendencies in Spark's professional and personal lives, of her sometimes self-defeating determinations, of the mental derangement that beset her in the early 1950s. I have also chosen letters that have allowed, with a minimum of editorial commentary, for what I hope to be a clear narrative or set of narratives to build.

Annotation

The decision to include only complete letters in the body of the text does produce some drawbacks. Chief among these is the obvious risk that it may leave out an awful lot of interesting passages contained within letters judged not sufficiently compelling to merit inclusion in their entirety. I have tried to circumvent this issue by including many such passages in notes at the end of individual letters, linking these wherever possible to relevant moments and movements in the letters of the main body of the text. If at times these links may appear tenuous, I must crave the reader's indulgence: some passages are simply too interesting to be omitted, or too important to future Spark scholars – such as, for example, her numerous mentions of what she has been wearing, or reading. My use of notes is intended to provide context for the letters to which they are appended, offering insight both into the matters being discussed and often into the character of the person with whom these matters are being discussed. By using notes I have reduced the need for a supporting apparatus – the explanations, biographical essays, contextual elucidations, and bibliographies that customarily freight editions of letters. I have tried, wherever possible, to allow Spark's own words to illuminate Spark's words.

Still, when these extracts in the footnotes become extended, a reader might ask: Why not give the whole thing? It is a question likely to arise, for example, in the case of lengthy passages from

Spark's letters to her literary agent John Smith. The answer is simple: any such extract comes from an even longer letter – in many cases, *much* longer – discussing contracts, foreign rights, percentages, dollars, pounds, amounting to a potentially dizzying quantity of *business*. During the height of her fame in the 1960s and 1970s, Spark had dozens of contracts on the go at any given moment; rather than breathe a sigh of relief at having agents competent in handling the minutiae of these contracts, Spark preferred to be on top of them herself, writing reams of prose that one might expect of a qualified accountant more than of an internationally renowned novelist. I have attempted to include, in the body of the text and the notes, enough of Spark-the-businesswoman for readers to appreciate how crucial this role was to her, as well as how distinct from her literary concerns and practice; any reader interested in accumulating more of the granular detail of Spark's business correspondence will henceforth know where to find it.

It may be apparent that in the notes I have not been egalitarian in my deployment of the letters of Spark's correspondents. The most obvious example of my discrimination is my neglect of Spark's single most significant correspondent, Derek Stanford. The NLS contains folders in which there are roughly five hundred letters sent by Stanford to Spark. The fact that Spark herself, in her autobiographical *Curriculum Vitae*, is breezily dismissive of these letters has not been the determining factor in my citing from them so rarely. Nor has the fact of their frequently being written on grubby scraps of paper in an illegible hand, or even the fact that most of them are (infuriatingly) undated. Rather, it is that they seem to me to shed so little light on what Spark writes in her letters to him, replete as they are with his ailments, his rhetorical turns of phrase, his hesitations, his tergiversations. By contrast, I have not hesitated to quote at length from figures whom Spark barely knew at the time she received their letters: an example is the long letter from John Updike received after he had read *The Prime of Miss Jean Brodie*; I include most of this letter not only because it is from an important figure in American letters, but because it illuminates the way in which Spark's career was being perceived in the moment it was taking

off. Similarly, I have quoted liberally from the letters to Spark sent
by Graham Greene and Evelyn Waugh, two major literary figures
whom she revered and who were generous towards her in the days
when she was not yet successful and famous. I believe that what they
had to say to Spark is of inherent interest, not just because they were
important writers but because they encouraged, and occasionally
criticised, in ways that were influential.

Where non-epistolary material can help explicate what is in the
letters – and behind the letters, in Spark's oeuvre – I have included
critics' views and insights in sometimes extended notes. So, for
example, I have lengthy notes on the *nouveau roman*, which was influential on Spark's fictions of the 1960s and early 1970s. I devote
space to a statement by Charlotte Brontë on her sister Anne when
what she writes seems so pertinent to Spark's own self and budding
career. I quote from Allen Tate's essay on *Madame Bovary* since Spark
reports that it was crucial in turning her from the writing of poetry
to the writing of fiction. I include a humorous passage from a letter
by James Kirkup because it gives something of the flavour of the era.
I include a long passage on celibacy in Roman Catholicism because,
while it was not entirely relevant to Spark at the time, later it will
play an important role in her life. I include a long passage from Paul
Scott's laudatory review of Spark's most recent novel, *The Bachelors*,
not only because it is helpful for understanding the wellsprings of
Spark's genius but because it signals a new era in her fame. And I include references to T. S. Eliot wherever they appear, not just because
of his importance to Spark as a poet but because he features in the
delusions from which she suffered during her mental breakdown.

Despite Spark's own penchant for prolepsis, I have tried where
possible in the notes not to anticipate: not to let the notes run ahead of
the narrative being told in the letters themselves. Exceptions to this
principle – more exceptions – arise where a significant response to
a Spark letter would otherwise go unmentioned or where an important thread would otherwise be left hanging. I have assumed that the
letters will be read sequentially. So, for example, a figure is generally
given some brief introduction the first time s/he is encountered. A
book being read or a first name being mentioned will not be noted

if the reference is clear from previous letters. The reader who finds a reference missing is invited to turn back to these previous letters. So, when Spark writes in a footnote to her letter of 1 September 1959 to Paul Allen 'C & J send love too', this is not annotated, as from the previous two letters it is clear that she is referring to the couple with whom she is holidaying, Christine Brooke-Rose and Jerzy Peterkiewicz. I give every figure their full name the first time they appear in the notes following a given letter, and in subsequent notes to that same letter I give only the family name. I have chosen not to give individuals their date of birth (and of death where pertinent) in the notes as I find that a proliferation of parentheses impedes ease of reading. It is in the index that the reader will find the dates of the figures mentioned in the volume – or of all that I have been able to obtain. Where a year is not specified in the notes, only the month, it is because the year is that of the letter which is being annotated. I have chosen to cite the King James Version of the Bible in the notes, having been assured by Penelope Jardine that it was the version that was most read and appreciated by her companion.

Throughout the notes and chronologies, I have abbreviated Muriel Spark's name to MS.

Presentation

It is hard (not to say impossible) to convey the variety and variegation of the material support of Spark's letters: the paper, the inks and their colours, her doodles, her tendency to use up every inch of the page – later, her playful use of the typewriter. I have included one example in facsimile of a particularly amusing lettercard (p. 184), but otherwise have included only the customary indications:

TLS	typed letter signed (and without the 'S', unsigned)
ALS	autograph letter signed (and without the 'S', unsigned)
APCS	autograph picture postcard signed (with brief description of the picture)

TLcc	carbon copy of typed letter
TL/AL draft	typed/autograph letter draft
s/	signed (on a typewritten letter)

So as to avoid lengthy repetitions, where Spark wrote on letterhead giving her own address, I have not signalled this. Where she uses official letterhead, such as that belonging to a hotel or a journal, I have simplified the address and indicated the use of letterhead in the descriptive note following the letter. The provenance of each letter is given also in the descriptive note (in abbreviation). As Spark not infrequently misdates a letter, and as her way of writing the date varies widely, the correct date (so far as this could be ascertained) as well as the name and location of the addressee are given in a standardised form in an editorial header; the one change made to Spark's own version of her address and date headers is that the full stops with which she sometimes ends the line have been deleted.

Spark uses single quotation marks and double indifferently; I have regularised these to single throughout. I have also regularised indentations. On the one occasion where Spark uses square brackets I have substituted for these curly brackets – { . . . } – so as to retain square brackets for editorial interpolations.

The principle applied in the presentation of the letters is that of 'clear text', which is to say the words as they were written down by the author, with no silent editorial corrections or emendations. But here again exceptions must be signalled. Spark is a stickler about punctuation and is furious when editors dare to interfere with her often idiosyncratic use of the comma. I have ventured to alter her punctuation in only one instance, though an instance that recurs: when she closes a parenthesis with a bracket and puts the full stop, comma, or semi-colon in the wrong place – inside the bracket when it should be outside, and vice versa. I have done this (and have been normative in venturing 'wrong place') because this is one irregularity that would cause a reader to be not only distracted but also, on occasion, confused.

Spark is an excellent but not infallible typist and speller. I have left her rare typos and misspellings, signalling them with '[*sic*]'; I judge it interesting that (in letters that will appear in Volume II), when writing to Alec Guinness to persuade him to act in a dramatised version of her novel *Not to Disturb*, she spells him – not once but repeatedly – 'Alec Guiness'. However, I do not judge it interesting that she regularly misspells the word 'embarrassed/ embarrassing/embarrassment' (using only one 'r'), and so after noting the first instance I have, in yet another exception to my rule, silently corrected it. Spark uses 'x'/'X' to signify 'kiss': sometimes in lower-case, sometimes upper, and sometimes (in handwritten letters) it is not always clear which; I have regularised all to lower-case. Spark does not attempt italics in her handwritten letters and typewriters did not offer this option. She therefore uses underline, as do her correspondents, either for emphasis or to indicate titles of works. I have converted these to italics throughout, retaining an underline in only one instance, where Spark uses a double-underline (in her letter to Derek Stanford of 25 September 1952).

Where there are additions to a letter in another hand, as for example in Spark's letter to Iris Birtwistle of 7 August 1950 where Derek Stanford added a postscript, these appear in italics. Editorial cuts from within quotations are signalled by ellipses within square brackets – [. . .] – while ellipses not within square brackets belong to the author of the passage being quoted.

The editing of a selection of a writer's letters is not an exact science, and any editor is likely to feel the weight of the letters that have been lost and omitted; the material letters that have been handled and admired but whose physical properties have not been represented; the allusions and references that have presumably been missed; the note that is either too long or too short (the reader who feels either over-informed or under-informed); the errors that have inevitably but unknowingly been incorporated; the principles that have surely been broken. When ticking off Alan Barnsley for in- truding on her work-time, Spark writes: 'you must remember that your first business in life is to give pleasure to the public through your writing'.[6] My hope is that enough of Spark's genius has been retained, enough of consistency and balance and accuracy maintained, to permit *pleasure* (rather than pedantry) to be paramount in any reader's experience of the present volume.

1. Letter to Derek Stanford, 7 June 1954 (HRC).
2. See letter to Frances Cowell, 5 June 1963.
3. Letter to Guy Strutt, 11 January 1987 (Lord Rayleigh Collection).
4. Letter to Muriel Spark, 15 June 1948 (NLS).
5. Letter to Constance Babington Smith, 6 July 1963 (NLS).
6. Letter to Alan Barnsley, late February 1962.

Acknowledgements

When I wrote to Muriel Spark in February 2005 to invite her to receive an honorary degree in May at the graduation ceremony of The American University of Paris, I hardly believed she would accept; I knew her age and that she was in poor health. Accept she did, promptly by fax, signalling that she would be travelling by car with her companion Penelope Jardine from their home in Tuscany. So it turned out that I was fortunate enough to spend a week with Penelope and Muriel during what was to be the last full year of Muriel's life. (I permit myself first names here, if not elsewhere in the present volume.) My first debt is to Muriel herself for the graciousness with which she coped with the demands of a graduation ceremony and with the large public event I organised in celebration of her work. I am not aware if she said anything to Penelope Jardine, who was soon to become her literary executor, to indicate that I might be a suitable editor of her letters. I had ten more years of work to do on the letters of Samuel Beckett, but I already had fifteen years' experience of labouring on letters; I was born in the same city as Muriel, and had left it at around the same age that she did; I was connected to America through my job, as she was through hers; I speak Italian and know Italy well; for years, I had been reading, studying, teaching, and writing on Muriel's oeuvre.

I like to imagine it was something of this mix of experience and competence that led Penelope Jardine to invite me to consider editing her companion's letters when my work on the Beckett edition was completed; but perhaps such choices have more to do with instinct than with competence. In any case, it is to Penelope that I signal my second debt of gratitude, as without her unfailing confidence in me the process of collecting and editing the letters would have been not only far less pleasant but not possible at all. Penelope has been informative both from a distance when I have been working in Paris and in person when I have visited her in Tuscany, which I have done regularly, sharing with her the fruits of my work as these emerged. Working with literary estates can be fraught; no editor could have asked for a more congenial context than that from which I have benefitted, thanks to Penelope's support. (These central acknowledgements, as well as all the ones that follow, relate to the entire project of collecting and editing Spark's letters: Volume I, here, and Volume II to follow.)

Nobody working on Spark, least of all anyone doing archival work, can fail to acknowledge a huge debt to her biographer Martin Stannard. His diligence in collecting materials was exemplary, and he has been generous in sharing them with me. It is from his archive, now in the National Library of Scotland (the NLS), that any scholarly work on Spark and her life necessarily departs. His detailed chronologies, as well as his biography, have been invaluable to what is presented here.

If the letters as transcribed are reliably accurate, then it is in no small measure thanks to the assistance I have received from that most patient of friends and literary editors, Gérard Kahn. He has read and reread my transcriptions, usually finding something to improve, to the point where I am now confident of their faithfulness. Editing can be a solitary, even isolating, practice; Gérard has ensured that I never felt alone when faced with an obscurely handwritten name or when I had to decide if a letter merited inclusion.

Several students and former students have assisted me in locating and transcribing letters. David Kammerman has been of huge help with transcription and with the year-by-year chronologies. Thanks go to Sarah Sturman for her work on early versions of letters to Derek Stanford; to Michelle Reilly; to Will Ihrig; to Chloe Elder and Lydia Wiernik Partenio for their sterling work in the NLS. Eugene

Manning has assisted me at the New York Public Library. Holly Isard has carried out very useful research at London libraries.

When I have been stuck for a reference and the internet has not yielded an answer, the 'phone a friend' option – or, more usually, *email* a friend – has been my principal resource. On matters connected to the Scottish literary scene, Alan Taylor has been an essential source of information; on the poets and poetry of the 1950s, I have turned regularly to Alan Jenkins; on art and artists, as well as writers, I have drawn on the capacious intellectual resources of Alan Hollinghurst; on medieval literature, I have fruitfully consulted my colleague Roy Rosenstein and his colleague David Raybin; on 1950s politics and the BBC, Neville Shack; on historical matters relating to the *Times Literary Supplement*, Russell Williams.

The representatives of several estates have been generous in offering me their time and knowledge: for the Alan and Dina Barnsley estate, Michael Barnsley and Mary Gabriel Vorenkamp; for the Iris Birtwistle estate, Pip Birtwistle; for the Philip Camberg estate, his daughter Vivian Philbin; for the Ian Hamilton Finlay estate, Alec Finlay and Hamilton Finlay's biographer Alistair Peebles; for the Alan Maclean estate, his son Ben Maclean; for the Howard Sergeant estate, his daughter Cherrill Sands; for the Frank Sheed estate, his granddaughter Mary Jo Middleton; for the Judy Sproxton estate, Nicholas Sproxton; for the Guy Strutt estate, Lord and Lady Rayleigh.

I have been assisted by Anna-Louise Milne and Alistair Milne in my search for information about Robin Spark's schooling; Chris Fuse has helped on Father Frank O'Malley; Joan Winterkorn has assisted on various estates; Brigitta Olubas has generously shared information on Shirley Hazzard; Madeleine Childs has helped on the International Ballet Company; Bruce Meyer on Howard Sergeant; Cairns Craig on Scottish context; Adrian Poole and Donat Gallagher on Evelyn Waugh; Sister Margaret at the Abbey of Santa Cecilia, Rome, on matters ecclesiastical; Lino Pertile on questions of theology; Nigel Leask on Scottish and Romantic literature. Barbara Epler at New Directions, Robert Hosmer, and Gabriel Josipovici have all been generous with their letters and their knowledge.

Turning to the public and university archives, my debts proliferate; but none is equal to what I owe the curator of the Muriel Spark Archive at the NLS, Colin McIlroy. The Spark Archive is massive and massively complex, and without his guidance I would have been lost, not just once but repeatedly.

At the American University of Paris, I have received the support of former President Celeste Schenck and, in the office of Academic Affairs, the assistance of Brenda Torney and Provost Hannah Westley; while, at the AUP Library, Sally Murray, Jorge Sosa, Lily Servel, and Isabelle Dupuy have all been inventive and supportive in tracking down even the most obscure article. Elizabeth Garver at the Harry Ransom Center, the University of Austin in Texas, has gone beyond the call of duty to be accommodating and helpful. Further thanks go to: the immensely helpful AnnaLee Pauls at Princeton University's Firestone Library; the very responsive and diligent Chloe Rushovich, Elly Crookes, and Kelly Collins at the Macmillan Archive; Elizabeth B. Scott at St Michael's College Collection; Rebecca Maguire and Jenna Effenberger at Yale University Beinecke Rare Book and Manuscript Library; Marc Carlson, Melissa Kunz, and Abigail Dairaghi at The University of Tulsa, McFarlin Library, Department of Special Collections and University Archives; Zoe Stansell, Khondaker Ahmed, and Andrew Gough at the British Library Manuscripts Reference Service; John Zarrillo at Georgetown University Library, Special Collections; Louise North at the BBC Written Archives Centre; Sarah Law at the British Film Institute; Justine Palmer at the Royal Literary Fund; Alison Carrick, Joel Minor, and Kate Goldkamp at Washington University in St. Louis, University Libraries, Special Collections; Ann Dinsdal at the Brontë Society and Brontë Parsonage Museum; Mandy Wise at the University College London Library Special Collections; Philip W. Errington at Sotheby's Department of Printed Books and Manuscripts; Joe Smith at the University of Notre Dame Archives; Sarah Pymer at Hull University History Centre Archives; Tiffany Charrington at the Poetry Society; Livonia Okello at the Society of Authors; Philippa Edwards at Stanbrook Abbey Library; Katie McDonald at the Royal Society of Edinburgh

Records and Archive; Maxwell Zupke at the University of California in Los Angeles Library Special Collections; Kathy Shoemaker at the Emory University Stuart A. Rose Manuscript, Archives, and Rare Book Library; Tara Craig at Columbia University Rare Book and Manuscript Library; Robin Darwall-Smith at University College Oxford Archive; Kyle A. D. Pugh at McMaster University Library William Ready Division for Archives and Research Collections; Elizabeth Pitkethley, Chaplain, and Alison Ray, archivist, at St. Peter's College, University of Oxford; Alison Dowle at HTB and Alpha International; Daniel Joyce at the Birmingham Oratory Archive; Michele Drisse at the University of Reading Museums and Special Collections; Fiona M. Donaldson at the James Gillespie's Trust Alumni Team; Andrew Isodoro at Boston College John J. Burns Library; John Wells at Cambridge University Library, Department of Archives and Modern Manuscripts.

I have been fortunate to be assisted by Georgia Glover, representing the Spark Estate's literary agency, David Higham Associates. And at the publishing house Virago, my thanks are due to the commissioning editor who took on the letters project, Donna Coonan, as well as to the current editor of Virago Modern Classics, Olivia Barber. In preparing the letters for press I have been greatly assisted by Zoe Gullen and Linda Silverman at Virago and by the immense experience and expertise of copy-editor Leigh Mueller.

I have endeavoured to trace and acknowledge the holder of the physical copies of Spark's letters. Where the effort has, on rare occasions, not yielded results, or where I have made omissions or errors, I would be glad to hear from the owners, and shall if possible make corrections in subsequent editions.

Abbreviations of Names of Works

CEN	*Church of England Newspaper*
CP	Muriel Spark, *Complete Poems* (Carcanet, 2015)
CV	Muriel Spark, *Curriculum Vitae* (Constable, 1992)
ITF	Derek Stanford, *Inside the Forties: Literary Memoirs 1937–1957* (Sidgwick & Jackson, 1977)
MSB	Martin Stannard, *Muriel Spark: The Biography* (Weidenfeld & Nicolson, 2009)
MSBCS	Derek Stanford, *Muriel Spark: A Biographical and Critical Study* (Centaur Press Ltd, 1963)
ODNB	*Oxford Dictionary of National Biography*
OED	*Oxford English Dictionary*
RS	*The Riverside Shakespeare: The Complete Works*, ed. G. Blakemore Evans (Houghton Mifflin, 1997)
TCD	*The Crooked Dividend: Essays on Muriel Spark*, ed. Gerard Carruthers and Helen Stoddart (Scottish Literature International, 1922)
TCSS	Muriel Spark, *The Complete Short Stories* (Viking, 2001)
TGF	Muriel Spark, *The Golden Fleece: Essays* (Carcanet, 2014)
TLS	*Times Literary Supplement*

Abbreviations of Archives

BBC WAC	British Broadcasting Corporation Written Archives Centre
BL	British Library
CamUL	University of Cambridge Library, Department of Archives and Modern Manuscripts
CBF	Collection of the Birtwistle family
CUL	Columbia University Rare Book and Manuscript Library
GULSC	Georgetown University Library, Special Collections
HHL	Houghton Library, Harvard University
HRC	Harry Ransom Center, The University of Texas at Austin
MA	Macmillan Archive
MBC	Michael Barnsley Collection
NLS	National Library of Scotland
NYPL	New York Public Library
PFL	Princeton University Firestone Library
PJC	Penelope Jardine Collection
RLFA	Royal Literary Fund Archive
SMCC	St Michael's College Collection
UCLA	University of California in Los Angeles Library Special Collections

1944

Muriel Camberg returned to the United Kingdom in March as Mrs Muriel Spark (henceforth referred to as MS), having emigrated to Southern Rhodesia in August 1937 to marry Sydney Oswald Spark. Her husband's psychological struggles revealed themselves not long after her arrival in Africa, and she began to file for divorce in late 1939, finalising it only in March 1943, by which time they had a son, Samuel (later known as Robin). With custody granted to his father, MS had to leave her son behind, having placed him in a convent school in Gwelo. She arranged a berth on a troopship from Cape Town in February 1944, daring the U-boats which were sinking many ships at the time, and arrived in Liverpool in March, setting off then to reunite with her family in Edinburgh. After only a few weeks, she left the relative safety of wartime Edinburgh for unfamiliar London, which was being regularly bombed. There, she took a room at the Helena Club in Kensington and registered for work with the Department of Employment, where a chance encounter with another fan of Ivy Compton-Burnett earned her an opportunity to interview for a job at the Foreign Office in Sefton Delmer's top secret 'Black Propaganda' operation, creating disinformation to broadcast to the enemy. Successful, MS was employed in the newsroom of the Political Intelligence Department as 'Duty Secretary' from early May until early October. Working in Delmer's offices in Milton Bryan, her job was to receive information from returning crews of Allied bombers, type up the messages, pass them on to Delmer, and liaise with the Foreign Office in London. In the last of these roles, MS made friends with Colin Methven, her contact at the Foreign Office.

TO SARAH CAMBERG, EDINBURGH, 30 MAY 1944

Box 2, Western Central District P. Office, New Oxford Street, London, W.1
30/5/44

Dear Mum,

I'm so thrilled about the news of Phil's baby. I am sure it has
brought me luck with Sonny, and that I shall have my baby here
soon. Won't it be grand?[1]

Please wire Sol 'Will welcome you and Sonny with pleasure' or
something like that. If only Sonny comes, he will at least be over here,
and S.O.S. poor devil can get a job. I don't wish him any harm. I can
help with Sonny, and I am sure he will be a source of great pleasure to
you. He is a little darling – so affectionate and lovable. I enclose 10/-
for the cable.[2] I am not badly off for cash, but have not much over after
Income tax and board etc. are paid. At least, I am independent which
I have not been for many years, which is something.

Well you have a lot to look forward to now, and give Phil and
Sophie my love. I'm sending a sleeping bag in Jaeger wool. Fancy
your having two grandsons! I hope you both live to see them both
grow up and make a success of life.

Best love to all,
s/Muriel

TLS. NLS.

1. MS's sister-in-law Sophie, wife of her brother Philip, had given birth to a
   son, David. MS is writing to her mother after her return to England from
   Cape Town in February 1944. Her son Samuel Harry Louis (here 'Sonny',
   later 'Robin'), born in Bulawayo on 9 July 1938, will not return to England
   until the following year.
2. MS refers to her former husband Sydney Oswald Spark (here 'Sol',
   'S.O.S.') as 'poor devil' because his mental health had so deteriorated
   since she had first met him that he had to be institutionalised frequently
   and was incapable of properly caring for their son, whose custody he had
   gained in the couple's divorce.
       As the present letter is a typed top copy, not a carbon copy, and is to be
   found in MS's personal archive, it is possible she did not send it (as Martin
   Stannard suggests in *Muriel Spark: The Biography* (henceforth in the notes
   MSB; Weidenfeld & Nicolson, 2009), p. 543 n. 49).

1945–1947

In March 1945, MS left her parent's home in Bruntsfield, Edinburgh, where she had been employed for three months by the Red Cross, and returned to London, determined to make her way as a writer. She saw much of Colin Methven who acted as her primary source of emotional and material support. Having had little contact with her mentally ill ex-husband over the previous two years, she was somewhat surprised to meet him when he arrived from South Africa with their son Robin in Liverpool on 23 September. MS set Robin up in her parents' care, then returned to London where she had lived through the end of the war, to try to make a living to support him; she restarted what would prove a long battle for custody of her son as well as for child support.

Through 1946, MS wrote poetry and took on various jobs in London, including for the British Council and for the journal *Argentor*, a quarterly put out by the National Jewellers' Association. She became friends with numerous poets, including those associated with the Poetry Society, of which she became a member early in the year. She published verse in the Society's journal, the *Poetry Review*, where she also won a competition, and in *Poetry of To-Day* published 'Three Thoughts in Africa'. No MS letters of substance from 1945 or 1946 have been found, however.

In April 1947, MS was appointed General Secretary of the Poetry Society and Editor of the *Poetry Review*; having vowed to modernise the publication's hide-bound traditionalism, she faced challenges from the start. In August, the first issue of the *Poetry Review* for which MS had full responsibility was published. She continued her battle with her ex-husband for custody of their child and for the allowance paid for Robin's support; she also had to defend herself against his suit that claimed unpaid costs in their divorce in Southern Rhodesia. At a September party given by her new poet friend Arnold Vincent Bowen, she met the poet and Editor of the journal *Outposts*, Howard Sergeant, with whom she began an eighteen-month affair that would prove intense and turbulent, not least because Sergeant was both married and possessive.

TO WILLIAM KEAN SEYMOUR, PEASLAKE, SURREY, 15 JULY 1947

The Poetry Society, 33 Portman Square, London, W.1[1]
15th July, 1947

Dear Mr. Seymour,

I enclose the book 'Boccaccio' which I told you about, for review.[2]

Yesterday I got hold of your collected works and I cannot tell you how excited I am by them. I had read some of your poems and heard you read them, but there are many others in your book which I had not seen or heard and which are giving me great pleasure.[3] I am wondering if you could be persuaded to give us another reading or to let us arrange to have your poems read at one of our 8 o/clock meetings.

Yours sincerely,
s/Muriel Spark
Muriel Spark
General Secretary

P.S. Perhaps you would let us have a poem for the 'Review'?
M. S.

TLS on Poetry Society letterhead. UTML.

1. MS writes on Poetry Society letterhead but was herself resident not in the flat that was supposed to come with her new role as General Secretary of the Poetry Society, but at the Helena Club at Kensington Gate, where she lived intermittently from 1944 and of which she writes in her autobiographical *Curriculum Vitae* (henceforth in the notes *CV*): 'The Helena Club was absolutely charming. It was my home in London from time to time over many years. We were mainly secretaries. [. . .] At the Helena Club two houses had been made into one. The Club was very spacious with an air of quiet but expensive elegance quite at odds with the humble price we paid' (Constable, 1992, p. 144).

   The previous General Secretary of the Poetry Society, Galloway Kyle, had declined to vacate the flat at Portman Square that was part of the Society's property.

2. William Kean Seymour was influential in the Poetry Society of which MS became General Secretary in spring 1947, at the same time as she became Editor of its principal publication, the *Poetry Review*. In *CV*, written some forty-five years later, she calls Seymour 'a born mediocrity' (p. 175). The book MS sent Seymour was almost certainly the biographical study *Boccaccio* by Francis MacManus, published by Sheed & Ward earlier in the year.
3. Seymour's *Collected Poems* was published by Robert Hale in 1946.

TO WILLIAM KEAN SEYMOUR, PEASLAKE, SURREY,
21 JULY 1947

Hind's Head Hotel, Bray, Berkshire
July 21, 1947

Dear Mr Seymour,

I am answering your letter from the above address because I am staying here for a week. This is not strictly a holiday but I am enjoying the long peaceful evenings – I go up to town each day.

Your poem is most amusing and will look well in the 'Review'.[1] I plan to break down the lamentable reputation the 'Review' has for being tradition-bound; also I want to cut out the awful letters of appreciation which appear in its pages along with similar twitterings.

I have brought your book here with me, and I fear Mr Harding's library, from whence it came, has lost it for ever.[2] I particularly like the poems which you loftily term your earlier, younger mood but have not noticed any which could really be described as a later, older mood.

It will be a great pleasure to discuss with you your next talk and reading. We are resuming in September; perhaps you and I might plan something for that month or October.

Yours sincerely,

(in a young and early mood),

Muriel Spark

ALS on Hind's Head Hotel letterhead. UTML.

1. Later in 1947, the *Poetry Review* will publish William Kean Seymour's 'Fama Semper Vivat', but as he published regularly in the journal, there is no certainty that MS is referring to this poem.
2. The poet and regular contributor to the *Poetry Review* H. W. Harding was Chairman and Treasurer of the Poetry Society.

TO WILLIAM KEAN SEYMOUR, PEASLAKE, SURREY, 7 AUGUST 1947

The Poetry Society, 33 Portman Square, London, W.1
7th August, 1947

Dear Mr. Seymour,

Your letter and poem delight me; I feel flattered that you should tell me of your holiday in such rare and vital speech.

Everyone here has gone on holiday, and with the 'Review' now in preparation I am incredibly busy and rather excited for it is the first number I have turned out on my own. The last batch of copy is to be at the printers' on the 16th of this month and although I would hate to badger so nice a contributor as yourself, would you please let me have your M.S. in good time?[1]

There are two books here which might interest you for a later review if you cannot include them in your current article. They are

'A Skeleton Key to Finnigans [*sic*] Wake'
    by Joseph Campbell and Henry Morton
and 'Paradise Lost and its Critics'
    by A. J. A. Waldock.[2]

I am sending them to you under separate cover, resisting the temptation to lure you into this office to fetch them.

The enclosed poem might amuse you, being one of my flippant Bray pronouncements.

Yours sincerely,
s/Muriel S.

THE BELLS AT BRAY

Let me inform the pious reed
In the seraphic river
What pagan bells infect my head
With ill-considered fever,
What indiscreet, unhallowed creed
Converts my heart for ever.

Belfry and steeple that reprove
The idle miscreant
May not deny this Druid grove
Its heathen river-chant,
Nor save the foolish world whereof
I am inhabitant.

Alas, henceforward it will be
A waste of lover's time
To woo an infidel like me,
Seduced by song and rhyme,
Kinswoman of a melody
And mistress of a chime.[3]

Muriel Spark

TLS on Poetry Society letterhead. UTML.

1. It is not known which piece by William Kean Seymour MS is referring to, or if he did indeed submit it in a timely manner.
2. *A Skeleton Key to Finnegans Wake* by Joseph Campbell and Henry Morton Robinson had recently been published by Faber & Faber. *Paradise Lost and its Critics* by A. J. A. Waldock had also just been published, by Cambridge University Press.
3. This poem will later be published in the *Poetry Review* (vol. 37, no. 5, September–October 1947); however, it will not be selected by MS for her collection compiled in 2003, *Complete Poems* (henceforth in the notes *CP*; Carcanet, 2015; in original US edition, *All the Poems of Muriel Spark*, New Directions, 2004).

TO WILLIAM KEAN SEYMOUR, PEASLAKE, SURREY, 21 SEPTEMBER 1947

The Poetry Society, 33 Portman Square, London, W.1
September 21, 1947

My dear William,

Arnold Vincent Bowen and some of his lovely disreputable friends have just left this office where they have been making noisy pronouncements about Realism in poetry. Realism to them usually means a dustbin but Vincent and I know that every fantastic image is real.[1]

On Friday A.V.B. took me to the Wheatsheaf which is a poet's pub and the first I have been to. Wide-eyed with awe I breathed the same air as the picturesque Tambimuttu upon whose shoulder rested the blonde hand of a slimmer and later Byron. Everyone seemed to be posturing in the Greek style. A scholarly girl arrived and took off her glasses whereupon Tambimuttu took off his tie, and this puzzled me somewhat.[2]

I went with funny Sir Eugen Millington-Drake to see the International Ballet do Swanlake [*sic*] on Saturday afternoon. This Ballet Company annoys me by making visible what should exist in the imagination of the audience if the dancing were expressive. For instance, in the last scene the retreating ballerina gave a passably convincing performance until a floodlit cardboard swan sailed across the gauzy background.[3] After the ballet I went to Vincent's party at his temporary flat where there were yet more poets. Howard Sergeant was the only name I recognised since he is one of my contributors but the rest were rarer plants.[4] We played a game in which someone picks a poem title out of a hat and everyone has fifteen minutes in which to write a poem upon it; the results were surprisingly good.

To-day, Sunday, I had Irene Brent for a duty lunch which brought me down to earth after my literary cavortings. I might as well tell you now the sad news that Margaret Rawlings is too ill to give her talk here on Friday the 26th and Irene Brent is coming instead. I had to put Irene in some time and the sooner the better. Really, she exhausted me, so clamorous is her personality. I felt she might easily devour me as well as her lunch. Poor Irene. I hope you will still come and bring your Rosalind on the 26th even although la Brent takes some listening to. We must discuss this on Wednesday night to which I am wildly looking forward.[5]

This letter was intended to answer your nice one to me but I have not yet said how delighted I am by your criticism of my poems. Bowen's cronies are not enthusiastic about my work and imply that it is too 'sheltered'. Ah well, we can't all be he-men.

Thank you, too, for the copies of the Chelsea paper which seems vital and many-eyed, due in no small measure to your book review.

Yours ever,

s/Muriel

TLS on Poetry Society letterhead. UTML.

Muriel Spark,
1948

1. MS admired the work of Welsh poet Arnold Vincent Bowen; his collection *Lyrics of Love and Death* was published in 1943. Of the 'disreputable friends' MS was meeting, Martin Stannard writes: 'The younger poets she was now meeting rejected both the social realism of early Auden, and the "Apocalyptic" school of Henry Treece, feeling their way towards a new engagement with anarchism and surrealism. "Neo-Romanticism" was emerging with one foot in European surrealism and the other in the English tradition of Wordsworth' (*MSB*, p. 83).

2. The Wheatsheaf pub, established in 1931 at 25 Rathbone Place, London W1, was a popular haunt for writers, among them George Orwell and Dylan Thomas; Tamil poet Meary James Tambimuttu, being also an editor, publisher, and critic, was an influential figure on the London literary scene.

3. Eugen Millington-Drake was a British diplomat who, during 1939–40, when he was British Minister to Uruguay, played a significant role in the Battle of the River Plate. In *CV*, MS writes: 'He took me frequently to the theatre, which I loved, and which his wife Lady Effie didn't care for. Eugen supported me entirely throughout the ensuing strife at the Poetry Society. He was a Vice-President' (p. 172).

   The International Ballet was a hugely successful company founded in 1941 by Mona Inglesby. The version of *Swan Lake* MS attended was choreographed by Marius Petipa and produced by Nicholas Serguïev.

4. Howard Sergeant was an active member of the Poetry Society who, in 1943, had founded the poetry journal *Outposts*. Though married at the time, he would go on to become, for about eighteen months, MS's lover. His letters to MS are numerous and voluminous; MS's to him, whose qualities he extols in his own letters, have not been found despite extensive research. The depth of MS's feeling for Sergeant may be attested to in her unusually frank poem 'A Letter to Howard' that will be published in the Autumn 1948 edition of *Poetry Quarterly*, whose first line runs, 'My love, full of wonder today I call you by everlasting'. Decades later, in *CV*, MS would recollect him very differently:

   > One big attraction of Howard was that he danced so beautifully I loved to go dancing with him and often did. Another attraction was that he was fairly manly. [. . .] Howard was a travelling accountant and was often away. He had been a staunch supporter of the *Poetry Review*, although often, I thought, rather too interfering. He was an extremely jealous man. [. . .] He swore eternal love but was upset because, for instance, I had told him that if any relationship interfered with my natural bond with my son I would break the relationship. (pp. 176, 180–1)

5. Irene Brent was an actress associated with the Poetry Society. Margaret Rawlings, Lady Barlow, was a successful stage and later screen actress

whose career began with the theatre company of the poet John Masefield in Oxford in 1927, and continued through the 1970s. The novelist Rosalind Wade was Seymour's wife.

TO JOHN GRADDON, LONDON, 25 SEPTEMBER 1947

[The Helena Club, 82 Lancaster Gate, London W.2]
25th September 1947

Dear Mr. Graddon,

It is by now a matter of common knowledge that Mr. Harding intends to press the Council for my immediate dismissal and that he is holding to their heads the threat of his own immediate resignation if this is refused.[1]

I do not wish to lose my position without being heard – I gave up a better one financially to take on this work because I believed in it – and I trust that the Council will give me leave to speak in my own defence before they make their decision.

I am quite willing to work peacefully with Mr. Harding and have no quarrel with him except on those occasions when I have opposed him because it seemed to me that his course of action was against the best interests of the Society. I have personal reasons both to fear and dislike him but would not let these influence my work which I think has been good and valuable, and on which I ask to be judged.

Please give careful thought to this and let me state my case before a decision is made. I am sure the Society would not wish to act unjustly; please, therefore, try to be present at the meeting of the Executive on October 3, when doubtless this matter will be discussed. A copy of this letter has been sent to Mr Harding.

Yours sincerely,

Muriel Spark
General Secretary

TLcc. PJC.

1. An influential member of the Poetry Society, John Graddon would suc-
    ceed H. W. Harding as the Society's Treasurer in October after Harding
    did, indeed, resign. From the moment she took up her role at the Poetry
    Society and the *Poetry Review*, MS faced stiff opposition to her attempts
    to modernise both. At the top of the typescript of the present letter is
    written, in MS's hand: 'This letter sent to all members of the Executive'.

TO JOHN WALLER, LONDON, 22 OCTOBER 1947

The Poetry Society, 33 Portman Square, London, W.1
22nd October 1947

Dear Mr. Waller,
   I have very great pleasure in announcing that you are the
winner of this year's Greenwood Competition, and congratulating
you upon your fine poem.[1]
   This is ready to go to print in Poetry Review. Will you come in
and look at the poem before it goes, and tell me if you would like
to make any changes in lay-out?
   Yours sincerely,
   s/Muriel Spark
   Muriel Spark
   Editor

                                   TLS on Poetry Society letterhead. BL.

1. John Waller became known as one of the 'Cairo poets', having been posted
    during World War II to the Ministry of Information in Egypt. He founded
    there the Salamander Society and launched *Oasis: The Middle East Anthology
    of Poetry from the Forces*. In 1948, he would be appointed a fellow of the Royal
    Society of Literature. In his *Inside the Forties: Literary Memoirs 1937–1957*
    (Sidgwick & Jackson, 1977; henceforth in the notes *ITF*), Derek Stanford
    wrote of him: 'In those early postwar days, Waller had not yet inherited
    his baronetcy, but was still very much the golden boy, wearing a belted
    teddy-bear overcoat like some actor-manager and knight of the stage. With
    his Oscar-down-from-Oxford manner, he appeared to have tailored his
    personality with such fine economy that only a silhouette of anecdote and
    gossip remained. I never heard him speak a serious word, nor do I recall him
    uttering a dull one' (pp. 168–9).

The Poetry Society administered the annual Greenwood Prize, awarded in 1947 to Waller's poem 'The Lovely and the Dead'. In a subsequent letter to Waller, on 22 December, MS will write: 'Perhaps you will come and read "The Lovely and the Dead" to us in the Spring? It has been usual to have reprints of past Greenwood Poems made in the style of the enclosed poem selling at 6d. per copy and I would like to know if you have any objection to our doing this' (BL).

TO ARNOLD VINCENT BOWEN, BIRKENHEAD, CHESHIRE, 28 OCTOBER 1947

[London]
28th October, 1947

My dear Vincent,

This is another reply to your letter.[1] I am busy getting the 'Poetry Review' out. Have many good names in the next one, amongst which are A. V. Bowen, Robert Armstrong, Roy Campbell and your Vivien [sic] Locke-Ellis.[2] Copy of my editorial will be coming in a day or two.

November 14th is going to be an exciting day for me and I am looking forward to coming. I will probably take Friday off so that I will reach you some time in the late afternoon. We have just had a new Treasurer appointed so will be paying all contributors at the end of this week. Mr. Graddon is the new Treasurer.

Congratulations on your poems in 'Northern Anthology'. I love 'The Soviet Sailors'.[3] Here are my two latest poems. First, a tribute to my old friend and mentor, E. Vandermere Fleming who died recently. He was one of my chief champions in the recent dispute and was never happier than when overthrowing the mighty and exalting the humble. The other is the latest Gray Book Series. I was not at Wigmore Street since I had to stay and do some work at the office but they very kindly telephone [sic] and told me the title they had pulled out of the hat and rang me 15 minutes later for the result. The name was 'Silence'. Let me know what you think of them.[4] I love your suggestions for my new lyric.

Howard Sergeant has taken it for Outpost and I hope to be able to change it as you suggest.[5]

I will write more fully later and answer all your questions but bless you in the meantime. Keep me posted with poems for 'Poetry Review'.

Love to you both,

TLcc. NLS.

1. Vincent Arnold Bowen had corresponded with MS since early in the year. On 19 July, he wrote, in response to poems MS had sent him: 'Each new reading reinforces my original opinion that (a) you *are* indeed a poet; (b) with tremendous possibilities [. . .] let me just end this untidy letter by repeating yet once more what I truly believe, – that *you have it in your power* to make your verse more precious to the human spirit, and that no one will look forward to that consummation more eagerly than your *sincere* friend and well-wisher [. . .]' (NLS).

   And in an undated letter, probably from August or September, he wrote: 'May Heaven prosper you now, & direct you in *all* yr endeavours, dear child of Poetry. If you hold fast to yʳ high ideals, The Poetry Society, so long moribund, must flash & flame into life at last' (NLS). Then, on 18 October, he wrote with suggestions on MS's verse and with a plea that she respond to his own poems.

2. Poets Robert Armstrong, Roy Campbell, and Vivian Locke Ellis were closely associated with the *Poetry Review*. The first of them was set to become one of MS's most active opponents at the Poetry Society.

3. Bowen published four poems in *An Anthology of Contemporary Northern Poetry*, edited by Howard Sergeant and published by Harrap earlier in the year: 'Lament', 'The Haunted Lover', 'November Leaves', and 'Twenty Soviet Sailors'.

4. Edward Vandermere Fleming's collection of poems *Waters of Affliction, and Other Poems* was published in 1934 by Chapman & Hall. MS's 'Silence' will not appear in her *Complete Poems*.

5. Bowen's suggestions for improvement of MS's 'Song' were not incorporated in the poem as published in Howard Sergeant's *Outposts* (no. 9, Winter 1947).

Herbert Palmer with George Fraser, 1948

TO HERBERT PALMER, ST ALBANS, HERTFORDSHIRE, 21 NOVEMBER 1947

The Poetry Society, 33 Portman Square, London, W.1
21st November, 1947

Dear Mr. Herbert Palmer,

I can see from your letter you are very angry indeed but first let me hasten to tell you that the Greenwood Report has not yet been published but will be in the next number of 'Poetry Review' – a copy of which will certainly be sent to you. In the meantime I enclose the current number and would be very glad to know what you think of it.[1]

We now pay contributors which I think is a long overdue ruling and I venture to think that the next number of 'Poetry Review'

will show a marked improvement in the standard of contributors
and a truer and more representative critical standard.

Now about your book 'Sword in the Desert', this was
discovered by the staff when Mr. Kyle retired and we were never
told to whom it belonged and we naturally thought that it was a
review copy belonging to the library. However, since it is yours I
hasten to enclose it now but, alas, it has the Poetry Society label
on it. If you do not want it thus mutilated we shall of course send
you a Postal Order for 6/-. We have another copy of this book in
our library, otherwise I would have kept it and sent you the money
in the first place.[2]

I would like to take this opportunity of saying how very much I
have admired your work from my student days and especially this
last book with its strange piercing and indeed swordlike power.
I am hoping you may approve of us sufficiently to send us a poem
for place of honour in 'Poetry Review' or perhaps an article of
your inimitably hellfire-raising variety.

I have set aside your 'Letter to the Editor'. Perhaps when you
are in London you will call in and see us, or write and send us
a poem.

Yours very sincerely,
s/Muriel Spark
Muriel Spark
Editor

TLS on Poetry Society letterhead. HRC.

1. Despite being one of its poets from the older, well-established generation,
    Herbert Palmer, a friend of John Masefield, was one of MS's supporters
    at the Poetry Society. The Greenwood Report was presumably related to
    the annual Greenwood Prize.
2. Galloway Kyle was Editor of the *Poetry Review* from 1915 until when MS
    took over the role in 1947. Palmer's *A Sword in the Desert: A Book of Poems
    and Verses for the Present Times* was published in 1946 by Harrap.

1948

MS's poetry, on which she laboured intently, was starting to appear in reviews including *Poetry Quarterly*, *Poetry Commonwealth*, and *Outposts*. Her volatile affair with Howard Sergeant continued, though it became increasingly clear that he was not about to leave his wife; from February, Derek Stanford was starting to be a presence in MS's life. MS was confidently and capably at the helm of the *Poetry Review*, while also writing for *Parliamentary Affairs*, though she faced unrelenting challenges to her position at the *Review* and the Poetry Society, particularly from Marie Stopes and William Kean Seymour. She parried repeated assaults on her position, riposting by letter, besting attempts in May to subject her to an inquiry designed to force her resignation; but eventually, in November, she was fired from her post. At the year's end, she left the Helena Club where she had been living since the war, and moved temporarily to the home of a supporter, Christmas Humphreys, while working to start a new journal, *Forum*. Throughout the year she battled with the tax office to have the child allowance allotted for her son Robin's upkeep paid to her, as the person who was actually supporting him; and, through lawyers, she unsuccessfully fought her ex-husband (who was acquitted in court of administering excessive punishment on a pupil in an Edinburgh school) to have Robin enrolled in a school near London.

TO J. HOLBERTON, RADNOR SCHOOL, REDHILL,
SURREY, 20 JANUARY 1948

[The Helena Club, 82 Lancaster Gate, London W.2]
20th January, 1948

Dear Mr. Holburton,
   Thank you so much for showing us round your school which
I think is a delightful one, and I am very pleased indeed to have
found so suitable a school for my small son.[1]
   Yours sincerely,

Muriel Spark

                                                      TLcc. PJC.

1. MS wished to have her son closer to London, and also farther from his
   father in Edinburgh whose psychiatric problems were unabating; while
   serving as a temporary teacher at Tynecastle School, he had been charged
   with assaulting a pupil, an accusation of which he was cleared in Edinburgh
   Sheriff Court on 13 February. MS, who was in a custody battle, will be
   prevented in her desire to place her son at Radnor School by Sydney Spark,
   whose solicitors, Furst & Furst, will write to MS's solicitors, Mackenzie &
   Black, on 12 May: 'We have today heard from him. He tells us that he has
   given the matter his careful consideration, and while he will be agreeable
   to send the boy to a Boarding School he insists that it should be in the
   Edinburgh area' (PJC).

TO WILLIAM KEAN SEYMOUR, PEASLAKE, SURREY,
3 FEBRUARY 1948

The Poetry Society, 33 Portman Square, London, W.1
3rd Feb. 1948

Dear William,
   Since you dislike letters typed by my secretary, I am writing
this letter so it needs must be briefer than I would otherwise
make it.

Your letter of 2nd February states your complaints very plausibly but you reconstruct past arguments to suit yourself I am afraid.[1]

Most of my lack of tact about which you complain has been brought about by your persistent questioning after I had answered your first question. However, in future, all reviewers must take my reasons or leave them. The phrase I used on Friday was 'You force me to be frank'. This was the result of your probing. You, in your letter, translate my words into 'You force me to be *brutal*'. So the distortion goes on. I am afraid I have been used to receiving and delivering criticism without comment or indignation, and cannot accustom myself to your subjective attitude.

What you said about Howard Sergeant having to confirm my acceptances is also distorted in your letter. The statement was an outrageous one which affects both Howard Sergeant and myself adversely.[2]

Your poem was not altered by me. I accepted it *on condition* you changed the last line. You did so, and in my view it was a change for the worse and so I asked if you would agree to leave it as it was. This is a strictly ethical manner of conducting an editorship.[3]

My kindness in consulting you about which books I should cut, at *great* inconvenience to myself, has obviously been treated as a kind of weakness on my part, giving you the feeling that you have a right to insult and direct me. Let me disillusion you right away: where Poetry Review is concerned I am quite inexorable and I will not be bullied into putting *anything* into that journal which does not please me, merely in order to placate a troublesome personality.

In conclusion I would like to answer the remarks you make about your 'articles being welcomed by Mr Kyle'. It must be apparent to you by now that all that was good enough for Mr Kyle is not anything like good enough for me, which is the reason why I have been entrusted with this job.[4]

As for your poems not wearing a 'new look', I have no

answer to make beyond that contained in my editorial article in
December 1947 Poetry Review.[5]

Your sincerely,

Muriel

P.S. I have been asked to the Poets' Club tea on Saturday & hope
to go. Will you be there? If so we might have a chat.

M

ALS on Poetry Society letterhead. UTML.

1. A carbon copy of William Kean Seymour's long typed letter of complaint,
   dated 2 February, is in UTML.
2. On 1 February, Howard Sergeant wrote to Seymour to lodge similar
   objections to MS's:

   > I am disturbed by your statement (to Muriel) that I am exercising my
   > influence upon the editorial policy of *Poetry Review* and acting as an
   > unofficial censor over work submitted. [. . .] One of the principal
   > conditions of my agreement with the Meridian Press Ltd. is that I
   > shall not give editorial assistance to any other poetry magazine. You
   > will, no doubt, appreciate that what you say might have dangerous
   > repercussions so far as I am concerned. [. . .] I do not know whether
   > it is any longer necessary for me to deny having exercised any influ-
   > ence whatever – but I feel that some apology is due. (UTML)

3. From the extant correspondence between MS and Seymour, it is not clear
   which poem is being discussed; the *Poetry Review* for February 1948 (vol.
   39, no. 1) published two: 'Admit Impediment' and 'Experience'. MS wrote
   to Seymour on 12 January after he responded to her wish for a different
   ending to his poem: 'I like your alteration very much. Far be it from me
   to start interfering with your poems but since a cat may look at a king
   may I say, in the softest of mews, that the new line does not scan, that is
   if you want it to repeat the form of the other three verses, and I am sure,
   although I may be wrong, that halt in metre spoils the poem though I like
   the sense better than the original line. Don't please think I am trying to
   be difficult but can you do something about it?' (UTML).
4. In 'The Politics of a Literary Magazine: A Study of *The Poetry Review*,
   1912–1972', Abby Arthur Johnson writes, of Kyle:

   > In the year before coming to office, he made a statement which
   > forecast the type of pressure he would exert. 'We should look for-
   > ward as well as backward,' he declared; 'in reality the latter is more

necessary than the former, and it is particularly essential in relation to a poet who may find the times too noisy, too self-centred and too self-righteous to heed him'. [. . .] In 1947, Muriel Spark came to 'the dark house in Portman Square' and took control of the *Review*. From her earliest editorials, she tried to sweep the ghosts from the pages of the journal. (*Journal of Modern Literature*, vol. 3, no. 4, April 1974, pp. 956, 957)

5. MS's editorial in the *Poetry Review* began: 'Cannot we cease railing at the moderns?' And it continued in this vein, mounting a stout defence of what was worthwhile in contemporary verse: 'Let us read and consider with open minds what the modern poets are writing, so that if we approve or condemn, we do so with dignity.'

TO MARGARET CROSLAND, LONDON, 9 FEBRUARY 1948

[The Poetry Society, London]
9th February, 1948

Dear Miss Crosland,

Thank you very much for letting me see a batch of your poems.[1] I have read them with great interest and whilst I like each one of them in part none, in my opinion, possesses throughout the 'charged' quality which distinguishes its opening. I do not know if you like or dislike to receive, unsolicited, any kind of individual reaction to your poetry but it is so seldom that poems as originally conceived as yours are submitted to me that I feel compelled to remark, albeit with diffidence, upon a surprising falling off of the poetic content at the end of your poems. This is, of course, merely an opinion and possibly an erroneous one.

Voyage is a really excellent poem with a decided air, yet I feel it disintegrates or miscarries in the last stanza through a sudden access of deliberation which destroys the effect of the spontaneity which you had achieved so far. I think the line 'This side of time' is an infidelity to the idiom in which you have conceived the rest of the poem. *Pimlico* I like too but expected a definite change in the trend of thought after Line 10 and this was not realised, although as I say, this is only a personal view; and possibly the poem was intended as a fragment.

I admire the phraseology of *Litany* but cannot find sufficient felicity in the pattern in which these phrases congregate and I do not think there is an excuse for the line endings in this poem. I like very much your imagery in *At Season's Turn* but this poem seems to lack an integral rhythm which is the very spirit of free verse.[2]

A great danger to competent poets like yourself is the temptation to allow work which can be improved upon to be published merely because journals will accept it on the strength of the many redeeming merits it possesses. The attractive technique embodied in your style and your reverence for the one inevitable, ultimate word make it all the more important that you should try to retain and express the inspirational fervour with which you begin a poem, until it is ended.

Perhaps you would let me know if you disagree with my remarks and in any case I hope you will send more of your work. If you wish to come and see me perhaps you would make an appointment with Miss Thomson, my secretary.

Yours sincerely,

Muriel Spark
Editor

TLcc. NLS.

1. Margaret Crosland was a prolific translator from French and Italian, as well as being an essayist and critic, publishing many of her translations and editions with the London publisher Peter Owen. Her collection of poems, *Strange Tempe*, was published in 1945 by The Fortune Press.
2. 'Voyage', 'Pimlico', and 'At Season's Turn' are all included in Crosland's *Meeting and Parting, New & Selected Poems 1941–2003* (Centaur Press, 2004); the line in 'Voyage' to which MS objects, 'this side of time', is retained. Crosland's poems were not published in *Forum*, which ran to only two issues, the second appearing in 1949.

TO HUGO MANNING, LONDON, 19 FEBRUARY 1948

The Poetry Society, 33 Portman Square, London, W.1
19th February, 1948

Dear Mr. Hugo Manning,

It was most encouraging to receive your letter yesterday with your two poems. May I keep both of them? I greatly admire all your poetry. You seem to have an aptitude for the sudden and deadly accurate phrase which gives your poetry the charged effect which I so like.[1]

I quite agree with your observations on revolution and change and I believe and hope this has already been achieved. I am now aiming at a really high standard of poetry and criticism in 'Poetry Review.'

Do please keep sending me poems from time to time, for it is only in this way that we can ever make something of the 'Review.'

Your sincerely,
s/Muriel Spark
Muriel Spark
Editor
Hope you can come to some of our readings.
M. S.

TLS on Poetry Society letterhead, with handwritten PS. HRC.

---

1. The poet, short-story writer, essayist, translator, and spiritualist Hugo Manning, a member of the General Council of the Poetry Society, was soon to become one of MS's close friends and supporters; their friendship would last until Manning's death in 1977. He worked night shifts for Reuters, as does the affectionately drawn character modelled on him in MS's 1981 novel *Loitering with Intent*. His poem sequence 'The Headlands' appeared in the *Poetry Review* (vol. 39, no.1, February 1948).

TO ALEX COMFORT, LONDON, 4 MARCH 1948

[The Poetry Society, London]
4th March, 1948

Dear Alex Comfort,

Thank you so much for sending me your two fine poems which
I would like to keep, if I may, for the April POETRY REVIEW. I
especially like 'The Tribal Deities.'[1]

It is kind of you too to offer to review and I would be delighted
if you would agree to do some books for us. I don't quite know
what type you would prefer but would be very pleased if you
would do a few of the better modern poets for the June number.
One I had in mind was Derek Stanford's new book MUSIC FOR
STATUES from Routledge and I expect others will be coming in.[2]

Again with many thanks for your encouragement.

Yours sincerely,

Muriel Spark
Editor

TLcc. NLS.

1. The physician, pacifist, anarchist, poet, and essayist Alex Comfort (who
   in the 1970s would become internationally famous for his manual *The Joy
   of Sex*) had been publishing poetry since the early 1940s. MS wrote to him
   on 1 March inviting him to 'send me a poem', adding: 'I am trying very
   hard to raise the standard of this Review and a poem from you would
   encourage me tremendously' (NLS). MS published both poems in the
   Poetry Review: 'By the Waters of Babylon' and 'The Tribal Deities' (vol. 39,
   no. 2, April–May 1948).
2. Comfort will indeed go on to write reviews for the *Poetry Review*.
   MS had met poet and man of letters Derek Stanford, a friend of her lover
   Howard Sergeant, through the Poetry Society. He previously edited, with
   John Bayliss, *A Romantic Miscellany* (Fortune Press, 1946), and published
   The Freedom of Poetry: Studies in Contemporary Verse (Falcon Press, 1947).
   Music for Statues was his first solo collection of poems.

TO DEREK STANFORD, HOUNSLOW, MIDDLESEX,
11 MARCH 1948

The Poetry Review, 33 Portman Square, London W.1
Editor: Muriel Spark
11/3/48

Dearest Derek,

I sent you a formal letter to-day, but am writing now to send you my poem about which I have so little confidence that I must give you some explanations.[1]

The last time we met you gave me the one inevitable explanation of bi-sexuality I had been searching for. This linked up in my mind with the image of the biblical Joseph whom I have always believed to be homosexual or bi-sexual – this would explain the resentment of his brothers, the nature of his dreams and his rejection of Potiphar's wife. Then, the other night, we spoke of Kirkup whom I had recently met and who seemed to me the most immediate personification of the Joseph conception. All this is in the *poem, I think.[2]

Hooray for Sunday!

Love,

s/Muriel

* I want to convey the vulnerability of the Joseph. Have I achieved it? M.

JOSEPH

You of my gentlest knowing O where is the radiant
coat of your bridehood, the father-gift when that
old gaunt first blessed and wrapped your limbs in gold?

Who shall enfold your groom and woman, loved and
lover until your separate selves will meet?
Shall the darling marriage and the handfast of many

colours compel your smile, manwoman
of gentleness, so less than the loud others
they are turned to naught in your most and mighty
      dreams.

Be fearful of the brothers, your violent
dealers of deception, your kin. O when
the merchants are moving past and the caravan,

manwoman of my gentlest knowing, be
fearful of the deep, the inescapable brothers
whose corn-sheaves fell in your fields, whose stars
      bowed down.

Muriel Spark[3]

TLS on Poetry Society letterhead. WUL.

1. Through the length of their correspondence, which will last for more
   than a decade, MS will almost always write to Derek Stanford in
   Hounslow. In *CV*, relations between them having long since soured, she
   comments:

   > Derek Stanford was a young critic and poet about my age. He was
   > as different from the macho Howard Sergeant as could be imagined.
   > Derek came from a respectable ordinary-class family. He was an
   > only child and lived all the time I knew him with his parents at 46
   > Lulworth Avenue, Lampton, Hounslow. He was amusing, very ec-
   > centric, short, frail and almost totally bald. [. . .] I didn't take any
   > notice, and rightly, when Derek wrote to tell me about his previous
   > sexual hang-ups, 'with men and women'. I felt his past was none of
   > my business. (pp. 186–7)

2. The poet, travel writer, and translator James Kirkup published his first
   volume of poems in 1947, *The Drowned Sailor*, with the Grey Walls Press,
   run by MS's friend Wrey Gardiner. In an undated letter, humorously
   signed 'Ronald Firbank', Kirkup will later write to MS of performing in
   King Lear:

I *wish* you could have seen me in 'Lear' — I *have* got *the* most beautiful legs, and I had them in sheer nylon tights of a hyacinth shade, with an enormous codpiece of mirror-sequins, all designed and lovingly executed by myself. I had such a *time*, keeping my seams straight, and oh, how deliciously cool nylons are in this hot, lowering weather! [. . .] I must confess I quite fell in love with you Muriel last time I thought you were radiantly lovely and one of the nicest girls I've ever seen. You were quite transformed, because I always used to think you quite dreadful, *before*. Would you mind if I lived with you, and Derek too, for a while, when I return to London. I'm sure we could arrange things very well and set up a very darling *ménage à trois* we would be like a nest of singing birds. I think you're utterly beautiful, and maybe you could *grow* to love me, if you don't already, for I realise I *do* have some strange fascination for girls, and boys like me are very loveable. What do you say? (NLS)

3. No record of the publication of 'Joseph' has been found; it does not appear in MS's *Complete Poems*.

Derek Stanford with Muriel Spark, early 1950s

TO DEREK STANFORD, HOUNSLOW, MIDDLESEX,
16 MARCH 1948

The Poetry Review, 33 Portman Square, London W.1
Editor: Muriel Spark
16/3/48

Dearest Derek,
   Please forgive me for plaguing you with my poems. Can you
spare time to look critically at my latest?
   Hope to see you soon,
   Love
   Muriel

BLUEBELL AMONG THE SABLES

   The visitor came clothed with sables,
   My dark and social friend.
   The afternoon prospered after its kind,
   But they bore me, those intimate parliaments.
   Those tea-times wear my heart away.

   So I took half my pleasure in the sables
   Which flowed across her arm, the chair,
         the floor,
   Sleek and fathomless like contemplative
   Living animals, the deep elect,
   In ceremonious most limp obedience.

   But the dark skins did move. She felt them creep:
   'My God! my sables!'
         Indeed they were alive with a new life,
   The sombre swiftly shot with quick and silver
   Fur within fur. It was Bluebell, my beautiful,
   My small and little cat pounding the sables;
   Flat on her spine she tumbled them,

Shaking their kindly tails between her teeth.
　'My furs! your cat!'

I said, 'No need for alarm.
Those dead pelts can't do Bluebell any harm.'
(I am a human female and do not possess any sables.)
Poor soul, this put her in the wrong;
As one who somehow fails the higher vision
She was meek: 'They cost the earth, my furs.'
I stroked the comical creature, she the sables;
So all came even.

And she said there was no damage, no damage.
It may be she had profit of the event.
As for myself, that moment was well spent
When I saw Bluebell pummelling the sables.
I have the image, the gratuitous image
Miserly seized: those sable wonders glowing,
An order of the profound earth, of roots
And minerals wrought soft in civil strands,
Defined in which, the sprite, like air and like
A dawn asperges, green-eyed Bluebell plying
The sensuous fabric with her shining pads.

MURIEL SPARK[1]

ALS on Poetry Society letterhead
with typed attachment
of poem. WUL.

1. 'Bluebell among the Sables' appears in MS's *Complete Poems* (pp. 74–5),
where MS misdates it by a decade, placing it as 'c.1958'; it contains variants, chief of which is the omission of the line '(I am a human female and
do not possess any sables.)'.

TO WILLIAM KEAN SEYMOUR, PEASLAKE, SURREY, 17 MAY 1948

The Poetry Society, 33 Portman Square, London, W.1
17th May 1948

Dear Mr. Seymour,

I have received your letter of the 14th May and I note what you say. I intend to deal impersonally and objectively with the many points you raise although I feel bound to say before proceeding further that some of them fill me with disgust.

That you are not an ally of mine in any dispute that may have arisen in the Poetry Society I am not, as you appear to imagine, in doubt. Nevertheless I do not propose to embark upon a private discussion with you, in correspondence, as to the advisability or otherwise of the suggested Enquiry. A poll has been decided upon and you will have a vote as well as myself and the other members of the Society. Your prayer for my resignation is understandable when I consider the third paragraph of your letter with which I shall deal next.[1]

I have not at any time outlined a plan to you for the replacement of my friend Mr. Weston Ramsey as Chairman of the Society. Such a statement is as you well know a deliberate lie and I would warn you most severely that there exists a law of libel of which I shall not hesitate to avail myself if further provoked. It is hardly likely that, if I were involved in any such despicable intrigue, I would come to you for support. Surely, if such were the case, I would have mentioned the scheme to Sir George Cockerill himself, to Mr. John Graddon, to Mr. Howard Sergeant, to Mr. Christmas Humphreys, to Mrs. Violet Adamson, to Mrs. Enid Van den Bergh, to Mr. H. K. Grant, all of whom are Members of the Council and upon all of whom I look upon as friends — yet I was in contact with all of these people on the day that you called at my office, and they will testify to the fact that Mr. Ramsey's name was not mentioned except in praise and sympathy with his difficult task.[2]

I have been giving some thought as to your motive for making such an outrageous allegation. It occurs to me that (a) either you wish to cause a division in the ranks of those you consider to be your opponents or (b) you wish to discredit me in the eyes of my supporters. Perhaps you had both of these objects in mind. I do not think, however, there is any possibility of the former problem arising. With regard to the latter, I am reminded perforce of a conversation I had with you some months ago in which you expressed your opinion that you yourself would like to be editor of Poetry Review. You also told me on another occasion that Mr. Kyle had made you an offer in this connection (which, if true, he had no authority to do). Can it be that you are intriguing to replace me? If so, you can imagine the effect your methods and motive would have upon fair-minded people who would hardly allow a man of your years, who has had ample opportunity to distinguish himself or otherwise, in the literary world, to take away the livelihood of a young woman with a child to support, who happens to be making a marked success of her work. – This is not self-praise; I speak from the knowledge of daily tributes I receive from intelligent people throughout the world. Our files are full of such letters.

Whilst we are on this subject I would mention that you have not in the past shown me the respect which is due to me and which has been shown me by other members, Council members and contributors. I have had reason to complain on several occasions of your manner of lifting and reading papers which happen to be lying upon my desk, and of giving instructions to my staff without my permission. Everything connected with this office is to run smoothly – on that I am determined, and with this end in view I feel compelled to ask you to observe the same procedure as is observed by all other members, Council members and contributors. I give below one or two suggestions:

(a) If you wish to see me, please telephone and make an appointment. With shortage of staff, it is impossible for me to see everyone who wishes to see me, without having first received notice.

(b) Will you please address me at all times as 'Mrs. Spark' and not by my Christian name.

(c) Since we are, as I have said, extremely busy and short-staffed, please do not call upon the Staff in working hours and take tea with them. Although they usually stop work for a few moments at tea-time, a visitor in the office prolongs this interval and disrupts the working scheme unduly. If you have books to leave or to call for, or if you wish to leave M.S.S. you can do this briefly, and of course, any other enquiry connected with poetry or the Poetry Society will be attended to by my Staff with their usual courtesy. But I do not wish work to be held up.

I make these observations merely because, as a servant of the Society I am concerned for the rights of *all* the Members and Subscribers, of whom there are over 3,000. Naturally, to spend an undue amount of time upon one particular member would be a violation of my duty, and as you are now a member of the Council and thus a servant of the Society yourself, I am sure you will appreciate this.

Yours truly,
s/Muriel Spark
Muriel Spark
General Secretary and Editor

TLS on Poetry Society letterhead. UTML.

1. At the Annual General Meeting of the Poetry Society that took place on 11 May it was decided by those hostile to MS – chief among whom were Marie Stopes and William Kean Seymour – that members of the Society should be balloted on whether there should be an inquiry into the resignations that had occurred since MS's arrival at the Society. In his letter of 14 May, Seymour, who according to Martin Stannard was known as 'Schemer Seymour' (*MSB*, p. 95), wrote: 'May I say in all sincerity that I was amazed also that you should canvass my support for your plan of "getting rid of" Weston Ramsey as Chairman and appointing Sir George Cockerill in his place. Apart from this being the height of ingratitude it indicated on your part a complete misconception of your capacity and duty as a servant of the Council' (NLS).

2. John Graddon was Treasurer of the Poetry Society; H. K. Grant was its Librarian; the list of 'Members of the General Council' of the Poetry Society appeared on the inside front-cover of the *Poetry Review*.

TO WILLIAM KEAN SEYMOUR, PEASLAKE, SURREY, 20 MAY 1948

The Poetry Society, 33 Portman Square, London, W.1
20th May 1948

Dear Mr. Seymour,

In reply to your letter of the 18th May, I can only say that this letter is obviously written for a larger audience than myself, and unless you cease these allegations immediately you will have to take the consequences.[1]

You will learn that the mere invention of dialogue cannot establish evidence, and I repeat that your statements are deliberate lies.

Yours sincerely,
s/Muriel Spark
Muriel Spark
General Secretary and Editor

TLS. UTML.

1. In his letter of 18 May, William Kean Seymour wrote to rebut 'the arrogant nonsense in your letter', and to refute the allegations MS had made. He concluded his letter: 'As a Vice-President and a leading Review contributor, and now as a duly elected member of the Council, I suggest that you do not attempt to browbeat me on this or any other point in order to make a case against me' (UTML).

TO MARIE STOPES, DORKING, SURREY, 29 MAY 1948

[The Helena Club, 82 Lancaster Gate, London W.2]
29th May 1948

Madam,

I have received your outrageously impudent letter of 27th May.[1]

My private affairs are no concern of yours and your malicious interest in them seems to me to be most unwholesome. You have no rights whatsoever to make enquiries about me – all enquiries necessary were made by those who appointed me and confirmed my appointment. I must say that your attitude fills me with contempt, as it would all right-thinking people.

I shall give you no information about myself. I would warn you most severely, however, that your statements are libellous and should you continue to repeat them my solicitors would be instructed to act against you.

Yours truly,

Muriel Spark
General-Secretary

TLcc. NLS.

1. In addition to being an influential scientist and an advocate of birth control and eugenics, Marie Stopes was an essayist, playwright, and poet. After a ballot of Poetry Society members concluded that there should be no inquiry into the earlier resignations at the Society, Stopes had begun to delve into MS's personal history in an attempt to discredit her, at which point MS had, on 25 May, telephoned her to ask her to desist. Responding to this call, in her letter to MS of 27 May, headed by her several titles ('D. Sc., Ph.D., F.L.S., F.G.S., F.R.S. Lit.'), Stopes wrote: 'as a Vice President and a member long concerned for the good name of the Poetry Society, I am fully entitled to be informed and to make enquiries about yourself. [. . .] I request you to inform me whether or not your husband divorced you so that I may have the facts correct' (NLS).

    Martin Stannard comments, of MS's reaction to the attempt to oust her: 'Those who offered false counsel and plotted against her, entered her private bestiary: Robert Armstrong; the Chairman, H. W. Harding; Seymour; Marie Stopes, the proponent of birth control. Muriel later lamented that Stopes's mother had not been better informed on the subject' (*MSB*, p. 82).

The present letter is written not on Poetry Society letterhead; of another such letter, MS explains in *CV*:

> I wrote the above, as I wrote all personal and semi-personal letters, on my own writing paper, because Robert Armstrong had raised the petty question in a council meeting, whether I used Poetry Society paper for letters to my supporters in the Society and therefore at the Society's expense. I could have pointed out that he wrote all his letters about his poems and Poetry Society business on Inland Revenue government paper, in other words at the taxpayer's expense, but I didn't feel I could sink quite so low. (p. 179)

TO HM INSPECTOR OF TAXES, MARYLEBONE DISTRICT, LONDON, 8 JUNE 1948

[The Helena Club, 82 Lancaster Gate, London W.2]
8th June 1948

Dear Sir,

I regret the delay in replying to your letter of 4th May as I informed you on the telephone I intended to do; I have been away on sick leave and have been unable to attend to this matter.

As I informed you in my last letter, my ex-husband had legal custody of the child until September 1945, when the child was sent home to me from Africa with instructions by telegram from the Ministry of Internal Affairs, Rhodesia, that he was to be handed over to me as his father was unable to look after him. On making investigations into the period of time over which my custody of the child was to operate, I was told (also by telegram) that I could keep the child until his father was able to support him, that is, to care for him and take actual custody.[1]

Now, since September 1945, and for about eighteen months before it my ex-husband has not had *actual* custody of the child. He was in a nervous disorders hospital in Africa from 1944–1945 and when he returned to Edinburgh in 1945 he was some months in a nervous disorders hospital. I am, and have been, supporting the child, and although his father is in receipt of a disability pension from the Rhodesian Government, which also includes an allowance for the child, he does not pass this money on towards the child's maintenance. I maintain that, since my ex-husband is still in receipt of a disability allowance from the Rhodesian Government, he is not in a position to care for the child in a proper manner and therefore, acting on the concession I received from the Rhodesian Department of Internal Affairs, the child remains in my custody. I am therefore entitled, morally and legally, to the child allowance. My ex-husband's statement that he is the sole supporter of the child is untrue. He does not contribute to the child's upkeep.

Yours faithfully,

Muriel Spark

TLcc. NLS.

1. On the conditions of MS's return to England from Rhodesia and on the custody of her child, see 30 May 1944, nn. 1 and 2.

TO SYDNEY BAILEY, PARLIAMENTARY AFFAIRS, THE HANSARD SOCIETY, LONDON, 4 JULY 1948

[The Helena Club, 82 Lancaster Gate, London W.2]
4th July, 1948

Dear Mr. Bailey,

I am sorry to have delayed the enclosed anthology for so long.[1] I had an unusual pressure of work which kept me busy in my spare time which I had reserved for your anthology.

Possibly this is too long. I have tried to make it as concise yet comprehensive as possible. In this case, will you either cut out what you do not require, or return the batch to me for shortening?

I have entitled the group Poetry and Government, because this allows a wider scope, but you may wish to alter it.

If this is what you want, I could let you have another series, perhaps concentrating upon a particular period, or an anthology of parliamentary prose.[2]

Yours sincerely,

TLcc. UTML.

1. Sydney Bailey, who will go on to become a notable expert and mediator in international affairs, had recently been appointed Secretary to the Hansard Society, and was Assistant Editor of the Hansard Society's journal, *Parliamentary Affairs*. On 10 June, MS wrote to him: 'I am very interested indeed to hear about the anthology you contemplate including in an early issue, and of course I should be extremely pleased to help you with this' (UTML).
2. Bailey will reply on 6 July to say that he has amended her title to 'Poetry and Politics', and to suggest that MS begin to collect material for a further issue of *Parliamentary Affairs*, concentrating on political poetry of a particular period (NLS).

TO HERBERT PALMER, ST ALBANS, HERTFORDSHIRE, 18 DECEMBER 1948

c/o Mrs. T. C. Humphreys, 58 Marlborough Place, St. Johns Wood, London, N.W.8
18th December, 1948

Dear Mr. Herbert Palmer,

How very nice of you to write me such a charming letter. I was greatly amused by your description of Hell and Purgatory which I think calls for a satyrical [sic] poem from your pen.[1]

We were all delighted with your company on Sunday night. I have seen the photographs and you have come out extremely well, and so I have ordered extra copies of these and will be sending you them as soon as I have them which will be some time after Christmas. The pictures will probably appear in Picture Post or one of the picture papers.[2]

I will write you in the New Year and let you know when the
next Forum meeting will be, and we are looking forward to
hearing you read again.

With sincere good wishes for Christmas,

Yours sincerely,

s/Muriel Spark

P.S. Since writing the above I have received your other letter. I
think Mr Gawsworth should know that the true position is not
as you have described. *I* made the position quite clear to the
editorial committee who took over the 'Review' (and for this
very purpose, I had an independent witness): *Both* articles (of
quite diffrent nature) were to be printed in the December P. R. in
honour of Emily Brontë's centenary.[3]

Almost at the last minute (as the Poetry Society records will show)
the size of the magazine was reduced from 80 to 64 pages. This meant
either taking Phoebe Hesketh's article out altogether, or cutting it.[4] I
was reluctant to do the latter, but made it *quite* clear to the editorial
committee who took over that it should go in the next issue. Beyond
that, I have no responsibility. Obviously, Mr Gawsworth has not been
told by the editorial committee that this has been commissioned.
I hope you will explain to him. Unfortunately, another writer has
complained to me that an essay which had been commissioned by me
has been returned as unsuitable by the new editor.

M. S.

TLS with handwritten PS. HRC.

---

1. In an undated letter to MS, Herbert Palmer drew a sketch of the prem-
    ises of the Poetry Society which included the upstairs flat that Galloway
    Kyle had refused to vacate when MS became Secretary: 'You see Kyle was
    upstairs gnashing his teeth in Hell – first time I realized that Hell can be
    up-above – and Purgatory was the ground floor, and Paradise, I suppose,
    out in the bloody street. Of course I have complained to Hell but Hell can
    only shower down more abuse – which doesn't help me at all. Now Johnny
    Gawsworth has taken over Purgatory – if he doesn't mind his step better
    I'll kick him up aloft to join his brother in Hell' (HRC).

    The poet and editor John Gawsworth (pseudonym of Terence Ian
    Fytton Armstrong) replaced MS as Editor of the *Poetry Review.*

2. After losing her battle with the old guard at the Poetry Society, MS was removed from her role as Editor of the *Poetry Review*. She moved out of the Helena Club in Lancaster Gate and temporarily into the home of a Society member who had in fact voted against her, the barrister and Buddhist proselytiser Christmas Humphreys. There she organised an evening, with the support of several of the writers who had resigned from the Poetry Society in protest.

3. In his undated letter, Palmer complained to MS for not having printed an article he had submitted on Emily Brontë and which Gawsworth had subsequently refused to publish.

4. Phoebe Hesketh, of whom Palmer says in his undated letter, 'I *know* to be one of the immortals', had been publishing poetry — nature poetry in particular — since 1939.

At the house of Christmas Humphreys, 1948, from foreground, left to right: Eileen Fraser (head), Eric de Mauny, Derek Patmore, unidentified (possibly Hugo Manning, or Sefton Delmer), Muriel Spark, Howard Sergeant, Derek Stanford, unidentified

1949

Despite being able to begin 1949 with a move to her own rented bedsit at 1 Vicarage Gate, Kensington, for MS the year began (and ended) with financial struggle. After a short-lived unhappy stint from February to May as Personal Assistant to Pearson Horder, a publicity consultant, MS resolved to try to earn her living exclusively through her writing. She continued work on her new magazine, *Forum*, whose first issue, which included poems by old supporters and newer acquaintances such as Iris Birtwistle and Hugo Manning, came out in early summer. She pitched various projects to publishers, including a complete works of Anne Brontë, a selection of Brontë letters, a selection of Jane Austen letters, an anthology of the work of William Wordsworth, and a selection of writings by Dorothy Wordsworth. Having joined the Society of Authors in March, she applied in October for a grant, and received £30 after recommendations from poets Wrey Gardiner and Herbert Palmer. Although MS successfully published poems and won awards for them, she complained to Derek Stanford about being obliged to neglect her poetry in favour of paying jobs. Her affair with Howard Sergeant ended, while Stanford went from trusted literary companion, confidant, and 'dearest friend', to lover; from this point they functioned as an intimate and professional duo. Having first corresponded with her in 1948, MS developed a closer friendship with Iris Birtwistle, a well-to-do Roman Catholic poet who generously supported her with everything from money and a typewriter to, later, gin, and handkerchiefs. Her tussles with her ex-husband continued: although he had not contributed to their son's upkeep in years and although MS was able to demonstrate her meagre income, he continued to demand payment for the outstanding balance on expenses associated with their divorce in Southern Rhodesia.

TO DEREK STANFORD, HOUNSLOW, MIDDLESEX,
6 FEBRUARY 1949

1 Vicarage Gate, W.8
February 6, 1949

Dearest Derek,

I enclose my latest, and when you have time perhaps you would
be kind enough to criticise, dissect and possibly exterminate it.
I usually pass an order of liquidation on every two out of three
poems I write, which is a great waste of energy. If only one could
learn not to write the ones that turn out to be duds. There must
be something in Mendel one could take an object lesson from,
although I don't know if it's a good thing to keep the poetic species
pure. What I mean is that if there were no bad poems there would
be nothing to compare the good ones with. Would there?[1]

I have been reading Eliot's essays this weekend – at least, the
ones on Poetic Drama and Dramatic Poetry, and Thoughts after
Lambeth and have made copious notes, which I dearly love doing.
The next article I am doing for Women's Review is on Eliot's
dramatic works and I find it interesting to see what he says himself
about dramatic poetry.[2]

Have you ever wanted to become a Catholic? I would, if I could
find Faith. I shall set out on a pilgrimage, I think, turning over
small stones and leaves, climbing rare mountains in Tibet and
making odd enquiries in public libraries, searching for Faith.

Do ring me during the week, and let me know if you are going
to Peter's.[3] Also, I would very much like to see your new poem.

All news when I see you,

Much love,

s/Muriel

P.S. Have you seen the current Poetry Review? – A long letter
from Mr. Brockway in answer to yours is included. I don't know if
Gawsworth showed it to you. It didn't arrive before I left the P.S.[4]

s/M.

TLS. HRC.

1. MS had moved house in late January. She later described her new lodgings: 'I was now living at No.1, Vicarage Gate, a short way up Kensington Church Street from Kensington High Street. The name of this rooming house was Eras House. I had a small single-bed room, a gas ring and a wash basin' (*CV*, p. 193).

    It is not known which poem MS enclosed.

    MS refers to the botanist Gregor Mendel, best known for his development of the three principles of inheritance.
2. T. S. Eliot's *Selected Essays 1917–1932* had recently been published in London by Faber & Faber.
3. MS is probably referring to Peter Owen, the co-founder of the publishing house Peter Nevill.
4. MS had published the work of the poet and translator James Brockway in the *Poetry Review*.

TO DEREK PATMORE, 25 FEBRUARY 1949

Forum, Stories and Poems, 1 Vicarage Gate, London, W.8
Editor: Muriel Spark
25/2/49

Dear Mr Patmore,

   I should have written you sooner to say that the European Affairs journal scheme did not materialise so far as I was concerned, as the proprietors were not willing (or able, eventually) to pay me enough![1] I have taken a more lucrative but less inspiring job in Public relations, and am carrying on with the Forum magazine.[2] This will publish short stories and poems, and either will be welcome from your pen. I don't know if you write short stories, but if you do I am sure they will be good ones and if you don't perhaps this will prove an incentive. With good wishes,

   Yours sincerely,
   Muriel Spark

                                        ALS on Forum letterhead. HRC.

1. Derek Patmore belonged to the group of poets who supported MS in her break from the Poetry Society. MS outlined the ambitious plan for a journal in a letter to Sir Ronald Storrs on 19 December 1948: 'The European Journal will be fortnightly review in 20 pages, the same size as The Spectator. It will have an editorial board who will shape the policy of the paper, Associate Editors representing each European country, and permanent correspondents in all European capitals' (NLS).
2. On 14 February, MS started working as a full-time assistant to the publicity consultant Pearson Horder. *Forum: Stories and Poems* was the new journal MS managed to establish, of which she was Editor (and later Co-editor, with Derek Stanford). Its first issue, published later in 1949, will include work by authors who had supported her at the Poetry Society and with whom she corresponded – among others, Iris Birtwistle, Roy Campbell, Wrey Gardiner, Robert Greacen, Hugo Manning, Derek Stanford, Herbert Palmer, and John Waller.

TO DEREK STANFORD, HOUNSLOW, MIDDLESEX, 20 APRIL 1949

Forum, Stories and Poems, 1 Vicarage Gate, London, W.8
Editor: Muriel Spark
20th April 1949

My dear Derek,

Have had a God Almighty row with Howard. He had such a lot coming to him & something went 'snap' inside me, as they say, and I rather let him have it.[1]

This time, I'm not sorry. I don't feel terribly upset and I don't want to revive the affair. One way and another, Howard's obsession for me wasn't a bit like love. He was beginning to resent any man telephoning me for any reason. I'm sure this wasn't good for him, and certainly not for me. And then there was this bloody nonsense about shooting up to Blackpool & expecting to find me sitting at home pining & wailing, on his return.[2]

Howard resented a lot that happened whilst I edited Poetry Review. I think I was unaware of this at the time, and took it for granted that he would help me, out of sheer goodwill. But I don't think he expected me to exploit his assistance – the contacts he gave me etc. – in the way I did. On the other hand I helped him, but only incidentally, for I really think, as I thought then, that he is a good writer.

What a mix up it is! On the whole, it is good we have had this row, for it *does* finalise things. I was beginning to behave in an unnatural way when I was with Howard. Also I thought the 'Don't tell Lionel' theme a bit overdone. (I hope Lionel makes him happy.)[3]

I suppose my fault has been selfishness. Howard needs a woman who will dedicate her life to him. I can't do this for two reasons 1) I have to earn a living for my son and 2) when I am not earning a living I want to write; and I am not prepared to submerge either of these activities.

Oh dear, what a lot I've written. I have to clarify things and to whom could I tell them, but to you, my dearest friend?

Howard said (but more crudely) that I am too self-opiniated [*sic*]. Is this so? If it is true, you must tell me, dear Derek. – I should never resent your telling me my faults, you would be so courteous always.[4]

Please come soon to see me. I don't want to encroach on your spare time, but if you *can* come, and won't feel bored, please do.

With love,
Muriel

ALS on Forum letterhead. WUL.

1. In his letter of 15 June 1948 to MS, almost one year earlier, Howard Sergeant was already anticipating the demise of their affair:

> I think that you believe you would be happier without me, but you are afraid of hurting me. Sooner or later, if that is the case, you will have to hurt me, so perhaps you should forget about my feelings in the matter and tell me now. There is already a great barrier between us and, of late, I have not had the slightest idea of what is going on in your mind. [. . .] I realise that it must be extremely difficult – after the nights and days of such exquisite tenderness we have known – for you to say frankly that you do not want me: Darling, be kind to me and truthful. Don't you really feel that it would be best to part?

Isn't that what you want and are afraid to say? It may be that there is someone else. You need not fear that I shall make it awkward for you if you tell me. In my present state I am distracted whenever I am not with you – but that is entirely because you make me feel so uncertain about you. I hate to have any suspicions at all. Yet how can I know that there is anything between us to which you acknowledge wholehearted loyalty when you leave me in such doubt. On some days you make me wonderfully certain; on others I am overwhelmed by a sense of loss. Every person you meet, in my fear, may be a potential danger. There may be no-one else now, but in *your* uncertainty about the future, the danger is always there: particularly when I know that you have Robin to consider and would, if you felt it for his benefit, marry without being in love. (NLS)

2. Sergeant's wife Dorothy and their infant daughter, Deirdre, lived in Blackpool.
3. Lionel Monteith was a close friend of Sergeant and was Editor of *Poetry Commonwealth*, which ran for eight issues between 1948 and 1951, and whose first issue included MS's poem 'Song of the Divided Lover'. Bruce Meyer, in his work devoted to Howard Sergeant, explains that Monteith had become the spokesman of the still-married Sergeant, charged with the task of stifling any ambitions MS might have to become his second wife. Meyer writes of the precise period of the present letter:

    Fearing that Spark would continue to press him for marriage, Sergeant asked Monteith to have dinner with Spark while he was away on business and to persuade her that marriage to Sergeant would not be a good idea. [. . .] As early as 1947, Sergeant had urged Monteith to throw cold water on Muriel's plans for marriage. In a letter of November 1947 from Glasgow, Sergeant instructed Monteith: 'If the subject comes up, I want you to bring all the weight you can against the idea.' (*Sergeant of* Outposts: *One Editor's Role in Post-war British Poetry, 1944–1987*: doctoral thesis at McMaster University, July 1988, 156–7; MacSphere)

4. Sergeant's recriminations would continue in his letter to MS of the following day, 21 April. After accusing her of presumptuousness and arrogance in her dealings with both the Poetry Society and the Forum group, he will continue:

    Your fiction of the Woman Menace is of course merely a rationalisation for yourself. You are well aware of your own disloyalty in so many ways that you have to invent this character as a belief of mine so that you can feel justified. In no sense, have you ever showed any

loyalty. Indeed your one concern has always been your own self
and everything & everyone else had to take second place. Please
do not attempt to provide me with an analysis of Love – Your sole
conception of it is selfish: indeed, it seems to me that you are quite
incapable of thinking beyond yourself. (NLS)

TO DEREK STANFORD, HOUNSLOW, MIDDLESEX,
20 MAY 1949

[Pearson Horder Ltd, Belgrove House, Belgrove Street, London]
Friday, 20.5.49

My dearest Derek,

   To-day my chief has not arrived.[1] He won't be coming in until
this afternoon. I am trying to write a poem but the poem will
not come because when I should have written it, I denied it. The
reason I denied it was because when I wanted to write it there
was work to do. So it goes on. It makes me angry to think of the
poems lost in this way. They might have been bad poems, but for
every dozen bad poems or so, there is a good one, and now the
good ones may never come.

   So you will understand I am sad to-day, and suffering from
loss of memory, in a way. I mean that the images won't come,
not that I don't remember what a table a chair or a telephone is. –
Sometimes everything has another meaning than its apparent one,
but today it is forgotten.

   This is 10 a.m. At 11 a.m. I will ring Colin.[2] At 10.30 I'll ring
Mrs Henderson and tell her I can't come for the weekend as she
wants me to.[3] Then I shall try to read Wrey Gardiner's book, not
thoroughly but here and there.[4] In fact, this morning I shall do
everything I can think of except that which I am paid to do. So far
I have read the Times Lit. Sup. and, as I said, tried to write the
poem. I wish I had brought some poems with me to type. I am
sucking a piece of cotton wool which I sometimes do for comfort.

   Dear Derek, I am so full of the sense of being a slave. I can
see years of slavery ahead of me. || Howard has just telephoned

and has nothing much to say. || It will be nothing but an oblique journey while I want to travel as the crow flies. Everyone else who wants to write feels the same, I suppose. I wish you would ring me but you will this afternoon.

One thing makes me happy. That is your friendship. You make my despair recognisable to me, which before was vague. This is a good thing because when I turn on it in rage I know in what direction to lash out. I have too often committed that characteristic crime of the female, which is to vent the results of frustration on those things and people which are not the source of frustration. I love to hear you speaking to me and to have your encouragement. What I wonder is if I can offer you any solace. My halting conversation must be irritating to you, because unlike you, I often open my mouth & say things which I haven't properly compiled. You help me to think more clearly, but how do I help you? With other men I have felt that what I can't offer in one way I can in another. I mean, that where my mind has failed to seduce, my body could do so. With you, I know that you have feelings for the body similar to yet different from my own, the difference being the differences in our sexes. So that when we lie together it is a happy thing because we are equal. When we exchange ideas, I fall short of you.

But you must know that I need you and love to be with you, and no doubt it is all much more complex than I can imagine. Howard always thought I was promiscuous and had always to be parading before a male audience. Actually, he was wrong, but he was deceived by my expression of a need to compensate for my other shortcomings. I think, somehow you understand this; at least you have made me understand it.

I am talking on and on in this letter, just like Wrey in his book.

Dear Derek, come and see me again soon. It gives me a wonderful sense of hope and release to think we may share things and be conspirators.

With love,

Muriel

ALS. HRC.

1. MS's employer Pearson Horder.
2. MS had met Colin Methven while living between wartime London and Milton Bryan, where she worked as Duty Secretary in the newsroom of the Political Intelligence Department; Methven was her telephone interlocutor at the Foreign Office, and soon became a close friend and confidant (as would, later, his daughter Deirdre, who had been evacuated to Canada). MS writes of her time spent with Methven during the war years:

> He was a good deal older than me and had been married and divorced twice. He was good-looking, always with a lot of effortless charm, but I think his health had been ruined by a serious wound in the First World War. He had a most dangerous-looking bullet scar in his neck.
>
> I didn't at that time want any romantic attachment, and so Colin, with his delightful conversation, his generous entertainments, his true affection and very sound advice, was always just right for me as he was. I know he enjoyed my company. (*CV*, p. 154)

Of the post-war years, MS writes: 'Colin was still, and was to remain, my principal moral support' (*CV*, p. 165).
3. Mrs Henderson has not been further identified.
4. A close friend of MS, the editor, publisher, and poet Wrey Gardiner founded *Poetry Quarterly* in 1939, as well as Grey Walls Press in 1940 (which later merged with the Falcon Press). MS is almost certainly reading his novel published by the Falcon Press in 1948, *A Season of Olives*.

TO SYDNEY BAILEY, PARLIAMENTARY AFFAIRS,
THE HANSARD SOCIETY, LONDON, 9 JUNE 1949

[Vicarage Gate, London]
9th June, 1949

Dear Mr. Bailey,

Thank you for your letter of 7th June. I shall be very pleased to prepare the next anthology for publication in your journal next year.

I am interested to note your December issue will be devoted to aspects of American government, and I am wondering if you would be interested in an anthology of American parliamentary poems. There are many lively and appropriate pieces in American literature. This is merely a suggestion, and I hope you won't mind my making it; if you think the idea a good one and can spare the space, it is something I should very much like to do.[1]

Yours sincerely,

Muriel Spark

TLcc. NLS.

1. Sydney Bailey will respond positively on 13 June: 'Your suggestion sounds most interesting, and I shall look forward to receiving your American anthology not later than 1st September.' And on 18 June, MS will write to Bailey: 'I shall be letting you have the American anthology before September 1st' (NLS).

TO DEREK STANFORD, HOUNSLOW, MIDDLESEX, 11 JULY 1949

1 Vicarage Gate, Kensington, W.8
11ᵗʰ July 1949

My darling Derek,

I can't begin my day's work until I tell you how greatly I love you. It is a feeling that increases as I know you better and I am very jealous to preserve my love for you.

How delightful this past weekend has been! I feel enriched in so many ways and can't imagine that you feel reciprocated. But if my love, affection and enjoyment of your company, please you, I feel happy and released from the bitterness you know I have suffered in the past year. When I told you that I am happier now than ever before, I meant not only that I have found the way in which I can best live, but also, that you are identified with fulfilment for me. For you know, had it not been for your insistence and encouragement I should not have been able even to begin the work which is making me so happy. From now on, whenever I have to do work I dislike – as no doubt will be necessary from time to

time – it will seem temporary and irrelevant so long as you are
allied to my cause.

I am your well-wisher and your intimate too, and although you
don't need encouragement I will give you it nevertheless.

Forgive the naiveté of this letter. I am just awake and, you
know, I always wake to innocence – which renders my words
sincere if not distinguished.

My love to my dear Derek,
Muriel

ALS. HRC.

TO DEREK STANFORD, HOUNSLOW, MIDDLESEX, CIRCA 19 JULY 1949

1 Vicarage Gate W.8
19 (?) July '49, 9 p.m.

Dearest darling Derek,

Still trying to come to terms with St. Swithin, but he is an
evasive old cleric.[1] Anyway, my thoughts are with you and your
sweetness to me to-day. My pink carnation, set in the tooth-glass-
of-many-functions is putting me off too, in a romantic way. But
that is not to say she is an anarchist. On the contrary she has no
social conscience – I think she is a tyrant like the figure of Pavlova
whom she brings to mind. The association arises from two things
I think: On the first and only occasion when I saw Pavlova she
wore a pink ruffly ballet dress, just like my carnation and for the
first time I experienced a sense of the deliberate cultivation of
artifice combining with natural expression. My friend Frances
and I both felt sick afterwards, which is my second reason for
associating my carnation with Pavlova, (although my sickness has
passed off now). –[2]

Silly letter that this is. I meant to tell you of my love for you,
and speak of your uniqueness. You are the first man I have ever
known closely who has recognised the essential isolation of human

nature; men usually do not like to see a woman as an island and attempt to land and set their flag upon it. I suppose most women want this, but in my experience I have always had to leave off tilling the ground or bringing in the harvest in order to build up defences. Whereas you, my darling, come to give me a hand with the fortifications and bring me lovely, exotic herbs to plant as well; and you are my most welcome guest.

Tomorrow I do penance for my frivolity by typing ten thousand words of Chap. II.[3] But tomorrow evening I hope you will be with me. Bring your review of the Romantics with you.[4] And I desire to have your completed poem placed before me with due ceremony. I shall take Gascoyne (in typescript) to bed with me tonight.[5]

With all my love,
Muriel

ALS. HRC.

1. Although in her letter of two months prior (see 20 May 1949) MS writes of 'when we lie together', Martin Stannard suggests that the eve of St Swithin's Day, four days prior to the present letter, was the date on which MS and Derek Stanford 'eventually became lovers' (*MSB*, p. 104).

2. MS writes in *CV* of the outings organised by her schoolteacher Miss Christina Kay, who was later to become a model for the character of Jean Brodie in *The Prime of Miss Jean Brodie* (who also takes her pupils to see the Russian prima ballerina Anna Pavlova): 'The most exciting of these outings with our beloved Miss Kay was to the Empire Theatre to see Anna Pavlova, indisputably the world's greatest dancer of her time. [. . .] Frances and I were now twelve years old. Both had already seen ballet-dancing, but we had never thought such dancing as Pavlova's and her *corps de ballet*'s could exist. We spoke of it together time and time again afterwards' (p. 65).

   Frances Niven (later Cowell) was to remain a friend of Muriel's for life, and there will be a rich correspondence between them following the research done in preparing MS's autobiography in the early 1990s. In *CV,* MS writes of her schooldays: 'for a while I had no chum, but soon I found another best friend, Frances Niven. I already knew Frances quite well. We were both deeply interested in poetry and imaginative writing of all kinds. From then, Frances was my closest friend all through my school-days' (p. 56).

3. On 24 June, MS wrote to Stanford: 'The idea of interpretation through events, letters and other accounts, on the one hand and through the works

of the author on the other, is a new one & I have come to think it is the best possible way of writing a life' (HRC). And on 3 July, she would write to Herbert Palmer: 'I have just completed a biography & introduction to the works of Anne Brontë together with Derek Stanford for Lindsay Drummond. They have now asked me to do a new life of the Brontës which I am trying desperately to get finished before their advance runs out' (HRC).

4. Stanford's review has not been identified.

5. MS may be reading David Gascoyne's collection of poems that will be published in 1950 by John Lehmann: *A Vagrant and Other Poems*.

TO DEREK STANFORD, HOUNSLOW, MIDDLESEX, 10 AUGUST 1949

1, Vicarage Gate, Kensington W.8
10 p.m. 10.8.49

My darling,

I can't go to bed without writing to tell you once more of my love for you, and I wish I could find sufficient ways in which to express it.[1]

To-day was so lovely and I hope you won't feel it misspent. It was a pity our visitors prevented us from parting properly, but hope you weren't too much delayed by our drinking interlude, nor put out by their arrival. I would rather have spoken about your poem; I am anxious about your finishing it as I think it is by far the most reflective and profound of your poems.

My darling poet, please believe my love for you and my resolution not to encroach upon your time if it is going to interfere with your proper work. Sleep well to-night, as I shall, for I know you have been with me and your presence remains. Everything in my heart is sweetness for you, and desire for your wellbeing. I long to be able to spend an unbroken period of time with you; surely, we shall be able to have our holiday together.

I must make a poem for you soon, to celebrate not only yourself but my own integration through you.

Tonight I wish you sleep, benison and balm, and wish only that

I could cover your face with my kisses before you sleep. Telephone
me soon and tell me you love me —
  Muriel Sarah

ALS. HRC.

1. Nine days earlier, on 1 August, MS began her letter to Derek Stanford:

> I am missing you to-day, and wondering about you – what you are
> saying and thinking. Are you happy or uneasy? I am happy that you
> stayed with me last night. Everything is all right now, with me.
>   My dearest, you *must* always trust me. I will *not* deceive you ever
> for I respect and love you in quite a strange and different way to any
> of my former love experiences. I am not deluding myself, for I know
> by my own reactions that I am *for* you in all that you do, without feel-
> ing any resentments at all, as I have, in the past, with others. (HRC)

TO HERBERT PALMER, ST ALBANS, HERTFORDSHIRE, 13 OCTOBER 1949

Forum, Stories and Poems, 1 Vicarage Gate, London, W.8
Editors: Muriel Spark & Derek Stanford[1]
13th October, 1949

Dear Mr Palmer,
    Derek has I believe written to you to ask if you are a member
of the Soc. of Authors, and if so, to ask if you would sponsor an
application on my behalf, to the Society of Authors for a grant.
I would be most grateful if you would do this, that is, if you feel
sufficient faith in my work.
    The position is that I have been living on my writing since
the end of June, and although I have had a lot of success I am at
present finding it very difficult to continue work on hand through
lack of funds. I was commissioned by Lindsay Drummond to
write a Life & Letters of the Brontës and also, (with Derek
Stanford) an omnibus volume of Anne Brontë's work. But before
I could complete the former, and after the latter was accepted,

other publishers announced similar titles and Lindsays' were not
willing to publish – although they were *very* pleased with the work
I had done.[2] Since June I have completed, with Derek Stanford,
a symposium volume of essays by younger critics, introduced by
us both – entitled 'Tribute to Wordsworth' – and this is being
published next spring by Allan Wingate. But the money I got for
my share in this book is not enough to cover my living expenses
while I complete further work on hand. [3]

This new work is a selection of Brontë letters for Grey Walls
Press – which will be paid for on completion; and I have also been
commissioned to write a middle-page essay in the T.L.S. on the
Brontës, but this, too, will not be paid until after publication.
Thirdly, I have prepared an anthology of American Political
verse for *Parliamentary Affairs* – but this will not be paid for until
December. I am also doing some reviewing for Life and Letters,
but although these things will eventually be remunerative, at
the moment I have not the wherewithal to complete the work
commissioned, and as I understand the Society of Authors have a
fund for the making of grants to authors in like circumstances I
shall apply to them if you will be so kind as to add your name to
Wrey Gardiner as a recommender.

I enclose a copy of Poetry Quarterly so that you may see my
recent work – a poem and an essay.[4] Please do not take this
request amiss, and I feel sure you will treat it as *confidential* – I do
not of course mind my friends knowing, but I have a few enemies I
would not care to satisfy in this way.

I hope you are well & writing more. Look forward to your book.
Best wishes
Muriel

                                    ALS on Forum letterhead. HRC.

1. In her letter to Derek Stanford of 1 August, MS scored out her own name
    as Editor of *Forum* and added a small sketch of a stick-woman next to a
    stick-man. Now, in official letterhead, she and Stanford are signalled as
    Co-editors.

2. After these two projects collapsed, in a letter of 25 August, MS proposed
    another to the publisher Lindsay Drummond, to be undertaken jointly by
    herself and Stanford: 'As we have been, for some time now, considering
    some reprints of 19th Century Classics, we are writing to enquire whether
    you might feel interested in a popular selected edition of the Letters of Jane
    Austen. We believe this work would have the double attraction of proving
    both a commercial success and of obtaining literary prestige' (WUL).
3. Forty years later, MS would recollect:

    > My first project with Derek Stanford was to edit a book on
    > Wordsworth to mark the centenary of his death in 1850. [. . .]
    > We found a sympathetic publisher in André Deutsch, then of Allan
    > Wingate, who impressed me very much by his intelligence and
    > courtesy. He went out of his way for us as if we were world-famous
    > authors instead of small-time beginners. [. . .] Derek and I earned
    > twenty-five pounds each for this book. My gross literary earnings for
    > 1949 totalled one hundred and twenty-nine pounds, five shillings.
    > (*CV*, p. 194)

4. MS sent *Poetry Quarterly*, no. 11 (Autumn 1949) which contained her poem
    'The Beads' and her essay 'Cecil Day Lewis'.

TO HERBERT PALMER, ST ALBANS, HERTFORDSHIRE, 22 OCTOBER 1949

1, Vicarage Gate, Kensington W.8
22nd October 1949

Dear M[r] Palmer,

Many thanks for your note & recommendation to the S.O.A. I
have forwarded this & am sure it will be effective.

Do try & keep better. To give way to despair at this stage would
be tragic, as I'm sure the publication of your book will bring you
renewed interest. We are all looking forward to seeing it & are
trying to get it for review.[1] I am still in bed & recovering slowly.
Derek has been looking after me & if it hadn't been for him I'd
have died, for I have no relatives & very few friends (mostly fair-
weather) in London.[2]

I am getting plenty of work in & hope to get down to it on
Monday. The Soc. of Authors have written in reply to my letter,

saying they are carefully considering my case & that a letter from *you* will help.

One thing worries me. I'm afraid I am going to have difficulty in getting a vol. of poems published. I have tried Routledge without success & my poems are at present with Chatto. Although I like critical work & must do it to earn a living it is poetry that is nearest my heart. It wounds me to have *no time* to write a poem when I want to. I suppose I am not unique in this respect. I would really rather see one book of verse of mine in print than all the other publications put together.

Do take care of yourself & try and get well again, for you can't be spared from the world of letters.

Best wishes from us both
Muriel

ALS. HRC.

1. In her letter of 17 October to Herbert Palmer, MS wrote: 'We were so distressed to hear of your illness and do hope you will recover soon from this vile malady. Some say shingles is mainly a nervous trouble – but of course who isn't nervous these days?' (HRC). Palmer's *The Old Knight: A Poem Sequence for the Present Times* was due for publication by J. M. Dent & Sons.
2. In her letter of 17 October, MS reported to Palmer: 'Shortly after writing you I succumbed with an infection of the chest & lungs & am now in bed with threatened pleurisy. Have always had a weak chest. Added to my present troubles this enforced cessation of work is worrying me considerably, particularly as the D^r's bills are mounting up. – I haven't been stamping my N. Health cards – can't afford it – so can't call on a N. Health D^r to attend me!'

TO HERBERT PALMER, ST ALBANS, HERTFORDSHIRE, 2 NOVEMBER 1949

1, Vicarage Gate, Kensington, London, W.8
2nd November, 1949

Dear Mr Palmer,

This is a hasty note to let you know that I have received £30 from the Society of Authors. Thank you very much for your efforts on my behalf, which I am sure were invaluable in obtaining this relief for me.

How are you keeping? Derek Stanford and I send our best wishes for your quick recovery & hope to have an opportunity of seeing you soon.

With best wishes & thanks.

Yours sincerely,

Muriel Spark

ALS. HRC.

1950

MS found herself in serious need of gainful employment, yet by
March she had given up her part-time position at the journal *European
Affairs*. She edited the second (and final) issue of *Forum*, contributed
regularly to journals such as *Public Opinion*, and submitted poems to
publications as far afield as Los Angeles. She was disappointed in her
hopes that her biography of the Brontës, commissioned by Lindsay
Drummond, would come to fruition; and that her proposal for an
edition of the complete works of Anne Brontë would be accepted.
Her most significant literary project required research into the life of
Mary Shelley, in preparation of a critical biography which she completed in September. She contracted with publisher Peter Nevill to
write a book on John Masefield and visited the elderly poet laureate
to gain his consent and cooperation. She celebrated the release of
Tribute to Wordsworth, co-authored with Derek Stanford, with whom
her relationship was deepening. She visited her family in Edinburgh
in March, holidayed with them at Morecambe in late August, and
moved flats to Sussex Mansions, South Kensington, in June. Her
financial precariousness towards the end of the year prompted her
to apply in November – unsuccessfully – to the Royal Literary Fund
for support.

TO DEREK STANFORD, HOUNSLOW, MIDDLESEX,
16 MARCH 1950

160 Bruntsfield Place, Edinburgh
16/3/50

My Darling-one,

How sad I was to part from you last night. I didn't sleep but
thought of you with much nostalgia. It was sweet of you to spill
me on the train fortified with gin which was much needed. Are
you missing me? Sweet love, have a good rest for you *must* be
tired.[1]

Robin is full of beans but *much* thinner after his illness. He has
exams at school to-day which I don't suppose he will do well in,
being excited about my coming. I'm going to see his head mistress
this afternoon to see if he can stay on at this school another
year.[2] The family were pleased to see me – have been boozing all
morning. I am getting a new watch *and* the new clock and am to
keep the money as I hoped.

I am seeking out a bonny present for you my sweet love whom I
need very much.

Rob. has been busy with his garden & has crocuses etc. actually
coming up. He knows about transplanting & things. He also
has a butterfly collection & a beetle collection. Also a pen-knife
collection. I suppose he is at the collecting stage.

I must go now & wash my ugly pan ready to face lame M^r.
Jameson – Robin's headmaster.[3] Tomorrow I shall try to see
Nelson's publishers for you never know.[4]

Darling my bonny boy, I do long to be with you again. I'll write
again tomorrow to tell you when I'll be coming. Will also *wire* you
as I may not know definitely tomorrow.

Have other news, quite good, to tell you when we meet,
dear love,

Think happily of your
Muriel

ALS. HRC.

1. In an undated letter written from Edinburgh, MS wrote to Derek Stanford: 'Have been trying to read but without much success. I miss my Boy & his patent-medicine-High-Altar (like the Aunt Léonie in Proust who kept by her bedside "everything that she needed for the performance, in bed, of her duties to soul and body, to keep the proper times for pepsin and for vespers")' (HRC).
2. Eleven-year-old Robin Spark was attending James Gillespie's Primary School, as his mother had before him. The head mistress of the girls' primary school was a Miss Bertha Mackay, and of the boys' school a Mr Jameson; MS seems to be preparing to see them both.
3. The word 'pan' signifies 'skull' or 'cranium' in Scots.
4. ThomasNelson was a publishing house founded in Edinburgh in 1798, specialising in books with a religious content. MS may have been seeking to interest the publisher in her proposal for a book of Mary Shelley's letters, a proposal she had already put to Macmillan Ltd, in a letter dated 21 January.

TO DEREK STANFORD, HOUNSLOW, MIDDLESEX,
17 MARCH 1950

160 Bruntsfield Place, Edinburgh
17.3.50

Bonny Boy,

Your letter woke me this morning, which was indeed the next best thing to finding you there. I didn't sleep well as my new alarm clock woke me at *4 a.m.* like the Lindfield one. The whole house had a cup of tea and went back to bed.

I think Nine, from what you say, is on the way to being all the things its printed 'manifesto' said it wasn't going to be.[1] Personally I feel stultified as a poet by its vogueishness and slightly vituperative spirit. I knew of course that Nine would proclaim the cocktail party as a great work of art – as immoderate as John Russell's condemnation. I'd like to read it again, but so far I still think that there are two ways of looking at it. 1) As a play someone has written in the mid-twentieth century, in which case it comes off in a mediocre way – that is, it is twenty years behind the earlier psychological plays, and attempts to reconcile psychoanalytical extremes – ending in nihilism – with the

Christianity of the gospels, though not of St. Paul etc. On another level, it preaches a moral favourable to matrimony. 2) The second way of looking at it I think is to see it as a marriage feast wherefor the funeral baked meats of Eliot's *Waste Land* are coldly furnished forth. For although the *Waste Land* meats were certainly baked for consumption at the funeral, at least they were hot.[2]

But I may change my mind on re-reading.

My best bonny, do you still miss me? I do, you. There is a wonderfully clear light to-day, a *moving* light blowing down from the Pentland Hills. But I can only half appreciate anything without you. We must go to the country soon.

Everything here goes quite satisfactory, with some prospects for the future that seem to have cheered up the family a bit. I have lots to tell you besides that I love you dearly as well you should know.

I saw Robin's headmaster yesterday & they have agreed to keep him on another year. They recommend an art school for him, very strongly, & seem to think he has talents in that direction. The idea suits Robin who is delighted to think he won't have to learn spelling any more. He has painted quite an interesting picture using some tins of enamel he found in the house.

I doubt if I can get away with grace before Sunday night, but will know tomorrow morning when some friends who are invited to tea on Sat. *or* Sunday are going to ring my mother to say which day. So I'll wire you sweetheart, tomorrow.

My best dear boy I do long to see your bonny face again. Think of me meantime with sweet thoughts.

Muriel

ALS. HRC.

1. Edited by the poet and translator Peter Russell, vol. 1, no. 1 of the journal *Nine* was published in October 1949. Immediately following its first Editorial appears 'A Message from T. S. Eliot, O.M.': 'You have asked me for a "message" for the first number of NINE. [. . .] What you really need is neither notorious names, nor a constant flow of new ones. You do not need, either, a "programme" – I note with pleasure that your circular does not contain a manifesto. The one thing necessary is a small number

of devoted writers working together – disagreeing about many things, but seeing eye to eye about humbug.' If not a 'manifesto', the Editorial did indeed develop a programme of sorts, if only by way of rejection of a certain view of poetry:

> The 'traditionalists', as they call themselves, have betrayed the tradition. Their roots go no deeper than 1880, their leaves and their flowers are only coated with the milk and the honey of the richest and sweetest past. They are a dowdy lot.
>
> And these sub-men have the temerity to hate. And the singers and dancers they have chosen to hate are the singers and dancers who have made immediate all that teeming past, and offered it in all its proud informing quality to those who had lost it, or never known of it. Joyce, Lewis, Pound, Eliot, Lawrence have been insulted, jeered at, oppressed.

2. T. S. Eliot's *The Cocktail Party* had been staged but not yet published when Peter Russell reviewed it in *Nine*, where he wrote, in 'A Note on T. S. Eliot's New Play': 'In spite of difficulties encountered by both audience and newspaper critics, the play was an outstanding success. Considering the fact that the actors neither knew their parts well nor even professed to understand them, only strengthens one's conviction that *The Cocktail Party* will take its place with others of Mr. Eliot's works among the great achievements of our time.' John Russell's review, 'Mr. Eliot's Comedy', which appeared on 12 March in the *Sunday Times*, concluded:

> Mr. Eliot is too big a writer to be judged by any but the highest standards; and there is in this play an element of patronage, a basic incuriosity, which suggests that consultation with eminent men of letters can never be a substitute for direct and affectionate observation of human life. 'The Cocktail Party' has been accepted by many as a profound commentary upon modern morals; but there will, I fancy, be others for whom it will call to mind the injunction 'Physician, heal thyself.'

Speaking of the speed with which his father's funeral was followed by his mother's remarriage, Hamlet remarks:

> Thrift, thrift, Horatio, the funeral bak'd-meats
> Did coldly furnish forth the marriage tables.

(*Hamlet*, I, ii, 180–1, in *The Riverside Shakespeare: The Complete Works*, ed. G. Blakemore Evans, Houghton Mifflin, 1997; all subsequent Shakespeare quotations are from this edition – henceforth in the notes *RS*)

TO GROVER JACOBY, EDITOR, VARIEGATION,
LOS ANGELES, 21 MAY 1950

1, Vicarage Gate, Kensington, London, W.8
21st May, 1950

Dear Mr. Jacoby,

I am delighted to learn of your new magazine 'Recurrence'
which I am sure under your editorship will prove an excellent
companion-journal to 'Variegations' [*sic*]. May I wish your venture
all success! Over here there is an increasing trend towards rhymed
and formal verse, and where it is not merely *pastiche* but embodies
contemporary feeling it is often successful.[1]

I have been writing little verse lately, being busy on my new
critical-biography of Mary Shelley, due out next spring. In the
Autumn my two Brontë books are appearing. I wonder if you have
seen 'Tribute to Wordsworth' – a selection of essays past and
present edited by Derek Stanford and myself, for the centenary of
Wordsworth's death. It hasn't been published in the U.S. as yet,
but I understand it is selling quite well there. I should always be
pleased to hear of your own literary activities, though I imagine
your editorial work takes up a fair amount of your time.

The enclosed poems may suit your new magazine, but if not I
may perhaps be permitted to submit others from time to time.

The mortality rate of poetry-publishing magazines has been
particularly heavy over here. You will have heard that Horizon
closed down; so too did The New English Weekly, with such a
personality as T. S. Eliot on its editorial board! The latest casualties
are Life and Letters, The Leader and News Review – the latter
did not, however, print poetry but most of the younger writers
reviewed there constantly. So, you see, we are particularly pleased
when American journals offer us their hospitality as you are doing.

With all good wishes,
Yours sincerely,
s/Muriel Spark
(Muriel Spark)

P.S. I must express my thanks to you for complying with my request in sending your cheque to my small nephew. This was a great help to me.[2]

    s/MS

TLS. UCLA.

1. Grover Jacoby inaugurated *Variegation: A Free Verse Quarterly* in Los Angeles in 1946; to this he was now adding *Recurrence: A Quarterly of Rhyme.*
2. MS's nephew David Camberg was nearly six years old at the time; an explanation for her asking Jacoby to direct the cheque to him is offered in her letter of 10 August 1951 to Jacoby, where she writes, 'I returned the cheque to my small nephew in the U.S. (he is now in Alabama) so it will no doubt go through my brother's account. I tell you this in case there should be any query. It is my only way of making a gift to the child, owing to current dollar restrictions' (UCLA).

TO IRIS BIRTWISTLE, HOGHTON, LANCASHIRE, 24 JULY 1950

8, Sussex Mansions, 65, Old Brompton Road, London S.W.7
24th July, 1950

My dear Iris,

First I was moving, then I was behind-hand with work and you know how it is. But I was delighted with your letter & hope through my lateness in writing I haven't missed you in London.[1]

Derek Stanford and I are esconced [*sic*] here in a large room & kitchen. Forum is behind time as usual & I doubt if we'll manage a number before late autumn when of course you shall have dozens of copies. Derek is writing a critical work on Christopher Fry whom he knew in the army, while I'm straining to finish a critical-biography of Mary Shelley for the end of September. So here I live half in the 19th century & half in the 20th & no time to read for pleasure which is galling enough. Yet in spite of poverty, debts and all the rest we console & encourage each other and are happy.

Now keep out of hospital if you can. I have a great fear

of hospitals with their barbarous hygiene and devastating systematicness and terrible cleanliness, and would advise all people I like never to enter one. Your experience at Asprey's reminds me of mine in a publicity office which nearly did for me.[2]

We both like all your poems and can't decide what to keep if we may be so selfish as to keep one for so uncertain a date as the next publication-day of Forum.[3] Will add our decision to the end of this letter. Are you preparing a vol? There's not much chance even for good poets these days but I think you might be successful in placing a vol as your poems have freshness. I haven't been, tho' I have tried about five publishers and have given up meantime as can't afford the packing, stamps, energy & time to send them out. I can get any amount of prose work commissioned but to offer poetry to a publisher is like giving processed cheese to T. S. Eliot or a decomposed herring to Rita Hayworth.

Ring me when you come to London. I shall be away betw. 19th & 26th August & at the end of September but hope to see you in between.

Best love,

Muriel

P.S. The typewriter ticks on as usual and I hope I can have it for a time to come tho' will render it up with grace as soon as you need it. Don't know what I would have done without it.[4]

We would like to keep 'I make reply in country terms' – a lovely piece.[5]

ALS. CBF.

1. MS had moved to her new address at Sussex Mansions a little more than one month previously – 'a furnished room in the flat of Mr and Mrs Andipatin, a fine couple from Mauritius' (*CV*, p. 197). Since 1948, she had corresponded and become friends with the poet, and generous benefactress, Iris Birtwistle through the *Poetry Review*, to which Birtwistle submitted poems; the typewriter on which MS was producing much of her work at this time belonged to Birtwistle; she was a staunch Roman Catholic (as distinct from an Anglo-Catholic) who came from a wealthy Lancashire mill-owning family.

2. Asprey was, and remains, a renowned manufacturer and seller of jewellery and luxury goods, to clients including the British royal family. Why MS refers to Asprey is unclear, as Birtwistle never worked there, whereas MS had been deeply unhappy with her speech-writing and publicity work for Pearson Horder.

3. MS published Birtwistle's poem 'Star of the Sea' in the first issue of *Forum*, and later in 1950 would publish 'Letter to a Sailor' in *Forum*'s second and last issue.

4. On 3 July 1949, MS wrote to Birtwistle:

> How greatly I enjoyed meeting you and some of your family! I wish you could have stayed in London longer & we could have arranged another meeting. First I must tell you about the typewriter. By now it is all mended up & ticks along like a little steam engine – for the modest sum of four pounds ten. I quite expected to have to spend much more on it & would have willingly done so. Therefore I am more than delighted to have the use of it for a time. I shall take great care of it, as you know. (CBF)

5. This piece will not appear in *Forum*.

Iris Birtwistle in Majorca

TO IRIS BIRTWISTLE, HOGHTON, LANCASHIRE,
7 AUGUST 1950

8, Sussex Mansions, 65 Old Brompton Road, S.W.7
7th August, 1950

My dear Iris,

August Bank Holiday & all it implies finds us both somewhat
weary, having no garden & the park no doubt looking like
Frith's Margate Sands.[1] The very name *Bank* holiday sounds
so grim don't you think; imagine what we've come to when
we have to celebrate a holiday because the banks close (or
so I suppose). Why can't we have a holiday for Counting the
Grass, or a Lie-abed Day or a Broody Day or anything that
means a proper holiday? Derek who takes the historical view
of everything would say the rot set in with Oliver Cromwell I
expect.

It was really nice to see you again and Derek declares his
partiality for yourself as much as for your poems. Will you come
and see us again soon, and we shall fetch Wrey and a few friends
to make a party? Will you bring gay Angela with you?[2]

It was cheering to have your letter and I'm enormously
delighted with the elegant hankies which you ought by no means
to have sent. Derek tells me they are classical hankies from the
literary point of view and right-wing from the political, since
all things must have a category but he's wrong because I am a
romantic writer and voted Labour in the last election yet dearly
love my new hankies.

That is good news about your poem in Tribune which we are
looking out for.[3] I hope you will let us see what you write apart
from contributions to Forum and tell us what you read because
we would like to know. My prose work prevents me from
reading as much poetry as I'd like but I try to read some for an
hour or two at nights and have just made the personal discovery
of Marvell, by which I mean I always knew he was there but only
feel the impact now. I'm sending you my latest poem which is a

light-weight moan of sorts based on Verlaine's poem 'Le ciel est
par dessus le toit' which he wrote in prison, and if you know the
story already forgive me for not being able to resist telling how
Verlaine was jailed for shooting his homosexual lover Rimbaud.
They had a mighty quarrel and after Verlaine had shot Rimbaud
in the hand they made it up but an hour later Verlaine was
provoked to seize the pistol again, whereupon Rimbaud fled in
mortal terror to the police & was full of repentance when it was
too late to stop the law from its course. But they were friends
again when Verlaine came out. At one time the two poets came
to England – that was in the 1870's. They took lodgings and kept
house in turns. One day Rimbaud leaned out of the window &
saw Verlaine coming along the street with a fish in one hand and
a bottle of oil in the other. Rimbaud hailed his friend with a hoot
of mirth and shouted What a droll figure you look, you should
see yourself coming up the lane with a fish in one hand and a
bottle of oil in the other. So Verlaine came indoors & threw the
fish at Rimbaud. Later Rimbaud went native in Abyssinia & died
of syphillis [*sic*], which killed Verlaine too. Great poets hardly
ever die of old age it seems.

I don't know now if I'm going to Morecambe or somewhere
else but will ring you if I'm near you between the 22nd and 29th
& if you're free we must meet somewhere. Take care of yourself
and try & keep out of the hands of doctors. But don't get cured
entirely as glowing health is bad for poetry – truly, I have been
nurturing a state of acute anaemia these many years because the
iron tablets which are always proscribed [*sic*] normalise my health
and destroy my imagination.

Yours affectionately,
s/Muriel

P.S. Dear Iris,

*I wish I could remember dates exactly. Muriel says that after the shoot-
up Verlaine & Rimbaud were friends once more. I'm almost certain that
they were not, even though they met once or twice to see if they could
find a way back to each other. In the interests of a rather inexact truth,*

Muriel has told me that I should add this; though if she ever discovers that I'm wrong God help my peace of mind & masculine 'respect' (a nebulous quality at the best of times).

   Your gin was a tippler's delight & solace to us. M. took it for her 'feminine ailment' & wept for an hour after Christopher Fry (who was visiting the next night) had left. She told me in broken accents à la Lady of Shallott, that it was her 'Great Sorrow!' but I secretly suspect that it was really an unrequited passion for England's greatest verse-dramatist (don't you agree — about the latter, I mean).

   Hope we shall see you anon.

   Best wishes

   Derek S.

VILLANELLE

Like poor Verlaine, whom God defend,
I see the sky above the roof,
And write my book till summer's end.

When tree, town, bell and birdnote blend
I feel, since summer sails aloof,
Like poor Verlaine, whom God defend.

Who went to jail but did not mend;
I taste the pity sure enough
And write my book till summer's end.

I see a tree, and won't pretend
I'm warped on that nostalgic woof
Like poor Verlaine, whom God defend.

But rue the crooked dividend
These days will yield of galley-proof,
And write my book till summer's end.

Therefore I see the sky and spend
An hour of lyrical reproof,
Like poor Verlaine, whom God defend,
And write my book till summer's end.

MURIEL SPARK[4]

TLS with handwritten Stanford PS,
and attached MS's poem 'Villanelle'. CBF.

1. In 1950, the summer Bank Holiday was not due until 26 August, and so either MS has misdated her (typed) letter or she is anticipating her lack of interesting prospects for the holiday.
    The painting by William Powell Frith to which MS refers is *Ramsgate Sands (Life at the Seaside)*, painted in 1851–4 and depicting a very crowded beach.
2. Angela Birtwistle (later Kirby) was the youngest of Iris Birtwistle's seven siblings; born in 1932, she would, like her elder sister, go on to be a published poet.
3. In the event, no poem by Iris Birtwistle was published in *Tribune* in 1950.
4. With the exception of a change of title to 'Verlaine Villanelle', and a comma added at the end of line 4, this poem is published unaltered in MS's *Complete Poems* (p. 11).

TO HERBERT PALMER, ST ALBANS, HERTFORDSHIRE, EARLY AUGUST 1950

8, Sussex Mansions, 65 Old Brompton Rd., S.W.7

Dear Mr Palmer,
    Here is Kathleen Raine's latest book tho' it is not her best. Many of her best earlier pieces are quoted in full in Derek's 'Freedom of Poetry'.[1]
    I also enclose proofs of a small selection of Emily Brontë I have made for Grey Walls & if you have time to read the introduction I should be very grateful for your comments. Please let me have the proofs back some time – there's no hurry for the books.
    We thoroughly enjoyed our two visits to you – everything from

the landscape to the conversation & do please thank Mrs Palmer
for her kind hospitality and welcome.

I am reading your 'Post-Victorian Poetry' – rather, I have just
started, and am much enjoying it. I shd. think this would be
a more valuable authority for my work on the Georgians than
Swinnerton's 'Georgian Literary Scene' which I consider evades
the specific question of poetry wherever it arises. It's a queer
thing, but many scholars who have wide social view of things fail
as critics when they come to consider *specific* manifestation of
society, such as poetry.[2]

I am interested, of course, in the social conditions that gave
birth to the Georgians & also their popularity, but the ultimate
question must be 'What is the value of the actual poetry?' Many
of the Georgians wrote competent poetry – all of them wrote one
or two poems worth preserving (in fact, it seems as if they set out
each to write an anthology piece or two), but none of them – I
mean the self-acknowledged 'Georgians' – wrote poetry of any
stature or were great poets.

Do you agree? And do you agree that there might be some root
explanation for it, in the fact that there were so *many* Georgian
poets and that in acquiring a certain 'mass' inspiration, inspiration
itself became diffused & weakened? – After all, there are many
more 'poets' writing to-day than even thirty–fifty years ago – yet
inspiration seems to become weaker & weaker in each.

Perhaps 'inspiration' is in itself an absolute, having its own
being, and limits – and, maybe, where it is concentrated on a few
poets instead of spread out over many, the results are fewer, but
greater, poets.

We are looking forward to seeing you again & hope you can
come to London before the winter sets in.

With best regards to Mrs Palmer from us both & renewed
thanks for your welcome to us.

Yours sincerely,
Muriel

ALS. HRC. Dating: from subsequent letters
dated August and from Herbert Palmer to MS.

1. Kathleen Raine's most recent book, published by Hamish Hamilton, was *The Pythoness, and Other Poems*.
2. Herbert Palmer's *Post-Victorian Poetry* was published in 1938 by J. M. Dent and Sons Ltd; Frank Swinnerton's *The Georgian Literary Scene* was published originally by William Heinemann in 1935, and was reissued by Hutchinson in 1950.

TO DEREK STANFORD, HOUNSLOW, MIDDLESEX, CIRCA 25 AUGUST 1950

[The Lake District, England]

This is presumably the field where Wordsworth fucked Dora.[1] After a long dive [*sic*] during which I longed for a piddle we reached the lake which is supposed to be 10 miles long. The driver pointed out a ruined castle en route also Kay Shoes Factory.[2] I am now going to see where W. f'd the leech gatherer but judging from the mist that obscures all, I should think it might have taken place anywhere unnoticed.[3]

    Love
    Sara[4]

> APCS showing 'Dora's Field, Rydal'. HRC. Dating based on MS's visit to the Lake District, between 19 and 26 August 1950.

1. MS was on holiday with her parents and son in Morecambe, from where she visited the Lake District, home to William Wordsworth (on whom she and Derek Stanford had recently written). Knowingly or not, she conflates the Dorothy who was Wordsworth's sister – with whom he was rumoured to have had an incestuous relationship – and the Dorothy who was his daughter, known as 'Dora', after whom was named the field that is situated next to St Mary's Church in Rydal and that is depicted on her postcard.
2. The K Shoes factory in Kendal was one of the major employers in the region.
3. Wordsworth writes of his – decidedly unerotic – encounter with a leech gatherer near his home in Grasmere in his 1802 poem 'Resolution and Independence'.
4. MS signs using her middle name (officially spelt 'Sarah').

TO P. H. NEWBY, TALKS DEPARTMENT, BBC, LONDON,
17 OCTOBER 1950

8 Sussex Mansions, 65 Old Brompton Road, S.W.7
17th October, 1950

Dear Mr. Newby,

I have posted my critical-biography of Mary Shelley to you, in typescript form. I don't know if you will want to read through it all – it's rather a hefty amount. Perhaps the first and last chapters of the biography, and some of the critical chapters will give you an idea of what I've covered.[1]

Will you please attach to the typescript, the Introduction, which you still have?

As the book won't be out until after the centenary, I would much like to give a Talk, saying something about her life and then enlarging on her works. In the book, of course I have gone into very great detail, as it is the first critical study of Mary Shelley; but I am used to writing in a more compressed form.[2]

I would be glad to have the t/s back as soon as conveniently possible, as it has to be sent to America.

Yours sincerely,
s/Muriel Spark
(Muriel Spark)

TLS. BBC WAC.

1. On 23 September, MS wrote to the Director of Talks at the BBC, enclosing her Introduction: 'I have just completed a critical-biography of Mary Wollstonecraft Shelley, which will be published next January in time for the centenary of her death on 1st February 1951' (BBC WAC). On 29 September, her letter was answered by P. H. Newby, producer at the Talks Department, who expressed his interest. After serving in World War II, Newby had written two novels, *Journey to the Interior*, published in 1945, and *Agents and Witnesses*, published in 1947, which together had established his literary reputation. He was recruited by the BBC in 1949 with a view to developing series of literary talks, and would go on to have a thirty-year career there, while continuing to publish his own writings.

2. Of MS's *Child of Light: A Reassessment of Mary Wollstonecraft Shelley*, Martin
    Stannard writes:

> *Child of Light* is a remarkable book – the first serious attempt to re-
> claim Mary Shelley's writings and influence from her more famous
> husband's shadow. [. . .] The book's general line of defence is to
> rebut the then dismissive characterisation of Mary as a dull and
> depressive companion for Shelley. Muriel cleans off this sludge of
> sexist varnish and restores a portrait of a woman of intellect, 'prac-
> tical, staunch, rational and broad-minded', courageous in the face of
> poverty, public abuse, her beloved father's insensitivity, the deaths of
> most of her children, and, of course, of Shelley himself. Above all,
> we see the artist, always observing, always reading, always talking,
> and talking to herself in her journals. (*MSB*, pp. 115–16)

TO THE SECRETARY, THE ROYAL LITERARY FUND, LONDON, 3 NOVEMBER 1950

8, Sussex Mansions, 65, Old Brompton Road, London, S.W.7
3rd November, 1950

Dear Sir,

I have heard of your literary fund, and I am applying to you,
since I am a writer in rather urgent financial difficulties.[1]

I am 32 years of age. In 1947–48 I was editor of the Poetry
Review and general-secretary of the Poetry Society, during which
time I made it a policy to publish younger, professional writers,
and to see that they were paid, which had not been the practice
hitherto. But ultimately this policy clashed with the views of the
Council, and I resigned.

I took a job with a journal, *European Affairs*, and in 1949 I was
commissioned by Messrs. Lindsay Drummond to write a biography
of the Brontës. I was also commissioned by them to edit and
introduce Anne Brontë's complete works. I retained my job and
worked on the books in my spare time. But Lindsay Drummonds
went into liquidation, and the books were never published,
although I had received an advance sum of £50 on the biography.

At the end of 1949, I was commissioned by Pen-in-Hand Books, Oxford, to write a critical-biography of Mary Wollstonecraft Shelley, to appear in February 1951 for the centenary of her death. I received £20 against royalties, and according to my contract was to receive a further £30 on receipt of the manuscript. While writing the book I became ill, and was unable to continue my job during the summer, though I managed to finish the book, working full-time upon it. I sent it to Pen-in-Hand in the middle of October, and on applying for my £30, I now learn that there is very little likelihood of the book appearing, as they are possibly liquidating. Added to that, a further book, a collection of Mary Shelley's letters, was to have been edited by me for Pen-in-Hand, for which I was to have received £25 on receipt of manuscript. But this, too, will not appear.

It seems incredible that four books should have been commissioned within so short a time, and suffer the same fate. But this is unfortunately the case. I am hoping to place my critical-biography of Mary Shelley with some other publisher, but this will take time. And meanwhile, I am very hard pressed for money, and, in fact, at present am living on borrowed money while trying to find a job. I am also, of course, trying hard to extract the £30 which is immediately due to me from Pen-in-Hand; but although I have been to the expense of a trip to Oxford to see a director of the firm, he did not keep his appointment, and I fear they have no money.

I have, however, done other literary work during 1949–50: a selection of the Brontë letters and an edition of Emily Brontë's poems, with introductions for Grey Walls Press. These books are now in production, and I have proofs. In collaboration with another writer, Derek Stanford, I edited 'Tribute to Wordsworth' which was published by Allan Wingate, and for which I received £25 as my share. For the books at present in production at Grey Walls Press, I am not to receive payment until they appear.

I have also been earning some money by reviewing in *Public Opinion*, occasionally in *The Spectator* and *The Times Literary Supplement*, and by several poems which have been published in

Public Opinion, The Fortnightly, World Review and *Poetry Quarterly.* I
have some reviewing on hand, and have been commissioned to
give a Third Programme talk on Mary Shelley in February, but I
shall not be paid for these, for some time.

My son, aged twelve, is, through unfortunate circumstances,
entirely my liability. He is at present living with my mother in
Scotland, but I have been unable to contribute towards his upkeep
and schooling for some time, owing to illness and the financial
disappointments I have mentioned. My mother is kind enough to
care for the child during my present difficulty, but the liability is
none the less mine.

I ought to mention that last year when I was in financial
difficulties through Lindsay Drummonds' failure to publish my
books, I received a grant of £30 from the Society of Authors, and
I did not think then, that I would be in an even worse position
this year. Nor would I have been, had not my publishers failed me
again. I have not approached the Society of Authors a second time,
since I have learned that their funds are very low, and feel it could
hardly be expected of them to come to my rescue once more.

I must apologise for the length of this letter, but wished to give
you full details; and I should be very grateful if you could place
the matter before your committee.

The doctor who attended me during my illness would give me
a medical certificate should you wish one; and some people who
know of my work and private affairs – Mr. Christmas Humphreys,
and Mr. Wrey Gardiner, editor of *Public Opinion* and director of
Grey Walls Press, have said they will write to you on my behalf, if
it will help. And I can also let you see the work I have done.

Hoping to hear from you,

I am,

Yours sincerely,

- s/Muriel Spark

(Muriel Spark)

TLS. RLFA.

1. Established in 1790 to help writers experiencing financial difficulties, the Royal Literary Fund gave support to such notable authors as Samuel Taylor Coleridge, D. H. Lawrence, James Joyce, and Dylan Thomas.

    Handwritten on the top margin of the present letter: 'Form sent – interview suggested Wed. 22 Nov. or Wed. 24 Nov. [*sic*] – 3.30 Committee 13 December. JSB'.

TO THE EDITOR, PUBLIC OPINION, LONDON, MID-NOVEMBER 1950

Old Brompton Rd., S.W.7

Kindness or Weakness?

Your correspondent, Mrs. Birrell, says that Nationalist policy in South Africa is to keep the native down, and that 'the native understands this sort of treatment. To him kindness is a kind of weakness.' That was not my experience, though I have heard the phrase often enough.[1]

My own observations are mainly drawn from S. Rhodesia, where I spent six and a half years, though I lived in the Union as well.[2] The Rhodesian native is even less 'advanced' than the Union native, whom your correspondent states to be 400 years behind the white man, and so I assume that my remarks are equally relevant. In all the time I was in Africa, I can honestly say that I never met a native who took advantage of a kindness. True, I was robbed of food, but I knew, and they knew that I knew. On the other hand, I experienced many kindnesses from natives. They struck me as being childishly simple, with an inexhaustible capacity for sitting in the sun and laughing at apparently nothing. I don't believe these people respond well to hard-handed treatment any more than children do.

    Muriel Spark

                    Letter published in *Public Opinion*, 17 November 1950.

1. Founded in 1861, *Public Opinion* was a journal to which MS herself contributed. The letter of Mrs Birrell, who gave a London address but signed

herself '*A South African*', was headed 'South Africa without Smuts'. In addition to what MS cites, she wrote: 'The native is about 400 years behind the
white man in civilization. This is the point that the Englishman does not
realise. There never could be, at this stage, equality between the white and
the black populations. If equal rights were given to the black population,
there would be black supremacy, resulting in chaos. [. . .] How can any
Englishman judge if he has not lived in South Africa?' (10 November 1950).
2. MS sailed for Southern Rhodesia, then a self-governing British Crown
colony, in August 1937; she left what was then named the Union of South
Africa in February 1944.

TO JOHN MASEFIELD, ABINGDON, BERKSHIRE,
28 NOVEMBER 1950

8, Sussex Mansions, 65, Old Brompton Road, London, S.W.7
28th November, 1950

Dear Mr. Masefield,

I have been a student and admirer of your work for many years,
and have long hoped to give permanent, published form to my
appreciation and studies.[1] Though I have been engaged on literary
work, I have not felt, so far, that the time was propitious for a
book on your work, by a younger critic. Now, however, in view
of a recent tendency for poetry to return to formal and lucid
expression, I believe an appreciative study of your achievements
would be especially rewarding to a younger generation of readers.

My publishers, Messrs. Peter Nevill, have agreed to commission
my proposed work, but I am, of course, anxious to obtain your
approval of my plan; and I trust you will not consider it presumptious
[*sic*] in me to add the following notes on the factors I hope to stress.

The first object of my book would be to show your uniqueness —
that is, to rectify the current critical theory which associates
you too closely with the 'Georgian' group of poets, than whom I
believe you to be a poet of infinitely greater imaginative vigour.

I should also hope to reveal the aspects of your art which
will particularly benefit those readers and students of poetry
whose appreciative sensibility has been conditioned by modern

criticism – by the close analysis of text, and the examination of
various ways of using language in poetry. On this subject, I feel that
it should be recognised that you are the first poet in this century
to adapt 'the very language of men' to poetry, and thus I should
attempt to trace the very strong influence which your diction,
subject-matter and forms, have exerted on this century's verse.[2]
I am particularly interested in your handling of conversational
language, and, although I do not know if such an observation will
commend itself to you, I believe that if you had not written the
opening stanzas of *The Everlasting Mercy*, certain passages of dialogue
in *The Waste Land* would have been expressed far differently. I should
also like to deal with the influences of past literature on your work.[3]

I should, of course, devote considerable attention to you as a
narrative poet, tracing the course of the English narrative poem
to the present time, and showing its complex development in
your work. And the fact that your narrative poetry is successfully
intended for the voice as well as for the eye, should profit a new
generation of poets and readers to whom broadcasting offers a
wide scope for spoken verse. On the question of your narrative
poetry, I feel that your innovations here, represent your primary
contribution to English literature; and that their strength lies
partly in the Chaucerian objectivity of your statement. Many
narrative poems in our language have failed, I think, because of a
subjective attitude on the part of the poet – a moralising attitude,
with the effect of sentimentality, which is absent in your works.

Another aspect of your poetry I should like to treat, is that
of you as a poet of sea-scape, since curiously, the Nature-poetry
of this sea-faring island has been mainly occupied with pastoral
themes. I would try to illustrate your profound knowledge and
love of the sea and all its manifestations, and to show how you
have brough [*sic*] sea and sea-faring to life in poetry, with the same
detailed observation as John Clare attached to the land.

These are but scraps and suggestions of what I have in mind.
The work would, of course, cover your shorter poems, your plays,
fiction, and your own pronouncements on poetry.

My publishers have suggested that a biographical section to the book would serve as a background or 'spiritual landscape' to the critique; but this will, of course, rest with your judgment.

I must apologise for the length of this letter, but I have been concerned to give you some idea of my proposed book, and would very much welcome your comments, with any guidance you should be kind enough to offer, and also your views on a biographical section.

I must apologise, also, for lengthening this letter still further by adding some personal 'credentials', since I am sure you have never heard of me.

My critical work (which Mr. Herbert Palmer has commended) and my poems, have appeared in journals which include The Times Literary Supplement, The Spectator, World Review, The Fortnightly, The New English Weekly, New English Review, Public Opinion (for which I review regularly), Life and Letters, Poetry Quarterly, Punch, and in some anthologies.

I have edited and introduced the following books:

'Tribute to Wordsworth' (in collaboration)

'Letters of the Brontës'

'Poems of Emily Brontë'

'Letters of Mary Shelley' (in collaboration)

and my critical-biography of Mary Shelley will be appearing next year. I am also giving a Third Programme talk on her novels.

I hope I have conveyed to you a little of my enthusiasm for your work (which dates from the time when, as a young schoolgirl, I heard you read in Edinburgh), and for the present project.

Hoping to hear from you,

I am,

Yours sincerely,

(Muriel Spark)

TLcc. NLS.

1. Appreciation of John Masefield's work, both the poetry and the fiction, had been in decline for some time, especially in literary and academic circles

appreciative of modernism – a decline that his appointment as poet laureate in 1930 had done nothing to mitigate.

2. MS adapts the central idea with which William Wordsworth opens his 1800 Preface to the second edition of *Lyrical Ballads*: 'The first volume of these Poems has already been submitted to general perusal. It was published, as an experiment, which, I hoped, might be of some use to ascertain, how far, by fitting to metrical arrangement a selection of the real language of men in a state of vivid sensation, that sort of pleasure and that quantity of pleasure may be imparted, which a Poet may rationally endeavour to impart.'

3. Of *The Everlasting Mercy*, published in 1911, David Gervais writes:

> It is certainly quite unlike most of the verse of the period. Its story of a reformed wastrel was widely admired and debated for its 'low' comic dialogue and its revelation of the more squalid side of rural life. The brutally realistic boxing bout is enough to cast doubt on the notion that Masefield was ever a 'Georgian' poet. The poem was attacked by clerics, but it was also recited in public houses in the East End of London – not usually an audience for modern verse. (*ODNB* online, 2013)

John Masefield, in a photograph given by him to Muriel Spark during their first meeting

TO JOHN MASEFIELD, ABINGDON, BERKSHIRE,
9 DECEMBER 1950

8, Sussex Mansions, 65, Old Brompton Road, London, S.W.7
9th December, 1950

Dear Mr. Masefield,

How very delightful it was to meet you and Mrs. Masefield on Wednesday – I did so very much enjoy my visit and our conversation, and trust I did not tire you both.[1]

I shall shortly be making a start on my book, which the publishers have asked me to complete by the end of August next; and I shall hope to send you a few chapters in the early spring, which I should much appreciate your reading and commenting upon. I suggest this, since I feel you can best tell me if I am on the right lines so far as goes my interpretation of the spirit and intention of your work; and perhaps you might also be able to advise me on points I might otherwise miss.

The biographical section I should perhaps leave to the last, although it would appear first in the book, as this will leave me time to read your new autobiographical work which I am very much looking forward to seeing. I had meant to mention that I would like to consider your book 'Wonderings' in its semi-autobiographical capacity – as a sort of modern 'Prelude', or voyage of discovery into the early stages of the creative mind.[2]

Your remarks on Swinburne interested me greatly. Though I knew he was a powerful driving force to the generation of poets in which you came to maturity, I had not reckoned him as any particular mentor of yours. Since returning to London I have been looking at Swinburne again, and I do see how he must have stood out as the prime liberator and manipulator of language and rhythms. His own peculiar style, and his thought (which I find it difficult to get a grip on) do not seem to me such influential elements, as does the fact that he revealed the *possibilities* of poetic language. Was it not this aspect of Swinburne which was mostly of value to you?

Perhaps one should not look too closely in a poet's work for evidence of what past literature has stirred him; for if he is a good poet the effects of his reading will have been assimilated by his own powers. But the questions absorb my mind constantly, of how the creative mind gets into focus, what distinguishes one type of poem from another, and what makes the miracle of a poem — questions that are no doubt unanswerable; still, one must try to answer them if one must. To return to Swinburne, I think perhaps he represents a different type of poet from yourself, the essential difference being that Swinburne, as I suspect, thought of *how* he wanted to say things before he thought of *what* he wanted to say; whereas you appear to do the reverse.

But my main task, in my book, will be to convey my conviction that your work speaks for itself, by trying to show in what way it does so. The only critique on your writings that I know of, which attempts this successfully, is the one in 'Post-Victorian Poetry' by my good friend Herbert Palmer. He says some good things there on which I must try to enlarge.[3]

I also meant to say to you how interested I am in your book 'On The Hill' where in some poems, notably the first, you seem to have developed a new style which blends the strange and the familiar into a visionary whole.[4] I do not know if you have written many poems later than these, but if so I shall look forward to seeing them.

Let me say again how greatly I appreciate your courtesy to me, and what real pleasure I felt in the hospitality of Mrs. Masefield and yourself. I shall cherish the kind gifts of your portraits and book all the more since they will remind me of my visit to you.

With my best regards to Mrs. Masefield, and good wishes for the full recovery of your health.

Yours sincerely,

TLcc. NLS.

1. John Masefield wrote to MS on 29 November to propose she 'should first meet and talk with me', adding, 'I am much honoured, that you should

wish to write about my work, and much touched that you should have read so much of it and continue its friend' (NLS). The visit took place on 6 December. Masefield had been married to Constance de la Cherois Crommelin since 1903. MS would later recollect her visit: 'Although I found his house rather cold – we each had a small paraffin stove by our chair at lunch – and there was no alcoholic drink, it was one of the happiest days of my life. I remember well the euphoria of the white, frozen landscape around the house. It was on this occasion that Masefield spoke those words that I was to remember later: "All experience is good for an artist."' (*CV*, p. 197).

2. Masefield's *So Long to Learn: Chapters of an Autobiography* will be published in 1952. His long poem, *Wonderings (Between One and Six Years)*, was published in 1943. The title of William Wordsworth's autobiographical poem, which went through several transformations between 1800 and 1850, was given not by the poet himself but by his executors: *The Prelude, or Growth of a Poet's Mind*.

3. On Herbert Palmer's *Post-Victorian Poetry*, see early August 1950, n. 2.

4. Masefield's *On the Hill* had been published the previous year.

TO IRIS BIRTWISTLE, HOGHTON, LANCASHIRE, 20 DECEMBER 1950

8, Sussex Mansions, 65, Old Brompton Road, S.W.7
20.12.50

My dear Iris,

What a poppet you are. We have distributed your cards with great pride & shall drink your health on Christmas Day.

I think my publishers are going to be salvaged by a larger firm & that the book will be published after all. But who knows?[1]

My new book is on – guess who? John Masefield. Now, he *isn't* an old reactionary as I'm sure you think & as I thought till I re-read him recently. Read *Dauber* if you're doubtful, also the opening stanzas of *Everlasting Mercy*, also his novels.[2] I went to see him and was terribly impressed. He is so courteous – I mean naturally so, in every gesture he makes. He was very pleased about the book (the one I'm doing on him) & promised to help – presented me with an inscribed vol. & 2 pictures of himself. Full of stories about his travels – he sailed before the mast & worked in a factory in America in his youth. A born story-teller. He isn't anti-modern-poetry as one might expect. Very devoted to Swinburne.

But I caught a cold there – he lives outside Oxford – from which I am just recovering. Derek has been nursing me though he caught it from me.

The author of 'Fair House of Joy' has just written me an appreciative letter about my review of his book in P. Opinion. I feel such a fraud – I should really be writing to *him* as an adulatory reader. I place criticism very low on the scale of creative literature.[3]

What is your news? Are you home for Christmas? And are you coming to see us?

Best wishes & love from us both.

    Yours affectionately
      Muriel

P.S. Dear Iris,

I feel that we must reassure you on one point i.e. that your verse isn't mere inhibition release stuff. The proof of this is that you talk about things as much as about yourself, even though the poet's ego peeps through the phenomena. Of course, everything with all of us begins with some kind of inhibition, but the further one travels from the first conscious pain, the better I presume one's art becomes – and your verse has voyaged a goodly distance.

         ALS with PS in Derek Stanford's hand. CBF.

1. MS is referring to her critical biography of Mary Shelley, *Child of Light*; on the bankruptcy of the book's publisher, see 3 November 1950. Pen-in-Hand Books will indeed be bought up by Peter Baker who will incorporate it into his briefly flourishing publishing enterprise (before he was imprisoned for fraud); and MS's book will appear in 1951 with his Falcon Press.
2. John Masefield's narrative poem *Dauber*, published in 1913, drew on his experience as a sailor.
3. On 8 October, MS wrote to Iris Birtwistle: 'Do you read fiction? If so, read "Fair House of Joy" by Dennis Parry which I have just reviewed &

think very good writing' (CBF). In a letter of 1 November, she stated: '*Nothing* seems to happen to you that doesn't make a poem, which is a sign of instinctive talent. My own work has to be induced & only arrives after days of labour, usually stilborn [*sic*]. The more prose I write, the less poetry. So bugger prose, if you'll excuse me.' She continued: 'I *do* like your self-definition "primitive romantic" – We shall cogitate this before writing you about the poems.' And she added: 'George Fraser once told me I was an "agitated classic" which I have been pondering upon ever since. Herbert Palmer says I'm just plain "difficult".

Fair House of Joy was published earlier in the year by Robert Hale; on 9 December, Parry wrote to MS: 'It is nice to be praised anyhow; but a great deal nicer when one can see that the praise comes from a person who has really understood the book and has very definite standards. Anyhow, you have encouraged me a lot' (NLS). What Parry then said speaks not to his own work alone: 'I have taken to heart your first paragraph about choosing abnormal characters. Essentially, I agree that it is an admission of weakness. It means that one has not (yet, anyway) confidence in one's ability to make normal ones interesting. Still, I think it is preferable – as you suggest – to being hideously dull about ordinary well-integrated types. There is too much of that, and very well it pays!'

1951

MS continued to publish poetry, including in *Poetry Quarterly*, the *Times Literary Supplement*, and the *Spectator*, and was commissioned by P. H. Newby of the BBC to give several talks, among which a broadcast on her birthday, 1 February, on Mary Shelley. She worked on her long poem 'The Ballad of the Fanfarlo' which she intended to serve as her 'central statement in verse so far', but for which she struggled to find a publisher. Finally, in autumn, after several hitches in the publishing process, MS's first singly authored book appeared: *Child of Light: A Reassessment of Mary Wollstonecraft Shelley*. Motivated not least by the cash prize, in October MS submitted an anonymous entry to the *Observer*'s short-story competition: 'The Seraph and the Zambesi'. Just before Christmas, she learned that she had won the prize, and the story was published in the newspaper, bringing her notoriety, and a certain amount of envy. MS was increasingly engaged with issues of spirituality and Christianity, and published letters in the *Church of England Newspaper*. While they maintained a relationship that mixed the professional and the personal, the literary and the amorous, a number of long, tender, amatory letters testify to the increased intimacy and growing bond MS shared with Derek Stanford; though they continued to maintain separate addresses, they functioned largely as a married couple.

TO DEREK STANFORD, HOUNSLOW, MIDDLESEX,
23 JANUARY 1951

8, Sussex Mansions, 65 Old Brompton Rd., S.W.7
Tues. 1.30

My Sweet Swyke,*

So very relieved to have your note – kept thinking of you
feeling rough, & wondering *how* rough & wishing to do something.
Popkin Derek, *stay in bed* another day *at least*. You got up too
soon the last time. Stay in bed till you're better, and then one day
more. It's the only way. All day tomorrow (Wednesday) I'll be at
Horders.[1] You are not to come out at night even if you feel well.
So *if* you're better come over on Thursday morning, if not stay
where you are. (If you are *really* better by Wed. night then darling
come & I'll console & nurse you.) But write me if you can so that
my little heart won't misgive.

Am seeing Wrey to-day as arranged & will sell your 2 books
and you'll be lucky to see the change. I'm all right for cash – me
mum sent me my usual pound which, if she continues to do so, I
shall soon be in a position to demand as a right. The old girl has
her points, best appreciated this side of the Tweed though.

Have finished my Mary Shelley & had to spend ages cutting
it down from 2,000 words. Am wondering if Horder is going
to 'try me out' on Wed. and then say 'sorry no good.' I don't
trust him.

Have found your Theodore Roethke after all.[2]

Have re-read The Cocktail Party and am prepared now to
concede you a few more points re. the quality of the verse. I
object rather, to the too-frequent use of service-staircases, first
in the Chamberlayne's flat & then in Reilley's rooms. I suppose
my objection arises from their suggesting something Jesuitical,
which offends my early Prrresbyterrrean environment. I see what
the Guardians are, I think. Edward mentions them first. I think
they represent God's Will which, as the play shows, Man's Will
attempts to counteract but never can successfully. Look up your

own copy & let me know what you think of this suggestion. (*Have you a copy?*)

Very interested in Winters after what you say. *Fetch the book.* You are not to tempt me & then deny me.[3]

Lovely boy, I am missing you dreadfully. Everything seems threadbare when you're not here and I can't eat properly because there's no-one to cook up things for. I had a lovely feast for Sunday & have been trying to eat it all up before it goes off but it nearly chokes me. I have my miscarriage to-day and am doing better than ever. Wish we could take the usual advantage of it.

No letters of importance except the one from you which I praise. Had my hair done. Am doing Masefield most of the time. Will start my wonderful notes system on it soon. Take heart and cough mixture regularly; and keep warm, and in mind your loving

Muriel

* See Middle-English Glossary[4]

ALS on Sussex Mansions letterhead. WUL.

Dating based on a (dated) letter to Stanford from

previous day containing similar information (HRC).

1. In her letter to Derek Stanford of the previous day, 22 January, MS noted: 'Horder wants me to work on Wednesday, just one day. I've said I'll go, as it will help the coffers' (HRC).
2. Theodore Roethke's second collection of poems, *The Lost Son and Other Poems*, appeared in 1948, but MS may be referring to Roethke's next collection, published in 1951, *Praise to the End!*
3. The most recent book by the American poet Yvor Winters was *Three Poems*, published in 1950, though MS may be referring to one of his earlier works.
4. The *OED* gives *swyke* as a variant of *swike*: 'In modern Scottish and northern dialect in the forms *swike, swyke, swick*, with the sense "cheat, deception"; also in Scottish phrase the swick of, the responsibility for (something blameworthy).'

TO DEREK STANFORD, HOUNSLOW, MIDDLESEX,
24 JANUARY 1951

8, Sussex Mansions, S.W.7
Wed. night

My own Boy,

That was a dear letter to send me. I had it waiting when I
returned from work – Peter had brought it over.[1]

But you must take every possible care of yourself and let others
do as much as possible for you. 'Flu is a treacherous thing and can
complicate easily. So darling let me prevail upon you to stay in bed
at least till Friday. The wind is cold again and I don't want you to
relapse. If the weather is fine at the end of the week, and you quite
better, then come, but not unless.

Now I'm glad you are of good cheer, for one thing that has
worried me is the thought of your feeling depressed and perhaps
unable to read or work. I have been fancying pastoral scenes too,
lately. There is a bit of Spring already, in the light – I mean the
colour of the light, not the degree of lightness. We shall love each
other at Shipton before long my darling. I am very well pleased
and content with our life. It is something I had not expected,
taking a form I had not imagined. None of the lives I imagined
came to anything, or if they came, were not desirable.[2]

For my news: I saw Wrey who was sorry about your illness
and sends his love. My essay, he told me, should have been 1500
and not 1700–1800 words – would I cut it down? – it *must* fit
in, etc. This I promised to do, but left him the copy I'd brought.
I discovered on counting the words per page in the new Public
Opinion, that 1700 is correct, but who was I to argue? So I
wasted last night cutting the thing down, rang him this morning
to make *quite* sure, only to find that, in the words of the master,
'I seem to have it mixed up – it *should* be 1700'. So all's well.[3]
Wrey *thought* he had brought the proofs of our reviews in P.Q. for
us to correct. But they weren't in his bag, ('I took them out so
that I'd remember to put them in' quoth he). What to do? – He

must have them by Monday next! – I suggested he got someone at
the Falcon Press-gang to post them. Wrey looked doubtful about
this. Eventually I said I'd give him a ring on Thurs. to say how you
were keeping & maybe we'd meet him at Crown Passage on Friday
& correct the things there.[4] But if you're not better sweetheart,
there's no point in my going. He'll have to post them. Hermann
Peschmann has got the American Anthology to review for P.Q.
anyway, so it's not much cop.[5]

My Robert Frost wasn't in yet, so I'll ring Cape's again
tomorrow.[6] I fetched back Wrey's novel which is really quite bright
in parts. His self-portrait is amusing, if you know Wrey. You are
in it – made to sound very successful somehow, – something about
your canary-coloured waistcoat that made me feel very lonely when
I read it, for I want to see you inside the canary waistcoat popkin.
Wrey stood me two ports as a consolation for your absence.[7]
The baby was christened at St. Martins-in-the-Fields and farted
all the time. Cynthia and five other of her relatives will inherit
£90,000 between them if a case pending in Chancery is won. The
money was left by an old relative who married a French Count,
to various charities which are now defunct. Some of the money
is invested in America, and the American trustees are trying to
make her intestate, in which case Cynthia will be a rich gal. Old
mother Gardiner is none too pleased at this news which has been
elaborated on for her benefit. Ma feels her chances of retaining her
grip on Charlie are being threatened; while he now refuses to see
her at all, even at weekends.[8]

A surprise-packet came from Iris this morning, may all earthly
joys attend her. Heavenly joys too. It was a present of a pound to
buy drinks, for some purpose undefined. Also, I may look upon
the typewriter as a gift and not a loan heretoforward. What all
this is in aid of, except her own sweet benevolence, I can't say,
except what can be gathered from her words 'There has been a
completely unexpected & overwhelming piece of luck in my life,
which will come into effect soon.' Now this may mean she is in
love; or is in love and getting married; or has inherited a fortune.
I hope it is all the lot.

Re my day at Horder. I did an article for him which seared into
my inner heart – all about goodwill in the factories – for some
man who was knighted for his factory, really. Still, there was no
unpleasantness apart from the actual work, and all's fixed for
Monday week. I'm to be paid as 'expenses' i.e. no tax. I suppose
he'll add today's wages on the cheque when he pays me. He
seemed cheerful about what I did. I must write a satire on these
industrial knights as soon as I get a little more horrible insight. On
the whole as it is work which I can vent *hate* upon, it is better than
being at 'Model' which was simply a corrosive bore.[9] At least hate
starts the juices working. Then the cash is very nice really. I got
away at 5.30 and apart from a slight pain in my little tripes, don't
feel too bad for it all.

What a blether I am. But my dear, if I don't tell you now I might
never, for I'm sure I'll be all day kissing and kissing you when
you come.

A copy of Envoy has arrived for you. Some work by Gertrude
Stein reprinted in it – why I don't know, also an essay on her. –
Was she Irish? Now what about sending them your Elizabeth
Myers, after they've printed your Darley?[10]

Gastons turned down both your books so I was foiled of my
gain.[11] (Have you considered the difference, as it occurs to me
now, between 'gain' and 'profit'? The word 'gain' was much used
in Victorian times by the impoverished gentility to deprecate
those who were 'clever' enough to make a profit – Charlotte
Brontë's friend, Ellen Nussey, was pleased that Charlotte made a
profit from her books, but said her publishers were too eager 'for
gain'.)

No more to tell you darling. I want you to be well and cheerful.
Get really well and please don't come out straight from bed. Mind
and get up about the house a little first. I love you so dearly. Write
if you can to your

Muriel

P.S. On Friday 10 a.m. I go to the B.B.C. Will be busy there till
noon I expect – will be home soon after 12.[12] After that will be in
all day. Those are my movements if you think of coming, which

I am not for, unless you can give a good account of yourself in
health. Can I send you anything?
   Love
   M.

ALS. HRC. Dating from visit to BBC on 26 January.

1. In her letter to Derek Stanford written two days earlier, 22 January,
   after encouraging him to write to her, MS added, 'You cd. address it c/o
   Nevills – or enclose it in a letter to them if you don't want the address seen'
   (HRC). In the present letter, Peter may be Peter Owen, whose publishing
   enterprise was Peter Nevill – he would soon launch the influential Peter
   Owen Books that would publish MS, and for which she would work – or
   possibly Peter Baker of Falcon Press.
2. MS and Stanford visited Shipton-under-Wychwood where Christopher Fry
   lived in June 1950, in connection with a book Stanford was planning on
   the dramatist; a return to Shipton was evidently being planned.
3. Wrey Gardiner was appointed the previous year to the post of Literary
   Editor of a new edition of *Public Opinion*, published by the *Daily Mirror*.
   MS's article would appear in February as 'Mary Shelley: Wife to a Genius'.
4. Gardiner was editor of *Poetry Quarterly*. Crown Passage, near Pall Mall,
   had been the home to Gardiner's Grey Walls Press, and was now home
   to Falcon Press.
5. MS is referring to *The Oxford Book of American Verse* which had recently been
   published. Hermann Peschmann, whose book *The Voice of Poetry, 1930–
   1950* will appear in 1952, did not review the volume in *Poetry Quarterly*, but
   he referred to it in the opening of his review of *Complete Poems of Robert Frost*,
   entitled 'American Countryman', which appeared in the same journal (vol.
   13, no. 1, Spring 1951).
6. MS reviewed *Complete Poems of Robert Frost* in 'The Complete Frost', *Public
   Opinion* (no. 4662, 30 March 1951; reprinted in Muriel Spark, *The Golden
   Fleece: Essays* (Carcanet, 2014; henceforth in the notes *TGF*), pp. 36–8).
7. MS may be referring to Gardiner's autobiographical work, *The Flowering
   Moment*, published by his own Grey Walls Press in 1949. There are indeed
   brief references to Stanford in it, though it may be MS's feelings towards
   Stanford more than Gardiner's sketch that make him appear 'very successful': 'Derek Stanford, *les yeux pochés* with hay fever, his cap folded
   with his newspaper and his manuscripts, is another shadowy shape in my
   afternoons. But he is becoming clearer in perspective as the weeks go by.
   [. . .] Derek Stanford's domed half bald forehead, large eyes and sensual
   lips are so very like the portraits of Shakespeare' (pp. 62, 81).
8. Gardiner's third wife was Cynthia Kortright. Charlie has not been further
   identified.

9. MS had been working occasionally as an editorial assistant for *European Affairs*, which 'was run by Elma Dangerfield, a clever English society woman, and Monty Radulovitch, a Montenegrin journalist who had written a book on Tito' (*CV*, pp. 192–3). Her 'Model' may possibly be an amalgam of the directors' names: *Mo-(d)-El*.

10. *Envoy: An Irish Review of Literature and Art* was established in December 1949, in Dublin, by its Editor John Ryan, with a focus on modernist and international writers; it would continue to be published until July 1951, ending with volume 5. Stanford had been working on the English novelist Elizabeth Myers, who had published three novels during the 1940s and who died in 1947. Stanford's article on the Irish poet and mathematician, entitled 'George Darley', will be published in *Envoy* (vol. 5, no. 18, May 1951).

11. Thomas J. Gaston was a book dealer occupying premises off Chancery Lane, Fleet Street, and later on the Old Kent Road; it paid cash to literary editors, reviewers, and publishers' sales representatives for books that had either been reviewed or were deemed unsuitable for review, selling them on to libraries at discount. Stanford's books were probably review copies entrusted to MS to sell there.

12. MS's appointment with P. H. Newby at the BBC was for the purpose of recording her talk for the Third Programme entitled 'Mary Shelley's Novels, *Frankenstein* and *The Last Man*', for which her fee was 20 guineas.

TO IRIS BIRTWISTLE, HOGHTON, LANCASHIRE, 25 JANUARY 1951

8, Sussex Mansions, 65 Old Brompton Road, S.W.7
25th Jan. 1951

My dear Iris,

Am overwhelmed by your kindnesses. Your cheque is a lovely surprise, and we'll drink your health. But you really ought not to have done this. And as for the typewriter, I *can't* really thank you enough. – Don't know what I'd have done without it, and have been meaning to ask you if you needed it. – Now, do let me look upon it still as a continued loan, so that if your own one gives way you can call on it. After all, you need a typewriter quite as much as I do. You're a dear girl to do these nice things.

We are in long debate as to the mysterious 'piece of luck' in your life which you mentioned. Our theories so far have been

(1) You are in love. (2) You are in love and getting married (3) your poems have been accepted by a publisher (4) you have won a poetry prize (5) you have inherited a fortune (6) you have made a wonderful antique deal. I hope it is all the lot, but unless it is a private thing we should like to know.

Derek is down with 'flu. First he was elated, then depressed, but getting better now. He sends his love, and purrs to hear your praise. Can we have copies of your new poems as we sometimes miss The Fortnightly & P.R. in the libraries. I like the sound of Apple Jane.[1]

Am starting a part-time job soon (3 days a week) which I loathe, but at least it's better than full-time. The job is publicity for several industrial firms – writing hypocritical speeches for the managing directors to make to other managing directors. But it's better to do something you hate than something merely boring, as hate stimulates the reaction.

Hope all the babes in the family are well, and that you thrive.[2] Let us know your good news if at all possible. *Many* thanks and love from us both,

Muriel

ALS. CBF.

---

1. The *Fortnightly Review* was founded in 1865 by, among others, Anthony Trollope; it continued publication until 1954. 'P.R.' is the *Poetry Review*. 'The Ballad of Apple Jane' will be published in *Poetry London*, edited by Meary Tambimuttu; it will later appear in Iris Birtwistle's posthumously published collection, *When Leaf and Note Are Gone* (Bugg Press, 2008).
2. Birtwistle will go on to adopt three boys but at this point had no children. MS is probably referring to her nieces and nephews.

TO DEREK STANFORD, HOUNSLOW, MIDDLESEX,
2 APRIL 1951

160, Bruntsfield Place, Edinburgh
Monday

Darling Boy,

Am now reclining on the bed whereon I first saw the light –
(alas as Sophocles said) – thinking of your sweet send-off to me
last night, and hoping your throat is better.[1]

They put me in a 1st class de luxe sleeper, complete with
washbasin, po, hangers & other super equipment all of which I
made use of; the po I made full use of. All are in good form here &
have got out the fatted calf etc. Robin is a joy. He's using delightful
expressions such as 'Women teachers are unpredictable,' and has
just told me the following story:

There were two brothers, one a thrifty man, the other a
spendthrift and drunk. The thrifty brother bought National
Savings all his life and the other brother just drank. The thrifty
brother now finds himself so heavily taxed that he has only a bob
left, while the licentious one is making a fortune by selling his
empty bottles.

Rob. & I went out today to order a 3/6^{d} kitten which we hope
to have on Thursday.

My friend the bookseller next door to us advises me not to go
to Douglas & Foulis as they are too dear. He thinks he can supply
all our wants very reasonably. So far he has unearthed 'A Life
Drama' by Alexander Smith and 'The Poetical Works of David
Gray' which includes 'The Luggie' – at two bob a time. He is
sure he has both Fred & Charlie Tennyson and also Horne, the
two Ebeneezers and Allingham in his back store, and will let me
have them later this week. This bookseller is the rarest character
in the neighbourhood, being knowledgeable on literary matters
from a somewhat biographical angle – what I mean is, that he
knows dozens of anecdotes about almost any minor or major
author you might happen to mention, but hardly ever ventures a

remark on the merits of their work. He is an old buddy of Gordon
Bottomley. I don't know this bookseller's name, and I have known
him too long now to ask.[2]

Am sleepy now, but pleased at my book purchases and quite
satisfied with my reception. I have partaken heavily of port
which adds to my somnolence. Despite the luxurious sleeping
compartment, I didn't sleep very well last night.

I long for you darling, and the consolation of your voice –
particularly do I feel this when those around me are intoning the
chorus of domestic, material, and altogether pernickety affairs in
order to take their own minds off the yawn in time between rising
and going to bed.

The week will pass and we shall be united again. If this weren't
in my mind just now, I would begin to spew already – even before
I have been properly scunnered. Maybe, this time, I won't be.

Take care of your throat, gentle Derek. Write to me soon and
often and think tenderly of your true love

Muriel

> ALS. NLS. Dating: MS took the night train on 1 April, and
> comments on her reading-matter in a dated letter two days later.

1. MS alludes, presumably, to the fate of Sophocles' Oedipus who returns,
    incestuously and tragically, to his mother's bed.
2. Douglas & Foulis were long-established Edinburgh librarians and book-
    sellers with a shop at no. 9 Castle Street. MS purchased the works of two
    Scottish poets: Alexander Smith's *A Life-Drama and Other Poems*, originally
    published in 1852; and *The Poetical Works of David Gray*, first published in
    1852–3, which contains the long narrative poem 'The Luggie'. Most of the
    further nineteenth-century poets mentioned here were interested, as was
    MS, in the possibilities of narrative verse: the brothers Frederick Tennyson
    and Charles Tennyson, Richard Henry Horne, Ebenezer Elliott, Ebenezer
    Jones, William Allingham, and Gordon Bottomley.

TO DEREK STANFORD, HOUNSLOW, MIDDLESEX,
4 APRIL 1951

160 Bruntsfield Place, Edinburgh
4th Apl. 51

Dear sweet Popple,

Thank you for the two dear letters – one yesterday, one today, the which have been sustaining me.

Poor Paul Potts – I resign him my title of the Unluckiest Girl in the World. But his Orwell book will be publishable surely after the time stated in the will has elapsed.[1]

Yesterday I went for a walk over the Pentland hills in strange weather – I stood in a patch of brilliant sunshine and saw snow falling a few yards away, driven aslant by a high wind. I enjoyed this solitary excursion and read my/our David Gray as I walked. To-day my curse arrived – nine days early. But I've been fighting it off with booze and some wonderful new tablets – Codein [sic] – which my mother produced. All's well so far. I was presented with a new radio to-day by my pa despite my protests that I'd rather have the money. However have been promised a fiver to go home with as well. Robin today told me the following:

> Ladies and gentlemen
> Take my advice,
> Take off your knickers
> And slide on the ice.

which is one of the milder rhymes current at school, I gather.

I read part of Bridges on Poetry this morning, but don't consider him anything like as original in thought as Masefield, nor as fluent a prose writer. Bridges is a closer analyst than Masefield. But this close analysing isn't a virtue to itself, in fact it is bloody vicious, unless accompanied by a strong sensibility – an *ear* and an *eye* for poetry, a feeling for the *touch, taste and smell of it*. Bridges half-heartedly attacks the scientist, but he's altogether too scientific. And not even originally so, as is I. A. Richards (all of whose theories are, in any case, the product of a fine intuition). In Bridges, the manqué philosopher met with the manqué philologist, and his poetry was the result.[2]

I am exhilerated [*sic*] by the amount of high dudgeon that is being disseminated up here on account of the Stone. My mother and father and all our neighbours – in fact all I have met, are ardently in favour of keeping 'our' stone in bonnie Scotland. I pointed out to my mother that her Sassenach blood should be boiling at the outrage perpetrated on Westminster Abbey, but she says, all the same, it is *our* stone. The newspapers are frankly and openly against the threatened arrest, from which no end of political consequences, disastrous to the Union of the Crowns will follow it seems.[3]

Dear sweetheart, only five more days and we shall be united again. I hope to get the books tomorrow morning. What a lot we shall have to look at and say, and what a cuddling and canoodling there will be. Keep well my love, for me.[4]

By the way, my face was very inflamed yesterday and my eyes suddenly became all-over bloodshot. This lasted a few hours. It is everyone's opinion here that I *did* have a slight dose of the measles after all, and these are the after-effects. However, I'm feeling fine and all symptoms have disappeared.

Gentle Derek, keep writing to me if you can. Yes, I would like *Capt. Margaret*, if not too expensive.[5] Write and let me know *by return* if there are any other books I can profitably purchase, as this is obviously the place to find them.

I'll tell you in good time the hour of my arrival when I hope to see the bonnie brown face of my love. Think sweetly
of your Muriel

ALS. HRC.

1. The poet Paul Potts had written about his friend George Orwell, who had died the previous year; but the final clause of Orwell's will (dated 18 January 1950) stated: 'in case any suggestion should arise I request that no memorial service be held for me after my death and that no biography of

me shall be written' (*The Complete Works of George Orwell*, ed. Peter Davison, Secker & Warburg, 1998, vol. XX, p. 237). Potts's writing would appear in the *London Magazine* in 1957 as 'Don Quixote on a Bicycle', and later in his book *Dante Called You Beatrice* (Eyre & Spottiswoode, 1960).

2. MS was almost certainly reading Robert Bridges's *The Necessity of Poetry*, where there is a section devoted to the 'Insufficiency of Philosophy and Science' (Clarendon Press, 1918, pp. 9–12); she judges his literary theories inferior to those of I. A. Richards, who published, among many other influential works, *Science and Poetry* (Kegan Paul & Co., 1926).

3. On Christmas Day 1950, four students from the University of Glasgow stole the Stone of Scone from Westminster Abbey where it had resided since it was taken from Scone in Scotland in 1296; it had formed part of the chair on which Scottish, and subsequently British, monarchs were coronated, and had thus become a symbol of Scottish nationalist aspirations. One week after the present letter, on 11 April, the Stone would reappear in Arbroath Abbey, only subsequently to be returned to Westminster Abbey in 1952 (and then returned again to Scotland in 1996).

4. In her letter to Stanford four days later, 8 April, MS will write: 'I have got a lovely series (6 vols) of Routledge's 19th cent. poets – for 4/- the lot. These include ample selections with biographical notes, of poets from Crabbe to Kipling.' After detailing the contents of the volumes she will add: 'I am so weary of my exile and will be overjoyed to get on the train tomorrow night. I've had very little time for reading – none at all for thinking. Robin is in his usual high spirits, and has only now got school holidays' (HRC).

5. The novel *Captain Margaret: A Romance*, by John Masefield (Grant Richards, 1908).

TO IRIS BIRTWISTLE, HOGHTON, LANCASHIRE,
22 APRIL 1951

8, Sussex Mansions, 65, Old Brompton Road, S.W.7
22-4-51

My dear Iris,

How very much we enjoyed your party and sorry we were that you were not staying in London longer so that we could meet again. We feasted on your eggs and wine, toasting you. And we were so glad to see you looking so well.

Tomorrow Derek & I go to Oxford to cover Fry's new play which is opening at St. Mary's Church – a religious festival play. Derek is writing it up for World Review, Public Opinion &

the C. of E. Newspaper while I am doing a short piece for the Spectator – probably unsigned.[1]

Did you have a good holiday in the country? This part of the week wd. have been better so far as weather in the south goes.

The proofs of my Mary Shelley book have started to come already from the new publishers.[2] Derek and I are making a selection of Mary S's letters for the same publisher & they hope to print it next year. We are doing our introduction in the form of a dialogue, which should be unusual if it fails to be anything else. We would very much and dearly like to dedicate the book to you, if you will accept it as a token of friendship.

Derek's book on Fry is expected any moment. I'm excited, Derek not.[3] Am enclosing your copy of Outposts with many thanks. May I keep 'The Spirit of Catholicism' a little longer? Have posted 'Thoughts for Meditation' to you, which please accept as a gift. (The 'Poverty', alas, *didn't* come from Hollis & Carter.) Derek sends much love along with mine.[4]

Affectionately,

Muriel

P.S. Regret smudges from my biro. M.

ALS. CBF.

1. MS's positive review of Christopher Fry's verse play *A Sleep of Prisoners* will be signed 'M. S.' when published in the *Spectator* one week later (27 April).
2. The new publisher was Peter Baker's Falcon Press, which had taken over Pen in Hand Press.
3. Derek Stanford's *Christopher Fry: An Appreciation* was to be published by Peter Nevill.
4. *Outposts* was a literary journal edited by Howard Sergeant. The highly influential *Das Wesen des Katholizismus* by German theologian Karl Adam was published in 1924; its English translation by Dom. Justin McCann, *The Spirit of Catholicism*, was issued by Sheed and Ward in 1929. *Thoughts for Meditation: A Way to Recovery from Within* was an anthology of writings selected and arranged by N. Gangulee, published in 1951 by Faber & Faber with an introduction by T. S. Eliot, in which he said of the chosen extracts: 'They are intended for everyone who is curious about those emotions, and states of soul, which are to be found, so to speak, only beyond the limit of the visible spectrum of human feeling, and which can be experienced

only in moments of illumination, or by the development of another organ
of perception than that of everyday vision' (p. 11).

5.   *Pleasures of Poverty: An Argument and an Anthology* by Anthony Bertram was
published by Hollis & Carter in 1950.

TO THE EDITOR, THE SPECTATOR, LONDON,
MID-MAY 1951

[Old Brompton Road, London]

Sir, – I have just seen Mr. W. P. Jackson's letter in *The Spectator* of
May 4, in which he forcibly points out my error in interpreting the
last scene in Christopher Fry's play *A Sleep of Prisoners*.[1]

First let me say that I readily apologise as Mr. Jackson demands,
to the author, producer and actors.

A mistake such as this is significant, however, the more especially
as I listened very attentively to the play, and did indeed see it through
to the end, which Mr. Jackson doubts. It is even more significant
when one finds that no less an authority than the dramatic critic of
The Church Times has made the same mistake. I do not know how this
critic arrived at his error, for he is unknown to me; but another critic
with whom I discussed the play was also under the impression that
Jonah and the Whale was the theme represented.[2]

Mr. Jackson mentions a 'programme-note by the author', on
the play. I take it he is referring to a short essay entitled 'The
Church as Theatre', not as he states, by the author, but by Michael
Macowan, which appears along with several others on various
aspects of drama. This I did not read. I was there to review the
play, and as we all know, that's the thing.[3]

I suggest that a little revision on the part of the author and a
more emphatic handling from producer and actors, might clarify
this last scene for future audiences.

Yours etc.,

M.S.

Published in the *Spectator*, 25 May 1951.

1. In her review of Christopher Fry's play in the *Spectator* (see 22 April 1951, n. 1), MS wrote: 'First the story of Cain's murder of Abel is presented. [. . .] lastly, Jonah and the whale. Each story is approached in a highly original manner with emphasis on its present-day significance.' In his response letter, Walter Patrick Jackson, then an undergraduate at University College, Oxford, wrote:

   > I feel that I cannot be the only one of your readers to have been mystified by your critic's discovery of the presence of Jonah and the whale in Christopher Fry's new play *A Sleep of Prisoners* which had its *première* in Oxford last week. One wonders if the critic bothered to see the play through to the end or even read the helpful programme-note by the author, which fully explained the significance of the four biblical stories which form the dream-sequence. While admiring the critic's ingenuity in replacing the Fry furnace by what he may have been thinking of as the Bridie belly, I feel that the distortion makes such nonsense of the play that an apology to the author, producer and actors would seem the least possible atonement. (4 May 1951)

2. The review, signed 'Davy Gam Esquire', appeared in the *Church Times* (27 April 1951), where the reviewer asked, 'was this an allusion to Jonah?' and admitted to be 'confused from the pews'.
3. The actor, TV director, and writer Michael Macowan was the producer of Fry's play.

   MS echoes Hamlet's hopeful lines:

   > The play's the thing
   > Wherein I'll catch the conscience of the King (*RS: Hamlet*, II, ii, 604–5)

TO THE EDITOR, THE CHURCH OF ENGLAND
NEWSPAPER, LONDON, LATE MAY 1951

London S.W.7

Sir, – Throughout all the correspondence appearing in your own and other papers concerning the Royal visit to the Pope, there has been an unspoken assumption that there is something about the aura of the Vatican which exerts an influence, perverse or otherwise, over visitors.[1]

What has not been remarked on is the salutary effect on the Vatican of continued contact with eminent Protestants.

Muriel Spark

> Published in the *Church of England Newspaper*, 25 May 1951.

1. MS and Derek Stanford were friends with C. E. (Clifford) Rhodes, an ordained minister who had been Editor of the *Church of England Newspaper* (henceforth in the notes *CEN*) since 1946, and who was progressive in his theology and his practice.

     On 10 May 1949, in the first British royal visit for several centuries, Princess Margaret of York spent time at the Vatican, where she met and talked with Pope Pius XII.

TO JOHN MASEFIELD, ABINGDON, BERKSHIRE, 26 MAY 1951

8 Sussex Mansions, 65 Old Brompton Road, London, S.W.7
26th May, 1951

Dear Mr. Masefield,

When your kind letter returning my typescript arrived this morning, I was just about to write and ask you please not to trouble with it until you were quite fit again. I do hope you are mending now, and that we shall see some brighter weather to encourage your return to health.

All you say interests me greatly, especially what you say about giving stories 'by word of mouth to living audiences.' That is a very important thing, I think. Some of my poet-friends complain that there are no living audiences left, but perhaps that is because we haven't tried to sway them *by word of mouth*. We are a dreadfully bookish age, I fear, with our footnotes to poems and highbrow allusions. The trouble is, once a major poet has got into the bloodstream of a generation, it is difficult for those who follow him to get rid of his influence. I was speaking to Herbert Palmer the other day, and he told me, as you did, that Swinburne was the poet who enchanted his generation. On us, T.S. Eliot has the same effect – I don't mean we read and enjoy him to the exclusion of other poets,˙ but that he provided a sort of revelation, and everything we write in the way of poetry seems guided by his work. For my own part I have decided that this is a phase which has to be first experienced and then transcended. For, although Eliot enjoys a great, and I think deserved fame, I believe poets will have to break away from his influence if they are to be heard. I would like to see a revival of narrative verse as a first step to being heard, for surely broadcasting is a good medium for it. At the same time there are some ways of writing which we shall have to retain from T. S. Eliot.

The people who are constantly denouncing our work as obscure, don't understand our problems. We have to address a disintegrated world. The world we draw our inspiration from is disintegrated. When we write a poem we are trying, in a manner, to write several poems at once and to speak on different levels and to make divided things whole. Our next job should be to do this and at the same time to make our meanings accessible, and I think this will come about through a rediscovery of form and the dramatic uses of rhetoric. That is but one reason why I am so drawn towards your own work.[1]

TLcc. NLS.

1. The remainder of this letter has not been found, either in carbon copy or in its original form; John Masefield typically did not keep letters sent to him. On 12 May, MS had written to P. H. Newby at the BBC in order to suggest a talk on Masefield: 'What I would like to speak of would be his importance as a narrative poet, and as a poet of the sea. The impact he made in the twenties was, I think, falsely grounded, and consequently his real merits have been overlooked. And I also feel he has been wrongly classed as a Georgian poet' (BBC WAC).

TO HOWARD SERGEANT, LONDON, 12 JUNE 1951

8 Sussex Mansions, 65 Old Brompton Road, S.W.7
12th June, 1951

Dear Howard,

Enclosed are the poems which I think you haven't seen.

The long one – The Fanfarlo – is my central statement in verse so far. Perhaps you might like to read it first before looking at the following notes, but first I'd like to draw your attention to the lines I have quoted from Baudelaire 'Samuel Cramer, who used to sign himself by the name of Manuela de Monteverde, or some such romantic folly – in the heyday of Romanticism – is the contradictory product of a pale German and a brown Chilean woman.' It isn't necessary to know Baudelaire's short story The Fanfarlo, as I have only lifted the characters, not the story, and these lines suffice to give the background.[1]

Regarding the poem, it is consciously intended, on one level as a plain narrative, using the border ballad style as the most natural one for me, and as a convenient one for narrative. On a deeper level, I have tried to make a commentary on the situation suggested in the epigraph. We find there that Samuel Cramer is a writer who signed himself by the exotic nom-de-plume of Manuela de Monteverde, and his romantic temperament is confirmed by this. We are also told that he is racially *different* – a product, as it were, of North and South – and in this I see the contemporary individualist – a divided being fitting into no *category*. He is in search of himself, when in my poem, I make him seek Manuela de Montaverde [*sic*]. My character, the steel chair, is not of course in Baudelaire; this character, and the little red light, etc., besides all the other inanimate characters, are representative of a mechanised, totalitarian age.

Part I of the poem deals with Samuel Cramer in search of himself, that is, of his ideal, Manuela de Monteverde. But the steel chair and his world have an ideal too, and this ideal is called Manuela de Montaverde [*sic*] too. Manuela is the humanist image.

To the world of the steel chair, which has become so completely mechanised that there is not even such a thing as pain, Samuel Cramer is No Man.

Part II of the poem brings in other types of humanity, all of whom in this new mechanised world are No Men. Still they testify to the glory of their Manuela de Montaverde [*sic*]; and in their statements I have attempted to echo ironically the words from the Shorter Chatechism [*sic*], in answer to the first Question: 'What is Man's chief end?' – 'Man's chief end is to glorify God and to enjoy Him forever.' These are types of meterial [*sic*] humanists. For all their oppression by the machine, they are still prepared to destroy each other in the name of Manuela de Monteverde.

Part III brings in Manuela de Montaverde [*sic*] himself, as well as The Fanfarlo, who is an important character in that she might be called one of the excessive gestures of Romanticism, an extension of Samuel Cramer as well as being a typical woman in her own right. Manuela's words ' . . . . I am a man / For whom the visible words exist' coming from a ghost, are supposed to be an ironic comment on Gautier's identical words.[2] Death is of course a symbol of Disaffection – he demands the renunciation of the material world, of the senses; he demands a blind and dark faith.

Perhaps there is too much repetition in the poem; I have used this because I think repetition a good thing if a poem is to be read aloud. The language is rather high-flown where Samuel Cramer speaks, but this is deliberate – I don't know if it comes off, though.

The other poems are mainly exercises in form. I am trying to work towards a lucid compactness before spreading out again.

Hope all this isn't a bore. You may quote any part of it if you think the poems worth mentioning. At any rate, please let me know what you think of The Fanfarlo. I don't see any possibility of getting it published, but am reading it at Ross Nichol's [*sic*] do, at Euston Road – maybe you'd like to come along. Derek is reading some of his latest poems too, some of which are very interesting.[3]

It was nice seeing you the other day and meeting Jean. Sorry you couldn't come back for coffee.[4]

Best wishes from us both,

> TLcc with MS's handwritten note detailing poems sent: 'Sent The Fanfarlo / Chrysalis / Shipton-under-Wychwood [etc.]'. NLS.

1. Howard Sergeant will choose not to publish 'The Ballad of the Fanfarlo' in his journal *Outposts*; it will find a publisher only in 1952 (and will be reprinted in *CP*, pp. 95–112). Charles Baudelaire's original in 'La Fanfarlo' reads: 'Samuel Cramer, qui signa autrefois du nom de Manuela de Monteverde quelques folies romantiques, – dans le bon temps du romantisme – est le produit contradictoire d'un blême Allemand et d'une brune Chilienne' (*Œuvres complètes*, ed. Claude Pichois, Bibliothèque de la Pléiade, 1975, vol. I, p. 553). MS's 'or some such romantic folly' is a mistranslation: the 'folies romantiques' refer not to Monteverde's name but to his occasional writings.
2. MS writes 'the visible words exist' but presumably intends 'the visible world exists', which corresponds to what appears in her poem and to what the poet Théophile Gautier is quoted by the Goncourt brothers, in their *Journal des Goncourt: Mémoires de la vie littéraire* (Bibliothèque-Charpentier, 1891, p. 182), as having said: 'Toute ma valeur, ils n'ont jamais parlé de cela, c'est que *je suis un homme pour qui le monde visible existe*.'
3. Ross Nichols was an academic, poet, and proselytiser of Celtic mythology and Druidry.
4. 'Jean' is almost certainly Jean Crabtree, who will marry Sergeant in 1954.

TO THE EDITOR, THE HUDSON REVIEW, NEW YORK, 29 JULY 1951

8, Sussex Mansions, 65, Old Brompton Road, S.W.7
29th July, 1951

Dear Sir,

I am enclosing an unpublished poem, the length of which I hope will not deter you from considering it.[1]

The reason I send it to you is because I have gathered from your pages that you are interested in work which illustrates a method of working, quite apart from the merits of the thing.

What I have tried with the enclosed poem is to develop a narrative genre which meets the allusive and symbolic requirements of modern verse. Whether I have succeeded or not, I felt that this should be attempted since straightforward narrative verse has become rather superfluous, due I suppose to the development of the novel. Yet I think the narrative poem has a potential future: old techniques of telling a story in verse can be adapted to the present more exacting need to tell, as it were, several stories at once.

The poem itself is intended, on one level, as a criticism of the romantic attitude. I look forward to hearing if you think it of sufficient merit to print.

Forgive me for going on and on about myself. As I have published very little outside this country I'd like to add that my work has appeared in World Review, Times Literary Supplement, The Spectator, The Fortnightly, Irish Times, The Listener, Life and Letters, Public Opinion, Poetry Quarterly, New English Magazine and other places.

My own publications (all critical) are:

Tribute to Wordsworth (edited in collaboration)
Child of Light (critical-biography Mary Shelley)
Letters of the Brontes (introduced & edited)
Poems of Emily Bronte (" ")
Letters of Mary Shelley (edited in collaboration)
John Masefield (critical work forthcoming)

Yours sincerely,
s/Muriel Spark
(Muriel Spark)

TLS. PFL.

---

1. As confirmed by MS's subsequent letter of 6 October 1951 to the *Hudson Review*, the poem sent with the present letter was 'The Fanfarlo' (PFL).

TO IRIS BIRTWISTLE, HOGHTON, LANCASHIRE,
19 AUGUST 1951

8, Sussex Mansions, 65, Old Brompton Road, S.W.7
19th Aug. 1951

My dear Iris,

Don't think me ungrateful for not writing earlier: as D. told
you I've been in a *state*.[1] The parcel you sent is quite the most
exciting news I have to report, so if you'll pretend you didn't send
it you'll be able to appreciate the fun and tryings-on I've had. I am
living in the house-coat and hate having to take it off. The blue
skirt and silk flowered dress I'm having shortened for day wear by
my landlady in exchange for an old umbrella. They are to be ready
for me next week. And the striped dress fits perfectly. Derek
has made off with the aertex blue shirt which on him has a natty
mediterranean effect. As you see I've hogged most of the parcel
and feel rather guilty at not leaving more for Miss P. Keir.[2] I've
even confiscated the blouses. But will pack up the coat and other
silk dresses in an anonymous parcel and send them off, hoping you
won't think me too greedy. Heaps of thanks for all these things –
my wardrobe was getting so *boring*, what there was of it, that
(do you know the feeling?) I would *look* at my few things and not
really *see* them. Now the element of surprise has returned to it,
besides bulk.

About my illness: it isn't really *an* illness but just a state where
I get this that & the next ailment. Had an operation on my gum
for an abscess a couple of weeks ago which should have cleared
up in two days, but it caused agony for ten days. Thanks so much
for thinking of your woman specialist for me. I don't think
that there's anything wrong with my innards except that I'm
chronically anaemic; am feeling better now in fact. But in case my
innards which have played up in the past, should do so again, may
I let you know & then you cd. introduce me to your vet? Some
months back I thought I shd. have to have it All Taken Away but
have recouped with the aid of iron pills.

To leave this nauseating subject and refer to another more
nauseating still, is it *really* true that Phoebe is to be published by
Heinneman [*sic*]? I'm sure it must be, first because you wouldn't
have said so otherwise, and second because that's just the sort of
thing that happens in life. So my question is rhetorical. I don't
attempt to disguise my envy (from a subjective point of view) and
disgust (from an objective one – because I think Phoebe's poetry
nothing short of *drab*). I suppose Heinemanns fell for the religion-
cum-birds, bees, and flowers subject-matter, which has been a
popular winner since Wordsworth, and also I suppose they liked
the regularity – lots of people judge poetry from the look of the
type on the page. Then, there's a certain amount of tum-te-tum
in her verse, which is also successful in persuading people they
are reading poetry. If I were reviewing her work (which I shan't)
I would say that same thing, so this is not just an overflow of rage
& frustration. I suppose Herbert Palmer helped her to place the
M.S. He is really cracked about her work.[3]

Why don't *you* try Heinemann's? I really think that you should,
in any case, try *somebody*. *I'm* trying various people at the moment.
Hand-and-Flower Press (who do the 1/- pamphlets) are looking
at my M.S. at present but have written to say they don't know if
they're going to continue publishing the pamphlets next year.

My Mary Shelley book shd. be out early in October at long last.
Have had a *time* with the portrait of Mary S. which turned out to
be unidentified, & at this late date the publisher wd. look at no
other. Have at last made a compromise.[4]

What good news about Barcelona. You must *absorb* and *write*
while there. Especially absorb, as the writing may come later.

We are going for 2 weeks in mid-Sept. to a cottage in Lindfield
part of which is rented to us by a kindly lady at a low rent. We
went there 2 years ago & were so engaged by the personality
of Miss Bassanno [*sic*] (the owner) that we spent many hours
fathoming out between us the Mystery of her Early Life. She is a
superior being, well-read, fiftyish and attractive, and friendly with
the Vicar whom she made us meet at her little cocktail-party. All
this I tell you so that you may be able to savour what more of her

personality we were able to convey when we wrote the following
lines, on our return.

> When Miss Bassano
> Played on the virginals
> Vastly the Vicar
> Envied those canticles.
>
> Soon Miss Bassano
> Played the bassoon
> Nice as a piano
> All the afternoon.
>
> Vastly the Vicar
> Envied Miss Bassano
> Playing the virginals
> And the bassoon.

It is called 'Air for Miss Bassano' but we should not like her to
see it as she would think us quite daft. But we are looking forward
to our holiday and meeting our Miss Bassano again. While there,
we shall be doing the Mary Shelley Letters which are for you as
you know, so you will be in our minds in Lindfield as we hope we
shall be on occasion, in yours at Barcelona.

We'll be back before your return from Spain, as plans stand at
the moment. So hope to see you in London then. Do give yourself
up to the sun and your own whims. Derek sends his best love.
(The books are not available yet but shd. be coming next week.) I
send my best love too & wishes for the most poetic of holidays.

Ever,

Muriel

P.S. Derek is agog about his forthcoming shirt and says I'm to
thank dear Iris for kind thoughts about his apparel and kind words
about his book.[5]

M.

ALS. CBF.

1. 'D.' is Derek Stanford. On 20 July, MS wrote to Iris Birtwistle, of her job at Pearson Horder: 'I wd. have written sooner but have just had a ghastly three-weeks at the public relations job I think I told you about. I've left never to return, as writing hack journalism for hateful people has left an awful scar on me. Sounds dramatic, but it's true. Couldn't write a thing of my own work for abt. a month. And now looking for a part-time job as dentist's assistant or shop assistant – something not connected with writing at all' (CBF).
2. Miss P. Keir has not been further identified.
3. Phoebe Hesketh, who lived not far from Birtwistle in Rivington, Lancashire, drew heavily on the local countryside for her poetry; her third collection of poems, *No Time for Cowards*, was due to be published in 1952 by Heinemann.
4. The first edition of *Child of Light* had no image on its cover; subsequent editions used the portrait of Mary Shelley painted by Richard Rothwell in 1840 (now in the National Portrait Gallery, London).
5. On Stanford's book, see 22 April 1951, n. 3.

TO P. H. NEWBY, BBC, LONDON, 31 AUGUST 1951

8, Sussex Mansions, 65, Old Brompton Road, S.W.7
31st August, 1951

Dear Mr. Newby,

Would you be interested in a talk on 'What has replaced narrative verse?' – supplementary to Richard Murphy's recent talk, 'Has narrative poetry failed?'.[1]

I enclose an outline of my idea, and hope you will think it worth doing.

Yours sincerely,

s/Muriel Spark

(Muriel Spark)

SUMMARY WHAT HAS REPLACED NARRATIVE VERSE?

1) Richard Murphy shows that narrative poetry lost significance because of a breakdown in fixed religious beliefs. The answer to the question, what has replaced narrative verse? can be found in Mr. Murphy's diagnosis.

2) A system of beliefs common to most of the population still operates, though they are not religious beliefs. These are beliefs in actual events (an ultimate manifestation of realism if you like) and people are most united when believing in national events such as the Derby, a royal wedding, a cup-tie – the sort of thing that once would have made a ballad. If they were put into a ballad now few would listen, not because the imaginative embellishments necessary to a ballad – to any narrative poem – are beyond the present range of beliefs. But the fact that a vast number of people *will* listen to a story on such topics is proved by the numbers who listen to a broadcast version of the Derby, the royal procession, a boat race, etc.

3) The narrative poem has been replaced by the broadcast commentary. The commentators are the present-day counterpart of the ancient bard who got up and gave utterance *con amore* as it were. The born narrator finds his vocation now in giving an eye-witness account of some big event instead of an imaginative account of the event. It is not a question of whether this is a good or a bad thing; the situation exists whereby, if we want to know something of the excitement transmitted by a story-teller in the past, we will find it in the excitement transmitted by a skilful commentator, who is no more than a story-teller himself. His story, like that of the ancient bard, needs to be commonly assumed as having a certain magnitude.

4) Why say this activity has replaced narrative verse? It has not replaced the novel.

My case is that narrative poetry is originally intended to be spoken to a large audience; the novel normally demands individual and silent reading.

5) Is there any relation between narrative verse and the broadcast commentary? I think there is, and fortunately the commentators are unconscious of it. The account of the last Derby, for instance, was certainly not done

in prose. That does not prove it poetry – it might be in a genre of its own. But it did contain some *elements* of narrative verse; they are technical elements, since the commentator is not creative. But technical qualities are none the less a very important part of poetry. These are among the elements I found:

1. verbal economy and intensity
2. a *dramatic* use of speech-rhythms, i.e. varying according to the mood to be conveyed.
3. a *dramatic* pattern of events – preparatory statement, suspense, action, climax and brief retrospective statement.
4. rhetoric

Now most of these things are enforced by circumstances, some are due to the skill of the narrator. I don't wish to examine the commentator's art, however, but its relation to the art of narrative poetry.

(This would need to be illustrated by short recordings of broadcast commentaries, compared with perhaps a few stanzas from John Masefield's Right Royal (1920) where, in the scene depicting the close of the race, the poet anticipates the modern commentator. Masefield is, incidentally, the last of the narrative poets in the old straightforward sense – when he writes about a fox he means a fox, not a symbol of persecuted mankind.)[2]

6) Speculations about the future of narrative poetry: I agree with Mr. Murphy's view, which, interpreted crudely, is that narrative poetry will be a sort of layer-cake, with the top layer for general readers and the subtler confections for the intellectuals, with variously flavoured strata for the in-betweens.

I think that narrative verse (I have chosen 'verse' as my subject rather than 'poetry' since I am concerned

with the technical aspects) will also absorb something
of the commentators' technique. It may be the use of
the present tense. It may be a certain breathlessness –
the one-word sentence, the short line – in the
rhythms at some points. Such prospects may not be
commendable to the reader of poetry to-day. However,
other times, other tastes. (At all costs, the suggestion
that he is a modern bard should be kept from the
modern commentator.)[3]

TLS. BBC WAC.

1. The talk by Anglo-Irish poet Richard Murphy, entitled 'Narrative Poetry
    Today', was announced in *Radio Times* for broadcast on 28 July: 'Richard
    Murphy talks about the decline of storytelling in poetry and suggests ways
    in which the narrative poem could be written today.'
2. In the conclusion of John Masefield's long narrative poem *Right Royal*
    (1920), the poetry itself, in its quickening of pace and gathering intensity,
    could be said to sound like race-commentary. One of Masefield's most
    famous long poems was *Reynard the Fox* (1920).
3. P. H. Newby will respond by letter on 11 September:

    Your suggestion is interesting but I wish I could believe it would
    resolve into something more (from the listener's point of view)
    than an amusing attitude to the broadcast commentary. The com-
    mentary and the ballad have something in common, no doubt, but
    they are listened to for very different reasons. I'm not convinced
    that the comparison could be pushed far, certainly not so far as to
    suggest narrative verse will absorb something of the commentator's
    technique. Thank you, however, for the suggestion. (BBC WAC)

TO IRIS BIRTWISTLE, BARCELONA,
10 SEPTEMBER 1951

Viking Cottage, Lindfield, N^r Hayward's Heath, Sussex
10.9.51

Arrived here yesterday to find all unchanged. Why should it be
changed after all, in 2 years when it hasn't changed in 200? We

have the whole cottage to ourselves as Miss Basanno 'has an old
lady' up the street whom she companionates. The cottage is full of
ancient & weird cupboards, rafters, and death-trap winding wood
stairs. There is a frog which snores in the garden. The apples fall
and give Derek the nerves. The dustman comes. The milkman
comes. The window-cleaner comes. The people next door have
got another baby just as I told D. they would. The man next door
has re-written 'War and Peace' in 10,000 words for the mob and
is very rich and clever not like us. But D. was clever enough to
get your Keith Douglas to review so you shall have it as a gift.[1]
Can we send it to Spain? We loved your cards & hope you anchor
somewhere after your own heart, far from the trippers. We are
here till 22nd Sept. Write to us if you can.

Love from both

Muriel

APCS showing 'Lindfield, Old Houses'. CBF.

---

1. *The Collected Poems of Keith Douglas*, edited by John Waller and G. S. Fraser,
   had just been published in London, by Editions Poetry.

TO IRIS BIRTWISTLE, BARCELONA, 14 SEPTEMBER 1951

at Viking Cottage, Lindfield, Sussex
14.9.51

My dear Iris,

How are you faring? We are awaiting your report of your next
port of call, hoping you have shaken off the English. Do you
know Amours de Voyage by Clough? All about the 19th century
English in Rome all very amusing. Clough is the only Victorian
I can stomach & that includes Wordsworth & Tennyson most
of the time.[1] We haven't had anything remarkable in the way of
weather, but are in love with Viking Cottage. Also with Lindfield
itself except for the old hens at Aramintas – which is the local arty

crafty tea shoppe where there are wee bits of pottery & pewter on wee shelves you know. They all meet there to discuss people like us. But Lindfield & Miss Basanno are pets. Here is an epitaph in the Churchyard (1768)

> Long was my pain, great was my grief
> Surgeons I'd many but no relief.
> I trust through Christ to rise with the just:
> My leg and thigh was buried fust.

But some idiot restoring the gravestone inscribed the last word 'fust' as 'first', being a know-all, & ruining the whole thing. Miss Basanno's 'old lady' i.e. Miss Helena Hall is very indignant about it.

We work hard, sometimes interrupted by people to see over the cottage, of which the verse enclosed is a memento of one occasion.

Write & let us know if you are not otherwise occupied, how you get on & what you think of Spain & the people.

Derek sports his posh blazer & I, everything from knickers upwards which came in our much talked-of & reminisced-about Parcels. I had one go in the sun with the bathing suit.

Best love & a happy time from Derek &
Muriel

NO MAN IS AN ISLAND – OH, REALLY?

> An old ma with her ancient daughter
> Came to view the cottage this September.
> We being tenants took nonchalent [*sic*] cover
> With books and pencils looking clever
> Wishing the beds were made. However
> They were escorted by the owner
> Into the garden, upstairs, all over.
> They tasted, smelt, looked, listened, touched every corner:

'This looks solid and the cupboards but mother
Doesn't like timber the lavatory's rather
Draughty the desk would have to go father
Died last spring we would rather
Have *his* desk.' Personally *we* would rather
Be dad than mum or daughter.

ALS with typewritten poem enclosed. CBF.

1. Arthur Hugh Clough's epistolary novel in five cantos, written largely in hexameters, published initially in 1858 in *Atlantic Monthly*, will remain one of MS's favourite poetic works.

TO THE EDITOR, THE CHURCH OF ENGLAND NEWSPAPER, LONDON, EARLY NOVEMBER 1951

8, Sussex Mansions, 65, Old Brompton Road, London, S.W.7

SIR, – I have read your discussion, under Commentary (*C.E.N.*, November 9), of the Pope's pronouncement on childbirth with deep interest. With your conclusions I am in agreement, but feel unhappy about the argument you use to refute Papal authority on this question.[1]

This is mainly based on the fact that the Pope is a celibate. I am sorry that you have brought in this question: first, because it has a very strong appearance of relevance, though, in fact, it is not relevant; and, secondly, because there is at present too little respect, and often a great deal of ignorant know-all contempt displayed towards celibacy. I am certain it was not your intention to convey such an attitude; but the fact that the question of celibacy has been introduced in your pages (as it has in the secular Press) does not help to remove this prejudice.

I do not think you could produce evidence to show that celibacy narrows the range of wisdom in human affairs of which a holy man is capable. Evidence to the contrary abounds. It might even be arguable in the present instance that the experience

of marriage limits the insight of a man, however devout, to a
personal sphere.

But surely the question is not whether a celibate or non-
celibate is qualified to pronounce on marriage relations, but
whether the Pope, a holy Christian, has spoken with the wisdom
and compassion with which he might have been expected
to be inspired. I agree with you that he has not done so. His
statement is unacceptable because it is contrary to the spirit of the
Gospels; and seems to proceed from the social politics of Roman
Catholicism rather than the ethics.

Muriel Spark

> Published in *CEN*, 16 November 1951, under the heading 'The Pope and
> Marriage Relations' and the sub-heading 'Does Celibacy Affect Judgment?'

1. The 'Commentary' given in *CEN* in its 9 November edition was prompted
   by an 'Address to Midwives on the Nature of Their Profession' delivered
   in October 1951 by Pope Pius XII, in which he spoke of 'the heroism of
   continence'. After stressing the enormous importance of 'the sex relationship', the article declares 'the Pope's pronouncement to the midwives
   of Italy a disaster'; it goes on to outline exactly why this was so, basing
   its – frankly blistering – argument on the failure of Roman Catholic universal principles to deal with the lived and historically varying conditions
   governing the lives of women and men, and not only or even mainly (as
   MS seems to suggest here) on the incredulity with which pronouncements
   made by a celibate pope will be received by sexually motivated individuals.
   The article concludes:

   > The pity of it is that the Pope has so far overstepped the limits of
   > common sense and the possible that his statements are irrelevant.
   > He has brought discredit upon the Christian Faith instead of honour.
   > Observing that Christianity is irrelevant and unpractical people
   > will fall back upon their old beliefs and habits, confirmed in them.
   > Their cynicism about Roman Catholicism in particular and religion
   > in general will increase and their last state will be worse than their
   > first. That is the harm this declaration has done.

TO IRIS BIRTWISTLE, HOGHTON, LANCASHIRE,
2 DECEMBER 1951

8 Sussex Mansions, 65, Old Brompton Road, London, S.W.7
2.12.51

My dear Iris

Your kind encouraging letter arrived in time to cheer me up
after reading the 1st review of my book in the Spectator. – Written
by a woman who, I think, is something academic at Oxford &
who as good as said it (the book) was a waste of paper. It made me
toy with the fancy that maybe I can do a profitable line, in future,
by expending a twelve-months' labour on the equipment of the
W.C.'s of Lady Margaret's Hall. This is sour grapes coming out,
not to mention coarse upbringing.[1]

I'm overjoyed that you don't think the book a bore. I've
changed my mind about so many things since I wrote it, that I
can't really have *faith* in it, if you know what I mean.

Do tell us about your ailments and if your tubes have recovered.
Coming back from Spain must have roused a protest from all
quarters of your frame I shd. think. About illnesses I am as bad
as Proust. They distress and fascinate me & I always want to give
them a life of their own. Derek of course is *the* one for ailments –
He uses a spray for his asthma which I tell him he would not
have to use if he went to Church, because it is merely a profane
manifestation of incense. But, as he says, who am *I* to talk?

Seriously, do take care of & coddle yourself. And let us see
what you are writing in the still watches.

Many thanks for your cheque & kindness in taking the books –
which I fear will find no other customers. As soon as they arrive
I'll inscribe them as instructed & post them off to you.

I still have your 'Spirit of Catholicism' which I have only
partly read & wd like to keep longer if I may. I like its calm
comprehensiveness.[2] Am trying to catch up with *devotional* reading
as well as theology. Have been reading Pascal in parts.

Do you know any work on the subject of angels (which attracts me)? I know abt. Aquinas' work. Has there been anything fairly recently?

Write soon & tell us you are better.

Best love from us both,

Muriel

ALS. CBF.

1. MS's *Child of Light*, which had just been published by Tower Bridge, was reviewed in the *Spectator* by a specialist on the Shelleys, the novelist, critic, academic, and sometime wife of Edmund Blunden, Sylva Norman (23 November). Her most damning statements on MS's book: 'Her own approach is often clumsy, sometimes ungrammatical, and singularly lacking in that sense of character that can illuminate actions from, as it were, behind themselves. [. . .] Her picture, ungratefully it may be, does not come to life.'

2. On *The Spirit of Catholicism*, see 22 April 1951, n. 4. Iris Birtwistle, who will become a major influence in MS's conversion to Catholicism, was herself, and remained throughout her life, a committed, if free-spirited, Roman Catholic.

TO IRIS BIRTWISTLE, HOGHTON, LANCASHIRE, 25 DECEMBER 1951

8 Sussex Mansions, 65, Old Brompton Road, London, S.W.7
Christmas Day 1951

My dear Iris,

We have just had a whopping great Xmas dinner followed by one of your delicious liqueurs – a Curaçao – in which we drank your good health.

So many thanks for the wire. It helped to pile on the excitement wh. you can imagine has been hectic. It all began last Wed. when a phone call came thro' from the Observer announcing the tidings which of course I couldn't believe – thought they had made some mistake. But no it was quite true, and here we are wallowing in riches. Do come quickly and celebrate with us – our party this time! I am to get the cheque at a lunch party on Wed. next – have never had so much before & of course will never probably have such fun again.[1]

Do you like my Seraph? A very Catholic one, Derek says.

Do write soon & let us know how you are keeping.

Derek sends love with mine, and best wishes for the New Year. Hoping to see you very soon.

Love

Muriel

ALS. CBF.

1. MS later recalled, in *CV*:

> In that year came the first real turning-point in my career. In November *The Observer* announced a short-story competition on the subject of Christmas. The first prize was two hundred and fifty pounds, quite a fortune in those days, with various secondary prizes.
>
> The rules were that the story should be not more than three thousand words, and the entry should be anonymous. The story was to be accompanied by an envelope signed by a pseudonym, the real name inside.
>
> I put aside my work on Masefield and wrote 'The Seraph and the Zambesi' on foolscap paper, straight off. Now I had to type it but I found I had no typing paper. I scrounged some from the owner of an art shop nearby in South Kensington, typed it out, put my pseudonym 'Aquarius' on the envelope and my name and address inside, and mailed it off to *The Observer* that afternoon. [. . .] Near Christmas, I had a phone call from Philip Toynbee of *The Observer*. My story had won first place out of the six thousand seven hundred entries. 'We thought it was written by a man until we opened the envelope,' said Philip. I don't know if I was supposed to be flattered by that.
>
> The story was published the following Sunday. I had by now met and liked the *Observer* editor and staff. The editor, David Astor, Philip Toynbee and Terence Kilmartin had been the judges. Just after midnight on the Sunday of publication, David Astor himself brought the paper to me. It was thrilling to have the newspaper delivered by the editor. (pp. 198–9)

TO P. H. NEWBY, BBC, LONDON, 28 DECEMBER 1951

8 Sussex Mansions, 65, Old Brompton Road, London, S.W.7
28th December 1951

Dear Mr Newby,

Enclosed is a short sketch – a parody on Eliot and Fry
combined – which I hope the 3rd Programme may be able to use.[1]

Maybe I should have sent it to the Drama dept. but as it is more
in the nature of criticism than drama I decided to submit it to
you. If I'm wrong, will you be kind enough to pass it to the proper
department?

With best wishes for The New Year,

Yours sincerely

Muriel Spark

ALS. BBC WAC.

1. MS's play was entitled *The Cocktail's Not for Drinking*. P. H. Newby will
    respond to MS on 2 January 1952: 'I was amused by your parody though
    I thought it a mistake to parody Fry and Eliot at the same time. However,
    as you guessed, it does not fall within my competence to judge it for
    broadcasting and I am passing it to drama department' (BBC WAC). In the
    Drama Script Reader's Report sent to the director Donald McWhinnie,
    the plot is summarised: 'The Duchess of Friskofer prepares a poisoned
    drink for her husband the Duke, it miscarries and they lose a butler.' The
    play's 'Construction' is given as 'Thin and rather pointless', its 'Dialogue'
    as 'Eliot-cum-Fry', its 'Characterisation' as 'Negligible', and under the
    section 'Remarks' it is given as 'A very forced bit of intellectual facetious-
    ness' (BBC WAC).

1952

At the start of the year, MS was contacted by John Smith from the literary agency Christy & Moore Ltd, who later became her first agent. Throughout the year, she published widely – articles, poems, reviews, stories – in journals that included the *Spectator*, *World Review*, *Variegation*, the *Norseman*, *Public Opinion*, and the *Church of England Newspaper*. In January, she entered into detailed discussion of the topic of predestination with Catholic priest Fr Ambrose Agius. She donated £50 to help with the cost of her son Robin's bar mitzvah, which was celebrated on 13 January. In January, also, her play for radio, *The Cocktail's Not for Drinking*, was rejected by P. H. Newby and Donald McWhinnie at the BBC. Before the end of February, she finished her book on John Masefield, and she visited Edinburgh, where she amused herself by reading Marcel Proust's *À la recherche du temps perdu*, a work she admired (and regularly reread, throughout the rest of her life). In May, she organised for Robin to start at Daniel Stewart's College in the autumn. In June, the Hand and Flower Press run by Erica Marx published her first collection of poems, *The Fanfarlo, and Other Verse*. In early summer, after much soul-searching and notwithstanding her lover's protestations, MS renounced sexual intimacy with Derek Stanford, as she prepared to be received into the Anglican church. In August, her story 'Daisy Overend' was published in *World Review*. In September, the Grey Walls Press published MS's edition of *Selected Poems of Emily Brontë* (though the book was made available only in 1953). On 7 November, MS was baptised at St Bride's Church, Fleet Street, and received into the Anglican church, by the Editor of the *Church of England Newspaper*, Clifford Rhodes.

TO MR F., EDINBURGH, FEBRUARY 1952

[Sussex Mansions, London]

Dear M^r F.

I write in reply to your letter of 28th January addressed to my
mother and father. I do so because they were recently very gravely
insulted by Mr S. O. Spark, and I feel that, in the first place,
they should receive the apology due to them, and which they are
themselves perhaps too patient and forbearing to demand.[1]

The incident, which has been reported to me from several
quarters, concerns a visit paid to my parents by Mr Spark last
week. In the hearing of my aunt and my son Robin, Mr Spark
called my parents among other epithets, 'thieves and robbers',
when they refused to hand over to him a small sum of money
which is the property of my son. I understand that my father was
obliged to remove Mr Spark bodily from the house, whereupon
your client continued to shout the words 'thieves and robbers' for
all the neighbours to hear. I understand that Mr Spark added the
remarkable request 'now sue me for slander'![2]

Now it must be clear to you that for a peaceful couple who have
reached their mid-sixties, who have lived over forty years in the
house they now occupy and who have always enjoyed the respect
of their neighbours, to be publicly called thieves and robbers is
most distressing, to say the least. Perhaps more serious, is the
effect on my young son of witnessing his father's behaviour.

My father, who has worked with the same firm for forty-five
years, and who would have retired last year had he not wished
the better to provide for my child, has often been called a fool for
working so hard at his age. But to be called a thief and a robber is,
I assure you, a new experience for him.

Before going on to discuss the substance of your letter, may I
suggest that you bring your influence to bear upon Mr Spark, and
try to persuade him to pull himself together, and to bind himself
over, as it were, to keep the peace, before someone in authority
does it for him. Meanwhile, the most charitable interpretation

we can put on Mr Spark's behaviour is that he is irresponsible and unable control [*sic*] himself.

This being so, is it likely that he is in a position to control other people's property? If only for this reason, I have advised my mother and father that it would be most improper and irresponsible to take away from my child the money gifts which he has received, and allow them to be put into Mr Spark's account as you are suggesting.

But apart from this, there is the question of general principle: you speak of Mr Spark's having been 'awarded the custody of the boy'. That was a long time ago, and meanwhile the boy has grown in health and happiness, he has been given love friendships and complete freedom in a good home; he has been sent to a good school and has been provided with private tuition as well. And has Mr Spark had anything to do with all this? The answer is, No.

Mr Spark has made no contribution to my son's upkeep for over five years. I am sure, therefore, you will realise that his title as a custodian of his child is merely a nominal one. In actual fact my mother has been the child's custodian & has fulfilled the task with unquestionable propriety, even to the extent of instilling into my son a sense of respect for his father!

There is another question of principle which supports my conviction that on no account should we give Robin's small sum of money away to Mr Spark. I understand the money gifts Robin recently received do not amount to a great deal.[3] I do not know the exact sum, as I write from London. Still, like his collection of stamps, his library, his soldiers, they are *his own*. They are his, to do what he likes with. We would not dream, of course, of allowing him to deal foolishly with this money, any more than we would permit him, say, to destroy his books. Fortunately, however, Robin is predisposed to be a reasonable boy, and he tells me he wishes to keep his money by him meantime. I hope that, and by proper guidance from my mother, who has been his guide for so long, he will gain a sense of responsibility from his use of this money. Personally I think he should be encouraged to buy such things as some of his own school sport equipment and he will no doubt want to do small act to help some less fortunate child. Now it seems to me that if these money gifts were to be removed from Robin, he would justifiably feel a great sense of injustice and a lack of confidence in himself. I am sure those friends who gave him the gifts meant him to keep them.

Furthermore, where would one draw the line in such matters? If this sum of money, insignificant in itself, were given to Mr Spark as a concession of principle, how do we know that he would not pounce on the child's library which we are carefully building up? What would prevent Mr Spark from seizing my son's wardrobe? According to the logic of what you are asking, my small boy's pocket-money, his sports' equipment, his savings, his stamp collection, his school books, his very bed – all of which my parents have provided – would be subject to confiscation by Mr S. O. Spark. And what is more serious, your client would demand the right to dispose of funds which we – my mother, my father and myself – have, by making various sacrifices, put by for Robin's immediate needs!

It is therefore with a sense of the chaos which would ensue from their granting Mr Spark's request, that I have to convey my parents' adamant refusal.

Regarding the first paragraph of your letter, my mother will shortly be sending you a statement of account, and she looks forward to receiving the settlement of it in due course.

Yours sincerely

AL draft. NLS. Dating from internal evidence.

1. Mr F. in this draft letter was one of Furst & Furst, the Edinburgh solicitors whose practice had been representing the interests of Sydney Spark, MS's divorced husband, since his return from Southern Rhodesia in 1945.
2. MS's father was Bernard Camberg (known as Barney); it is not known to which aunt or 'aunt', in the strict or loose sense of that term (the loose being common in Scotland at the time), MS is referring.
3. Robin Spark had received gifts for his bar mitzvah that took place on 13 January, including from the money won by his mother in the *Observer* short-story competition: 'My son, who to my parents' satisfaction had decided to be a Jew, also got fifty pounds to pay for a party for his bar mitzvah' (*CV*, p. 199).

TO DEREK STANFORD, HOUNSLOW, MIDDLESEX,
27 FEBRUARY 1952

160, Bruntsfield Place, Edinburgh
27.2.52

My own Boy,

Are you recovered from your tooth, I wonder? I have been
thinking about you at intervals during the day, hoping the
dentist didn't have one of those sudden accesses of professional
excitement, over your tooth, whereby they forget that the tooth
has a patient attached to it.

The journey was not too bad considering there was snow on
the line, holding up the train most of the way, and considering
my Gothic travelling companion. The latter snored heavily – so
heavily I wonder she could sleep thro' it. When the noise got too
loud I dropped my book heavily on the floor whereupon she would
wake & shut up for ten minutes or so. I was fascinated by her
travelling & sleeping gear – many pillows of different sizes to place
(apparently) under different parts of the body; lots of Germanic
'Frau's' equipment in small bags with string; an efficient-looking
vacuum flask dating from about 1920, a pair of hand-knitted
slippers, a large roll & butter which my Goth ate holding it with
both hands. When she went to wash, I was not surprised when
from the depth of a stout leather carrier, an alarm clock went
off. Whatever was in the violin case on the rack began to play. As
for me, I got a *wash* in a 1ˢᵗ class (conceded me by our attendant
friend).

Robin is full of fun & girls' curves. His favourite reading at
the moment is The Illustrated London News and Men Only
which I consider quite balanced. He is pleased with your poems
& is learning one by heart. I ventured to suggest they might be
beyond him for the present, but he assures me such is not the
case. I will let you know as soon as I know myself, which of these
inflammatory verses he has committed to memory.

Ruth is a darling black and white kitten, rather unpopular with my mother. She is so eager to please & anxious to play, I'm sure she is aware of being undesired.

I am bringing home an armchair and possibly an ottoman, also a carpet, which should make us more comfortable. Other items may be added. I won't actually be 'bringing' them but they will be sent by rail.

I came across my two earliest poetry notebooks to-day – 1929–30 and 1931–32 or 33, which amused me. At the age of 11 I had far more metrical variety at my disposal than I have had since. Some of the subject-matter was inspired by school travel-talks. Hence, one of the poems is on Egypt, another on Switzerland. Will bring these back with me, when I return, my own dear boy, to your bonny bonny self.[1]

Will write tomorrow. Meantime, keep my love with you, and be consoled by my thoughts of your tooth.

Adieu and love,

M.

ALS. WUL.

1. These notebooks will become a major source of resentment towards Derek Stanford in the late 1980s and early 1990s when MS is researching for her autobiography and is unable to find them. She will accuse him of having pilfered them and then sold them to American university libraries (see *CV*, p. 188).

TO HM INSPECTOR OF TAXES, LONDON, 6 MAY 1952

[Sussex Mansions, London]
6th May, 1952

Dear Sir,

I enclose my Income Tax return and allowance claim for the year ended 5th April 1952. As you will see I have made a loss of £50.15.6. working as a full-time writer during the past year.

As publication, and consquently payment, of some of my work is delayed, and as I am, like most authors, having rather a hard time, I wonder if you could let me know if I am due for a rebate on tax paid previously?

I enclose details of my income and details of expenses. As you will know, stationery & telephones – indeed, most things – are higher this year than last.

Yours sincerely,

(Muriel Spark)

TAXES 6 MAY 52

Earnings from full-time authorship. April 5th 1951 – April 5th 1952

	Details			
Public Opinion	. . . .	£9.	9.	0
The Spectator	. . . .	2.	12.	6
" "	. . . .	1.	1.	0
Public Opinion	. . . .	7.	17.	6
" "	. . . .	11.	0.	6
Spectator	. . . .	2.	2.	0
World Review	. . . .	2.	2.	0
World Review	. . . .	4.	4.	0
Grey Walls Press	. . . .	25.	0.	0
		£ 65.	8.	6

Expenses April 5th 1951 – April 5th 1952
incurred in the course of full-time authorship.

Travel	£15.	0.	0
Stamps (approx 5/6 a week including Air Mail to America with reply coupons)	14.	6.	0
Stationery (letter paper & notebooks)	12.	0.	0
Carbon-paper (approx. 6d. a week)	1.	6.	0
Typing paper (approx 5/- a month)	3.	0.	0
Typing ribbons (4/11d. a spool – one every 2 months)	1.	9.	6

Cleaning & repairs to typewriter	4.	10.	0
Light & heating (8 hrs a day for ½ year)	20.	0.	0
Telegrams & telephones (trunk, tol [*sic*] & local)	4.	5.	0
Subscriptions to literary societies			
connected with my work			
The Bronte Society		10.	0
The Society of Authors	2.	12.	6
Subscriptions to periodicals connected with my work;			
Times Literary Supplement, World Review	2.	5.	0
Entertainment of Editors and Publishers	35.	0.	0
	£116.	4.	0

TLcc. NLS.

TO HM INSPECTOR OF TAXES, LONDON, 18 MAY 1952

[Sussex Mansions, London]
18th May, 1952

Dear Sir,

Thank you for your letter of 16th May.

With regard to the prize awarded me by *The Observer*, I was given to understand that this was not taxable. I should point out that the sum of this prize was £250 (not £100 as you say in your letter) for a short story by me, the first I had ever written.

Should the inclusion of this sum in my income make me liable to tax, I should wish to appeal against its inclusion, for the following reasons:

The prize was not, in any sense, professional earnings. Indeed, there was a considerable outcry when I was awarded the prize, that it had not gone to a professional short-story writer. There was an article in 'The Bookseller' complaining bitterly of this fact.[1] In 'The Observer' of 30th Dec. 1951, it was clearly stated, in connection with this prize, that this was my first short story.

I am not a short story writer. I am a critic and biographer. I doubt if I shall ever have another short story published. The only *creative* writing I do is poetry. I went in for the competition much as one might enter for a crossword puzzle contest, and no-one was more surprised than myself when I won it. And, as I say, I had to put up with a great deal of criticism on the grounds that I was not a 'professional short-story writer'.

I hope you will be assured that, in setting out the above, I am not trying to avoid paying my just share of tax. The year in question was a particularly hard one, and I had to live on borrowed money (and a low diet!) for the most part. I am hoping to take a part-time job to tide me over until the fruits of my labours appear.

Yours sincerely,

(Muriel Spark)

P.S. I don't want to go into unnecessary details but to give you an idea of how long writers like myself have to wait for payment and publication, I would mention a book I completed in the Autumn of 1949. It was accepted by the publisher at that date, but has not so far appeared. This is holding up payment due to me on publication by the publishers, and also payment from an American publisher who has accepted the book. This book is 'Letters of the Brontës'. I have, besides this, five other books, all of them commissioned or accepted for publication, awaiting publication. Royalties, as you know, are not due till some time – often a whole year – after publication of a book.[2]

TLcc. NLS.

1. The article in the *Bookseller*, signed 'A student of fiction', conveys its author's outrage at being unable even to begin to understand MS's story 'The Seraph and the Zambesi', and decides that 'it appears that the judges were looking for something amateurish'. Of the judges of the competition, the 'student' writes: 'They were disappointed in not finding a literary counterpart to the Douanier Rousseau, but if it was amateurishness they sought, then surely they have succeeded' (5 January 1952).
2. MS's imminent publication was in fact of her first collection of poems, *The Fanfarlo and Other Verse* (Hand and Flower Press). On 4 April, she wrote to

Iris Birtwistle: 'Did you know Erica Marx is doing a separate vol. of my
poems – paper-backed pamphlet but not in the pamphlet series – I don't
know why. She is charging 3/6 for it whereas the pamphlets "proper" are
1/-. I think the title poem – a long one called "The Fanfarlo" helped to get
the book taken. It will be out this spring' (CBF).

TO ROBERT GITTINGS, BBC, LONDON, 11 JULY 1952

[Sussex Mansions, London]
11.7.52

Dear Robert Gittings,

I have just seen your interesting article in World Review.
Will you forgive me if I question you on one point, which
possibly I have no right to raise, and again, which I have perhaps
misunderstood?[1]

What I understand, maybe wrongly, by your denunciation of
friendly critics of Christopher Fry who have got their facts wrong,
who have invented etc. is Derek Stanford. Naturally of course I am
touchy about everything that concerns Derek. I ought to say, too,
that I am writing this without previous consultation with Derek.
I haven't even had the opportunity of discussing your essay with
him yet as I have just got back from Edinburgh. So if I am wrong
in thinking you mean Derek I can only ask you to forgive me.

But if you do mean him, I must say I am a little niggled by your
phrase 'on the strength of a few friendly drinks or a day in the
Cotswolds, to look into the poet's mystery as if they were God's
spies.' If you mean Derek, you really *are* wrong, and for these
reasons.[2]

Derek does not base any of his critical standards on any
'knowledge' he may have of a poet's personality. You must know
this if you have read any of his work. He makes distinctions and
draws comparisons from his experience of life and literature,
and of course his conclusions may be right or wrong. He has
a philosophical turn of mind and is apt to categorise writers
philosophically, which many critics do, and many do not. In

addition, I know he likes, where possible, to take the poet's personality into account when defining the type of writing in question, but he does not use this as a means of judgment. In this sense, Derek is a follower of Herbert Read whose criticism I know he particularly admires.

Now I don't think you can honestly say that Derek has attempted to 'look into the poet's mystery' (by which I take it you mean his work) – in any arrogant manner, nor that his attempt to discover, where Christopher Fry is concerned, the poet in the man, is his only critical resource.

But if it were, you are still not right in saying 'on the strength of a few friendly drinks and a day in the Cotswolds'. First, Derek did know Christopher in the forces, and I am sure he has nowhere tried to pretend he is better acquainted with Christopher than he is. Secondly, Derek did not spend a day in the Cotswolds with Christopher, he spent only an hour or two with him at the most. Derek and I stayed about two days in Shipton at that time and I know that when Derek met Mr. Fry there he got a unified impression of the man, the poet and the place. I am sure you have sufficient imagination to recognise that such a thing is possible. And you must be aware that Derek's understanding of Christopher Fry or any other poet, in the personal sense, has nothing whatever to do with the number of years he has known him, the number of times he has met him. When I say 'the personal sense' I mean in so far as the permanent personal essence which Derek always looks for in a poet, is to be related to the poetry. Thirdly, in any case, whenever Derek has written on Christopher he has consulted him.* And I think Derek discussed a lot of things with him on several occasions in London; sometimes I was there at the time.

Please don't think that, because I have raised this question, I consider it an important one so far as your article is concerned. The reply to the editors of World Review is what was needed. At the same time, I don't think your favourable remarks differ *in kind* from those of other favourable critics as you seem to suggest. I mean, that if other favourable criticism might have been harmful

to Mr. Fry, then so might yours, and the good thing is that it is
not harmful. To return (as I can't resist doing) to Derek again,
any element of 'harm' in his work is in fact mildly operative
against himself: you may not have thought of this, but it is true
that Christopher Fry was for a long time, and may still be for all
I know, unpopular with 'intellectuals'. Derek's point of view is
intellectual, but not in inverted commas, so to speak; in other
words he follows his own taste. His admiration for the work of
Christopher Fry is on the whole disapproved of by 'intellectuals',
not that Derek cares at all.

I hope you will accept my apology if I have jumped to a wrong
conclusion, just as I think you will say frankly if it is Derek you
refer to. And if I am wrong, you must put it down to my partiality
for him.

Yours sincerely,

(Muriel Spark)

* I don't mean by this of course that Derek has offered his work
for supervision.

TLcc. NLS.

1. Robert Gittings's article 'Christopher Fry' appeared in *World Review* (New
    Series 41, July 1952). Gittings had been friends with Christopher Fry
    since his schooldays; since 1940 he had worked as a writer and producer
    at the BBC, and published his first book of poems, *Wentworth Place*, in 1950
    (Heinemann).
2. Derek Stanford and MS visited Christopher Fry at his home in Shipton-
    under-Wychwood the previous year in preparation of Stanford's book
    Christopher Fry: An Appreciation.

TO ROBERT GITTINGS, WEST BROYLE HOUSE, CHICHESTER, 29 JULY 1952

8 Sussex Mansions, 65 Old Brompton Rd., S.W.7
29th July 1952

Dear Robert Gittings,

Many sincere thanks for your letter and for putting my mind easy on the subject of the Cotswolds and the drinks. When I told Derek I had written to you he pointed out that thousands of people go to the Cotswolds and they all drink and he further informed me that I had missed the point of your article, and that women are all the same. So you see my stock is not very high over this business at either end. Please accept my apologies.[1]

However I was right in that you attribute inaccuracies to Derek and having gone so far I feel bound to go further and say something on the question of inaccuracy where he is concerned.

First, if he has been inaccurate I can say quite assuredly that this is not because he has 'invented' (your term) facts but because of misunderstanding.

Second, to give you an example of how such inaccuracy can arise, I would like to speak of the example you cite in your letter, of Derek's alleged inaccuracy. You say 'to attribute to Mr. Fry without his permission, a rather silly dance-lyric, which was, in fact, the joint work of other members of the Non-Combatant Pioneer Corps, does seem both inaccurate and harmful'. Now, your statement is inaccurate. I remember, in this very room, Derek mentioned the lyric to Mr. Fry in connection with his book 'Christopher Fry, an appreciation'. C. F. tried to recall the exact words of the tune. Of course Derek made no formalised application for permission to use it but Mr. Fry did not express a wish that it should not be used, nor did he say that the lyric was the joint work of several people. Later, when he saw Derek's book in typescript form he did not ask for the removal of the lyric and he did not speak of his part-authorship. Later on Derek found the original version of the lyric, it is in C. F.'s writing. Mr. Fry had given it to Derek to publish in the Company magazine of which D. was the editor. That's the history of Derek's insertion of the lyric in his book. I agree with you that it is silly: that's its chief charm to my mind. And how can it be harmful if it has done no harm?

Please do not interpret this as a retort to your statement. I have gone into these details only because you chose this example, and, more important, because you will see how easy it is to get the facts wrong. One other point on this score since you are, understandably, keen on accuracy and take your critical stand by it: The section of the military of which both Christopher Fry and Derek were members was not as you say, the 'Non-Combatant Pioneer Corps'. From January 1941 onward it was officially called the 'Non-Combatant Corps'. Before that it had been called the 'Non-Combatant Labour Corps'. The word 'Pioneer' seems to be, I fear a belligerent wish-fulfilment fantasy emanating from the scholarly cells of Amen House.[2]

I don't say all this in order to prove that Derek is always accurate. My own conviction about any inaccuracies his books may contain is that they have arisen from misunderstanding. Certainly not from a will to invent. Of course I believe he is always ready to be put right as to facts.[3]

Finally, I hope I am correct in interpreting the last sentence of your letter in a strictly particular sense. You say, 'I need hardly add that the article was submitted to Mr. Fry, and discussed fully with him, before it was sent to the Editor of *World Review*.' Now, although I am sure the other readers of World Review would have had twenty fits if they had known of this, I don't myself say you were wrong in this particular case. Your words 'I need hardly add' did lead me to wonder, though, if you considered it right in general for a critic to submit his criticism to the author on whose work he is writing. Surely you don't mean this. Such an unusual proceeding would be the death of honest criticism, would it not? But I don't deny there are times when a critic feels it would be advantageous to have the author's opinion on what he writes, if the author can be bothered.[4]

Please believe me when I say that your letter has removed my suspicions of ill-will, and I hope you will accept this in the same spirit.

    With kind regards,

    Yours sincerely,

TLcc. NLS.

1. Robert Gittings responded to MS's letter of 11 July on 23 July, writing, of his mention of visits to Christopher Fry: 'Quite categorically, it does not refer to any visit by you, Mr. Stanford, or, indeed, anyone else, to Mr. Fry's former home at Shipton-under-Wychwood' (NLS).

2. Amen House was the home of Oxford University Press in London. In his response to the present letter, Gittings will write, on 30 July: 'Thank you for putting me right over "pioneer". I must absolve the O.U.P. though, as it arises from my own vague recollection of Christopher himself using the term' (NLS).

3. MS would come to revise this judgement in *CV*, where she says, of Stanford and of this exchange with Gittings in particular:

> He was bookish with scholarly leanings, but, as I found gradually, and later to my cost, wildly and almost constitutionally inaccurate. [...] Derek Stanford's main fault as a critic was inaccuracy. It brought in a great many complaints. A book he wrote on Christopher Fry was challenged publicly by Fry's friend, Robert Gittings. I was so sorry for despondent Derek that I wrote to Gittings a sort of defence, but I was on the losing side. Robert Gittings pointed out that a silly dance-lyric had been attributed to Fry, which in fact was not his work, and recommended me to feel concern that Derek's published works be accurate. It was often small facts, dates and titles that Derek couldn't get right. (pp. 187, 189)

4. In his letter to MS of 30 July, Gittings will write:

> Your last paragraph raises a very interesting point. I think my answer is: Yes, if a critical article contains much biography, as distinct from purely textual criticism, and particularly if it quotes hitherto un-published material, then the critic certainly owes an obligation to his subject to show him the article. I don't think it will shackle free criticism, and I do think it does away with the least chance of inac-curacy or misrepresentation, which, as you rightly say, may creep in through some purely accidental misunderstanding. (NLS)

TO DEREK STANFORD, HOUNSLOW, MIDDLESEX, 25 SEPTEMBER 1952

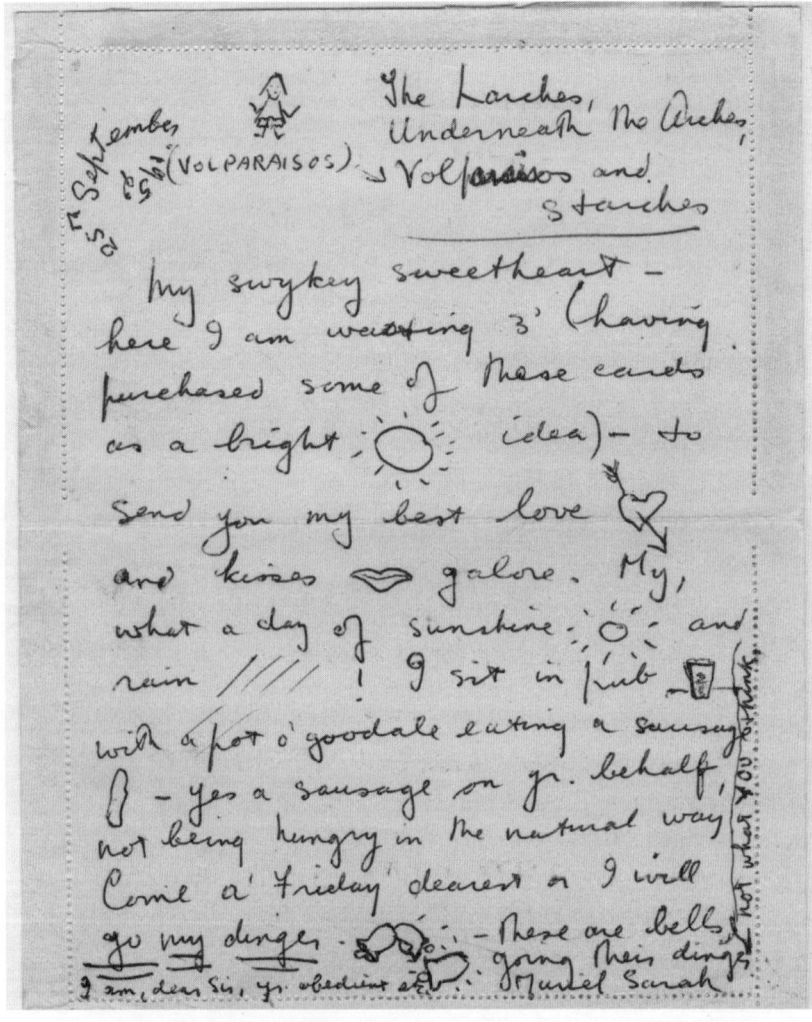

The Larches, Underneath the Arches, Volparaisos and Starches
[Sussex Mansions, London]
25th September, 1952

My swykey sweetheart – here I am wasting 3' (having purchased some of these cards as a bright [doodle] idea) – to send you my best love [doodle] and kisses [doodle] galore. My, what a day of

sunshine [doodle] and rain [doodle]! I sit in pub [doodle] with a pot
o' goodale eating a sausage [doodle] – yes a sausage on yr. behalf,
not being hungry in the natural way. Come a' Friday dearest or I
will *go my dinger* [doodle] – these are bells going their dinger, not
what YOU think.

I am, dear Sir, yr. obedient etc.

Muriel Sarah

ALS. HRC. Place from postmark.

TO THE EDITOR, THE CHURCH OF ENGLAND
NEWSPAPER, LONDON, LATE OCTOBER 1952

8 Sussex Mansions, 65 Old Brompton Rd., S.W.7

Sir, – I was interested to read the Rev. A. Johansen's article, in
last week's *C.E.N.*, about his conversations in Russia. But I regret
that so much of the article was occupied with those inventories
of statistics, which visitors to Russia seem so prone to bring back
with them.[1]

Recently, I heard a report of a visit to Moscow by the Authors'
Peace Appeal: it was the same old thing, three thousand of this
and seven hundred thousand of that. What these authors were
doing with their creative insight and critical faculties I don't know.
They said that enough trees had been planted in the Soviet to go
three (or was it three thousand?) times round the earth. It would
take fifteen minutes to demolish a building. What sort of trees and
buildings, what quality and kind of people did the planting and
demolishing they did not say.

No doubt the Russian people know the statistics of their daily
life better than we know ours, and when questioned are inclined
to answer in terms of numbers. But a visitor from the Church
might be expected to look for the essence beyond these answers,
and to discern how Christianity is revealed to the people – in
what form, to what degree, of what quality. For it doesn't help
us much to understand our fellow-Christians in the Soviet Union

when visitors depart speaking the language of the humane-liberal tradition, and return, dazzled with percentages, to address us in the language of economics.

Muriel Spark

Published in the *Church of England Newspaper*, 31 October 1952.

1. Reverend A. Johansen's article was the cover story in the *CEN* of 24 October: 'Casual Talks in Moscow Streets: What Ordinary Russians Told a Visitor about Religion'.

TO DEREK STANFORD, HOUNSLOW, MIDDLESEX, 26 OCTOBER 1952

8, Sussex Mans.
Sunday 26 Oct 52

My Dearest Own Boy,

A note to ask you to forgive me, as I know you will do. Your exasperation about my going on abt. my play is justified & I can see that now, & will try not to go on about it. My present panic comes from doing so much on spec. & getting nowhere. Not an *excuse* for panicking of course. I had hopes of my 'Cocktail' – all washed up. Hopes of my essays – washed up so far as I can see. Hopes of my 'Pearl Miners' – the same hopes of my review in Observer – ditto.[1]

I am getting as bad as Ian. Perhaps I wasn't nice enough about Ian's last letter & this is a judgment.[2]

Yes, I'll do my play for a week. I think it a good idea. In fact your suggestions were all good. What I was moaning about I don't know, except that I'm out of sorts, not being able to go to Church. Read, for my expostulation about the delay, not a diatribe against old Rhodes, but against the circumstances – hardly as you say a Xtian attitude. I think I had better start attending St. Mary Abbots' a-Sundays, don't you?[3]

Dearest, be my friend. I have to live in the world & have a sense of the insecurity of the world – much more so than before. I knew I would have to face insecurity when I decided on the security of God. Now, of course, it is difficult to remember my gain, being so beset everywhere with my loss – not the least of which is the loss of our love's most lovely communion. At least, not being able to go to Church shows me where I stand. If I can only find God in Church, then something's wrong with my faith, which I have hopes of putting right. Converts are always unbearable at this stage, I've heard. Don't take me for a model of Xtianity . . .

All my love,

Muriel

Hope you will ring again. Am sure you will.

xxx

ALS. HRC.

1. MS is referring to her unfinished play *Warrender Chase*, elements of which will re-emerge in her 1981 novel *Loitering with Intent*.

   On MS's play *The Cocktail's Not for Drinking*, see 28 December 1951. On 10 January, Donald McWhinnie at the BBC Drama Script Unit returned the play to MS: 'Unfortunately we have been unable to find a place for it in the programmes' (BBC WAC).

   MS's poem 'The Pearl-Miners' will be published the following year in *Poetry* (September 1953; *CP*, pp. 24–5).

   On 16 September, MS wrote to David Astor, Editor of the *Observer*: 'I would love to write something for you and am working on one or two things now which you may like. The subject of your new essay comp. sounds delightful: too elusive for me, I fear, but I'm doing an essay on Noses' (NLS). On 23 October, Astor replied: 'I do hope that it won't be long before we find the right sort of formula for your contribution – I am sure it is only a matter of time' (NLS).

2. 'Ian' is the Scottish poet and artist Ian Hamilton Finlay whom MS knew through Derek Stanford.

3. The reason MS was not able to visit her usual church, which was St Augustine's in Kensington, was almost certainly because she had been advised she was living in sin with Stanford; she had resolved to become chaste – to renounce 'our love's most lovely communion' – and be baptised into the Church of England by the Anglican priest and Editor of the *CEN*, Clifford Rhodes. St Mary Abbots Church, also in Kensington, had a particular significance for MS and Stanford, as Martin Stannard explains:

'Its graveyard had been her garden in Vicarage Gate days. Muriel and Stanford had once lain on their backs in the grass there and composed a joint verse. There she had sat happily alone among the tombstones with notebook, pencil, sandwiches and cigarettes, puzzling out her own poems' (*MSB*, p. 134).

TO DEREK STANFORD, HOUNSLOW, MIDDLESEX,
9 NOVEMBER 1952

[Sussex Mansions, London]
Sunday 9/11/52

x

x x x

x

x[1]

My dearest Derek,

  – A statement of my thoughts, darling, while you are not here to talk back. Such is the mean advantage I take.

  As you know, I wish we could be married & fully enjoy our love in more ways than that of which we are at present deprived. And I wish, of course, that we could be married in Church if it were possible. The fact of *being* married would, for my part, give a fuller meaning to our relationship. What I'd *prefer* to do, would be to wait, as we are, until you gave full inner assent to a Church marriage. But in any case I don't even know if you are able to assent to a civil marriage.

  I'd prefer to wait, but as I said, I have this family problem pressing on me. I regard it as providential (for them) that they were prevented from coming and hearing our emergency story. I know it would have shaken them up a great deal. Especially Robin, who has imbibed their conventional outlook & their morals. He would have suffered a grief. So would my father. I don't know about my mother – she would have had many conflicted feelings of sorts. Anyway, I've come to regard the inflicting of grief on my parents – especially on Robin, as something I should not do. You are thinking

on the same lines as regards your parents, I know — in fact you
put the idea into practice long before I thought of it. Remember
that their generation have a different code for women than for
men. I feel it slightly humiliating to have to suit my actions to the
reactions of my parents, whose company is on the whole tedious,
and by whose *conscious advice* I would not be guided. I am guided
simply by the fact that it is in my power to cause them pain, and
that I must not do so. This is the pressure to which I am subject,
and I am asking you to accept the problem as yours. And I couldn't
possibly resent it if you declined to accept it; you must judge for
yourself whether, for you, it is really a problem.

What I want to avoid is further rash-decisions, last-minute
actions and palpitating frictions on our part, should my people
decide to come to London. Sooner or later they will come. When
they do, if we are still together, living, outwardly, as man and
wife, I would like us to be living *thoroughly* as man and wife, and
in fact to *be* man and wife. I am tired of putting them off, and so
are you. We are past the stage of hiding & concealing. There is
no way of making them understand that we are living celebately
[*sic*], without in any case, paining them. I mean that, even if we
told them the absolute truth — that we are living celebately [*sic*]
until you are consciously — and I, too, spiritually — prepared for
marriage — even if we told them this, we cannot evade the fact
that we are known as 'M^r & Mrs Stanford' & that this fiction has
to be respected in these quarters. I am not too happy about this
myself, so could hardly expect them to take it easily. And the
dominant feeling in Robin's mind that his mother was up to no
good, I couldn't bear — not only because of his *opinion* of me, but
because of the effect such a feeling would have on himself. If we
were married, I would not hesitate to admit that we had formerly
lived together & in fact would consider it a salutary human
example for Robin — it wd. broaden his outlook to know that
there is a time for fallibility and a time for putting it right (i.e.
when it *becomes* fallibility). He might not be able to understand
this at once, but in any case he *would* understand that we were
married.

There are several things we can do, as far as I can see, and I
think you will probably suggest other things too. Don't forget,
by the way, that I love you dearly and won't love you the less,
whatever you suggest. We could get married in a Registry Office,
fairly soon, which would merely legalise the man-and-wife
relationship between us, which we have already acknowledged.
From my own particular viewpoint, which I don't know if you
share, this would *also* be spiritually acceptable to me; I mean that,
the Church accepts such a marriage; this is a charitable attitude
on the Church's part, – at least it seems so from my point of view,
because it allows for theological & spiritual reservations on the
part of either party, or both. You may not regard a civil marriage
as more than a civil contract, and you are not required to do so; it
would be, if that is your view, no more than a legal confirmation
of what we have affirmed; that we are man and wife. In all senses,
then, we could truthfully say, 'We are married.' Another course
would be to get married in Church (and if we were married
civilly, I would always hope that we would eventually be re-
married in Church). This would depend upon the extent to which
you were prepared to equate your real spiritual perceptions with
the Christian religion; and it would depend on your frankly telling
the officiating minister of your *special* interpretation of the service,
and of all your reservations. I, too, would have to submit my
interpretations & reservations. It would depend, then, on whether
these were acceptable to the priest. If it were Rhodes, I think he
would accept us to the fullest extent of his conscience, which is as
broad as the Church itself.

But maybe you won't want to or feel able to accept this problem
of mine – which is only part of the general problem of our living
together in the society in which we find ourselves, and in the
spiritual state in which we find ourselves – perhaps you will not
be able to consider my problem yours. Would it be advisable,
then, for us to find some other place, where I could live alone
as a single person, until we discovered a way of life? My whole
heart revolts against it. I hope darling I will not be condemned
to living apart from you. I am not sure that bitterness against all

the circumstances which had brought it about (not yourself, my dear) – against the pressure which had set me apart from you, would not overwhelm me. I would have to pray for courage to contend with it. For you know I treasure you and all that you do. If you cannot accept my problem, darling, do this for me: assure me that it is for your spiritual good. Make me understand that, if I must live apart from you, it is because you would be wronging yourself to marry me. If I fully understood this to be the case, if it *is* the case (which I *trust* not) – if I really understood that your development & welfare was involved, I could accept our parting with less suffering & resentment of the circumstances. For, it would be no pleasure or solace or grace to me to be married to you, if it got into the way of your spirit. Believe me, my own boy, I am really sincere in saying that. If it is wrong for us not to be married, then I know it would be by far the more wrong, for us to be married to your spiritual – or intellectual – detriment. I know, too, that such a marriage would do me no good. I would deteriorate.

But I'm not at present trying to anticipate too much. I have a trust, and that is, that all will be well – which platitudinous sentiment I base simply on my present endeavours to be very honest. You know my tendencies to force issues. Well, I have tried to tell you that I am being forced, and naturally am asking you to be forced along with me. What is natural, however, is not always fair. Forgive me if I am unfairly placing you in a spot. I can't say that I'm *not* taking advantage, in asking you this, of your love for me, because *of course* I am doing so, and I take these liberties, from my love for you, too. And who knows? – you may be in complete sympathy with my predicament, and wish to involve yourself with me in it, and *yet* be unable to actively comply, for some reason you are not fully ready to formulate. I am not, in my proper senses, obdurate against any such objection, if you make it, because I would know you were sincere, and I know that we are not rational beings entirely.

Now, pray for guidance, dear, to your Prime Mover or whatever. Trite advice, but it's all I will presume to give, not wishing to be thought of as a Claudel, any more than you are a Gide, you dear thing that you are.[2] Eight pages, I see I've written. It's enough to cook my goose re. matrimony, I shd. think. If only they hadn't told me to go on, go on, go on! My love & blessings, from your

Muriel

Sunday 9th 11 '52

A *postscript* my own boy.

Throughout the foregoing, I have not written of my duty to you. I am not forgetful of it, though. That is why I am unable to say to myself 'I must do this – or else that' – far less say what *you* must do. My duty to you is very great. You have behaved responsibly towards me. All this, quite apart from our love. You are, in fact, a highly responsible being. It is just that you have not so far seen your way to *acknowledge* the responsibility – which you have, in fact, observed. Usually, with men & women alike, it is the other way round. They get married and acknowledge responsibility, then fail to observe it.

You see my uncertainty? With your permission, I was going to speak of this to Rhodes, if he could give me a time.

I am at present considering the extent of my responsibility, in *observance* to you. I have to be your love & your helpmeet. I have to deny myself a few material things which I would otherwise thoughtlessly acquire. (Later, I might have to face real need, I know.) I have to keep my will under control – quite the opposite of suppression. You are ahead of me in these things, these actions & attitudes.

I am ahead of you, I submit, in that, I see that you are, by your actions, in favour of the marital responsibilities between us – but you will not have it acknowledged by us.

My own responsibilities to you, at the present time, do not differ at all, I think, from those I would undertake on marriage. Now is my time to realize them, and darling, I am trying to do so, along with the troublesome doubts about Robin's claim on my

conduct. – This makes it difficult for me always to speak to you as
I should, in full freedom. Especially, you know, on the phone, it's
not easy to convey both a dilemma *and* goodwill, tho' indeed I feel
them both.

Don't think I spend all my time thinking about these things.
I work hard, and of course you know that. My play no longer
oppresses me; it will be done in good season. I will do my work
as it comes to me, and am thankful that I am getting work to do.
Things have not been all black recently – There was my story
accepted by Norseman, my essay by World Review. I have got
the Newman from the Observer & the Paul Jennings book: At
least these are commissioned. It seems as tho' my Bronte Letters
will be safe with Nevill's. We have our Mary Shelley and my
Masefield – some returns from both next year, if all goes aright.[3]
You see, I do not despair & I'll try to do my duty to us both by
working hard. Thanks to you, I have got over my panic about the
play; I have this grandiose conception of it's being composed in
Time-Eternal. No other time, quite seriously, would be suitable
at all, for such a project as I have in mind re that play (& no doubt
it will see the boards but in Eternity too!).[4] I want you to do your
work. On my conscience, I may as well tell you, is that Fry album
which you would not possibly have done, had your responsibilities
towards me not required the money. My feeling about the album,
personally, is that it is a good book. But I am conscious of the fact
that *you* would have preferred not to write it. I see myself as the
indirect cause of your going against your preference, (as well as
being the one who suggested it, if I remember).[5] I would not wish
you to write anything you were not fully in assent to, again, not
for anybody's sake. Do not do the Emily Brontë at all, my sweet,
if you do not want to, really. But I think you do want to, on your
own terms & in your own way. I will start mine, all being well,
in January – that's a promise. (So is the black coat not-to-be-worn
until the Spring.)

Needless to say, I am not posting this letter. My twilight
cogitations must not be read when the morning light cracks
down on your lone Osterley bedroom. You are such a *terrible boy*,

really. What a piece of work is Derek Stanford![6] But I know fine,
that you would not be loveable at all to me were you cut to the
simple proportions of the 'marrying man' or I, for that matter,
to the 'marrying girl'. Part of my duty to you, I think, is *never*
to try to make you conform to an entity within the limits of my
understanding. You see, I ask you to explain yourself, but I don't
expect fully to understand you, ever, in this life. Nor you me. If
we were constant beings by nature, like angels, it would be easier.
But we are flux, mere flux. No, not 'mere' flux – necessary, right
& proper flux. Let us, then, fluctuate in each other's direction
from time to time & create a bit of harmony and joy; as indeed has
happened heretofore.

Now, as to my being shoved into a single room with nothing but
my righteousness to console me, do you think I like the idea the
more I think of it? No fear, and neither do you. And I don't like
the ancestral voices prophesying calamitous wailings & breast-
beatings from Edinburgh, either.[7] And neither do you. Besides, I
am not making a Hamlet out of Robin, if I can help it & neither
are you. So rack yr. loaf, my love, & meantime I'll stave off the
Border-sallies.[8]

Let me tell you something else, while about it. I am only a wee
thing but I'm a woman, in case you've forgot. Therefore, consider
yourself, my snooty-pie, as not yet accepted. On principle,
you would have to propose to me *three times* before you were
accepted, if at all. It is my due, as a bonny girl, and I deserve
no less. Furthermore, each proposal is to be framed in different
phraseology, & a lot depends on the same. Also on deportment &
general demeanour. Even then . . . . . . but you are quaking already
& I am your garrulous
    Sarah

                                                    ALS. HRC.

1. In the handwritten original of this letter, MS's 'kiss' symbols form a clear
    Christian cross; MS had been baptised two days previously.
2. Paul Claudel and André Gide were close acquaintances from 1899 and

continued so for more than ten years before they became adversaries; among the sources of their animosity was Gide's refusal of Claudel's attempts to convert him to Christianity (and Catholicism, in particular).

3.   The story recently accepted by the journal the *Norseman* was 'The House of the Famous Poet'; it will be published in 1952. On the essay that MS submitted to *World Review*, on Allen Tate, receipt of which was acknowledged on 31 October (NLS), see 10 February 1953. It is not known where – or indeed if – MS's review of Paul Jennings's *Even Oddlier* was published; her review of the biography *Newman's Way* by Sean O'Faoláin, 'An Exile's Path', will appear in the *Observer* (30 November). By 'our Mary Shelley' MS refers to what will become *My Best Mary: The Selected Letters of Mary Wollstonecraft Shelley*, which will be published by Wingate in 1953.

4.   In a letter to Derek Stanford sent three months earlier, on 17 August, when discussing her play in progress, MS addressed what will become one of the key motifs of her fiction, the relation between an open future and predestination: 'Warrender Chase progresses steadily towards the abyss prepared for him. I feel like Mister Calvin. Think of me sweet heart, with my play, my anxiety about you & my two pathetic bottles of milk standing unsucked in the kitchen' (NLS).

In his *Muriel Spark's Early Fiction* (Edinburgh University Press, 2021), James Bailey writes of the unpublished *Warrender Chase* that exists as notes in the NLS:

> Drafted in 1952, the play is a ludic and frequently absurd meditation on mortality, spectrality and the significance of one's life's work. The surname of the eponymous protagonist, Spark writes in her notes for a supplementary *précis*, is itself meaningful: Chase is an author consumed with anxiety as he seeks with mounting desperation to bring innumerable creative endeavours to completion. [. . .] Perhaps Chase's 'tragedy' is that death catches up with him before his work is done. Spark, like her protagonist, never finished the job, and the play remained uncompleted. (p. 35)

5.   Stanford followed up his critical work *Christopher Fry: An Appreciation* with a book intended for a broader readership, to be published in 1952 by Peter Nevill: *Christopher Fry Album*.

6.   MS *did* post the present letter. Osterley is part of the Borough of Hounslow where Stanford lived with his parents at 26 Lulworth Avenue. MS is perhaps alluding to the French term *enfant terrible*; she then borrows from William Shakespeare's Hamlet, who explains his melancholy state to Rosencrantz and Guildenstern: 'What a piece of work is a man, how noble in reason, how infinite in faculties, in form and moving, how express and admirable in action, how like an angel in apprehension, how like a god!' (*RS*: *Hamlet*, II, ii, 303–7).

7. MS adapts from Samuel Taylor Coleridge's 'Kubla Khan':

   > And 'mid this tumult Kubla heard from far
   > Ancestral voices prophesying war!

8. MS alludes to the remarriage of Hamlet's mother Gertrude, which is
   the principal source of Hamlet's melancholy at the start of Shakespeare's
   tragedy.
      By 'border-sallies' MS is referring to raids made across the Scotland–
   England frontier by the Border Reivers, as recorded in the Border Ballads
   of which MS was immensely fond.

TO IRIS BIRTWISTLE, HOGHTON, LANCASHIRE, 2 DECEMBER 1952

8, Sussex Mansions, 65, Old Brompton Rd. S.W.7
2nd Dec. 1952

Dearest Iris,

I've been wanting to write you for so long. I do wish you were
here, so that I could pester you on the phone again. I had to put
aside all letter-writing & also my play, which I passionately want
to get on with, to try & do something for the Observer. They
keep writing me letters & sending books for review, but so far
have only printed 1 review & 1 'shorter notice'. They didn't like
my acrobats piece. I did another on Noses for them which they
liked, & asked me to re-write, which I did, ages ago; & haven't
heard anything more. So bugger the Observer, from now on. I
think they think that as they 'discovered' me they can get me to
write for their wastepaper baskets forever after. But I've done
a new Christmas story for the Church of England Newspaper –
appearing this Friday. Will send you a copy.[1]

As to my news, personal. Derek & I have been living in grand
celibacy since you left. I haven't told Derek that I'd mentioned the
possibility to you, as he's rather touchy about it, & I don't want
to hurt him unnecessarily. But I'll tell him, after I've posted this,
that I *have* told you, in my letter. We are getting along very nicely
at the moment, but dear Iris, I'm so uncertain about the future.

At first we left the question of marriage open, & then I decided, maybe wrongly, that we should have a time-limit, partly because I hate uncertainty & partly because my parents & Robin are sure to turn up in London some time. I have managed to put them off for years, and they sense something, I know. And I don't feel inclined to put them off any more. They are dreadfully provincial-minded & would be horrified to find us together – and if we explained that we were living quite chastely, they might be even more horrified, if they believed it at all. It's Robin I'm thinking of, particularly. I don't want him to be upset, as he would be, having been under my mother's conventional influence for so long. So D. & I decided on 19th March as a date by which D. can make up his mind whether he can marry me.

But once or twice since then, I've been a terror to Derek. It *niggles* me, Iris, to think that after almost four years of being called his wife, for his convenience, as well as my own, I've now got to wait till he makes up his mind about putting the thing into practice – so that on 19th March he might say yes or he might say no. It ought to be *me*, (by my feminine reckoning) who says yes or no. Still I've only got myself to blame, and I do love the bastard. However, I've been intimating to D. that I'm not at all sure if I *will* marry him, whatever he says. This upsets him a lot. So I have decided to swallow my pride & chuck this line, & just wait & pray for the best.

Derek has a good case, anyway. He points out that I was quite content to live with him in an unmarried state & that I made the decision about celibacy. He can't be expected to change his attitude on fundamentals, just when I choose to change mine. Actually, he didn't hesitate about our physical parting, when he knew my feelings, and he didn't think of leaving me, as many a man might have done. I know he is trying to come to terms with the idea of marriage & his mind doesn't respond well to pressure. He is quite a pet, as you know.

Keep all this to yourself, won't you? Except, remember me in your prayers, please. Both of us.

I was baptized on Nov 7 at St. Bride's, Fleet Street, by Derek's

friend, C. O. Rhodes (who edits the C. of E. Newspaper). He is
rather too low-church for me, but Derek is so strongly against
Anglo-Catholics, that I thought it wd. be helpful to D. if I didn't
continue with the priest I had been seeing.[2] Derek was very
pleased about this & was one of my sponsors at the baptism! But
I'm still attending the services at St. Augustine's (the Anglo-
Catholic place) – as the form of worship is a delight, & much more
normal than these bleak Protestant outfits. Next thing is to get
confirmed. Derek isn't confirmed & says he doesn't want to be.
But if we get married he wants it to be in church, not in a registry
office. He's a mass of paradoxes – an extremely religious soul,
dear Iris, make no mistake.

Well, that's my news. I wish I could come & see you, but as I've
to go to Edinburgh (in order to keep them from coming here) for
a week this month, I wouldn't manage it till January. Can I come
in January please?

I liked your poems enormously – but not the conversion one,
so much. Derek sent them back to you before I had a second look,
so would you lend them to me again when next you write? I have
done one – which I'll enclose if I can type it out this afternoon. If
not, will send it in my next. The little room is my sanctuary, and
just at this time, I couldn't have kept sane without a room all to
myself, you dear thing. By this time next year, I may be alone, in
another room all to myself – but who knows?[3]

Give your mother my love. I do hope all turns out well for her.
She is so charming & so brave & so *composed*, quite a model for me
in my upheaved state.[4]

How good about the Christmas cards! Am looking forward to
seeing one at Christmas. Why don't you write your autobiography
& retrieve the family fortunes? You *could* do it. Your prose is
just the sort of thing – if you kept to the style of yr. letters. An
autobiography about yourself & your family amorphously on the
fringe – you would remember heaps of things, *as* you wrote,
about yourself & the emergence of the poetic instinct etc. – things
that you can't, maybe, place at the moment. Then there's the
Wren phase & the amusing side & the awful side. *Do it*, you old

Iris, because you ought to do something more than snatching
a week here & there to type the bottled-up poems. Even if the
poems have to wait for a bit, it's often a good thing, because they
lie fallow & then come up again later. If autobiography doesn't
appeal to you, then do a novel & give it three hours a day steady.
What cheek I have telling you what you ought to do, but really I
look upon you as a writer by vocation & on your poems as part of
your job in life, not just a spare-time outlet. And I suggest prose,
because it doesn't at all militate against the poetic vision, & in fact
it needs the poetic vision; prose is something, (if it's a long work)
that needs to be done every day, & it's something that will sell,
and I think you'ld enjoy the doing of it. But I may be wrong.

   Love to all the expectant mothers & particularly the youngest,
whom I remember with affection, as she bubbled in from her
school that day we first met. Give kind words, too, to Mrs Jowett.[5]

   Love to your dear self. Write soon; (circumspectly, as I know
you will!).

   Muriel

ALS. CBF.

1. The *Observer* will publish MS's 'Eyes and Noses' on 18 January 1953; the
    CEN will publish 'The Leaf-Sweeper' on 5 December.
2. MS refers to her Anglican priest at St Augustine's Church, Roy Foster.
3. It appears that Iris Birtwistle, who was wealthy and well connected, was
    instrumental in finding MS her lodging in Sussex Mansions.
4. Birtwistle's mother was Mary Muriel Marwood. According to Birtwistle's
    son Pip Birtwistle, 'It is from her that IMB got her staunch Catholicism
    and faith' (email to the editor, 1 May 2023).
5. By 'expectant mothers' MS probably refers to Birtwistle's younger sister
    Angela Kirby, whose first child will be born in 1953, and to Glen Craig –
    wife of one of Birtwistle's brothers, Michael Albert Astley – who was also
    pregnant. Mrs Jowett has not been further identified.

TO DEREK STANFORD, HOUNSLOW, MIDDLESEX,
16 DECEMBER 1952

[Bruntsfield Place, Edinburgh
16 December 1952]

Boozie woozle – This is what transpires from taking Chianti
with your Anty, booze w. yr. flooze & wine w. yr. clandestine.
You overlook the pills whats you shouldov-took, you trouble yr.
Cousin Jess to send yr. Lozen-jez. The which I trust you will
receive a-Monday by the post the fust.[1]
 Sarah with her love and kisses

 ALS. HRC. Dating from dated lettercard written the same day.

1. MS wrote in a separate lettercard the same day: 'The ground is slippery
   here: everything white. Did you miss me? Indeed I did you, in my lone
   cabin. All is in good fettle here. Robin thrilled with his book. Am hasten-
   ing to get this off before the post leaves & am enclosing the pills (which
   I seem to have brought by mistake) in another envelope.' In her PS, MS
   added: 'Sorry, darling, about depriving you of the pills. It meant, psychologically, I wanted to bring your sleep with me' (HRC).

TO DEREK STANFORD, HOUNSLOW, MIDDLESEX,
17 DECEMBER 1952

160, Bruntsfield Place, Edinburgh
17-12-52

My own darling,
 So many thanks for your 2 bright shiners. Poor H. P., & sweet
you, going to see him. I hope you were well wrapped up &
managed to leave him with some of your own cheer.[1] I wrote to
him with pleasant fond records. Have had awful nights – little
sleep – but otherwise am quite recovered & feeling very well. Is
it all right by you if I arrive back next *Tuesday* instead of *Sunday*?
I'll tell you for why: Robin is in a quandary about being bullied

at school. Being a *wee* boy, there is very little he can do, bar the unthinkable act of reporting his tormentors to the High Places. So we held a council of war & decided to have a party to which those he can count as *friends* are invited. They are to be regaled with ice-cream, toffees, crackers, games, & all manner of flipperties, yum yum. So that when it comes to pass, next term, that Rob's enemies advance, he will be consolidated by his own gang. Some of them have asked him to parties, so it all looks likely. However, I wd. like to stay & preside – let me know if you can spare your engaged girl, darling. They are being very nice to me, & I am getting some work done, for a wonder. Any nice letters? Or only rejects? Will write you a proper letter for tomorrow's post. Bless you my love,

Muriel

A new story being planned, entitled 'The Four Pearly Shadows'.

ALS. HRC.

1. 'H. P.' is Herbert Palmer. In her letter to Derek Stanford two days later, 19 December, MS will write, 'Hope you are none the worse for yr. mission to St. Albans' (HRC).

1953

After Christmas in Edinburgh, MS returned to London and worked intensively on short stories, poems, essays, and reviews, including a response to Allen Tate's 'The Man of Letters in the Modern World'. With no resolution to her life with Derek Stanford, she took further distance from him, moving out of Sussex Mansions to a small furnished room in Queen's Gate Terrace. On 2 April, she was confirmed at St Augustine's Church and took her first Anglican communion. She read broadly in John Henry Newman's writings while working part-time at Nevill's publishing house, and put the finishing touches to five short stories. In April, *My Best Mary: Selected Letters of Mary Shelley* (co-edited with Stanford) appeared. She deepened her acquaintance with a number of Catholic figures who would remain important to her: Christine Brooke-Rose and her husband Jerzy Peterkiewicz, June and Neville Baybrooke, and the publishers Frank Sheed and Maisie Ward. Sheed commissioned from her a book on Job and another on T. S. Eliot (neither of which she would complete). By mid-June, her *John Masefield* was published, and she had completed her part of *Emily Brontë: Her Life and Work* (also co-edited with Stanford, and published later in the year). In August, MS covered the Edinburgh International Festival for the *Observer* and the *Church of England Newspaper*, producing an important review of Eliot's play *The Confidential Clerk*. Throughout the year, her health was deteriorating, exacerbated by her use of the amphetamine Dexedrine. In October, MS left the flat in Queen's Gate Terrace to return to even more modest accommodations in Sussex Mansions. Her essay on Proust, 'The Religion of an Agnostic: A Sacramental View of the World in the Writings of Proust', appeared in the *Church of England Newspaper* in late November. But by the end of the year, in addition to the religious crisis she was experiencing, MS was nearing mental collapse, causing her to seek treatment from a Dr Lieber. She spent Christmas in the company of Roy Foster, an Anglican vicar at St Augustine's with whom she was close.

TO IRIS BIRTWISTLE, WROXTON, OXFORDSHIRE,
4 JANUARY 1953

8, Sussex Mansions, 65, Old Brompton Road, S.W.7
4th January 1953

My dearest Iris,

So many things to thank you for, not the least your prayers.
Don't think I'm ungrateful, for I've thought of you often & feel
happy in the knowledge that you're *there* & wish us both well.

I do hope the New Year will bring you and your mother more
settled circumstances. I do admire the calm way you take all these
upheavals.

Now, let me know when I can come and see you, because it wd.
be something for me to look forward to, if you're not too wearied
with visitors by now. A mid-week couple of days would be best for
me, but I can manage any week-end, except 17th–18th Jan. Would
a Monday & Tuesday following that, be any good to you? – Say
Monday 19th or Monday 26th. If you prefer later in the week, it's
O.K. for me. Just suggest whatever day best suits you.[1]

Derek feels that we shouldn't visit together in the circs. &
I think he's right. I was grateful & amused & happy at your
circumspect generalisations in reply to my last, you clever girl. All
things seem to be working slowly towards our marriage. Derek
talks about 'the wedding' from time to time, when not pressed on
the point. *Men*! But *I'm* unsettled, really, & my work's suffering –
I've started so many new projects & haven't finished any. However
I have resolved to start no more till these are finished. Will you
please pray, dear Iris, for the following practical benefits for me:

1) spiritual discipline
2) imaginative discipline
3) that I shall stop thinking about myself so much.

You're the only person I know who understands that prayer can
be specific & practical. I don't know anyone else who wouldn't
think I was morbid & neurotic if I asked them to pray for things
I need, just as I might ask them for a letter of introduction

to someone. But I know you're a sensible girl & a practised
petitioner & of good repute in the heavens; so give me a good
recommendation.

Have just acquired a booklet called 'A Devotional Calendar
for Catholics'.[2] Do you know it? It's very useful, but of course it
wouldn't be me if I wasn't critical about something. This time,
it's the hushed, awed, solemn, soulful *tone* throughout that makes
me wonder if it is really Catholic. There's nothing wrong with
the actual instructions for each day – e.g.: *Jan 4*: 'Pray that the
Sweet Name of Jesus be loved and honoured' . . . etc; or *Jan 10*:
'Pray for Wisdom to follow Christ'. – This is all good & helpful
& instructive. But nowhere, throughout the whole year, do I
see 'Pray for insight into how funny I am & the knowledge that
some of my frantic antics are enough to bring the heavenly house
down.' Now, Iris, it is not *Catholic* to exclude this luminous truth,
which has been revealed to so many of the Saints, that human
behaviour, at its most earnest and sincere, is often very funny by
eternal standards. I'm not suggesting that the Holy Angels rock
with mirth at the tragic self-betrayals of humankind. But tragedy
is tragedy, and all that seems tragic is not so – I think this is true
because I've arrived at it, personally, through literary satire; and
since it appears to be a verity to me in one sense, I have to express
it in religious terms. So I really miss the element of self-mockery
which is absent from this Catholic Calendar.

Tell this heretic your views, please. Maybe you'ld like to see the
publication. Will send you a copy.

I enclose, meantime, a new poem which no-one will print.
Opinion wanted here too please, from you both.

All love & hoping to see you before long,

Muriel

ALS. CBF.

1. MS did take to visiting Iris Birtwistle in Wroxton, whence she will write
to Derek Stanford on 14 July: 'There I am having snoozed my head off all
afternoon in superluxurious surrounds, in between talk talk talk about the

Catholic Faith, the which, in its Anglican version I uphold singlehanded. Have got the curse & am a bit the worse for the wear; otherwise am soothed considerably by acres (or very near) of green lawns & woodlands' (NLS).

2. *A Devotional Calendar for Catholics* had been published annually since 1925 in London by Talbot & Co.

TO ALLEN TATE, MINNEAPOLIS, MINNESOTA,
10 FEBRUARY 1953

8, Sussex Mansions, 65, Old Brompton Road, London, S.W.7
10th February 1953

Dear M[r] Tate,

I send a commentary on your recent article in 'World Review', in which you may be interested.[1]

I'm glad of this opportunity of saying how greatly I appreciate your work, having become an early addict through 'The Limits of Poetry'. It would be a welcome thing if more of your poetry & prose were published here.[2]

Yours sincerely,
Muriel Spark

MR. TATE gives a satisfactory statement of the position and responsibilities of the present-day writer. (The writer, that is, of literature purporting to be durable, in which sense I use the term throughout.) The writer's task is 'to preserve the integrity, the purity, and the reality of language, wherever and for whatever purpose it may be used', and this is achieved 'by means of discrimination, through choice, towards an end'. Being concerned with the practical implications of this proposition, I deduce (perhaps reduce, as Mr. Tate seems to imply my deductions) from his essay, a further proposition:

That, in order to write well, the writer to-day must live virtuously.

I am aware that any supporting arguments would be more forceful if made by a better writer and a more virtuous one.

However, if the proposition is true, then I would be a better writer, if more virtuous.

The proposition applies to writers to-day, obviously not to those of the past. The reason is that, for our time, the controlling theme of all good writing is virtue. It has been imposed on us by history; it is not simply the duty of writers to see all problems as moral ones; they cannot avoid the theme. A novel about life in the Sahara or an ode to the West Wind, composed now, happens to fail if the controlling theme of virtue is not implicit. (Nor is it likely to succeed if this theme is *explicit*.)

At other times, the writer's proper concern to balance current fallacies with his own unbalance imposed on him the themes of Rebellion, Aesthetics, Theology and so on. At all times the best writing was done by those who had truly experienced their subject; who were able to bring the refinements of their experience to bear on their verbal discrimination. In proportion as they have had access to the theme to be expressed, the best writers have always had access to the language; a relationship existed between a personal assent to the theme (often the practice of it) and the language of it.

For writers, 'experience' must mean a deeply-felt, intensely-perceived condition. The alliance between experience and expression is assumed, these days, where the subject-*matter* of a work is concerned; to write a book about Italy, the writer is expected to have lived in Italy.

But good writing to-day, on Italy or anything else, does not emerge except under the compulsive theme of virtue. The writer cannot avoid the necessity of experiencing virtue. A relationship exists between virtue and the practice of letters, but no real relationship exists between the practice of virtue and the practice of letters.

Previously, it was not necessary to practise, say, rebellion – to live as a rebel – in order to write within the theme of rebellion. Inward assent was enough; though from this assent, outward tokens of the rebel (as with Shelley) were manifest. Virtue, however, differs from other themes in that it requires not only personal assent, but personal practice, or it is not virtue.

I have heard it said that writers to-day do in fact live virtuously, because they cannot afford to do otherwise. It need hardly be said that not being able to afford bits of vice here and there between work is not assent to, and practice of, virtue.

It was comparatively easy for writers in the past to dedicate themselves to beauty, social order, theology, and the rest of it. We seem to be required to fall in love with virtue, which has been shelved from one generation to another, being supremely difficult to practise; and it has landed onerously on us.

I am writing, of course, as a literary critic, not as a moralist; nor am I zealous for the souls of literary people. Neither am I passing on a handy hint that it pays writers to be virtuous, for, by its nature, virtue cannot be practised as a means of perfecting one's art; it can only be practised to its proper end, and about whether this end is the glory of God or the glory of humankind, there is much debate. The truth of the one or the other conviction may possibly become apparent, not by argument, but by their respective fruits. But I suggest that, so far as the 'end' towards which he 'discriminates, through choice' remains unspecified, the writer's understanding of his theme remains accordingly vague.

As he is a custodian of the meaning of language, for himself and everyone else, the writer has nothing for it, as I infer from Mr. Tate, but to practise virtue to its proper end, and if he does not know the proper end, it is his responsibility to find out. Perhaps he can do this only by attending to his *particular* responsibility, which, Mr. Tate says, is discrimination. But since the fact is that, on the whole, writers to-day write poorly, since they do not seem able to discriminate, there is the possibility that they interpret their *particular* responsibility too exclusively. If, through discrimination, the writer is to 'preserve the integrity, the purity, and the reality of language', he must not only experience the corresponding realities of his theme; he must understand towards what end he experiences and discriminates.

ALS with attachment of letter/commentary to
the Editor of *World Review*. PFL.

1. The poet and influential literary critic Allen Tate, a professor at the University of Minnesota, had converted to Catholicism in 1950. In *World Review* he published 'The Man of Letters in the Modern World' (October 1952). MS's response was published as 'Reflections on Mr Tate's Article', in 'Letters and Points' in *World Review* (January 1953).
2. Allen Tate's *On the Limits of Poetry – Selected Essays: 1928–1948* was published by The Swallow Press and William Morrow & Co. in New York in 1948.

Allen Tate

TO DEREK STANFORD, HOUNSLOW, MIDDLESEX, 19 MAY 1953

1, Queen's Gate Terrace, S.W.7[1]
19-5-53

Well dear Boy – what have I got to say to you, having decided, thro' an excess of loving thoughts to pen this card? Take it as a news sheet from eternity; as of course there's no news in eternity, that happy country without a history. There, the News of the World comes out blank from the press of a Sunday.[2] There the poems are unspoken, unthought, unpublished. Think of that my joyable friend, and ponder no more that pristine territory so traditionally by intellectuals pondered.

Yours exceedingly,
EXALTER PATER[3]

ALS. HRC.

1. MS leads with her new address, to which she moved in March. Martin Stannard writes: 'The move to Queen's Gate Terrace was to a tiny, sparsely furnished room. She bought a kettle, a chest of drawers, a Catholic prayer book, and thirteen volumes of Newman' (*MSB*, p. 139).
2. The *News of the World*, published from 1843 to 2011, had in the early 1950s the biggest circulation of any Sunday newspaper in the United Kingdom.
3. 'Exalter Pater' is standard in neither classical nor ecclesiastical Latin.

TO DEREK STANFORD, HOUNSLOW, MIDDLESEX,
6 JUNE 1953

1, Queen's Gate Terrace, S.W.7
6th June 1957[1]

Dearest Sulker,

This is not a moan or a plea or a protest but a declaration of bumf.

1) You say we should not *think* of each other as lovers. Right.

2) You say we should think of each other as friends. You say this with a long face which seems to mean '*only* as friends' i.e. not '*exclusively*' but '*merely*', i.e. you seem to think we have been reduced to the meagrest possible resource of human relationships.

3) You must have taken leave of your senses because

4) The best part of our relationship is our friendship. As lovers we were all right on the sexual side but hopeless on the intercommunication side of lovers' minds. In some respects of

course we have got worse in this way, as we are both changing our minds.

5) Our friendship is not just the bit of salvage from the wreck. It is the best part of the ship. The rudder has gone overboard if you'll excuse my metaphor and so has the mast if you follow. But as the ship is anyhow in harbour what use is there pretending we haven't a meeting ground?

You are supposed to be the one that prizes friendship. Well you will bloodywell have to put up with mine as I am your friend
Muriel

ALS. HRC.

1. It may be that the '7' in the address misleads MS into writing '7' in the date directly beneath it. The discussion of celibacy, as well as MS's address, yields 1953 as the true date of this letter.

TO FRANK SHEED, SHEED & WARD LTD, LONDON, 28 JUNE 1953

1, Queen's Gate Terrace, S.W.7
28th June 1953

Dear Mr Sheed,

Very many thanks for your kind letter, and for 'The Legacy'. I have read it once & am really very intrigued; it seems to contain the elements of several poems – e.g. the lines on p.21

'I came forth like Lazarus and wept to look upon
Mere roofs of the suburb in mists of the morning.'

– There is a *completed* poetic idea in this, don't you think? It suggests, not only the drab prospect as Lazarus saw it, but that he hadn't, somehow, been ready for death in any case; if so he wd. have known how to praise life. I don't know whether this speculation is valid or not, but I find the lines very satisfying. I hope to read the whole poem again more carefully in the next two weeks, & will review it in the S.S.T.A. journal. They welcome Catholic books by the way & though it's an educational paper, they review general literature; it goes to 3,000 secondary school teachers! – Quality, let's hope, in place of quantity.[1]

About the Pauline privilege: this is really very kind of you. Your statement of the case is accurate, except that some qualification seems necessary about A's insanity; I mean, I don't know if he is officially 'incurable'. We have had high hopes from time to time & he was even discharged on two occasions. But he had to return to the mental home, where he still is. I suppose an accurate statement would run as follows: (you will probably want to condense it) –

'A. & B., neither baptised, married in a colony before a magistrate. There was insanity in A.'s family, of which B. was not aware, at the time of the marriage, shortly after which, the insanity began to manifest itself, in the form of violence.

There is one child of the marriage, now aged 15.

B. left A. after three years, taking the child. A. was not yet under treatment for mental trouble. B. sought a divorce on grounds of cruelty, but no such grounds were valid under the law (Roman-Dutch) of the colony, at that time (1940). After a further three years' separation, and much urging by B. & her friends, A. divorced B. for desertion. The same year, A. came under treatment for a mental disease (a complication of paranoia I believe) and has been under treatment, except for the 2 occasions mentioned above, ever since. He was sent home from S. Rhodesia, under custody, in 1945, & is now in a hospital in Edinburgh. B. was baptized Nov. 1952.'

That's the story, with a lot of unnecessary detail I daresay. But if, according to the Church, I am still married to him, the state of separation would have to continue, as he is really quite murderous, poor soul.[2]

My friend, Derek Stanford, asks me to thank you for your efforts on our behalf. He gets on famously with my son, which of course adds to his status as a prospective husband. But he may yet be spared me as a wife. We shall see.

When I was told I couldn't remarry, I did wonder, you know, if there were not some good purpose in an otherwise meaningless situation. Do you think my remaining single might have some alleviating effect on 'B.'s' health? Or is this a superstition? However, it isn't a legal point, and, as you see, I have written the long letter which I promised, last time, to spare you.

Many *many* thanks for so kindly coming to our assistance, and I look forward to knowing the results of your enquiries.

Yours very sincerely,

Muriel Spark

Sorry I couldn't type this letter, to make it more legible. After 11 p.m., one can't behave like a woodpecker, in furnished rooms!

ALS. Private collection.

1. The Catholic lay theologian and author Frank Sheed was the founder, with his wife Maisie Ward, of the New York publishing house Sheed & Ward Ltd, which specialised in books on Catholic themes. In his *Muriel Spark: A Biographical and Critical Study* (Centaur Press Ltd, 1963; henceforth in the notes *MSBCS*), Derek Stanford writes: 'Mr. Frank Sheed of Sheed and Ward became her friend about this time. As a speaker for the Catholic Evidence Guild, he would address all and sundry from a rostrum in Hyde Park. I remember how we were once rewarded for our attention, on a cold wet Sunday afternoon, by omelettes cooked by Mrs. Maisie Ward in their flat above his office near Covent Garden' (pp. 59–60). On 21 June, MS wrote to Sheed: 'I did so much enjoy our luncheon meeting; thank you very much. It was specially pleasant to me, as I hardly ever meet a person of letters who is also a Catholic and of human sympathies, all at once' (Private collection).

   The Legacy, a poem by Michael Mason, had just been published by Sheed & Ward; MS would review it for the *Journal of the Scottish Secondary Teachers' Association* (October 1953).

2. The 'Pauline privilege', based on 1 Corinthians 7: 10–15, has been interpreted as giving permission to divorced partners of a marriage who were not baptised at the time of their marriage, and who have subsequently been baptised, to enter into a sacramental marriage – that is, with the full blessing of the Church.

   By 'A' MS refers to her former husband, Sydney Oswald Spark; by 'B', to herself.

TO CLIFFORD RHODES, THE CHURCH OF ENGLAND
NEWSPAPER, LONDON, 4 JULY 1953

1, Queen's Gate Terrace, S.W.7
4th July, 1953

Dear Mr Rhodes,

About your welcome articles & comments on the African
problem: I am not writing this as a 'letter to the ed.', because I'm
not sure if the following suggestion is entirely, or partly, or at all,
practicable. But if you see any sense in it, you might like to use the
suggestion in some part of the C.E.N.

From the secular & religious press, I gather that Christians are
deeply troubled by a feeling of helplessness in the face of obvious
wrongs done to natives of Africa, because the Christian protest
evokes the monotonous answer, 'But you have to *live* here before
you can judge the thing aright.' This is an answer which is difficult
to demolish by argument, for the simple reason that we don't
live there; and it may be that many people suspect that some
mysterious quality adheres to the circumstance of living in Africa,
whereby the elementary Christian obligations towards our fellow
men, are no longer binding.

Looking back on a six years' residence in S. Rhodesia, and six
months in Capetown, during the years 1937–1944, I do not find it
difficult to see how the illusion arises, that being on the spot alters
the principle, not merely the practiced manifestation of Christian
duty. The idea that the African is a species apart from, and
inferior to, the European, is thoroughly blended with the whole
current of life; and so, even those Europeans who would reject
the proposition as a conceived idea, are bound, in fact, to act upon
it as a preconceived and accepted idea. The thing is insidious, it
becomes second nature. As a symptomatic example, it may be
worth recording that during the years I spent in Africa I only once
heard an African referred to as 'a man'; this was in a magistrate's
court, and the momentary surprise I felt at hearing the term
applied to 'a native', made me realise how deeply imbedded was

the general notion that Africans do not come within the category, 'man'. And yet, not one Rhodesian whom I met would think of denying the fact that an African is a man, if the question were put to him. But the question does not arise in the assumptions which rule the everyday life of the European, and according to which an African is something other than a man. Under the influence of this all-pervasive attitude, I believe, for my own part, that living on the spot would be the first requisite for judging the African problem wrongly.

Christians in Africa, who are aware of a vast social guilt in this matter, are faced with the tremendous difficulty of correcting an assumption which is held unconsciously by the majority of fellow-whites, most of whom would give no allegiance to the principles they practise every day, if they were presented personally with a formulated version of them. In such a situation the white Christian, however conscientious, can hardly avoid being bogged down by the system within which he is working, and which operates on an irrational basis. No wonder he, too, is inclined to say, 'You can't deal with the problem unless you actually live here'.

Christians outside Africa have rightly been vociferous in their protests. These have been effective, it seems, so far as no real apologist has arisen to justify the blatant injustices done to the African. Some have refuted the Christian charge, explaining that racial discrimination in the normal sense means paternal benevolence in Africa; and they add that anyway, you have to live on the spot. But there has been no positive enunciation of principles (discounting the trite sophistry of the politicians). This is because the European residents in the countries concerned do not want to consider the principles involved; to do so would cause discomfort to their consciences, and to act upon principles, however warily, would cause practical discomforts.

The Christian in this country, then, is frustrated by the irrational nature of the problem. The sermons and speeches and protests seem to receive general approbation here, and a considerable response in Africa. And yet the system proceeds

as usual, beyond the reach of reasoning, a great ruthless
determination that things in Africa shall not be otherwise
than thus.

It might seem that any hope of a more decent attitude to
Africans, depends on the courageous actions of individuals who
have settled in the territories concerned, and who have not
allowed themselves to be doped by social habit into thinking that
things are not too bad. Such individuals are, however, very few.
They are easily deported on the grounds of stirring up trouble.
They can, in fact, very easily stir up trouble and violence. If there
were more of them, it would not be so; especially if they did
not form a party, and thus make a minority issue, standing for
principles instead of enacting them as a matter of course. I mean,
that these, [illegible, several words] British families who depart
from these shores to settle in African territories where the natives
are still in an elementary stage of development, are not out of
reach. They have not yet been conditioned to the local methods of
dealing with Africans, and a campaign directed towards educating
these emigrants might be more fruitful than the constant passing
of censorious Resolutions by Christian bodies.

From my own observations while living in Africa, I came to
the conclusion that the new arrivals from the home country very
swiftly settled down to the normal routine of exercising what any
sane person in this country would call harshness. In fact, the older
settlers were infinitely more considerate to the Africans than were
the later immigrants who, newly arrived from a hard-pressed
environment, were suddenly presented with a dazzling array
of servants and underlings, black in colour and willing to sleep
together on the floor of a hut at the bottom of the yard. These
masters and mistresses were otherwise kindly and well-meaning
people; they did not think of withholding assent from such an
engaging mode of life, practised so universally by the white
population.

I do not know if the situation has changed very much. It
seems unlikely, in view of the prevalent unrest. A propagandist
campaign, appealing to emigrants, indoctrinating them, and

explaining the problems ahead of them in their dealings with Africans, might at least influence a few families in each batch towards propagating the Christian attitude, by their example. At the most, it might help to stop the rot.

It is probable, of course, that the emigrants get numerous hand-outs from Government information departments, telling them what to expect and how to conduct themselves when they reach their destination, etc. If so, there will certainly not be any information, in this literature, as to the conditions under which the African really lives, no hint that he might live better, or learn to be a better man. It needs a Christian body to make a purposive effort to get at the new settlers before they leave the country – as soon as the passage is booked, and on the boat, both before it leaves and during the voyage. It would need lecturers versed in the customs of the territories concerned, and it would need buckets of money. Also, there would be official opposition, and here the only hope would be for a national newspaper to support the campaign, on 'ethical' if not on specifically Christian grounds. But at least a Christian body might initiate some such drive, so that the Christian basis of the principles in question might be established from the start.

As you know the set-up amongst the Christian groups who feel urgently about Africa, better than I do, you may think the scheme impossibly mad. I haven't assembled the case very well, but if you think anything useful might be extracted, do please extract & use it, otherwise scrap the letter.[1]

All kind wishes,

TLcc. NLS.

---

1. In his letter to MS written two days later, 6 July, Clifford Rhodes will respond: 'I brought your suggestion before the Africa Committee of Christian Action, and they thought it a very good one. The next thing is to work out ways and means' (NLS).

TO JOHN DAVY, THE OBSERVER, LONDON, 25 JULY 1953

1, Queen's Gate Terrace, London, S.W.7
25th July, 1953

Dear Mr Davy,

About my suggestion, the other day; I would like to write some pieces for the Observer on the sidelights of the Edinburgh Festival.[1] The performances and celebrities would not interest me directly; I'd like to concentrate on the unofficial civic side of the affair. The Edinburgh scene can be quite amusing at these times, and I would probably want to write more as a barbarian seeing the sights than as a thirster for the culture. (Without trying to throw contempt on the Festival, of course.)

The functions presided over by the City Fathers are cause for contemplation, if one is free to be slightly irresponsible.

The places of pilgrimage, such as Mary Q. of Scots' apartments at Holyrood, as well as the pilgrims, would be pleasant to write about, especially in places associated with events of debatable history, open to anyone's speculation. The men who act as guides are a joy, very Scottish, very severe.[2]

Usually, there is an influx of European youth, who camp outside the city. These are the visitors who endear themselves most to the citizens, because their presence proves the earnest uncommercial motives of the occasion. It is felt that a poor Belgian student is inevitably more appreciative than a wealthy Harvard boy. The rich visitors from the U.S. and the colonies pep up the trade, of course. Some of them, particularly the Americans who have toured the Continent first, try to haggle with the small shopkeepers, but there has always been a strong resistance to haggling in Edinburgh.

Some of these aspects of Festival-time, I would like to present in the form of reported conversations. I very much enjoy telling a story by using exaggerated dialogue.

It might be amusing to interview Ivor Brown in Edinburgh for the Observer, at crosspurposes.[3]

It is difficult to be more explicit in advance, but I'm sure I would find many other things, perhaps better ones, to write about, once I was there. These suggestions are based on my previous experience of the place and people during the Festival, when I wasn't observing them for a special purpose.

I don't know if the tone I have thought of adopting sounds too flippant from your point of view. There are more serious sides to the subject which you might not otherwise cover; for instance, Edinburgh's real passion for European culture combined with the nationalist leanings – a manifestation perhaps, of the traditional 'auld alliance' attitude.[4] But I doubt if I would be the person for this aspect. I would prefer to keep to a lighter vein, if you think the suggestion worth while.

I would be staying with relations in Edinburgh, but as I won't be going unless for this purpose, I would need my train-fare, which is about £7.

Will you let me know if you feel I could do something on these lines suitable for the Observer? Many thanks, anyway, for considering the idea.

Yours sincerely,

TLcc. NLS.

1. The journalist John Davy was Science Editor at the *Observer*.
    The Edinburgh International Festival had started six years previously, in 1947, with a view, in the wake of World War II, to promoting cultural understanding and fostering international cooperation and harmony through the arts.
2. Holyrood Palace, the reigning British monarch's residence in the Scottish capital, contains the chambers where Mary, Queen of Scots, lived between 1561 and 1567; there she, a devout Catholic, debated with the Protestant John Knox, and there she witnessed the death by stabbing of her secretary David Rizzio – an event which has drawn tourists to the chambers ever since they were opened to the public.
3. Ivor Brown, a vocal opponent of modernism with culturally conservative views, was Drama Critic at the *Observer*; 'at crosspurposes' as he would, therefore, have been interviewed by his own paper.
4. The Auld Alliance, which began formally with the Treaty of Paris in 1295, cemented association and mutual support between Scotland and France; it had (and may continue to have) influence on Scotland's civic life, its architecture, and its cultural openness to Continental Europe.

TO DEREK STANFORD, HOUNSLOW, MIDDLESEX,
27 AUGUST 1953

160, Bruntsfield Place, Edinburgh
27th Aug. 1953

My dearest Boy,

I haven't written before because 1) I am out of my element &
consequently a little troubled, and 2) sheer lack of time. But of
course you are in my thoughts so often as I wish to assure myself
that there *is* another world besides this incredible one of Art-
Success & Successful Artists. Before I tell you about my doings, let
me say that I have decided that my only hope of an integrated life, is
to exist on a level which is to most people, entirely backward. The
'here and now' as it is lived by most intelligent people bewilders
me. *I can't grasp what is actually happening in the present tense.* I can't
follow the evidence of things which come to pass. When I come
back I'll tell you what I have come to think is the meaning of 'Life
Everlasting' and 'World Without End' – for the present, I'll only
say that I think the meaning lies within temporal experience, and
that anyone who slips unawares into the habit of directing their
intelligence towards Life Everlasting, finds it awfully difficult to
keep up with the normal intelligence of well-informed people.

Consequently, my darling, I am not making much shape with
my coverage of the Ed. Festival. Really, I am at sea. It *is* beyond
my intelligence to grasp what is happening. No-one else seems to
be troubled to grasp what is happening, they go to the places &
see the things & are able to tell their friends all about them. Not
so me.[1]

Well, I have probably taken on too much. There is a Press
Office here which is most depressingly haunted by journalists full
of confidence and bad feeling – I am sure about the bad feeling,
& can't put it any other way. The Press Officer himself is nice
& helpful. He produced my Confidential black ticket & heaps of
others. Nice Arthur Dowle sent me a letter to say I'm representing
the C.E.N. & asking for all facilities for me –[2] Why couldn't the

Observer have done this? However, press tickets are to be had for
the asking. I feel I must go to the things which the C.E.N. wd. be
interested in rather than my own choice. And for the Observer I
am just making scrappy notes here & there. Have put aside Sunday
& Monday to write the articles in, which is cutting things a bit
fine. As I have to wait for the Eliot play on Tuesday I will finish the
Observer by Wed. Robin is moaning because I have no time for
him, so have agreed to wait over until Thurs night. If all goes well
I'll be back on Fri. morning (4th).

This has been my programme & is what I've planned also.

Wed 26th Aug. – Picked up tickets & information leaflets at
the Press Office. Spent the day in telephone boxes making
appointments to see people about youth camps etc. What a
weariness! Got one hour's sleep in & then went to Glyndebourne
Opera – La Cenerentola (a most amusing Cinderella comedy)
which I really enjoyed. The ugly sisters stole the show.[3] After this
I shook off the Daily Worker critic who had sat next me & who,
despite his thirty-bob seat, grumbled much that his paper had
been slighted by not getting a 1st night ticket. More of him anon.
Suffice it to say I was cheered up by him in a novel way – I mean
at least he was something to *reflect* on, the wee horror. Well,
having made my escape I proceeded to the Festival Club for which
I had been given one of the complimentary tickets with which
journalists are wont to light their cigarettes, they are so plentiful.
(Incidentally, this lavishness makes me wonder why needful things
like books are not made available freely to people like us. – A sign
of my backward understanding of life.) There at this enormous
vulgar Kardomah of Civic hospitality, I met with the Greacens
& Hellstrom [sic].[4] They had promised me information, you see.
However, I was able to enlighten Hellström of several interesting
events & sights of which the B.B.C.'s publicity dept. had kept him
in ignorance. And I was able to give the Greacens answers to some
of their questions concerning my plans, which seemed to be of
kindly interest to them, although they are not themselves staying
on. Patricia suggested some alternative things which I might see &
do, for no reason, that I could see, but that they were alternatives.

Robert had kindly stored up some 'sayings' & local folk-lore,
which he passed on & for which he deserved the thanks I gave
him, though the point of these respective items still escapes me.

To-day I saw Sir P. Laird & wife. A dreary business. A fruitless
business. They were the hosts but I did the entertaining in so
far as I gave them something to discuss afterwards & possibly to
deplore. A limited couple.[5] You see I am uncharitable, but it seems
that as I am here for business I ought not to devote my time to
visiting the sick, so to speak.

To-night I was to have gone to the Rome Symphony Concert,
but have swapped my ticket for a 'fringe' event, as it is
called – Norman Nicholson's new play, yclept 'A Match for the
Devil' – something for the C.E.N. I think. This afternoon I went
to a Unesco film about good works among the Siamese & the
Mexicans on the part of Latin Americans – quite good but ruined
by stirring incidental music & sentimental talkie-talk.[6]

I met McLellan (the publisher so-called). Got some sidelights on
the Nationalist approach to the Festival. McLellan of course in kilt.
Lots of ideals. I felt like saying 'Why didn't you bloodywell pay
my friend Ian & stop talking about the Culture of the Folk?' But I
didn't want to waste myself on argument – only to get his approach
to this feast of international sweetmeats.[7] The Daily Worker man
found me again but alas I lost him, I can tell you, within two ticks.

Tomorrow morning (Friday) I go to the sight-seeing tourists'
paradise – the historic bits of masonry which [sic] our brethren
pack their trunks in all four corners of the earth, with a view to
ultimately beholding. Tomorrow night, the Tattoo – a military
parade high up on the windy & frozen castle esplanade. Also on
Friday, a Civic garden party.[8]

On Saturday I betake me to the European Youth Movement,
its camp – half an hour's ride from here. They will take me
round. They will permit me to witness their discussion groups
at work & to hear their lectures. They will give me lunch. They
will put me on the bus which will return me in time for a recital
at St. Giles' Cathedral. In the evening, the Trojan Women and a
bawdy 16th cent. Scots play (refabricated by an Edinburgh Univ.

student) entitled 'Philotus' – author anonymous. This is a student production. What's more, they promise to tell me what they think about the Festival.[9]

There is the service at St Mary's Cathedral on Sunday. And then I start writing articles till Tuesday night – the Confidential Clerk. Hope to finish the Observer article by Wed. mid-day. To give myself a treat, I have taken a press ticket for the Spanish ballet on Wed. night. This is, I hope, going to be exclusively a pleasure, & I will not review it nor write about the audience, no, not anywhere.

Thursday next I am keeping for Robin & at night I'll travel back to my sweet boy. Are you weary with this list? Well, imagine me, little love, actually fulfilling the thing. I am a bit happier now for having written you all this.

The brighter side is that, far from there being too little for me to say, there is too much. The weary side is that I can't get at the notions a really bright journalist could hit on. And the worst side is that there is too little time for me to make much of an article for the Observer; not only will it be too abstract – not enough of the dazzling concrete – but it won't be well or happily written. The C.E.N., on the other hand, will be but a scrap-heap of notices.

I should never have taken it on, little dear.

Added to my troubles, my mother is making a bit of an 'atmosphere' – to the effect that I have come to enjoy myself amongst my smart friends & high-placed successes, & would not think of bringing them home to our humble dwelling lest I should be veritably shamed before all my smart friends, etc. Also, that I am having a good time & taking no notice of any of my less sought-after relatives & her own acquaintances who 'want to see me'. (Why don't they go to the Zoo for their 'seeing'?) But my old woman sweetens up from time to time. I haven't really time to explain every morning how it is – that it's all a job to do, etc. I just beetle off out. When it comes to the writing bit, I may go to the Festival Club, where there is a decent writing room, & keep out of the family's way.

As for Simone Weil – I doubt if I can get much done to her, just yet. To think that I nearly brought Anne![10]

Now sweetheart, I was much moved by your going to see the railway line. When, in the state described above, I read that you were on this pursuit bent, I praised the Lord that such a dear spirit exists, for it is a glimmer of hope to me that this hell will not last for ever, to know that you are testifying to the life of my own kind of normality. I feel you are upholding my spiritual household for me. Let me see the poem you will certainly have written or will write.[11]

The family were inconsolable at having missed your Forest Guy both nights. The wireless has gone wonky & is away being repaired. Between ourselves, it is – apart from their disappointment – a good thing for me. To have had Ted Rae [*sic*] on my infrequent periods in the house – or Music While you Work before I go out in the morning, would have been just about the end.[12]

They speak much of you & hold you in high regard. You are to have ever such a Fairisle pullover with all the wonders that the Shetland Isles can muster. But this is a close secret. I betray it so that you can drop me a hint, before my mother places the order, as to the colours you would prefer to be omitted from the scheme. But she is determined to put her plan into effect & will not be dissuaded by my references to 'a few books, instead'; so it is only a matter of guiding her taste – without dampening her vision of the finished product.

Say a prayer for me, my own dear. This will soon be over & I'll be back at my rightful tasks again. I do not spend much, that is one comfort to me. What I spend, I will charge up to the Observer wherever possible.

Will send you the results of my labours as soon as they are composed. Probably won't write you again before then, but you keep writing to me, my lovely friend. Now I need your letters, more than ever.

Much love from your
misfitted
Muriel

ALS. WUL.

1. In *CV*, of her visit to her home city, MS recollects: 'I was thoroughly undernourished. When I went to Edinburgh for *The Observer* to cover the Edinburgh Festival in 1953 I felt thoroughly ill, and hardly knew what I was doing' (p. 200). On 22 July, Iris Birtwistle wrote to her to express concern for her wellbeing: 'Really, we were worried about you . . . . . . far too pale, far too thin' (NLS). MS was already suffering from the strain and effects of overdosing on amphetamines that would, within months, lead to a serious mental collapse, accompanied by hallucinatory delusions.

2. By 'Confidential' MS refers to T. S. Eliot's comic play in verse, *The Confidential Clerk*, which was due to premiere at the Edinburgh Festival, which MS was keen to review, and which would soon play a significant role in her delusions.

   Arthur Dowle signed himself as 'Asst. Editor' of the *Church of England Newspaper* when writing to MS with his corroborating letter of 25 August (NLS); he had read Modern History and then trained at Westcott House, Cambridge, and would go on to become Chaplain of St Edward's Church, Cambridge.

3. The Glyndebourne Opera production of Gioachino Rossini's *La Cenerentola* played for seven performances at the King's Theatre.

4. Kardomah is credited as Britain's first coffee-house chain, and there were Kardomah Cafés thriving in many major cities in England and Wales throughout the first half of the twentieth century.

   The Irish poet Robert Greacen did freelance work for *Tribune* as well as the *Times Literary Supplement*; he was married to Patricia Hutchins, who published *James Joyce's Dublin* with Grey Walls Press in 1950.

   Gustav Hellström worked on radio programmes for the BBC in London in the 1950s.

5. Sir Patrick Ramsay Laird was then Secretary of the Department of Agriculture for Scotland. What linked him to MS and Derek Stanford has not been established.

6. The Fringe, which runs alongside the official Edinburgh International Festival, started in the same year, 1947.

   A Match for the Devil by Norman Nicholson, a writer better known for his poetry, was to premiere at the Fringe, drawing its plot from the Old Testament Book of Hosea; it would be published in 1955 by Faber & Faber.

   The UNESCO-funded 'One World' documentary *World without End* was directed by Paul Rotha and Basil Wright.

7. William ('Bill') McLellan was a Glasgow publisher of books and journals, known for favouring, in the 1940s and 1950s, writers sympathetic to Hugh McDiarmid, but not known for his generosity in paying his authors.

   On 24 August, MS wrote to Stanford of Ian Hamilton Finlay's latest work:

Here is Ian's new piece. I like it very very much. It is the sort of story that the London birds *will not* call a story. They say there is no action; but the action takes place in the author's consciousness, conveyed in each phase of realisation. Ian is profoundly a poet. I prefer his prose to his poetry, and also to his painting. This is because he has the poetic vision but not much sense of the medium in painting and verse. I think poetic vision has always to humble itself before the medium so that the medium can exalt it finally. In prose, Ian seems well away. (HRC)

8. The Royal Edinburgh Military Tattoo began three years previously, in 1950, as part of the larger festival, taking place on the esplanade of Edinburgh Castle; it proved instantly popular with tourists.

    MS mentions 'Civic' in order to distinguish this party from the more famous Royal Garden Party hosted by the reigning monarch in the grounds of Holyrood Palace. The invitation came from 'The Lord Provost, Magistrates and Council of the City of Edinburgh and The Council of the Edinburgh Festival Society', to a party to be held 'within the grounds of Lauriston Castle' (NLS).

9. The Edinburgh University Theatre Company (now named Bedlam Theatre) staged Euripides' *The Trojan Women* (in Gilbert Murray's translation) and *Philotus* (possibly based on *Philotas* by the Elizabethan–Jacobean dramatist Samuel Daniel) between 26 and 31 August, with Jack Ronder (who would go on to be a screenwriter for cinema and television) as producer.

10. At least three books by the French thinker, mystic, and activist Simone Weil were published in English translation between 1952 and 1953, by Routledge & K. Paul: *Letter to a Priest* and *The Need for Roots: Prelude to a Declaration of Duties towards Mankind*, both translated from the French by A. F. Wills; and *Gravity and Grace*, translated by Emma Craufurd.

    MS was considering writing a biography of Anne Brontë.

11. In his letter to MS of 27 August, Stanford recounts paying a visit 'to reconnoitre St Albans Abbey Station and environs', a place of special romantic significance to him and MS: 'But just as I was hoping to immerse myself in a fine green nostalgia of chemin-de-fer d'antan, my eyes were presented with the following menace.' What follows is a representation of a sign indicating that the railway line was closed (NLS).

12. No record has been found of 'Forest Guy'. If, as MS implies, it was a work for radio, its broadcast by the BBC was neither announced nor registered.

    Ted Ray was a comedian whose show *Ray's a Laugh* ran from 1949 to 1961 on BBC Radio's Home Service. *Music While You Work* aired at 10.30 a.m. daily on the same channel.

TO FRANK SHEED, SHEED & WARD LTD, LONDON,
20 SEPTEMBER 1953

1, Queen's Gate Terrace, S.W.7
20th September 1953 (which I see is the Eve of St. Matthew)

My dear Frank,

That was a most enjoyable meeting for me on Friday last. It was extremely kind of you both to put me so warmly at my ease when I was so late. I had been particularly vexed and worried as it was my first meeting with Mrs Sheed, but I quickly forgot everything except your two selves and my most restorative lunch![1]

I did enjoy meeting Mrs Sheed – I suppose she is tired of hearing people remark on the beauty of her eyes – it could hardly go unnoticed. I wouldn't mention this if it were just an adornment, – but the light and expression of her eyes struck me very warmly. If I had been in a less stupid state (having had only 3 hours sleep after working late) I would have liked to ask her something about her approach to St. Matthew, for I'm slowly working through him – not for work but 'personal improvement' – in an attempt to get some light on 'The Kingdom of Heaven'. Following your own method, I'm trying to piece together what we know about the Kingdom of Heaven. The wonderful thing about St. Matthew is that with his Kingdom of Heaven theme (which he expressly states as his 'theme', – where he writes ' . . . this gospel of the Kingdom of Heaven') he leads up to the Blessed Sacrament. After its institution by Our Lord, St. Matthew does not mention the Kingdom of Heaven again, although the preceding narrative is brimming over with the phrase. So, in this series of 'meditations', I find that all St. Matthew cites of Our Lord's words on the Kingdom of Heaven, do really say something about the Sacrament.[2]

There's a tendency today to teach that Heaven is a 'state' not a 'place'. This doesn't satisfy me. It is a Place with all sorts of qualities we don't usually associate with the concept 'place'. But as it is Place, it follows that nowhere that we know of in this world is a true place. At least, so I think. This explains a feeling of 'elsewhereness' which most of us feel at times, & that's why, (isn't it?) we are traditionally said to be 'in exile'. There's probably nothing new in this. Only, it's new to me. Any heresies you happen to spot, you may put down to the fact that I have expressed myself clumsily! Or put them down to Plato.

As you seemed tickled by that quotation about our appearance in the last 3/10[ths] of a second, I send you a copy, in case you wanted to quote it anywhere. We seem to be the 11th-hour Labourers of the Parable, quite literally! Our Lord also assumes this role for us, perhaps.[3]

All very good thoughts – and also to M[rs] Sheed, with many thanks.

Yours ever –

Muriel

P.S. When are you next speaking at Hyde Park? I help with the Children's Service between 3 & 4 p.m. on Sundays. If you speak after 4pm I'll be there with my friend Derek next time, I hope.

ALS. Private collection.

1. Frank Sheed was married to, and ran his publishing house with, Maisie Ward, who was herself a prolific writer and lay preacher.
2. Citing from Matthew 24:14 – 'And this gospel of the kingdom shall be preached in all the world for a witness unto all nations; and then shall the end come' – MS appears to identify the Kingdom of Heaven with the Blessed Sacrament (or Eucharist or Holy Communion), and to imply that such an identification is justified by the way in which St Matthew's narrative about the Kingdom of Heaven leads to the institution of the Eucharist. The Kingdom of Heaven and the Eucharist are, however, quite distinct: the Eucharist repeats *sacramentally* the historical sacrifice of Christ on the cross, whereas the Kingdom of Heaven is the Kingdom of God. Perhaps MS sees in the Eucharist or Sacrament a pledge of future glory in heaven that allows it to be conflated with the Kingdom of Heaven: through the Sacrament, being born again in Christ, the believer is led to a state of personal, intimate fellowship with God, thus to the Kingdom of Heaven.
3. MS refers to the Parable of the Labourers in the Vineyard in Matthew 20, which has been interpreted as giving encouragement to those who convert to Christianity late in life.

Frank Sheed

TO DEREK STANFORD, HOUNSLOW, MIDDLESEX,
27 SEPTEMBER 1953

1, Queen's Gate Terrace, S.W.7
27-9-53

My Bonnie Dearest – Here is the C. of E. review so that you can
see the wee toad's attitude for yourself. To discuss it was difficult
without your having seen it.[1] My point about Rhodes was only
that it's unusual for an editor to have a play reviewed by a critic,
and then, a fortnight later, to have the previous *review* torn to bits
by another critic. As you'll see, K. R.'s piece *isn't* about the *play* –
it's about my notice of it. So I stand by the fact that this would
generally be regarded as unethical – provided that the editor had
not in the meantime had cause to doubt the entire justice of the

earlier review. Rhodes may well feel this way. On the other hand, we know Rhodes isn't the 'usual' sort of editor. He's extremely magnanimous in his handling of contributors. He has this reputation for intellectual generosity even in the Anglo-Catholic set-up. Fr. Hannah told me ages ago that, after his book had been attacked in the C.E.N., he went to see Rhodes, who gave him a complete free hand to reply.[2] So he's probably quite unaware of anything outside the proper course in this case. (I'm not going to raise any objections to him, unless he mentioned it to me, when I would explain my attitude as friendly-like as poss.)

Therefore don't think I've got it in for Rhodes. I only stressed the point on the phone as you didn't quite understand, not having seen the nature of the article. As for the piece itself, I'm not going to answer it, possibly out of pride, but so far as *policy* apart from motive is concerned, this is a case where I can begin a policy of not answering any attacks whatsoever, unless they are positively libellous, or unless it is simply a matter of a reviewer mis-quoting me. On a question of misinterpretation or sheer malice or ignorance, I don't see how one can ever defend oneself adequately, unless one were absolutely certain of the perfect truth of one's utterance, which is never. Besides, there isn't time for it, my own love.

I would really prefer you not to write a 'letter' yourself – I'll tell you for why, my bonnie friend. You haven't seen the play – & who knows, when you do see it you may think my piece about it a little cock-eyed – though you'll certainly find it more meaningful than our friend. Should it come to a show-down (you having written) you wd. find your position difficult to support if you hadn't seen the play.

I don't really think, between ourselves, K. R. disliked it as much as he says. He is pouring out another sort of dislike, poor soul. He gets awfully mixed up where – you'll notice – he suggests that Eliot didn't intend any meaning, only adaption [*sic*] of verse to the modern theatre. – Which presumably implies that Eliot approves of meaningless plays in the modern theatre so much that he takes the trouble to adapt verse for the purpose!

What a life! Robert Greacen has been round to show me his

Masefield piece on the French service. (Just a re-hash of some of my book, with mention of my book incorporated – which is O.K.) He came to borrow typing paper & to ask me to come & give the child her supper & put her to bed tomorrow night, as he & Patricia are both lecturing. I supplied the paper, but courteously declined the second honour. Apart from the fact that I don't consider my time my own at present – as I owe you so much money, – even if it were my own, I don't consider that the relief of authors is 'good works', unless they are poor or ill, or called away on an emergency. What say you? – I know Patricia was kind when I was ill, but we've put a lot of kindnesses their way since then. Robert stayed an hour & a half tho' I didn't encourage him greatly. His Noel Coward will be out in a fortnight.[3] Coward is 'touched' that an intellectual shd. write about him, has ordered vast quantities to distribute amongst friends, has organised a campaign to send people round bookshops buying copies & ordering more, and seems to be all that a critic could require, except really worth writing about. Robert isn't under any illusions – only glad that the book looks likely to sell. In considering Fry's unhelpfulness, it's consoling to remember that he *is* a valuable poet. By the way, did you see an article in today's Observer about the new anti-hanging book by three M.P.'s. It deals with the case of the man who confessed to a murder 'because he wanted to be a hero' – the one Fry quotes in *The Lady's Not*.[4] Well, the curious thing is that though another man was hung for the murder (in 1946), four years later this man (Rowlands) actually *did* commit a murder of exactly the same type – and was acquitted as 'crackers' (possibly to save face, as it seemed likely he really did the first after all[)]. Would it be possible to find some *actual* guilt in Thomas's (in The Lady) nature – even though the facts of the later crime, in 1950, were unknown to Fry? – I mean, could he have followed the nature of the case, so intuitively, that Thomas has a real 'crime' like Rowlands? It might be Thomas's war-guilt which was the reality, or did he kill something symbolically when, escaping with Jennet, he released the rational mind on the world, like Prometheus with his fire. – It was a gift or benefit for mankind, but also a murder, in the Promethean sense, of part of

Zeus. He reduced the power of Zeus, in the way that Thomas,
releasing Jennett [*sic*] in her representation of the rational mentality,
necessarily reduced the power or 'hold' of God, which, without
reason, was exercised by faith.

In this Promethean analogy, there are some striking
resemblances between Fry's story & Aeschylus. The myth itself
is less relevant than Aeschylus' rendering of Prometheus as the
inventor of rational arts & sciences:

> Thy Godlike crime was to be kind,
> To render with thy precepts less
> The sum of human wretchedness,
> And strengthen Man with his own mind.[5]

And as such, Aeschylus approves of him. Isn't Thomas's 'crime' —
if there is a real one, psychologically speaking, just this? Fry's
attitude is the same as that of Aeschylus to his hero, though aware
of something demolished in the process.

I don't think Fry had consciously followed the Prometheus
play — do you? — Even if there *is* an analogy to be drawn, as I
personally feel. The story of Prometheus is so archetypal that
direct acquaintance with the play need not be supposed.

I thought of suggesting this analogy to you for consideration, as
you might find it worth your while to look at Aeschylus' play. If
you found something really Promethean in *The Lady*, it is a useful
form of reference to an international public. All the European
birds know what the Promethean symbol stands for. It is part of
the literary critics' Esperanto, as it were.

It all depends on whether you feel Thomas committed any
'crime' which could be called psychologically 'real' — as his
factual prototype did, in the realm of fact. This was, of course,
subsequent to the first confession — as if they were determined to
make the confession true.

Is this far-fetched? In any case, it does not affect the
Promethean analogy if that is of any interest in itself.

I wish I had a copy of Fry's play — but I remember most of the *movements*. There's a lot in the words, which are like the sort of thing 'Prometheus' gives. I have a good work here on Aeschylus with a chapter on 'Prometheus' which you can see. But I haven't this play either.

Jennet would seem to represent both the stolen gifts and a type of Prometheus herself – a telescoped figure. But she does give the impression, in the play, of being an *intuitive vehicle of rationalism* – not rationalism itself. (Of course 'rationalism' is only a slapdash definition of what she stands for.) She seems *very* like the character Io in 'Prometheus' – the only real mortal in the play, though her father was a *river-god*. The others were Titans, or figures of antiquity, like Fry's mediaevals – a different race, almost. Io alas defies Zeus & is an outcast.

Note, too, the resemblance to the myth in the fire symbol. The lady was truly not for burning – that fate was for the old order, from which the fiery brand was stolen and imparted to the human race which, ultimately, has its share of 'burning'. The vehicle – the brand itself – lives for ever & ever.

Zeus in the play is forced to compromise, as the officials in *The Lady* were forced to connive at the escape of Jennet, by sheer embarassment [*sic*].[6]

The most striking thing about the comparison is the attitude of the two poets. Both are on the side of the 'criminal' on account of his *humanity* or *humaneness*. Both start off on the note of 'crime' and 'guilt'.

Prometheus is chained to his rock, his crime already accomplished, in Aeschylus. But this is only the technical aspect. The course of the story is analogous. Compare Prometheus' plight with Thomas's, where the latter says

> A world unable to die sits on and on
> In Spring sunlight . . .[7]

It is the *monotony* of this living hell which makes both characters similar in their type of suffering.

Zeus is accused in a manner in which (I seem to remember)

Thomas accuses God – or what he stands for in *society*. But
Prometheus retains his reverence for 'the gods', like Thomas.

Incidentally, Nicholas telling his mother that he has killed the
brother, is a very Greek trick (I don't remember if anything like
this occurs in 'Prometheus'). – In Fry's comedy, of course, it isn't
taken seriously, but it is just as symbolically important as were
those weird 'misinformations' in Greek tragedies.

Against my argument we must admit Thomas's misanthropy
as against Prometheus' love for humankind. But Thomas's
misanthropy is akin to Prometheus' disgust with Zeus – both are
measured from a basic humanitarianism.

The book I mentioned, with the chapter on 'Prometheus' has
this passage:

'Euhemerism {or the reading of 'history' from legend}, ancient
or modern, rationalized the Titan into an historical personage,
now a governor of Egypt, now an astronomer, now the founder of
alchemy.' It is this last which, if I'm on the right track, Fry uses as
a symbol of the gift Thomas released for mankind.

This book, by an American scholar (H. Weir Smith), has a whole
range of references to Promethean interpretations in European
literature. I think Fry's play can be placed within this group.[8]

It would make an essay, if you are at all impressed – which
you could call The Lady & Prometheus, or something like. No
acknowledgments to your wee pet wd. be necessary or desirable –
that's part of the pact. Must go to bed now, or I'll start looking up
Shelley – who was more likely to have conveyed any Promethean
suggestion to Fry than Aeschylus.

One last note. Prometheus himself is not the rational-
empiricist. He is a myth-maker, one of those whom Thomas
describes (Your book p.155) as the 'We' . . .

> . . who have given you a world as contradictory . . . .
>   etc . . .
> A conscienceless hermaphrodite who plays
> Heaven off against hell, hell off against heaven[9]

In fact this is a perfect description of the world of Prometheus as Aeschylus portrayed it in the play. Prometheus does not himself fully come under the new dispensation which he has founded by his gift of the rational faculties. He is not to be equated with his gift, nor is he any longer wholly part of the old order. He is, in a sense, the old order bound to the new, but not wholly identified with it, as Thomas is bound to Jennett [*sic*].

The imagery of 'the spheres' as one might say, throughout *The Lady* has much in common with the cosmic poetry of *Prometheus*.

In fact, my own love, take it from your sleepy girl that, although the Promethean typology of Fry's play is not the *only* interpretive clue, it certainly represents 'a reading'. Prometheus himself might well have said 'since opening time I've been / propped up at the bar of heaven and earth'.[10]

Blessings for you my best boy. I am going to say my prayers not forgetting one for your poor throat – & tuck me in.

All love & kisses too

from

your

Muriel

P.S. This gives me a new slant on Fry – something to justify his language as a suitable one for drama. Aeschylus is famous for his 'Fry' language. Always inventing words, too. Quite a boy, he was, and most unpopular with the intellectuals. At least, to start with . . . . 'Is he sound?' said they. (Of course I'll use Thomas as a type of *Job* – but not at length.)

xxx

P.P.S. In case you think of suggesting that I shd. do an essay on these lines – the answer is no fear. / Uneconomical / C. Fry for you. / Anne & the Bk. of Job for me. /[11]

Love, love, my best one

M

Bring the measurements! for vescot. xxx xxx xxx[12]

ALS. HRC.

1. MS's review of T. S. Eliot's *The Confidential Clerk*, entitled 'The Wisdom of Mr. T. S. Eliot', appeared in the *CEN* on 11 September. In it, MS wrote 'It is a Christian play; it contains Christian teaching and elaborates Christian ideas, some of which are to be found in the Book of Wisdom.' It was with this Christian interpretation that the second reviewer, Kenneth J. Robinson (MS's 'wee toad'), took issue. His article appeared in the same journal on 23 September, entitled 'Eliot? – I Strongly Disagree', and had a subtitle which ran: 'Our Dramatic Critic, Mr. Kenneth Robinson, offers an opposing point of view to Miss Muriel Spark, who discussed Mr. Eliot's new play – "The Confidential Clerk", in her "Edinburgh Festival Diary" in the "C.E.N.".' Robinson stated that 'any one who tries to interpret Mr. Eliot's play in the light of Christian doctrine is wasting his time'.

    In his response to the two articles, which were sent to him by Clifford Rhodes, T. S. Eliot will reply, on Faber and Faber letterhead, on 30 September:

    > I have to thank you for your letter of September 11th, and for kindly sending me the copy of the *Church of England Newspaper* containing a critique of my play by Miss Muriel Spark. I should have acknowledged it as soon as I read it, for it struck me as one of the two or three most intelligent reviews I had read. It seemed to me remarkable that anyone who could only have seen the play once, and certainly not have read it, should have grasped so much of its intention.
    >
    > The article by Mr. Robinson was also interesting, and it is very healthy that there should be differences of opinion. (NLS)

2. Walton Hannah, an Anglican priest who later converted to Catholicism, published his controversial critique of Freemasonry, *Darkness Visible: A Revelation & Interpretation of Freemasonry*, in 1952 with Augustine Press.
3. Robert Greacen's *The Art of Noël Coward* was about to be released by the Hand and Flower Press.
4. *Hanged – And Innocent?* by two MPs strongly opposed to capital punishment, Reginald Paget and Sydney Silverman, had just been published by Victor Gollancz, with an epilogue by MP Christopher Hollis. The review in the *Observer* (27 September 1953), entitled 'Three Doubtful Cases', was signed 'A Lawyer'.

    As its epigraph, Christopher Fry's *The Lady's Not for Burning* has:

    > 'In the past I wanted to be hung. It was worth while being hung to be a hero, seeing that life was not really worth living.'
    > *A convict who confessed falsely to a murder, February 1947*

    MS confuses the names involved in the murder case: Walter Graham

Rowland was accused of having murdered Olive Balchin in Manchester in October 1946, was convicted, and was hanged in February 1947. David J. Ware confessed to the murder while Rowland was in Strangeways Prison; he later attempted to murder a woman in 1951, and was judged criminally insane; this led to speculation that Rowland had in fact been innocent.

5. MS cites from Lord Byron's 'Prometheus' (lines 35–8).
6. MS regularly misspells 'embarrassment/embarrassed/embarrassing', using only one 'r'. As signalled in the Editorial Principles, further instances have been silently corrected.
7. MS quotes from Act I of *The Lady's Not for Burning*, using Derek Stanford's *Christopher Fry: An Appreciation* (p. 67) to do so.
8. MS refers to Herbert Weir Smyth, *Aeschylean Tragedy* (University of California Press, 1924, p. 96).
9. MS quotes from Stanford's quotation from Act II of the play.
10. MS quotes Thomas in Act I of Fry's play using Stanford's book (p. 219) to do so.
11. MS was working on a biography of Anne Brontë and, for Sheed & Ward, a book on the biblical figure of Job and a book on T. S. Eliot; none of these books would be completed in their projected form.
12. By 'vescot' MS may be referring to Stanford's waistcoats, for which she had a penchant (see 24 January 1951).

1954

The year had scarcely begun before the loss of grip on reality that MS had been experiencing became more severe, announcing a mental breakdown produced – or accelerated – by her consumption of the amphetamine appetite-suppressant Dexedrine. She was treated for her symptoms which included the paranoid delusion that she was being written to in code. She persisted in trying to write books on T. S. Eliot, Anne Brontë, Jane Austen, and the biblical figure Job, but found herself unable to complete any of them. From January, with encouragement from Catholic friends, Iris Birtwistle in particular, MS was under instruction for her conversion to Roman Catholicism. On 1 May, she was received into the Roman Catholic Church at Ealing Priory; on 30 May, she was confirmed. After some delays, her edition of *The Brontë Letters* was published by Peter Nevill. By May, she had been taken on by her first literary agent, John Smith of Christy & Moore Ltd, to whom she sent stories. In July, she spent a week at The Hermitage, attached to Stanbrook Abbey in Worcestershire, where she seriously considered becoming a nun. In August there was a first exchange of letters with Alan Maclean, at the publisher Macmillan Ltd, who expressed an interest in MS's stories. In October, MS went to a guest house at The Friars, Aylesford, in Kent, where artists in difficulties were welcome; she soon moved into a cottage which she renamed 'St Jude's Cottage', where she would remain until mid-1955. She became friends with Alan Barnsley (pen-name Gabriel Fielding) and his wife Dina, and grew closer to novelist Christine Brooke-Rose and her husband Jerzy Peterkiewicz; she was assisted financially by generous contributions from David Astor of the *Observer* and Graham Greene, who from October was supporting MS with what she called a 'stipend'.

TO THE EDITOR, THE LISTENER, LONDON,
17 JANUARY 1954

50, Old Brompton Road, London, S.W.7
17th January 1954

Sir,

While appreciating your reviewer's favourable comments on the
critical-biography of Emily Brontë by Derek Stanford and myself,
I feel it necessary to correct some points on which the book is
misrepresented.[1]

Referring to Mr Stanford's part of the book, your critic states
that he accuses of inadequacy all former Brontë critics. This is
not the case. He cites particularly the excellent criticism of Emily
Brontë by Lord David Cecil, Sir Herbert Read, Charles Morgan
and Phyllis Bentley. The critics whom he deprecates are of the
sentimental 'Brontë-lover' school, to correct whose attitude was
the purpose we both shared.

In dealing with the biographical section for which I am
responsible, your critic says I advance a theory which is hardly
tenable, representing this with something which is not my theory,
but a not-quite accurate version of one of my many propositions.
In the logic of which your critic ends by disputing my supposed
'theory' with my own argument! The impression is given that I
have arbitrarily swept aside certain evidence given to Mrs Gaskell
about Emily's character, and that I hold the view that the Brontë
family were unaware of any strangeness in Emily's character at
an early stage. The proposition in question is that Emily Brontë's
development is obscured by the attribution to her early years of
qualities which did not emerge till her last years; to support this I
show that what was said about her at the time by people who knew
her was different from what was said after she became famous,
by people who had known her. Mrs Gaskell, who had not known
Emily, does not come into this particular argument. My method
of tracing Emily's development exclusively from documents
relating currently to her life and from her own autobiographical

statements, gives an incomplete picture of Emily, as I repeatedly stress. The 'legendary' aspect drawn from later hearsay has also to be taken into account; but it is not to be misapplied to a stage in her life at which her powers had not developed.

I regret the necessity for answering your critic at this length, but prefer if possible to be discredited with the fallacies which I express rather than those which I do not.[2]

Yours etc.,

Muriel Spark

Love dearest

In a hurry

x

M.

TLcc sent to Derek Stanford with handwritten PS. HRC.

Letter published in the *Listener*, 28 January 1954.

1. MS is responding to the anonymous review that had appeared in the *Listener* of *Emily Brontë: Her Life and Work* by herself and Derek Stanford, published in late 1953 by Peter Owen.
2. In a response published in the *Listener* immediately following MS's letter, '*Our reviewer writes*': 'My point was (and still is) that the people who "knew" Emily Brontë were mostly not alive when she "became famous", so they could not have spoken about her differently then.'

TO DEREK STANFORD, HOUNSLOW, MIDDLESEX, 24 MARCH 1954

50 Old Brompton Rd, SW.7

Tues 24-3-54

Bonny dear

— So sad at your non-arrival, I light a candle & say a Rosary for you. I also read the Gutch — a priceless document, we must peruse it together one day when you are up to it.[1]

My bonny love I do hope you are not weathered under in a painful degree. Only hoping that your absence means that you are taking precautions against a threatened relapse. I had lunch with Frank today. He advises me to get ahead with the *Job*. He swears he always wanted the *Job* to be done first anyway & was never keen on the Eliot book. I will have to see about more money from him before long, alas. My decoding activities have quite eaten in to the advance.[2]

But no more of this. I am on the mend, with heaps of yeast tablets per day and a good resolution re. sleep etc.

Now I won't discuss the thing much. I may hand it to a cryptographer. *Job* is the thing to concentrate on. Let's hope the author hasn't been 'getting at' me over the centuries. I reckon he *has* you know.

You didn't guess, did you, that your wee thing was really the author of *Job* reincarnate? Well, keep on not guessing so my sweet.

Tomorrow morning I have my instruction at *11*.[3] Tomorrow afternoon I go to my 2nd viewing of the Conf-Clerk, – my last attempt to reconcile the many mysteries – tho' indeed I am now quite disinterested in the motive – only in what I can personally get out of it by way of self-knowledge.[4]

I will be back here by 5 p.m. Do come over sweetheart and see me if you can. The hearth is swept – all is spick & span.

Much love & blessings on your health & good works. Be hopeful, dearest,

Muriel

I will leave the house about 10 am. tomorrow should you want to ring me. But will hope to see you here at 5 p.m. or as soon after that as poss.

ALS. HRC.

1. Reverend Charles Gutch was an Anglo-Catholic who campaigned on behalf of the poor during the Victorian era, and whose *Sermons*, to which MS is probably referring, was published in 1898.
2. In *CV*, MS writes of her breakdown, post-dating it somewhat:

   I was already embarked on a study of Eliot. Frank Sheed of Sheed & Ward commissioned a short book.

So I continued my Eliot studies. But in 1954 shortly after my reception into the Church of Rome something strange occurred. Something strange was not surprising, because, foolishly, I had been taking dexedrine as an appetite suppressant, so that I would feel less hungry. It was a mad idea. (p. 204)

Martin Stannard elaborates:

For some months she had been innocently popping Dexedrine, then readily available from chemist shops to assist dieting. It seemed an ideal drug to get her through this difficult time: she economised on food, lost weight, and her wits were sharpened for those long working nights: three books to write, reviews, poems, letters, and reading, reading, reading. Theological and aesthetic ideas jangled around the anxieties about Stanford, her family and, not least, the attempt to live on a tiny and erratic income.

Then, shortly after she began instruction, around 15–20 January 1954, something went badly wrong. Her friends noticed the trouble before she did: T. S. Eliot, she insisted, was sending her threatening messages. His play was full of them. Some were in the theatre programme. Obsessively she began to seek them out, covering sheet after sheet of paper with anagrams and cryptographic experiments. (*MSB*, pp. 150–1)

3. On 24 January, MS wrote to Iris Birtwistle: 'It has just turned 3 a.m. This Sunday morning & I am "cleaning up" with a view to wending my way across the road to bed. But I must write first to tell you I have started my instruction – now on to the 2nd week & progressing with due delight.' She continued, further into the letter:

It seems there is a 'spirit afloat' as Newman said of the Oxford Movement. And truly, I wouldn't be surprised to see a mass-exit of Anglo-Catholics from the C. of E. into the Church of Christ, any time shortly. We must all have been thinking on the same lines lately. (CBF)

4. On MS's first viewing of Eliot's *The Confidential Clerk*, see 27 August 1953; and on her published review of the play, see 27 September 1953.

TO DEREK STANFORD, HOUNSLOW, MIDDLESEX,
26 MARCH 1954

[Old Brompton Road, London]
26-3-54

Bonnie my dear,

I miss you very much & pray for your being better in due
season. I hope your long winter's woes are brought to a head
by this temporary sucumbing [*sic*]. You should listen to Ye olde
Sparke's Wisdom & leave the cold-cures alone, then you'd have
one dose & be done with it. My instinct is all against those bottles
of yours but bless you sweet heart, they may be the thing for *you*.
Did you get on all right at the dentist? I keep up my Rosary for the
same & the days I neglect it I get a twinge of the toothache – s'
truth.[1]

Now as you're abed a few prayers on my behalf will come in
handy, for sick persons get special favours, don't you forget.

I rang Iris yesterday morning but she'd just left. Spoke to Ma
who seemed a trifle coldish as yet. But Iris rang in the evening as
requested, full of love & good sayings. – A most forgiving girl, I
feel quite reconciled with her now. Meantime, I'd got your letter
with Eliot's enclosed – I was full of joy over this, just what I
wanted.[2] Now I feel released from a very real bondage & can make
use of the experience. The real deliverance is the feeling that I can
discover things about myself independent of the 'code' – things
that I didn't intuitively find among the anagrams but which I hope
will come to light in my mind & in fact have already done so. But
the awful part was not really knowing what sort of illusions I had
to face. Now I've eliminated one possible illusion I can tackle the
rest as planned. From the moment I decided to enter the Church I
felt less tongue-tied & befuddled. All the same, you must question
me sometimes pet, as you advised Fr. Foster.[3] I know you do this,
lovely, when you can't understand me, but do so when you think
you *can* understand me. I'll tell you more about this anon.

I told Mrs Andipatin about ourselves, and of course she knew already tho' didn't say so. What delicacy that woman has! They both love & admire you dearest so don't feel embarrassed. They understand the set-up & are the finest sort of people. I hope you don't mind my speaking to them without consulting you, but it had to be done sometime & I took the simplest opportunity that turned up.

As to Eliot's reply, I don't think you should answer it as he seems to be busy. I don't want you to feel you are compromised, and am sure you are not – it was obviously a work of mercy on your part, & as for myself I don't mind whether he thinks me a fool or not – the main thing was to get the thing clarified for my health's sake. I smiled at his allusion to the 'author' of the code. – I'm sure now it's a matter of my own choice. I suppose he gets a lot of mad letters. He says nothing about the Greek. The Greek is there. No matter, I have other things to concern me. I may return to it later when I've refurbished my Greek & after the *Job* is done.[4] Many many thanks my darling for this service. Am on my way to the bank to face the worst. Hope to get my Observer review done this week. Good luck about your Tablet book. I'd like to have a squint at the Swift when you've done it.

P.S. Send me my mother's letter when next you write. I'd like to see it. My Brontë is out but no copies yet. Have no interest in it really.[5] Love,

M.

Keep in good heart & mind. Blessings on your work. Iris is coming up on Friday week (this day week i.e.).

Love, love, to you.

M.

ALS. HRC.

1. With hindsight and its questionable benefit, MS writes in *CV*:

    Derek Stanford's letters are full of his ailments, whether from hypochondria or from genuine illness, let us not split hairs. The fact is that phrases like 'The worst has happened. I am in bed with a cold' and 'My doctors say that I must avoid the night air' abound. It so happened that when I recently came upon one of Derek's unopened letters addressed to me so long ago, I said to the friend who was helping me to sort them: 'I bet it's about his health.' Sure enough, the note begins: 'The worst has come to pass, and here I am still in bed on Monday morning.' (p. 186)

2. On 19 March, T. S. Eliot wrote to Stanford:

I have just returned from abroad, and find a mass of correspondence awaiting me, but as your enquiry seems from your second letter to be urgent, I will answer it at once, as it needs but a brief answer. If there is any code concealed in *The Confidential Clerk*, I shall be interested to know what it is. From the precedent of Bacon having written the works of Shakespeare, and Queen Victoria having written *In Memoriam*, I should expect the code to disclose the name of the author of the play. (NLS)

3. From 1950 to 1965, the Reverend Roy Foster was Anglican vicar at St Augustine's Church, which MS was attending.
4. In *CV*, of the most delusional period, MS writes:

As I worked on the Eliot book one night the letters of the words I was reading became confused. They formed anagrams and cross-words. In a way, as long as this sensation lasted, I knew they were hallucinations. But I didn't connect them with the dexedrine. It is difficult to convey how absolutely fascinating that involuntary word-game was. I thought at first that there was a code built into Eliot's work and tried to decipher it. Next, I seemed to realize that this word-game went through other books by other authors. It appeared that they were phonetics of Greek, and were extracts from the Greek dramatists.

This experience lasted from 25 January to 22 April 1954. (p. 204)

5. *The Brontë Letters*, edited and introduced by MS, had just been published by Peter Nevill.

TO IRIS BIRTWISTLE, WROXTON, OXFORDSHIRE,
13 MAY 1954

50 Old Brompton Road, S.W.7
13th May 1954

My dearest Iris,

How very sweet of you to add to my blessings – I couldn't ever repay your kindness tho' the loan were repaid ten times over. The extra £10 is particularly helpful in view of one of the usual setbacks of my trade which occurred this week – I must tell you of this, it has its funny side. I had put all my own work aside for the past 10 days to correct some dreary proofs of a most exacting technical book for Falcon Press. Laboured I at this wretched thing with my newfound Catholic diligence day & night, night & day. Took the job along to Falcon, and found the Receiver in possession of the building, the staff gazing at each other with a wild surmise tho' not too despondent about the prospect of their wages. What cheered everybody up was the Receiver himself. They had expected some grave solid and judicious gent of middle years, and were lined up, hearts pit-a-pat, to greet the same. But a mere youth turned up, much more embarrassed than they could ever be, and there he is, master of the show, doling out his signature for every sixpence which departs from the petty cash. The debate among the staff is whether he is aged 15 or 16. The Directors have the worst of it of course, apparently they are fabulously comitted [*sic*]; Peter Baker who owns the firm has gone into a nursing home. If the firm can be salvaged Wrey Gardiner will return, I hear. This is confidential, if only for the sake of my own claim! – Once it gets known that the firm is on the rocks my nine pounds-odd won't stand a chance among the incredible sums demanded from every printer in the kingdom.

So I was enormously grateful for the extra sum, and especially Iris, I must tell you that all I ever receive from you has a unique fruitfulness. This isn't a superstition – I really think an awareness of the intention which accompanies the benefit helps one to use money to good advantage. For instance – when you let us have a large sum of money before, I was able to have the extra little room to myself; my own room for the first time for nearly four years. And it was there that I began to think out my position in peace and was able to decide on a real course of conduct on independent lines. This is between ourselves of course. Derek is more and more coming to realise the rightness of our parting. I know you pray for him, as you have done for me; you must continue this loveliest favour of all for both of us.

I'm writing a metaphysical lyric for Iris and Damian which seems to be taking a likely shape. Can I know the colour of his eyes please? – For a real poetic reason, less trite than it sounds.[1]

Kiss the mite for me, and remember me with love to your mother. Do say if you can come to my Confirmation, it would be delightful, and I think wd. encourage Derek to be present. He is awfully shy about public worship, which is understandable. The genuflexions and reverent attitudes that Catholics take for granted often put a strain on people used to the hushed Protestant reserve, even if they admire the Catholic traditions and like to 'watch' the services. I think D. feels a little this way, but of course don't altogether know his mind. However, you if anyone, could persuade him to come to the Confirmation – and if you can't manage to come yourself, please urge him in passing, next time you write, to support me with his presence.[2]

I must away and work. Let me know your latest news, and how soon you are to be officially adopted by Damian.

Bless you and best love,

s/Muriel

I'm highly pleased about Bob & Teresa's verdict on the Bronte. The Masefield has gone off to them. Many thanks for this. You are quite the best customer for Spark books![3]

TLS. CBF.

---

1. In an undated letter that enclosed money, probably sent in April, Iris Birtwistle wrote to MS to describe her adoption of her first child, Damien

(so spelt), whom she had found in a parlous state of health; she asked if MS would accept to become the child's godmother (NLS).

2.   How rapidly MS's religious sensibility had shifted towards convergence with Birtwistle's: as recently as ten months prior, MS had still been encouraging Birtwistle towards the Church of England, to which she had herself then recently converted. On 18 July 1953, she wrote to her friend:

> I'm sorry I wasn't able to answer all your questions about the Catholic Faith in England. Why not consult the Anglican Priest you told me about? I'm sure he wouldn't be put out – quite the opposite – however holy he is. Holiness, in fact, is just what is required for such a task. Not only am I not holy, I am not sufficiently informed to answer your questions adequately, being so recent a convert. But the Priest – any Priest – will make these things quite clear, if you are prepared to listen, of course. I'm sure you would be willing to listen, as you're so keen in your questions – just like myself, before my conversion. And of course, one continues to discover new and wonderful things about the Faith. [. . .] I am sure you realise how much I hope you will be drawn, in God's own way, to the Church of England, though I wouldn't myself venture to disturb you, and only advise you to proceed, because of your interest. (CBF)

3.   In the same undated letter (probably from April), Birtwistle sent a cheque to cover the cost of MS sending a copy of her *The Brontë Letters* to her friends Bob and Teresa Travis, residents of Hoghton, Lancashire.

TO DEREK STANFORD, HOUNSLOW, MIDDLESEX,
31 MAY 1954

50, Old Brompton Road, S.W.7
31st May 1954

Dearest Brother Mine,

It seems sad not to be seeing you till Wednesday – and then only to spend our time together with other people.

Let us get rid of Wrey at an early hour, skip the party and spend the evening in peace, shall we? – If you will let me know your mind on this some time on Wednesday morning I will ring Rosamond & give the excuse of pressure of work.[1]

I would like to tell you, too, how very greatly I prefer your company to anyone else's I know. It isn't only that we have so much of an intimate past in common. From my point of view, now that I've been a Catholic for some months, I feel a stronger-growing need of your type of mind, one of *honest doubting*; honest doubts are the very life-blood of faith to me. St. Thomas says, 'Those who wish to discover the truth should previously, that is before they set to work, doubt well; that is to say, they should examine thoroughly what is to be doubted.'[2]

Now, as an Anglo-Catholic, I found the company of Catholics invigorating, for it expressed a testimony to those supernatural aspects of life which I knew to be realities, but to which I did not find myself bound by in Anglicanism. Well, I have benefitted by their example & prayers, but I must say that as Catholicism takes shape within me, I find myself moving away from the attitudes of my Catholic friends. Not that I disapprove of their temper of belief, on the contrary I've every reason to be grateful for its influence. But having gained so much, I don't wish to lose what I have already been given as a gift of grace – a certain belief in the value and reality of sensible experience. Individually, all my Catholic friends are rational partakers of life to a more or less degree. But get them together in a majority outside of a church, and a tacit understanding that the fantastic and the real are one and the same, somehow superimposes itself upon the company, except where the subject of morals is concerned. On morals they are perfectly clear. On questions of the Faith, who is clear? – For this very reason it is necessary to bring to all considerations of Faith the salutary criterion of personal experience (i.e. of the mind & soul – not merely emotions). I am not verging here on a doctrine of Private Judgment, as you know.[3] As with morals, so with faith – there is a body of doctrine which Catholics believe and are bound to believe; this is merely practical, because not all tenets of the Church, whether of morals or of faith can possibly come within the personal inward experience of the individual – a lifetime could never exhaust the experience of everything believed; but it is because of knowledge in part that one can take on trust – as in most matters – the authority of that which

logically coheres with what is known. When I say that questions
of the Faith require that test of personal experience which enables
people to discern morals reasonably, I mean to consider the point
in the light of the obvious fact that questions of the Faith *are*
discussed; not, amongst Catholics as to whether they are true or
not – nor alas, are they considered as to how and why they are
true in such and such a circumstance.

What I find amongst Catholics, when they congregate, then, is
an insufficient clarity on the above distinctions. The enthusiasm
of a very real belief obscures that very reality, in fact; one is
impressed by the enthusiasm while it lasts, but it must be admitted
that after such a session one's mind has remained unused, the
reflective understanding of the subject is no further advanced.
Suppose, for instance, it is a question of Our Lady. There is no
doubt amongst the company as to the reality of Our Lady, and
of her practical effects on the world. It is a question of how and
why. But will they discuss how & why? – They will not, although
probably they think that is what they are doing. One witness will
speak of a miraculous cure done in the presence of her aunt –
very true certainly; another will recall a period of history when
devotion to Our Lady was at its most rife and interesting. Who
will discuss why, at that particular time, this devotion flourished?
Who will have taken the trouble to investigate the inner life of the
aunt, since she certainly witnessed the miracle – and who, with
more courage of conviction, would give an accurately-observed
account of the *psychology* of the aunt, even within the limits of an
unscientific observer? If I had an aunt who had seen a miracle, I
would want to know what had taken place previously in her life
and mind so far as that was possible; this is necessary for two
reasons: to assess the merits of the claim and, if these are satisfied,
to assess the method by which the lady was prepared for such an
event, and the reason, in her particular case, for it; – the 'how' &
the 'why', in other words.

These examples are cited typically – they are the sort of
illustrations given by Catholics to a discussion of Our Lady. But
as to a general discussion which calls for 'personal' testimony

in a more intellectual sense, this is not forthcoming amongst
the Catholics we know. Of course the intellectuals like Victor
White are eminently readable on these lines; you and I can
discuss such a question in 'personal' terms by reference to our
personal experience of literature for example, and we know a
little mythology as understood from the modern psychological
point of view. (I mean, we can speak of Demeter, for example, as
a psychological and therefore ever-present phenomenon as distinct
from a figure of ancient folk-lore.)[4] What would be interesting
would be to come across a Catholic doctor or lawyer or farmer
who, from the inside understanding and with the terminology of
his profession, could express the fact of the Blessed Virgin and her
works. But it is precisely from such people that we get, instead
of a personal reflection on the subject, a statement that on such
and such an occasion, such and such a thing happened as a result
of Our Lady's intercession — with elaborations on the statement,
but no exploration of the experience from the vantage-point of a
particular calling in life. And of course Our Lady is not the only
question. I think on the whole Catholics — particularly perhaps
in a non-Catholic country — tend to be unconsciously always on
the apologetic, even amongst themselves. There is an inbred fear
of betraying the Faith, possibly justifiable in former times, but no
longer so in this respect. Even the Papal Encyclicals are very far in
advance of the common practice. On the question of the scriptures,
for example, the Encyclicals say, go ahead, investigate everything —
the dates, the text, the literary form. But the superstition about
scriptural studies creeps in even amongst scriptural scholars, with
the exception of the very eminent. (Knox, who is popular in tone
only as an apologist, is very sound & accurate in textual scholarship,
and he is not always considered quite the thing by Catholics.)[5]

I know it is very much human nature I am reviewing when thus
I pin-point Catholics; but in the average intelligent Catholic, the
limitations of human nature take a form which I feel it a need to
avoid participation with, and a duty to oppose by pursuing the
revealed facts of experience without fear or guilt. I am of the type
of Catholic who must take recourse to the living waters of the

defining mind. And what is the defining mind, but the mind that
'doubts well'? There can be no definition without doubt, unless it
be an intuitive act of definition, in which case we must return to
doubt in order to verify the intuition. Doubt may be said to be a
process of defining – it is not a fixed principle, by its nature.

Doubt, allowing for the fluctuations imposed on the mind by
our moods, moves towards one or more objective, sometimes of a
conflicting nature. Disbelief on the other hand, if it is honest and
not confused with doubt, is a fixed principle.

For instance take the experience claimed by a number of people
that they have seen flying saucers, I doubt it, I don't disbelieve it.

Now, what I doubt is not the experience, for it is verified by
sufficient numbers. I doubt (a) whether, if the object exists, it is
a flying saucer – perhaps it is something else; (b) whether, if the
object exists, it exists materially (as a space-vessel) or psychically
(as the second apparition of Hamlet's father, 'seen' by Hamlet
but not by his mother) or spiritually (as the first appearance of
the Ghost in Hamlet, witnessed by three independent observers
and so, in dramatic terms, a *'real'* ghost); as regards the two
latter distinctions of my doubt, the question is whether – if the
phenomenon is not a material one – it is a projection from within
the minds of the subject or an imposition from without; (in the
former case, if it is a psychical apparition, one would expect a
large number of people not to 'see' the object simultaneously with
those who do 'see' it – as in Hamlet's second ghost-vision). And
further, I doubt (c) whether in fact the object is real – it may be
a fantasy of the imagination; that is, there may be no such thing
as a 'psychic reality' – for not all psychologists are agreed about
the reality of psychical objects of experience, and hence the
experience may be without an object – purely subjective.

This is to illustrate my conception of doubt. It seems to me
that doubt presupposes the existence of an experience and moves
towards an objective definition of the experience, not simply
by defining the object as that which has been suggested by the
experience itself, but by defining in successive stages the 'how and
why' of the experience.

Disbelief, however, discounts experience. To say I disbelieve in flying saucers, would mean (a) that I did not believe that the people who claimed to have seen them, saw them; or (b) that I did not believe that the experience was honestly undergone – i.e., that it was not true experience. Thus, a man might, seeing his neighbour very excited & hearing him describe flying saucers, fool himself that he too had seen one, only the other day, and hardly noticed it! If one were convinced that the testimony of those who have seen flying saucers was the result of rumour & suggestion & exaggeration, one could say, therefore I disbelieve in flying saucers. And on the grounds that they conflicted with known and universal experience, if they did so, one would disbelieve and not doubt.

As a further example of the difference between disbelief and doubt – the one concerning experience, the other concerning definition of an accepted experience, take the case of Father Divine, the American negro who claims to be God.[6]

I do not doubt only, that he is God, I disbelieve it (a) on the prejudicial grounds of my religion, for his claim conflicts with a known experience of God in that religion; and (b) because his claim conflicts with a known experience of mankind; he cannot be God, as he is not only human but fallible also in his doctrines (his followers are all forbidden sexual intercourse, and their death when it occurs, is a disgrace & due to some lapse in discipleship) which opposes the natural order – no marriage, births, etc. Now it will be argued, do I, disbelieving in Father Divine's divinity, disbelieve in his experience and in the experience of his followers? The answer is, yes, I do not disbelieve that there exists an experience felt by the man, and defined by him as god-ship; I don't disbelieve that the followers have an experience of the man which they define as his divinity. But I disbelieve that the experience is in fact commensurable in his case, with godship, in theirs with his divinity, – just as the disbeliever in the experience of flying saucers will fix it as a principle that the subjects of the experience are under the influence of suggestion and not true experience. In fact the 'experience' here works on revivalist principles. It is *stirred up*. – This is no more true experience than are the 'experiences'

of drunkenness – and no less! So I disbelieve in the experiences
of Divine & his sect – they are not true experiences, the test
of which is that in order to claim it, they have to deny the true
experiences of maternity, family life, death.

I disbelieve in Methodism, because 'Methodism' is not to be
confused with the practise [sic] & worship of Methodists only. It
is an intellectual concept among other things and must stand the
test of intellectual experience, just as 'Catholicism' has to do.
When I say I disbelieve in Methodism I deny the experience of
total human participation, mind-logic, body-obedience, spirit-
worship, etc. to be present in Methodism. I do not deny that
Methodists experience God, I do not even doubt it. In speaking
of Methodism's insufficiency as a concept, I mean that it does not
enjoy the universal status in this capacity, that a known condition
like 'fatalism' enjoys.

Where does this lead me? I've been trying to say that doubt
starts off by accepting an experience – if it's a personal doubt,
then the experience will be a personal one, and with an objective
a given proposition – someone else's experience, the doubt will
be impersonal. But the experience is accepted as a true one. In
disbelief, the experience is rejected as a false or insufficient one
as regards the measure of its claims. Doubt is never fixed, never
at rest until it finds truth by *defining*. Now it seems to me, that
Catholics, who start from the point of advantage of accepted or
personally known – whether inward or outward, emotional or
intellectual – experience, which is their body of beliefs more
intensely and firmly held than in any other expression of human
or divine society – Catholics should understand the value of *doubt*
more than anyone else. For it is not the experience of Christ,
of the Saints, of the Church or her dogmas, nor their personal
understanding of God that they are doubting. Those doubts that
torment us, as to whether or not we are doing right or wrong
in this or that particular, are, in fact, too greatly scrupulized
over by religious people. They admit, quite rightly, of doubt
where personal morals are concerned; but not in faith. No-one
who doubts whether, in given circumstances, a certain action

was compatible with Charity, would be accused of doubting
that the virtue of Charity is good, or of disbelieving in it.
But few Catholics would care to discuss whether, in certain
circumstances, the Communion of Saints penetrates certain other
human affinities – that of kindred minds throughout civilized
history – that of kindred souls outside of family relationships –
the affinity of blood relations where there is otherwise nothing
in common – the affinity of man with the soil and with animal
creation.[7] Catholics are scared stiff of the Holy Ghost, and that's
the truth, though the Church teaches far otherwise. It was St.
Thomas who took the pagans, and heretics and infidels as his
sources of truth, as well as the former Fathers – who constantly
provide him with confirmation of his assertions of truth from
pagan sources.[8] All the great doctors & mystics have understood
doubt. And to understand doubt a little, is to welcome the society
of a true and devout doubter.

No more for tonight. Needless to say, I consider myself a loyal
Catholic withal.

Love to you from

Muriel

P.S. 'Charity believeth all things' – that is experience, 'endureth
all things' – that is doubt, for Charity also 'hopeth' and 'beareth'
all things: It carries all things towards its object – in doubt is
Hope & Charity. – But publish it not in the streets of Askelon.[9]

ALS. HRC.

1. Rosamond Batchelor worked as an editor at Sheed & Ward Ltd, for which
    MS was engaged to write on both Job and T. S. Eliot; at the start of the
    year, Batchelor's translation from the Polish of Leon Maks's *Russia by the
    Back Door* was published by Sheed & Ward.
2. MS had in fact received her confirmation the previous day, Sunday 30
    May, in a ceremony which, despite her best efforts to persuade him, Derek
    Stanford did not attend. She interprets the doubts of Thomas the Apostle –
    Doubting Thomas – rather than citing him directly from the Bible, where
    he appears principally in the Gospel of John.
3. The Doctrine or Right of Private Judgement is a key concept of the
    Protestant Reformation which asserts that everyone may – indeed

should – read the Bible for themselves, and make their own judgement on interpretation of scripture; as opposed to the Church of Rome, which asserts its own sole authority and infallibility in scriptural interpretation and judgement.

4. Victor White was a Dominican priest and close follower of Carl Jung who corresponded with him and visited him in Bollingen in 1946, and who would, as MS would also, review Jung's 1952 book *Antwort auf Hiob* that was then being published in English as *Answer to Job*. (See 'Victor White and C. G. Jung: The Fateful Encounter of the White Raven and the Gnostic', in *New Blackfriars*, vol. 62, no. 733/734, July/August 1981.)

   The Greek goddess Demeter, usually associated with grain and agriculture, was also celebrated in the Homeric 'Hymn to Demeter' which tells of the abduction of her daughter Persephone by Hades, ruler of the underworld – and of her subsequent rescue.

5. MS refers to the English Catholic convert, priest, translator, radio broadcaster, and prolific author – of, among other things, detective stories – Ronald Knox, whose biography would later be published by MS's supporter Evelyn Waugh.

6. MS refers to the Black American preacher and spiritual leader known as Father Divine.

7. Though understood variously by the different branches of the Christian church as 'part of the 9th article of the Apostles' Creed', the Communion of the Saints, according to *The Concise Oxford Dictionary of the Christian Church*, 'is usually interpreted as the spiritual union existing between each Christian and Christ, and so between every Christian whether in Heaven, Purgatory, or on earth' (ed. E. A. Livingstone, Oxford University Press, 2013).

8. MS may be referring to what is recounted in the third-century apocryphal book *Acts of Thomas*, which tells of the Apostle's missionary activities in Syria and India.

9. MS loosely cites 1 Corinthians 13 on charity which 'Beareth all things, believeth all things, hopeth all things, endureth all things'.

   The port city of Ashkelon was a site of conflict between Israelites and Philistines, leading David to include mention of it in his lament for Saul and Jonathan (in 2 Samuel 1: 19–20): 'The beauty of Israel is slain upon thy high places: how are the mighty fallen! Tell it not in Gath, publish it not in the streets of Askelon; lest the daughters of the Philistines rejoice, lest the daughters of the uncircumcised triumph.'

TO DEREK STANFORD, HOUNSLOW, MIDDLESEX,
5 JULY 1954

c/o Mrs Wilson, The Hermitage, Callow End, N^r Worcester
Monday 4th July

Dearest Cranford-Stanford,

Many thanks for your farewell-card on Sat. and your hail-card
this morning. Quite a link with the past, the latter.[1]

I've come to the conclusion that distance in time can very well
be reckoned spatially. For here, there is both clock-time, everything
punctually reminded by bells – and time-not-our-time; also, time past.

I haven't had more than a few sniffs round the countryside so
far, owing to my being required at the Abbey – a few green stops
from the door of this pleasant 18th century dwelling.

I saw the Lady Abbess on Saturday shortly after I arrived. A
young woman – in her early forties, most English; regal so far
as her office is *worn*; simple so far as she's a nun; intelligent &
a straight-talker in the 'English family' tradition. A good face,
neither ascetic nor unspiritual. Apparently she hasn't been in
office long. Her predecessor was very old, very famous, – Dame
Laurentia – a sort of oracular sage, much consulted by the
agnostics & aetheists [sic] of her time. – Bernard Shaw made many
a trip to consult her about it and about [sic], I gather.[2]

Well, the present Abbess was elected last September – by
the community, i.e. the nuns themselves & seems to have been
specially chosen for her non-extremist ways and a distinction of
her own which doesn't attempt to rival the beloved departed.

They are an enclosed order. This too was chosen by themselves.
They could have been an out-&-about set of nuns – apparently the
Benedictine abbey in Wales is not enclosed. But at Stanbrook they
are most particular about a) the ancient traditions of the calling and
b) their Englishness. They boast a sort of public-school trust in the
Community – a too close prying into the inner lives of the nuns is
here unheard of. Not, apparently, like *other* convents, unnamed.

Various nuns are sent to speak to me (through grilles of

course) – chosen I imagine for their assessing powers as well as their entertaining capacities. Dame Mary – she's a born psychologist. Dame Bede is the Infirmarian, or nurse, very practical, very untrained. They do not greatly care for trained nurses – that is, the hospital variety. For their own needs, they want less of the lump-of-flesh attitude & more of the comforting type of approach. For epidemics & broken bones, ex-rays [*sic*] etc., well there's always Worcester hospital where the National Health is understanding enough to provide private wards for the nuns. – This is inserted to give you a general picture – but, back to personalities.

Dame Felicitas is the librarian, a scholar & a lady. With her, I've had a pleasant passage. She has most interesting opinions about things. On Anglican writing, for example, she absorbs with respect the type of book which establishes the Anglican raison d'être on, say, the Little Gidding experiment, which, frankly anti-Roman, may be (in the sort of writing she has in mind) supported by the Reformation Fathers – Hooker, Andrewes, Taylor, etc. That, she feels, is a clear-cut case.[3] What she cannot abide – and really I am with her – is the attempt to range round the Early Fathers – Jerome, Augustine and the like for an Anglican context. I think, even from the non-Roman point of view, the messiness of this approach is inclined to impair the value of Anglicanism, since there's no doubt it has a value. The C. of E. as *it is at present* could learn a lot from this lady.

But cutting across her definitiveness in this direction – and giving her point of view an attractiveness to those interested in the wider realm of Christian thought, is her theory of the English Character in general, and its origin. That which established, she claims, what we call the English Tradition – liberality of thought, the will for tolerance, stability & practical judgment – the whole school of virtues deriving from St. Gregory the Great whose influence was profound & unifying. (It was he, as you know, who sent St Augustine of Canterbury to revive the Faith in England.) His *Pastoralis curae*, translated by Alfred the Great, was distributed in 800 copies – what you might call a bumper edition for those days. She has lent me a copy of a new American translation of 'Pastoral Care', so I'm now about to put the theory to the test. This same Dame Felicitas together with the late Abbess 'discovered' the earliest known Gregorian M.S. some time back. The librarian from Worcester library came to consult the worthy dames as to a piece of ancient script which he had unbound from the wrapping of an old book-binding, & that same turned out to be an 800 B.C. MS of great worth to scholar-pilgrims throughout this globe.[4]

Well, well. The aforesaid Dame Mary – the psychological one – is a psychologist by nature, not by learning. She understands the harmonies of their religious life when expressed in humane terms. The whole life centres round the recitation & chanting & singing of the Hours. Their raison d'être is the Divine Office. Thus, while they are contemplative by definition, they are not contemplative in the Carmelite sense. They do not, for instance, go in for prayer-instruction except in a general way. – No 'exercises' and 'points'. Instruction in Latin and Greek are substituted so that the nuns may know that which they sing at their Lauds, Matins, Terce, Sext, Nones and Compline. She explains that the life at first seems to be the very opposite to what it is. The day is broken up into small periods – scraps of routine activity. It is only when these become as habitual as breathing, that the daily newspaper and the Gospel for the day begin to harmonise together. Things do, she asserts, cohere, under a small patch of sky, as it does no-where else in the world; the importance of this, being that a coherence in one small area forms a hub to control what goes on at the circumference. The Rule of St. Benedict is adhered to with modern allowances, but as strict as possible. Life is rigorous & tough for new people, especially smokers of whom they have a number.

Besides the Offices which is the main work of the convent, they do weaving & painting; sew their own habits, scrub their own floors, do their own gardening. They are encouraged to spend as much time out of doors as possible. Spacious grounds, but of course they don't go out of the grounds at any time.

That is the general outline, so far. I'm hoping to have more to discuss with you when I see you a-Thursday. Perhaps I'll have had time to see the Severn River which is not far off & to make a trip to the Malvern Hills, also nearby.

The countryside is gorgeous, but the weather forbids long

walks. There are no picture p-c.'s to be had in the village, but I will probably get some at Worcester if my interviews permit a morning's absence.

I have been lent a large pile of Job books – incl. St. Gregory – from their library. As good a monastic library as any in England, they say.

I've learnt something about the other Orders, but it is certain that it would be Benedictine for me if anything. The vows are not the usual 'Poverty, Chastity & Obedience' but 'Stability, Conversion of Life, and Obedience'.

Now to mundane matters. Can you please put me in the post *right away* £2 as I will need them & can't cash a cheque easily. Will give you the money on my return. I have to send Robin £1 for his birthday on the 9th of July (Saturday) so will have to post it before I leave on Thursday. The other pound I may need, as the taxi-fare from Worcester is 10/- – rather more than I'd calculated. I hope to get my Observer cheque by Monday week, which will tide me over. Pray for my piece to get into next week's Observer so that payment will be included in the cheque. I will pray for your term & have already remembered you in the Masses. To be given a Mass is a very good & effective prayer, especially in this holy place.

Remember to send a card to Robin – with a small remembrance if you can afford it dear, but anyway a card.

Bless you my poppet & think good things for me. I'll let you know when I'm arriving on Thursday – we'll have a return celebration.

Best love from your aspiring pal –

Muriel

ALS. HRC. Dating: in her subsequent letter to Derek Stanford, MS corrects the day of her son's birthday to *Friday* the 9th, indicating that in the present letter she was one day out; the Monday previous to the birthday was 5 July.

1. MS writes from the guest house linked to Stanbrook Abbey, the Benedictine monastery for nuns which at the time was the most populous in England,

and where she was spending one week's holiday. She combines Derek Stanford's name with the name of the novel, *Cranford*, by Elizabeth Gaskell, whose work she and Stanford had previously proposed to anthologise.

2. Elizabeth Sumner, then forty-three years old, became Abbess at Stanbrook Abbey after the death of Abbess Laurentia McLachlan in August the previous year; Dame Laurentia had been Abbess since 1931 and had established a reputation for her leadership, her publications, her interest in Gregorian chant, her spiritual wisdom, and her friendships with such figures as George Bernard Shaw and Sydney Cockerell.

3. Between 1625 and 1646, the extended family of ordained deacon Nicholas Ferrar lived in a manor at Little Gidding in Cambridgeshire, following their interpretation of the rites and rituals of the Church of England and the Book of Common Prayer. Their Little Gidding Community (as it later came to be known) was accused by the Puritans of being a 'Protestant nunnery' and was raided and closed by Oliver Cromwell's soldiers in 1646. T. S. Eliot revived interest in the surviving church, and the ideal it emblematised, in his 1944 poem 'Little Gidding', last of his *Four Quartets* in which he writes:

> You are here to kneel
> Where prayer has been valid

and

> So, while the light fails
> on a winter's afternoon, in a secluded chapel
> History is now and England.

MS refers to the influential sixteenth-century advocate of Anglicanism Richard Hooker, author of *Of the Laws of Ecclesiastical Polity*; to the bishop and anti-Puritan advisor to the monarch Lancelot Andrewes, whose *Ninety-Six Sermons* were published posthumously in 1629; and to the classical scholar, theologian, and Presbyterian minister John Taylor, whose *The Scripture-Doctrine of Original Sin*, published in 1740, sought to rebut the Calvinist doctrine of original sin.

4. MS muddles her facts. The manuscript that was discovered, or more precisely *identified*, by Dame Laurentia in or around 1907 was in fact the earliest surviving example of Paterius's anthology of the writings of Pope Gregory the Great's writings. The fragments of manuscript had been brought by Canon James Wilson, librarian of Worcester Cathedral. Dame Felicitas Corrigan, not born at the time of the 'discovery', was then working on her book *In a Great Tradition: Tribute to Dame Laurentia McLachlan*, which would be published by John Murray in 1956 (personal communication from Sr Margaret Truran, Abbey of Santa Cecilia, Rome, 23 November 2023).

TO DEREK STANFORD, HOUNSLOW, MIDDLESEX,
5 JULY 1954

c/o Mrs Wilson, The Hermitage, Callow End, N^r Worcester
4th July 1954

My dearest Cranfordian,
   I missed the post with my other epistle today & though I
sent it by Epress [*sic*], I doubt very much if you will get it before
Wednesday. This would make it rather risky to post the £2; it
might not reach me on Thursday morning unless you were able to
catch an early mail. Which things being so, I'll leave the matter
to your discretion. Only £1 will be needed now, as, foreseeing
the difficulties, I sent a cheque to Robin. His birthday, the 9th, is
on the Friday (not the Saturday as stated beforetimes). He will be
sixteen!! Well, bless him, I hope to be assured of his wellbeing in
the most obvious eventualities, before taking any step Stanbrook-
wards, though fain would I join them without delay – at least
I would like to join them next year. But as I told you & I think
you'll agree, I can't just vanish behind the grille not knowing what
would befall him as regards maternal care should my mother die
before he reached maturity. The call of God is strong in the pure
& simple form of the service of a religious life, but then God is in
Robin too – more clear to me than to a stranger. So it's a matter
of abiding the providential answer. To ignore this problem would
be, I feel, to tamper with Providence, don't you think?[1]
   Meantime I'll try to keep in touch with Stanbrook. Tomorrow
or next day I'll send you another descriptive epistle & the
'characters' of the next batch of nuns.
   Much love from your
   aspiring Muriel
   ALS. HRC. Dating: this letter written on the same day as the previous one.

1. On what she calls 'Holy Saturday 1954' (3 April), MS wrote to Iris
   Birtwistle: 'Did Derek tell you my secret plan? That is something to work

for – it may take two years. What do you think?' (CBF). The plan was almost certainly the one elaborated here: that she should enter orders and become a Benedictine nun.

The role of Providence was much on her mind as MS recovered, slowly, from her breakdown; it was even informing her literary-critical judgement when she wrote to Derek Stanford one month previously, on 7 June, about a favourable review of *The Brontë Letters*:

> Blush I more to read Norman Nicholson's piece in Time and Tide – very favourable indeed – and to think how I slated his play! Mea culpa . . . but it wasn't much of a play. Do read Time & Tide – a long piece. He feels there's something creative about the book – which of course I like, and ascribes this to a mixture of Providence, the Brontes and myself, which is decidedly agreeable. The feeling that a job of editing can be a creative work is very important – but hardly any critics bother to weigh up the selective part of the editing of popular selections. (HRC)

TO ALAN MACLEAN, MACMILLAN LTD, LONDON, 2 AUGUST 1954

50, Old Brompton Road, London, S.W.7
2nd August, 1954

Dear Mr. Maclean,

Thank you for your letter of 30th July, and for thinking of me in connection with a novel.[1]

I have not made any plans to write a novel. At present I am working on a critical study for Sheed and Ward, and when this is finished I hope to do a little purely creative work.[2] I have considered the novel form as a possibility, and your letter encourages me towards the idea. But I could not attempt a long work without a sum of money in advance of royalties. I do not know how you would feel about this.

I should say, also, that I am obliged to offer Sheed and Ward my next proposed work. But they publish very little fiction, and I think they would let me write a novel for another publisher.

If this position has any likelihood from your point of view I would be glad to discuss it with you some time. But in any event,

I appreciate your kind interest, and am sorry for my inability to offer you a completed novel at the present time.

Yours sincerely,

s/Muriel Spark

TLS. MA.

1. In 1952, MS met the novelist and editor Tony Strachan when he came to work at the Falcon Press, 'who was to become a lifelong friend' (*CV*, p. 199). Four years after the present letter, on 15 July 1958, she will explain to Alan and Dina Barnsley the role Strachan played at Macmillan: 'In the most disinterested way he has been promoting my work for the last five years or so. I never see or hear from him between one Macmillan party and another. Unknown to me he got Macmillan interested in my writing a novel. Quite disinterested; he doesn't even seek the credit. He has apparently been trying to place my things in Europe as well. Most unboastful, not like us' (MBC). It was Strachan who recommended MS to Alan Maclean, who had recently become an editor at Macmillan; Alan Maclean's career at the Foreign Office had been curtailed when his brother, the spy Donald Maclean, defected to the Soviet Union in 1951. At Macmillan, he would become a highly influential editor, working there until his retirement in 1984, becoming over the course of his career Director of both Macmillan and Pan.

2. MS refers to her unfinished study of Job.

Alan Maclean

TO DEREK STANFORD, HOUNSLOW, MIDDLESEX,
5 AUGUST 1954

[Old Brompton Road, London]
5th Aug

Dearest Boy,

Don't worry about me, please. I have put away the Anne, and
whether I will feel differently about its value (for me) or not later
on, I won't think about now.[1] I am doing my book on Job and
already feel more at peace with my soul. I know you won't hold
my defection against me when it was so obviously necessary to
my health. I felt, today, that I was dying. I've got to the stage
now where the rightness of a work or otherwise, for myself, is
absolutely essential if I'm to write anything at all. So be patient my
dear, I am not out of the wood yet. But do realise, as I know you
will, that I am not well and am trying my best to recover. My plan
is to try and stick to my *Job* and do nothing else in the literary line
until it is finished, unless my funds run out. I won't think too far
ahead but must just keep frugally on.

I'll give you back most of your Anne money, and the notes if you
fix up with Robt. Hale, or decide to get another collaborator. I'd
really rather you did this, for I hate to think of your work wasted.

Dear love, I *am* sorry for this. But I am not any more beset
with a gnawing anxiety and a fear of what I was trying to do. I
feel there are three good things done to-day, The Last Man & the
Mary Shelley withdrawn and the Anne put away. True, I have
taken on the Jane Austen but I don't feel oppressed at all by this –
I feel it's justified enough by the unique 'to and from' letters plan.
But when I come to do it, if I feel this sense of despair I'll have
to pay back the money, with God's help.[2] Anyway, it's clear that
I'm paralysed as a writer unless I write according to this queer
dictatorial sense I have; the thing I *can* express seems to be the
right thing – what I *can't*, is 'wrong'. Well, there it is.

I don't know how I will manage even now, but I love *Job* and
one must write with love. A passage in Charlotte Bronte's memoir

of Anne caught my attention to-day – where she said that Anne wrote Wildfell Hall out of a sense of duty & *hated* writing it, but would pursue it. It struck me as the way to death. I don't say it is, or was in Anne's case. But it struck *me* in that way; that if I continued, I would go on to a death of some kind. So, dear, I had to stop; and yould [*sic*] be the first to advise me so.[3]

I thought I would tell you right away how I'd decided, and that I feel very much better. I'll be in a better condition after a rest from work next week with Robin, and more free from worry.

See you Sunday. Send me your encouragement & love, dear. Pray for me.

Affectionately

Muriel

My love to your Mother. I hope she is better.[4]

> ALS. HRC. Dating: the contents match the letter
> of 9 August 1954 to Alan Maclean.

1. On 2 June, John Smith of Christy & Moore Ltd, Literary Agents, who had recently taken on MS and Derek Stanford, wrote to MS to say that the Lutterworth Press might be interested in a book on Anne Brontë, to which MS responded the next day: 'The main selling point is that Anne is the only one of the Brontë sisters on whom no single work has been written – no biography nor critical book, and very few essays. She is dreadfully neglected in all writings on the Brontes. We could – with encouragement – complete the work very soon' (WUL). Then on 19 July, Smith wrote, 'when I lunched with Robert Hale he expressed quite considerable interest in the possibility of a book on Anne Bronte' (NLS). Robert Hale founded his publishing company of the same name in 1935.
2. MS had prepared an edition of Mary Shelley's *The Last Man* for publication by the Falcon Press, which went into receivership before the book was published; she sought through her agent Smith to have *Child of Light* republished, and published better, but he was not encouraging. MS had undertaken to prepare an edition of Jane Austen's letters for Peter Owen, who had set up his own publishing house, Peter Owen Ltd.
3. In what builds into almost a manifesto of what MS was determined not to let happen to her and her art, Charlotte Brontë wrote:

> 'The Tenant of Wildfell Hall', by Acton Bell, had likewise an un-favourable reception. At this I cannot wonder. The choice of subject

was an entire mistake. Nothing less congruous with the writer's nature could be conceived. The motives which dictated this choice were pure, but, I think, slightly morbid. She had, in the course of her life been called on to contemplate, near at hand, and for a long time, the terrible effects of talents misused and faculties abused; hers was naturally a sensitive, reserved, and dejected nature; what she saw sank very deeply into her mind; it did her harm. She brooded over it till she believed it to be a duty to reproduce every detail (of course with fictitious characters, incidents, and situations) as a warning to others. She hated her work, but would pursue it. When reasoned with on the subject, she regarded such reasonings as a temptation to self-indulgence. She must be honest; she must not varnish, soften, or conceal. This well-meant resolution brought on her misconstruction, and some abuse, which she bore, as it was her custom, to bear whatever was unpleasant, with mild, steady patience. (Anne Brontë, *Agnes Grey with A Memoir of Her Sisters by Charlotte Brontë*, John Grant, 1907, pp. 8–9)

4. In *CV*, MS writes of Derek Stanford's parents: 'I felt his past was none of my business. I also felt his parents were none of my business, although he was extremely cagey about them – I never knew why' (p. 187). Notwithstanding, MS did occasionally write to and receive letters from Stanford's mother, Ada.

TO ALAN MACLEAN, MACMILLAN LTD, LONDON, 9 AUGUST 1954

50, Old Brompton Road, S.W.7
9th August 1954

Dear Mr Maclean,

Thank you for your letter of the 6th. It is most kind of you to suggest my submitting a collection of short stories.

I wish I could send something for you to read and consider. The difficulty is, that I'm not really satisfied with the few stories I have written – not more than twelve, some of which I think not worth keeping. In fact, there is only one story which I feel comes off – one which you may have seen, entitled 'Harper and Wilton', it appeared in one of John Pudney's collections. This is only a light piece of about 800 words, but it seems to say what I wanted it to say and no more. Some of my other stories have perhaps more potential value but I regard them as 'unfinished' work. Instead of trying to revise them, I would prefer to wait and see how they look beside any other stories I may write in the future.[1]

These details are by way of an explanation which I feel I owe to your very welcome encouragement, and you will know that I'd gladly respond to it if it were possible to do so. I could not ask you to commission a book of stories, not only because you might reasonably hesitate to take such a risk, but because, also, I'm not sure when or how I would propose to write them. I think, too, this applies to a novel. On thinking over this question, it seems to me that if I have any creative gift at all, I could not employ it to fulfil a fixed obligation; and although I suggested an advance on royalties as a means of realising the idea of a novel, I think, now, that this would be impracticable in my own case. For instance, I couldn't even give you an adequate outline of the theme of a story until I had written it!

I hope you won't think this excessively fussy. But in fact, lately I have been withdrawing some of my past work from possible new markets, and retracting as far as possible on speculations for the future, in order to keep my interests clear for the book I am writing at present for Sheed and Ward. It is a work on the Book of Job, and if I had my choice, I would confine my plans to getting a better knowledge of this subject than I can spare time for at present, since *Job* is more important to me, really, than any novels or stories which may or may not emerge.

This will give you an idea of how I am placed with my work, so you will know there are real grounds for my negative attitude towards your proposals, attractive though they are. If I should write a novel, and find myself free to offer it to you, I shall certainly do so.

Yours very sincerely.
Muriel Spark

ALS. MA.

1. Despite what she advances here, MS had in fact sent her stories to John
    Smith to ask him to place them, and he had responded on 28 May to say,
    'I have enjoyed the stories tremendously and best of all like LADIES AND
    GENTLEMEN, LAVISHES GHAST and DAISY OVEREND' (NLS).
    'Harper and Wilton' was published in *Pick of Today's Short Stories*, no. 4
    (ed. John Pudney, Putnam & Co., Ltd, 1953; reprinted in Muriel Spark,
    The Complete Short Stories (Viking, 2001; henceforth in the notes *TCSS*),
    pp. 171–6).

TO DEREK STANFORD, HOUNSLOW, MIDDLESEX,
3 NOVEMBER 1954

The Friars, Aylesford, Kent[1]
3.11.54

Dearest Poppet,

The Dylan broadcasts duly received. I haven't been able to settle
to any one complete piece yet; I begin to get interested, then my
mind strays. I think, for Dylan's prose, one must be emptied of
care, receptive.[2] I am enjoying an article by Auden in Encounter
on the master–servant relationship in literature. You must see
this – I'll fetch it to you. Auden's criticism has one peculiarity
which reveals the poet: his tendency to illustrate his points with
apparently irrelevant quotations; so that you have to penetrate his
personal mystique, almost, in order to really get his point. That
is, he makes himself clear in prose, but when he quotes by way of
illustration, one realises that he is illustrating something deeper or
else he is not illustrating a point at all, but making a further one.[3]

The furniture arrived yesterday. Due to a misunderstanding
arising from the likeness between the names of Maidstone and
Maidenhead – fortunately discovered before the van left London,
the estimate was increased by £2 – still very cheap however. A
certain wee Mary Evans from Swansea (not, as I first thought,
Under-Milkwood) busied herself in the loading of books into a
cupboard, where they are to repose during decoration-operations.
I busied myself with the brewing of teas and Nescafés. In both my
rooms, the ceiling and walls were being painted ivory, in a new

kind of waterproof paint. The living room was in the hands of Jimmy, a wee Irishman who is deaf and obliging. He lives on the estate as a general handyman. Conversations with Jimmy are of a poetic, irrational substance.

'Good morning Jimmy' you say.

'Is that so?' says he 'God bless ye then.'

'Do you take sugar in your tea, Jimmy?'

'No' says he, 'only two lumps.'

Meanwhile he beams, always beams.

The bedroom walls were being painted by a nun in land-girl breeches. We had great difficulty in persuading the removal-men that she was a nun. They never would have thought it, they said. But they were carted off to the castle for lunch, and left with the pleasantest possible impression of nuns and Roman Catholics in general.[4]

The cottage is too good to be true. It's unbelievable luck. There is a pleasant woman next door whose function it is to see to everyone's material needs on the estate. She has bedrooms for any-one who wants to come to stay. Only a few bob. You must be my first visitor darling.

I need very little new furniture. It's surprising how much I have & how well everything fits in.

I must tell you about the Barnsleys when we meet. They are agog to meet you. Both very charming and quite athirst for literary company in the way that writers are at the first-book stage. Many amusing anecdotes re. Erica Marx. He is a G.P. & she a very sweet woman.[5]

I rang Robin to tell him about the cottage. But he won't come for Christmas, only the following week. Ah well! The excuse now given by my mother, & Robin too, is, 'We thought you were going to be ill at Christmas'! Said I 'Don't build up your hopes on *that*. Never count your chickens before they are hatched.' I face the fact that it is a dirty trick, and make the best of it. I refuse to blame Robin & have proposed to meet him at the station on his way to his opulent relations. He seemed delighted.

On All-Saints Eve there was a grand liturgical torch-light

procession through the village. All the non-Catholic inhabitants
turned out to watch. The men took off their hats respectfully as
they do when a funeral passes, only this time it was the statue
of Our Lady (a lovely little 15ᵗʰ cent. carving) and the relics
of Sᵗ Simon Stock, which were borne past. The Friars sang
the litany of the Saints and the Salve Regina. The rain stopped
exactly for the period of the procession & started again just as
the relics were taken into the chapel. There was a midnight
mass followed by a real Feast of the Saints. Everyone went to
bed with queasy stomachs & slept in late next day. The Prior
institutes these things – he's dramatic in a quiet way, I think. The
villagers themselves are quite friendly to the Catholics – for the
community & pilgrimages are good for trade, besides being quite
unobjectionable. But the local Protestant Truth Society birds have
caused some anti-Catholic stirs. They call the Prior The White
Devil.⁶

Well sweet Derek, I do wish you were here or would come
on a day-visit soon. Life is not without its crosses. I have a trying
lady who has come here to be converted; an ancient art-teacher
with *definite* ideas about Art. Now she *will* denounce all modern
art in the sweeping Munnings style.⁷ I annoy the old dear by
refusing to argue seriously: hence she suspects I'm as amused as
I am. But otherwise, one is forced, in particular cases, to defend
a modern work which is *not* good. I don't personally care for all
the 'modern' work done here – but not everyone has the right to
attack it.

This gem of a lady is, by the way, much troubled because
Catholics won't say yea or nay to the proposition that dogs have
souls & go to heaven.

Says the Prior, 'Look always to God. If you could see God you
would understand all about the dogs.'

See you Friday, love. Chancery Lane station, isn't it? – at 2.30.
Love & blessings
Muriel
I'll bring the stories for Graham Greene.⁸

                                                    ALS. HRC.

1. In October, MS moved to The Friars, the guest house attached to a Carmelite priory at Aylesford, near Maidstone in Kent, that was welcoming to Catholic artists in difficulty, as part of her plan of recovery from her recent breakdown; she will remain there until mid-1955, making occasional trips up to London. In an undated letter, probably from 27 October, she wrote to Derek Stanford: 'A note to say I have seen the cottage & decided on it. Will tell you the pros & cons later. Meantime, at £1 per week it will, at the least, be a cheap place to store my things, as I have to move anyway. At best, it is a bonny wee home *in potentia*. I will arrange to move my things by van on Wednesday if possible' (HRC). MS was decorating and furnishing the house she found on the priory grounds in preparation for moving into it; officially named 'Red Cottage', she called it 'St Jude's Cottage', after the patron saint of lost causes.

2. On 18 June, MS wrote to Stanford:

> I'm much encouraged that you seem satisfied with your style in Dylan, as it's a bad habit we both have to deprecate our own work indiscriminately. One ought to be able to say when a piece of work is pleasing, even if one's own. Now I'm anxious to see Dylan. What do you make of the line that returns to my mind sometimes 'After the first death there is no other'? Among other connotations, this suggests to me the Christian idea of 'first death' in the individual – the conversion. In one of the Apochryphal [*sic*] N.T. books, one of the early Xtian writers has words to this effect. 'After the first death, the second death is harmless'. Of course, in Dylan's poem, I hardly think he had this in his intention; more likely he refers to the Fall, death being its consequence to the human race. But the two ideas are not unrelated. (HRC)

   On BBC Radio, several recent broadcasts were devoted to Dylan Thomas who died the previous year, as advertised in *Radio Times*: 'A Visit to America: Recorded on the eve of his departure for the U.S.A., and a few weeks before his death' on 22 August on the Third Programme; 'A reading of his poems arranged and introduced by Louis MacNeice' on 25 August on the Third Programme; 'a dramatised reading of Thomas's *Under Milk Wood*', with Richard Burton as First Voice, on 24 September on the Home Service.

3. W. H. Auden's essay 'Ballam and the Ass: On the Literary Use of the Master–Servant Relationship' appeared in *Encounter*, July 1954.

4. Allington Castle, originally built in the twelfth century and rebuilt in the sixteenth and seventeenth centuries, was bought by the Carmelites in 1950 and was linked to nearby Aylesford Priory.

   By 1944, the 80,000 women volunteers in the Women's Land Army had come to be known as 'land girls' since they worked frequently in agriculture; their 'uniform' often included 'land-girl breeches'.

5. Alan Barnsley, who published under the pen-name Gabriel Fielding, was a

general practitioner in Maidstone, including at Maidstone Prison; his first book, a poetry collection entitled *The Frog Prince and Other Poems*, was published in 1952, and his first novel, *Brotherly Love*, appeared in 1954. When MS met him, he was working on his novel *In the Time of Greenbloom*; in *CV*, MS describes him as 'a very good novelist' (p. 207), and in a letter to Martin Stannard from 21 May 1995 she writes, of this period: 'I was encouraged to write creatively by Tony Strachan mainly, also by Alan Barnsley, the Braybrookes, David Astor, editor of *The Observer*, Philip Toynbee' (NLS). Dina (Edwina) Barnsley and her husband converted to Catholicism in 1954, during which year and subsequently MS visited them regularly.

Having fled the Nazis in France with her partner, the painter Mariette Lydis, Erica Marx, niece of Karl Marx, founded the Hand and Flower Press in 1941 in Aldington in Kent, specialising in 'Poems in Pamphlet' selling at one shilling each, which published MS's first book of poems, *The Fanfarlo and Other Verse*, in 1952.

6. On 25 October, MS wrote to Stanford: 'The Father Prior is returned. As the rumour had it, he's a charmer. He swears that all his Friars and Brothers are Saints. Says if I write children's stories he'll set up a printing press here & print 'em. (Not *my* children's stories, alas, I fear – but I might try. If you have a copy of Oscar Wilde's children's stories lying about . . . .)' (HRC). The Irish Carmelite Father Malachy Lynch was the first Prior at The Friars, where he was responsible for much of the rebuilding that went on after the estate was acquired. In the notes accompanying his 'Little Requiem for Father Malachy', John Taverner wrote: 'To have known Father Malachy is a great privilege. He was a very simple man, no great intellectual, his scholarship was of the Spirit and its range as vast. My encounters with him were not all that frequent, but a few minutes with him were enough to tell you that you had encountered something rare. As someone has said, we know and we do not know, yet know all we need, that here is a man we and the world are better for having' (www.wiscmusicclassical.com/work/8513/Requiem-for-Father-Malachy--John-Tavener/; accessed 20 November 2023).

7. The popular painter, known particularly for his equine paintings, Alfred Munnings, friend of Winston Churchill, David Astor, and John Masefield, was known for his opposition to modernism. He had been President of London's Royal Academy from 1947 when, at the Academy's annual banquet in 1949, he delivered a fierce, and somewhat inebriated, attack on modern art in general and Pablo Picasso in particular; the speech was broadcast by the BBC, which received numerous complaints at Munnings's frequent use of the word 'damn'.

8. An appeal had been made by Stanford to Graham Greene to fund support for MS during her time at Aylesford. Martin Stannard elaborates on the generous response: 'Greene's film-production company agreed to pay her

£120 in six-monthly instalments in return for a non-existent script and, with a rent of just £1 a week, her fund stretched ahead as a living wage for more than a year' (*MSB*, p. 162). In her letter of 25 October, MS remarked to Stanford, 'Lovely news about Graham Greene's 1ˢᵗ instalment of stipend!' (HRC). In a later response to Stanford, on 14 December, Greene would write: 'I came up to London from the country for a few hours yesterday and read Mrs Spark's short stories. I thought they were extremely alive and interesting and I feel glad I have been able to be of some help to her' (NLS).

TO DEREK STANFORD, HOUNSLOW, MIDDLESEX, 9 DECEMBER 1954

St Jude's Cottage, Allington Castle, Nʳ Maidstone, Kent
9/12/54

Dearest Pumpkin,

Many thanks for yrs. to hand. Also for the service of putting my poem into the workings of destiny.

I have written a brief note to Frank to say I'll ring him on Monday. I really must start writing thank-you letters to my list of donors; one every now & again will make the effort less worrying.[1]

Bluebell has walked over this page with her sooty paws. She has the impudence to cock her tiny snoot at all but the top of the milk these days. She has suddenly realised that she is of Middle-Eastern extraction, not just ordinary Anglo-Cat descent (no theological inuendos [sic] are inuendoed [sic] here!)[2]

I can imagine Neville would talk to himself. *How* nice.[3]

Bluebell is now on my shoulder. I have to sit hunch-back to accommodate. Her eye is on my pen. She thinks I am making these scratches all for her amusement & is crouching fierce-like. She thinks the papers on my table are arranged as toys for her. My masterpieces in the making!

I have read Brighton Rock. How simple & stark it really is! A weakness in Pinkie's fictional character is, I think, where Gr. Greene has inclined to show him *emphatically* as a product of an evil environment. But the same type persists in the new

Utopian environment. A good start in life for the kids doesnt [*sic*]
necessarily mean the elimination of the Pinkie menace.[4]

Well sweet, I must to bed. Will ring you on Monday. Keep very
well & warm.

Much love,

Muriel

xxx

ALS. HRC.

1. Appeals had been made for financial support of MS not only to Graham
    Greene but also to David Astor and to Frank Sheed, and by Alan Barnsley
    to Evelyn Waugh.
2. The gift of a kitten was made to MS by her neighbour Miss Martin; the
    name Bluebell had figured already in MS's poem 'Bluebell among the
    Sables' (see 16 March 1948).
3. The Catholic writer and editor Neville Braybrooke, with his wife June (who
    published under the name Isobel English), had been friends and supporters
    of MS since getting to know her in the *Poetry Review* circle in the late 1940s.
4. Pinkie is the evil antagonist in Graham Greene's 1938 novel *Brighton Rock*.

Alan and Dina Barnsley

1955

Still resident at St Jude's Cottage, where she adopted a cat she came to love, and named it Bluebell, at the end of January MS wrote to Alan Maclean at Macmillan that her short stories were turning into a novel. The drafting of this novel, MS's first, occupied her through the year; it was typed up in November, having undergone a title change, from *The Loving of Mrs Hogg* to *Holiday of Obligation*. In February, Maclean wrote to MS to propose an exceptional £100 advance on her unwritten novel, to be disbursed in two £50 tranches, terms more than acceptable to MS. Defying a depression lingering from her mental collapse the previous year, MS wrote articles for the *Tablet* and a review of Carl Jung's *Answer to Job* for the *Church of England Newspaper*. She received financial support from the Scottish author A. J. Cronin and the Catholic publisher Frank Sheed. In June, she sent Maclean the first five chapters of her novel and applied to, but did not win, the Tom-Gallon Trust Award with her story 'Miss Pinkerton's Apocalypse'. In July, she wrote her important story 'The Portobello Road', which she submitted later in the year to Maclean's new *Winter Tales* collection and for which she received £50. In August, she left St Jude's Cottage and took up lodgings in the house of Tiny Lazzari, who went on to become a close friend, at 13 Baldwin Crescent, Camberwell, London, where she would be resident for most of the next ten years.

TO DEREK STANFORD, HOUNSLOW, MIDDLESEX, EARLY JANUARY 1955

[St Jude's Cottage, Allington Castle, Kent]
Monday

Dearest love,

I am in bed this morning, with a hot bottle and my books & papers around me.

Bluebell has had a scrambled egg with baked beans, seeing today isn't *every* day.

She has been watching the birds in the snow outside the window, like a theatre-goer, participating in the action without actually taking part. She gets awfully worked up over the bird-palaver, for she imagines herself, a phantom-puss, stalking amongst them. This, if you follow me, gives rise to pity and terror, terror and pity, which causes Bluebell to waggle her hind quarters and emit the sound of 'Bree-up' in a small squeaky tone. Bluebell has also been playing Weezabaws. I shout 'Weezabaw', whereupon she arches her back and springs onto my pillow with a mad glare in her eyes. As she knows it's only a game, her next move is to snuggle into my neck with a long, loving and satiated purr.[1]

I am trying to do my review for the Tablet, hence my stay-abed programme. I need to relax while doing this work, as it is really a very exacting task for me. I am resolved to take on no more reviews, however tempting.[2]

My novel proceeds fairly well. Try to obtain a football coupon for me please. Do you know of a handy book about *smuggling*?[3]

I haven't been quite so well this week, but am told not to expect an absolutely steady recovery. At least my 'symptoms' are becoming less vague and more easily describable. I think this means that my powers of self-observation are becoming more precise, rather than that the symptoms are becoming more pronounced. Once one is able to grasp these things clearly, they are more easily dealt with.[4]

Miss Martin was thrilled with your letter, and had to ask me to decipher part of it. There is no doubt, Bluebell owes her recovery to wee Marty who would deny herself much more than I could for the sake of an animal. She doesn't like her own animals to be thought of as 'animals' as a general rule. Sometimes she says 'I'm not going to allow *my* cats to be tormented by *animals* (i.e. other cats)'. And, when the pigeon at the Friars was eaten by a dog, she declared, 'I'm not giving them any more of my birds to be eaten by *animals*'. But occasionally she refers to her cats and birds as 'my animals'; in this case she is using the word in a partly figurative sense, as a mother will speak of 'my chicks' or the father of 'the young cubs', and both will refer to their children as 'the kids'. So, Miss Martin: 'The animals.'

I was glad to have your letters, and pictured the joyful scene at the distribution of presents. As I envisage it, the affair was ritualistic, like the distribution of Ashes, or the Asperges. A participation. Bless you all.[5]

Looking forward to Wednesday.

Love & kisses,

Muriel

> ALS. HRC. Dating: MS is at St Jude's Cottage, having returned from Edinburgh on Monday 3 January, so probable date is 3 or 10 January.

1. Derek Stanford will later write:

> Muriel Spark carries with her an imaginary train of maids-in-waiting, courtiers and graces. It is difficult to reconcile this picture with that of an ink-stained editor putting the Poetry Review to bed after an orgy of pasting-up; or with that of her singing her 'Weary Song,' after some day of persistent frustration, to the 'Gothical' words of
>
> Weeza-weeza-ba,
> O Weeza-weeza-ba
> O Weeza-weeza-ba
>
> – each line in higher key. (*MSBCS*, p. 67)

He will add, in a footnote, of the identification of the Weezaba with the Magi in the Bible: 'Pronounced WEEZAR-WEEZAR-BOR. The "Weezaba," along with "The Gladank," and "The Flate" are strange creatures which feature in Muriel Spark's poem *The Nativity*, published, with some omissions, in *Poetry Quarterly*.'

2. MS was sent several poetry books to review by Maryvonne Butcher at the *Tablet*; but what she in fact wrote and submitted was a piece about The Friars called 'In Kent and Christendome' that was gratefully received by Butcher, who responded: 'that is a charming piece and just what we wanted. It is a delight to deal with someone who does things professionally!' (NLS). This article will appear in the *Tablet* on 12 February.

3. The smuggling of diamonds becomes a theme of the novel MS is writing.

4. MS's health was being supervised by Dr J. Lieber of Weymouth Street, London, who had prescribed the medicine Largactil (chlorpromazine) which, new on the market, was being used to treat psychosis, schizophrenia, and paranoia; it comes with a panoply of undesirable side effects.

5. The rite of Asperges consists in the sprinkling of the church congregation with holy water. MS wrote to Stanford from Edinburgh on 31 December 1954 where she was celebrating – or tolerating – her own family Christmas: 'I am very bored. On Wed. evening I listened to one of Pamela Hansford Johnstone's [*sic*] Proust-reconstructions, in which was repeated Proust's remark to the effect that often those to whom we are attached by fate or choice can be the greatest source of boredom to us' (HRC).

TO DEREK STANFORD, HOUNSLOW, MIDDLESEX,
20 JANUARY 1955

St. Jude's Cottage [Allington Castle, Kent]
20-1-55

Dearest Boy,

Your letter received and prayers offered for the ailments of G. Tickell & yourself.[1] You must always let me know how matters proceed for those I pray for, so that I can offer thanksgivings or further importunities as the case may be. Some say that thanksgiving is due whether the prayer appears to be answered or not, since prayers always *are* answered in *some* sense. But my own view is different. Let's keep our minds clear as to what has happened & what has not, from *our* point of view – that's what *I* say. Otherwise the whole performance of petition & thanksgiving becomes perfunctory. What is your view?

My neighbour immediately next door, Mrs Bell, is reputed to be a spiritualist. She is small and fat and surprised. She stands in the road outside our cottages, with her plump parsnip legs astraddle and as you come out of the door her eyes say 'Goodness me!' Then, in her fluting trill she tells you about herself, though you have heard it before. 'My husband was in the Merchant Navy, you should see his paintings. Mr Bell married me eighteen years ago but now he's a decorator doing outside work. I'm the second wife y'see. Would you look at Mr Bell's novel that he wrote? I said to Mr Bell, as Mrs Stark is an authoress – It's called 'Murder on the High Seas' a real good story. Mr Bell was away during the war, we've been here fourteen years. Anything you want, Mrs Stark, come and ask. I'm always in a muddle. I hate cooking. My sister worked in a high-class restaurant and she's a good cook, she was only married three years ago. Mother's been dead three years, she used to come and stay. My sister's husband courted her twelve years. Mr Bell always says to her 'Well, he had to get to know you *didn't* he?' – Mr Bell likes a joke. I've lost the lid of my dust-bin, it's under the snow.'

Bye-bye till Wednesday – chophouse at 1.[2]

Much loving of sweet Derek

from

Muriel

Thank you for the stamps & Ted's most useful letter. I will probably quote the relevant portions verbatim – work it in. Wouldn't Ted be pleased![3]

ALS. HRC.

1. The translator Geoffrey Tickell is described by Martin Stannard as being one of the 'bachelors' whom MS frequented in London, and 'an obsessive theatregoer and literary scholar' (*MSB*, pp. 181, 555 n. 13).
2. MS is planning a trip to London, yet five days previously, on 15 January, she wrote to Derek Stanford:

I've got a nice long stretch of peace & quiet – my *Job* article going nicely, and my novel to proceed with when that's done. The cottage is warm and snug. I made an expedition to the shops away up on the London Road this morning, to lay in supplies against a possible ice-blockade. I enjoyed the walk hugely – was wrapped up in many thicknesses. On that particular road there are wide stretches of apple-trees on one side, & bare ground, undivided into fields, on the other. A few wooden cabins, black against the snow. At some parts the walk looked like a Canadian scene, at others like a Russian. One expected sleigh-bells and fur caps and perhaps a pack of avid dogs to turn every corner. (HRC)

3. Ted has not been further identified.

TO ALAN MACLEAN, MACMILLAN LTD, LONDON,
31 JANUARY 1955

St. Jude's Cottage, Allington Castle, nr. Maidstone, Kent
31st January, 1955

Dear Mr. Maclean,

I wonder if your readers have reported on my short stories?[1]

As I think you know, my earlier plan to make these the basis of a book of short stories has developed into the writing of a novel. I must apologise for this change of intention; when I came to consider means of integrating the story collection the ideas began to materialize in the form of a novel; it is taking shape quite nicely.

I should be greatly assisted if you would commission the novel, regarding my stories in the light of my potentialities as a novelist, not as material for a book.

You mentioned when I telephoned that it is not your usual practice to commission a work of fiction. For my own part I would not have thought it desirable, had I not actually started writing a novel for which I have a definite prospect as to its form and theme. I would have preferred to offer you the book on completion as I believe I promised in our previous correspondence. But I am now obliged to ask you to consider commissioning the book for the following reasons:

After a breakdown in health last year I have had to set aside the biblical criticism on which I was employed, to give up my part-time job, and to limit the book-reviewing and articles by which I formerly earned my living. I am advised to proceed with the novel, but I am not permitted to work more than two or three hours a day, and apparently must continue on these lines for some months. In the meantime I am being assisted financially by Mr. Graham Greene and Mr. David Astor, the editor of the Observer (both of whom, I know they won't object to my saying, think very well of my work).

In these circumstances I feel it necessary to find a publisher sufficiently interested in my work to make an advance payment for the novel and so facilitate its progress. This has always been my arrangement with publishers of my previous books of biography and literary criticism, but I realise, of course, that a different principle is involved in the case of fiction.

I should be grateful if you would give early consideration to this letter together with the stories, and let me know your reaction one way or another as soon as you can.

Yours sincerely,

s/Muriel Spark

TLS. MA.

1. MS wrote to Alan Maclean on 25 October 1954:

> I hope the enclosed stories will interest you. As I haven't got them all conveniently in typescript, I have marked the places in the books where some of the stories have appeared.
>
> There is only one new story amongst these. I have some still to revise, and hope to write others during a convalescence which I am spending in the country. They may not be your sort of stories, of course, but I hope they are, and in any case much appreciate your offer to read them. (MA)

TO ALAN MACLEAN, MACMILLAN LTD, LONDON,
3 FEBRUARY 1955

St. Jude's Cottage, Allington Castle, nr. Maidstone, Kent
3rd February, 1955

Dear Mr. Maclean,

Many thanks for your letter of the 31st.[1]

Would £100 be a convenient sum? This would enable me to complete the novel by the end of the year with ease. If the amount is agreeable, it could be payed [sic] in two sums – say £50 now and another £50 in June.[2]

Should you not wish to publish the novel, what would be the terms of repayment?

I am very happy to know that you like my stories, it is most encouraging.

Yours sincerely,
s/Muriel Spark

TLS. MA.

1. Alan Maclean had replied to MS's letter of 31 January the same day:

> Yes, we have indeed read your stories and like them very much. We are definitely interested in your work and, of course, in the novel on which you are now engaged. I believe that we shall be prepared to advance you a sum of money but, before suggesting this to our Chairman, I shall be grateful if you could give me an idea of how much you will need.
>
> As you know, we do not as a rule commission novels and you will realise that it is a different matter commissioning biographies, specialist books by experts, etc., etc. However, I think that if we were to make you an advance and you, in your turn, gave us first refusal of the novel, all would be well. (NLS)

> On 1 February, he addressed a memo to the directors at Macmillan Ltd – Daniel and Maurice Macmillan, Rache Lovat Dickson, and Thomas Mark – to propose giving an advance to MS: 'I know that she would like to come to us but I also know that there are one or two other publishers who

would like to have her, e.g., Heinemann and Cape. If you should decide
that she would be a worthwhile investment, I will get in touch with her
again at once' (MA).

2.   On the same day as the present letter, 3 February, two days after her thirty-
seventh birthday, MS wrote to Derek Stanford: 'heard from Macmillans.
They "like my stories very much", are "definitely interested in my work".
They would advance me a sum for first refusal of the novel (without actually commissioning it), depending on how much I would need. I think I
will ask £100. They might think this too high, but they can but say so. As
the money would presumably not be repayable in the event of their turning
down the novel, I don't think I could ask for more' (HRC).

TO DEREK STANFORD, HOUNSLOW, MIDDLESEX, 5 FEBRUARY 1955

St. Jude's Cottage, Allington
5-2-55

Dearest Boy,

Your letters gratefully received. I hope the weather treats you
right, or at least finds you stoically indifferent and weezabaw. Will
you read Thud fall the apples in the autumn night a-Sunday? I
always get a weezabaw frisson when I say that line into my strange
head.[1]

I have finished my Allington piece. It is now being O.K'ed for
accuracy by Holy Joan, and will be despatched anon to the Tablet.

Macmillans have come access [sic] with the weezabaw a treat.
I asked for £100, suggesting £50 now and £50 in June: this was
a safeguard against panic. With the whole £100 in hand, I might
have got thro' it before the novel was well enough in my grip, and
that's the sort of thing that sets me back. Was I right?

Well, they reply with a jovial 'yes' and a cheque for the
first £50. In response to my plaintive query as to the terms of
repayment, should they decide not to publish the novel, nice M^r
Maclean writes, 'In the mournful event that we do not want to
publish your novel, we shall lock you up in a tiny room on the top
floor here and feed you on old catalogues.'[2]

My plan, with your approval, is to place the £50 in the Post

Office and withdraw £2 a week towards expenses. I think we
should keep it separate from the 'getting-better' money, don't
you? I can then regard it as earnings for my 2–3 hours' writing
a day. It will reduce my getting-better needs. Let me know on
Wednesday what I'm to do with the cheque – Bank or P.O.

Luncheon on Wednesday will be weezabaw on me.

I haven't heard from Frank Sheed but if neither of us has heard
by Wednesday I can give you the cheque for £11 right away
without waiting. I meant to ask what Frank wrote. Did he sound
quite amiable?

Pray for the good progress of The Loving of M[rs] Hogg. I've
given myself a year to do it; Macmillans are quite satisfied with
that.[3]

What a lucky girl I am. What a sweet Boy you are.

Much love from

your jollified

Muriel

The despatching of our Angels was effective, wasn't it? How
rapid they work! Thank you for the loan of yours.

ALS. HRC.

1. MS may have in mind lines from Alfred, Lord Tennyson's 'The
    Lotus-Eaters':

    Lo! Sweeten'd with the summer light,
    The full-juiced apple, waxing over-mellow,
    Drops in a silent autumn night.

2. To Alan Maclean's jest MS will respond, in her letter of 5 February: 'I think
    I will be able to let you see how the novel is progressing about half-way
    through the year. This will be a safeguard against a sinister fate in your
    top floor lock-up' (MA).
3. Mrs Hogg is a key character in the novel MS is writing, whose working
    title at this point is 'The Loving of Mrs Hogg'.

St. Jude's Cottage, Allington Castle, nr. Maidstone. Kent
12th Feb. 1955

My own Boy,

Here are the last two stanzas: best I can do. They may at least
suggest something better.[1]

Bluebell goes on Monday to be sterilised poor little thing. I
wish it hadn't got to be. She has got a crush on Miss Martin's
black eunuch, by name of Beauty. The other Holy Beasts at
Allington are yclept Snowy and Mike. Bluebell prefers Beauty
because Snowy is proud and Mike is aged. Beauty, on the other
hand, is frisky up to a point and, being one year old, is able to
teach Bluebell a thing or two. She copies everything he does and
if she doesn't do it right he rolls her over and over. He watches
her intently when she runs up the lilac tree. 'Bluebell' I say, 'Big
Brother is watching you.' And sure enough, he springs up and
cuffs her one.

There was, up to this morning, another cat at Allington, by
name of Micky Bell – the property of my neighbour Mrs Bell.
Micky Bell was the terror of Allington. He was black & white
with fine green eyes. When one of the cats approached Micky
always acted playful and neighbourly. Then woosh! – he would
spring at them and bite huge chunks out of them. Two cats have
had to be destroyed because of wicked Micky Bell. After the last
attack on Beauty, however, Miss Martin conferred with Mr Bell.
(Poor soul, she was shattered about her cat's condition.) So M^r
Bell said 'Just take Micky away when no-one's looking and have
him put to sleep.' So Miss M. got up bright & early to-day, and
with the aid of Mrs Berridge, the remaining cottager, put poor
Micky in a basket and promised him a nice ride. They sneaked off
to Maidstone where, at the S.P.C.A. establishment, Micky went
to his last sleep. All is quiet at Allington now, but so far *M^rs* Bell
hasn't missed Micky. What's going to happen then I don't know.

We are all lying low and saying nothing. Mr Bell is doing his garden, guiltily and ever so carefully. I bet he is being ever so nice to Mrs Bell this weekend.

It is a sad story, but the world had to be made safe for Bluebell, Beauty, Mike and Snowy.

I don't think Mrs Bell will *ever* become a Catholic now!

I see in an article in the Tablet that Hugh Sykes Davies, describing Cambridge poets talks of 'a nostalgia that hankers after elegance . . . a touch of Teddy-boy poetry.' Well, well, I'd like to see the poetry, wouldn't you? All the student verse looks much the same to me these days. But I like the sound of Teddy-boy verse.[2]

My novel is going fairly slowly – days on, days off. One gets used to it, acquires patience. Louisa Jepp flourishes of course.[3] Nice to hear about the PEN meeting & Robert's devilry.[4]

It will be nice seeing Wrey, I hope we can. We promised to go to Rosamond in the evening. I wonder if we can ask the company to avoid ghost stories? They are not advised for me, but I don't myself feel particularly put out by them. Fr O'Malley warned about the dangers, at the moment, of discussing the dream-world. Hope you won't think this is a fuss . . I wd. like to be like everyone else but want to get better & so take no risks.[5]

Heaps of good love,
Muriel

Thanks pct for fixing up the Dong for me. You're a sweet one.[6]

ALS. HRC.

---

1.   The identity of these stanzas has not been ascertained.
2.   In an article just published in the *Tablet* (12 February), entitled 'The Cambridge Climate: Ideas in a University', Roland Hill wrote of contemporary life in the University of Cambridge, citing Hugh Sykes Davies, Fellow of St John's College: 'Today there is bewilderment, "nostalgia that hankers after elegance, archaic dandyism – a touch of Teddy-boy poetry".' In a letter to Derek Stanford written one week later, 19 February, MS will conclude (mentioning her close friend the novelist Christine Brooke-Rose and the critic and poet Bernard Bergonzi):

I've been reading thro' the poems sent me by the Tablet. My, how dreary, on the whole, they are! With the exception of Poetry from Wales, which contains a few nice pieces, there's nothing really to come up to the work that was published by the young say six years ago. Christine's poem is interesting of course, and Bergonzi has a sort of consistency of mood. But how ennervated [*sic*] it all is, how hard the poets seem to have worked on their verses! Tearing them out of their livers & hearts, and after all, are they worth it? In my view, Art is nearer to Play than Work, however serious the theme. Art is to the artist what play is to children, and play is very serious to children. (HRC)

3. Louisa Jepp is a character in the novel MS is writing.
4. Stanford was an active member of the writers' association devoted to freedom of expression, PEN; Robert is likely to be Robert Greacen.
5. In *CV*, MS writes:

> As soon as I stopped taking dexedrine the delusions of the word-game stopped. But I felt ill, as I had felt at Edinburgh the previous year. I found a friend in Father Frank O'Malley, a kind of lay-psychologist and Jungian. He didn't think I needed to go for psychiatric treatment, but I saw him often. (p. 205)

Father Chris Fuse, then a student of the Rosminians (and currently parish priest of St Peter's Catholic Church, Cardiff), writes of Father O'Malley:

> I was a student member of the community when Father Frank O'Malley was the parish priest. He had a wide clientele of those he listened to with his professional Jungian skills. He did mention years later that the famous Muriel Spark had come to consult him. Father Frank had been headteacher of Grace Dieu Manor Preparatory School in Leicester before arriving as Parish Priest at Ely Place, London. He told me that his psychological training had helped him understand some of the background to problems which the youngsters occasionally presented. (Email to the editor, 6 May 2023)

6. 'Dong' was a term shared by MS and Stanford signifying 'doctor'.

"Bluebell" Snark

St. Jude's Cottage, Allington Castle, nr. Maidstone, Kent
27-2-55

Dearest Sozzle,

Bluebell is reviving, after some days of extremity. It was enteritis, says the vet. The other cats have been banished from her infectious presence, much to the distress of the eunuch Beauty, her pal. However, Beauty slipped in to Miss Martin's top room, where Bluebell is, to-day, and Bluebell gave a ten-minute purring concert. She then began to wash herself. The vet has been calling every day with a bottle of glucose & other restoratives, which she feeds to Bluebell through her side. Poor Bluebell hates it, but with the aid of Miss Martin's day & night nursing, spoonfuls of glucose & water, etc., she has pulled thro' the worst. She still can't be brought home but must stay in Miss Martin's cosy circular room, for fear of catching cold en route. Meantime the other cat, being banished and bored, has attacked one of the pigeons, the which I have been nursing in my cottage. It roosts on the mantelpiece and leaves its droppings bye [*sic*] and large.

When the animals are all recoverd [*sic*], Miss Martin and I are planning to keep a she-goat on my patch of ground, so that we can have goats' milk and live to a long long age. I don't know if this is much incentive from my point of view, but I'd like to have a goat. Miss Martin plans to coax one *gratis* from a local farmer.

Last night, at Miss Martin's, the ten o'clock news opened with the words, 'Mr Butler says that sterling has recovered.' 'Oh,' said Miss M., 'I didn't know he was ill!' When the matter had been explained to her, she collapsed into a cackle of mirth, and when this had subsided, she pointed out, 'I thought he said that *Stalin* had recovered, so I thought he must have been ill.'[1]

I seem to be brighter this week, and tho' Bluebell's indisposition occupies me, I seem to be getting on nicely with my novel. Slowly, of course, but satisfactorily.

The enclosed letter from Oklahoma came to-day. I wonder if he has taken into account the special arrangements made by letter? Will discuss this with you on Wednesday.[2]

I wish I had remembered to bring the book on Jung for you. Too late now, but I'd like to see your review. I'm not so struck on mine, now I've re-read it, but it's certainly an improvement on my first draft.[3]

Did you hear G. Fraser the other night? I'm afraid I do not like his public personality at all, – it is less than his talent as a *reviewer* – I do not call him a *critic*, for a critic would have a greater power of self-criticism, and would not betray himself on points of small vanity. We all possess our vanities of course. One can't say that George is more vain than anybody else. But he *betrays* his vanity most lamentably. A good critic conceals it from the world.[4]

My electricity bill has arrived – three months' – £3-10/-. Not too bad for the winter, really.

Fetch me your copy of OTHER VOICES please, it sounds most dreary in the interesting sense. I am interested in Nevill's [sic] reviews, and will follow them up in future. One can never quite say how his mind ticks. He is very much of the adult school-boy in a nice way.[5]

The snows have fled; Julie the sow has returned in farrow from the hog; the grown-up cats are prowling for moles and the squirrels are poking their heads out of doors after the pigeons. The magpies peck the cap off my milk-bottle each morning and suck the top cream, and, as Horace says, 'the fields no longer blench frozen under a film of rime.'[6]

Best love sweetheart

from

Muriel

P.S. Please bring Oklahoma letter with you a-Wednesday, so that I can reply some time to his naturalistic courtesies. M.

ALS. HRC.

1. Rab Butler had been Chancellor of the Exchequer since 1951; faced with economic challenges, including rising inflation, he had recently raised the bank rate. Joseph Stalin died in 1953.
2. MS was in correspondence with Savoie Lottinville of the University of Oklahoma Press, which altered the title of her edition from *The Brontë Letters* to *The Letters of the Brontës: A Selection* when it published it in 1954; he had expressed an interest in publishing the book of Jane Austen's letters that MS had proposed to – but in the event would not – edit.
3. In a postscript to her letter to Derek Stanford of 19 February, MS wrote: 'I shall bring you the Penguin "Introduction to Jung" – it has a useful glossary which will make it easy for you to summarise the *Job*' (HRC). Both Stanford and MS were reviewing Carl Jung's *Answer to Job*, published in 1952 and in English translation in 1954. MS's review will appear in *CEN* (15 April 1955; *TGF*, pp. 192–7).
4. G. S. Fraser participated in *Literary Opinion*, no. 8, with a talk on 'Reviewers and Critics', broadcast by the BBC Third Programme on 18 February.
5. By 'Nevill' MS probably intends Neville Braybrooke.

Other Voices was a weekly journal published in London by Ralph Rumney, whose first issue came out on 21 January.

6. In 1950, MS corresponded with L. R. Lind of the Department of Latin and Greek at the University of Kansas, to whom she had submitted translations from Horace for publication. Her translation here is from Odes 1:4 (reprinted with variants in *CP*, p. 117, under the title 'To Lucius Sestius in the Spring').

TO FRANK SHEED, SHEED & WARD, NEW YORK, 23 MARCH 1955

St. Jude's Cottage, Allington Castle, nr. Maidstone, Kent
23/3/55

My dear Frank,

It was sweet of you to write, and I don't know how to thank you for so much kindness. I'm extremely grateful for the cheque for $100, and most anxious to start really *earning* it. 'Job' will *have* to be a *very good* book, that's the only solution.

Fr. O'Malley doesn't want me to return to Job studies as yet. All his other advice has proved wise, and so I think will this, in the long run. I stretched a point by writing an article on a book by Jung on Job for the C. of E. Newspaper. The editor likes it a lot, but the effect on myself was rather mournful. Fr O'Malley said 'Didn't I *tell* you . . . etc.' So I leave Job unfinished for the time being and regard the constraint as a mortification, wondering sometimes whether it's you, Frank, or me who's being mortified!

I'm sure I am getting better. The process of recovery isn't perceptible from day to day – and this is the most difficult part. It calls for something like faith. One can only judge by comparing one's condition over a number of weeks with what it was three or four months ago. When I look at things in that light I can see an improvement, and my friends can observe this better than I can, of course. Also, I'm beginning to take an *objective* interest in my state of mind. I feel the experience of a breakdown really can be *used* profitably; certainly it widens one's capacity for sympathy. At times, I've seemed to return to an earlier stage of development – been a child again, wanted to run out to play. This can be a glorious experience, or a horrifying one, according as one is, or isn't, able to reflect upon it. My reflective powers are growing stronger, and this is a good sign.

Enough about myself. You must tell me more about your feeling for Australia. I can understand your need to be *actually there* from time to time; it can't be satisfied by imagination only, or memory only. I think you must have a strong sacramental sense – your own bones have to participate in your love for Australia.[1] I don't myself feel like that about Scotland, my birthplace, but I feel a great desire to visit the Holy Land before I die – and without waiting too long, as I won't have begun to live till I've visited the Holy Land; this is because of the Jewish side of my origins. I haven't much interest in the modern political Israel, but I'd dearly love to see the land of my forefathers both of the spirit & the flesh.

When shall we meet and discuss these and other endearing topics? Do let me know when you are back, and are free to see me.

Many, many thanks, once more.

Love,

Muriel

ALS. Private collection.

1. Frank Sheed was born in Sydney and spent the first two decades of his life in Australia.

TO DEREK STANFORD, HOUNSLOW, MIDDLESEX, 7 MAY 1955

Allington Castle [Kent]
7/5/55

Dearest Pimpernell,

Many thanks for your 2 notes. I say a Hail Mary for the successful touching-up of your 1st lecture. I see Eliot has done a paper on Authors & Critics (see leader T.L.S.) but his complaints

are addressed to the New Analysers so far as I can see, not to
boys who lecture in churches. I got a letter from Christine saying
couldn't I make it a Wed. or Thursday one of these weeks. Well,
so I shall, after your lectures are completed.[1]

I got a sweet note from your Mama, heard all about the hats,
and that both men actually said she had not done wrong in
choosing them.

Got *Bluebell & Sables* back from New Statesman, with a note
'Sorry for delay but I've been away.' So charming. However, I am
not disappointed of any high hopes, since I didn't entertain them.
We shall try the Listener. I've got an Income Tax form – how I
can fill in what I haven't earned I don't know. We shall have to
take counsel together on this, or maybe get advise [*sic*] a-Tuesday.

My book is *definitely* going to be entitled *HOLIDAY OF
OBLIGATION*. 'Mrs Hogg' was too cramping a title, whereas
Holiday of Obligation fits in perfectly with what I'm actually
writing. And a fitting title too for a book written during a 'holiday
of obligation'. What do you think of this title?

I got the Curse a week early, due to this Largactyl I think.[2]
Still, the drug does have a *certain* effect. I don't feel my inward
sufferings so acutely – 'my sorrow, my sorrow' as I used to call it
when we had the sherry at Lindfield & the wine at So. Ken. in the
early days. Well, I feel it less, which is a good thing tho' I would
be reluctant to become altogether numb, for fear of losing the
pity for others that comes of self-pity which has become a bore.
My book is going well. Another 3,000 words, and I shall have
done half. Then I'll type it for inspection by Macmillans and also
yourself.[3] Can I have the chance of reading Ian's story? He is really
very *strong*, must be.[4]

Poor Neville has had that nice article returned by the swine of
a Prior (*not our* Fr. Prior) at Hartley. I don't know if they are going
to insist on payment, but I hope they do. If we can see them a-
Tuesday, it would be nice. Maybe June will ask me to stay over but
I won't count on it, so we won't go if we're very late away from
Uncle Rhodes.[5] I'm looking forward to seeing Uncle Rhodes. My
Job article is a great success with the sisters. My garden flourishes

and the seeds are beginning to shoot.[6] Bluebell has been eating
daffodils, and sipping the water out of their vase in preference
to milk. I got Gravity & Grace from the County library. Simone
decidedly demanded too much from herself & the human race in
general; no-one should demand more than God does. God only
wants the whole individual, body and soul. Simone wanted to
give body & soul and the kitchen stove as well. Self-sacrifice with
knobs on, in other words, and even then, self-sacrifice is an aim of
perfection, a ripeness, achieved by slow degrees in due time and
course. It is not fitting to serve God with apples green & tart.[7]

   Much love from

   Muriel xxx

ALS. HRC.

1. T. S. Eliot addressed the Authors' Club, London, on 13 April. The editorial
    in the TLS of 6 May 1955 cited Eliot's talk: 'What I have to say might be
    called the Author's Complaining against Critics. Not *my* complaint against
    my critics, but my complaint on behalf of authors against some kinds of crit-
    icism.' The unsigned report (by G. S. Fraser) of the talk stated: 'The tone
    as much as the statements [. . .] should teach other critics useful lessons.
    The tone is one of urbane modesty; the statements both preach and practise
    the critic's most important and hardest task at all times – the task of con-
    centration on the relevant.' The talk is reproduced in *The Complete Prose of
    T. S. Eliot: The Critical Edition, Volume 8: Still and Still Moving, 1954–1965*, ed.
    Jewel Spears Brooker and Ronald Schuchard (Johns Hopkins University
    Press and Faber & Faber Ltd, 2019, pp. 53 61).
2. On Dr Lieber's prescription of Largactil, see early January 1955, n. 4.
3. MS wrote to Derek Stanford on 22 April: 'I'm not feeling well again to-
    day. *Very* low. These relapses must be expected.' She went on: 'My novel
    is going quite well – I've done another 3,500 words. At the end of May I'll
    stop writing & start typing (which means, for me, practically re-writing)
    so that I'll have something to show Macmillan's by the end of June.' She
    added: 'Sometimes I lose my confidence, like to-day. Mind you bolster it
    up for me' (HRC).
4. Ian Hamilton Finlay's story to which MS refers was probably 'Peasants',
    which remained unpublished until it became, in the 1960s, a play of the
    same name. Hamilton Finlay was struggling during this period in both his
    professional life and his private – hence the need to be strong.
5. Of the period, in *CV*, MS writes: 'I had a great many Catholic friends; I
    suppose one is naturally drawn to others of like beliefs. My sponsors when

I was received were June and Neville Braybrooke, both very good writers, who lived at Hampstead. I loved to visit them; they were brimming with intelligence and wit' (p. 203).

6. In a letter to Stanford sent from Allington, undated but probably from April, MS wrote:

> I have been rather tired, but faring quite well. The best of this life in this weather is that every now & again you can put down your work & take a turn in the sun. The countryside is on the doorstep: you don't have to walk before you come to your 'walk', if you see. Everything is aflourish now – daffs & crocuses & popping buds. A magnificent long-evening sky, not too technicolour. The Italian Garden is breath-taking at twilight. The little lily-ponds. The cypresses. The castle nestling below. You really must try to come soon, my dear. (HRC)

7. MS had been interested in the life and work of Simone Weil for at least two years (see 27 August 1953, n. 10), and would go on being interested. *Gravity and Grace* contains writings on spirituality selected after Weil's death by her Catholic friend Gustave Thibon; in it, for example in her chapter on 'The Self', Weil outlines her aim for 'the destruction of the I' and 'redemptive suffering'. Weil died in Ashford, Kent, in August 1943, at the age of thirty-four, of causes that are still the subject of debate but which are agreed to have been linked to the privations she imposed on herself during her short lifetime.

TO NEVILLE BRAYBROOKE, HAMPSTEAD, LONDON, 20 MAY 1955

St. Jude's Cottage, Allington Castle, nr. Maidstone.
20th May 1955

My dear Neville,

As a final attempt, I rang the Hartley Prior to-night, hoping to speak him into reason – pointing out my embarassment, etc., and your difficulties and niceness in the circumstances etc. But he would have none of it. The essay was unsuitable, too flowery, bad English (!!)[1]

I asked if he could see his way etc. to send £5 etc. Says he 'Not me. He's had more than he was entitled to already.' (!)

So I let rip and told him a bit of my mind. Said I: 'Catholics should not behave as if they were above the law.' Said he: 'If the essay was unsuitable I'm not obliged to pay.' 'You are by law, I said; if I was Mr Braybrooke I would insist on payment. Moreover' I said 'the essay is delightful.'

'That's only your opinion' said he.

'Not at all' I said, 'several distinguished writers of our acquaintance think it admirable and so does that lady who has to do with Hartley.'

I also said it was rather disgraceful to take a week of your time, as you are so poor.

'If he's able, why's he poor?' he asked, cloddish.

'Why are the Carmelites poor, if they preach the truth?' said I.

'S'not the same thing,' he said. 'Not at all.'

'Yes it is. Everyone who does something disinterestedly is poor.' I said.

'Who asked him to be a writer?' he said, the nasty little blob. 'Why doesn't he get a job like anyone else?' – The usual third-rate chatter.

'That's his business,' I said. 'He hasn't asked *you* for anything. *You* are indebted to *him*.'

I told him that I was not going to write on Hartley for the Tablet, now; that I thought Hartley was a very queer Catholic set-up ('Only your opinion,' he said. 'It doesn't count with me.' To which I replied, 'It counts with a number of others.') These last remarks were irrational of course, but on the whole I do think a place takes its tone from the authority in charge. Well, Neville, that's all I can remember of the conversation, just hot from the 'phone. It doesn't help you much, I'm afraid. But if I could have used some persuasive, I would have done so; he just wasn't having any. Other items I recall were when I said 'I feel that Mr Braybrooke should appeal to the Father General.' 'Tell him to do so' he said, 'tell him to write to Rome.' 'I doubt if he would' I said. 'He's too nice.' I also said 'You are very ungracious.'

Throughout I kept my voice fairly low & reasonable, though he got rather roused I'm afraid.

Seriously, if you felt like appealing to the Father General of the

Carmelites, I'm sure you would get some payment. But perhaps you'ld rather let it lie.

Truly, I am so sorry about the whole thing. I knew he was a brutish sort, but didn't think he was quite so unpleasant, and certainly didn't dream he was so hard and stupid.

Alan Barnsley has your MS. He is bringing it over on Saturday (tomorrow) and I'll put it in the post to you separately, if I don't include it with this.

Another thing I've remembered: He said a lot of scornful items about poverty, to which I kept replying that he was most irreligious in his attitude to poverty. This, in fact, seems to me to be the crux of the matter. If you had been rolling in riches, he would probably have loaded you with more. At least, he'd have been polite.

I do hope you manage to sell the essay for publication. Let me know how things go.

I couldn't ring on Tuesday, wasn't free before the evening, when you were to be out. But I'll ring this coming Tuesday. If you would like to put in at Derek's lecture, we could all have lunch together afterwards. But if that's impossible, maybe we could meet for tea and talks.

I've been staying with Alan & Dina. Dina is expecting a baby. They are awfully sweet. A. & D. like your essay & commiserate with you over the misfortune.

Blessings and all hope for better news, Love to June, hoping she fares well in health & work

Muriel.

P.S. I am to meet a girl who is helping me with typing at 5.30 or so on Tuesday, so if we don't meet before then, perhaps later?
P.P.S. I think you would have nothing to lose by telling the Prior of Hartley that your piece is being broadcast on Radio Erin – this, in view of his telling Mrs Spark that the 'English was bad'! – or something to that effect. It will at least make him a little more humble.

M.

ALS. NLS.

1. Neville Braybrooke had apparently, through MS, been commissioned to
    write an article for the Hartley Priory which was attached to the Oratory
    of St Francis de Sales in Hartley, Kent. Carmelite Friars had been estab-
    lished at the Oratory since 1937. Neither the identity of the Prior nor the
    content of Braybrooke's article later broadcast on radio in Ireland has been
    established.

TO DEREK STANFORD, HOUNSLOW, MIDDLESEX,
9 JUNE 1955

[St Jude's Cottage, Allington Castle, Kent]
Thursday
Corpus Christi

Dearest Love,

I have been wondering how you got on at your meeting, how
the questions were answered, and are you duly elected to the
council of the Elect?

Bluebell is incredible. She actually cries for a game & indicates
by many subtle almost-human means, what sort of game –
whether the shoe-cupboard game, or that which pertains to
pellets of paper, or a mere frisk with my red pen.

I had a tooth out this morning – at least the stump of that
tooth. It had to be. I walked into a dentist's establishment in the
first street I came to – a Mr Welch. He is sixty-odd, has been in
practice for 30 years in Maidstone. He tells the following story:

Being on some civic council with the Canon of the local Catholic
church, they are on matey terms. One night, after a sitting, the
Canon suggested recourse to the pub. 'Thanks,' said Mr Welch,
'but I'm a tee-totaller.' The old Canon patted him on the shoulder,
'My boy,' he said 'you don't know what you're missing.' 'Well,'
said the dentist, 'you're a batchelor [sic], aren't you, being a Roman
priest?' 'Yes' said the Canon. So Mr Welch patted him on the
shoulder, 'Father, you don't know what you're missing,' said he.

We had a chat about sex & sin after my painless extraction.
Mr W. is of the opinion that no-one can judge anyone else, since
everyone has a '*kink*' of some sort!

I meant to ask you if you could bring or send the little article by Peter Clough – the bright nephew of Sister Theresa – which we were perusing at the Barnsleys. I think you had it tucked into a book. Do hope it isn't astray.[1]

Alan sent me the prescription with a brief note to say he'd been busy, which is O.K.[2]

I am touching up Chap. 3 – taking out small phrases which might make the Baron 'overdone'. I am taken with your conception of the Baron – it's what I was trying to convey ultimately – only thro' Caroline's eyes he is, at that stage, a 'disapproved-of' character, one who evokes suspicions. You will see how everyone falls under suspicion from everyone else, in a sense, throughout the story. I don't mean the characters are suspected variously of wrong-doing necessarily, but of being other than they are. Human judgment is fallible – that's the accepted viewpoint.[3]

It was lovely seeing you again on Wednesday. Hope you are none the worse for the wet nasty weather. Looking forward to seeing you a-Tuesday. 1 p.m. at the Cumberland. If you have no other plan, I wd. like to drop in at the C.E.N. some time to see that tape-machine.[4]

I have thought of the opening sentence of my last chapter. It begins, 'Sir Edwin Manders was once very young.'[5]

Best of luck with your researches into the fortunes of the young poet whose name I can't remember (John Ban??lam??) but whose history is so tempting to enquire into.[6]

† love,
Muriel

ALS. HRC. Dating: Corpus Christi fell on Thursday 9 June in 1955.

1. Peter Clough and his article have not been further identified.
2. As a general practitioner Alan Barnsley was in a position to give prescriptions.
3. The Baron Stock is a character in the novel MS is writing, in which Caroline Rose, a recent convert to Catholicism who believes she hears the noise of typewriters, is the protagonist.

4. The Cumberland was 'the hotel opposite Hyde Park, in Oxford Street, you know', as MS describes it in a letter of 20 April to Derek Stanford in which she suggests they meet there (HRC).

   The 'C.E.N.' is the *Church of England Newspaper*; reel-to-reel tape recorders were rare in 1955.

5. While Sir Edwin Manders remains a character in MS's novel as published, this sentence does not remain as the first of its final chapter.

6. The poet whom MS recalls as 'John Ban??lam??' has not been further identified.

TO ALAN MACLEAN, MACMILLAN LTD, LONDON,
16 JUNE 1955

St. Jude's Cottage, Allington Castle, nr. Maidstone, Kent
16th June, 1955

Dear Mr. Maclean,

I am sending by separate post the first five chapters – about half – of my novel *Holiday of Obligation*. I shall probably want to revise some of this, so please don't regard it as finished in any way.[1]

I am enjoying writing the book and hope you will like it so far. And of course it would be encouraging to have another cheque from you.

Yours sincerely,
s/Muriel Spark

TLS. MA.

1. The novel when published will contain nine chapters.

TO THE TOM-GALLON TRUST, THE SOCIETY OF AUTHORS,
LONDON, 23 JUNE 1955

St. Jude's Cottage, Allington Castle, nr. Maidstone, Kent
23rd June, 1955

Dear Sirs,

I would like to submit the enclosed story, *Miss Pinkerton's
Apocalypse*, for the Tom Gallon Trust Award.[1]

Other of my short stories have appeared in the following places:

The Observer, Christmas 1951; World Review edited by
Desmond Fitzgerald, August 1952; Heinemann's collection
of Observer Prize Stories, 1952; The Norseman edited by J.
Lehmhuhl (2 stories during 1953); Church of England Newspaper
edited by C. O. Rhodes, December 1952; Pick of To-day's Short
Stories edited by John Pudney, 1954; Chance (a Cambridge
magazine, now defunct) 1953.

I have published some books of literary criticism, biography and
poetry; this accounts for my small output of stories. But after a
serious breakdown in health last year I have been advised to give
up reviewing and criticism, which was proving rather a strain,
and to concentrate if possible on creative prose. I am at present
writing a novel in which Messrs. Macmillan are very interested.

My financial position is extremely precarious. After the
breakdown in health last year I had to give up my part-time job
in London and am obliged to live in the country. I have been
receiving financial assistance from Graham Greene and the editor
of the Observer, David Astor, both of whom like my work, as
well as from one or two other literary people. I am still receiving
medical and psychiatrical treatment, I think with some success,
but I do not foresee being able to earn much money for some
months. My only regular form of income is 32/6d. a week from
the National Health. Macmillans gave me £50 to help me start my
novel, half of which is completed; I think they will let me have
another £50 on this account shortly.

I understand that one of the conditions of the award is that the recipient must devote his time to fiction. This is, in any case, my intention for the future; the doctors advise me to avoid literary criticism on any large scale, and to stick to fiction to which I am more naturally inclined.

As I am hoping to return to London at the end of this year, the Award would be of great practical help and encouragement to me.

If you would like any further details I should be glad to let you have them.

Your faithfully,
s/Muriel Spark
(Muriel Spark)

TLScc. HRC.

1. The Tom-Gallon Trust Award was (and remains) an annual award for a short story, administered by the Society of Authors and financed by a bequest made by Nellie Tom-Gallon in memory of her brother, playwright and novelist Tom Gallon.

TO DEREK STANFORD, HOUNSLOW, MIDDLESEX, 1 JULY 1955

St. Jude's Cottage, Allington Castle, nr. Maidstone
1ˢᵗ July 55

Dearest Pet,

Your letter most welcome, also the jolly passage about Charlie, which I had seen but failed to take a note of, to my subsequent regret. So 'twas an act of grace to copy it out for me – quite my sort of image, is Charlie, and I've no doubt I will utilise him anon.[1]

One or two most pleasant reports: *1ˢᵗ* Macmillans – my cheque for £50 duly received & deposited in P.O. A letter from them, also, *commissioning* a story of 7,000 words, for the princely sum of £50. They hope it won't interfere with the novel, they say – but I truly think it will make a welcome change for me at this stage. I will be free to publish the story in Britain or America *before or*

after publication in their 1956 edition of 'Winter's Tales'. This
latter anthology has some distinguished contributors in the 1ˢᵗ
number, due to appear this autumn. We must try & get it for
review. I attribute this good fortune to my special intentions at
last Wednesday's Mass. It Pays to Advertise one's wares among
the Saints & I trust that your good commodities will be similarly
received.

I haven't thought of the theme of my story, but already I have
the feeling of it. The first sentence is:

'One day in my young youth, at high summer, lolling with my
lovely companions against a haystack, I found a needle.'[2]

Write to me quickly & say what you think of this opening.

This means, I think, that I should put off London holiday until
after Robin's visit, definitely. By then I hope the story will be
written & I can get some Kensington 'atmosphere' for the novel.

Now another piece of interesting news is that Robin is going to
a camp in *Sussex* (after his camp in Ireland) with his Jewish youth
club. That will be from 1ˢᵗ to 14ᵗʰ August & he hopes we'll visit
him there. He doesn't say what part of Sussex, but shall we make
that our Sussex trip, wherever it should turn out to be?

After the 14ᵗʰ he will be free to come to me. I propose to
borrow a camp bed so that he can stay for a few nights & maybe
you can pay a visit here about that time so that we can take him to
the Barnsleys one day. After a few days here I propose to make my
trip to London – a few days with Robin & about ten more days in
London on my own 'holiday' – which I hope the story-money will
more than justify. Will you please pray well that my story *comes to
something*. I am not free of the fear that my efforts won't add up to
anything at all.

Do hasten to get on with your own story. I send all good
blessings on your Balzac introduction.[3]

Mʳˢ Wyndham was extremely sweet: a softer & happier edition
of Daisy Overend – and of course a younger generation – under
30 I think. I will tell you when we meet of the house, the
grounds, the dogs, the kids, the conversation which was in many
ways a treat. ('Is one allowed to smoke in Chapel?' etc.) She

seemed to me a strange mixture of rich luxury and child-like simplicity. David Astor (apparently her 'rich' relative) had his first son a month ago & is delighted about it, being blessed with 2 daughters already. So next time you have occasion to write, you must mention our pleasure at this news.[4]

Well darling, this lucky-news-bearing letter has just been interrupted by Maria, who bears a dish of strawberries & cream for me, by what excellent fine inspiration, who can say? My nursing efforts have been appreciated, I guess.

Bluebell washed herself all over when she heard Macmillans letter read out to her, tho' it was not her usual wash-time. She shares my tin of salmon to-day. Friday is fast-day for me, feast-day for Bluebell.

I must now set about composing a letter of thanks & acceptance to nice Mr Maclean. I wondered after leaving you on Wed. if I'd thanked you properly for drafting out the letter for David Astor – my resolution not to ask what you'd written made me drop the subject but I appreciated your doings in this connection most heartily.

See you Wednesday at 1 p.m. in the pub by Chancery Lane station.

Best love till then,

Muriel xxx

ALS. HRC.

1. Charlie has not been further identified.
2. This sentence, with small variants, does indeed open the story MS will later publish, entitled 'The Portobello Road', of which Martin Stannard writes: 'Muriel had found her mature voice, had cured herself of the babel in her head. In her collections of stories, she always placed "Portobello" at the front, as though to acknowledge it as the first perfect fruit of her imagination' (*MSB*, p. 171).
3. Derek Stanford was writing an introduction to his selection of passages from Honoré de Balzac's essay *Petites misères de la vie conjugale*, which was being translated by his friend Geoffrey Tickell; it will be published as *Pinpricks of Married Life & The Physiology of Marriage* (Neville Spearman, 1957).

4. MS had visited Cliveden House in Buckinghamshire, built in the seventeenth century and belonging since 1893 to the Astor family. Mrs Anne Wyndham was the cousin of David Astor, Editor of the *Observer*. On the grounds of Cliveden House stands Octagon Temple, built in the eighteenth century and converted later into a chapel. Daisy Overend is the focus of the narrator's attention in a story named after her which appeared in *World Review* (August 1952), where she is described as being 'small, imperious, smart' and 'the flower and consummation of her kind'. The narrator continues: 'Very charming she was. A tubular skirt clung to her hips, a tiny cap to her hair, and her hair clung, bronzed and shingled, to her head, like the cup of a toy egg of which her face was the other half. Her eyes were considered to be expressive and they expressed avarice in various forms; the pupils were round and watchful' (*TCSS*, p. 229).

Richard David Langhorne Astor was born on 28 April.

TO ALAN MACLEAN, MACMILLAN LTD, LONDON, 1 JULY 1955

St. Jude's Cottage, Allington Castle, Nr. Maidstone, Kent
1st July, 1955

Dear Mr. Maclean,

Thank you very much for your letter of 28th June enclosing your cheque for £50, and also for your letter of 30th June.[1]

About the novel: I am not sure that the incidence of 'voices' hasn't been overdone in the first part of the book. The voices are essential to the story, but only as a contributory factor. If you as a reader get the impression that the voices are going to constitute the main theme, this may indicate some over-balance which it will be easier to adjust when I have drafted the remaining chapters. I am glad to have your reaction, and happy to know that on the whole you like what I have written. I expect to finish the novel by the end of the year.[2]

There is no hurry to return the first five chapters, but I should like them back some time, in case of revision being necessary.

I am delighted to know of your Winter's Tales, and will be happy to contribute a story. I have one in mind to write, and this will be a good occasion to have a few weeks' change from the novel. If I let you have the story in the early part of August will that be convenient? Thank you very much for this kind offer.[3]

Yours sincerely,

s/Muriel Spark

TLS. MA.

1. Alan Maclean replied to MS's previous letter on 28 June:

    We have now read the first five chapters of your novel, HOLIDAY OF OBLIGATION, and are happy to say that we like them very much. The only thing which slightly worries us is the 'voices'. You have no doubt got these fellows under some sort of control, but we rather hope that they are not going to dominate the whole novel. Otherwise we are delighted with what you have done, are sure that the second half will be as good as the first and have pleasure in enclosing our second cheque for £50. (NLS)

2. In *CV*, MS writes:

    From the aspect of method, I could see that to create a character who suffered from verbal illusions on the printed page would be clumsy. So I made my main character 'hear' a typewriter with voices composing the novel itself. (pp. 206–7)

3. In a letter of 30 June to MS, Maclean outlined his plan for what would become Macmillan's annual *Winter's Tales* series:

    We are publishing for the first time this year a collection of twelve short stories by authors of varying degrees of establishment. [. . .] We are now getting together the material for the next volume, to be published in the Autumn of 1956, and we wonder whether you would care to write one of the stories.

    We are aiming at an average length of 7,000 words per story but this is not a rigid requirement. We can offer a fee of £50 and each story will be illustrated. (MA)

TO DEREK STANFORD, HOUNSLOW, MIDDLESEX,
4 JULY 1955

St. Jude's [Allington Castle, Kent]
4.7.55

Bonny Pet,

Your letter was extra welcome this morning. After a day of
very good encouragements some demon or maybe guardian spirit
deflates my mind most painfully, so that I feel my hand paralysed
against my work, see no hope for myself, against all contrary
evidence. I was very doubtful if the opening of my story 'meant'
anything at all – it was just one of those stray ideas without
any 'situation' hanging on to it. I'm still not sure what, if anything, I can write, but your encouragement resolves me to use
this opening as the secret heart of my story whatever it shall be.
There are two factors necessary to my well-being – the sort of
encouragement that Macmillans & my patrons can give, and the
encouragement that can only be given by *those who know*, other
writers, a good critic. An honest word of praise from such is great
balm in my present state for I've very little confidence to fall back
on. For the actual writing none but the Holy Ghost can help me. I
am hoping to do a bit of my novel until the story crystallises more,
I think it *will* now. After all, these are early days.

I have been reading The Moonstone by Wilkie Collins – a most
absorbing story, wonderful technique in many respects. For my
liking too much narrative, not enough dialogue – but that's his
chosen medium, there is no real artistic objection to it, only one
of personal taste.

Well, I've been very up & down – more down than up really, as
you will guess.[1]

In the overwhelm of good news I forgot to add that the National
Health have increased my stipend to £2 a week. Let the Spiritual
Health thrive as well and I'll be most content.

Could you lend me a vol. of Dylan Thomas's short stories? – I
think they would stimulate me now.

I pray hard for the success of your Balzac and your Ghost
Story, – you dear administer of Grace.
Much love till Wed. at 1 at the pub
from
Muriel

ALS. HRC.

1. MS will write very few letters between the present one and the letter she
    writes six months later, on 14 January 1956, to Alan and Dina Barnsley,
    where she will offer what may be some explanation of her uncharacteristic
    reticence: 'I have been much oppressed recently by the general lacrimae
    rerum. Darling Derek has been my solace. Figuratively speaking, there is
    a great conspiracy going on against me, but actually speaking I cannot at
    all believe it, not at all at all. It is a terrible thing to be incapable of really
    believing in one's paranoiac feelings' (MBC).

*Graham
Greene,
1959*

TO GRAHAM GREENE, LONDON, 4 DECEMBER 1955

13, Baldwin Crescent, Camberwell, S.E.5[1]
4th December, 1955

Dear Mr. Greene,

I am grateful for your kind letter and helpful suggestions. I will try the people you mention and see if they have any part-time work to offer.

It is reassuring to know I may apply to you for advice about the placing of my novel. I think Macmillans want to publish it but they are bothered about one section which they haven't yet specified. I may be able to revise it if their objection is reasonable.[2]

I have recently had a story accepted by Botteghe Oscure, which is cheering news.[3]

I am looking forward to reading 'The Quiet American'.[4] Also, to meeting you in the New Year when you can spare a time. I do take it very kindly that you should give my affairs so much consideration.

Yours sincerely,

TLcc. NLS.

1. Martin Stannard writes of MS's change of address:

> Muriel left Allington Castle in August 1955, grateful for its respite, impatient to be gone. After eight months the haven of her cottage had become a prison. The retreat was provincial – full of prying eyes, too cosy. She longed to reconnect herself to the normality – and anonymity – of the metropolis. The decision to go was made in July, shortly after she completed 'Portobello'. Father O'Malley had a niece, Teresa Walshe, who lodged with a Catholic landlady. It was one of the best introductions Muriel ever received. 'Tiny' Lazzari was a vivacious, chirruping Irish widow with a Cork accent, small of stature, big of heart. No. 13 Baldwin Crescent was her own house. She lived on the ground floor, her son, his wife and their two children on the first. The third was for tenants, including Teresa. Muriel occupied a pair of cramped attic rooms adjacent to a kitchen, and looked out over the back garden. [. . .] Muriel could sit in silence at her desk, staring at the patch of lawn, or walk down

the road and turn a corner into the noise. She loved it, and stayed there for eleven years, gradually colonising more of the house. This was her British base when she went to work in New York during 1962, and remained her London home until she left for Rome in 1966. (*MSB*, p. 172)

2. In his letter of 2 December, Graham Greene wrote:

    I am delighted to hear that you are better and I do hope that Macmillans will publish your book. Perhaps they are not quite the publisher for anything weird and if you have trouble there don't hesitate to ask advice on another publisher. At the end of a misspent life one has quite a lot of experience.
        I will certainly speak to anybody I can about the possibilities of a part-time job, but I am going to be out of London until the end of next week and again for Christmas. Perhaps early in the New Year you would come and have a drink and I could find out exactly what you had in mind, apart from reading. Don't hesitate to use my name in approaching, say, Tom Burns of Burns Oates, or Jonathan Cape or A. S. Frere of Heinemann's, in the meantime. Hamish Hamilton, too, might be worth trying and again say that I suggested it. (NLS)

3. Founded in 1948 and edited by Princess Marguerite Caetani, *Botteghe Oscure* was an international literary journal published in Rome, for which Giorgio Bassani had been the Editor, succeeded by Eugene Walter (who will become important in MS's life in Rome during the 1960s); it was with Walter that MS corresponded about the publication of her story 'The Portobello Road' (which will appear in 1956 in *Botteghe Oscure*, no. 18).
4. Greene's novel *The Quiet American* was about to be published by Heinemann.

1956

With *The Comforters* completed, but still not contracted to Macmillan, who sent it to five readers for reports, and still not settled in its final title, the year was one in which patience was required of MS. She took on work in January reviewing for Graham Greene's company, and from late February worked part-time for publisher Peter Owen. After being paid for a BBC broadcast, she sent one of her numerous cheques to her son Robin, who had finished school at Daniel Stewart's College. She worked on her long story 'The Go-Away Bird' but failed to convince Alan Maclean to publish her stories. In March, she finally received a contract for her novel from Macmillan, and on the 15th of the month met Maclean for the first time. She proposed to Peter Owen a selection of the letters of Cardinal Newman, to be prepared by Derek Stanford and herself. In April, after trying out further titles to her novel – *Characters in a Novel*, *Types and Shadows*, *Shadow Play* – she lit on *The Comforters* as its definitive title; publication was set for early the following year. Evelyn Waugh offered a positive notice for the novel's blurb ('brilliantly original and fascinating'), as did, later, Graham Greene ('one of the few really original first novels one has read for many years'). The novel was bought by the publisher Lippincott, in Philadelphia, for US publication. MS wrote on her fellow native of Edinburgh Robert Louis Stevenson for the *Journal of the Scottish Secondary Teachers' Association* and composed an article on St Monica, mother of St Augustine. Late in the year, she started on her second novel, *Robinson*, and penned the following humorous self-portrait: 'Born in ice cave of southern Tyrol year 609 B.C. of centaur stock, mother descended Venus. Muriel Spark rose from the waves as is well known. Demands fabulous fees' (*MSB*, p. 177).

TO GRAHAM GREENE, LONDON, 1 FEBRUARY 1956

13, Baldwin Crescent, Camberwell, London, S.E.5
1st February, 1956

Dear Mr. Greene,

Thank you for sending me the Polish translations, and for your very generous cheque.

I am enclosing the reports which I hope are satisfactory. I should always be glad to do any further work for you, and of course, another time, would not expect such large payment.[1]

I am still looking out for a job either in the secretarial or editorial line. The main difficulty is getting part-time work. I have decided to take a full-time job if I can get one. It was most kind of you to speak to Mr. Frere for me.[2]

Macmillans have taken my novel.

I did so much enjoy the Quiet American. I read it at Christmas and it had a happy cooling effect. And I was delighted to see my neglected friend Clough in the epigraph. It struck me that his hero (in Amours de Voyage) was not unlike yours (I mean the narrator in your book).[3]

Yours sincerely,

TLcc. NLS.

1. In his letter of 19 January, Graham Greene wrote: 'I am enclosing herewith two Polish translations in MS. and a book of Polish short stories printed in English – BALTIC TALES. Would you please read these for me and let me have a report on them. I am enclosing a cheque for £30 in payment to you for this service' (NLS).
2. In her letter of 14 January to Iris Birtwistle, MS wrote: 'Do come soon before I get a job. I am looking for a part-time one, very difficult to get but at least, thank God, I'm fit enough now to take it on. Did Derek tell you I had written a novel which Macmillans are going to publish? It is a true nervous-breakdown production, quite crackers really' (CBF).

   Alexander Stuart Frere had been Managing Editor at Heinemann since 1929 and worked with many of the twentieth century's most eminent writers.

3. The epigraph to *The Quiet American* is lifted from *Amours de Voyage* by Arthur
    Hugh Clough, long a favourite of MS's:

> I do not like being moved: for the will is excited; and action
> Is a most dangerous thing; I tremble for something factitious,
> Some malpractice of heart and illegitimate process;
> We're so prone to these things, with our terrible notions of duty.

The hero-narrator of Greene's novel, Thomas Fowler, is highly critical of the burgeoning American intervention in French Indochina (later
Vietnam). The relations between verse and narrative, and between heroism
and scepticism – relations crucial to MS's own developing practice – are
explored in 'Arthur Hugh Clough, *Amours de Voyage*, and the Victorian
Crisis of Action', where Stefanie Markovits writes:

> Writers skirmishing over the relative roles of action and character in
> literature redefined heroism and influenced the development of the
> novel as a genre concerned with character and states of conscious-
> ness rather than deeds.
>   Nowhere is this battle more visible than in the generic tensions
> of Victorian narrative verse. And nowhere is the question of gen-
> eric hybridity and its relationship to the proper roles for action
> and character in literature demonstrated more beautifully than in
> Arthur Hugh Clough's *Amours de Voyage* (written 1849, published
> 1858). Clough referred to this poem as his 'five-act epistolary tragi-
> comedy, or comi-tragedy,' but in many respects the work, written
> as a series of letters composed in (mock) epic hexameters punctuated
> by lyrical elegiacs in a narrative voice, is also novelistic. (*Nineteenth-
> Century Literature*, vol. 55, no. 4, March 2001, p. 446)

TO ALAN MACLEAN, MACMILLAN LTD, LONDON, 20 FEBRUARY 1956

13, Baldwin Crescent, Camberwell, London, S.E.5
20th February, 1956

Dear Mr. Maclean,

   I am sorry to importune you but I should really be so grateful
for a contract for my novel, the more pressing part of which is, of
course, the further cheque in advance of royalties. Do you think
you could manage this some time this week? I would take it very

kindly if you could. If you could point out to your directors that the ms. was delivered three months ago or more, and accepted by you two months since, and that I have revised it as suggested, perhaps they won't think this unreasonably hasty.[1]

I am hoping to get started on my new novel THE GO-AWAY BIRD early in March, and I hope you will be interested in it. As I think I told you, I have to have an advance on royalties before I can start a book, and as you were kind enough to encourage my first novel in this way I should be grateful if you could do so again, on the same basis (£50 to start with and a further £50 in the middle of the year). The only difference I would like to suggest is that on this occasion I should not submit the chapters half-way through the book. I think I can compose better by writing straight ahead and then revising on the typewriter. I don't think you will object to this, as you did not really insist on seeing the first part of my other book.

The scene of THE GO-AWAY BIRD is Southern Rhodesia where I spent six years. (The Go-away bird is a real bird which is common in Rhodesia, – it says 'go'way'; in my novel the 'Go-away Bird' is also a human character.) I am going to write it in the first person for a change. I have high hopes of the book turning out well. I hope it sounds tempting.

Let me know what you think of all this, please when you have time.

Hoping you survive unfrozen, and with best wishes,
Sincerely,
s/Muriel Spark

TLS. MA.

1. On 12 December 1955, Alan Maclean wrote to C. P. Snow, whose work Macmillan published, for his view of the novel MS had submitted, saying: 'I wonder if you would be kind enough to read this first novel, TYPES AND SHADOWS by Muriel Spark. I think you read the first five chapters some months ago and we gambled to the extent of £100 on the book. One or two of us have read it here, and I shall be extremely interested to know what you think of it' (MA). Five readers' reports were solicited by Maclean,

and all recommended publication, while noting the oddball nature of the narrative and the special talent that had produced it (MA). C. P. Snow's report concluded: 'In general crackpot talents are not my cup of tea at all, and I only really like novels which have at least one foot on the ground. Miss Spark is nowhere near the ground at any point; she is even more crackpot than, say Stevie Smith, to whom she has a certain resemblance. But she has a very real talent of its kind (Miss Spark – Stevie Smith also); some of the writing in this book is razor-edged; and I feel that real talent is so rare that we probably ought to publish it.'

TO DR H. J. L. ROBBIE, DANIEL STEWART'S COLLEGE, EDINBURGH, 13 MARCH 1956

13, Baldwin Crescent, Camberwell, London, S.E.5
13th March, 1956

Dear Dr. Robbie,

I have heard from my son, Robin Spark, that he recently had the opportunity of discussing with you his possibilities for the future.[1] As I think he told you, he is himself very keen to study medicine. I understand that you do not think this feasible.

I understand also – and of course, fully accept – that you do not feel able, on the strength of his marks, to recommend him for a science course. But in view of his obvious keenness to study medicine, I am wondering if there is any other course of study which you might recommend, and which would assist towards obtaining a University entrance for medicine.

You will understand that I do not wish Robin to undertake work beyond his capacities. But he has maintained a consistent idea about medicine for the past two years, and as his father has guaranteed the financial side of this venture, I do not wish to oppose the boy's leanings. Robin himself fully recognises the difficulties in his way, but he is very anxious to have a try.

I should very much welcome your comments, and any suggestions you may feel able to make towards the possibility of his reading medicine.

I should like to take this opportunity of thanking you and

Robin's teachers for the interest and encouragement shown
to him.

I am very conscious of many initial disadvantages which my
son has to over come [sic], and have been greatly impressed by his
general development while at Daniel Stewart's. I am especially
grateful to you, as I am not myself able to see very much of him,
and although Robin is in the excellent care of my parents, I feel
that much of his good progress generally, is due to his school
environment.[2]

Yours sincerely,

TLdraft. NLS.

1. H. J. L. Robbie was Headmaster of Daniel Stewart's College from 1946
   until his death in 1964. In his *Supplement to A History of Daniel Stewart's
   College 1955–1970*, David Rintoul writes: 'That the school came first with
   Dr. Robbie is certain, and also that he had a remarkable knowledge of the
   boys he governed – some must have thought that he had spies in every part
   of the city. He expected much of his boys and his staff, and more from
   himself. He was really at heart a shy man, who shrank from familiarity'
   (published by the college, 1971, p. 113).
2. In the Epilogue to *A History of Daniel Stewart's College 1855–1955* by J.
   Thompson, the mission of the school is given:

   > We make whole men, or try to make them, failing sometimes from
   > the flaws in the boy, or his home, or ourselves, but not losing sight of
   > the end. We have nearly all our boys from the age of five (few other
   > schools have them so long) and we might stamp them in one mould,
   > identical in speech, tastes and shibboleths as so many schools do. But
   > we have never tried to do that, and, I hope, never will. Our best
   > are identical in these ways only – that they are Christian; that they
   > learn to distinguish right from wrong and to prefer right; that they
   > are adequately learned, have begun to work independently and are
   > endowed with saving commonsense; that their bodies are matched
   > to their minds; and that they are not boorish. In other things our
   > toleration permits a great diversity: there is room for all kinds of
   > heretics. These are not original virtues, but they are worth setting
   > down, for they link us to our past. Toleration apart, they are the
   > qualities we have aimed at in Scotland for nearly four hundred years.
   > (Published by the college, 1971, p. 107)

TO PAUL ALLEN, LONDON, 15 MARCH 1956

13, Baldwin Crescent, Camberwell, S.E.5
15th Mar. 1956

Dear Paul,

I should have written earlier. Your nice long letter was
very cheering and I'm glad to know you have London Mystery
Magazine more or less to yourself. I hope the printing hold-up will
soon be over, and look forward to seeing the L.M.M. – I've never
looked into a copy, – I don't think so, at least.[1]

Yes, by all means keep the Leafsweeper till next Christmas
in case it will be suitable then. I have just written another story
which I am trying first on the Cornhill.[2] But I haven't so much
time now, having started work with Peter Owen at the end of
February. I do three days a week, – Mon., Wed., and Friday.
The other days I'm usually reviewing, or so exhausted, merely
brooding on what is past or passing or to come.

The decor at Peter Owen's would amuse you – you must look
in some time. It is like a scene from a play of the thirties. Bare
boards, upturned packing cases of wood & cardboard for working
purposes, old bits of sacks and sheaves of tattered manuscripts.
Peter, who is quite nice really, rushes in and out at a pace.
Sometimes bits of the set collapse, and the Owen drama is held up
while we heave things into place again.[3]

My novel, now reverted to its former title 'Types and Shadows'
won't be out till Spring 1947 [*sic*]. I want to start on another, but
so far haven't had any more money from Macmillans, so really
can't afford to. I'm *very* happy to know you have started *your*
novel. I do hope you will keep on with it, the main character
sounds fascinating and very true to one's experience. Is he going
to become involved in any situation in spite of himself, or does
he reduce experience to abstractions throughout? I should like to
read any part you may have ready.[4]

I do hope we can meet soon. I have been waiting for payments
for some of my work, to arrange a party. But in the meantime do

fix up with Derek a night when you will be free to come and have coffee, and tell us more about your novel. Or ring me up any time, it will be jolly to see you again. I much enjoyed your Christmas party, and it seems strange how the weeks have flown since then.

Best wishes in the meantime,

Yours ever,

s/Muriel

TLS. NLS

1. MS had met the Irish writer Paul Allen through Derek Stanford in 1954. He is described by Stanford as 'a modern language graduate from Trinity College, Dublin, who became literary editor of *Courier* and the *London Mystery Magazine*' (*ITF*, p. 201). MS's fondness for Allen, who would later be identified as one of her 'bachelors', is attested to in a letter she will send to his son Peter Allen on 17 October 2003 when she learns of Paul's death: 'I remember him as a young man and it is very difficult to part with old friends. I always have the very fondest memory of Paul, of his sister and mother. We had very good times together. I will remember him fondly.' She added: 'Thank you for sending me a copy of his speech. He was an exceptionally talented Irishman and I hope that his speech will be received just the same, and appreciated' (PJC).

2. In typewritten notes on Martin Stannard's copy of the present letter, Allen wrote: 'The Leaf Sweeper eventually appeared in THE LONDON MYSTERY MAGAZINE. MISS PINKERTON'S APOCALYPSE was published in COURIER. I was on the editorial staff of both magazines. [. . .] I first met Muriel with Derek Stanford at a teashop in the Strand. The Courier Office was in Grand Buildings, Trafalgar Square. Thereafter, we had some fine evenings of wine and poetry, only ended when Spark and Stanford parted company' (Private collection).

    MS's stories were not published in the *Cornhill Magazine*.

3. In his obituary of Peter Owen, Ion Trewin will recollect:

    > Muriel Spark, an early editor who had yet to publish her first novel, recalled in her memoirs working part-time at Peter Nevill and then in Owen's first formal office in Old Brompton Road, South Kensington. She was also secretary, publicity assistant and proofreader, which meant, during her time, books in translation by Hesse, Cocteau and Pavese, which were an education to her and 'a joy'. The offices, she remembered, were bleak – 'one light bulb, bare boards, a long table which was the packing department'. Owen was always retreating to his own tiny office to take phone calls from

his uncles, one of whom worked at Zwemmer, the Charing Cross Road booksellers, and gave his nephew intellectual advice. The other was a psychiatrist.

Owen in turn remembered Spark as a brilliant shorthand typist and as very efficient. She also had literary taste and judgment. She brought Samuel Beckett to Owen's attention, but he was not convinced (this was before *Waiting for Godot*). 'Beckett was getting on for 50, had never made it,' he recalled. 'We had a choice between Beckett and the Japanese [author] Osamu Dazai. Muriel said, can't we do both? I said we can't afford both, and chose Dazai.' (*Guardian*, 1 June 2016)

4. MS is probably referring to Allen's autobiographical story 'Neutrality', which will become part of his (unpublished) novel *The English Boy* (see 16 July 1957).

TO ALAN MACLEAN, MACMILLAN LTD, LONDON, 17 MARCH 1956

13, Baldwin Crescent, Camberwell, S.E.5
17th March, 1956

Dear Mr. Maclean,

Thank you very much for your nice hospitable luncheon session the other day.

I am enclosing the signed agreement for my novel. The only alteration is in the title (from 'Characters in a Novel' to 'Types and Shadows') and hope this will be all right.

I am hoping to write an additional section, an envoi, which I am chewing over at the moment. I might get it done over the Easter holidays, and I will let you have it some time after that.

About the stories: I am sending (separately) another four, which, together with 'The Portobello Road', make thirteen in all. I have listed them on the attached sheet, so that you can see whether you have them all.

I should very much like you to consider these stories as, at least, the basis of a book. I have had more success with stories, so far, than with anything else I have written. (The Observer prize helped a lot, and I think that should also help to sell the stories.)

I think you may already have had an opinion on some of the stories, and I should be glad if you would consider this collection as it stands. I could add three or four, or perhaps one longish 'conte' if the work were commissioned.

You know my position: I can't do much creative writing unless I have an advance on royalties first. It would be an enormous help if I had an advance on the stories, and then I might be able to get along gaily with 'The Go-away Bird'.

I do much appreciate your encouragement so far. What a bore it is to have to go on about money as if it were one's main concern! However, I'm sure you understand how I am placed.

I look forward to hearing what you think of the stories. I think the latest one 'Come Along, Marjorie' might especially interest you.

Many thanks for all your good efforts on my behalf, and again for a very pleasant lunch.

Best wishes,

Sincerely,

s/Muriel Spark

List of stories by Muriel Spark

Daisy Overend
The Seraph and the Zambesi
The Pawnbroker's Wife
The Twins
Harper and Wilton
The Pearly Shadow
The Leafsweeper
The Portobello Road[1]
Ladies and Gentlemen
Miss Pinkerton's Apocalypse
'A Sad Tale's Best for Winter'[2]
The House of the Famous Poet
Come Along, Marjorie

TLS. MA.

1. A note in MS's hand next to 'The Portobello Road' reads 'W.T. for 1956' (where 'W.T.' stands for 'Winter's Tales'); an additional story title has been added in pencil – 'The Thing About Police Stations', the story being presumably the one enclosed with the next letter to Alan Maclean, dated 31 March.

2. In an undated letter (of which only a fragment survives) from some time earlier in the year, MS wrote to Alan Barnsley:

> I have taken to Sherlock Holmes recently – beautifully styl*ised* – no artistic *style*, & verbally rather attractive & pure in parts. I have started a story called 'A Sad Tale's Best for Winter' – taken from *A Winter's Tale* as of course you know (The Hell you did!). It is a continuation of the story that Shakespeare's character never finished, only getting as far as 'There was a man dwelt by a graveyard.' The theme of my story is roughly the proposition that corruption is a very low activity but the contemplation of corruption very high. (MBC)

TO ALAN MACLEAN, MACMILLAN LTD, LONDON, 31 MARCH 1956

13, Baldwin Crescent, Camberwell, S.E.5
31ˢᵗ March 1956

Dear Mʳ Maclean,

The verdict of my friends – with which I agree – is that 'Shadow Show' won't do. It reminds one of a circus, and I am not sure that there wasn't a film by that name. For a different type of book, of course, the idea is good.

I don't really think we can do better than 'Types and Shadows'. 1) It has the advantage of being accurate. 2) No-one need feel squeamish about using a phrase from a hymn – it is not Holy Writ. 3) In any case it is not an accurate translation of St. Thomas' 'et secundum Documentum . . . etc.', it is merely a comparatively recent English version which has gained currency.[1] 4) Other books have titles with sacred associations and are apparently unobjectionable on that account. (vz. Graham Greene 'the Power & the Glory'.)

Do let us stick to 'Types and Shadows' unless, of course, you hit on a *very* much better title. I am open to considering anything, but think *T & S.* is the best we have yet.

Best wishes.

Sincerely,

Muriel Spark

P.S. Another story enclosed to add to the collection.[2]

ALS. MA.

1. The notion of the *type* is described in *The Concise Oxford Dictionary of the Christian Church* as: 'In theology the foreshadowing of the Christian dispensation in the events and persons of the O[ld] T[estament]. Just as Christ could refer to Jonah as the symbol of His Resurrection, so St Paul found in the Israelites' crossing of the Red Sea the "type" of Baptism (1 Cor. 10: 1–6). Typology was much used in the early Church.'

    MS attributes to St Thomas Aquinas the medieval Latin hymn 'Pange lingua gloriosi corporis mysterium', which contains the lines:

    > Et antiquum documentum
    > Novo cedat ritui.

    In 'Of the Glorious Body Telling', a translation by John M. Neale, these lines become:

    > Types and shadows have their ending,
    > For the newer rite is here.
    > (*English Hymnal*, 326: Oxford University Press, 1906)

2. The extra story is 'The Thing About Police Stations'.

TO FATHER DESSAIN, BIRMINGHAM ORATORY, 10 APRIL 1956

13, Baldwin Crescent, Camberwell, S.E.5
10th April, 1956

Dear Father Dessain,

Father Caraman, S.J. has given me your name and has suggested that I write to you as Newman's executor.[1]

I am preparing a selection of Newman's letters, in conjunction with another editor, Mr. Derek Stanford, for publication by Peter Owen and subsequently by the Newman Press in America. Mr. Stanford, who is an Anglican, is selecting and introducing the letters up to 1845, and I am dealing with the letters of the later years. I am a Catholic.[2]

The selection as a whole is not to be a large one. We have been so far assisted by Father Caraman who has lent us a number of manuscript letters, some of which are hitherto unpublished, and some of which I should like your permission to use.

I have not yet made a start on the selection but I would be greatly assisted in doing so if I had, first, your kind permission to use material from Ward's *Life and Letters* (1912), and secondly, if I had some idea what, if any, copyright fee would be required. Longmans tell me that the work is free so far as they are concerned.[3]

The terms of our contract limit us rather stringently as regards copyright fees, and we have to allow for copyright requirements on any unpublished material we may, with your kind permission, use.

I trust you will appreciate that I cannot, as yet, specify what material I wish to use from the Ward volumes, but if you could give me a rough idea of your position with regard to these volumes, and also your usual copyright fees for unpublished letters (providing, of course, the use of them had your approval) I could let you know my exact requirements later.

I hope you will make it convenient to see me at Birmingham Oratory some time later on. This is merely a preliminary to our starting the book, hoping for your assistance, so that we may be able to judge the limits of our choice of letters.[4]

Yours sincerely,

TLcc. UTML.

1. Cardinal John Henry Newman was a key – perhaps *the* key – writer leading to MS's conversion to Catholicism, as she states in *CV*: 'In 1953 I was

absorbed by the theological writings of John Henry Newman through whose influence I finally became a Roman Catholic' (p. 202); his writings would remain hugely important to MS even as she took her distance from the institutions of the Catholic Church. Ian Ker concludes his entry on Newman in the *ODNB* (2020): 'Certainly the most significant Roman Catholic theologian of the nineteenth century, Newman has also come to be seen as the most seminal of modern Catholic thinkers. Within the English context, he was the most important Anglican theologian since Hooker, as well as being one of the great Victorian prose writers.'

The introduction to Father Charles Stephen Dessain's *The Mind of Cardinal Newman* states: 'Father Stephen was lavish in the amount of time he gave to assisting scholars with their books and theses. Newman scholars the world over also stand indebted to him for his editing of the Letters and Diaries of John Henry Newman. Twenty-one volumes covering the whole of the Catholic period of Newman's life saw the light of day under his editorship' (Catholic Truth Society, 2017).

In Dessain's 1960 article 'The Newman Archives and the Projected Edition of the Cardinal's Letters', he is described as 'the superior of the Oratory of the Immaculate Conception, Edgbaston, Birmingham, and editor of the forthcoming edition of Newman's letters' (*Catholic Historical Review*, vol. 46, no. 1, 1960).

Father Philip Caraman, SJ (Society of Jesus) was the Editor of the Jesuit periodical the *Month*, where he was encouraged by such Catholic-convert writers as Evelyn Waugh and Graham Greene. He was helpful in MS's conversion, and to him, on 1 June 1954, MS wrote, 'I was confirmed on Sunday last, the 31st May' (NLS).

2. On 13 February, MS wrote to Peter Owen: 'Derek and I have pleasure in enclosing the scheme of our proposed collection of Newman's Letters. I am sure you will find it a worthwhile proposition, and we look forward to hearing from you' (Private collection). Newman was received into the Catholic Church on 9 October 1845.

3. MS refers to Wilfrid Ward, *The Life of John Henry Cardinal Newman, Based on His Private Journals and Correspondence* (Longman, 1912).

4. Five months later, on 18 September, MS will write to Paul Allen: 'I am finding the Newman letters absorbing but very hard work, especially as I have to break off to go to the office daily. I could get thoroughly immersed in the subject of Newman, perhaps it would overwhelm me if I didn't have to do other things. I will have to make a trip to Birmingham Oratory soon, to see about copyright. Fr. Dessain? is looking after Newman's affairs now. – Do you know him?' (NLS).

TO ALAN MACLEAN, MACMILLAN LTD, LONDON,
22 APRIL 1956

13, Baldwin Crescent, Camberwell, S.E.5
22nd April, 1956

Dear Mr. Maclean,

I have thought of a very good title for my novel. It is THE
COMFORTERS. This pins down my main theme. It seems
to satisfy the need to cover all the various strands in the novel
without laying stress on any minor ones. It should be a better
selling title than any we have had so far.[1]

Do please write and agree with me. I don't like 'Shadow Play'. I
do like The Comforters.

I am sending two additional pages to be inserted at the end.
I had hoped to make it longer, but I don't want to say more
than I want to convey. Anything else would be padding. I
hope you will like this. I have tested the reaction of a friend,
who thinks it rounds off the novel well, – suitably dramatic
and explanatory. I have followed your advice in attempting
to make Laurence more effectual and to pick up some of his
characteristics.

I don't want to insist on galleys if this will delay the production.
But if you do go straight into pages, will you please ask your
printer to follow my own punctuation? My style of punctuation is
unorthodox at times, but I mean it so.

Another point which I would like you to reconsider: the
deletions we made from pages 141–143a. My friends are mostly in
favour of leaving this passage in the book. I should like to do so,
because it throws further light on the Manders' household as well
as elaborating Mrs. Hogg's younger days. I think the objection of
mild indecency is covered by Caroline's remark on p.143a. But I
leave the decision to you.[2]

Do ring me at Peter Owen's if there is any point you wish to
discuss. I am working there full time at the moment.

It is exciting to know the novel is going into production now.
Many thanks for all your efforts.
Best wishes,
Sincerely,
s/Muriel Spark

TLS. MA.

1. In *Muriel Spark, Existentialism and the Art of Death*, Cairns Craig writes:

> Job is the symbol of faith as a daily trial and as a daily refusal of the
> temptations offered by his 'comforters'. The Book of Job was to be
> equally important to Spark: her first novel was titled *The Comforters*,
> enigmatically invoking Job as the context for a narrative of religious
> conversion. (Edinburgh University Press, 2019, pp. 7–8)

> James Bailey explains further, in *Muriel Spark's Early Fiction*:

> The reason for the title's suitability can be deduced from the con-
> tents of the author's notebooks, which reveal that her work on
> the novel coincided with two detailed reviews of books about the
> Book of Job, written by Carl Jung and T. H. Robinson respectively.
> Spark's commitment to completing these reviews, of which only
> the former was published, was perhaps a way of compensating for
> her own failure to submit a monograph on the subject, which had
> been commissioned by the publishers Sheed & Ward (Stannard
> 2009:143). Both reviews fixate on the same theme: Job's intol-
> erable *comforters*, whose solipsistic behaviour exacerbates their
> friend's present suffering. 'The harm Satan did to Job seems trivial
> in comparison with the crushing afflictions which we actually see
> in progress,' she wrote in the review of Jung's book. 'He appears
> surrounded', she continued, 'by a conspiracy of mediocrity'. (p. 41)

2. MS was successful in retaining the passage, which runs from p. 146 to
    p. 148 in the Birlinn centenary edition.

TO ALAN MACLEAN, MACMILLAN LTD, LONDON, I MAY 1956

13, Baldwin Crescent, Camberwell, S.E.5
1st May, 1956

Dear Mr. Maclean,

I send chapter 7 in which the deleted passage occurs. The deleted passage begins at 'Mrs. Hogg's tremendous . . ' on p.141 and ends at 'only a gargoyle' on p.143a.

As I consider it, the more I think this passage should remain.

1) It is part of the 'mythos' of the novel. Mrs. H. is a kind of sprawly Behemoth. An excessive figure.

2) Mrs. Hogg's early life is elaborated here. The Manders' household is more fully revealed. Laurence's childhood is returned to; and the only mention in the novel of his brother, killed in the war, occurs here. In fact, the narrative needs this passage.

3) It gives an example of Caroline's 'voices' which are otherwise hardly present in Part II of the book.

4) Objections of obscenity are met by Caroline's remarks on p.143a. It is clear, at least, that Mrs. H.'s breasts have been deliberately exaggerated.[1]

5) From the technical point of view, Mrs. H. represents a sort of 'gargoyle'. I think gargoyles are always necessary. See Caroline's remark on p.143a. where she concludes that Mrs. H. is 'Not a real-life character . . only a gargoyle'.

Please do consider these arguments. If you still don't like the passage, then leave it out. Arguments don't always signify.

I ought to mention that I think most of your readers, who objected to this part, saw it before it was toned down (by my inserting the comments etc. of Caroline).

I hope I have made all this clear. I am typing at breakfast time with an eye on the clock.

Please return this chapter when convenient.

All the best,

s/Muriel

TLS. MA.

1. In her reader's report on the novel, dated 9 March, Mona Andrade commented: 'Why the slightly indecent harping on the size of Mrs. Hogg's bosom
   and the variety and shape of her brassiers [*sic*]? It is very off-putting! As Mrs.
   Hogg is a witch one somehow doesn't see her as an elderly Jane Russell' (MA).

TO ALAN MACLEAN, MACMILLAN LTD, LONDON,
19 OCTOBER 1956

13, Baldwin Crescent, Camberwell, S.E.5
19th October, 1956

Dear Mr. McLean [*sic*],

On the question of the blurb, it really is a most difficult book to
pin down to a few words. I think, in fact, that the jacket cover with
its book-within-a-book motif has got hold of one of the main factors.[1]

I am sending a revised blurb, done by Derek Stanford who
knows my work well. Perhaps you could consider this in
conjunction with your own?

There are one or two points which I think might profitably be
brought out, and I think the second blurb covers them.

1) From the sales point of view, the Observer prize, which was
rather my widest success.

Also, the fact that tho' it is my first novel, it isn't my first
book.*

2) The Chinese box book-within-a-book construction.

3) I would prefer it to be called an 'eccentric' novel than a
'crazy' one, as I think the latter may give an impression of gaiety
more than occurs in the novel. What do you think?

4) I would rather the fact of the grandmother's 'criminal gang'
wasn't mentioned, because this is part of the plot & ought not to
be revealed.

Perhaps you would let me know what you finally decide on,
tho' in fact I am not at all exacting about these things, for the
book will ultimately have to rest on its own merit.

If you have a spare advance copy of the book, Alan Barnsley will
send it to Evelyn Waugh to see if he can get a word of praise.

Hope to see you on Wednesday,

Best wishes,

Sincerely,

s/Muriel Spark

* I once gave you a list of books 'by the same author' for inclusion on one of the prelims. I think you gave it to one of your production or publicity people. Would you like another, or would you rather omit this item?

TLS. MA.

1.   On 3 June, MS wrote to Alan Maclean: 'Here is a draft blurb, but please alter it, or scrap it altogether as you please. I thought it best to mention the Observer story as a selling point. If you think the blurb excessive in any way please tone it down' (MA). And on 14 October, she wrote to him: 'Thanks, too, for the pull of the wrapper which I think is quite excellent. It has been much admired by those who have read the manuscript. Do please convey my thanks to the artist' (MA). The jacket to the first edition of *The Comforters* creates the effect of *mise en abyme* by including, twice, in shrinking proportions, the original cover, which features the cartoon of a woman holding a diamond.

Evelyn Waugh, 1951

TO ALAN MACLEAN, MACMILLAN LTD, LONDON,
6 NOVEMBER 1956

13, Baldwin Crescent, Camberwell, S.E.5
6th Nov. 1956

Dear Mr. Maclean,
  I enclose the copy of Evelyn Waugh's letter to Gabriel Fielding.
  Yours very sincerely,
  s/Muriel Spark

(1956)

Piers Court, Stinchcombe, Nr. Dursley, Glos.
Oct.29

Dear Mr. Fielding
  Thank you for sending me Mrs. Spark's remarkable book.
  The first half, up to the motor accident, is brilliant. The second half
rather diffuse. The mechanics of the hallucinations are well managed.
These particularly interested me as I am myself engaged on a similar
subject.[1]
  Mrs. Spark no doubt wants a phrase to quote on the wrapper and in
advertisements. She can report me as saying: 'brilliantly original and
fascinating.'
  Please do not trouble to acknowledge this
  Yours sincerely
  E. Waugh

TLS. MA.

1. Evelyn Waugh was working on his novel *The Ordeal of Gilbert Pinfold*. His
    letter to Alan Barnsley / Gabriel Fielding is reproduced in *The Letters of
    Evelyn Waugh*, ed. Mark Amory (Phoenix, 2009, p. 540). In *CV*, MS writes,
    of Waugh's reaction:

       To his friend, Ann Fleming, he wrote

I have been sent proofs of a very clever first novel by a lady named Muriel Spark. The theme is a Catholic novelist suffering from hallucinations. It will appear quite soon. I am sure people will think it is by me. Please contradict such assertions.

On publication of my novel Evelyn Waugh was extremely generous, writing a most interesting essay on it in the *Spectator*.

Recently I asked Evelyn Waugh's eldest son, Auberon (Bron) if he remembers his father's reaction on getting those proofs of *The Comforters* while in the middle of writing his *Pinfold*.

All I remember [wrote Bron in reply] is him singing the praises of it, and saying how curious it was that you should be writing about the same sort of experience at the same time.

His attack, of course, was brought on by a mixture of chloral and bromide, yours by dexedrine, which should have the opposite effect to chloral and bromide. The sentence which jumps out from Evelyn Waugh's review is surely: 'It so happens that *The Comforters* came to me just as I had finished a story on a similar theme, and I was struck by how much more ambitious was Miss Spark's essay and how much better she had accomplished it.' (pp. 207–8)

Further praise will come from Graham Greene, who will write to Derek Stanford on 31 January 1957:

I did read Mrs Spark's novel with great interest while I was in Canada but I am afraid did not realise that you needed a quotation as it were for use. I had really meant to write to Mrs Spark herself saying how much I had enjoyed her book – which is one of the few really original first novels one has read for many years. (NLS)

1957

After the long wait, *The Comforters* was published by Macmillan in February and by Lippincott in the US in August, in both cases to favourable reviews. MS resigned from her job at Peter Owen but applied (unsuccessfully) to the post of Editor at *London Mystery Magazine*. In February, she was contacted by Rayner Heppenstall of the BBC who hoped to broadcast her work – the start of a long and fraught relationship. MS sent him her radio play 'The Party through the Wall', which was accepted, with changes, and broadcast in August. In late March, she was contacted by Rachel MacKenzie of the *New Yorker*, to whom she sent several stories, none of which was accepted. From January to July, MS worked on her second novel, *Robinson*, which was contracted to Macmillan in November. In May, and again in repeat in November, *The Comforters* was discussed on BBC radio by critics including Angus Wilson and Frank Kermode. In June, she changed literary agencies to Pearn, Pollinger & Higham where the novelist Paul Scott became her agent, while in the US, for Harold Ober Associates, the literary agent Ivan von Auw – who would go on to become a close friend and her single most important agent – began to handle her contracts. In June, *Letters of John Henry Newman*, edited by MS and Derek Stanford, was published by Peter Owen. MS received her first letter – fan mail – from playwright John Van Druten, which started a rich correspondence ending only with Van Druten's sudden death in December. MS spent a fortnight in Edinburgh in late summer, while her son Robin started on two years' National Service. From autumn, MS worked on her third novel, *Memento Mori*, and in October sent its opening chapters to Scott, her agent. In December, she read Doris Lessing for the first time, with whom she would later correspond.

TO ALAN MACLEAN, MACMILLAN LTD, LONDON,
2 JANUARY 1957

13, Baldwin Crescent, Camberwell, S.E.5
2nd January, 1957

Dear Alan,

I hope you have had jolly festivities. I have been in Edinburgh which to me is like being in another century partly, rather a traumatic experience.

All good wishes for a happy New Year!

I enclose a list of people to whom I would like my book to be sent. Is publication date settled for 7th February?

Anyway, I am asking a few friends to come for a drink on February 7th, and hope you will be able to come and adorn the occasion, for without you it would, like the book, be incomplete. Any time after 7.30. A bus from the Oval will bring you to Flodden Road, then first left into Baldwin Crescent. Do come.

I have started *Robinson* which the beautiful Lippincott money will allow me to give some time to, and if Macmillans' should make me an advance on the same terms as for *The Comforters*, I ought to be able to write the book this year in peace.[1]

I believe Derek told you how much we both enjoyed David Daiches's *Two Worlds*. If you could let me know roughly when review copies are going out I shall ask for it somewhere, as I should very much like to write a piece on it.[2]

All good wishes,
Yours sincerely,
s/Muriel

P.S. Two lists enclosed.

1. 'With author's compliments'
2. Suggestions for your review list.[3]

Let me know if the former is too long.

TLS. MA.

1. In *CV*, MS writes: 'Alan Maclean had found for me an American publisher, Lippincott. I was now able to give up my job with Peter Owen and write creatively, full time. "*The Comforters*", wrote Lippincott in May 1957, "has caused a very agreeable stir among all of us who have read it." That is exactly the sort of thing a first novelist wants to hear from a publisher' (p. 211).
2. The autobiographical *Two Worlds* by Scottish literary historian and critic David Daiches, just published by Macmillan, tells of his childhood between the two world wars, of his schooling, and of his father who was the Chief Rabbi of Edinburgh.
3. The second list is not extant in the Macmillan Archive. The first list contains the names (in this order) G. S. Fraser, Paul Allen, Graham Greene, Robert Greacen, Hugo Manning, T. Christmas Humphreys, Howard Sergeant, The Rev. F. O'Malley, A. J. Cronin, Neville Braybrooke, Colin Wilson, Evelyn Waugh, Herbert Read, Princess Caetani, Dr Alan Barnsley, Derek Stanford, The Hon. David Astor, and Edwin Muir (this last, MS indicates, to receive a copy without the author's compliments as not a personal acquaintance).

TO MAJOR NORMAN KARK, NORMAN KARK PUBLICATIONS, LONDON, 20 JANUARY 1957

13, Baldwin Crescent, Camberwell, London, S.E.5
20th January, 1957

Dear Major Kark,

I have heard from my friend Paul Allen that he is leaving you, and I understand there will be a vacancy on LONDON MYSTERY MAGAZINE. I do hope that you will consider me for the job, for which I think my experience and interests are specially suited.[1]

Perhaps Paul Allen has told you something of my abilities: I have worked in publishing for many years, and especially with success on magazines – the most notable among them being POETRY REVIEW which attracted a great deal of attention during my editorship.

You will know that I have contributed both to LONDON MYSTERY MAGAZINE and COURIER.[2] In 1951 I was awarded first prize in *The Observer* short story competition. My stories appear in most of the prominent journals and anthologies here and in America, the most recent being *Botteghe Oscure* and Macmillan's *Winter's Tales*. I ought to mention that I am known predominantly as a 'mystery' writer.[3]

My latest book – a novel – which has received extremely high praise from Evelyn Waugh, is appearing next month from Macmillan, and is also being published by Lippincott in America. My former books have been works of literary criticism and have been very well and widely reviewed here and in America.

I am at present an editor for a London publisher who is very satisfied with my work, and I also review regularly – mostly short stories – in *The Observer*. I am most attracted and intrigued by the possibilities of the LONDON MYSTERY MAGAZINE, for I feel that my critical and creative talents would find full scope in that editorial medium.

Mr. Graham Greene, who knows my work, has said that I might mention his name in connection with any application for a job. Perhaps you would let me know if I may come and see you?

Yours sincerely,

TLcc. NLS.

1. Major Norman Kark is described in the headline to his (unsigned) obituary in *The Times* as 'Advertising man who lit up Trafalgar Square and published one of the century's glossiest magazines'. The article elaborates:

   > Kark had long been smitten by the romance of Fleet Street, and he used his advertising profits to fulfil his publishing dreams. In 1938 he founded a quarterly called *Courier* ('A Norman Kark magazine'), notable for its wide-ranging content, its impressive design using colour photography and illustration, and its exceptionally high quality of production. He edited every issue himself. [. . .] *Courier* was never less than expensive, and more often than not showed little or no profit, but Kark kept it going until the 1960s. At its height after the war, his stable also included such titles as *Bandwagon* and *To-Day*, as well as a fashion journal and a tractor magazine. Gradually all folded save *London Mystery* (later *Selection*), which he continued to edit until he was 86. (17 April 2000)

2. In *London Mystery Magazine* (no. 31, December 1956), MS published 'The Leaf Sweeper'; in *Courier* (no. 25, July 1955), she published 'Miss Pinkerton's Apocalypse'.
3. In both instances, the story published was 'The Portobello Road'. One year earlier, on 9 January 1956, MS wrote to 'Dear Countess Caetani' (rather than the more accurate *Princess* Caetani): 'I am writing to you to ask if I can have payment for my story THE PORTOBELLO ROAD as soon as you can possibly send it.' She added, pointedly: 'I am convalescent and do really need the money' (Private collection).

TO ALAN MACLEAN, MACMILLAN LTD, LONDON, 18 FEBRUARY 1957

13, Baldwin Crescent, Camberwell, S.E.5
18th February, 1957

Dear Alan,

I am sending you the first two, and part of the third chapters of my new novel. This is a rough draft and may be quite changed, finally. But I think it will enable you to see the drift and style, and I do hope you will like it and want to know what comes next.

I would prefer not to send any more odd chapters, it is better to write straight on without stopping to type the work, which will in any case finally need revision. Will you be able to put in a strong recommendation for me, on the strength of these pages?

I would like to write the novel during the spring and summer, continuously from now, and should have it ready in September.

Do let me know what you think of this portion, and perhaps we can meet and discuss it.[1]

I have made a map of the island, which, if reproduced would have to be done by a professional artist.[2]

The story is to be more straightforward than the Comforters so far as plot is concerned. It will probably be a shorter book, but I can't yet say for certain.

This is my only typed copy, and as it differs from the original

manuscript – having been touched up a bit – please guard it with
your life. Shall I know your reaction soon?

I am just about to write a notice of TWO WORLDS which has
been sent to me for review.

See you soon,

Best wishes,

s/Muriel

TLS. MA.

1. Alan Maclean will respond to MS's chapters, on 11 March: 'I think that
   they are most intriguing and I certainly want to know what comes next.
   It all looks very promising and it is excellent news that you think you may
   be able to finish it by September' (MA).
2. The original of MS's map of the island of Robinson that lends its name to
   her novel is not extant in the Macmillan Archive; but a copy of it will be
   sent with her letter of 19 July 1957 to Alan Barnsley (included here); the
   version which appears at the start of the published novel will be an almost
   exact replica of MS's sketch.

TO RACHEL MACKENZIE, THE NEW YORKER, NEW YORK, 7 APRIL 1957

13, Baldwin Crescent, Camberwell, London, S.E.5
7th April, 1957

Dear Miss MacKenzie,

Thank you very much for your letter of March 28, in which you
speak so kindly of my story 'The Portobello Road'. I am so glad
you enjoyed it.[1]

I should very much like to submit work to THE NEW
YORKER, and indeed have been thinking of doing so. Do you
ask for first world rights? I have one or two stories which I think
are of NEW YORKER standard, and which have had a limited
circulation in English publications of a non-national nature. I could
send these, together with some unpublished work. I also have a
story in progress which may interest you.

Perhaps you would let me know about this, and also your length limit?[2]

Yours very sincerely,

s/Muriel Spark

Muriel Spark

P.S. My first novel, which has been well received here, is to be published by Lippincott this year.

TLS. NYPL.

1. Rachel MacKenzie had joined the highly regarded magazine the *New Yorker* after teaching literature at various colleges in the US, and would be Fiction Editor there from 1956 to 1979. She worked with and encouraged many of the era's great writers, including Isaac Bashevis Singer, Harold Brodkey, Bernard Malamud, and Philip Roth. Her obituary in the *New York Times* cited Singer's reaction to her death in 1980: 'I consider her the greatest editor who ever lived. I think that American literature and literature generally has lost a giant, one of the last people who understood literature thoroughly from the beginning to the end' (30 March 1980).

   Although MS will first publish a story in the *New Yorker* only in 1960, and although her relations with MacKenzie will quickly sour, the correspondence between editor and author shows how actively MacKenzie cultivated MS's interest and her subsequent commitment to MS's work. Further on MS's relation to MacKenzie and the *New Yorker*, see Lisa Harrison, '"The Magazine That Is Considered the Best in the World": Muriel Spark and the *New Yorker*', in *Muriel Spark: Twenty-First-Century Perspectives*, ed. David Herman (Johns Hopkins University Press, 2010, pp. 39–60).

2. MacKenzie will reply on 22 April:

   > It's good news that you are interested in letting us see some work. You ask about rights. What the New Yorker buys is all U.S. and Canadian newspaper and magazine rights, but we have a policy against using material that has been published, even when circulation has been extremely limited. I'm afraid we'll have to wait for the story in progress, unless you have unpublished pieces you think might interest us.
   >
   > We have no arbitrary policy on length, but we put such a premium on brevity that we pay twice the rate for the first 2000 words of a manuscript as for the remainder. If you read the magazine, however, you know that the range in length is great. (NLS)

TO PAUL ALLEN, HAMPSTEAD, LONDON,
16 JULY 1957

13, Baldwin Crescent, Camberwell, London, S.E.5
16th July, 1957

My dear Paul,

It was a great joy to read your story NEUTRALITY, and although I hope this is the first chapter of an autobiographical novel, I think it is quite self-contained enough to be published as a story, in fact, just what a first chapter should be. And as a piece of writing it is very arresting indeed, touched with *genius*, an unmistakeable touch which I can't easily define but always know when I come across it. I like the merging of the real event with the fantasy in the child's mind, so that the reader is aware of the distinctions in his own mind, and the unity in the child's. It is very subtle and very well written. Have you sent it to John Lehamann [*sic*], or to the Cornhill as we suggested? I think you should. And also, that you should use this statement as a microcosm, expanding in later chapters.[1]

I am keeping this copy, but will let you have it back if you should want it, when I see you.

It was a happy evening when we called on you. You must ring soon, and we shall have a Sunday evening together.

My book, ROBINSON, is now being typed by a typist. I am writing a story called THE GO-AWAY BIRD to complete my collection, and after that hope to have a rest, and to go to Scotland for a short holiday. Robin will probably have to do his National Service soon.

I have just read MR WESTON'S GOOD WINE for the first time, and am delighted by it. Do you know it? I mean to get some more T. F. Powys books.[2]

All good wishes to Igor – we may see you both soon,[3]
Best love,
s/Muriel

TLScc with typed and autograph annotations by Paul
Allen, and a copy of 'Neutrality' enclosed. NLS.

1. After being Managing Director of the Hogarth Press, John Lehmann set up, with his sister the novelist Rosamond Lehmann, his own publishing house which ran from 1946 to 1953. In 1954, he founded the *London Magazine*, which MS seems to consider an appropriate venue for Allen's work. The *Cornhill Magazine* ran from 1860 to 1975, publishing literary work by an array of celebrated writers. In 1957, its editor was the Lord Byron scholar John 'Jock' Murray.

   In his notes made on Martin Stannard's copy of the present letter, Allen wrote:

   > I think I was lodging with friends at 5 Denning Road, Hampstead and Muriel and Derek came there out of the blue and I was delighted to see them. They often came to Hampstead, probably to see the Braybrookes in Gardnor Road where I attended a very good party with them.
   >   I wrote a series of Irish sketches accepted by W. L. Webb for the Guardian. Muriel was most enthusiastic and encouraging. She persuaded me to show them to both Peter Owen and her own publisher Alan McLean [sic] of Macmillan's. The title she suggested was THE ENGLISH BOY but the Ms was too short for publication as a novel. These publishers decided that I was an essayist and not a novelist but Muriel continued to encourage me.

2. *Mr. Weston's Good Wine* by T. F. Powys was published by Chatto & Windus in 1927.
3. Born of a Russian father and an English mother, Igor Chroustchoff served as a rifleman in World War II and was part of MS's literary circle in London after the war. Derek Stanford will write:

   > Two final names to be mentioned here: Paul Allen [. . .] and his friend Igor Chroustchoff whose father had married Peter Warlock's mistress some time before she committed suicide. Igor celebrates his birthday on Keats's nativity, to which 'season of mists and mellow fruitfulness' he attributed his elegiac nature. Igor remained an agnostic though he had submitted himself for instruction at Farm Street. Muriel said she had these two friends in mind when she wrote *The Bachelors*. (*ITF*, p. 201)

   Later, on 15 May 1959, MS will write to Chroustchoff: 'Are you away for Whitsun? I hope you are translating Laforgue I could not do as you do – maintain an interest in literature without turning it to personal account – but I honour the activity in you & really don't know anyone else who doesn't make a career of it' (Private collection).

   Later still, in 1961, MS will ask Chroustchoff to help her to arrange her archive and papers, then find reasons for this not to come about.

TO JOHN VAN DRUTEN, THERMAL, CALIFORNIA,
17 JULY 1957

13, Baldwin Crescent, Camberwell, London, S.E.5
17th July, 1957

Dear Mr. Van Druten,

It was so nice of you to give Lippincott those kind words, and permission to quote them. I hope you did not mind my suggesting that they refer to you. Since I had your letter I'm afraid I have been showing it off considerably, and really, such encouragement means a great deal to me.[1]

I have just finished reading *The Widening Circle* which I found altogether absorbing; it has set me thinking on so many subjects. I was particularly interested in your belief that 'the best authors never allow hatred or dislike to appear towards their characters.' This is a problem which I find very tantalising. To me, a character one really hates is likely to be the most interesting creatively, and one comes to hate such a character with a kind of savage love. I believe it is a danger – and bad art – when an author hates, and thinks himself justified, righteous. Perhaps the answer is, to make one's fierce prejudices an obvious idiosyncrasy on the narrator's part? I speak, of course, as one trying to master the practical problems of fiction – and perhaps within the limits of satire. As you say, the greatest art sees human nature dispassionately.

I share your sense of awe and fascination for murders. Do you know of the Christie case of about 1950? It had something archetypal about it, like Elizabethan drama. I followed it with horrible avidity day by day – he had put about five corpses under his floor-boards, and let another man hang for one of them – up to his last statement from the condemned cell: 'The cooking here is excellent'. And yet he wasn't the arch-villain type, but a pathetic little soul. When he was asked, did he commit each of these murders? – he continually answered, 'I must have done.'[2]

I am also an addict of *Rebecca of Sunnybrook Farm* and the water-lifts (still in operation) at Folkestone.[3] And of course, I was greatly interested in your chapters on your religious position, particularly in your sense of God's penetration of the world. I could wish you were a Roman Catholic – but that is because I am a Roman Catholic, and it is only my way of wishing you well, as an oriental might say, 'May you live a thousand years!'[4]

My second novel is just finished. I hope you will like it.

With all good wishes, and many thanks for your kindness,

Yours sincerely,

s/Muriel Spark

TLS. NYPL.

1. John Van Druten wrote to MS on 14 April to offer his 'warmest possible congratulations' on her 'extraordinary' writing, which he first encountered in the short story 'The Portobello Road' in *Winter Tales*, no. 2:

    It was a story that fascinated and amazed me, both with its turns of plot, and its very remarkable writing.

    I tried then to find out more about you, and was rewarded by getting your poems 'The Fanfarlo'. These had very much the same effect on me. Now I have just finished your novel 'The Comforters', which has moved and stirred me in just the same way. (Though I do wonder a little about its title – WHO are the Comforters?) (NLS)

    The English-born Van Druten emigrated to the US in 1925 after *Young Woodley*, his first play, was banned by the Lord Chamberlain for its depiction of the love felt by a schoolboy for his headmaster's wife; he subsequently enjoyed great success in the US and the UK with plays that included *The Voice of the Turtle* (1943), *I Remember Mama* (1944), and *I Am a Camera* (1951). His autobiography, *The Widening Circle*, was published in 1957 by Charles Scribner's Sons. He wrote to MS from the A. J. C. Ranch which he had bought with his then partner Carter Lodge and the British actress Auriol Lee.

    On 21 May, MS wrote to Alan Maclean to whom she had forwarded Van Druten's letter: 'I wd. make a copy myself but find it curiously embarrassing to type out fan letters addressed to myself. I suppose this is a twisty form of Pride' (MA).

2. John Christie was a serial killer responsible for the deaths of at least eight individuals; three of the bodies of his victims were found behind the wallpaper in a kitchen alcove, and his wife's remains were found beneath floorboards. He was arrested on 28 March 1953, tried, convicted, and

hanged on 15 July the same year.
3. *Rebecca of Sunnybrook Farm* by Kate Douglas Wiggin was published in 1903.
    Installed in 1885, the Folkestone Leas Lift is a funicular railway that
    employs water and gravity to transport passengers from the seafront to
    the town's promenade above.
4. The review by Lewis Nichols of *The Widening Circle* in the *New York Times
    Book Review* remarked: 'Books are discussed, and such delicacies as sweet
    corn and shad roe, and Mr. Van Druten's own gropings for a religious faith.
    The effect is like listening to an extremely pleasant soliloquy by a man who
    knows what he feels but who would not dream of imposing his feeling on
    anyone else' (13 October 1957).

John Van Druten

TO ALAN BARNSLEY, MAIDSTONE, KENT, 19 JULY 1957

13, Baldwin Crescent, Camberwell, S.E.5
19th July, 1957

My dear Alan,

Thank you very much for sending the prescription for Derek. It was most thoughtful of you, and your kindness alone will cheer him up. I shall probably see him tomorrow, and give it to him. He has been laid up with a cold, to add to his troubles.

I have just finished the fascinating account of Mr. Pinfold's purgatory, and I hope with all my heart that he goes straight to heaven when he dies, for purgatory apart, he writes so well. I was struck by the similarity of the experiences described in the book to my own real ones – for instance, where Pinfold imagines his tormentors to be a band of 'guardians' as in the Cocktail Party. I should think a lot of people will recognise their symptoms, for there isn't much differentiation between minds when they are bats. It can make a good adventure story in retrospect, though.

Now I am going to call myself a member of the Joan of Arc school of writers. It is only right & proper that we Catholics should hear voices and see visions. Did you ever see the nice review Evelyn Waugh wrote of my book? I thought it really kind – I mean, to take so much trouble to understand it – and kind of you, too, to send it to him in the first place. I enclose the review, but please return it for it is a treasure.[1]

I send also, a map of Robinson. It is an island, 84 sq. miles, in the Atlantic owned by a man called Robinson. Alan Maclean is not keen on printing the map as end-papers. But the book really needs it. He says maps annoy people – they have to keep referring back. What do you think?

I'm so glad you are to have three months for writing. That is something to look forward to, and you are sure of getting your book finished in that time. It really is rather a strain having to write *all* the time, I find.

I saw Christine and Jerzy last night. He told me such a funny story about his childhood in Poland, during the first war. A band of great Cossacks raided the village, and one of them raided the church. He emerged with a great deal of loot including a chasuble embroidered with white lilies which he wore over his uniform, and thus garbed, mounted and galloped away. Jerzy's grandfather hastily places his hands over the child's eyes lest he should witness the sacrilege, but he was too late, Jerzy had seen all.[2]

I should love to see your mother's children's book.[3]

Love to Felicity and all her relations,[4]

Ever affectionately,

s/Muriel

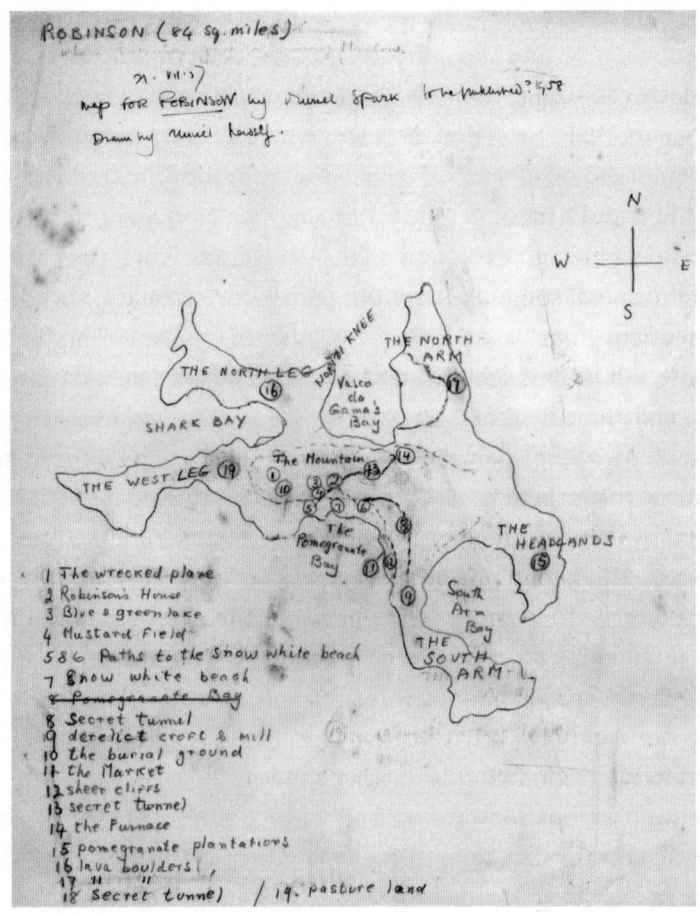

TLS with hand-drawn map. MBC.

1. MS refers to Evelyn Waugh's *The Ordeal of Gilbert Pinfold* and to Waugh's review of *The Comforters* (see 6 November 1956).
2. MS refers to Christine Brooke-Rose and her husband, the Polish-born novelist, poet, and translator Jerzy Peterkiewicz.
3. Alan Barnsley's mother, Katherine Fielding Barnsley, was a distant descendant of the novelist Henry Fielding (from whom Alan Barnsley derived his pen-name); her novel for children is *Mr Paley – Dog About Town* which will be published in November by Hutchinson.
4. Felicity was one of Barnsley's daughters; her 'relations' comprised her four siblings.

TO JOHN VAN DRUTEN, THERMAL, CALIFORNIA, 18 AUGUST 1957

13, Baldwin Crescent, Camberwell, London, S.E.5
18th August, 1957

Dear Mr. Van Druten,

I was delighted to have your letter which arrived just as I was leaving to spend some days in Kent with Gabriel Fielding whom you mention. In private life he is Dr. Alan Barnsley – a medical doctor – and he and his wife are my greatest friends. Alan has had an enormously interesting life, which is to say he lives very intensely. All those characters in his book, including the mother, are drawn from the life. He is hoping one day to give up his practice so that he can concentrate on writing. He is also the doctor for Maidstone prison, and one way and another he seems to act as a magnet for strange experiences. He was delighted to know you had read his last book. I have asked him to let you know about his mother's plays; I think only one was successful in any sense. She is over eighty now, has just written a children's book which is to be published soon, and is writing a novel.[1]

I am to have my first dramatic effort broadcast on the 23rd. It is a short half-hour play. I wonder if you would be interested to see the script? Writing for the wireless was an exciting experiment – one becomes very sound-conscious, while writing, because of the need to concentrate on aural effects and at the same time suggest a visual effect.

I have also come to the end of my summer's work, the novel and a long short story which is to be published with a collection. I am hoping Lippincott will take them also, and I will see that you have copies. I feel, when I have come to the end of a long literary work, limp and useless. I wonder if you have that experience? For a few weeks I seem to forget a lot of my knowledge, and when I meet people, don't know what to say to them. This is the case with me, whether the work is good or not.

I was most amused by your account of meeting the Crippen son.[2] The other day when I was with Alan Barnsley in his car he had to call in to the prison. A man rushed up to us when we stopped inside the gates, and Alan introduced me to him. 'Doctor', said the man, 'you must give me this lady's name and address so that I can get in touch with her when I come out of here.' Later, Alan told me the man is doing twelve years for three attempted murders! They have tried him in one jail after another, and now are trying the more liberal treatment of Maidstone prison. It seemed quite clear to me the man was mad. Very excitable and crazed-looking.

Have you read Evelyn Waugh's new novel, 'The Ordeal of Gilbert Pinfold'? I should like to know what you think of it. It has a 'voices' theme similar to that in my first novel. I don't think it among the best of Waugh's books, for it is too much of a straight case-history to be a work of art, but it is very amusing.

I do hope you will be coming to England soon, and that we can meet. My coming to America is most unlikely at the moment, unless I should have some swoop of success – one never knows. But you come to England, and come and see me at Camberwell.

All kind wishes,
Yours sincerely,
s/Muriel Spark

TLS. NYPL.

1. John Van Druten wrote to MS on 24 July expressing his admiration for Alan Barnsley's novel *In the Time of Greenbloom*, though he added: 'I was not sure, at the end, just what it had all been about, and what the last section was trying to express' (NLS). In his study of the work of Barnsley/Fielding, *Searching Brightness: The Achievement of Gabriel Fielding* (Shoestring Press, 2023), Paul Binding writes, referring to the novel's protagonist, the author's 'virtual alter ago, John Blaydon':

> *In The Time of Greenbloom* is in six strictly sequential sections, each so organically centred on a particular situation with its own commanding personal interchanges and dominant images as to have its own irreducible experiential identity. [. . .] In the last section of the novel, 'Island Summer', set on Anglesey, it is Greenbloom who makes John appreciate that his very unhappiness is a reason for continuing life rather than abandoning it. (Hence the best of all reasons for the novel bearing the title it does.) [. . .] John in truth though cured of his suicidal wishes does not wholly understand what Greenbloom has been trying to inculcate into him, only an important measure of it. But it is left to readers (especially to those who absorb the succeeding book) to realise its truth. (pp. 80, 116, 119)

    Katherine Fielding Barnsley's play for children, *The Great Big World*, described in the *Evening Standard* (28 December 1921) as 'a delightful fantasy', was a success in 1921. On her book for children, see letter of 19 July 1957, n. 4. Her novel in progress would not be published.
2. Dr Crippen was accused, tried, and hanged for the murder of his wife in 1910, on evidence that has since been disputed. In his letter of 24 July, Van Druten explained that living near him in California was Crippen's son Hawley Crippen, and that he had unsuccessfully tried to meet him, fascinated as he was by 'his father's duality'.

TO DEREK STANFORD, HOUNSLOW, MIDDLESEX,
21 AUGUST 1957

13, Baldwin Crescent, Camberwell, London, S.E.5
21ˢᵗ August, 1957

My dear Derek,
    I met Father O'Malley the other evening when I went to visit Teresa, and he advised me to write to you, which accordingly I am very pleased to do.[1]

I hope you are keeping a little better. I was sorry to hear from
Wrey Gardiner that you still had occasional trouble with your
stomach. Fr. O'Malley said he would drop you a line and will be
very pleased to see you for a chat; he knows of cases with your
symptoms and so might even be able to advise you.

Alan Maclean took me to see Edith Sitwell last night. She holds
court at the Sesame Club each evening at six, and dispenses gin
with grapefruit juice and ice. She was really quite a charmer and
very amusing indeed, both consciously and unconsciously.[2] She got
to know a gangster-killer in America who (according to her) was in
reality a public benefactor. As she told the story she kept on mixing
up her idioms – e.g. 'The gal took the stiff . . . . etc.' She told a
wonderful story of her father. A cousin of the Sitwells had written
to his wife (the Sitwells' mother) a letter signed 'Your Tenant and
Well-wisher', informing her that old Sitwell kept a scarlet woman.
After about a week the wife informed him of this letter, though
she herself knew it was a hoax. The old man was furious, and had it
pinned up outside the police station – all about the scarlet woman,
etc. – offering a reward for anyone who disclosed the offender. The
young Sitwells took great pride in this unusual form of publicity.
Dame Edith asked me to come and see her again, but I shall be
gone to Edinburgh. There was a very young blond poet whom she
had just taken up, hanging on her every word. There was a curious
mixture of sycophancy and genuine respect for her, among her circle
of guests. Alan Maclean has her taped, he says she is very shrewd
and sees through everything. I also got that impression. I also got
the impression of her being very warm and kindhearted and *un*-
selfish, besides, of course, being egotistical. A curious complexity,
altogether. She looked very splendid in a gold tunic shot with opal.

I had such a dreadful experience in Church last Sunday, I fairly
took a turn. A man with a very strong *smell* was placed next me.
He kept fidgetting [*sic*] about and brushing against my coat, but
I was praying away and trying to avert my nose from the smell.
When we sat up just before the Sanctus, he still kept fidgetting
[*sic*], and then I noticed he was exposing himself. It is a dreadful
thing for a girl to see in Church when her mind is elsewhere.

However, when I made rapidly to depart, the man saw that the game was up and said, 'Sorry miss, sorry miss,' as he was escorted up the aisle by the sidesmen.

I hope your work is going very well. I am doing nothing special at present. I am going to Edinburgh on Saturday. My mother said she would write to you, and hopes you will be better soon. I shall be returning about the first week in September. I am rather tired, and look forward to the rest.

Teresa asked me to send her love. She is getting much better, though she has had a bad time. Mrs. Lazarri [*sic*] is away in Ireland just now, seeing her daughter who has been ill.

I got a fairly snooty letter from that Dessain saying that the Newman is not an original letter. I wonder if he could be wrong?

Good wishes,

Love,

s/Muriel

TLS. HRC.

1. On Father O'Malley and Teresa Walshe, his niece, see 4 December 1955, n. 1.
2. During the 1950s, Edith Sitwell, who had converted to Catholicism in 1955, lived at The Sesame Club, 49 Grosvenor Street, in London's Mayfair. In a piece entitled 'A Drink with Dame Edith', written for publication in the *Literary Review* more than thirty years later, MS will expand upon her evening with Sitwell, where she describes it as an antidote to her unpleasant first experience with her new literary agent Paul Scott, who, she felt, acted insultingly towards her and her new novel, *Robinson*:

> Inevitably, I came out with my experience that very afternoon with my agent, showing her how he had flicked my typescript at me with his thumb and third finger. She took an intense interest in the story. 'My dear,' she said, 'you must acquire a pair of lorgnettes, make an occasion to see that man again, focus the glasses on him and sit looking at him through them as if he was an insect. Just look and look.' She showed me with her own eyeglasses, which were hanging on one of the chains around her neck, how it was done. (*TGF*, p. 150)

TO DEREK STANFORD, HOUNSLOW, MIDDLESEX,
22 AUGUST 1957

13, Baldwin Crescent, Camberwell, S.E.5
22 Aug. 1957

My dear Derek,

I was very pleased that you liked the *Go-Away Bird* and thank
you for your critique. As far as style is concerned I had a vague
'French' style in mind. I think one of the things I wanted to
convey was the destruction of innocence.[1] Another aim was
to contrast different social groups, and so demonstrate how
illusions are destroyed – I mean, such illusions as Colonials hold
about the home country; and also, to show the selfishness of the
individuals.

I have just finished reading *Herself Surprised* and myself am
surprised by its high quality, considering one does not hear a
great deal about Joyce Carey. I thought his language, or idiom,
perfect for the narrator, and the whole extremely subtle. Just at
times I thought it sentimental – Royzie's dying in a workhouse,
for instance, but perhaps this is just my anti-Dickensian prejudice.
If you should come by Penguin editions of any of his other novels
please do not forget me, and I shall return them in good order.[2]

I was very pleased to have *Good Behaviour* into which I have been
dipping with pleasure. I hope to read it through on my holiday.[3]

I am leaving on Saturday morning, and will be in Edinburgh for
ten days or a fortnight, if you would like to write. I hope you will
write to my mother as usual. No-one, she declares, understands
her so well as you, and I believe she is right.

I am making an effort with the story *The Black Madonna*, but it
goes slowly, for I think I have written rather too much in the past
few months, and need a rest.

I hear you were at St. Albans and hope you were refreshed
by that good place. I should like a trip there before the chill of
autumn sets in. I was sorry to hear you had a bad cold, and hope it
has cleared up.

By the way, I have not seen June and Neville since last I saw
you, nor heard from them. I feel better to leave well alone.

Poor Bluebell's skin seems to be taking a bad turn again, though
she does not scratch. She flourishes only in the steady sunny
weather – a true daughter of Persia.

I enclose *Theology*. Please forward to Fr. Brocard when you have
perused it.[4]

I should be pleased to know what you are writing & how your
novel progresses. Patricia is writing a novel, I hear.[5]

Best love,

Muriel

P.S. Who is the author of 'Pale Horse, Pale Rider?' I remember
reading it, in Africa, when it was published in Penguin New
Writing, and was highly impressed.[6]

ALS. HRC.

1. When asked in 1998 by Martin McQuillan about a possible influence of the
nouveau roman on her work – the term had been coined earlier in 1957 to
cover the work of several French writers of the time, mostly published by
the Éditions de Minuit – MS responded: 'I was thinking the same thoughts
that they were thinking, people like Robbe-Grillet. We were influenced
by the same, breathing the same informed air. So, I naturally would have a
bent towards the *nouveau roman* but in fact I was very influenced by Robbe-
Grillet' ('"The Same Informed Air": An Interview with Muriel Spark', in
Theorizing Muriel Spark, ed. Martin McQuillan, Palgrave, 2002, p. 216).
     In 'Body and State in Spark's Early Fiction', Michael Gardiner writes:

> Her first novel, *The Comforters*, turns to the anti-realist *nouveau roman*,
> particularly Alain Robbe-Grillet's *Les Gommes* (1953, tr. 1966). *The
> Comforters* picks up on the way the *nouveau roman* had shaken the
> stable and discrete perspective of classical realism, to leave narration
> open to viewpoints that change according to the object described –
> a powerful comment on the universalist certainties which reached
> their zenith in logical positivism. *Nouveau roman* theorists described
> a destruction of myths of depth and of cinematic ideologies of
> perception programmed to arrange objects relative to the observ-
> ing eye giving us the sense that the visible world belongs to us as
> consumers. The *nouveau roman* looked, in other words, for a less
> mimetic and more didactic method, less dependent on apparently

intuitive certainties and so more actively critical. (Michael Gardiner and Willy Maley, eds., *The Edinburgh Companion to Muriel Spark*, Edinburgh University Press, 2010, pp. 28–9)

Further on the influence of the *nouveau roman* on Spark's work, see James Bailey, '"Drama[s] of Exact Observation": Spark and the *Nouveau Roman*', in *Muriel Spark's Early Fiction* (pp. 103–41).

2. Joyce Carey, the author of more than fifteen novels, whose work dealt extensively with Africa, was born in Belfast and died in March 1957; his novel *Herself Surprised*, first in his 'First Trilogy', was published in 1941. MS will later collaborate with his son, the musician Tristram Cary, on musical adaptations of her work.

3. MS was reading Harold Nicolson's *Good Behaviour: Being a Study of Certain Types of Civility*, published by Constable in 1955.

4. The then monthly (now bi-monthly) journal *Theology* was edited by the Anglican priest Alec Vidler. August's issue was volume 50, no. 446. MS had come to know Father Brocard Sewell at Aylesford monastery where he was a friar. He is described by Martin Stannard as 'A worldly fellow who ran a press and founded a literary journal, the *Aylesford Review* (1955–68). Later he started the *Antigonish Review*. Both were well regarded as "little magazines". He also had, Neville Braybrooke thought, "a real vocation to get on with very tarty girls and remain a very religious man at the same time"' (*MSB*, p. 162).

   Fiona MacCarthy's obituary in *The Guardian* portrays a man of vast literary appetite and talent, as well as of broad and often controversial acquaintance: 'Brocard was a stalwart companion, with a celibate's antennae for the sexual and emotional upheavals of his friends. Têtes-à-têtes in out-of-the-way tearooms were his speciality and he amazed my teenage son by demanding two double vermouths in a pub. He once made the comment that "perhaps most of us have, at least potentially, something of the decadent in us"' (2 April 2000).

5. In January, Derek Stanford had begun to write a novel whose working title was 'Goodbye Bohemia: An Idyll'. In it he dramatized his relations with MS, who is portrayed as the character Susan and who, Stannard judges, 'is regarded as an accessory'. Of the unfinished work, Stanford would later remark (to Stannard) that he '"felt even more of a silly bugger than he had taken himself to be"' (*MSB*, p. 113).

   Patricia Hutchins published *James Joyce's Dublin* with Grey Walls Press earlier in 1957; no record has been found of the publication of her novel.

6. *Pale Horse, Pale Rider* by Katherine Anne Porter recounts the experience of suffering and survival during the 1918 influenza pandemic. It was published not in the Penguin New Writing series but rather in the Winter 1938 edition of Louisiana State University's *Southern Review*; in 1939, it was collected in an eponymous volume, along with two other of Porter's short novels, and published by Harcourt, Brace & Company.

TO DEREK STANFORD, HOUNSLOW, MIDDLESEX,
27 AUGUST 1957

160, Bruntsfield Place, Edinburgh
27ᵗʰ Aug, 57

My dear Derek
   Thank you very much for your letter and most impressive
article. I was pleased with the review.[1] I think your point about
Newman's extremism quite a considerable one, but would add
the observations that 1) while in the R. C. Church he preached
moderation to many, including the *Rambler* group, and indeed
tried to represent in himself a via media between the Ward
faction and Acton's group; 2) he himself was, I think, irked by
any imposition of moderation upon himself while an R. C. He
complained of being put on the shelf, which I think meant just
that his views about so many things were regarded as outré or
extreme; 3) Can a man who brings great new ideas to the world
and his age, avoid being, in some aspects, an 'extremist'? I think,
if I may say so, your argument is not fully supported in your
reference to the other members of his family and their religious
turns. I mean, unless you think of the Church of England at that
particular time, as representing a norm from which they all, with
the exception of the daughters, departed. The religious lives of
Frank & Charles were fairly typical of middle class families at that
time.[2] The C. of E. was even then in flux (many say, so it should
always be). I think, too, that if Newman's extremism is to be
proved by the actions of his family, you cannot leave the daughters
out of account. The daughters of Evangelical families were usually
the very first, if they took a religious turn, as N. said, to depart
from their Mother Church, drawn by the spiritual vitality of other
sects.
   You make a good point in your letter to the editor, about
Lead Kindly Light. Of course, the bird may have meant that N
was 'prophetic' at the time of writing, but if so, he should have
said so.[3]

I think your article very good indeed. So much of what you say of Newman's character is true, and any tendency to suppress this material, or overlook it, can not ultimately serve his cause, or lead to the best being got out of Newman's work.

My mother was delighted to have your letter, especially as she is very upset at the moment. We are having a sad time of it with Robin. He has all of a sudden — with alarming suddenness — turned against us all. He accuses Grannie of ruining his life, and says, once he leaves home for the Army he will never return, etc. I won't go into it all, but we are trying to be as nice to him as possible. There is no doubt in my mind that he is undergoing a breakdown. His father has been seeing him every day for the past three months, and I think has been a bad influence, both consciously and unconsciously, (for morbidity is contagious). Poor Robin, he is like Prince Hamlet, making the wildest accusations against my mother & me. I suggested to him he might have overworked, and strained his nerves, but of course he flared up — what was I trying to suggest? etc . . .

Perhaps you will remember Robin & all of us in your prayers. I am staying here for a fortnight, and really feel I should try to stay as long as my mother needs me. Now that she has lost her friend Peggy she has no-one to confide in. My father is very good. He keeps quiet & tries to say nothing — as indeed we all do — to start Robin off. It is all a bit of a nightmare. I intend to do some work if possible. It is the only way to keep steady.

I saw — with Robin — *The Admirable Chrighton* [sic] — which was a charming period-piece-film, but not nearly so good as The Importance of Being Earnest. Barrie had a streak of vulgarity in his act — or, I should say, a basic mean untruthful touch (which emerges as whimsy) — which Wilde never had so far as his act was concerned.[4]

We are going into the country by bus to-day — all four of us — hoping that Robin may cheer up. You never know, he may get over this.

I hope all goes well with your work. Let me see the poems, I should like that. I hope you will continue your novel.

I was very pleased to know of your Middleton Murry in Essays in Criticism & hope it has success at other sources too.[5] And that you are keeping in with the Jesuits!

Best love,

Muriel

P.S. If you feel like dropping Rob a casual line, please do so, of course, not mentioning the present trouble.

ALS. HRC.

1. It is not known which article MS was sent. *Letters of John Henry Newman*, edited by MS and Derek Stanford and recently published by Peter Owen, was reviewed by A. J. Cornwell in the *Tablet* (24 August 1957).
2. John Henry Newman had two younger brothers, Francis William (Frank) and Charles Robert.
3. It is not known to which journal Stanford had written.
4. J. M. Barrie's 1902 comic stage play *The Admirable Crichton* became a film (for the second time) in 1957, directed by Lewis Gilbert and starring Kenneth More and Diane Cilento. Oscar Wilde's 1895 play *The Importance of Being Earnest* was adapted for cinema by Anthony Asquith, the film being released in 1952 starring Michael Redgrave and Edith Evans. For a further and different assessment of MS's debt to J. M. Barrie, see Cairns Craig, 'Muriel Spark and J. M. Barrie', in *The Crooked Dividend: Essays on Muriel Spark*, ed. Gerard Carruthers and Helen Stoddart (Scottish Literature International, 1922; henceforth in the notes *TCD*), pp. 103–25.
5. Derek Stanford's essay 'Middleton Murry as Literary Critic' will be published in *Essays in Criticism* (vol. 8, no.1, January 1958).

TO DEREK STANFORD, HOUNSLOW, MIDDLESEX,
30 AUGUST 1957

[Bruntsfield, Edinburgh]
30th Aug. 1957

My dear Derek,

I am glad to say we are all very much jollies. Robin seems to have got over his turn. I bought him a nice little portable wireless as a prize, only hoping that the Fates will readjust my bank balance.

Have you seen the Pelican *Victorian Prose* edited by Kenneth & Miriam Allott? In their biographical notes (p.310) they say of Newman, 'He is the only Victorian preacher whose sermons are certainly literature.' And they recommend '. . . the neglected collections of *Sermons*.' Should you feel like distilling this information blande et suaviter into Peter Owen's ear, please do so, it might pep up his ideas on the subject.[1]

I stopped in bed all yesterday and wrote the remaining 5,000 words of The Black Madonna which I am going to attempt to sell to *Winter's Tales*.

I have a loan of an old typewriter which I sold to a sucker who lives nearby several years ago for twelve pounds. Now I dare not raise my voice against it.

I am quite pleased with the *Black Madonna*, it is my contribution to a) the coloured question and 2) the new upper-prolly art. If you would like to see a carbon, let me know.[2]

I shall be here all next week. Robin is going away next week to the seaside for a holiday with his father. I hope this won't upset him again. I expect the idea of the call-up looming ahead is depressing for a youth.[3]

I look forward to seeing your poems & hearing your news.

The weather here is cold, damp, bleak. I have forgotten to bring Ian's address, and forget the name of the people he stayed with before, so can't trace him. If you let me have it I will try to look him up.[4]

I had a card from Neville to say they are off to Italy. They enjoyed *The Party through the Wall*. June's novel *Every Eye* is appearing in French and possibly Italian.[5]

I hear from friends of my mother who have relatives in London that there were some radio press notices of the play, but I haven't seen any, of course. Have you? The rehearsals, to which I went, were quite a palaver. They start early in the morning & go on all day, on the date of the broadcast, till they do it live on the air. Rayner is infinitely patient, and the actors struck me as being rather stupid, on the whole. Rayner was asking for you, perhaps you will be seeing him. I like him very much, the more I see of him.[6]

Love,
Muriel

ALS. HRC.

1. *The Pelican Book of English Prose: 5. Victorian Prose 1830–1880*, edited by Kenneth and Miriam Allott, was published by Penguin Books in 1956.

   A book consisting of a selection of Cardinal Newman's sermons had been proposed by Stanford and MS to the publisher Peter Owen.

   MS borrows the Latin 'blande et suaviter' from the episode in Newman's life when he was officially to be permitted to establish himself in Oxford but unofficially to be prevented from doing so. In her introduction to *Letters of John Henry Newman*, she writes: 'While permission was granted for the mission to proceed, the Bishop of Birmingham was given a secret instruction by Cardinal Barnabo, the Prefect of Propaganda, that in the event of Newman himself going to reside at Oxford, he should be "blandly and suavely" recalled' (p. 143).

2. In the closing pages of 'The Black Madonna', a white couple give birth to a Black child, after praying for a baby to the Black Madonna in their local church; the story deals with racism, class, and how these incite varying kinds and intensities of snobbery.

3. National Service in the UK's armed forces started in 1947 and would end only in 1960; all able-bodied men between the ages of seventeen and twenty-one were required to serve for a duration of eighteen months.

4. Ian Hamilton Finlay.

5. The first broadcast of a radio play by MS, *The Party through the Wall*, took place on the BBC Third Programme on 23 August.

   June Braybrooke's *Every Eye*, issued under her pen-name Isobel English, was published in 1956 by André Deutsch, winning praise from, among others, John Betjeman and Stevie Smith.

6. The novelist and poet Rayner Heppenstall, who worked as a writer and producer for BBC Radio for twenty years from 1945, was instrumental in encouraging MS to write for radio, as MS mentions in a letter of 2 March to Alan Maclean: 'I had a letter from Rayner Heppenstall asking me to write for sound broadcasting. I shall be seeing him in the next few days. In the meantime would you send him, c/o Features Department., B.B.C., a copy of THE COMFIES, and I may be able to persuade him to do a programme from it, with lots of voices and noises off? I will tell him it is coming to him' (MA).

When her radio plays are later published along with new stories in *Voices at Play: Stories and Ear-Pieces*, in the book's introduction she will explain: 'The plays were written at the suggestion of Mr. Rayner Heppenstall for the Third Programme' (Macmillan, 1961, v). In an internal BBC memo dated 28 May, Heppenstall wrote: 'This script, originally commissioned for the next series of "Writing for Radio", is now complete and has been accepted. [. . .] Muriel Spark has not written for broadcasting in this way before. She is a gifted writer and she has now taken to writing exclusively for a living. I had, I think I may say, built up in her a good deal of interest in the medium, and the script she has written seems to me quite first-rate' (BBC WAC).

Derek Stanford offered this portrait of Heppenstall:

> Muriel's most interesting non-Catholic friend at that period was Rayner Heppenstall, a literary all-rounder who set a personal stamp on everything he wrote. He had come her way in his capacity as a Third Programme producer, having suggested to her that she write some playscripts for radio [. . .] Heppenstall himself I found of interest. He had transformed prejudice into a system of thought all his own. I loved to hear him fulminate against the South as being compact of snobbery, simony and sodomy. The best of England, according to him, lay North of the Wash (Heppenstall was born in Huddersfield). The natural religion of the English people – as opposed to the Establishment – was to be found in non-conformist chapels, or in the faith of old Yorkshire and Lancashire families. He liked to parade this point of view, though he himself was a rationalist agnostic. (*ITF*, pp. 201–2)

TO DEREK STANFORD, HOUNSLOW, MIDDLESEX, 2 SEPTEMBER 1957

160, Bruntsfield Place, Edinburgh
2nd September 1957

Dear Pumpernickel,

Many thanks for your plump epistle. I read my mother that piece of it which pertained to Robin's 'being a person of fine parts' and thus more susceptible than the grosser orders of being; and she expresses herself greatly consoled by these words, and declares that Derek speaks like a Judge.

Robin has gone off to Dunbar with his father for a week. Dunbar is a seaside resort. We are saving your letter for his

return. We are hoping that the sea air will refresh him. His
moods continue to veer, but I think my attitude to him has a
more settling effect than my mother's, although my mother is in
many ways the more devoted. I simply say to him, 'Robin, you're
a pain in the neck,' and such like, while my mother is inclined to
weep. It is difficult to describe the course of Robin's antagonism,
or its type, in a letter, but it doesn't resemble anything I have
experienced before, and I can only observe certain new attitudes
(new to him) which are his father's too; whether this is something
latent in him now appearing, or whether it is merely an influence
lately acquired, I don't know. He will be called up quite soon, and
I think it a good thing for him to get away from *everybody*.

My main worry, really, is my mother. She takes these things so
badly – makes the great mistake of putting all her hopes on Robin
or (as previously) my brother. She has a powerful loving nature,
very sacrificial, and simply lays herself on the altar. Fortunately,
she can treat me as more of a friend because she does not dote
upon me quite so much as on the male progeny.

All this between ourselves. It is quite a study, if one does not
become overwhelmed, but only partially involved. I sometimes
wonder what histrionic pictures are passing through my mother's
mind when she says, e.g. 'All the Citizens of Edinburgh would
arise to deny Robin's accusations.' – I suddenly see a mediaeval
matriarch at the head of a procession, the Mayor and Corporation,
and a theatrical group of 'citizens' as in a Shakespearean historical
play. Robin seems to know by instinct the way to get her down.
He says things like, 'Well I'll say this, at least, you've supplied me
with good food,' as if it were a boarding house.

Of course I have been pushing on with my work as much
as possible, as I don't think I can contribute very much to any
argument. Robin rang up the evening he arrived at Dunbar, and
apologized. The poor boy is in a nervous state, doesn't know quite
what he thinks, and, as I say, it may be the best thing for him to
get away from his family for a while. My father, by the way, is
marvellous – takes no part at all in any of the transactions, simply
reads the paper.

Did I thank you for Joyce Cary's *A Fearful Joy*? I shall treat myself to this very soon.[1] I have just finished typing my *Black Madonna*, and sent it off to Macmillan for Winter's Tales (I hope). I enclose one of a new batch of cuttings (which please return) about the reprint of The Comforters, which I think is somewhat apocryphal. I have written to ask Alan Maclean whether this is to be interpreted in the literal or the diplomatic sense. I didn't know it had been reviewed on Woman's Hour, did you?[2]

Also enclosed is a cutting from the Times re. Ronald Knox. I thought the anecdote in the last paragraph might be useful. If you have a spare carbon of your article I should *very much* like to have it. Do you want me to return the Newman article in the C.E.N.?[3] I am enclosing my Black Madonna & would like it back when you have read it, as I shall probably send a carbon to America. Would you think this suitable for the Atlantic Monthly or New Yorker? If you would be kind, and send me the address of the *Atlantic Monthly* I would be most obliged. I did not bring my ref. books or equipment, for I did not intend to stay so long. I shall be back, I think, on the 10th.

I wonder if I could try Evergreen Review with certain fantastic items like Pawnbroker's Wife & House of the Famous Poet? I would not really call them 'previously published' – at least I could get away with it, I think – since they have only appeared in the Norseman. Many thanks for this handy tip. When I return I shall send some things, including Lavishes Ghast.[4]

I was not thinking of Kenneth Allot [*sic*] being anything special, only of a Pelican Book being an impressive thing to Peter. He would judge it the authority of authorities, my dear, but I leave it to you.

Thank you for Ian's address. I suppose he has no phone number? Anyway, I shall call, some time, and send in my report.

Among my batch of press cuttings is one signed Maryvonne Butcher – but it is in German! In the same batch she reviews June's book Every Eye. I am dying to get it translated to see what Auntie Maryvonne has been saying about us. No-one of our acquaintance here reads German – besides, it might be so *bad* I wouldn't like to let my mum down in front of her pals, should she find one of them to translate it. Do you know of any educated person? If so, perhaps I could send it to you for translation.[5]

I think what you say of religious inertia very good, especially as it applies to Newman. In other ways it may be analogous to 'Industrial inertia' – an economists' term – where you find an industry (such as the potteries in the midlands) continuing in a place long after the natural resources (such as the clay, etc.) have been exhausted.

My mother sends her dearest love. She will write you when she settles down a bit. I hope your tum behaves.

Best love,

Mollie Moonflower

P.S. It might be a good idea, eventually, for you to publish a vol. of essays called 'obituaries', – i.e. articles written on various writers immediately after their death. – I think these would have, necessarily, a particular *tone*. You have Middleton Murry, Dylan Thomas, Wyndham Lewis, Joyce Cary, etc. – What do you think?

P.P.S. I wd. like to know that your novel progresses.

ALS. HRC.

1. Joyce Cary's *A Fearful Joy* was published in 1949 and reissued in Penguin paperback in 1955.
2. *Woman's Hour* was (and remains) a feature of BBC Radio.
3. MS is probably referring first to the obituary of Ronald Knox that appeared in *The Times* on 26 August; then to an unidentified article by Derek Stanford; and finally to a page in the *CEN* of 23 August that included a review of *Letters of J. H. Newman* by R. E. C. Houghton and a long article about Newman by Stanford entitled 'An Un-English Leader of the Oxford Movement'.
4. All three are short stories.
5. Maryvonne Butcher's article 'Eine neue Generation englischer Schriftstellerinnen?' appeared in *Dokumente für übernationale Zusammenarbeit*, vol. 4, 1957, pp. 370–2.

TO JOHN VAN DRUTEN, NEW YORK,
5 SEPTEMBER 1957

[Bruntsfield Place, Edinburgh]
as from 13, Baldwin Crescent, Camberwell, London, S.E.5
5th September, 1957

My dear Mr. John van Druten,

I am in Edinburgh with my parents at the moment, and your
two letters have been sent on to me. How kind of you to send that
first review! I am delighted with it, perhaps most of all because
Lippincott are at present considering two new manuscripts of
mine – the novel and the book of stories – and favourable reviews
may have a favourable influence upon them.[1]

I still find a certain difficulty in getting my type of work past
the publishers, to the public. Once the work is published things
are much easier, for it seems to appeal to quite a lot of people, and
then the publishers forget their earlier complaints and hesitations.
I had enormous difficulty with Macmillan over 'The Comforters',
they wanted me to change it, said it was far too odd, etc. Some
of these criticisms may be true, of course, but one can't change
a whole book – and also, I feel I must try out my own forms
of expression. Well, after the critics began to praise the book
Macmillan said they always knew it would be like that, etc.
Now, it has all begun again. They say my new novel is all right,
but nothing like the last one, etc . . . But the fact is, I don't ever
want to write a book which is 'like the last one'. However, this
is just one of those obstacles in life, and I appreciate all the more
encouragement such as yours, for I feel you are receptive in a
special way to new ideas and forms in literature.

I too, was profoundly disturbed by MISS LONELYHEARTS,
it is a desperate sort of book, the dead end of cynicism. I haven't
read Nathaniel West's other writings.[2] I have just been reading
Joyce Cary's HERSELF SURPRISED which I thought very
impressive, and am going to read more of his work.

I was sorry to know you had been ill. Your letters sound so

jolly, I am sure you must be on the mend, and do hope to hear of your starting a new play on one of the themes which have been teasing you.[3]

I have an idea going round my mind for a new novel called MEMENTO MORI. Everyone in it is over seventy. I have written the opening pages, but don't at all know where it is going to lead. I wish to experiment with the time-factor, or rather partly to ignore it, so that a character who may have died at one stage in the story is represented, say two weeks later, as carrying on his normal life; and yet, the character would not be a ghost. My main problem is, whether I should make clear to the reader what I am doing, or simply let the irrationality be an accepted thing. I think the irrational is acceptable if it is consistent. I hate to ram home my ideas with explanations. Perhaps I may send you a few pages when I get further on with it, to let you see better what I mean?

It is kind of you to look at my short play. It was very favourably received, but I noticed lots of flaws which I think I could avoid in a second attempt. I am sending it to you by separate post.[4]

I am 'Mrs.' Spark, having been married a long time ago to a man who turned out to be a mental case. I was divorced from him very shortly afterwards. He is still in a mental home, and my mother sees him occasionally, though I am advised to keep out of the way. – This by way of explaining the 'Mrs.' but I do not mind being addressed 'Miss' or 'Muriel', whichever you prefer.

My parents' home here in Edinburgh is rather jolly but fairly fantastic, I will tell you all about it some day. It is rather a relaxation for me to come here. The Festival has been on, but I have not been to any concerts or plays, for honestly, I need a rest from 'culture' occasionally. I have been buying clothes, of which I am very fond.

I do hope you will be quite well soon.

Yours very sincerely,

s/Muriel Spark

TLS. NYPL.

1. With his letter to MS of 30 August, John Van Druten enclosed the review of *The Comforters*, signed 'M. L.', which had appeared in New York in the *Saturday Review* (31 August 1957) and which concluded: 'This is the author's first novel, though she has written considerable criticism and poetry, and it displays a degree of polish not customarily found in an initial effort.' Of the review, Van Druten wrote: 'It is actually quite nice – almost very nice – though its placement in the magazine is not as good as the book deserves, and I do not feel that sufficient tribute or attention has been paid to your talents' (NLS).

    George Stevens, Managing Editor at MS's American publisher Lippincott, wrote to Rache Lovat Dickson at Macmillan, also on 30 August:

    > Our edition of THE COMFORTERS by Muriel Spark is just out, and while it is early in the game to say anything about its prospects, we do seem to be starting out with indications of a good press. Next Sunday's Times Book Review has a very favorable review indeed, the last paragraph of which reads as follows: 'THE COMFORTERS, in fact, has two prime qualities. It is both enjoyable and memorable. Trend-watchers are advised to note the name of Muriel Spark. Before very long they may be able to boast that they read her when.' Also, the *Saturday Review* gives it a very nice, though inconspicuous, notice. We shall hope for the best. (MA)

2. Nathaniel West's novella *Miss Lonelyhearts* was published in 1933. In his letter of 23 August, Van Druten wrote: 'And this morning I started MISS LONELYHEARTS and am deeply shocked by it, and by its writing. And I just don't know where to turn next' (NLS).

3. In his letter of 23 August, Van Druten wrote that he had been seriously ill for about nine months and that, although he was recovering, he was finding it difficult to write:

    > I have had thoughts for possible new plays, but they will keep denying themselves to me at the last. Either they turn into nice well-made conventional plays, which are no longer of any use to me – (the same is true of novels: a good novel is no good to me any more – I found that out over ANGEL by Elizabeth Taylor, just finished – a book has to be a novel AND something else, some sort of extra and odd experience. Your novel was. So few are.) – or they refuse to spread themselves into that other dimension that I need. (NLS)

4. The play MS wished to send was *The Party through the Wall*.

TO DEREK STANFORD, HOUNSLOW, MIDDLESEX,
7 SEPTEMBER 1957

Edinburgh
7-9-57

My dear Chopsticks,

I return your Betjeman piece which is perceptive, well-written, and delightful in its choice of quotation.[1] You say much in short space. I was struck by the resemblance of his verse to some Georgian poetry – I think in the subject matter. But he is not afraid to *pile it on*, and not sentimental like the Georgians. They were fond of urban scenes and place-names without fully exploiting the poetry of these items. If I had a book of Georgian verse here I could be more specific about the poets. I like very much your adherence throughout to the text in hand, without being tangled up in it. Those extremely textual critics make me think of a fly being caught on the fly-paper, whereas the critic should be a bee alighting on a flower, & making off with the pollen, without damaging the flower. Well, you are my best bee as an essayist, and as Procurer of Books from Time and Tide, for which I am uncommonly grateful.[2]

I was pleased with your reaction to the *Black Madonna*, for I was not too sure of it. I have sent it to the New Yorker as a first go. Many thanks for the addresses, and for the tip about the New York Review. I shall have a big sending-out when I get home.

I laughed at the Archbishop's trick on the Religious Press, and also at your own crack against Their Graces in your obituary of Ronald Knox.[3] You do not say if we can have the Maryvonne review translated. I will try Christine & Jerzy if you know of no reader of German.

I heard from Herbert Corby, now in New York, who sent me some advance cuttings of The Comfies now published there. The reviews are good. Herbert is very amusing in his sardonic Cockney way, about the habits of the natives. Polish waitresses keep telling him how to speak English. He calls it a 'great illiterate adventure'.[4]

I have been asked to speak to the University of Birmingham English Club in December, on some subject of literary interest. They pay travelling & overnight expenses but *no fee*. Therefore, I think, no. What do you think? It would take me a week to prepare a paper, and unless I hit on some subject which I could sell later as an essay, it would be rather an expensive affair. Any advice & suggestions welcomed.

Robin returns from his holiday tomorrow. He telephoned several times & seems to be enjoying the sea-side part of it, but finding his father a handful. I think he needs more companionship from boys his own age & will get it in the army.

We had a lot of ladies to tea the other day – the prospective legatees of the Will. It was an absolute corker of an occasion. The old housekeeper said, 'Weel, Mʳˢ Camberg, when I got yon' letter from yon' lawyer I said to mysel' 'Weel, the deil's aye guid tae his ain'.' (i.e. 'The devil's always good to his own.') There was also a wee hunchback called Mary who has been left £50. She declared herself to be 'fair awa' wi ma'self.' This Mary is a great favourite of Robin. Apparently she lavishes sweets and presents upon him, which is embarrassing for my mum, for Mary is getting on in years and only a 'working girl.' But, as Mary says, 'I may be defor-r-rmed but I'm aye guid to the bairns.' My mother is tickled by Mary, because she makes free of the best houses in the town, and is received where grander persons are refused, and no-one dare close their doors to Mary, even if they would.

I called on Ian but found him out, and so left a note.⁵ I went in fear & trembling because Rose Street is one of our eighteenth-century narrow alley-ways, and the razor-slashings & bag-snatchings that go on in Rose Street, you would not believe. However, I emerged unscathed. Ian rang up while I was out & had a chat with my mum. He rang again this morning (& found me in), but apparently he is living out of Edinburgh at the moment, so whether we can arrange to meet or not I don't know. He is to ring again tomorrow. He sounded rather depressed, but says he is quite well.

I had dinner last night with Alison Foster (former English

mistress whom you met once at the Poetry Society). She told me an amusing tale about a relative of hers who tried to persuade a worthy old aunt in Aberdeen to accompany him to one of J. M. Barrie's plays. 'He's a good playwright,' he said. 'Aye, Willy,' said the old lady, 'but he doesna' come o' good stock.'[6]

I return on Tuesday, by day, arriving 4.20. I will let you know how I fare with old Ian.

Best love,
Lotus Lolliepop

ALS. HRC.

1. Derek Stanford's writing on John Betjeman will give rise to his 1961 publication, *John Betjeman: A Study* (Neville Spearman).
2. *Time and Tide* was a weekly British magazine founded in 1920, publishing many writers whose work MS read.
3. Stanford's obituary of Ronald Knox, possibly unsigned, has not been found.
4. MS published work by the poet Herbert Corby in the January–February 1948 issue of the *Poetry Review*.
5. Ian Hamilton Finlay.
6. As a schoolteacher at James Gillespie's School, the 'indefatigable and enthusiastic' Alison Foster (as MS describes her in *CV*, p. 60) had been instrumental in encouraging MS's budding interest in writing poetry. She stayed in touch with MS, writing to her of her own nervous breakdown in the early 1950s.

Muriel Spark, 1960

TO DEREK STANFORD, HOUNSLOW, MIDDLESEX,
12 SEPTEMBER 1957

13, Baldwin Crescent, Camberwell, S.E.5
Sept. 12. '57 Feast of Our Lady's Birthday

My dear Pussboots,

You have not sent me WILLIAM BLAKE & OUR LADY, of
which I have the highest anticipations, I also hope to see THE
FORTUNES OF ROMANTICISM when available.[1]

I returned to find the four biographies from T & T awaiting me.
The [*sic*] are my tweenie books (i.e. in-between, as the in-between
maid was called Tweenie). I shall read them twixt other work.[2]
Apparently the report about my reprint was incorrect, but the
book has been reviewed twice more on the BBC – once on the

Home & once on Women's Hour. I didn't hear either and didn't care much, but I'm glad it is being canvassed to all classes.[3]

Ball of Tower Bridge is giving some trouble – says I still owe him an option – (P. P. & H. were trying to re-claim the book from him). I have the impression that when we wound up with him we settled the option question. Have you any recollections of our transactions? I should be grateful for them. I have unearthed a letter from him in which he says 'I feel that in all the circumstances it would be better to sever my association with you and your husband . . .' which is as good as declining any further books, don't you think? If a publisher says he wants to sever his association with an author, obviously he doesn't want any more books from the author. 'Husband' by the way is none other than Pussboots himself, and which honorary title I have tactfully explained to Pearn Pollinger.[4]

I saw Ian at last, at the top of a winding stair, very murky and Russian. He sat there at the table like a cross between a character in Chekov and a working-class Glaswegian, waiting for his 'tea', being cooked for him by Lesley. Lesley is a slim, pale, coffee-bar-type girl, very agreeable and consumptive looking, but not very interesting. I think she falls for Ian's old jaw about the artist and his Needs. He spoke of Marion, rather sorry for her. He did not say much of Janet. He said, with a sort of mischievous grin, that he had written you a letter, 'awful mixed-up', and didn't know what you'ld think of it.[5]

He got better but has had a relapse; is nothing like so bad as he was at first, though. He chucked the clinic, but is going back when it re-opens, but he is going to ask for a male psychiatrist. He feels too 'considerate' towards a woman to be able to tell her what he feels, – which I think is a sign of his being not too ill. He gets £4.2.0 a week from the N.H. and N.A.B.[6] He is moving this week to a new flat which is very posh, with frigidaires [sic] and what not. Lesley is moving there too, I don't know what the set-up is. We talked about the Festival & agreed it had very little to do with us. His new address is

11, Belford Mews, Edinburgh 4.

He lent me The Ballad of the Sad Café for which I was most grateful. If you know this rare item, do tell me your thoughts on the same.[7]

I rang Wrey, and heard that Cynthia has departed with retinue to her mother to think things over. A very good idea. Wrey wants me to visit him, but I fear for my virtue, and will probably make some excuse to meet him outside.

Robin returned much the better from his holiday. He confided in me that my mother 'gets on his nerves' a bit with her strange predictions and dream-warnings, her lamentations over my brother, her showing-off of him (Robin) to all the callers – who are, I must admit, a lot of 'tickets'. It took *me* a long time to appreciate the ménage. Unfortunately, Rob exaggerates – which is understandable, he wants to drive home his point. He claims that my mother is the cause of his failing his exams, which really I don't believe. My mother has been far more considerate to Robin than she ever was to my brother & me. However, Rob is making himself cheerful & waiting for his army call-up, which I daresay is a cloud hanging over him. I have no doubt the sea-side holiday saved him from a breakdown, for he was really very tense before he went away, and was much more relaxed on his return.[8]

Thanks for the tip about Brontës as Teachers. I shall adopt this suggestion & send it for approval. I would never have thought of this in a hundred years.[9]

Many congratulations on your Commonweal acceptance. Do cultivate them. I too am completely at the service of our Cousins Across the Sea who seem to appreciate girls & boys like us, and who send nice words as well as nice dollars.[10]

Bluebell came to meet me with a great fuss from which she has not yet subsided. Full of licks and purrs. And *cunning*. Whereas she was eating dutifully any old thing from M^rs L & the girls – scraps, etc., she will touch nothing but the most expensive cat-meat and mince from me.[11] Which just goes to show that even the cat sees a softie in

your loving
Mollie Moonflower

P.S. Rob & I treated ourselves to a wee offering for you – we hoped it would not be too loud. – Sent under separate cover.

ALS. HRC.

1. These two pieces, probably books Derek Stanford intended to write, were not published.
2. MS reviewed four books for *Time and Tide* (19 October 1957): Ursula Bloom, *The Elegant Edwardian*; Ernest H. Shepard, *Drawn from Memory*; Peter Bull, *Bulls in the Meadows*; G. D. Roberts, *Without My Wig*.
3. MS refers to reviews of *The Comforters* on BBC Radio.
4. MS's relations with F. N. Ball of Tower Bridge Publications, which first published MS's Mary Shelley biography *Child of Light*, had become acrimonious in 1951. After MS left John Smith – only later to return to him – Pearn, Pollinger & Higham became MS's literary agency.
5. Ian Hamilton Finlay was living in a flat in Nicolson Street, Edinburgh. The writer and translator Lesley Lendrum was a close friend who assisted him in his work. The artist Marion Fletcher had married Hamilton Finlay in 1947 (with Hugh McDiarmid as best man), though by 1957 the two were no longer living together; they divorced in 1961. The American Janet Sideman resided in Scotland between 1956 and 1959, working some of the time at the School of Scottish Studies, and was in a relationship with Hamilton Finlay between 1957 and 1958.
6. The 'N.H.' is the National Health; Hamilton Finlay had moved to Edinburgh from rural Perthshire the previous year in order to seek treatment at the city's Davidson Clinic for his nervous anxiety and agoraphobia. The 'N.A.B.' was the National Assistance Board, established to administer the National Assistance Act of 1948, which itself was designed to help those not covered by previous acts through national insurance contributions, such as the physically disabled, the homeless, and unmarried mothers.
7. Carson McCullers's *The Ballad of the Sad Café* was published in 1951.
8. On 15 October, MS will write to Dina Barnsley: 'I have been seeing Robin off to Aldershot where he starts his N. Service in the R.A.M.C. We had a jolly evening together before he left. He is going through a very *accusing* phase & says I am a rotten mother just to see how I take it. When I say, yes, you're right, chum, can't you try to cover it up so's no-one will guess? – he cheers up and is ever so loving' (MBC).
9. 'The Brontes as Teachers' will become the title of an essay MS later publishes in the *New Yorker* (22 January 1966; *TGF*, pp. 114–20).
10. Stanford's article 'From Engagement to Indifference: Politics and the Writer – In Britain, Cautious Coexistence' will be published in the American Catholic journal *Commonweal* (7 March 1958).
11. 'Mrs L.' is Tiny Lazzari, MS's landlady in London.

TO JOHN VAN DRUTEN, NEW YORK,
23 SEPTEMBER 1957

13, Baldwin Crescent, Camberwell, London, S.E.5
23rd September, 1957

My dear John,

Thank you so much for your jolly letter, and also for the most impressive N.Y. Times book review. I have another very good one from the N.Y. Herald Tribune – this, and those you kindly sent me are all I have seen so far.[1]

I am delighted to know you have started a new play, and so proud to be told of it so early on, and to be given a glimpse of how your mind works. I am greatly attracted by the idea of your probably arranging the scenes in a different sequence from that in which they were written. The poetic-logical order of things is not always compatible with their chronological order, it seems to me. I do wish you a happy writing of your new work, and hope to be told more of it, if it does not worry you to speak of a work in progress.

I am going through a period when everything seems to be going wrong in small ways. I have got used to these phases: after a while everything goes right. But, for instance, a man has just been enquiring about the television rights of The Comforters, but my agents have lost the contract so couldn't say on the spot whether the rights were free or not. However, this will sort itself out, and I doubt very much if the book would televise anyway. Another thing that happened the other day, I went to get my hair trimmed; I usually wear it fairly long, but asked the girl to take a bit off. Now the moment she had the scissors in her hand I saw in the mirror a sort of orgiastic look in her eyes, and all in a moment she was shearing off great lumps. I said nothing, I was mesmerised, and she was standing upright, you know, while I was sitting, which always puts one in the wrong. So I said nothing, but just let the horror work out its course. I now have a short cut, and feel light headed and like Samson with all the virtue gone out of me.

And then, again, there is another contract which the agents have lost . . . it is quite incredible, but true; normally they are quite efficient. All will be well when my Good Phase returns.

I have had to put aside *Memento Mori* for a while to do book reviews and another little broadcast piece. I wonder what you will think of the one I sent you? Do tell me truthfully what you feel.[2] The new one is to be called THE INTERVIEW, and that is really all I know about it so far. I have a vague *interview*-like cloud of experience on which I want to work. I usually think about this cloud-like thing for a while, and then become more lucid when I have a pen in my hand. I would rather be getting on with my novel, but this promises quicker returns, which I can't overlook as yet. I have a sense of providence in these matters, and feel that if the novel has to wait it will be all the better for it.

I have several books of short stories for review – nothing exciting, so far. There is a collection of Frank O'Connor's, which I find pleasant reading, and it is quite a world of its own, but he seems to say the same thing over and over again. I can't understand a writer wanting to do this. There is another book of fables by a girl of fifteen, which I haven't looked into properly yet, but they don't seem to me very special. It is quite a phenomenon of our age, this craze for teen-age writers. I wonder if you ever read Colin Wilson's *The Outsider* which enjoyed great fame here? He was twenty-four when he wrote it. I have met him several times, and he always is bubbling over with his super-man ideas, and is so self-important that he simply isn't offensive, but rather sweet. You just sit back and let him babble on.[3]

Do you know a novel called THE DESPERATE ART by a young ex-patriate American, John Rosenberg? It has been out some time, but I mention it because it contains this extra-dimensional quality which you admire. The prose is rather peculiar, very consciously elevated. It has a cumulative effect, and the whole thing is rather striking. Do let me know if you can't easily get a copy, and I will send you mine.[4]

Well, it is great fun to be writing 'my dear John' to John Van Druten to whose letters I very much look forward.

All good fortune for your new play.

Yours ever,

s/Muriel

TLS. NYPL.

1. The review of *The Comforters* by Aileen Pippett in the *New York Times Book Review* began: 'Here is a brilliant first novel gaily dedicated to the proposition that things are not always what they seem – and to its corollary, that a good way of hiding anything is to display it openly' (1 September 1957). In her review in the *New York Herald Tribune*, Martha Bacon enthused: '"The Comforters" is a book that simply exists in space like a good abstraction and it is always interesting and often hilarious' (1 September 1957). She concluded: 'And tap-tap-tap goes the novel, the loose ends tied up neatly, no characters arbitrarily introduced, and the prose as fine and shiny as a summer day.'

2. MS had sent *The Party through the Wall*.

3. MS's review of Frank O'Connor's *Domestic Relations* will appear in the *Observer* (6 October 1957). The teenager's book of fables has not been identified. Colin Wilson's *The Outsider* was published in 1956 in the UK by Gollancz and in the US by Houghton Mifflin; it had already proved immensely popular.

4. John Rosenberg was part of the circle of friends that included the Braybrookes, at whose Hampstead home MS probably met him. His first novel, *The Desperate Art*, was published in London in 1955 by Longmans, Green, & Co. He was to prove important in the further decay of MS's relations with Derek Stanford as it was through him that Stanford met a young American woman with whom he fell in love. Martin Stannard writes of Rosenberg:

> John, a New York Jew by birth, was an Anglophile agnostic, novelist, reviewer, script reader and publisher who later became a distinguished TV drama producer [. . .] The Rosenbergs had attended Muriel's parties at Baldwin Crescent. [. . .] John Rosenberg was trapped in the drudgery of script-reading and report-writing for MGM who rarely bought anything. [. . .] Despite producing five novels and a biography of Dorothy Richardson, he always felt frustrated as a writer. (*MSB*, pp. 195, 197, 556 n. 59)

TO ALAN BARNSLEY, MAIDSTONE, KENT,
23 OCTOBER 1957

13, Baldwin Crescent, Camberwell, London, S.E.5
23rd October, 1957

Dearest Alan,

I was thrilled to know you approve of CRUSOE, and do hope
you will enjoy the whole.[1] I feel very much more settled after
seeing McLean [*sic*] and your excellent Thayer

> (I love Thayer
> For he's Lord Mayor,
> He's classy, he's glad & he's good.
> Oh, I love Thayer
> The best purveyor
> Of delicate doggie – food.)[2]

To continue. Well, it was a wonderful day for both of us, and I am
really very grateful, easier in my mind, and able to continue with
my difficult detective story, which is not quite my sort of thing –
only I'm determined to try it, as an exercise.[3] I'm sure 8DAYS
will be your best ever. You can't expect to have an exciting day
and then continue as if nothing had happened – you will soon be
sailing along again, very dear Alan, talented Alan.[4] I am looking
forward so much to seeing you both again on Monday week.
Meantime here is a poem which I found last night in a book of
Early English Lyrics:

> Adam lay ibounden,
>   Bounden in a bond;
> Four thousand winter
>   Thoght he not too long;
> And all was for an appil,
>   An appil that he tok,
> As clerkes finden

Writen in here book.
Ne hadde the appil take ben,
  The appil taken ben,
Ne hadde never our lady
  A ben hevene quene.
Blessed be the time
  That appil take was.
Therefore we moun singen
  Deo gracias.[5]

It is on the theme of St. Augustine's *felix culpa* ('O happy fault, that merited such a Redeemer!'), adapted to Our Lady.

Here is one that gives me a frisson:

I have set my hert so hie
  Me liket no love that lowere is,
And alle the paines that I may drie,
  Me thenk hit do me good iwis;
For on that lorde that loved us alle
  So hertely have I set my thowght,
It is my joye on him to calle,
  For love me hath in balus browght.
  Me thenk it do iwis.[6]

And this one I can't understand, but love; am sure you will too:

I stond as still as ony stone,
The grace of God than he will send.
All thing may not cum anone,
But wane God will it may amend.
  Lex is leyd adowne,
  And *veritas* is but small;
  Amor is owt of towne,
  And *caritas* is gon with all.[7]

I think it is a Christian-realist-stoic piece, very unusual for the
period, really, in tone. It is austere, like Chance in 8Days.

And to end the anthology:

> As I up rose in a morning,
>   My thought was on a maide ying,
> That song aslepe with her lulling
>   Her dere sone, our Saviour.
>
> As she him toke all in her lap,
> He toke that maiden be the pap,
> And toke therof a right god nap,
>   And soke his fille of that licour.
>
> To his moder than he gan say,
> 'For this milk me muste deye;
> It is my kind therewith to play,
>   My swete moder, my par amour.'
>
> The maiden freely gan to sing,
> And in her song she made morning,
> How he that is our heven king
>   Shuld shed his blod with grete dolour.
>
> 'Your weping, moder, greveth me sore;
> But I wold deye, ye wern forlore.
> Do way, moder, and wepe no more!
>   Your lulling lesseth my languor.'[8]

How natural religion was to the middle ages! Some of the Mary–
Infant poems, like the last one, seem to me to cut right across,
or rather to redeem, the Oedipus tangle in civilized man. Let me
know what you think of these poems, and whether they please
you, for they are sent as a present, in gratitude for your friendship.
   Would you please send me the correct version, and the source

if you know it, of that little rhyme you recited, ending 'Ivan will strangle you soon.'? I would like to quote it as a chapter heading. I am having verse chapter headings for Memento Mori. I have been thinking a lot of what you told me about the Institutions for the aged, and the patients' fear of making too much of a nuisance. I think I can use this theme, it would strengthen my book.[9]

I loved meeting Godfrey and think he is perfect, and will go straight to heaven to pray for us all in purgatory.[10]

Dear Dina – best of love, dear, till Monday week, and congratulations on Alan's success. I will send you some more poems soon if you would like them.

Heaps of love to you both,
s/Muriel

TLS. GULSC.

1. On 15 October, MS wrote to Dina Barnsley (comparing herself to Christine Brooke-Rose): 'I have been very good, as a good friend, and haven't sent ROBINSON, because I thought it might be off-putting to Alan. That was nice of me. I judge by myself – Christine finishes a novel within *5 weeks*! This gives me a quite unreasonable sense of panic – I feel I'm getting nowhere, plodding along with my reviews, etc., for a living. It is all unreasonable, because it's the quality that counts ultimately, not the speed of writing. I will send *Robinson* whenever you say, *yes*' (MBC).
2. Mr Theyer was a representative of Alan Barnsley's publisher William Morrow, to whom he had introduced MS, at the publisher's London office, in the hope of advancing her commercial prospects. At the meeting (as reported to the editor on 13 May 2024 by Barnsley's son Michael, who had heard this from his father), Theyer delivered a lecture on how selling books was similar to selling dog food and how prices had to be kept low. After the meeting, MS remarked to Barnsley: 'I don't know how he could be so rude about your books!'
3. The story MS was writing becomes 'The End of Summer Time', which will be published the following year in *London Mystery Magazine*, 37, June 1958; on the advice of her then agent Bruce Hunter, MS will later rework this story and give it the title 'Chimes', publishing it in 1995 (*TCSS*, pp. 256–61). Of it, on 17 May 1958, she will write to Derek Stanford: 'Thanks for the Mystery Magazine. I am proud to say my story was *so suitable* (i.e. bad) that they haven't, for once, seemed to change a word' (HRC).
4. Alan Barnsley was working on a novel whose provisional title was *Chance*

in 8 Days; it will be published the following year by Hutchinson under the title *Eight Days*.

5. MS cites an anonymous poem from E. K. Chambers and F. Sidgwick, eds., *Early English Lyrics, Amorous, Divine, Moral & Trivial* (Sidgwick & Jackson, 1926, p. 102); in line 8 she changes 'Wreten' to 'Writen', and throughout her letter she omits diacriticals which were hard to reproduce on a 1950s typewriter.

6. Anonymous, in *Early English Lyrics*, p. 155.

7. Anonymous, in *Early English Lyrics*, p. 161. At the editor's request, the following (unpunctuated) version of the poem has been provided by the medievalist David Raybin:

> I stand as silent/motionless/meek as any stone
> [In the hope] that God will therefore send his grace
> All things don't always happen immediately
> But when God wishes, they may be relieved
> *Law* is overcome
> And *truth* is meagre
> *Love* is gone out of town
> And *charity* is gone with the rest

8. Anonymous, in *Early English Lyrics*, p. 141.

9. As published, *Memento Mori* will not contain chapter headings in verse such as the present – unidentified – one. On 17 October, MS wrote to her new literary agent Paul Scott: 'I am glad you like the beginning of MEMENTO MORI. I am gathering information about the Senile Wards in hospitals. They fascinate and terrify me. I visualise myself one day occupying a bed as Granny Spark. You would be Granpa Scott . . .' (NLS).

10. Godfrey Barnsley, one of Alan's older brothers.

TO ALAN AND DINA BARNSLEY, MAIDSTONE, KENT,
1 NOVEMBER 1957

Kidney Wood nr. St. Albans[1]
Friday

Derek & I are sitting in the wood sheltering from a shower. We have built a fire and have an umbrella hung above our heads on a low tree, and sit on a w'proof, very snug. Not bad, we say to each other for two old crones of 39.[2] What a nice letter from you – I think your criticism the most sane I have heard so far.

You are right about descriptive passages not being my thing – on the question of structure, this is my particular way of doing (viz. Fanfarlo from Beaudelaire [*sic*], etc.). I use a form – story-bookish, almost childish, but archetypal (viz Robinson Crusoe) & put it into use for my own situations. If you go on doing something weird like this long enough it has an eventual effect. But how nice of you to like Robinson – no-one has praised it so much – only moaned about explanations. You must tell Alan Maclean what you feel about it, loves. I think I might have to make it mid-week, but will let you know in good time. Longing to see you.

Derek sends love with mine.

xxx

M.

BLESSINGS FOR 8 DAYS

We went to MONET exhibition & now see only mauve grass & trees.[3]

ALS. MBC. Dating from postmark: (Saturday) 2 November 1957.

1. The city of St Albans was important for Derek Stanford and MS during their early romance; MS also travelled there to visit Herbert Palmer. Less than two months later, on 8 January 1958, MS will write to Alan and Dina Barnsley:

    Let us all go to St. Albans one day in the spring. I wish to live there one day. St. Albans has the most wonderful civic sense of any town in England. The air of antiquity and monastic scholarship never leaves it, and even the modern part of the town is well set out. St. Albans is a centre of the 'Michael-force' as the occultists describe it – a sort of psychic centre. So it should be, for St. Alban was Britain's first martyr. My mother was born & brought up quite near by in Watford, where we used to go for summer holidays. And so I feel at home there. (MCB)

2. MS was aware that the Barnsleys had doubts about her ties to Stanford. On 15 October, she wrote to Dina:

Derek is very good. I will not hear a word against him. He is in a touchy psychological state at present, and knows it. My role is merely to be companionable and to ask no questions. We go for walks in the country some times, but don't meet so often as we did before. I have simply no resentment for Derek. After all, Dina, why shouldn't I show sweetness and patience to an old friend? This is always the woman's privilege. Then, again, how many men of Derek's persuasion would be content with a relationship without sex? – He never infringes on my principles in this or any other respect. And then, I enjoy his company; we share a lot. F^r Brocard did not give me the impression that he thought our meeting a bad thing, but as you say, he probably thought of the old unsatisfactory two-way pull between us. (MBC)

3. An exhibition of the paintings of Claude Monet took place at the Tate Gallery in London between 16 September and 5 November.

TO DEREK STANFORD, HOUNSLOW, MIDDLESEX,
19 NOVEMBER 1957

[Camberwell, London]
19.11.57

Dearest Bonny,

I am so relieved that you got home safely and without too much effort. I am delighted with your gallant attentions en route, and awed by your resources after an exhausting evening.[1] It prompted a little poem:

FAITH AND WORKS

My friend is always doing Good
But doubts the Meaning of his labour,
While I by Faith am much imbued
And can't be bothered with my Neighbour.

These mortal heresies in us
Friendship makes orthodox and thus
We are the truest Saint alive
As near as two and two make five.[2]

I am trying to rush through my reviews so as to have a day free
when the sun shines and you feel free for a walk. The jacket cover
of Robinson has arrived. MacM. are not too pleased with it, and
want my opinion.[3] I think the idea is very good – an aerial view
of the island with the wrecked plane in the form of a tiny cross
which is also the cross at the end of a rosary which twines itself
round the title. The background is blue-green and the island and
lettering etc., a sort of Carmelite brown. The symbolism isn't
very clear, though, unless you are a Catholic. The beads look like
ordinary blobs. The island is too tiny.

Best love, poppet, hope to see you soon.

Love,

s/Doulzin

TLS. WUL.

1. The often-sickly Derek Stanford was recovering from a bout of Asian flu.
2. Seven months later, on 12 June 1958, MS will expand, to Stanford, on
    her view of faith:

> I do so agree with you about the 'God-inspired,' and with your
> saying 'If people bowed in their spirits to God they would not be so
> keen to appropriate His voice.' In fact I have come to think that God
> wants us to use our *own* voice more than anything. There is a type of
> mind that attributes everything to either God or the Devil. A young
> priest once complained to me of this in the Prior of Aylesford, and
> remarked that it left no initiative or responsibility to the individual.
> And it is true that the 'God-inspired' are the most irresponsible of
> people. Especially those who consider themselves as Mystics. Most
> of all I distrust the equation (implicit but real) of the Mystic with
> the Superman. St. John of the Cross for instance, takes quite the
> opposite view. (HRC)

3. On 10 November, MS wrote to Stanford from the Barnsleys' home in
    Maidstone: 'Macmillan are doing Robinson in early summer after all,
    which is a relief. Alan & I are working on the blurb, but have had no suc-
    cess so far. If it doesn't come off perhaps you will have a go?' She added:
    'I haven't done a stroke of work this week & feel much refreshed, less
    depressed, and in good spirits to start again' (HRC).

TO ALAN MACLEAN, MACMILLAN LTD, LONDON, 20 NOVEMBER 1957

13, Baldwin Crescent, Camberwell, London, S.E.5
20th November, 1957

My dear Alan,

Thank you very much for the exciting signs of *Robinson*'s future.

About the jacket: I like the idea, but don't think the design is strong or unified enough. If the artist retains the rosary perhaps he could make it more lifelike, less abstract? I am not sure that anyone but an Ould Papisher like me or an Anglo Young Man like you would recognise the rosary as it is; people may think it represents merely the course of the plane. But I shall be quite content if you decide to use this design.[1]

About the blurb: Derek has been to work on it, and I have touched it up. We have tried to combine both drafts. I enclose the result, together with Alan's draft, so that you can see what has been done. I hope this will be more or less acceptable, but again, leave it to you.[2]

Derek sends his love. We must arrange to meet for a drink some time soon.

Keep well,

Yours ever,

s/Muriel

P.S. I return the second Third Programme review of The Comforters, so that you can quote from Angus Wilson. If this copy is to spare I should like to have it back.[3] Also enclosed is a review in Yale Review from which you might like to quote. May I have this back in due course?[4]

TLS. MA.

1. Alan Maclean must have taken MS at her word, as *Robinson* will appear the following year with its cover just as MS describes it.
2. Alan Barnsley had drafted a blurb for the novel, which Maclean described,

in a letter to MS of 19 November, as 'a little too literary for the average
Blurb and Catalogue Reader' (MA).

3. The repeat of the broadcast on 'Recent Novels' aired on the BBC Third
    Programme on 7 May, featuring discussion among Angus Wilson,
    Christopher Salmon (representing the Talks Department at the BBC), and
    the literary critic and academic Frank Kermode (who will go on to become
    one of MS's most significant champions and whose first contact with her
    work seems to have been in preparation of this programme). Wilson
    remarked, of *The Comforters*: 'I think it's a remarkable picture of a commu-
    nity – a minority community – in this country and in this particular case
    a middle class and Roman Catholic community, some of them converts,
    some of them born Catholics, and to me, as always, the fascinating thing is
    that you here have very typical English people who are yet separated from
    their ordinary counterparts, pagan and Protestant counterparts, by the
    fact that they hold this minority belief' (MA).

4. *The Comforters* was reviewed by Martin Price in the *Yale Review* (vol. 47,
    1957–8).

Muriel Spark in Baldwin Crescent

TO JOHN VAN DRUTEN, THERMAL, CALIFORNIA,
21 NOVEMBER 1957

13, Baldwin Crescent, Camberwell, London, S.E.5
21st November, 1957

My dear Johnnie,

How are you getting on with your new play? I should have
written to you before but have been both busy and depressed –
busy with work I don't like, and depressed about doing it. But I
have thought about you a lot, hoping in fact, you would write to
me first.

Your last letter was about my radio play. I think you are right
about my having done that sort of thing before. But I was so
taken up with handling a new technique I hadn't any room left for
original thought. The reception of the play was rather comical.
The listeners hated it and the critics loved it.[1] This situation seems
to be my lot in life, for Lippincott tell me the reviews of *The
Comforters* have been enthusiastic, but nobody is buying the book.
I have told them that the critics' influence always prevails in the
end. I hope I am right, for this is just my sales talk to persuade
them to take my next novel, which in fact they have done. Have
you ever experienced a complete dichotomy between the critics'
and the public's taste?[2]

Now how are you getting on with your new play? I should like
to know about it if you have time to write. You had also started
the dramatisation of a murder novel. Can you do this without
adding your own ideas?[3]

The work I have been doing, which I dislike doing in bulk,
is book reviewing. There is usually an Autumn rush and then
everything quietens down at the end of the year. I wonder if you
ever see the *Observer*? I review for them, and they are also running
a series called 'Best Sellers of the Century' – articles on books like
'The Green Hat' and 'Sorrel and Son'. I am to do 'Gone With the
Wind' which I am now re-reading. It is quite a book.[4]

I have only done two chapters of my third novel MEMENTO

MORI about which I told you. Lippincott are contracting for it on the strength of the two chapters, and so I shall be getting down to it again soon. Meantime I have been collecting information about our various systems of dealing with old homeless people. It is a transition period, and many old people, if they haven't got relatives to visit them, still have a rough time. My friend Dr. Barnsley (Gabriel Fielding) is giving me considerable help and information.[5]

I stayed a week with the Barnsleys recently. He is finishing his third novel now. It is to be called EIGHT DAYS, and describes an eight-day visit to Tangier by a prison doctor. What I have seen of it is very powerful – he has that masculine *drive* which I can't get into my work at all.[6]

Have you come across *The Letters of John Henry Newman* which I edited in conjunction with another writer, Derek Stanford? It was published recently by Newman Press. I don't really know if it would interest you unless you are attracted by Newman. The main point of interest in the book is that the Anglican letters were edited by Derek Stanford who is an Anglican, and the Catholic letters be [*sic*] me, a Catholic. This arrangement has never been tried before, and it seemed to be quite successful. We may do another Newman book, but there is a great deal of work in it, and little reward.

My son has now gone to do his National Service. He is 19, I am 39. It is a solemn thought. He is stationed at Aldershot and sometimes gets leave at the weekends to come to London. I have never seen very much of him, for he has been brought up by my parents in Edinburgh. He is very jolly, and full of notions for bettering the world. He wants to study medicine, and has quite a good working brain, but gets stumped at the exams.[7]

All good wishes,

Yours ever,

s/Muriel

TLS. NYPL.

1. In his letter to MS of 27 September, John Van Druten thanked MS for the script of her radio play, and recalled that MS had said she 'never wanted to write a book that was like another book. Especially not like a former one of yours.' He went on:

   > it is too like the two other things of yours that I know. The voices from the Comforters, and the dead characters from the Portobello Road story. I seemed to recognise both right away.
   >
   > This does not, of course, make it bad – but it does weaken its effect on me. I have read this before. I think it is well done, though a little under-characterised . . . but God help anyone with a half hour only in which to do it all. I do feel a certain jumpiness in it. I think it is good, and I am afraid I want it to be better, that is all. I am sorry. (NYPL)

2. On 2 November, MS wrote to Lynn Carrick at Lippincott: 'You know, I don't think it will be long before my work starts selling well. The main reason for this optimism is the consistent praise of the critics. I have seen before, and yourself will know, how the influence of the critics prevails on public taste – and often with a more lasting effect than perhaps a year. And I feel, now, that I am in my best creative period, and hope to do some good work' (NLS).

3. Van Druten would attempt to reply to both questions in his letter of 1 December, his last to MS, written less than three weeks before his death.

4. On 25 October, MS wrote to Derek Stanford: 'I am to do Stevie Smith's poems for next week, which gladdens my heart for I am a Stevie fan. Also a review of cat books. I don't know how I shall get through all the reviews, and doubt very much if they will print the half. That's always what they do when they get an influx of books – place large commissions for reviews, and then can't find space for them. But of course I make no moans' (HRC).

5. On 26 September, MS wrote to Paul Scott: 'Within the next few days I shall be sending you the first two chapters of my new novel MEMENTO MORI for submission to Macmillan' (Private collection). And on 12 October, she wrote to Stanford: 'I have a letter from Paul Scott to say that Maclean can't put up my chapters to his board until I have written half the book. He says Maclean is "enchanted" with the two chapters. I am pretty sure, from what Maclean said when I met him, and by the date of Paul's letter, that Mcl. has not even read it. Well, well. I shall write the book, I think, and then sell it to the highest bidder. This is my very down period. Pray that it goes up soon' (HRC).

6. To this suggestion, Van Druten will respond in his letter of 1 December: 'Don't be silly – wanting a masculine DRIVE to our style – what on earth would you do with it, any more than with great masculine biceps? God knows what each writer needs, and allots it to them' (NLS).

Seven months later, on 15 July 1958, MS will write to Alan and Dina Barnsley:

> I should be able to read through EIGHT DAYS by about the 25th if you can let me have the proofs by then. I should not keep them long. That is, if you really think I can help you – I don't feel, myself, that I could make any but minor suggestions now you have reached this stage. It is rather like the situation of my English mistress and me. You have got past the stage where anyone can say a word or phrase is 'right' or 'wrong' – it depends so much on what is right or wrong for your unique style. (As when Peter Ustinov, at school, was asked who was the greatest composer. He answered 'Mozart' and was told he was *wrong*, it was Beethoven.) But I shall enjoy reading EIGHT DAYS, that's certain. (MBC)

7. On 12 October, MS wrote to Stanford: 'I have a letter from Robin in which he says "Now that I am here things don't seem too bad and at least I am going to try and make the best of my national service; but one thing is certain I would never, never sign on as a regular – the two years will be quite sufficient." I think this as sweet as can be' (HRC).

1958

On 1 February, MS celebrated her fortieth birthday. She spent time in the early months of the year discussing with Alan Maclean the contents of her first collection of stories, *The Go-Away Bird and Other Stories* which Macmillan would publish in November. In April, Rayner Heppenstall expressed interest in an adaptation for radio of *The Comforters*. In May, Derek Stanford wrote to MS about his new love interest, and for the remainder of the year the correspondence between the two was tense, turning acrimonious; the plan they had to collaborate on *Newman by His Contemporaries* had fallen apart by the end of the year. At the end of May, MS was obliged to defend herself physically from Rayner Heppenstall's drunken sexual advances. In May, the BBC broadcast MS's radio play *The Interview*, and in June, 'A Tribute to John Masefield', to which MS contributed. Also in June, *Robinson* was published by Macmillan, to generally favourable reviews. By July, *Memento Mori* was completed. In August, MS's beloved cat Bluebell was sick and needed to be put down. In July, her literary agency finalised a change of its name from Pearn, Pollinger & Higham to David Higham Associates Ltd. In September, MS retreated to The Friars at Aylesford to work on her new novel, whose title she already knew: *The Ballad of Peckham Rye*. Graham Greene wrote from Cuba in October calling *Memento Mori* 'your best book'. In the same month, *Robinson* was published in the US. In December, Paul Scott announced that he was going part-time at David Higham Associates so as to spend more time on his own writing.

TO ALAN BARNSLEY, MAIDSTONE, KENT,
13 MARCH 1958

13 Baldwin Crescent, Camberwell, London, S.E.5
13th March, 1958

My dear Alan,

A note to tell you I have had a charming letter from Evelyn
Waugh about *Robinson* in which he commends its originality and
the dialogue. He makes a number of very sound verbal criticisms
which, alas, it is too late to benefit by.* I have written to thank
him. The criticisms have a useful general application to my work.[1]

Thank you for sending him the book. I shall pass his letter to
the American publisher, criticisms and all. I think they will be
impressed.

I am working very hard, hoping to put all aside and start
MEMENTO MORI on Monday next. Four chapters are
completed and I am hoping to get the first draft down during the
spring months.

All good wishes,

Yours,

s/Muriel.

* so far as 'Robinson' is concerned – the book has gone to press.

TLS. MBC.

1. Evelyn Waugh wrote to MS on 9 March:

> It was very kind of you to send me the proofs of *Robinson*. It is a
> highly original tale. I hope it will prove popular.
>
> Since this is an uncorrected copy perhaps it is officious to men-
> tion some *corrigenda*. On pp 2, 66 and elsewhere 'transpire' is used
> wrongly. p 43. An Americanism: 'did not have' for 'lacked'. p 190
> 'if or how'. 'How' is redundant unless qualified by 'still less'. p 145.
> for 'mouth' read 'mouths'. p 162 'too near by'; an Americanism.
>
> I do not know whether you had the intention of mystifying the
> reader. It was plain to me from the first that the blood was goat's blood.
>
> The dialogue is good. (NLS)

TO FATHER BROCARD SEWELL, AYLESFORD PRIORY,
KENT, CIRCA 24 MARCH 1958

[Camberwell, London]

My dear Father Brocard,

Thank you for your letter – most interesting. We shan't fall out over Fascism, I think. I know very little of political theory, and I judge politics according to their fruits.

I don't at all feel it my duty as a Christian to go about liking everybody regardless. There are still Fascists and Mosleyite fellow-travellers about; I can't abide them. All the Fascists or semi-Fascists I have known have been cranks or thugs. I have had opportunities of observing them. How well I remember the Fascists of the thirties strutting about in their black shirts and mouthing their eloquent nothings! During the war I worked in the Political Intelligence department of the F.O. – a minor job, but I was able to observe the Fascist mentality at close quarters. I can't like or respect the type of character which is drawn to Fascism.[1]

You, as a priest, of course, must necessarily see human souls in a different light – and I myself would be the last to deny to a Fascist or a Communist the *human* respect due to every soul born into the world. But I am obliged, by my calling, to take note of character, of psychological types and varying mentalities; this, as you know, is not an amoral process. And I observe of Fascists that they are subject for satire. I have one in my current novel. I will go further than this to explain my point of view, and say that every such type which engages the creative mind intensely is, in fact, a part or projection of the writer's own personality. If, as a writer, I satirise a Fascist I satirise a part of myself. Now, I am not pleading the special case of a writer.

I make no distinction between the writer in myself and the rational being – some of my work has 'irrational' content but that is a different thing – because there is no such distinction. The slightly mystical point I have made above is merely to show you that I don't speak about Fascists without thinking why I do

so. And I think this factor has always to be taken into account
when we express likes or dislikes – it does not only apply to the
writer. But I do not think this should deter us from saying with an
honest mind what we like and dislike, provided our reasons are
sound and our observations of sufficient range, and our experience
direct.

Like you, I don't vote. Politics bore me, and I am not even
sure I approve the Vote for Women, though my grandmother
was a suffragette. Max Beerbohm frivolously calls himself a Tory
Anarchist and I think that would as near as possible describe my
politics if I had any. I am always attracted to the liberal *mind* in my
friends. But one or two 'liberal' Catholics I know seem merely to
make it an excuse for taking liberties.

The Newman book, which we shan't be starting till late
summer, is to be NEWMAN BY HIS CONTEMPORARIES.
I think, don't you? that it is important for the understanding
of Newman to know the criticisms and comments to which
he was subjected during his lifetime, for all his best thought
and writings, and possibly his actions, were called out by
contemporary opinion. The book will comprise extracts from the
press and from journals, books of essays, memoirs, etc. My part
will be biographical and Derek's critical – a rough distinction.
Any suggestion you may make will be welcomed by us both.
Macmillan are to publish it. They have given us very generous
terms – more than double what we received from Peter Owen;
this means we shall have more time to spend on the book, and to
give more care to it than to Newman Letters.[2]

Did you see Sean O'Faolain's review in the Observer of a book
on Newman by Fr. Louis Bouyer? The review is very amusing,
espially [*sic*] the bit where he speaks of Newman's experience with
the Church in Ireland. ('They had the faith. They gave him the
works.' – This may be an old chestnut to you but it is new to me.)
I can send you the review if you would like to see it.[3]

I am looking forward to seeing Mr. Neame's poem. THE
EUROPEAN is of no account, so far as I have heard & seen. But a
poem is a poem is a poem . . . .[4]

Kindest wishes,

Yours ever,

TLcc. NLS. Dating by Stannard based on
25 March 1958 response to this letter.

1. In the 1930s, Father Brocard Sewell was a member of the British Union
   of Fascists, headed by the British politician Oswald Mosley, though he
   would later voice views that were too liberal for the Catholic Church,
   particularly on the issue of contraception, and would eventually be
   removed from Aylesford Priory. He wrote to MS from Aylesford on 25
   February:

   > Can we really say, 'I do not like & cannot respect Fascists?' I can
   > understand the proposition: 'I do not like & cannot respect *Fascism*'
   > (as long as the latter is clearly defined & given an exact meaning).
   >   I hope we shan't quarrel on this. [. . .] Sir Oswald now lives in
   > Paris. Probably in 50 years' time – if we are not all destroyed be-
   > forehand – someone will 'discover' his very remarkable book 'The
   > Alternative' & will put the ideas into practice while concealing their
   > source & calling them 'The New Conservatism' – or something of
   > the kind – 'Conservative Socialism' perhaps! (NLS)

   The 'F.O.' is the UK government's Foreign Office. MS writes of her
   wartime experience in *CV*:

   > The job was wonderfully interesting. I played a very small part, but
   > as a fly on the wall I took in a whole world of method and intrigue
   > in the dark field of Black Propaganda or Psychological Warfare,
   > and the successful and purposeful deceit of the enemy. [. . .] Black
   > propaganda was distinct from the BBC's white variety. Black took
   > up the position that we were loyal Germans devoted to the Führer.
   > From that point of view the news was presented in such a way
   > that the Germans got the impression that they were listening to a
   > German station. This was a camouflage for subtle and deadly anti-
   > Nazi propaganda. (pp. 147, 148)

2. On 27 September 1957, MS wrote to Peter Owen: 'Derek and I have a
   scheme which we are sure will be a success. We are calling it: NEWMAN:
   BY HIS CONTEMPORARIES. – A biographical and critical Portrait'
   (HRC). This project will be abandoned by MS.
3. Seán O'Faoláin's *Observer* review of *Newman, His Life and Spirituality* by Louis
   Bouyer was entitled 'Saint John Newman?' (26 January 1958).

4. *The European* was a magazine published between 1953 and 1959 which echoed the views of, and was bankrolled by, Diana Mosley (née Mitford) and her husband Oswald. In his letter to MS of 25 February, Fr Brocard wrote: '*European* often prints good stuff.' With his letter he enclosed the poem 'The Jansenist' by Alan Neame, adding of him: 'He is not a "Fascist" (are there any today?), but views sympathetically Sir Oswald Mosley's new policy of "European Socialism" – economically a synthesis of Distributism and Syndicalism.'

TO DEREK STANFORD, HOUNSLOW, MIDDLESEX, 27 MAY 1958

13, Baldwin Crescent, Camberwell, London S.E.5
27-5-58

Dear Old Chum,
   Your 2nd letter just received. (Also delayed by wrong postal address – please note, pet.)
   How jolly nice of you to write your protests. I am *delighted* & hope they are both printed. I have been quite put off my stroke, pussle, but now feel fully supported. Rayner has an idea that it was anti-*him* but I think they just didn't understand the play & were looking for a deep Third Programme message & meaning in it.[1] Rayner said to tell anyone who objects to the Critics to write to the Features Dept of the B.B.C. itself & make moan in that quarter. But you have done quite enough already and we shall see what happens.[2] Do let me see the nice consoling piece you have written on *Robinson* in W.R.[3]
   Many thanks, once more, for chivalrous intervention which is most gratefully received by your loving
   Polly Parsnip[4]
   Price-Jones [sic] had better watch out . . .[5]

ALS. HRC.

1. MS's play *The Interview* first aired on the BBC Third Programme on 21 May, produced by Rayner Heppenstall. The *Radio Times* listing announced: 'The scene is a large flat off Knightsbridge, on a foggy afternoon.

A great deal of imagination is exercised by Dame Lettice Chatterton, a former political hostess, and her secretary-companion, Miss Bone, who is entered for a General Knowledge Quiz' (18–24 May). In an internal memo recommending the play to the BBC, Heppenstall had written: 'I think that she shows a quite specific gift for thinking in terms of the blind medium, and I would certainly like to get her a bit more scope' (18 November 1957, BBC WAC). And in a further memo advising the Third Programme as the rightful place for such a play, he wrote: 'She now offers a further idea, to be called "The Interview", and to be done at a length of 45 minutes. It is to have the same kind of inherent controlled craziness of "The Party through the Wall", but without recourse to supernatural agents. I very strongly recommend the commissioning of this' (6 December 1957, BBC WAC).

MS's susceptibility to hostile reviews receives mention in a letter to Derek Stanford from one month earlier, 26 April:

> I spent an evening at Rayner's this week and we had a long chat about the terrible men in the northern hills of Britain who wear skirts. We spoke also about the injustices of this vale of tears, and how the reviewing system probably works. I put forward the view that while the system does admittedly allow of corruption, it is rather like a General Council in which the truth ultimately emerges in spite of intrigues & Cardinals. He thought this interesting, but commented that it is a classical and Catholic view, while he himself was inclined to the Protestant. I must say, for myself, a bad review does cause me to Protest, if it is a bad review of my own work, and especially if I suspect malice behind it. (HRC)

And on 21 May, MS wrote to Stanford: 'I *am* sorry you missed my play, which was attacked by critics very badly. I do not like them one bit. Others of good judgment send me good reactions & encouragement. The Observer had quite a good review of it' (WUL).

2. On 22 May, MS wrote to Stanford: 'The Critics on Sunday are discussing 'The Interview' & I expect they will tear it limb from limb. Did you hear it? If so, what did you think of the new ending? I had to write it in a hurry one morning as it was suddenly discovered that the piece was too short for the time allotted. I thought it improved the play. The actors took it rather too seriously – feeling, I think that it must have deep meaning, being a 3rd Prgm. piece. I would rather they had larked about a bit' (HRC).
3. Stanford was writing for *Women's Review*.
4. The reconciliation of MS with Stanford, signalled by her sign-off, was welcome given their recent spat, attested to in MS's letter to him of 17 May, in which she wrote:

You must be a very Gloomy Dane if you think I don't think you have ever done anything in the way of 'offices rendered' for me. I have always given you the credit for goodness in dozens of ways. – I can't mention all here, because I don't know what you really have in mind, the only objection I had was to your saying you had 'maintained my name' in such a context as to suppose I had such a dreadful bad name that you were full-time employed on maintenance work!

There is no point in duelling by letter. I have no grudge against you – except a bit, I must say, for a certain amount of rudeness & inconsiderateness to me since just before Easter – but even that I have really *forgotten* & condone by the knowledge that you have not been well & were probably (one must always allow for this) provoked in some way that I am not aware of. (HRC)

5. Alan Pryce-Jones was Editor of the *Times Literary Supplement* from 1948 to 1959. MS had possibly seen the anonymous *TLS* review of *Robinson* that would appear in the 27 June issue, or she is anticipating its tenor. The review begins: '*Robinson* is a finely written, suggestive, and irritating book.' And it concludes, condescendingly: 'Miss Spark has real talent and a vivid imagination (though it is a trifle misty at the edges) but so far she appears to be using these gifts to tease and to mystify rather than to enlighten and explore; so what in fact lingers in the mind is not some satisfying aesthetic pattern or overall impression but individual felicities here and there.'

TO DEREK STANFORD, HOUNSLOW, MIDDLESEX,
5 JUNE 1958

13, Baldwin Crescent, Camberwell, London, S.E.5
Thurs Corpus Christi '58

Dear Hep-Cat,

Have just returned from Mass to your letter. Thank you kindly for seeing my point of view re. Rayner. I do not object to what he thinks of my clothes, etc., but to his presuming to say it. He has rung to ask me along, but I do not feel like doing so without first explaining my objections, and I do not feel like explaining my objections lest I go to extremes and answer offence with offence – e.g. I have thought of saying: 'Since when were you an authority on women – what evidence?' But this would be a reflection on dear Margaret — which is no way out. Of course he claims to have been drunk & not to remember what he said.[1]

But why should I bother, anyway? He is not my problem, but if anyone's, his wife's. I can't and ought not to take on the sorting out of psychological difficulties in married men. More and more I see the virtue, in my friends, of sheer good manners, and after that a certain reserve. It may be a fault in me, but I feel too with Alan Barnsley as with Rayner, that they intrude where Angels fear to tread, in the domains of my soul where they have no right or place. And they *are* married men.

(I am speaking to you as to an Uncle!) You yourself are delicate in these matters, you are not one to attempt rape on a mystery, or violate what is beyond reason, either by word or action. I trust to observe the same by you, my dear, and do not, you see, ask you to explain much that is beyond my understanding. I do not even attempt to explain these unknown factors to myself: whatever construction one puts upon such mystifications is bound to be too simple, and so fallacious. The all-too-simple and idle method is to ascribe unpleasant motives; I would rather err in the opposite direction, and indeed, I feel deeply that the happier constructions are always nearer the truth where you are concerned, because you are an old and tried friend.[2]

To return to Rayner, if it doesn't bore you: A hint from you that he must show more respect will come in very handy. For my part, I have frequently lectured him with great indignation about his rudeness to you. *He* explained the same by the theory that you were both competing for my attention, and remarked that it would be better for him to see us both separately. I left him in no doubt that he alone, in my opinion, was the offender. Any rudeness on your part was nothing if not provoked.

Thank you for your further thoughts on *Robinson*. I think them most interesting, and reflect that, if the disappearance of the island symbolises the loss of romance, the story itself fails to produce sufficient *sense* of romance. It is true January says at the end 'there are things about the island of which I have not told you – etc.' or words to that effect. But why are they not told? (This bears out a criticism of Rayner's – in one of his sane intervals between insults – that the book falls between two categories: the Epic and the Comic.) Perhaps you may see some consoling objection to my criticism; but I am not really satisfied with the book, and am in some trepidation about its reception.[3]

You missed a treat in Palmer on the wireless giving forth on Masefield. He was magnificent. I hope to go and see him soon.[4]

I do your story between-times. I have passed the half-way mark of my novel & am trying to speed up. I think (but I always think) this is the best so far.[5]

I should be glad to know what you said about The Potting Shed, and am delighted at Greene's reaction. Please send samples.[6]

Love & blessings

Tessa Toothy

ALS. HRC.

1. Margaret was Rayner Heppenstall's wife.
    On 1 June, MS wrote to Derek Stanford:

    I had a remarkable passage with Rayner yesterday. He came to lunch and brought gin on which he got tight. Then I had to literally struggle for my honour – a real hard tussle and me terrified all the time Mrs. L. would overhear. I was bloody angry, particularly as he said some aggressive things, and refused to leave. Eventually I got him on his way, staggering up the Crescent at 7 p.m., after which Teresa came and calmed me down with aspirins, she having had a similar experience with a bloke a few nights ago. Rayner rang this morning to apologise but I froze him off. He keeps saying he wants to meet you. If you see him you can tell him I am bloody angry – because what makes it all the more rotten is the fact that he is in a position to give me work on the B.B.C. and so should be more careful about taking advantage. He wouldn't be my type in any case. (HRC)

    In an undated letter to Stanford probably from 10 June, she will expand: 'Rainer said offensive things, not about my work (which might have been at least understandable) but about the clothes I wear, my appearance, and the food I gave him for lunch! That is why I feel so annoyed at his damn cheek alone. As you will quite understand' (HRC). And in a further undated letter to Stanford, written not long after, she will write:

> I saw Rayner last night, largely so that the family would not wonder what was amiss on my abrupt absence. He is out to make amends & as I have now made my feelings quite clear to him – and he claims it was an isolated incident while under the influence – I reckon best to say no more; don't you think so? (HRC)

2. In an undated letter from late May, MS responded to Stanford's announcement that he was in an intimate relationship with a woman:

> Your information about your feelings for Delilah does not surprise me particularly – for I have always been careful to avoid intrusion into your life with your other friends, and have no possessive feelings – and so I think it a little out of proportion to suggest that I might be taken by surprise by any news of you whatsoever in that respect. (HRC)

3. On 4 February, MS had written to Alan Maclean: 'What will the fate of ROBINSON be, I wonder? Sometimes I like it and sometimes I don't – and then I think if I were a critic I would say "This is a novel with a map. The map is very nice."' (MA). On 18 May, she wrote to Stanford: 'I have a hostility to Robinson just now and hate being reminded of the book. If I can pluck up courage I'll get it to you. (Publication of the book is 26th June.)' (UV). And on 12 June she would write to Stanford: 'Pray also for a respectable reception of *Robinson* on the 26th. Bad reviews put me off my work. On the other hand I do not expect rave-notices for a novel which is, by intention, a light-weight' (HRC).
   At the end of *Robinson*, the eponymous island sinks into the sea.

4. On 4 May, MS wrote to R. D. Smith at the BBC to say 'Thank you very much for your letter of 30th April and for thinking of me in connection with your tribute to Masefield. I shall be delighted to contribute' (BBC WAC). On 1 June, the BBC Home Service broadcast 'Greetings to John Masefield on his eightieth birthday: A celebration with comments and quotations from many admirers'. Contributors included Herbert Palmer and MS (*Radio Times*, 1–7 June 1958).

5. MS was editing Stanford's story entitled 'The Dug-Out Boat'. Her own novel in progress was *Memento Mori*.

6. Graham Greene's 1957 play *The Potting Shed* was produced in London in February; Greene thanked MS for her response to it in a letter of 6 March, adding, 'When are you going to produce another book?' (NLS).

TO DEREK STANFORD, HOUNSLOW, MIDDLESEX,
18 JUNE 1958

13, Baldwin Crescent, Camberwell, S.E.5
18.6.58

Dear Popkin,

Here is your Dug-Out, much re-shuffled, snipped and scored.[1]

It was necessary to simplify it. The outline of action, as it stood, was too complicated for a story, though it would have made a novel. Consequently I have taken out B & K as characters altogether. I think they are unnecessary to the main theme although, of course, they introduced more psychological interest. This means you can still refer to Dorothy as 'D.', which I think is suited to the diary form. (It was, I thought, unlikely, anyway that he would write about K in his diary – unless he intended it for publication.)

The grip of the old man on the younger must work slowly. At first, the old man would be a bit of a bore – but not too much.

I have made the old man's name Singleton – he himself experiences the *creature*. Otherwise you have too many stories within stories – (again, all right in a novel).

Read it through as I have pasted it up and let me know what you think of it. At least it is reduced in length. I do hope you are satisfied at least with some of the changes.

I enclose the rejected pages in case you want to piece them all together in your original style again.

All best thoughts to you dear,

Affectionately,

Pipkin

ALS. HRC.

1. In an undated letter to Derek Stanford sent in the five weeks prior to the present letter, MS wrote:

I have been doing some of the 'Dug-Out' – it will be one story, not
two as I thought possible at one time. But you may be able to use
some of the deleted passages for another piece. But will you please
supply *names* for 'D', 'K' and 'B' – This, I think, is important, as it
would concretise the story. If you find it difficult to name B (who
I believe is a male character) why not use an ambiguous name like
Evelyn or Bobbi? Let me know of this, little dear. My main objective
is to reduce the length of the story and at the same time to clarify it
by having fewer people telling stories about other people, who tell of
other people and so on. Perhaps Singleton's story, because it depends
so much on sense-evidence, should be in the first person. I am much
enjoying this task which I do at odd minutes. (HRC)

TO ALAN MACLEAN, MACMILLAN LTD, LONDON,
30 JUNE 1958

13, Baldwin Crescent, Camberwell, London, S.E.5
30th June, 1958

CONFIDENTIAL

My dear Alan,
   The only reason that the question of libel in connection
with Come Along Marjorie has occurred to me is that, the last
time I mentioned a religious house (the retreat-house called
St. Philumena's in The Comforters) a number of lay-residents
at a Carmelite priory, The Friars, Aylesford, Kent, took St.
Philumena's to mean themselves.[1]
   I was already aware that The Comforters was disapproved of
in that quarter, but had assumed this was some Catholic question
of faith and morals, or something like that – one never knows
how individual Catholics are going to interpret faith and morals.
It was not until a year after publication of the book, in February
of this year, that I learned the real nature of their objection. The
objectors, I think, number four at the very most. They don't
resemble any of the characters in any of my books or stories,
unless there is some secret resemblance which they themselves
discern.

Consequently, I wrote to a priest friend of mine at The Friars, making it clear that my 'St. Philumena's' was not based on the priory at Aylesford; and I invited my critics, through him, to quote chapter and verse. In his reply my priest friend seemed quite satisfied and quoted from the Beggar's Opera:

> If you censure the age
> Be cautious and sage,
> For everyone cries 'That was levelled at ME.'[2]

None of my critics, of course, mentioned libel; it was merely a verbal and voluble objection to the book — lots of gobble and gabble, among a few people.

This will explain why it did not previously occur to me to anticipate a similar interpretation of *Come Along Marjorie*, by the few lay residents of The Friars. (The clergy there are quite reasonable and I don't think are likely to be hostile to anything I may write. The Prior was not keen on *The Comforters*, I gather, but liked my last Newman book.)

Now, what worries me is this: While I was staying at The Friars in the autumn of 1944 [*sic*] an incident did occur rather similar to that described in *Come Along Marjorie*.

An elderly woman who had been resident there for some weeks suddenly decided not to speak. She kept it up for some time. I heard that doctors had been brought in, without success. Then she went on hunger-strike. Finally, the asylum people came and took her away.

I enclose a pamphlet which describes The Friars.

My story was written a year or two after my stay at The Friars. I would feel justified in denying that it was 'based on' the incident at Aylesford. So many incidents in one's real and imaginative life go to make up a story, it is impossible to pin the basis down to one of them. My writing is never strict reportage.

Some differences between my story and the incident described above: —

My story is about an Abbey in Worcestershire, a twelfth century foundation, whereas The Friars is a religious house, not an Abbey, in Kent, founded in the thirteenth century.

My story places the Abbey on the site of an ancient Temple of Mithras. No-one so far has suggested that The Friars is built on the site of any ancient temple.

The priests in the story are monks, and the superior is an Abbot; whereas the priests at The Friars are friars, and the superior is the Prior.

In the story they wear white habits, whereas the friars wear brown. (White cloaks for dressed-up occasions.)

In the story the action takes place 'just after the war', whereas the incident referred to above took place in 1954.

In the story Miss Pettigrew is tall with dark hair. The lady who went on hunger-strike at The Friars was, if I remember, frail and grey, and pale.

In the story Miss Pettigrew is made to say to the narrator, 'The Lord is risen'. The unfortunate lady at The Friars did not speak to me at all, nor to anyone else.

In my story I call some of the lay residents 'The Cloisters' and I speak of an annexe. The lay residents at The Friars are known as 'The Courtyard'; and, when I stayed there, there was no annexe (although I believe an annexe has more recently been built).

The characters Jennifer and Squackle-wackle in my story do not correspond in any way that I know of, to anyone resident at The Friars at the time I was staying there.

The Abbey in my story is situated in 'the town', whereas The Friars lies outside a small village.

These are all the possible differences I can think of. But in general, the atmosphere of my story is, I think, different from that at The Friars.

I should be sorry if my *Marjorie* was abandoned merely because of the murmurings of a handful of cranks. You must understand that lay-workers, especially women, resident in a monastery, half-isolated as they are from the world (without wholly leading the life of religious) — isolated both psychologically and geographically, are particularly prone to imagine insults and ironic barbs and blisters. I'm afraid they incline to look for trouble; possibly in order to liven things up.

Be assured, however, that there is no deliberate malice or libel on my part against anyone in *Marjorie*. It is a sympathetic story. But I thought it only fair and prudent, since hearing of the objections to my innocent *Comforters*, to give you this information.

I have marked this letter 'confidential' for obvious reasons – but you will of course, show it to your colleagues and lawyer if necessary.

And of course, if you think further alterations to the story might be advisable, just let me know.

Yours ever,

s/Muriel

P.S. I think I should add, I think it most unlikely that the people at The Friars would bring action, even if they thought they had a case. As regards the woman in the incident, I don't think her case is unique enough; I understand the symptoms are fairly common.

TLS. MA.

1. On 'Come Along, Marjory', see 17 March 1956 in which MS hopes that Alan Maclean will enjoy her recently completed story; Maclean was preparing MS's first volume of stories, *The Go-Away Bird and Other Stories*, which Macmillan would publish later in the year and which includes 'Come Along, Marjory'.
2. The priest to whom MS wrote is likely to have been Fr Brocard; however, when contacted by Martin Stannard, he responded that he did not have the letter in his possession.

TO ALAN AND DINA BARNSLEY, MAIDSTONE, KENT, MID-1958

[Camberwell, London]

Dearest Alan & Dina,

Thank you so much for your generous acceptance of Memento. All I need at this stage is for my book to be loved and this is just the impression you give me.[1] I do hope all goes well

with Dina and that Dina dear, you won't overdo things when
you get up. We must arrange lunch out on Sunday otherwise – if
this is not fixed beforehand – I for one will bust up the party &
refuse to come.

I wish you could give me some advice about how to start
adapting The Comforters. I have made three false starts. It is
an involuted book, very difficult to grip hold of. But I am glad
it's dedicated to you because it is highly thought of amongst the
Finicky Few, and Evelyn Waugh cared so much for it. Can't you
think of a starting-point, you Dina lying in bed there, you lazy
thing? Perhaps you can pray & an idea will descend upon me?
Actually a draft has already been made by a BBC producer, called
Christopher Holme, but I am obliged to re-write, or write a new,
opening & to cut his draft by half.[2]

This is awfully good practise [*sic*], of course, in case I should
want to write a play (or get a job on the BBC as a script writer,
should Macmillan fail to come across with the slosh). Talking
of slosh, I have thought of a new novel I may write next year.
I want to deal with the puritanical hypocricies that are going
about in our society, and having dealt with Death in Memento
(Death being a rude word in some circles) I now want to write a
novel called 'Money'. I think one could have a lot from writing
about this particular 'rude word'. I would have to get up the
subject – study banking etc. and find out what debentures
mean, & that sort of thing. But the human side is well within
my power. I think Money is a theme which comes nicely within
my specially religious orbit. Write back immediately and tell
me what you think of 'Money' for a title – and the general idea.
Not a word to a soul. (or rather, please tell everybody, since
that's what you'll do in any case.) You must tell me all you know
about stockbrokers. The book will not be *against* money – only
exploring the idea on a large canvas! I am not mentioning this to
Macmillan or Paul yet, as I don't quite know if I am going to do
it, & don't want to be tied down.

Alan, I am longing to see the first of the new Greenbloom. You
will have it all down, 1ˢᵗ draft, within 3 months. The opening

sentence is enchanting. Man, you're so talented it takes my breath away.

Lots of love to the younger set & to yourselves

xxx

Muriel

ALS. MBC. Dating: *Memento Mori* recently completed; BBC adaptation of *The Comforters* broadcast on 17 December 1958; before the 'quarrel' with Alan Barnsley.

1. Having just completed her novel, on 12 June MS wrote to Derek Stanford, glossing Aristotle's description of the emotions requiring catharsis in the performance of tragedy:

    > I think I have something of *pity* and *fear* in Memento Mori. I think you will like it best of all my work, if I can get it done. 'The pain of being human' as you say, forces itself upon the imagination when one is dealing with the aged. It is, in a sense, an exercise of the imagination in the tragic human position. I do so intensely *feel* the pain of being human that perhaps I am inclined to 'laugh it off' in my work too much. (HRC)

2. The writer for radio and theatre Christopher Holme, then Assistant Head of Features at the BBC, had, with Rayner Heppenstall, proposed an adaptation of *The Comforters* for radio; on 20 February, in a memo to the eminent radio producer Douglas Cleverdon, he explained:

    > The author is herself keen on the idea and would help with any interpolated material or rewriting.
    >
    > In some preliminary work on this story, which in a way anticipates Pinfold, I have conceived a great enthusiasm for it in terms of radio. It is a Chinese Box affair, a novel written about herself by a writer on The Modern Novel who has an hallucination that someone is writing a novel about her. [. . .] The right length would be 90 minutes. The action is quite exciting enough to sustain that length. It has a full measure of the ingredients, crime, mystery, detection, which hold popular audiences in other Services for a 90-minute spell. (BBC WAC)

TO PAUL SCOTT, DAVID HIGHAM ASSOCIATES, LONDON,
19 JULY 1958

13, Baldwin Crescent, Camberwell, London, S.E.5
19th July, 1958

Dear Paul,

I gave Alan Maclean his copy of MEMENTO MORI yesterday.[1]
We did not discuss terms of publication but he volunteered the
opinion that, on the strength of my past two books, and the
reviews they have received, the new novel should be published in a
much bigger way, and generally pushed ahead.[2]

I think this looks promising as regards terms. Perhaps you
would discuss these with me when you have read the book?[3]

I think Alan knows by now that I do not welcome suggestions
for constructional changes in my work. But if any of these are
forthcoming I would consider them only after terms had been
discussed and agreed.

Yours ever,
s/Muriel

TLS draft. NLS.

1. After a distinguished military career during World War II spent mainly
   in India, Paul Scott joined Pearn, Pollinger & Higham in 1950; the literary agency changed its name to David Higham Associates in 1958. Scott
   had worked as an accountant for Falcon Press in 1953 and MS may have
   met him then; she certainly met him in 1957 when he made an adverse
   impression on her because of his dismissive response to *Robinson* (see 21
   August 1957, n. 2).
2. MS wrote to Dina Barnsley on 30 June: 'Robinson had a splendid review
   in Spectator, and also in Time and Tide. A middling one in T.L.S. Good
   in Observer and Sunday Times. So altogether Macmillan are dripping with
   pleasure and also, I think, surprise. Pray now, for those still to come –
   New Statesman, Listener, Manchester Guardian. That will about complete
   the important ones' (MBC).
3. Despite her misgivings, MS had made fast progress on *Memento Mori*. On
   1 June, she wrote to Derek Stanford, 'I have done just over a third of my
   novel, which is rather behind schedule' (HRC). And in an undated letter

to Stanford, probably from later in June: 'My novel creeps on. Entering the bones of old people is an ageing process. I begin to talk with a cracked voice, and consider getting the printer to set up the type rather shaky' (HRC).

MS's sense that this was to be the most appreciated of her novels to date would soon be borne out by one whose opinion mattered greatly to her, Graham Greene, who would write to her from Havana on 27 October: 'Many many congratulations on Memento Mori. Verily your best book' (NLS).

Muriel Spark with Paul Scott at the signing of Memento Mori, *1959*

TO PAUL SCOTT, DAVID HIGHAM ASSOCIATES, LONDON, 5 AUGUST 1958

13, Baldwin Crescent, Camberwell, London, S.E.5
5th August, 1958

My dear Paul,
  I would like to tell you again how much I enjoyed THE MARK

OF THE WARRIOR. First of all the actual writing, it is so
good; this always conditions my approach to a book. I think
the reason why one wants to talk about a novel after it has been
read really depends on the prose, and I think style is always the
main persuasive. To me, the formal 'game-of-chess' style of the
WARRIOR is absolutely right for the theme. If the book had been
about real warfare it would have needed a different style.[1]

As a story I like it tremendously; much stronger than THE
MALE CHILD.[2] I like the planned construction as if the book
itself were an exercise of war. You know I admired the handling of
the female characters in THE MALE CHILD. THE WARRIOR
must have been much more difficult; I should think it is more
difficult to portray a predominance of male characters all distinct
from each other, than where the characters are mixed. Ramsay
is awfully good, particularly the way he develops from the youth
who first meets Craig to the terrifying organiser. He seems to
squeeze all the *woman* out of himself. One sees him more and
more through Craig's eyes as the book develops, and one wants
Ramsay to go on and on in this terrifying way just to see how
far he can go, although the process is bound to kill him in some
way. When I commented to you on his being called 'Ramsay' this
was not meant as a criticism. It simply accentuates the difference
between this army environment and what one would expect to be
his normal personality; and the very fact that, as you say, the use
of the surname is a real convention, gives an extra impression of
the psychological pressure upon him (I mean where he is called
'Ramsay' throughout by the *narrator*. I see Craig calls his brother
'John' and the Company call each other by first names).

I wish there had been more Esther at the end to balance the
beginning.

I did enjoy the book very much, Paul. It is the only book I have
read for pleasure this year, and it was an enormous pleasure.

Best love,
s/Muriel

TLS. UTML.

1. Although later in his career, and especially posthumously, he will enjoy huge critical and commercial success, notably with the publication of his *Raj Quartet*, for now Paul Scott was trying to make a career for himself as a novelist while continuing his work as a literary agent. His novel *The Mark of the Warrior* had been published by Eyre & Spottiswoode earlier in the year.
2. *A Male Child* was published in 1956, also by Eyre & Spottiswoode.

TO DINA BARNSLEY, MAIDSTONE, KENT,
14 AUGUST 1958

13, Baldwin Crescent, Camberwell, SE5
14th Aug 1958 Vigil of the Assumption

Dearest Dina,

I do hope your bronchitis is clearing up and baby safe & snug.

I have just had Bluebell destroyed. She had a complication of diseases – as fast as one thing cleared up she fell sick with another. She was costing me weekly £1 – likely to last through the winter at this cost & still remain sick. I thought it unbecoming a Catholic in my position to spend a pound a week on a cat (or in any position; unless the cat was a pedigree investment). For a long time I had been hanging on to her against advice from all quarters, as I had a sort of mystique about her. But I think this is plain silly. However, this morning I saw that her eye was infected from her bad ear. Simultaneously I read in the paper about a mother who neglected her baby & gave it away to a neighbour, but fed the cat on the best – said she preferred cats. I decided then to call in the vet with his box of tricks. When she was dead the vet opened out her ear and showed me that it was loaded with pus. She had been unable to breathe for weeks through this infection & did not respond to pencillin [*sic*] really well. This ear had been giving off an awful smell. I have been going round with a cloth soaked in disinfectant, cleaning everything.

The only thing I'm sorry about was the vet not allowing me to stay in the room while she was being killed. Having made the decision I wasn't in the least squeamish & could easily have witnessed her last end. I believe they sometimes struggle a bit.

When the vet called me in, there was Bluebell lying stretched on her side on the table. She was not quite dead. The vet was feeling her fading heart-beat. One of her tiny paws was twitching slightly. Her eyes were open, popping upwards & glazed. I think during the course of the destruction their legs must twitch quite a lot. It is like an anaesthetic, only an overdose. She made no sound.

I gave Bluebell a last gentle stroke & the vet's assistant lifted her up by her four legs (upside-down) and put her in a bag. This bag had once held my hats. It was a large paper carrier. I had to empty my hats out of it quickly when the vet demanded 'something to put her in.' They carted her away in this bag.

Please keep this letter as I may want to refer to it some time for a story.

I feel very relieved, especially after seeing the state of her inside ear.

I have had a letter from Lippincott. Lynn Carrick (the chief man there) says he has read Memento with 'utter fascination', & thinks it is 'wonderful & unique'. I was a little worried about the American reception of the book, but I can now relax on that score.[1]

Still pressing on with The Comforters. The actual hours I have put in on it are very few, but the anxiety is large.[2]

Any chance of your coming up next week? I hope to have a party before I go away in September & want you & Alan to come. The date largely depends on you.

Write soon & tell me you are better.

Best love

Muriel

ALS. GULSC.

1. MS had met Lynn Carrick, with his wife Virginia, for lunch in London in July. A graduate of Princeton University, a former captain with the Marine Corps during World War II, Carrick had been appointed director of Lippincott's New York office in 1948. Later, in 1961, he will move to London where for two years he will be Lippincott's European representative, during which time he will see more of MS. On 12 August, he wrote to MS: 'MEMENTO MORI reached us on Friday and I read it over the

week-end with utter fascination. It is wonderful and certainly unique. I can't help wondering how you came to know so much about the aged' (NLS).
2. MS is referring to her attempt to adapt *The Comforters* for radio (see mid-1958 to Alan and Dina Barnsley, n. 2).

TO ALAN BARNSLEY, MAIDSTONE, KENT, CIRCA AUGUST 1958

[Camberwell, London]
Post – Telephone

Dearest Alan,

I pray for 8 DAYS, its splendid and inevitable success. You do not realise how the pattern of your life is reflected with blessing in your work. It is expansive, has magnitude, just like your own character and household. You simply don't realise how rare & distinguished this type of writing is in these days, when writers live in smart little box-rooms, have no children, meet each other & each other in pubs & pubs, catty as catty, small as small. Their vision is likewise.

I wonder if I have expressed what I mean?

I am sure you can't go wrong, for you are disposed towards the magnanimous light, and your time is well spent, however it may appear, whether doctoring or writing. A time to sow & a time to reap. Your books, like your family & whole environment are the kindly fruits of the earth. All are part of your *talent*.

I do look forward to seeing you on Tuesday. Bring 8 DAYS, do, if agreeable to you to do so. I should love to hear some of it.*

God bless you,

Muriel

* I have been praising it far and wide. Derek & I were discussing (re. Greenbloom) the other day, how one cannot forget your novels, while other novels, one can't remember!

ALS. MBC. Dating from letter to Alan and Dina Barnsley of 15 July where MS says: 'I should be able to read through EIGHT DAYS by about the 25th if you can let me have the proofs by then' (MBC).

TO ALAN MACLEAN, MACMILLAN LTD, LONDON,
14 SEPTEMBER 1958

The Friars, Aylesford, Kent
14th Sept 58

My dear Alan,

This is an excellent wrapper. Some commentators have
wondered if the Gothic lettering is right. Perhaps my name, at
least, might be plain-lettered? I think this might help to mitigate
a *slightly* too funereal note in the conception (since the book is
not entirely tragic by nature). However, I leave it to you, and am
really very delighted with it.[1]

I spent 10 days in Scotland & am now staying here for a while.
It is a place of great beauty & there are not too many Catholics at
this time of year. If you were to come down on a week-day and
hear the Friars at their plain-chant, you would simply fall into the
patient welcoming jaws of Rome.

Yours,
Muriel

ALS. MA.

1. On 30 July, MS wrote to Alan Maclean of the cover:

> I wonder if it is necessary to include an autobiographical note? If
> so, perhaps we could take out the bit about exciting adventures.
> Also, 'Political Intelligence Dept . . .' – this was intended to sound
> mysterious & intriguing but it seems a bit silly to push this line now.
> Would you put in somewhere 'was received into the Roman Catholic
> Church in 1954'? – This is really a milestone event. (MA)

The dust jacket to the first edition of *Memento Mori* retains the gothic
lettering for the title and the author's name, and shows a skeletal hand
reaching down towards a telephone.

TO DEREK STANFORD, HOUNSLOW, MIDDLESEX,
23 SEPTEMBER 1958

The Friars, Aylesford, Kent
23-9-58

My dear Derek,

Your letter has been sent on to me here where I shall be staying
until Monday next. Everything is very much changed for the
better at The Friars. The tone has been raised unmeasurably & it
is better organised. I am in one of the new annexe rooms – off a
long corridor painted pale green. In this they have copied my St.
Philumena's in *The Comforters*, as I pointed out when I came. (The
book pre-dates the new building!)

I was glad to hear from you and to know more plainly how
things stand. I think (and I think Macmillan would agree) it would
be inadvisable to attempt collaboration by correspondence. Of
course, a great deal of our collaborations have been done partly
by correspondence & separately, but then we were meeting fairly
regularly & were able to compare notes & exchange books etc. I
think *Newman by his Contemporaries* would be a book in which our
two sections must overlap considerably & the difficulties of the
book alone would be too great if we didn't meet.

I don't think, from what you say, we should meet until you are
quite better, and have lost your fear of the tummy-ache. I can't
help being slightly amused – though very sorry for you – at this
new vision of myself as the girl what gives them the gripes. I think
quite plainly we are not in a position even to discuss the book
until you are better, and I suggest we get Paul to ask Macmillan
for deferrment [sic] of six months. This will bring the delivery
date to July–August next. As the book is not a 'dated' one, there
should be no difficulty. I suggest we tell Macmillan that you have
been having stomach trouble (or 'nerve' trouble if you prefer
it) and are slackening your pace for six months. They are very
reasonable & very pleased with me at the moment & so I would
anticipate no objections from them.[1]

Alternatively, if you feel it would be an embarrassment to you to ask for this concession, we could approach Macmillan with a view to your doing the book alone. In this case I would want to retain a fair proportion of the advance to compensate for time spent & loss of publication; this could be agreed upon between you & Paul & I would then pay him back whatever sum you had agreed upon.

I am *perfectly happy* to proceed on *either basis*.

I think there is an excellent chance of the book being commissioned in America, but we had better get the authorship question clear before Paul proceeds to offer it.

Cheer up, little dear. Everyone has a nasty patch from time to time. I do not think you have anything radically wrong with you and in fact I think (from your letter) that you may be already on the mend. I hope you can get treatment if you really need it, but don't let them mess you around at all.

My poor little Bluebell is dead. I had six agonising weeks of her last illness. It was a curious disorder, a complication of diseases, so that as fast as we cleared up one thing she contracted another. She went to a vet to stay for a week. He (unknown to me) kept her *in a cage*. I retrieved her. She then couldn't walk & had got 'flu. The R.S.P.C.A. blamed me for trusting the vet, who was apparently not fully qualified. They admitted, however, that the public are easily defrauded by these unqualified vets, and that the law is to blame.[2] Bluebell recovered somewhat after much nursing and visits from a qualified vet. Her coat improved and she began to eat enormously. One of her last actions was to steal my Sunday dinner lamb chop while I slept thro' the innocent night. Then her glands swole [sic] up (as they had been doing before) all over her body. Penicillin was of no avail. Her ear began to suppurate. The vets considered her to be senile & were surprised to learn she was only 3½ years old. Poor Bluebell just fell to bits. At length her eye was affected. I summoned my courage and the vets. They brought two little boxes, one for Bluebell's death-bed and one for the lethal anaesthetic. They put me out of the room 'in case she should struggle.' I wanted to tell them that I would prefer to stay with my old friend, struggle or no struggle, it was the least I could do. I felt it mean to leave her and avert my gaze as if nothing was happening to her. But I did not want to prolong the performance by argumentation so I went out for a few moments. Then I was called back, and there was Bluebell full-stretched on the table with her eyes glazed and popping (a muscular reaction, I am told). The vet was feeling her heart and told me she was not quite dead. Her little paw was moving very faintly, then it stopped. The vet's assistant demanded 'something to take it away in.' The vet himself opened out Bluebell's ear to show me how it was loaded with terrible pus. I emptied my hats out of a large carrier bag and held out the bag for Bluebell. The assistant lifted her by her four legs upside-down. I gave her a last stroke and pat. He dumped her in the bag & I realised she was really dead. I was terribly upset but at the same time relieved that she was out of her suffering, not the least of which had been the dreaded injections, tooth-extractions and other unnatural performances upon her frail little body. She had got into a state of cringing whenever she heard a footstep at my door, lest it should be a cruel vet. I keep seeing her little smoky shape insinuating itself amongst my papers. I can't but think there is a form of perpetuity for the spirits of such animals as have become a part of the human heart, as Bluebell was.[3]

Well dear Derek, let me know more about what you are writing & how you progress in health. I am immensely grateful for your good work on Ace Books & hope fervently it will come to publication in paper-back for my Comforters.[4]

I shall be glad to know what you think of my suggestions for the Newman book, so that I can re-arrange my next working plans accordingly. At all events, there is no need for you to worry about the book, as you see.

I will pray for you and others here will say prayers for you too.

Love,

Muriel

ALS. HRC.

1. In his letter of 21 September to MS, Derek Stanford wrote, concerning his delay in progressing with the project of a joint book on Cardinal Newman:

> But, chief of all, my reason for deferring a meeting was the purely selfish fear I entertained concerning how any disturbance between us would react back upon me with this terrible pain and sickness in my stomach. I have come to fear bad recurrences of this: the last time we met I was laid up for a whole day with dreadful agony, continued vomiting & all the other trimmings. The worst of this is: that it clearly isn't something we do to each other deliberately. It is just a reaction which may overtake me, & over which I have no control. I'm at last trying to arrange for psychiatrical treatment through the National Health Service – a devious & tortuous approach, but I barely feel I can afford another path. (NLS)

2. Founded in 1824, the Royal Society for the Prevention of Cruelty to Animals was (and remains) the UK's largest animal welfare charity.

3. MS will write again about Bluebell, in an article entitled 'Ailourophilia' published in *Book Week*:

> If I were not a Christian I would worship the Cat. The ancient Egyptians did so with much success. But at least it seems evident to me that the domestic cat is the aristocrat of the animal kingdom, occupying a place of quality in the Great Chain of Being second only to our aspiring, agitated and ever-evolving selves. [. . .]
>
> I never got used to Bluebell's loveliness. When I woke in the morning to see her sitting, a sheer Act of Praise, on my dressing-table, surely waiting for some life to happen, I would gaze at her with awe and with awe.
>
> She was never exactly an ailourophobe but she grew to prefer human society to that of cats. At parties, she was gifted with the art of disappearing to nowhere from time to time. She was also greatly endowed with ESP. She would sit on my manuscripts if what I had written was any good, but if she stepped over the notebooks with her fastidious pads, I knew there was something wrong with the stuff. She came when called, but not invariably. Her sympathy, when she chose to exert it, was original and profound. She would brood comically over my wrongs, and, on occasions of rejoicing she quickly caught the spirit of the thing, sometimes taking a silly turn, leaping high, and landing with four legs outspread like a wonky new-born lamb. There was no end to Bluebell's virtues. (27 December 1964; *TGF*, pp. 166, 167–8)

4. In his letter of 21 September, Stanford reported having had conversations with a representative of the publisher Ace Books with a view to their pub- lishing *The Comforters* in a paperback edition.

TO DEREK STANFORD, HOUNSLOW, MIDDLESEX,
29 SEPTEMBER 1958

13 Baldwin Crescent, Camberwell, London, S.E.5
29.9.58

My dear Derek,

   Many thanks for your lovely Bluebell poem. It made me
feel very sad for Bluebell again. I hope you can place this 'In
Memoriam' in some worthy spot.[1]

   I saw Michael Swan who is staying at Allington Castle & he
was able to come out with me.[2] There is a case would turn your
heart over. His story is a terrible one. He 'tells' it as best he can
by writing odd words, with difficulty, both of his hand & brain,
on a slate. His physique & appearance are perfect. His only spoken
words are Yes, No, and Terrible. Sometimes, when hard pressed
to make himself clear he pronounces a word like 'Maidstone',
which makes me feel his difficulty is partly only psychological. He
told me his brain was 85% impaired. His *mind* is in good order &
he understands all conversation. The *functioning* part of his brain
is affected. I have told him to ignore his 85% loss & concentrate
on exploiting the 15% which he actually possesses, to the utmost.
He is not a believer, but goes to some of the Catholic services.
He is taking lectures in art & has done some drawings which are
excellent. Those done with his right hand, which is completely
numb, are better than the left-hand ones. He uses both hands with
great difficulty. He showed me the wound in his throat and at that
moment I understood for the first time those images of Christ
displaying his Sacred Heart. The mystery of Michael's suffering
is terrible. He has been told he will never write again – the
'automatic' writing he showed me was quite incoherent. 'Despair'
he wrote on his slate when I had read it. Someone at Allington
suggested he should try to make himself useful by feeding the pigs
& chickens. Michael refused. I pointed out there was a complete
misunderstanding at the best of times among people. Poor
Michael lit up & smiled, shaking his hands above his head at this.

It was the only time I saw him smile.[3] He is staying at Allington where Archie Colquhoun is librarian (the Sisters have gone & it is now a guest-house). Michael has lots of friends in London, & probably is well looked after. His tiny mother, aged 76, was with him part of the time & doing her best to be cheerful. Alan goes to see him occasionally. There is absolutely nothing anyone can do except pray for him, and anyone in a sensational way, I know.[4]

I do hope your psychiatrist will be of tremendous help to you. I shall pray for you (and for the psychiatrist). Let me know how you fare & be patient with yourself. At all events, your work is not impaired, my dear, as I see from your beautiful poem.

As regards Newman, I would not find it possible at all to do the book by myself. I think we had better request Macmillan to postpone the delivery date for six months & then review the position. What would you like Paul to say to Macmillan? I am sure they will not want elaborate explanations. We could say you are a little run-down, or simply that you have been advised to take things easy for a while. Paul feels, that we should say something this month. Alan Maclean is sure to ask how Newman is getting on & it would be best to answer suitably to all concerned.

Best wishes for your recovery.

Love,

Muriel

ALS. WUL.

1. Derek Stanford's sixteen-line poem is entitled 'Lines for a Little Cat'.
2. During the 1940s and 1950s, the novelist, essayist, and critic Michael Swan moved in literary circles that included many of the acquaintances of Stanford and MS; his daughter Anna Swan was the goddaughter of his close friend Alan Barnsley.
3. In *Statues without Shadows*, her account of the lives – and tragic deaths, her father by suicide, her mother by drug overdose – of her parents and of her own troubled upbringing, Anna Swan writes:

> It was late December 1957. My father was thirty-four and at the height of his success. [...] My father ought to have been plan-ning his next trip, unpacking his books or shopping for Christmas

presents. Instead, he took the Tube from South Ken to Piccadilly Circus. He booked a room in a seedy hotel in Coventry Street, ran a bath and cut his wrists and throat with a razor blade. [. . .] The loss of blood and oxygen to the brain caused severe neurological damage that left my father with the symptoms of a stroke: paralysis down the right side of his body and aphasia, which erased most of his vocabulary. Meticulous and methodical as he was, he forgot to place the Do Not Disturb sign outside the door. It saved his life but I doubt he would have thanked the poor chambermaid who found him. He never regained his command of language; for a writer it was a slow death. (Sceptre, 2005, pp. 176–7)

4. It is likely that the librarian was Archibald Colquhoun, the translator of Italian literature, best known for his translation of Giuseppe Tomasi di Lampedusa's *The Leopard*. Though this identification has not been confirmed, Colquhoun did have a connection to the Benedictine order, having gone to school at Ampleforth College which was founded by Benedictine monks and sits on the grounds of Ampleforth Abbey in Yorkshire.

Michael Swan's mother was Gwendolyn Davies Hyde-Clarke; Anna Swan describes her as 'Diminutive, dainty and invariably dressed in black' (*Statues without Shadows*, p. 22).

TO ALAN MACLEAN, MACMILLAN LTD, LONDON, 6 OCTOBER 1958

13 Baldwin Crescent, Camberwell, London S.E.5
6th Oct. 1958

My dear Alan,

About the change suggested by Lippincott to MEMENTO MORI: I take it they object only to the phrase 'Mr Owen . . . short for Cohen', and not to the fact that he is a Jew. I think I should have a Jew in MEMENTO, and surely it would be unfair to exclude them from the telephone calls – in the sense that they are as sensitive to death as anyone else. I suggest calling him 'Mr. Jack Rose' which indicates a Jew and yet is not exclusively a Jewish name. Will you ask Lynn Carrick if this will do? If so, I'll alter proofs accordingly.[1]

Yours,

s/Muriel

. TLS. MA.

1. The elderly characters in *Memento Mori* receive anonymous telephone calls telling them, 'Remember you must die.' The name Jack Rose was indeed adopted for the published novel.

TO DEREK STANFORD, HOUNSLOW, MIDDLESEX,
8 NOVEMBER 1958

13 Baldwin Crescent, Camberwell, London S.E.5
8th Nov. 58

Dear Derek,

Thanks for your note.

Your kind words about Alan & Dina are very welcome – and I must say refreshing as you disparaged Alan so drastically to my mother and father recently. It was embarrassing for me. They (my mother and father) naturally wondered why I went to stay with such a creature as you depicted & were alarmed really, by your account.

While on this subject, as you are in a reflective mood – I say it without irony at all – you may care to reflect on the embarrassment caused me by your revealing to my parents that I had had a nervous breakdown. As you very well knew, this was effectively concealed from my parents and Robin at the time, and it has caused me some difficulty to explain, and shock and surprise to my parents. However, I have coped with these difficulties up to a point, but it has been painful – not the least painful being the realisation that you were prepared to do these unnecessary things behind my back when I had shown you nothing but kindness.[1]

However, I put this down to your illness, and am prepared to forget it.

As regards the financial question; I only raise this because of course it is nice to know you are in a rather better position than I had the impression you were. It makes the idea of the Newman commitment easier to cope with. I can't afford – now that I have to contribute towards my parents and Robin besides keeping up my flat and supporting myself – to repay the money I have largely earned. Alan tells me you are quite prepared to do the book by yourself. This will be best, if Macmillan are agreeable. *I* couldn't do *all* Newman – only the part I signed for, and under the original arrangement for collaboration.[2]

Alan tells me good news of your impending marriage. I think this is fine, and am delighted you have made these plans. Also that you are now in a position to support a wife – it must give you a sense of achievement. I do wish you had told me of this sooner. Of course it is no business of mine. But I am always interested in your welfare. And of course, so far as this concerns our Newman book – from your previous letters I've had the impression that you weren't able financially, as well as in health, to meet your commitments. And, quite frankly, the prospect of having to give you financial assistance worried me. I'm very relieved you are now on your feet, and looking forward to a settled future.

I hope you don't mind my mentioning the Newman before time. But as you had discussed it with Alan I suppose you are able to discuss it with me without effect on your health. I hope so. You don't sound worried at all, by accounts of a cheerful nature I have from Igor and Paul and other chums.[3]

Of course, I don't want to let *Macmillan* down. That's a real anxiety; they have paid out two hundred and are entitled to have their book or the money back, and of course I hope, as Alan says you will, that you'll let them have the book and that you'll do well with it here and in America.

Best wishes once more. I'm dining with the Rosenbergs on Monday and perhaps they will tell me all about your news. *You* can't do better than Delilah. It is a grand idea. Do you plan to live in America?[4]

Yours,
s/Muriel

TLS. HRC.

1. That MS was having trouble with her son even before Derek Stanford's intervention is attested to in a letter sent to June and Neville Braybrooke one month earlier, on 4 October, where she wrote: 'I wish I could settle down to a routine attitude to poor Rob. I am either irritated beyond endurance or falling over myself to make up to him' (NLS).
2. MS refers to *Newman by His Contemporaries* which she had proposed to

produce with Stanford and which had been contracted to Macmillan by Alan Maclean.

3. Igor Chroustchoff and Paul Allen were prominent among MS's 'bachelors'.
4. Stanford was betrothed to – but in the event would not marry – an American relative of John Rosenberg who was studying in the UK; she has not been identified beyond her first name, Delilah.

TO DEREK STANFORD, HOUNSLOW, MIDDLESEX, 30 NOVEMBER 1958

13 Baldwin Crescent, Camberwell, London S.E.5
30 Nov 58

My dear Derek,

Thank you very much for your telegram and message which I much appreciated.

I don't know how much the reports have been exaggerated, but Alan Barnsley did not speak in malice or at least conscious malice. It did seem to me that I had been deceived by you from the beginning of this year especially, (when my diary entries testify to my bewilderment). It is perhaps really more important that you shouldn't deceive yourself on this point, because I myself don't bear any resentment to you – merely making it plain that I have only gradually become aware, from reports at second hand, of the explanation for much that puzzled and hurt me at the time. I think I was patient and kind, at least I hope so. And, as I say, reports are maybe highly exaggerated; and as regards our literary collaboration – which to me depended on the *status quo* of our friendship – I still don't know what you had in mind when making further plans & then suddenly again breaking communications. May next year see your restoration to health, the least of my good wishes.[1]

Muriel

So glad by your letter you like the stories. Comforters being broadcast on 17th Dec.

M.

ALS. HRC.

1. Notwithstanding the emollient tone of MS's letter of 8 November to Derek
   Stanford, the combined effect of his having, as MS saw it, betrayed the
   secret of her breakdown to her family, kept secret his engagement, and
   avoided meeting her throughout the year, had taken its toll. To this had
   been added a report of a visit made by Stanford to Alan Barnsley with a
   view to writing an article about Barnsley and MS – an article he would
   indeed write, and which when published will lower him yet further in MS's
   esteem (see 21 January 1961, n. 1).

1959

In late February, MS announced to Alan Maclean that she had finished *The Ballad of Peckham Rye*, which he swiftly contracted to publish. In March, *Memento Mori* was published in the UK to excellent reviews; by 9 April, Paul Scott could announce that nearly 3,000 copies were sold. In April, MS gave her first major interview, to *Books and Bookmen*, and was deeply unhappy with the printed article. Invited in April to contribute a story for *Queen* magazine, she wrote 'The Dark Glasses', which was accepted in October and was also offered for inclusion in *Winter's Tales*. Macmillan struck a deal with Penguin Books for paperback publication of MS's work. In May, *Memento Mori* was published in the US. MS submitted 'The Dry River Bed' to BBC Radio in June and went on holiday to Wales where she began serious work on her fifth novel, *The Bachelors*, based loosely on her London acquaintances. She received several requests for stories, including from *Vogue*. In late August, she took a five-week trip to Austria with the novelist Christine Brooke-Rose and her husband Jerzy Peterkiewicz, from where she wrote to one of her 'bachelors', the Irish writer and teacher Paul Allen. When on holiday, she completed two stories: 'A Member of the Family' and 'The Ormolu Clock'. Her work was contracted for translation and publication in several countries, including Germany, Sweden, and Norway. In October, Paul Scott announced he would be retiring from David Higham Associates, causing MS to consider changing literary agencies. In December, the theatre director Christopher Holme proposed adapting *The Ballad of Peckham Rye* for radio.

TO ALAN MACLEAN, MACMILLAN LTD, LONDON,
15 JANUARY 1959

13 Baldwin Crescent, Camberwell, London S.E.5
15th January, 1959

My dear Alan,

I much enjoyed last evening, it was very jolly.

I have been trying to recall faithfully the origins and reasons for writing various books. The enclosed accounts are fairly accurate, but they seem to me rather unsuitable and of course, too long – and also vaguely egoistic in tone, as suggesting the books are important enough to warrant all this chewing over.

I wonder if you could help me by underlining any parts or phrases which might be suitable for Fortnums' customers – or by any other suggestion?[1]

I am really finding this rather difficult. Even the enclosed accounts seem to suggest a far more serious *intention* in my work than I think I have. (If the achievement turns out to be 'serious' that is another matter.) But for Fortnums' purposes I feel something more light and airy would be wanted.

By the way, I can now let you have back the proof of Jane Duncan's book. Do you want it? I didn't really take to the breathless style but quite see the book will have a public.[2]

I haven't quite finished John Wain's novel of which you gave me a proof. I think it is a bit clumsy for Wain. For instance, in the opening George Links is a figure of satire and quite funny. But by chap. 3 you are induced to think and feel *with* him. And so it's neither one thing nor another. I am especially sensitive to this particular flaw because I do it myself. I am always waiting for some critic to pounce on it.[3]

Thank you again for your nice party. I enjoyed meeting Christopher Burney.[4]

Yours ever,

s/Muriel

TLS. MA.

1. Alan Maclean had organised for MS to sign copies of *Memento Mori* at the Piccadilly department store Fortnum & Mason, and had asked for an account of the origins of her novels; this account has not been found either in the Macmillan Archive or in the Muriel Spark Archive in the NLS.
2. MS was almost certainly reading either *My Friend Muriel* or *My Friends the Miss Boyds*, both of which were published in 1959 by Macmillan; Alan Maclean must indeed have seen a public for the work of Scottish novelist Jane Duncan as she would be offered a – remarkable – seven-novel contract the same year.
3. John Wain's novel *A Travelling Woman* was published by Macmillan in 1959.
4. Christopher Burney served in the Special Operations Executive during World War II; after capture, he survived fifteen months of solitary confinement in Fresnes prison, then deportation to Buchenwald concentration camp. His account of his experience, *Solitary Confinement*, was published in 1951 and republished by Macmillan in 1961, when MS reviews it; she will judge it 'a classic among war-time memoirs', adding: 'What I find most moving and intriguing about this study in solitude is its simple, almost casual assertion of a quite startling fact: that it was possible to retain a still centre of personal order in the immediate vicinity of prolonged chaos' (*Evening Standard*, 26 August 1961).

Muriel Spark signing copies of Memento Mori *at Fortnum & Mason, 1959*

TO DEREK STANFORD, HOUNSLOW, MIDDLESEX,
2 MARCH 1959

[Camberwell, London]
Monday

Dear Derek

Thanks for note. I believe they are very good at the Middlesex,
so Robin will not be seeing his 'present' for a long time yet. But it
was a nice thought.[1]

If it is gall stones they are taking out get them to keep them for
you in a jam jar, as many people do. It is a moot point whether
such stones & appendices & suchlike are counted as part of one's
natural body at the Resurrection. For instance, what has happened
to my appendix since it has been removed & will I rise again entire
without it? There is also the question of first teeth & the extracted
second teeth. Do we rise again with two sets? So hang on to
your stones, in case. Also warn them against removing any other
fittings whilst the mood is on them. Best of luck, anyhow.

    from

    Muriel

ALS. HRC. Dating from postmark on envelope.

1. The Middlesex Hospital treated patients from its opening in 1745 in the
Fitzrovia district of London until its closure in 2005.

    This is the last letter – or at least the last dated letter – from MS to
Derek Stanford in the principal archive of his letters from MS, at the Harry
Ransom Center; MS did write to him at least once more (see 21 January
1961), and she continued to receive occasional letters from Stanford,
including, for example, a delightedly enthusiastic response to his reading
of *Memento Mori* in April. Martin Stannard views this letter as terminal:
'The letter says two things simultaneously: "Get well soon" and "Get lost"'
(*MSB*, p. 203).

TO ALAN MACLEAN, MACMILLAN LTD, LONDON, 25 MAY 1959

13 Baldwin Crescent, Camberwell, London S.E.5
25th May, 1959

My dear Alan,

I have been thinking very hard about the paragraph in 'Peckham Rye' which we discussed.[1]

I really can't fit it in at an earlier point without upsetting other factors in the composition of the chapter – factors like the time-variations. And I don't want to start the book with this passage, for it would emphasise one intention at the expense of others.

The piece itself seems to me rather confusing, because the various alternatives it presents do not arise again in the novel. I don't know why I wrote it in the first place.

And now I'm a bit worried, because I like to follow your suggestions which are usually very helpful to my work. But I'm sure you won't mind if I follow my own strong instinct here. I would prefer to delete the passage altogether. Or, if you should think it essential, the paragraph could be left where it stands – perhaps preceded by a space?

I enclose pp.1–12 and p.233. May I have these back when the corrections have been transferred to your own copy, please? I shall have to send the new version to Lippincott.

I hope you enjoyed the Scarborough festival if festival it was!
Yours ever,
s/Muriel

TLS. MA.

1. It is not known to which paragraph MS is referring, probably deleted from the published edition of *The Ballad of Peckham Rye*. Surprisingly, no letter by MS has been found that contains mention either of the writing of *The Ballad of Peckham Rye*, composed between December 1958 and March 1959, or of the novel's submission to Macmillan. However, Alan Maclean did write to MS on 17 March to say: 'This is just a formal note to say that

we are delighted with the book, and definitely want to publish it' (MA). And, more revealingly, on 16 April Maclean wrote to Lynn Carrick, his opposite number at Lippincott, to explain why he thought so highly of the novel – and of the novelist:

> We think that it will have a very definite appeal here, whacky though it is. The problem of Youth, Juvenile Delinquency, Teddy Boys, etc., is very much in the public eye, and Peckham Rye is a part of London which is connected with various fables and bits of romantic near history. It is not, in my opinion, as satisfactory a book as MEMENTO MORI, but it is completely different. She is now going to review novels each week for the Observer for a period of three months, and, after that, is going to settle down to another longer novel to be called THE BACHELORS. This, of course, is only a project at the moment, but I believe that THE BALLAD OF PECKHAM RYE may do very well in between.
>
> As you say, she is very definitely an individual genius and I rather doubt that she is capable of writing to order. We feel that she is something very rare and now that her talents are beginning to be properly recognized, we think that everyone concerned will be rewarded. (MA)

TO ALAN MACLEAN, MACMILLAN LTD, LONDON, 28 MAY 1959

13 Baldwin Crescent, Camberwell, London S.E.5
28th May 1959

My dear Alan,
My holiday address is (from Monday 1st June)
c/o F[r]. Brocard Sewell, O. Carm.
St. Mary's College,
Tregeyb [sic],
Llandeilo,
Carmarthenshire.
My hosts are Carmelites, who don't come under my present Papist ban, since they themselves are like-minded.[1]
A man from Time Magazine was here to-day taking photographs. He made me pose pouring out tea, as Americans like a domestic touch, he said. I said, if you want to be realistic,

brother, you can take me washing up. No, he said, tea looks both domestic and sinister, kind of.[2]

Now, why should tea look sinister? And if it does, why pick on me? – However, I did as bid.

All good wishes,

Yours ever,

Muriel

ALS. MA.

1. St Mary's College in Tregib was a minor seminary set up by the Carmelites, dependent upon the larger St Mary's College in Aberystwyth, Wales.
2. *Time* did not run a feature on MS during this period; the identity of the photographer remains unknown.

TO ALAN MACLEAN, MACMILLAN LTD, LONDON, CIRCA MAY 1959

DEAR MISTER MACLEAN

ME AND MY PALS UP PECKHAM UNDERSTAND THAT YOU ARE DEBATING TO PRINT A BOOK ABOUT US BOYS BY A CERTAIN LOW SQUARE NAME OF SPARK WELL WE JUST WANT TO LET YOU NO GENTLE THAT IF SAME IS DONE YOU BETTER LOOK OUT FOR THAT HANSOM MUG OF YOURS WE CARVED UP PLENTY LIKE YOU IN OUR TIME YOURS COLLIE AND TREV[1]

AL in capital letters without punctuation, date, or address. MA.

1. The prevalence of gang violence and knife crime had been highlighted by Graham Greene's 1938 novel *Brighton Rock* which MS had read five years previously (see 9 December 1954). The dust jacket to the first edition of *The Ballad of Peckham Rye*, which Macmillan will publish in March 1960, and to which it had already committed, announces:

In the dance-halls of Camberwell, in the back streets of Peckham, in the residences on Denmark Hill and even on the Rye itself, the comic/satanic influence of Dougal Douglas is felt. [. . .] Among many others affected are Collie Gould and Trevor Lomas, leaders of their gang. [. . .] *The Ballad of Peckham Rye* is a novel of constant movement, written with brilliance, wit and perception. Muriel Spark's genius for combining truth with dazzlingly funny fantasy has never been better displayed – and readers of *Memento Mori* and her earlier books will know how good that is.

TO PAUL ALLEN, LONDON, 21 AUGUST 1959

Gasthof Antonitsch, Ferlach, S. Kärnten, Austria
21 Aug 59

My dear Paul,

We have been having a lot of rain, but quite a lot of sunshine too. You would love S. Kärnten, it has high, huge Gothic mountains and yet the people are so gentle. Perhaps if one lived among them always they would seem a little sugar-sweet.

I have learned quite a lot of German sentences and can ask for English cigarettes with filter-tips, wine, liquors, coffee, the loan of a typewriter, the price of typing paper and heaps of other things. Christine & Jerzy can speak fluent German, so they help me out.[1]

Bleiburg, where C & J spent a month & I only a week, was a noble little town full of exotic though decaying architecture, very Slavonic in influence – all pastel-painted & v. effective against the mountains. This is just a few kilometers from the Yugoslav border & they say – it is their favourite joke – that Tito is sending the bad weather – for the clouds do come over from Yugoslavia.

Christine & Jerzy are sweet to be with. We are all working v. hard all day. C. writes her novel & J. his play & I my novel – we write in various cafés, and everything is so cheap we can live like lords & ladies on very little. But I miss my batchelors [*sic*] very much, it is strange to be alone in a country with a married couple & without men friends of my own.

We avoid the English in Ferlach which is more touristic than Bleiburg, but an extremely attractive place with lots of wild walks and a huge dry river bed, (exactly like the one I envisaged in my play) leading far into the mountain. It is dry, full of boulders & huge colourful weeds, even in the floods, since the river has been diverted for the local water supply.[2]

There is a circus-fair coming here next week. On the whole S. Austria is very like Wales, though on a larger scale. When I was in Wales we had bad weather & a local fair, and here we have the same. C & J seem to think this is a frivolous observation.

Dear Paul do write & let me know how you are getting on with your writing & your life, & how your mother & Stephanie are liking the new flat.[3]

My next address – after 2nd September – will be
Strandhotel Obis,
Seelach,
Klopeiner See,
Süd Kärnten.

I have written a short story and 1½ chapters of my new novel The Batchelors [*sic*]. It is a new experience to be writing of London when London is 'abroad'.[4]

Give my love to Igor & Brian & to your mother & Steph.[5]
Love from
Muriel

ALS. NLS.

1. MS had been invited by Christine Brooke-Rose and Jerzy Peterkiewicz to join them on their holiday – MS's first on the continent of Europe. S. Kärnten is also – and perhaps better – known as South Carinthia.
2. MS's play for radio entitled *The Dry River Bed* had gone into rehearsal at the BBC on 17 June. MS will include it, in 1961, in her *Voices at Play* (pp. 87–109).
3. Stephanie was the younger of Paul Allen's two sisters.
4. The story was 'A Member of the Family' which is set in Bleilach, 'A lake town in Southern Austria'; in the story, the character Trudy remarks; "'it's all rather like Wales'" (*TCSS*, p. 111).
5. The journalist and actor Brian Parker, who would go on to be a successful

director of television programmes for the BBC, was a friend of Paul Allen and MS.

TO PAUL ALLEN, LONDON, 27 AUGUST 1959

Gasthof Antonitsch, Ferlach, Süd Kärnten [Austria]
27 Aug. 59

My dear Paul,

It was truly lovely to have your letter – one of very few I have been receiving, since my normal mail isn't being forwarded – and it is so full of your personality, I feel you are sitting with me on the terrace of this Café Gabi where I have begged! a sheet of fine paper to write to you.

The real Kärnten weather has come upon us – strong sunlight from early morning onwards & warm nights. The mountains glitter range upon range – very Alpine & visible only in this good weather. In the rain, one can only see the nearest mountains which overhang the town. It's a wonderful sight to see each town's church steeple rising beside its mountain. These steeples are onion-shaped, very Slovene, all over S. Austria.

I am learning German fast & get quite annoyed when I find a shop-keeper who can speak English. I like to feel my way in the tongue, however haltingly. To-day I was able to direct a couple of *Austrians* on a motor-bike the way to a certain mountain pass, so am very proud of my few German phrases. When I get stuck I make signs – the people are very amused & helpful.

Christine & Jerzy are very busy every day with their work but we meet for meals & are getting on famously. I am v. frivolous compared with them & don't take my writing so seriously. Of course I have more time. Jerzy goes back to his teaching at London Univ. at the beginning of term & Christine is going to look for a job. (But I've written a story & 2 chapters of my novel.)

Both send their love. Jerzy was pleased by Brian's appreciation of his book & amused that he is like Hugh Maguire – he accounts for this by the fact that he, too, was at a Jesuit school.[1]

Dear Paul I marvel at your Cardinal Richelieu, it is an exquisite piece & *robust* as well. Many congratulations – it is really most attractive & strangely moving. C. & J. haven't seen it yet – they both avoid reading while writing – but I'll let them see it when they pause for breath.[2]

Do write again & tell me more about Edgell Rickword whose poems I have had a great admiration for.[3]

I am glad you are feeling your English side a bit more & writing with your Englishness. Both sides are valuable & need to be exercised & nourished.[4]

Are you missing me a bit? How good it would be if you were here to enjoy the newness of everything with me!

The Stockwood cuttings are fascinating, for we see no papers here.[5] The Mass here is very beautiful – a dialogue Mass, partly in the vernacular, so it is not unlike a high Anglican service! A little boy reads the Lesson.

I am at the end of my paper. I'm sure there are heaps of things I've forgotten to say – will think of them when the envelope is sealed. Dear Paul, I write a very poor letter compared to yours. We will be here until 2nd September. I think I gave you the next address. Anyhow, do write soon. Love to all & esp. to yourself for writing so charmingly to

Muriel.

There is a frightful voyeur in the window just opposite mine. He sits with field-glasses & stares into the room! I've lodged a complaint, feeling v. embarrassed & English-spinsterish. He is a great fat brewer, but I think Frau Antonitsch will be a match for him.[6]

Save up some of the Eng. summer till I return so that we can sit outside that pub in Kensington where we went on our last meeting.

How is Steph's hussar?

ALS. NLS.

1. Jerzy Peterkiewicz's new book is likely to have been *Isolation: A Novel in Five Acts*, published by Heinemann in 1959. In notes to this letter made at Martin Stannard's request, Paul Allen explains that Hugh Maguire had attended, with him, the Jesuit Belvedere College in Dublin, and that this shared background gave him some resemblance to Peterkiewicz; Maguire was a violinist and concertmaster.

2. Allen's article 'Cardinal Richelieu's Anemones' appeared in the *Guardian* three days previously, on 24 August.

3. The *Collected Poems* of the poet and critic Edgell Rickword, closely associated with Communist politics and the *Left Review* of which he was founder and Editor in the 1930s, was published in 1947.

4. Allen was Irish by birth.

5. Mervyn Stockwood was appointed Bishop of Southwark, London, earlier in the year; while the precise cuttings sent to MS have not been found, what appeared in the *Guardian* of 24 August may be representative: on its front page, the paper carried the headline 'Dr Stockwood Cancels Priest's Licence', with the subtitle '"Form of Roman mass used," Prayer Book disregarded'. The inside pages reported on further controversies provoked by the bishop, including his endorsement of the Family Planning Association.

6. Frau Antonitsch was the owner of the hotel bearing her name where MS and her friends were staying.

TO ALAN MACLEAN, MACMILLAN LTD, LONDON,
1 SEPTEMBER 1959

Ferlach, S. Kärnten [Austria]
1st Sept. 1959

My dear Alan,

How very kind of you to send me the excellent information about epileptics! It arrived miraculously & unexpectedly just when I had reached the point in my novel where it is most needed. Thank you for taking so much trouble, I'm extremely grateful. The case histories are fascinating & a bit terrifying, especially where they report 'he has become more sociable & cheerful' etc. as a result of the drug. I mean, it makes one feel a bit uneasy about cheerfulness & so on.[1]

We are nothing if not cheerful now that we have fine weather again, we are soaking up the sun & feeling v. luxurious.
Jerzy & Christine are honeys to be with & we get on together

marvellously — which is rather unusual for writers, even tho' old
friends. The Jerzy's are writing far more industriously than I am, for
this is my first continental 'abroad' & I'm fascinated by practically
everything & am learning to speak German v. nicely — according to
J & C who are practised travellers & can even speak Icelandic.

These Carinthian towns are just on the borders of Yugoslavia,
surrounded by woods & mountains, v. savage & Gothic. The
towns are v. Slavonic in character — onion-shaped steeples &
oddly-constructed houses with lots of balconies & gables & lovely
useless towers. You would like the Kärnten Mass — it is rather
like an Anglican service, all in the vernacular & a bit *lower* in form
than the Anglo-Catholic Mass. The congregation recites the Ten
Commandments after the sermon & before the Creed. A small
boy reads the lesson & gospel (unheard-of in a London R. C.
church).

Everything is terribly cheap. We are living like lords on about
fifteen bob a day. Tomorrow we are going to a more posh lake
town to spend our last fortnight in style.

I don't know how my novel is turning out — at this stage it
seems a bit *dull*. But I think your epileptic articles will be a
stimulant. I've written a new short story & am doing another one
about the owner of our hotel here in Ferlach — a mighty Frau who
is a great power in the place & who recognises no equal except the
mountain range that separates herself from Tito.[2]

I do hope you have had, or are going to have, another slice of
holiday. Alan dear, thank you again for being so kind & helping me
with my book. I have the notes spread out on the café table where
I come to write, & am full of ideas.

Lots of love from
Muriel
C & J send love too.

ALS. MA.

---

1. The issue of epilepsy is raised in the opening pages of the novel on which
   MS was working, *The Bachelors*, as one of its central characters, Ronald

Bridges, 'could not leave alone any opportunity to try himself on the question whether his epilepsy would one day affect his mental powers or not' (p. 5). On 28 August, Alan Maclean wrote to MS:

> I understand that once a man has been diagnosed as an epileptic (both grand and petit mal), he will not be employed in any job where an attack might endanger him or other people, e.g. driving, stoking, etc. I have not been able to find any definite rule about the professions, but I gather that he would not be able to teach in schools. It seems, however, that with the use of barbiturates many epileptics do not have more than one or two attacks a year and can, therefore, lead active and normal lives. (MA)

2. This second story will become 'The Ormolu Clock' which, on 17 September one year later, will become MS's first story to be published in the *New Yorker* (*TCSS*, pp. 341–9).

TO PAUL ALLEN, LONDON, 5 SEPTEMBER 1959

Strandhotel Obis, Seelach, Klopeiner See, S. Kärnten [Austria]
5th Sept' 1959

My dear Paul

The church clock at St Kanzian is striking eleven at this moment, and we get up so early it seems that half the day is gone. St. Kanzian is the nearest village to the lake town where we have come to spend our last two weeks. We are still near the Yugoslav frontier and all the inscriptions on the gravestones of the church are in Slovene, as are those on the great stations of the Cross inside the Church. The café terrace where I am sitting now, under huge trees, faces the old church where one senses such a long unbroken religious past.

Dear Paul it was lovely for me to find your letter waiting for me when I arrived on Wednesday. We had been travelling since six in the morning, & had been very rushed as the alarm clock had let us down, as they always do. However we were in high spirits and bought fourpence-worth of gin on the way to settle our queasy stomachs. After that we had a long Germanic argument with the hotel management about our rooms, for Seelach is a touristic place and everyone is on the make, as in Brighton, etc.

I read to Jerzy your passage about the Jesuits and he was greatly interested.[1] Both C. & J. are just now coming to the end of their work, and I have completed all I want to do, and so we hope to have our last ten days workless, sheer holiday. It is very cold just now but we hope for fine weather on Our Lady's birthday, the 8th. Jerzy promises a return of the sun on that day. But even under a cloudy sky the lake is a great delight. I see it first thing in the morning from my window with the mountains in the background and a few brave bathers dotted along the shore.

You say such warming things about me, – dear Paul I am so often up and down by turns I sometimes take a great dislike to myself. And then I wonder how disinterested all my labours really are. I have a horror of losing sight of my first vision which has enabled me to write whatever I had a mind to, without thought of reward. This holiday has been a good experience, because we are living humbly and cheaply – the Jerzys' [*sic*] know how to do so on the Continent – and yet so happily. I should have hated to go to the smart places and met the same sort of people one might come across at the Ritz. I don't think anyone can say they have travelled at all if they have only been to the tourist centres. I feel you are one of those who have kept their vision intact & I think you wouldn't know how to lose it.[2]

You would like the Kärnten Mass. The congregation sings or recites throughout while the rite is going on at the altar. In some ways it is as if a Methodist or Congregational service were in progress in the pews and an R.C. one at the altar. But this is not a total analogy, for the unity of the service is quite clear. The congregation in Ferlach recited the Ten Commandments, in the vernacular, after the sermon and before the creed. They had a procession in commemoration of a year when the village escaped the Plague – their forefathers had taken a vow which they still keep. J. & C. told me that the sermons were extremely good – I was able to follow a little of them. One Sunday the subject was Angst and its folly. The next Sunday it was Death, as in Memento Mori. So now I have a resolution to consider the lilies of the field.[3]

I am thinking of you now preparing to return to school on

Monday and your giving out the spirit like the schoolmaster in your story. I hope it will be a happy term for you, Paul. The more spirit you give out the more you retain, that's the thing about spirit I think.[4] I find my writing, if I do it well, enriches me if it doesn't anyone else. You must wear your grand new clothes as a sign of your confidence, and I'm longing to see you in them.

I haven't written to the Heppenstalls, except a post card. I don't really know why, but some inward voice has prevented me from doing so. Perhaps this is sheer impoliteness. Am so glad you wrote to Lindy, she will appreciate that. Perhaps Rayner is a bit of a mystic, but without a religion I don't know if the word means anything. He can be so amusing at times & at other times conveys the abyss.[5]

I have now done 4 chapters of The Bachelors, have established all the characters & am now going to leave it alone till I return to London and attune my ear to London phraseologies. I wrote a little story for Vogue, but my best effort I think is a story I have just finished called 'The Ormolu Clock'.[6] It is all about the owner of our guest house in Ferlach, and her mighty character, and how she dealt with the old voyeur who tries, each season, to upset her guests. She is (in my story, I mean, for I have greatly enlarged her) an ambitious pagan, or perhaps not quite pagan – more like one of those terrifying women of the Old Testament – Judith, Miriam, Esther.

I have grown very fond of Jerzy & Christine in our weeks together. We are old friends but it is rare, and rather good, that writers should agree so well in proximity. We largely understand each other's ways & that is the great thing.

Next week when we have put away our work we shall walk and, I hope, sun-bathe and read. I have read most of the English books we brought with us, but I am saving up Joad's *Guide to Modern Thought*. I wonder if you know it?[7]

Our date for returning is the 17th.

Thank you dear Paul for offering to meet me, but the time of arrival at Cromwell Road would be uncertain & it would be fairly late in the evening. But will you ring me on the Friday if you are free to do so? I shall want to hear from you as soon as ever possible.

I hope your mother is gay as ever & liking the new flat.
Stephanie does right to be choosey about her men friends. There is
nothing like setting yourself a high standard & then even the less
likely types begin to live up to it. (This sounds like real Woman's
Page advice!)

What a long rigmarole this is.* But let us have a longer &
livelier talk when we meet again.

Meantime, lots of love from

Muriel

Do write again if you have the time.

* and I see my handwriting has degenerated in the process, like
  that of a true graphomaniac.

ALS. NLS.

1. In the margin of Martin Stannard's copy of this letter, Paul Allen wrote:
   'Jerzy and I both attended Jesuit colleges. Catholic topics were all the rage
   with us throughout the whole M.S. circle' (NLS). Allen's letter to MS has
   not been found.
2. Asked by Stannard if he sensed MS's fear of loss of artistic vision, Allen
   responded (on Stannard's copy of the present letter): 'No, she was always
   joyful and charming though, of course, one sensed inner conflict.'
3. MS cites Matthew 6: 28–9 (or possibly a similar passage in Luke 12: 27):

   > Consider the lilies of the field, how they grow; they toil not, neither
   > do they spin:
   >   And yet I say unto you, That even Solomon in all his glory was
   > not arrayed like one of these.
   >   Wherefore, if God so clothe the grass of the field, which to day is,
   > and to morrow is cast into the oven, shall he not much more clothe
   > you, O ye of little faith?

4. Allen was returning to his teaching post at St Olave's Grammar School,
   Tower Bridge, London.
5. Allen noted at the end of Stannard's copy of the present letter: 'Rayner
   and Margaret Heppenstall were Muriel's good friends. Lindy and Adam
   were their teenage children. I gave Lindy advice about going to France.
   Igor and I had many conversations with Rayner and collected his books. He
   disapproved of Muriel's success and contract to Macmillan's. He expected
   her to be a more independent artist.'
6. The 'little story for Vogue' was 'A Member of the Family' (*TCSS*, pp.

111–22). On 15 September, Jean Leroy of MS's literary agency David Higham Associates will write to MS: 'This is just to report that I read A MEMBER OF THE FAMILY which I enjoyed very much and which I certainly want to send across to America. [. . .] When I talked to Penelope Gilliatt of Vogue the other day, she told me she simply adored your story – so all's well there' (NLS).

7. *Guide to Modern Thought* by the influential and popularising philosopher C. E. M. Joad was originally published by Faber & Faber in 1933; it was subsequently republished regularly.

TO ALAN BARNSLEY, MAIDSTONE, KENT,
23 SEPTEMBER 1959

13 Baldwin Crescent, Camberwell, London, S.E.5
23 Sept. 1959

My dear Alan,

Take Alice Dawes, who is 24 & a diabetic since the age of 12. And take Patrick Chase – characters in The Bachelors – her lover, aged 54. Patrick has a plan to murder Alice, and he is in a position to carry it out. His habit is to give Alice her insulin injection every day. He plans to substitute water or some ineffectual fluid (?) for the insulin.[1]

Please ∴ tell me tell me 1) how long it would take, in probability, for Alice to die if deprived of insulin.

2) Would Alice have fits?

3) Would they resemble epileptic fits?

4) Would Alice *know* that she was being deprived of insulin? Or might she merely feel weaker & weaker.

A further complication from the medical point of view is that Alice is pregnant.

From the criminal point of view I think the obvious difficulties could be overcome (such as the question why Alice doesn't ring up her doctor when she becomes ill. Answer: she is alone in a chalet on a Swiss mountain with Patrick, etc. etc.).

This is not to be an achieved murder: but I must have a watertight plan of intention in Patrick's mind.

Please reply in such a way that it could be quoted in the actual novel. That is — a verbal answer from a doctor to Patrick's enquiry. (Doctor not in a position to give subsequent evidence about Patrick's enquiry.)

What a lovely September to return to! I am trying to pick up the threads of my novel, which I haven't touched for some weeks.

Let me know your answer, like a great dear. Indulgence of 700 years for this + a prayer for the Pope.

All love to childers & parents

from

Muriel

ALS. GULSC.

1. Alan Barnsley was well placed to give answers, being a doctor in general practice. Patrick Chase will have become Patrick Seton when *The Bachelors* is published; Alice Dawes remains Alice Dawes.

TO ALAN MACLEAN, LONDON, 20 NOVEMBER 1959

13, Baldwin Crescent, Camberwell, S.E.5
20th November 1959

My dear Alan,

I'm addressing this to you at First Street tho' it's about my work, because I think you understand me & I need your advice & don't want you to think me grumpy or officious.[1] It's the general question of giving interviews & it arises because I was rung up to-day at a quarter to two and questioned about myself as regards 'Peckham Rye' by a Mr Elliot who was *very* civil but who hadn't read the *book*. He telephoned at Mr White's suggestion.[2]

I don't at all want to complain about this occasion, or about Mr Elliot or Mr White. Only I've been thinking quite a lot about my personal difficulties in being interviewed, & how to overcome them & be reasonable & co-operate with your publicity

arrangements. Would it be possible for you-all not to give my
telephone number to anyone? — You could then ring me yourselves
first, or perhaps a better course would be to ask interviewers to
write — so that I can consider whether I want to speak to them or
not & if so, make a suitable time?

I know some authors have excellent answers off pat any hour
of the day or night. But I'm not up to that. On the other hand I
sometimes *like* answering reasonable questions about my writings
& the relationship of my life to it. But I find it v. difficult, since
I see life complexly, *suddenly* to answer questions of a personal
nature, — I need time to think. And it's difficult to speak to
strangers when one's mind has been on something else. Then, as
you know, 'clever' interviewers can sometimes appear offensive
& it's clear that you as publishers can't & don't always support the
author if something goes wrong — I'm not in the least suggesting
you should, since it may be the author's fault — only perhaps
therefore the decision to give interviews shd. be left with the
author.

Please don't take this as a moan against Mr Elliot. He was
perfectly nice & I told him what I could, but rather as if I were
broadcasting from Venus, you know. (Mr White must get me a
copy of any report before it appears.)

But for the future, do you think my suggestion a reasonable
one? Would it annoy editors to be asked to write to me first to
ask for an interview? — I don't want to annoy editors or seem
pompous. Dear Alan if this won't do *please* suggest something
else. I'm sure it's simply a matter of our getting things straight —
my recognising your needs as publishers & your recognising my
limitations. And please don't be offended by my writing to you
about this — it isn't personal & I think you are sweet.

Love from
Muriel

ALS. MA.

---

1. Alan Maclean lived in First Street, Knightsbridge.

MS's prevailing mood may perhaps be judged by an account of herself given in a letter to Dina Barnsley written four days later, on 24 November: 'I am in a doldrum & telling myself life is all doldrum – depression is the norm & anything else is a nice surprise. I am sick of writing novels. (But just try stopping me!)' (MBC).

2. Dennis G. White was head of publicity at Macmillan. Mr Elliot has not been further identified. MS may have been anticipating the extra attention she would be receiving, not least from the other side of the Atlantic. She wrote to Rachel MacKenzie on 1 November: 'I am very thrilled by your news about "The Ormolu Clock", and delighted that I have made the "New Yorker" at last. You have been so kind and encouraging all along, and I hope now to be able to do my best stories for you' (NYPL). And Maclean wrote to MS on 10 November: 'I am returning with thanks your story, "The Ormolu Clock". I think it is excellent and a worthy story to start your association with the New Yorker. We all send you our congratulations' (MA).

TO CHRISTOPHER HOLME, BBC, LONDON, 31 DECEMBER 1959

13 Baldwin Crescent, Camberwell, London S.E.5
31st Dec. 1959

Dear Christopher,

I am sorry about the bother, but I'm sure you will work it out with Rayner. I am assuming you will be doing the adaptation & wonder what you think of the idea of my writing lyrics for songs? – it is only an idea & I may not be able to manage it. But I mention it in case it appealed to you & then you could indicate where these could come in.[1]

Yours
Muriel
Best wishes for 1960!

ALS. BBC WAC.

1. MS had written to Christopher Holme on 6 March 1958, when her 'new novel' was *Robinson*: 'I am very pleased to know that you like my new novel. I was afraid you would not, as I wrote it with the part intention of doing

something quite different from The Comforters. It is very encouraging to know of your interest in The Comforters. I thought your adaptation very good and do hope the Third will respond favourably' (NLS).

On 4 December, Christopher Holme wrote an internal BBC memo proposing to adapt *The Ballad of Peckham Rye* for radio. On 10 December, he wrote to MS to propose meeting so as to discuss the adaptation; and on 21 December, he wrote a BBC memo to say: 'The idea is that I should block out a skeleton adaptation from the book and that Mrs. Spark should fill it in with new, specially written dialogue etc., where necessary. We are proposing to make some fairly radical departures from the original plot and perhaps even use a different first title for the programme' (BBC WAC).

1960

In March, Macmillan published *The Ballad of Peckham Rye* to excellent reviews and sales. MS wrote *The Danger Zone* for radio, and she collaborated until October with Christopher Holme and the composer Tristram Cary on a musical adaptation of *The Ballad*. By July, MS already had a clear idea and title for her sixth novel: *The Prime of Miss Jean Brodie*; she worked on the novel in free moments for the remainder of the year. In August, *The Ballad* was published in the US. Disappointed by the retirement in March of Paul Scott, for whose novel *The Chinese Love Pavilion* she wrote an enthusiastic blurb, MS withdrew from David Higham Associates and returned to her former agent, John Smith. In July, she took her son Robin to Nice for an unsuccessful week-long holiday. In September, she enjoyed her first *New Yorker* publication, with 'The Ormolu Clock'. In October, she submitted a piece to the BBC's Woman's Hour, which was broadcast as 'My Favourite Villain: Heathcliff'. The musical adaptation of *The Ballad* was broadcast on the BBC on 7 October. Macmillan threw a launch party for the publication of MS's fifth novel, *The Bachelors*, which came out on 13 October; the reviews were excellent. On 13 November, MS wrote two bitter letters to Alan Maclean accusing him of lying to her and failing to support her work; he stepped down as her editor, to be replaced by his superior, Rache Lovat Dickson. Despite the spat, she submitted to Macmillan a collection of her stories and radio plays, 'Stories and Ear-Pieces', for publication, and expressed to her new editor the desire to visit the 'Holy Land'. She travelled to Edinburgh for Christmas and New Year, with her Edinburgh novel, *Jean Brodie*, not yet finished.

TO CHRISTOPHER HOLME, BBC, LONDON, 9 JANUARY 1960

13, Baldwin Crescent, Camberwell, London, S.E.5
9th January, 1960

Dear Christopher,

Thanks so much. I am delighted to know you agree about the lyrics. The idea is getting a grip on me and I think it rather exciting.

I don't want to trouble you before you are ready. Only when you have time, please will you think about the following and let me know your views?

Frankie and Johnny ballad: I might find it difficult to do the whole story in this form as it would be so much a replica of the prose version which I've already written. But I should be able to do a ballad-piece to begin and end the story.

Occasional lyrics: The type of lyric I have in mind may be indicated by the notes enclosed. These would be songs illustrating the characters and situations. I have almost completed the 'Street Song of Nelly Mahone' and thought of a tune for it – but this may not be what you wish.

Does the general idea appeal to you? I think what I have in mind would probably work out as a sort of 3rd Pgm. *musical* rather than a play with music.

I am working on my novel mainly just now; it should be finished by the middle of February.[1] But if you can give me the go-ahead I can be working on the lyrics in between-times.

Yours,
s/Muriel
Muriel Spark
Do please say, if these ideas are all wrong.[2]

TLS. BBC WAC.

---

1. The novel in progress was *The Bachelors*.

2. Christopher Holme will respond enthusiastically on 15 January, starting his letter, 'I think you have hit it exactly for a start' (BBC WAC).

TO RAYNER HEPPENSTALL, BBC, LONDON, 22 JANUARY 1960

13, Baldwin Crescent, Camberwell, S.E.5
22nd Jan. 1960

Dear Rayner,

I somehow got the impression that Interception would not be wanted.[1]

Interception will probably have to be postponed again because 'Ballad' has now taken priority with my time and attention.[2] I can't promise Interception for April if you want a good job done on it. I'll have to spend more time and labour on 'Ballad', in its new form as a musical, than was originally allowed for, if I'm to make a good job of that.

A sub-title for Interception would be 'An Arrangement of Place'. As you know the plot has departed from the original synopsis, and turns on discrepancies of place-sense. The scene is a mountainous district. Two groups of people. The older set, Welsh-accented and round-eyed, are conscious of living safely in Wales. The younger group grow up to speak with foreign accents and are slit-eyed; they are conscious of living dangerously on a mountain border of Eastern Europe. And so, if the title could be conveniently changed from Interception to The Mountain Range, perhaps that would leave me more scope for development of plot; in this case a sub-title might be 'A Vision seen through Narrowed Eyes', unless you can suggest something better.

Yours,
s/Muriel

TLS. BBC WAC.

1. The previous day, 21 January, Rayner Heppenstall wrote to MS to say – with prescience, given that indeed the script would never be written: 'To my secretary over the telephone yesterday, I understand, however, you to have said that you regarded this as now once more in abeyance, and indeed, doubted whether the script would ever be written' (BBC WAC).

2. On 17 January, MS wrote to Christopher Holme of her work on the musical version of *The Ballad*: 'My music sense is quite undeveloped and I have only thought of the tunes to help me get the words and rhythms of the lyrics. But I haven't done much so far, and perhaps I am a bit precipitate. I think perhaps now I had better wait for your first outline, and then we can see what type of lyrics we want and where they can go' (BBC WAC).

   And on 20 January, again to Holme, she added: 'Possibly I *was* thinking and still *am* thinking unconsciously of the Bomb – everything seems to point that way' (BBC WAC). Also under consideration was a stage version of *The Ballad* by Clive Exton; having read his adaptation, MS will write on 6 February to John Smith, the literary agent to whom she had returned after leaving David Higham Associates: 'I think, now, I am willing to have a shot at it myself. Nobody could get quite what I mean – and I was prepared for that – but I think another hand in it would more widely diverge from my own than one could accept. If I do it myself there will be no question of having to decide on the *theory* – whether Dougal is a devil or not, etc. I'll just *do* it' (WUL).

TO ALAN MACLEAN, MACMILLAN LTD, LONDON, 5 FEBRUARY 1960

13, Baldwin Crescent, Camberwell, London, S.E.5
5th February, 1960

My dear Alan,

I thought, after all, you might like just to see the arrangements with A.B.C. television, which I have accepted. Please will you return the letter?[1]

I hope I didn't give you the wrong impression by saying I'd have to tell them what to ask & what not to, etc. It is only family affairs that have to be avoided, so that no offence is given to my son or to my former husband who has had a very rough time and is only now beginning to recover his health. But there's no need for you to be concerned with this. In fact I think it better if I tell the interviewer briefly what to avoid – I haven't ever found any of them unco-operative on this score.

It sounds quite fun, doesn't it? I suppose I shall be at the technical rehearsal while you, in London, are passing round the collection.

Your Sever,

s/Muriel

TLS. MA.

1. On 4 February, Guy Verney, producer at ABC Television (UK), wrote to MS 'to confirm that we would like you to appear in our programme, THE BOOK MAN, to discuss your new book, THE BALLAD OF PECKHAM RYE'. The terms he offered: 'For appearances in THE BOOK MAN we offer a standard fee of 25 guineas, plus 1st class travelling expenses, and 2 guineas subsistence for the night in Birmingham' (NLS).

TO RAYNER HEPPENSTALL, BBC, LONDON, 27 MAY 1960

13, Baldwin Crescent, S.E.5

27th May, 1960

Dear Rayner,

This is now completely revised and it's the utmost I can do. Once I've finished a thing to my own satisfaction it's impossible for me to re-enter the creative state in which I wrote it. You would find, if I did any more to it, that the lines would be more and more *out of character* – this as a result of my being unable to re-live the creative conditions in which I wrote the play.[1]

I think the insertion of the song and the other dialogue insertions throughout do give more body to the scenes with the young people. But I don't want these scenes to be too lush, they are austere.

Honestly, I think you will make a jolly good production of it. Any questions I can answer to help you with the production, of course I'll be glad to do my best.

See you soon,

Yours,

s/Muriel

TLS. BBC WAC.

1. On 9 April, MS wrote to Christopher Holme: 'Thank you so much for
    the completion of the first draft of "The Ballad".' She added: 'It may be
    better to condense the dialogue rather than cut, and I'll work this out with
    Rayner and see what he has to suggest' (BBC WAC). And on 12 April, she
    wrote to Rayner Heppenstall: 'As I said at the beginning, I am no good at
    adaptation and can re-write, or write new dialogue, only if told *where* to
    do it. [. . .] I have to start a new novel on May 15th, and so am fairly free
    and easy to work on this before that date' (BBC WAC).
        In turn, Holme wrote on 11 May to the composer Tristram Cary who
    had been chosen to write the music for the production:

    > This draft has now been cut down to length but it has not yet got
    > Muriel's contributions. As she and I discussed it rather fully, how-
    > ever, before I cut it, it will show you how our minds are working,
    > and give you a chance to jump in now and make any suggestions of
    > your own for structural or other changes before we go any further.
    > She will, I think, have already written some 'lyrics'. (BBC WAC)

TO PAUL SCOTT, LONDON, 3 JUNE 1960

13, Baldwin Crescent, Camberwell, S.E.5.
3rd June 1960

My dear Paul,
    Thank you for a lovely afternoon & for doing plumb-work.
I didn't intend this – only wanted an opinion or so – but was
delighted to have the problem solved.
    I hope my blurby piece for you is acceptable to the publishers on
both shores. I *do* love The Chinese Love Pavilion. You have set out
my tribute very nicely.[1]
    See you soon.
    Lots of love,
    Muriel
P.S. G thinks 'instantly' should be 'constantly' – or should it? –
but not importantest[2]

THE CHINESE LOVE PAVILION

MURIEL SPARK writes:

I love *The Chinese Love Pavilion*. It is enchantingly exotic, sensuous and colourful. Everyone should read it. There is an unusual
and fascinating handling of sex, but to me the most interesting
element in this book is its *high romance* which has so long been
debased in the English novel. In *The Chinese Love Pavilion* this
quality of romance is excitingly elevated; Mr. Scott proves that
it can be done. He has effectively laid on great heady splashes
of colour, sensuality and exoticism, and this is a thing most
serious novelists are rightly afraid of doing. The author has
succeeded by a method of gradual enticement of the sober
reader into his glamorous world where all five senses become
intensified, and also by the contrasting austerity of the central
character who in his long absence from the scene mysteriously pervades the book. The element of fantasy is instantly
chastened by the realistic detail – it is all vividly provable: this
is Malaya in the year of the Japanese surrender, these men are
the actual military in their post-battle slump, and these girls of
the Love Pavilion are undeniably there and nowhere else.

M.S.

ALS with typed blurb. HRC.

1. Paul Scott had officially retired from his role as literary agent at David
   Higham Associates, a move which prompted MS to leave the agency; but
   he continued to take an active interest in MS's affairs. His novel *The Chinese
   Love Pavilion* was due out in the autumn.
2. 'G' may be Gabriel Fielding (Alan Barnsley).

TO CHRISTOPHER HOLME, BBC, LONDON,
21 JUNE 1960

13, Baldwin Crescent, Camberwell, London, S.E.5
21st June, 1960

My dear Christopher,

I enclose your top copy of 'The Ballad' with the new insertions
and some alterations to the text.

The insertions have been placed according to Tristram's ideas
for his music, so that one section can merge naturalistically with
another.

You may find the 'ballad'-pieces a bit odd but I think they will
work in all right with the background music. I think Tristram has
suggested that they should be chanted or spoken. Some of them –
such as Nelly's and Dougal's – could be sung, since these would
not require professional voices. On the contrary, Nelly's ought to
be a terrible voice, and Dougal's should be quite spontaneous –
hardly singing at all.[1]

But do let me know what you think of the script now. I am
sending Tristram the batch of insertions and will also make the
alterations on his copy of the text when next I see him. I thought
some of his musical ideas were quite brilliant.

Yours ever,
s/Muriel
Muriel Spark

TLS. BBC WAC.

1. Christopher Holme will reply the following day, 22 June: 'I'm delighted
   with your songs and other insertions. I laughed aloud sometimes when
   reading them' (BBC WAC).

TO PAUL SCOTT, LONDON, 1 JULY 1960

13, Baldwin Crescent, Camberwell, S.E.5
1ˢᵗ July 1960

My dear Paul

Thank you once more for your kindness. I do so much look forward to your piece on me and am really touched by your wanting to do it & especially, I'm keen on being presented as a bit more of a Square than is currently supposed.[1]

Thanks, too, for news from Alan. Of course it will be best in early October & with both A. & Lovat Dickson out of the way the bk. might have a chance – tho' I shan't say so.[2] I'm avoiding Alan at the moment because, well-meaning tho' he is, I can't bear his ringing me up to apologise for not ringing me up (thus implying that I've been sitting with palpitations by the 'phone) or else ringing me up to suggest that he might ring me up next week to suggest that we might meet if he has a free day . . . etc. My landlady has got his measure now & has told him I'm hardly ever in & David H. (whom I saw to-day), has also suggested that I'm rather busy just now. So that's why I'm so grateful to you, among other things, for finding out about publication date.[3]

D. Higham Assocs. were all in a state of Paul-intoxication this afternoon. You seem to have made them very happy & Jean especially shed a maternal tear & assured me there was 'no-one like Paul,' which I heartfeltly reciprocated. Sheila W. showed me the marvellous spread in the Bookseller for the Love Pavilion. How good that is! I love the girl. All the blurb is just right, too. It is going to be hugely successful, I know.[4] It cheered up my day, as I had been very staggered by a nasty stab from Heppenstall. I think David & Jean will put it right. Really, I will have to cultivate some new chum on the BBC, because Rayner is altogether too neurotic (for a neurotic author to deal with, I mean).[5]

I will look out for Venetian Red.[6]

What did you think of The Fathers?[7]

Your children's holiday was the Feast of St. Peter & Paul. S. Michael lives in October.

I gave a party the other night at the request of Tom Maschler, so that he could meet young men with new manuscripts or at least new men with young manuscripts. There were 5 bachelors in all, with Tom in his element as Publisher, tho' not a bit bumptious.[8] He has got himself a white Sunbeam Alpine to go with the job. One of the guests asked me, did I make the mayonaise [*sic*] myself? I said, of *course* (tho' it was bought in a carton at Lyons' Corner House). And now he has written 'the food was delicious – mayonaise [*sic*] was *excellent* – always *the* test.' And so I feel the fraud that I am.

Dear Paul I shall be thinking of you now really into your new novel. I am so proud of you.

Ring me whenever you feel like having a chat about anything or nothing.

Best love,

Muriel

Derek Stanford is married, but I don't know to whom![9]

I have a copy of Charles Wrey G's book & you may borrow it if you would like to, later on.[10]

ALS. HRC.

1. In his letter to MS of 30 June, Paul Scott proposed to write a review of *The Bachelors* for Bill Smith, Editor of *Books and Bookmen*, the journal which would, in October, be featuring his own new novel *The Chinese Love Pavilion*.
2. Horatio Lovat Dickson, known as 'Rache', became a director at Macmillan in 1940, and General Manager in 1941; he was Alan Maclean's superior, therefore, at the publishing house.
3. MS's relations with the literary agent David Higham had been strained from the moment Scott left the agency, and particularly in anticipation of the publication of *The Bachelors*.
4. Jean Leroy was a director at David Higham Associates; Sheila Watson had started at the agency as a secretary, then risen so she could take over many of Scott's clients when he left the agency; she would herself leave, to co-found the literary agency Bolt & Watson, and after that a yet further agency, Watson, Little.

5. MS was awaiting a response from Rayner Heppenstall to her play *The Danger Zone*, and three days later, on 4 July, would write him a 'formal note' to remind him of what she judged to be his remissness – a reminder to which he will not take kindly (NLS).

6. In his letter of 30 June to MS, Scott wrote: 'The children had a holiday the other day (yesterday, Feast of St. Michael I think.) [. . .] Have also just read for Secker a tremendously good novel by an American-Italian P. M. Pasinetti, called *Venetian Red*. I hope they publish. They ought to.' Secker & Warburg would indeed go on to publish the novel, in the author's own translation, in 1961.

7. Allen Tate's only novel, *The Fathers*, originally published in 1938, was reissued by Scott's own publisher, Eyre & Spottiswoode.

8. Tom Maschler had recently moved from the publisher Allen Lane to take over at Jonathan Cape, whose founder died in February.

9. Derek Stanford had married Margaret Holdsworth, who published poetry under the name Margaret Philips.

10. Charles Wrey Gardiner's new book, just published by Rupert Hart-Davis, was *The Answer to Life is 'No'*.

Rache Lovat Dickson with Muriel Spark at her home in Baldwin Crescent

TO PAUL SCOTT, LONDON, 16 JULY 1960

13, Baldwin Crescent, Camberwell, S.E.5
16th July, 1960

My dear Paul,

This is just a rush note – I'm leaving tonight for a week in Nice with Robin – to say thank you for your two letters & for everything & for being your own self.

I went and had a row with Alan. He told me I was nuts and suffered from delusions. I told him he was insolent. We are now moving back into more placid waters, though.

You are not so brave as me, because I've actually bought my gaudy outfit for Nice. A pair of revealing slacks, and a wildly expensive sloppy top to cover up the revelation.[1]

I had lunch yesterday with Charles Wrey. I'm in his book. He's depressed because Rupert Hart-Davis has turned down his new book.[2] Cynthia had a seventh on the way, but had to get rid of it on a psychiatrist's advice. She hated this. She works ten hours a day making lampshades for less than five pounds a week, to keep the kids. Her comm. traveller lover comes at weekends and gets waited on for thirty bob. Charles is living with a Beat kid who is writing something for New Authors. He is still the same, very lovable and as unblameable as a cloud.

Fantastic goings-on all week on the telephone about a proposed film of THE BALLAD by a producer called Ken Annakin whom I met yesterday.[3] He wants to raise the cash to do the film. Dougal is to be an Indian and teach his landlady how to make curry. The gangster character, Trevor, is not to be a gangster, but a fine normal chap. Dougal gets married to his girl in the end. In spite of which I like Annakin, and think he's got some sensitivity and good notions. However, words like six hundred, six thousand, forty thousand, a hundred and fifty a week, have been floating through the blower all week. I said, what does it boil down to, please? – I'm a writer living in Camberwell, S.E.5., and I look to earn my keep when I've got something in black and white. They said, we

have to discuss all this together, and then we'll discuss it further
with you again when you get back from Nice. Meanwhile, they
said, you can be thinking about it in Nice. Thanks, I said, I was
just wondering what I was going to think about in Nice.

You shall have sharksin [*sic*] trunks if it comes off, I promise
you, dear Paul.

Book Soc. meeting is on 19th July. Alan says Tony Godwin
'isn't very hopeful' about me. I don't see why he should be. If they
didn't take your lovely LOVE PAVILION well, I give up.[4]

I'm going to pack now. Lots and lots of love,
s/Muriel

TLS. HRC.

1. In his letter to MS of 13 July, Paul Scott wrote, referring to *The Bachelors*
    and his own *The Chinese Love Pavilion*:

    > We are coming out more or less together. Ours will be the best
    > books of the month. Ours will be the best books of the Autumn. We
    > shall drip with mink, diamonds (you) Italian silk suits and sharkskin
    > bathing trunks (me). I picture me somewhere in the sun which is
    > why I choose silk suits and sharkskin trunks. I find after 20 years
    > of not caring a damn about how I look or what I dress in (between
    > 17 and 20 I was a bit of a peacock) I am looking with an upsurge of
    > interest at the shops in Regent Street, Shaftesbury Avenue etc., I
    > think I'm probably a teddy boy at heart. I lust after Italianate short
    > jackets and tapering trousers. The only trouble is the waistband. I
    > carry at least an extra stone of weight there. But I shall be able to
    > afford expensive massage and steam baths. (UTML)

2. Charles Wrey Gardiner's book, rejected by Rupert Hart-Davis whose
    publishing company had just published *The Answer to Life is 'No'*, appears
    never to have found a publisher.
3. The English director Ken Annakin had been making feature films since
    1947; in 1957, he directed *Across the Bridge*, based on a story by Graham
    Greene, and most recently directed *Swiss Family Robinson*, with John Mills
    and Dorothy McGuire in the leading roles.
4. The Book Society, which ran from 1929 to 1969, was a book sales club;
    Book Society Choices guaranteed sales of at least 10,000 extra copies.
    The publisher Tony Godwin was working for the Book Society, and had
    recently been recruited by Penguin Books; in this latter capacity, he

undertook to publish MS's first four novels, as Alan Maclean confirmed to MS in his letter of 4 July (NLS). In his letter of 13 July, Scott wrote: 'Alan MacLean's secretary writes to me this morning to say that "we are now planning to publish The Bachelors on October 13th and that they will keep me informed of any pleasant developments". Whether the latter still means the Book Society or not I don't know, but I feel rather that the Book Soc must have had their meeting, and said no' (UTML).

TO MARGARET STORM JAMESON, LONDON, 25 JULY 1960

13, Baldwin Crescent, Camberwell, London, S.E.5
25th July, 1960

Dear Storm Jameson,

Your very kind letter was waiting for me when I got back yesterday from holiday. I'm absolutely delighted that you think so well of my work. Thank you very much for mentioning me to Blanche Knopf.

I'm tied up with Lippincott for my next two novels. They have been rather agreeable to me so far – for instance, they've taken on my vol. of short stories, which can't be much of a commercial proposition for them. But of course, Knopf are a marvellous firm, and it's very nice to know of their interest in me, for the future. I've told my agent, David Higham.[1]

Many heaps of thanks, once more,

Yours,

s/Muriel Spark

TLS. HRC.

---

1. The prolific English journalist and novelist Margaret Storm Jameson had, in April in the magazine *Housewife*, published a very positive review of *The Ballad of Peckham Rye*. She wrote to MS on 21 July to say: 'I have just had lunch with a very old friend of mine, Blanche Knopf, who asked me what English writers were truly worth her trying to get hold of. I could think only of you and one other, a man whom she already publishes' (NLS).

TO PAUL SCOTT, LONDON, 8 AUGUST 1960

13, Baldwin Crescent, Camberwell, London, S.E.5
8th Aug. 1960

Very dear Paul,

I'm so very happy about your wonderful tribute. I mean it truly when I say it's quite the most welcome compliment I've ever received on my work, and the most perceptive of all I am trying to do. I never feel deeply satisfied with mere praise, but I am deeply satisfied by your understanding, and the care and attention you've given to the new book. It will be an invaluable asset to its publication. I'm very, very grateful for your putting the book on this level.[1]

1951 is right for the Observer comp. Publication date is Oct.13, not 14 – but I shouldn't worry about that. It's all such a lottery, but now I hope the reception of the book does justice to your faith in me, dear Paul.

I wrote a brief note to D. H. on Saturday and was careful to say that it was a question of my needing more personal attention for my type of work, and to add that, since I'd happened to reach the decision in his absence, it was no reflection on any other member of the firm.[2] To-day, he rang me himself, and I was a little more explicit on the question of his always being too busy. I thought it might be useful for himself to know this. But I was anxious to avoid recriminations and heated arguments (which I felt were lurking in the offing). Now, Paul, he swore that he had discussed this Penguin thing in detail with me. That's simply not true. Goodness me, everyone makes mistakes, but honestly I can't deal with people who will never admit a mistake. I hope I always respect a man's pride – but vanity in a purely business relationship comes hard to respect; one needs a more personal and loving relationship to make it easy to take another's vanity and display one's own. So I told him that he simply hadn't discussed the Penguin thing with me, but that in any case my reasons for leaving were more general, and that his ways and system were different from mine. He said he had toothache. I said I was (and felt it) very sorry. He said he'd been thirty-five years in the business. I said, yes I know that, David. He said, you're always changing your mind – there was to have been a 3-novel agreement with Lippincott, but you changed your mind about that. I said, yes I know. Finally, he said, well I've tried to do the same as Paul did for you – there's been no change in the system, he only dealt with your books. So I said, well Paul was always very generous with his time, and never *seemed* so busy as you do, and would always advise me about anything I asked. And I do realise you're a very busy man. So we left it at that, and I've agreed to see David Bolt on Wednesday to discuss what's outstanding, so that all is done as friendly and smoothly as possible.[3]

It is entirely sweet of you, Paul, not to be offended with me. I think you see it is a matter of David's personality being very uncongenial to me – not on this one occasion but really, ever since you left. My landlady observed that I was always *afraid* to ring him up about anything. I'm always afraid of people who don't really listen to what one says, and of people who are not quite straight in the sense that they shift their ground in such an obvious way that one's intelligence is insulted. I don't overlook the fact that I'm a difficult customer, myself.

This is all for your own ears, and I feel I owe you personally the most explicit reasons I can give for my moving from D. H. I haven't overlooked the fact that it was you, at D. H., who saw to it that my novels were properly paid for and put on a decent footing at Macmillan. It was a tremendous thing to do for me. And I know, without asking for your assurance, that you wouldn't want me to be worried away from my writing, as I have been, out of a sense of gratitude. I must be grateful in a more positive way.

All I hear about THE CHINESE LOVE PAVILION is very thrilling. That makes me as happy as a lark.

Hooray for Picasso. Ring me and say when.[4]

Admiringly, gratefully & lovingly,

s/Muriel

TLS. HRC.

1. Paul Scott wrote to MS the previous day, 7 August, to say, 'Here is copy of what I'm sending to Bill Smith of Books and Bookmen for his October issue (out end Sept)' (UTML). In his review, as published in *Books and Bookmen*, Scott did not hold back in his praise of MS:

> This month Macmillan will publish her new novel, *The Bachelors*. This makes five novels in three years. I believe she has done more outstanding work in a short space of time than any living writer. [. . .] The wish to be entertained is rooted in vitality and curiosity; the need not to escape so much as to peer inquisitively into other people's lives. It would be a pity if an author as capable of satisfying that wish as Muriel Spark were to be hampered from communicating with a large public by undeserved trade labels suggesting the opposite of lively. She properly credits you with an earthy intelligence which is a match for her own, tells you a story you want to listen to and makes it seem no more difficult than having a good gossip.
>
> In the Spark world tedium never sets in. [. . .] In this new novel she changes our conception of London which is suddenly and surprisingly full of men too mean, or lazy, frightened, selfish, worried, poor, unlucky-in-love to marry: and we shall look at the bachelors we actually know with renewed interest. We shall look at them and wonder whether, unchained as they are by wedlock to this world, their thoughts and aspirations move prematurely towards the next, as Mrs. Spark implies: perhaps only a woman could have noticed that there is something disembodied, not quite *of* this two-by-two-into-the-ark world, about the adult, unmarried male. [. . .] And in a world which tends to be grudging of enthusiasm I should like to stick my neck out and say that Mrs. Spark may be a clever woman but is not clever enough to trick me into thinking her genius is only talent of the highest order. (October 1960)

2. 'D. H.' is David Higham, head of David Higham Associates.
3. David Bolt had been an agent at David Higham Associates since 1958; he would later leave, with Sheila Watson, to establish Bolt & Watson.
4. The world's largest-ever retrospective of Pablo Picasso's work had opened at the Tate Gallery in London in June.

TO JOHN SMITH, CHRISTY & MOORE LTD, LONDON, 29 AUGUST 1960

13, Baldwin Crescent, Camberwell, London, S.E.5
29th August, 1960

My dear John,

Heaps of thanks for your letter and for Macmillan's ad. which looks quite nice.

I have written to David Bolt in the exact wording of your suggested letter, which I think leaves no doubt about what I want.

As you suggest, I am ignoring D. K.'s extraordinary scrawl. Speech is silver but silence is golden, my mother always says.[1]

Do please watch out for this Board of Alan's – they love to blame their Boards, don't they? You know I'm a bit disturbed about their recently changing their first intentions for The Bachelors – or so it seems; also, by this new theory of dear Alan's, that I'll turn out one after another novel, like Snow, and get my break-through in the course of time, etc. It sounds doom-like to me, because I generate my own talent at my own pace and can't undertake to keep pace with them. Can they keep pace with me? And anyway, I've been writing for 12 years, so no-one can say I haven't got patience.[2]

I don't give options to Macmillan – did you know that? But I like them so much in most respects, and of course I have a personal friendship with Alan which makes things very much easier. I shouldn't like to leave them. It's only that I'll feel a bit frustrated while writing The Prime of Miss Jean Brodie (new novel) if it is going to be regarded as just another bit of churn-out. See how things go when Alan comes back – and Paul will get-together with you too if you think it necessary or helpful. At least I know, now that you've got control, that the publisher won't be put off by bulldozer tactics![3]

The new story is well on its way, I hope to finish it tonight. The New Yorker letter is enclosed so that you can see how things

stand. I have written to tell Rachel MacKenzie about you, and
have promised the new story very soon.[4]

Heaps of grateful thanks,

Yours ever,

s/Muriel

TLS. WUL.

1. 'D. K.' was Daniel Keel, who in 1952 founded MS's Swiss (German-
   language) publisher, Diogenes. In her letter of 15 August to John Smith,
   MS wrote: 'Very many thanks for assistance with Daniel Keel. I feel he
   will take this hint' (WUL).
2. On 6 August, MS wrote to John Smith: 'I'm longing to know what you
   think of THE BACHELORS, particularly as you don't seem to be represented in it.' She continued: 'I think Macmillans' plans for publishing it
   are rather good, don't you? It would be nice, if you're speaking to Alan, if
   you could tell him how happy I am about all that' (WUL).
       On C. P. Snow and Macmillan, see 20 February 1956, n. 1.
3. This is the first mention in MS's letters (that have been found) of *The Prime
   of Miss Jean Brodie*.
4. The new story was 'The Father's Daughters' (in *TCSS* pp. 133–43).
       Smith was not the only writer whose work MS will promote to Rachel
   MacKenzie at the *New Yorker* – on 9 February 1962, for example, she will
   write to Alan and Dina Barnsley: 'What I want to tell you now is that Miss
   Rachel Mackenzie of the New Yorker is enthusiastic about your writing and
   would love to see some pieces, so do send her anything you have' (MBC).

TO KAY DICK AND KATHLEEN FARRELL, LONDON, 16 SEPTEMBER 1960

[Paris]

Here I am at last. It's wonderful. Hope you are both well. See you
soon.[1]

Love,

Muriel

APCS showing 'Paris, La place du Tertre et le
Sacré-Cœur'. HRC. Dating from postmark.

1. The journalist, editor, and novelist Kay Dick, and her partner the novelist Kathleen Farrell, had been friends with MS since the early 1950s. Here, MS records her first stay in Paris.

TO MOLLIE LEE, BBC WOMAN'S HOUR, LONDON,
9 OCTOBER 1960

13, Baldwin Crescent, Camberwell, London, S.E.5
9th Oct. 1960

Dear Mrs. Lee,
    Here is the little piece on Heathcliff which, as you had announced it, I have set about enjoying very much to do. I hope you will like it and that it's what you want for your programme.[1]
    Looking forward to seeing you on Wednesday next,
    Yours sincerely
    s/Muriel Spark
    Muriel Spark

                                                          TLS. BBC WAC.

1. On 10 September, MS wrote to Mollie Lee who worked for *Woman's Hour* at the BBC: 'I look forward to talking about my nightmare-figure, Heathcliffe [*sic*] & hope to start re-reading Wuthering Heights on my return from Paris on the 20th — so you should have the script well in time' (BBC WAC). 'My Favourite Villain: Heathcliff' begins: 'Heathcliff of *Wuthering Heights* is quite the most fascinating villain I have encountered in fiction. He's an arch-villain — there's no doubt at all about his evil nature. And yet he is not repulsive.' The article approaches its conclusion with words almost as applicable to MS's own fiction (past and to come) as to Emily Brontë's: 'I think we do occasionally come across the type of person Heathcliff represents — the obsessed spirit which infects everyone around it, the moral blackmailer, people of terrifying psychological influence; and of course, in ordinary life, one is best out of their way' (*TGF*, pp. 121, 123). MS's 'little piece' will be broadcast on *Woman's Hour* on 12 October.

TO EVELYN WAUGH, COMBE FLOREY, SOMERSET,
14 OCTOBER 1960

13, Baldwin Crescent, Camberwell, London, S.E.5
14th October, 1960

Dear Mr Waugh,

I have been reading & re-reading your very heartening letter for which, & for all your past encouragement, I can hardly thank you enough. You will know that yours is the opinion I value most of all. I am overjoyed.[1]

I don't know how The Bachelors will sell; my last books have sold about 8,000 copies in England, but rather more in America – my publisher there is very optimistic. Meanwhile I am fortunate in living out of the way in Camberwell, where expenses are small & I can enjoy a rich & famous feeling.

Macmillan are delighted by your letter and your very kind permission to quote from it. They are doing so, I believe, in their first advertisements this week-end. I am most grateful.

Yours sincerely,
Muriel Spark

ALS. BL.

1. On 11 October, Evelyn Waugh wrote to MS:

> How do you do it? I am dazzled by *The Bachelors*. Most novelists find there is one kind of book they can write (particularly humorous novelists) and go on doing with variations until death. You seem to have an inexhaustible source. *Bachelors* is the cleverest & most elegant of all your clever & elegant books. I have no idea how wide your success has been up to date. I suspect that you are still the sort of writer whom people rejoice to introduce to their friends; *Bachelors* shall take you clear through that phase into full fame. May you enjoy it.
>
> If your publisher wants a puff for you before the reviews appear he can quote 'I am dazzled by *The Bachelors*' and anything else in the foregoing note of homage. (NLS; reproduced in *The Letters of Evelyn Waugh*, p. 624)

TO KAY DICK, LONDON, 28 OCTOBER 1960

13, Baldwin Crescent, Camberwell, London SE5
28th Oct. 1960

My dear Kay,

This is sweet of you & I would have sent you one of my own copies had I but thought of it. My brain has been quite gone with all the *bloody* publication trials. Macmillan have under-printed, as usual & will probably be out of print soon. Would you be an angel & enquire for the book in *your* shops & let me know if they are available?[1]

I am longing for Pierrot. Everyone who knows of the book is longing for it. You have a *classic* there, I'm sure of it. I'm looking forward to the party.[2] Going into a shell now for a few weeks but hope to see you very soon.

Lots of love,
Muriel

ALS. HRC.

1. MS is worrying over the availability of *The Bachelors*.
2. Kay Dick's study of the eponymous figure of Pierrot, who features in *commedia dell'arte* and pantomime, had recently been published by Heinemann.

TO ALAN MACLEAN, MACMILLAN LTD, LONDON, 28 OCTOBER 1960

13, Baldwin Crescent, Camberwell, S.E.5
28th Oct. 1960

Dearest Alan,

Welcome home, and heaps of thanks for your post cards and messages. I hope you had some fun out of the trip besides hard labour. Longing to know all the ins & outs & to see what you look like now you are launched on a soaring biz-gent's career.

I have your letter but can't make head or tail of it. However,
I accept your apology. But I'm not going to discuss any more
business with *you*. It's a waste of time because you are a perfidious
Highlander who would never have got a job in these parts after the
'45 rebellion. And now you have set yourself up as an international
publisher.[1]

Myself, I am setting up for a playwright, commissioned by the
New Theatre.[2] If successful I shall be able to scatter the royalties
from my quaint little books like chicken feed. Meantime, dear, see
that you sell a few copies to keep me out of the clutches of your
quite horrid rivals, and also because the Inland Revenue have now
caught up with me.[3]

Let's meet soon.

Lots of love,

s/Mu

TLS. MA.

1. Discontented with the print-run of *The Bachelors*, MS was ceasing to have
   faith in Alan Maclean's management of her affairs at Macmillan.
2. On 25 October, MS wrote to Paul Scott:

   > Am being commissioned to write a play next year for the New
   > Theatre manager, Donald Albery. Other tenders are being received,
   > but we think we like *him*. I am so sick of publishers, that real *honest*
   > crooks such as haunt the theatre would be a lovely change. (IIRC)

3. That MS was feeling pressured to advance on *The Prime of Miss Jean Brodie*
   is made clear in a letter of 1 October to John Smith:

   > As soon as the radio fuss and the Bachelors fuss is over I want to
   > devise some means of keeping eight weeks clear so that I can write
   > my current novel. It has been depressingly put off for one thing &
   > another. You must help me, John, to devise some scheme of with-
   > drawal. (WUL)

TO PAUL SCOTT, LONDON, 29 OCTOBER 1960

13, Baldwin Crescent, Camberwell, London, SE5
29th October 1960

My dear Paul,

   Saturday has come at last, it is the day I have said I would 'start'
my novel again and put aside worldly things. I have been longing
for this particular Saturday & it heaved a sigh of relief in my ear
when I woke this morning & realised that the Day had arrived.
To start my novel again I have only to get it out & live with it for
a while, so of course I shall probably not write anything today,
only 'start' it. My first thought is to write to you & wish you
well with *your* new work. Also to tell you that your letter has
had a very desirable effect upon Macmillan. Alan is back – he
wrote immediately to apologise & to say it wasn't his fault, it was
someone else's – and he quite agrees that the 'target' was 10,000
copies. I think we must allow them their little Foreign Office
substitution of the word 'target' for the agreed figure – since they
know what we mean & they know that we know what they mean.
Also Maurice Macm. writes this morning 'delighted that the
Bachelors has broken the 10,000 barrier.' 'I *am* glad,' he says, 'that
everything is now straightened out.'[1]

   It is like a surrealistic play, Paul dear, and I only record these
consequences of your letter to show you how effective it has been,
and in what awe you are held, & how grateful I am. I think Alan's
surprise (at the 2nd reduction) was genuine & that he *was* let down –
and Maurice Macm. of course is in politics, he was only a stand-in.

   Now I am going to doctor my new cold which of course
descended upon me to-day in my relaxed condition. Not that I care.
You were reviewed with me in the Scotsman, I was so proud.[2]

   Best of luck & remember that I'm always available for you any
time, tho' so far it has been so much the other way round.

   Love to you both
   Muriel

                                        ALS. HRC.

1. MS had already written to Paul Scott on 25 October to complain that, having promised a print run of 10,000 copies of *The Bachelors*, Macmillan had printed only 7,000. On 27 October, Maurice Macmillan (son of Prime Minister Harold) wrote to MS: 'I *am* glad that everything is now straightened out; and delighted that the Bachelors has broken the 10,000 barrier. Somehow it has an almost mystic significance that figure, like 40 in a man's age. After 10,000 one can cease to be polite to publishers and even insult literary agents! After 40 alas is different; it is the age when *grown up* young *girls* start to get up when one comes into the room and people ask which war one's medals refer to' (NLS).

2. The unsigned review that appeared under 'New Novels' in the *Scotsman* (15 October 1960) was appreciative of both novels. Of *The Chinese Love Pavilion*, the reviewer wrote: 'This is a novel rich in texture, imaginatively worked and impressive in its flow of dramatic incident.' Of *The Bachelors*: 'This is more than a survey or analysis: it is an X-ray mercilessly incisive. [. . .] Miss Spark's originality and talent becomes more and more apparent.'

TO ALAN MACLEAN, LONDON, 13 NOVEMBER 1960

13, Baldwin Crescent, Camberwell, London, S.E.5
13th November 1960

My dear Alan,

I wonder if you can tell me – and perhaps you will have to ask yourself – what it is about me that makes you tell me lies, or at least mislead one with evasions.

I don't have this trouble with anyone else with whom I have to deal, and it quite honestly puzzles me.

Is it because you *want*, basically, to vex and upset me? If so, my dear Alan, I can't play that game with you. I am only a born 'victim' up to a very limited point. And that point has been reached. If you look back on the numerous occasions on which you have – and you *know* you have – deceived me about publishing matters, can you see *why* you have done so? I don't believe you are a fundamentally dishonest type, and this is what puzzles me.

Perhaps you think my books get more praise than they deserve, and have an instinct, deliberate or otherwise, to scare me off? Perhaps you resent *my* mushroom-like growth in reputation & consequent change in personality? – I know that these phenomena do cause resentment in others. Or perhaps you feel that, since you 'discovered' me, you ought to have some say in the pace and mode of my development?

Have I offended you?

Do I irritate you?

Do you feel, obscurely, that all my work is a hoax and a hoodwink?

Do you think I am some sort of personal threat to you?

For God's sake, Alan, – I love you like a brother & admire you in everything you do except that you are *not straight* with me.

If you have the means of bringing my talent to light, then why on earth aren't you the first to promote it? Why do you foster my work with one hand & blight it with another? Why is it that other publishers see the value of my talent & are eager to exploit it, while you have to be bullied all the time into a minimum effort which turns out, usually, to be even less than the minimum of what was promised? It is not *me* I am asking you to foster – it is my work in life which, in its small way, has got something in it. Gifts are *not* democratically bestowed – neither are the difficulties accompanying them; but perhaps herein lies the cause of offence?

Well, if we can't work together at least perhaps we'll be friends. So.

Love

Mu[1]

ALS. MA.

---

1. It is debatable which of the two scolding letters to Alan Maclean, both dated 13 November, was written first: this, the more personal handwritten one, or the longer typewritten one that follows here.

TO ALAN MACLEAN, MACMILLAN LTD, LONDON,
13 NOVEMBER 1960

13, Baldwin Crescent, Camberwell, London, S.E.5
13th November, 1960

Dear Alan,

You said you were advertising my book in the Sunday Times
and announcing the Television Choice *prominently.*

You promised me you had taken out one of the books which you
had planned to advertise, and that there remained only John Wain
and myself.

This has not been done.

I am *tired* of your ridiculous lies, your broken promises, your
complete waste of my time in discussions, when everything
agreed upon is set aside by you in the most casual way.

Maurice Macmillan assured me in a letter that my book would not
go out of print, and now it is on the way to being out of print. This is
not his fault, it was yours, for not leaving adequate instructions as to
what had been agreed between yourselves and my agents. The whole
history of the publication of The Bachelors has been a betrayal.

You have now ordered 3,000 copies to be reprinted. In view of
the vast attention the book has received from reviewers, and the
Television choice, I expect you to sell these copies by the end of
the year. I have ascertained that any publisher in his senses could
do this. What steps have you taken to see that this is done, so that
they obtain the full benefit of the Christmas trade? What steps
have you taken to see that the book does not go out of print again?
Have you ordered a third printing? I understand that ATV have
arranged special display cases in the book shops for their monthly
Choice. Have these been exploited?

Your publication of my books has been selfish. You have been
interested in obtaining the prestige and glory for yourselves and have
neglected the commercial side in a really shocking way. Of course it
is not necessary for you to make money out of my particular books,
you make your profits from an aggregate of books. But it is necessary

for me to sell my particular books, and if you do not do so I have no alternative but to go to a publisher who will treat me fairly.

If you have the least interest in publishing further books of mine you will now start an intelligent advertising and sales campaign for The Bachelors which will ensure that the present wreck of publication will be saved.

I am very tired indeed of having to explain to people who come to me with demands on my time, in the belief that I am a successful celebrity, that my books make more noise than money. These people have every right to do so – various organisations, for instance, have every right to expect that I should entertain visiting novelists from abroad, or go and give talks. My family has every right to expect that I should share my success with them. These are extensions of my personality and natural responsibilities which I would willingly accept, but it is not generally recognised that my publishers have let me down time and time again, that they are not interested in exploiting the reputation my work has gained for me. I am tired of people telling me how well Macmillan have done for me, when in fact Macmillan have done badly for me and I have done well for them.

Your policy is cramping and stifling my vital development as a writer. I am tired of living in an attic. I do not intend to write attic literature all my life. I have glorious things to be written, unlimited creative potentialities, a brimming talent to be expressed. I do not boast of anything I have written, I leave that to the critics and readers; it is no boast. But I do claim a unique vitality as a novelist, and there are many good publishers who are only too eager to foster my talent and see that I have the leisure and environment to fulfil it.

Please reply officially. I have always been happy to accept your privately written apologies; but this is not privately addressed, it is meant for you as publishers. You may of course write to me privately if you wish, but my conscience towards my work will not be satisfied until I have this position straight with Macmillan.

Yours,

s/Muriel.

TLS. MA.

TO PAUL ALLEN, LONDON, 17 NOVEMBER 1960

13, Baldwin Crescent, Camberwell, London, S.E.5
17th Nov. 1960

Dear Paul,

I see I am going out to Hampstead to a party on Sunday & quite forgot. I'm so sorry about this.

Could we make an arrangement to meet when we see each other at Brian's party on Thursday next?[1] Perhaps I could come to you first & we could go out for tea. Shall I come to you about 5 o'clock & then we can go to the party together?

I like M[r] Pusey & M[rs] Killey very much, it made me laugh a great deal, because of its cartoon-like outlines of the situation. I should put 'Catholic Church' instead of the Church (which the vicar has joined), otherwise English readers may be confused. I love 'he had the dogged strength of one who walks in many processions behind the cross' and of course I think of Don Harvey that day. *Please* do a story about that, called 'The Water Pilgrims'. If you don't, I will. I would like to capture the moment where the humble pilgrim gets restive & starts taking charge & 'helping Father'. *Please* do it. Remember the fizzy-pop drinks on board & the voice over the loudspeaker telling us of the last journey of the great Martyr. It is all so vivid in my mind, & *your* story brings it back to me.[2]

Shall I see you on Thursday then!

Love

Muriel

ALS. NLS.

1. Brian Parker.
2. Two months earlier, on 10 September, MS wrote to her literary agent John Smith to promote Paul Allen's work: 'This is Paul Allen's manuscript — most of the pieces have appeared in the Guardian. The writing appeals to me tremendously. I think it will to you.' She went on: 'He is not satisfied with this & is writing a novel called "The Usurpers" now. But I think this has a character by itself' (WUL).

In written response to Martin Stannard's question about the story which made MS laugh – 'In one of your stories?' – Allen responded: 'Yes, but lost'. Commenting on the outing which MS describes here, Allen wrote: 'Paul went by boat from Chelsea to the Tower of London with Muriel and a group of pilgrims following the route of St. Thomas More. Admitted to the martyr's cell, Muriel prised out a piece of the wall and put this relic into her handbag and they were hustled along by their head prefect for the day, Don Harvey, a London barrister and the friend of Alan Barnsley (Gabriel Fielding), both ardent Catholic converts' (note written on Stannard's copy of the present letter; Private collection).

TO PAUL SCOTT, LONDON, 17 NOVEMBER 1960

13, Baldwin Crescent, Camberwell, SE5
17th November 1960

My dear Paul,
 Don't read this until you have a moment to deal with frivolities as there is nothing in it but japes & jinks.
 The worm (ME) turned on her publishers. I said I was tired of living in an attic & writing attic literature. I needed to live up to my position (and all that lah-di-dah). I was brimming with good things to write, said I, but Macmillan's selfish policy (taking all the credit & making no commercial effort) was cramping & stifling my talent.[1] I said far more. A very indiscreet letter written at the still point of anger. (You know how an accumulation of upsets are more drastic in effect than one real blow.)
 The result is that the directors offered to come & see me in my attic in their Daimlers & Jaguars. I didn't submit them to quite that dramatic penance, but went in & saw them instead, with John Smith. First, however, I went to Marshall & Snelgrove & fitted myself out with a Paris model dress at 28 gns.[2]
 So in we went. (I said 'Do you mind if I take my coat off?' – because I wanted them to see the dress.) Lovat Dickson immediately said that they had ordered a 3rd printing of the Bachelors, bringing the total print up to 13,000.

John spoke up nobly & reasonably, almost as if inspired by *your* spirit.[3]

They have offered the following:

£1,000 a year (minimum) guaranteed for 3 or 4 years, novel or no novel (& regardless of terms).

They to buy a house which I will pay them back for, off royalties.

Or they will take out an insurance policy for £5000 payable in 15 years.

They are giving me another £500 advance on the Bachelors to show that they mean business.

Their advertising & promotion to increase, provided I give them an option. (This to safeguard themselves against my going elsewhere on the strength of their build-up.)

I think I will accept the £1,000 a year, as this is in any case what I'd ask for my next book & it will ensure their sales effort.

I'm also going to ask Lippincott to guarantee the same. (This is irrespective of all my other jobs & the income from them.)

Also, I'll be on the look-out for a small house.

So by the spring I hope to enjoy more leisure & be on the way to pleasant surroundings.

Let me know how funny you think this is.

The main thing is that I feel released from the compulsion to 'keep my eye' on their publishing methods. Let *them* worry about making my living.

But how wrong it is that one should have to *make a din* for one's normal needs.

Alan, meanwhile, has washed his hands of an author who has so little taste that she has to explain to the directors that she hasn't any private means. Very lowering. It seems I'm to deal with Lovat Dickson from now on.

The trouble is I'm fond of Alan, but alas, was never quite Foreign Office enough for him. I *did* explain my predicament to him & how difficult it was to live up to the 'successful celebrity' status that everyone thinks I hold. But he only coughed & said yes.

The new dress is beautiful & poetically worth it. Tell Penny it is wool crepe, v. fine, figured in brown & red, lined with silk throughout.⁴

    Blessings & lots of love from your loving

    Mu

Your letter since received. Any more old larks & it will *definitely* be *Fred*. Oh, how I hope your film comes off, it is a great film project.⁵ You really can't look back now, anyway. Paul, it is a clear road ahead for you tho' that is always the most difficult thing to realise at the time, the moment when you see daylight at the end of the tunnel & then there's a bend in the tunnel so that the daylight goes away for a short time. But really, you know it's there. I love to think of The Birds of Paradise – what a title! Now you must justify your retreat, take your stand by it. There is nothing upstage about practising your art & thinking of yourself as one who must be kept away from:

> Weave a circle round him thrice
> And close your eyes with holy dread
> For he on honey dew hath fed
> And drunk the milk of Paradise.*⁶

There is *some* truth in it. Then you'll emerge from your labours & talk big business & everyone will be scandalized!

    Gratefully & lots & lots of love,

    Mu

    * Do your Birds suckle their young? I hope so.

ALS. HRC.

1. On 14 October, MS wrote to Paul Scott of her work in progress: 'But *The Prime of Jean Brodie* is going to have a more happy home, I'm convinced. Cape's would offer anything in the world for it, – but I'm not too sure of them. Heinemann? Rupert Hart-Davis? Longmans? John Smith is for careful deliberation. So am I. But it seems that Macmillan are *out*' (HRC).
2. The department store Marshall & Snelgrove operated from its imposingly grand headquarters – since demolished – on London's Oxford Street.

3. John Smith, MS's literary agent.
4. Penny, Scott's wife, had published her first novel, *The Margaret Days*, under the pseudonym Elizabeth Avery, the previous year.
5. Scott's letter to MS containing the reference to 'Fred' has not been found. In her biography, *Paul Scott: A Life*, Hilary Spurling writes that Scott was 'being wooed (inconclusively as it turned out) by his very own film producer' but does not name the producer (Hutchinson, 1990, pp. 237–8).
6. *The Birds of Paradise* was the title of the novel on which Scott was working. MS quotes from Samuel Taylor Coleridge's 'Kubla Khan', in which the poet, if successful in his attempt to capture the exotic, in a blessing or a curse which alienates him from the diurnal world, is transformed into a mage.

TO ALAN MACLEAN, MACMILLAN LTD, LONDON,
21 NOVEMBER 1960

13, Baldwin Crescent, Camberwell, London S.E.5
21st November 1960

My dear Alan,

I am so very much happier now, that I'm just wondering if it is *sensible* for us to meet on Thursday to chew over things w. our lunch?[1] Please believe that I have no *resentment* towards you — *far from it*. But I am a little afraid of involving myself, and *you too*, in any thing approaching an argument at this stage. Last week's crisis was the result of an accumulation of anxieties, not just one tiny event; and it left me quite considerably shaken. Now that the situation has been saved & everything's on the mend, hadn't we better let sleeping dogs lie for a few weeks? Later on we can wake them up and see how funny they look! You have my word for it, as one who is supposed to be a professional humourist, that there *is* a funny side somewhere.

I *think* this will be your feeling too, but if there is anything which *you* feel urgently requires saying, that is of course a different matter, and in this case I'm perfectly prepared to discuss & to respect your point of view — indeed, I respect it already.

But if you are happy to accept things as they are, and me as a friend as I am, without further analysis at present, then I'm absolutely happy to accept you as you so admirably are. And I think we can agree that perhaps it would be sensible for me to go on dealing with Lovat Dickson for the time being, if he is willing to deal with me?

I need not say that I am sorry if I have offended you. I hear of your enthusiasm for my work from right, left & centre which makes me feel so good-o. So I hope to remain in your *good books*.

Love as ever,

Mu

ALS. MA.

1. On the previous day, 20 November, MS wrote to Rache Lovat Dickson who, it had been agreed at Macmillan, would take over the handling of MS's work: 'Thank you for the good news about your forthcoming advertisements of The Bachelors. And I am very reassured by your third printing of the book. It will be so nice for me to be able to forget about the problem of sales, and leave the ways and means to you – because, as you know, my own problems as a writer are quite enough for me' (MA).

    MS will explain the origin of Lovat Dickson's first name to John Smith two weeks later, on 3 December: 'According to "Who's Who" Lovat Dickson's name is Horatio Henry. "Rache" (which you were wondering about) is therefore short for Horatio. I don't blame him, do you?' (WUL).

TO LYNN CARRICK, LIPPINCOTT LTD, NEW YORK, 21 NOVEMBER 1960

13, Baldwin Crescent, Camberwell, London, S.E.5
21st November, 1960

My dear Lynn,

I am in the process of reorganising my arrangements with Macmillan, so as to provide more economic security for my future. Mr. Lovat Dickson has made some good suggestions which my agent and I are considering at the moment. The most immediately practical of these suggestions is that Macmillan guarantee a sum of £1000 a year for something like three years. Now I am writing to ask if you will do the same.

I won't go into all the details of my circumstances unless you would like me to do so. I will just say that, first, a peculiar sort of interim period has occurred in my career, whereby private and public demands upon me as a 'successful' writer are not commensurate with my financial success – unless I *work too hard*. Secondly, I have a real need, which deeply affects my work, for a slightly more expansive way of life and a home of my own. At present I live in an attic flat. It is quite a pretty attic, but still it cramps me and I am conscious of it colouring my outlook, and consequently my writing; there are certain things I want to write which I can't conceive of my doing properly in this particular environment. I am hoping to start buying a small house next year.[1] Thirdly, I should like to be able to feel that, if necessary, for the sake of my work and my health – both go together – I could lay down my pen for one whole year without worry. I don't suppose I could really keep away from my writing for as long as that, but I should like the security to be able to do so.

I think Macmillan's offer is a very good one. My present rate of earning (by working definitely too hard) is three thousand a year, and, since I am saving to buy a house, I don't want to fall below this figure. This money comes from lots of sources besides my books. I could count on subsidiary rights and odd jobs to provide a thousand pounds in the course of a year, and if I could count on a thousand from you also, I should feel secure.

Of course, I feel sure that my books will soon be earning far more than this, and am full of bright plans for my work. What I need are more suitable conditions in which to carry out the plans, more scope and leisure and less financial pressure.

So please do try to agree. Will you, at least, discuss it with John Smith and Macmillan?

All good wishes,

Yours ever,

TLcc. MA.

1. MS will not move house, still less buy her own house, but will rather move early the following year *within* the house of her landlady Tiny Lazzari. On 7 February 1961, she will write to June and Neville Braybrooke: 'I am *moving* into the large middle flat in this house – it means re-wiring & decorating & furnishing-up most elegant. All papers etc in a turmoil' (NLS).

Window display of The Bachelors

1961

By 4 January, *The Prime of Miss Jean Brodie* was completed. On 8 January, MS appeared on ITV's programme *The Bookman*. Having read *Jean Brodie*, Rache Lovat Dickson wrote to MS: 'I do congratulate you most warmly, and congratulate myself on having the luck to publish it. You have created an addition to the characters of English literature. How clever you are!' (MA). In February, Macmillan officially offered MS the possibility of an annual salary and a mortgage on a house – an offer she considered, then declined. In late March, she travelled to Haworth Parsonage in Yorkshire to record a piece on Emily Brontë for BBC TV, which aired on 16 April. She wrote to Terence Kilmartin at the *Observer* in April to decline further reviewing activity in favour of creative work. The BBC expressed an interest in an autobiographical chapter (which eventually would become the story 'The Gentile Jewesses', after first serving as the opening of the novel MS was planning, *The Mandelbaum Gate*). She employed one of her 'bachelors', Igor Chroustchoff, to organise her papers, then found reasons to make his task impossible. On 25 June, she flew to Israel, spent five days at the trial of Adolf Eichmann for the *Observer*, but found herself unable to write of the experience. While she was away, *Voices at Play: Stories and Ear-Pieces* was published in the UK to positive reviews. On 6 July, she passed through the Mandelbaum Gate into Jordan to continue her visit to the 'Holy Land'. On her return journey she stopped in Rome, visiting the city for the first time, and upon arrival in London fell into a depression. On 25 August, *The Go-Away Bird and Other Stories* was published in the US. Exceptionally, the *New Yorker* contracted to publish an abbreviated, 40,000-word version of *Jean Brodie*, which appeared in its issue of 14 October, followed by UK publication of the full-length version on 30 October; reviews were mixed. MS was interviewed for the BBC by Frank Kermode. In November, she wrote angry letters in an attempt to withdraw from her contractual obligations to Macmillan, initiating a dispute that lasted for two months. Between late November and mid-December, she retreated to The Friars, Aylesford, where she completed her play *Doctors of Philosophy*.

TO HERBERT PALMER, ST ALBANS, HERTFORDSHIRE,
4 JANUARY 1961

Edinburgh
4th Jan. 1961

Dear Herbert Palmer,

Your letter, which I was *very* happy to have, has been forwarded
to me here where I have been for some weeks while finishing a new
novel. It was lovely to hear from you. I haven't been in St. Albans
for years. Derek walked out on me and married Another.[1] So I am
Married to my Art. Your photograph is delightful & I love your cat,
I go crackers about cats. I have suggested to Rayner Heppenstall
that we both make a trip to see you after I get back to London some
time later in January. *You* are not Percy Mannering in my novel, I
make up all the characters out of my head.[2] But sometimes peoples'
conversations stick in my ear, which is like a wireless receiver,
and I don't know where the words come from. In any case, Percy
Mannering is the best character in the book, and head & shoulders
above the others for guts and charm & so if you resemble him in any
way you should be quite pleased. Try to get my 'Ballad of Peckham
Rye', it is one of my best. I will look out for The Singing Years, (a
good title).[3] I am sorry to hear of Mrs Palmer's decline, but if she
is happy in her own world that is all that can be desired after such
a difficult last few years. She has always seemed to me very sweet
& gentle. I look forward to hearing your new poems, and am glad
to hear the old ghosts have risen again. What was wrong with *Two
Fishers* though?[4] I never read modern poetry now, I read *Skelton*. *You*
have got a lot of Skelton. My novels are very Gothic in conception,
and you have to understand that before you can understand the
novels. I hope you get over your operation successfully but perhaps
will manage to see you before then. Meantime, many many thanks
for your delightful letter & best wishes for the New Year.

Lots & lots of love from
Muriel

ALS. HRC.

1. MS used to visit Herbert Palmer in St Albans with Derek Stanford; on Stanford's marriage, see 1 July 1960, n. 9.
2. In his long letter to MS from one week before, 29 December 1960, Palmer wrote, of Rayner Heppenstall, that he was 'surprised that a man for whom I seem to have done so much should never have lifted a finger to me from his throne of glory' (NLS). Percy Mannering is a character in MS's first novel, *The Comforters*.
3. In his letter of 29 December 1960, Palmer asked MS if she might review a book by a friend, Rosina Graham. He indicated it as *The Singing Years*, which will not have facilitated MS's offer to 'look out for' it, since, when it was published by Robert Hale later in the year, its author was identified as R. G. Graham and its title was *The Singing Days: The Last of a Medieval Town*.
4. In his letter of 29 December 1960, Palmer, now eighty years old, wrote of revising his poem 'Two Fishers', originally published in his first collection, of the same name, in 1918: 'My literary capacities have declined for everything except revision of my own poems, especially my early long poems – and there I have had the strangest and most uncanny returns of my old inspirations, so that I have been able to make masterpieces of *Two Fishers*, *Two Foemen*, and *The Wolf Knight*. Every weakness and error has been pointed out to me as it were by a ghost in spite of present-day difficulties in making contacts. At any rate the Artist has now completely triumphed.'

TO RACHE LOVAT DICKSON, MACMILLAN LTD, LONDON, 19 JANUARY 1961

13, Baldwin Cres. Camberwell, SE5
19th January 1961

Dear Rache,

I was overjoyed to have your message & letter & to know that you think so well of Miss Brodie. Thank you for such a quick & warm reaction to it, I needed it very much.[1]

Looking forward to seeing you next week,

Yours ever,

Muriel

                                                              ALS. MA.

1. No letters have been found in which MS expands upon her composition of what was set to become her most famous and commercially successful

novel, *The Prime of Miss Jean Brodie*. But on 29 November 1960, MS wrote
to Rache Lovat Dickson: 'I am going to Edinburgh on the 10ᵗʰ to polish
off Miss Brodie' (MA). On 2 December, she wrote to him: 'Miss Brodie
is turning out to be quite jolly, I think, & comic as you like it. I have
had a lot of interruptions but I think I should have a quieter time of it in
Edinburgh. What date would it be nice for you to have it by, for publication next autumn?' (MA). On 4 January, from Edinburgh, she continued,
to Lovat Dickson again: 'This is first to let you know I have finished my
new novel & am just getting it ready for the typist. I do hope you will
like it – you will have it quite soon' (MA). And on 11 January, she wrote
to John Smith:

> Here I am back again and at the moment giving myself up to a mild
> session of social whirl.
>   I am thoroughly exhausted after the novel. It is to be ready for
> final checking at the week-end and so I hope to do a postman's round
> on Monday. One copy to you, one to Observer, one to Macmillan.
> Perhaps yours could go off to Lippincott when you have read it for
> better or worse, if these arrangements suit you? (WUL)

TO DEREK STANFORD, HOUNSLOW, MIDDLESEX, 21 JANUARY 1961

13, Baldwin Crescent, Camberwell, London, S.E.5
21st January, 1961

Dear Derek,
    Thank you for your letter. I have now read your article under
'Evelyn Cavallo' in *The Critic*.[1]
    I was puzzled and concerned to learn from my American
publisher that an article 'by Evelyn Cavallo' had appeared in which
'Muriel Spark' figured prominently. How was I to know that the
culprit was old Fagan the Pagan (the last pseudonym to which you
laid claim, if I recall aright)?
    Evelyn Cavallo is certainly my pen name. I have written in The
Observer under this name which, as you know, I invented in my
poem. The poem specifies that this character may be of either sex,
not, as you say, exclusively male. I am sure that if I ever said this
was an image of you it was plainly a joke.

I am sure that in using the name you had none of the guile which the poem also specifies as an attribute of Evelyn Cavallo. But I suggest it was rather thoughtless of you to use this pseudonym since an outside observer might easily assume that I was myself the author of the article; this would obviously be embarrassing.[2]

So please do not use Evelyn Cavallo any more, and we will leave the matter like that.

The article itself has amused me, it is very vivid.[3]

Yours ever,

s/Muriel

TLS. Private collection.

1. Derek Stanford published 'Gabriel Fielding: A Portrait' in the December 1960–January 1961 issue of the American journal *The Critic: A Catholic Review of Books and the Arts*. Before writing the present letter, the very last that has been found from MS to Stanford, MS had believed the author of the article to be Alan Barnsley / Gabriel Fielding himself, as she outlined in a letter of 11 January to John Smith:

> Now Gabriel Fielding knows that this is my name. He knows the poem, and I have spoken to him of 'Evelyn Cavallo'. It is difficult to see how he himself could have written an article (which I haven't yet seen, of course) called 'Gabriel Fielding: a Portrait' unless he is doing a self-publicity stunt.
>
> What I must tell you, however, is that this is just the sort of thing he would do. And moreover, wouldn't hesitate to implicate me in the very thing. Obviously, an article which (as it would seem from Lynn's letter) praises 'Muriel Spark' and yet is written by 'Evelyn Cavallo' would be quite damaging, and I could be accused of trickery and self-publicising at a later time. (WUL)

2. The first four lines of the second stanza of MS's three-stanza poem run:

> Therefore, therefore, Evelyn,
> Why do you assert your so non-evident history
> While all your feminine motives make a mystery
> Which, to resolve, arise your masculine? (*CP*, p. 62)

On the same day as the present letter, 21 January, MS wrote to John

Smith: 'I have heard from Derek Stanford who owns up to the Evelyn
Cavallo article. He says he didn't know Evelyn Cavallo was my pen name
and chose it from my poem because I had once said the poem was an image
of him, in a sense' (WUL).

3. Much of Derek Stanford's article consists of a comparison of MS and
   Gabriel Fielding, as novelists, as characters, as Catholics:

> Meeting Fielding first in Muriel Spark's presence, I fell to thinking
> how the two of them represented different aspects of the Catholic
> mind. Both of them were converts of recent standing, and both were
> keen to explore and possess the Faith they had now made their own.
> But this keenness was expressed by them quite distinctly. While
> Fielding was all enthusiasm, all omnivorous excited interest, Muriel
> Spark was deftly analytic – set on knowing the precise truth to be
> learnt. [. . .] About him, as about his fiction, there dwells an all-
> enveloping aura of warmth. Just as Muriel Spark's fiction reflects
> a fastidious chastity of spirit, so Fielding's writing and personality
> radiates an embracing *agape*. (pp. 19–20)

TO JUNE BRAYBROOKE, HAMPSTEAD, LONDON, 12 MARCH 1961

[Camberwell, London]

I am *so proud* of you. Congratulations on your well-deserved
reception. It is a great moment. What pleasure Four Voices will
bring to readers! It is superb.[1] Love from your warm admirer
  Muriel

> APCS showing an illustration from *Dogs*, a book for children by Eric
> Leyland. Private collection. Date and place from postmark.

1. The novel *Four Voices* by June Braybrooke / Isobel English had recently
   been published by Longmans. MS had already congratulated Braybrooke
   in a letter of 19 February (misdated by MS as 19 February 1960): 'Surely
   it will be a winner, any reviewer must feel its merits from the first
   page on. There is not a false note, and there is a flesh-and-blood quality
   to balance the nervy-feeling prose which I so much *like*. Best of luck
   with publication, June dear' (NLS). In an earlier letter to her, dated 9
   August 1958, MS wrote: 'You are one of the very few *artists* among all

the writers I know' (NLS). And MS's fondness for Braybrooke's writing will not fade: in a letter written nearly forty years later, on 14 December 1999, after June Braybrooke's death and on hearing that her novels were to be reissued, MS will write to June's husband Neville offering, to serve as a blurb: '"The novels of Isabel [*sic*] English were one of the great pleasures of my youth and their re-issue will certainly bring joy to my old age. She is an exquisite writer; her humour is subtle and her thoughts moving"' (NLS).

TO TERENCE KILMARTIN, THE OBSERVER, LONDON, 29 APRIL 1961

13, Baldwin Crescent, Camberwell, London, S.E.5
29th April, 1961

My dear Terry,

I really am terribly sorry about the short story books. I have tried to review the three best ones – Mary Lavin, John Bates and Marcel Aymé – but have simply drawn a stubborn blank in trying to write about them.[1]

I feel very guilty at having hung on to these books so long, because for some time I have experienced a curious resistance to critical work and have only been able to write with ease on a creative level and to talk with ease in public on the question of the creative process. I'm afraid I hung on to the books drawn as always by the glamour of appearing in the Observer, and in the hope that when I had moved into my new flat I should be able to do a substantial story-book round-up for you.

But now this is absolutely out of my control and I can only ask you to believe it. I think it arises from an inner need to conserve my energy for my creative work after five years of rather intense work – eight books, dozens of reviews, stories, radio plays and talks. I hope this doesn't bore you, but I feel I owe you some explanation for defecting, and I want you to have the true one. Without the Observer, I would probably never have been a writing-animal at all. And so you know I am grateful.

May I let you know as soon as the spirit moves me to

write reviews again? I have no doubt that this blank is just a temporary one.[2]

Shall I bring the books, or send them in a taxi, or will you send for them?

Do think of me kindly.

Yours ever,

TLcc. NLS.

1. After serving in World War II with David Astor, who later became owner and Editor of the *Observer*, Terence Kilmartin was Literary Editor at Astor's newspaper from 1962 until he retired in 1986, later becoming renowned for his translations from French, and in particular his revision of Charles Scott Moncrieff's translation of Proust's *À la recherche du temps perdu*.

    Mary Lavin's *The Great Wave and Other Stories* had recently been published by Macmillan. No book by a John Bates has been identified for this period; possibly MS had been asked to review *Now Sleeps the Crimson Petal and Other Stories* by H. E. Bates, published in 1961. Marcel Aymé's *The Proverb and Other Stories* was also published, in translation, in 1961.

2. On 28 February, MS wrote to Rachel MacKenzie: 'One of the things I have quite been able to do as a result of all the New Yorker generosity has been to give up reviewing. I have never enjoyed it, really, but even when it wasn't necessary from the financial point of view, I always had qualms & second thoughts about turning it down. Now, however, I turn it all down' (NYPL).

    On 25 March, she wrote to John Smith seeking his help in extricating her from a commitment she had made to Frank Sheed to write an introduction to a book on religion in the Victorian novel:

    > My dilemma is really a nervous-exhaustion one. I *can't* do anything at all until I have moved into my flat. The work involved in the flat is quite considerable. I am longing to write something creative & the truth is I simply don't want to do this introduction – there is a fortnight's hard labour in it. On the other hand I feel indebted to Frank Sheed. (WUL)

    And on 6 April, she wrote to John Smith: 'I have got everything for the flat now except a coffee table & a dining table. Both are essential but have decided to call a halt to spending. So I am making do without my tables. It is an Unfinished Symphony. Come & see it soon' (WUL).

TO CHRISTINE BROOKE-ROSE, LONDON,
LATE APRIL 1961

Camberwell [London]
Saturday

Dearest Teeny

I finished your proofs just as my own arrived, which is an
Omen, of what I don't know, except that you & Jerzy & I have a
definite intertwining destiny.[1]

Now I think The Middlemen is a smashing success, it is packed
with latent hysteria which so wonderfully reveals its *cause* in the
last chapter. I get the impression that all the agitation & frustration
that goes on throughout the book are as much a product of things
to come as of things which have been. I think this is a profound
psychological truth – that disturbed minds are to be explained not
only by their personal or racial past but by their future as well,
physically speaking.

The ending is a triumph because it is so naturally & inevitably
the end of a long course, and there is the right *mystery* about the
last days of your people, it is not just a crude Judgment, there is
a sense of peace – I thought it very moving indeed. I admire your
detail in the body of the book, it is as obsessive as Robbe-Grillet
but not leading into a circular nowhere like his 'Jealousy'.[2] This is
your most serious book in my opinion, for it compels discussion
outside the literary considerations of form and style. It is a true
Satire. I have been discussing it with myself for hours. You have
made a good character of Stella for she is an innocent in the book,
the others are not innocent in that way. Very few novelists can do
an Innocent with a care for individual portraiture and the truths
of human nature. Every book should have a beginning a middle
and an end, I believe it, and you have done a true English Satire
about a society concerned with middles & neglectful of beginnings
& ends in their waking lives; and your beginnings and ends are
spread throughout the body of the novel, between the lines, and
explicitly revealed in the climax.

These are non-organised observations, but I am full of admiration. I don't go into the charm of the writing & its wit because these are self apparent & act as a beautiful persuasive.

I think this will be popular & successful on all levels, it can't fail to appeal to intelligent readers, and the others will be moved & delighted in spite of themselves.

Now I send congratulations and love, for yourself personally & also for what you've got in you.

Two misprints you may have overlooked in your other set of proofs.

p.43 line 3 'non'

p.91 'Arkright' spelt 'Arkwright' in middle chapter.

Lots & lots of love

Muriel

ALS. HRC. Dating: Martin Stannard dates this letter
to late April 1961; Christine Brooke-Rose's
The Middlemen was published later in 1961.

1. MS had received the proofs of *The Prime of Miss Jean Brodie*. On 28 January, she wrote to John Smith: 'I met Jerzy and Christine for lunch on Thursday last and heard the great good news which is so nice for them, for Macm., for you and for me' (WUL). Macmillan had committed to publishing Jerzy Peterkiewicz's novel *The Quick and the Dead*, which would appear in print later in the year. Christine Brooke-Rose's novel *The Middlemen* would also be published later in 1961, with Secker & Warburg.

    On 12 April, MS wrote to Rache Lovat Dickson:

    > Actually, my author's note for JEAN BRODIE was really intended for reviewers and interviewers, so that they shouldn't assume that it is an autobiographical novel and get it into that literary category. I haven't drawn more on my own experience for this novel than for any other novel. (MA)

2. Richard Howard's translation of Alain Robbe-Grillet's *Jealousy* was published by John Calder in 1959. On MS's broader relation to the *nouveau roman*, see 22 August 1957, n. 1.

TO RACHE LOVAT DICKSON, MACMILLAN LTD, LONDON, 25 MAY 1961

13, Baldwin Crescent, Camberwell, London SE5
25th May 1961

My dear Rache,

Here is the beginning of my novel 'The Gentile Jewesses'; it is an autobiographical chapter & the rest of the novel refers back to it.[1] But I think you will see what I am about. Do please tell me, as soon as you can, what you think of this. I have a scheme of how the whole book will shape but must go to the Holy Land. I want it to be a *religious novel* & entertaining as well. A really religious novel hasn't been done for a long time.[2]

It was so nice seeing you the other day.

Yours ever,

Muriel

ALS. MA.

1. On 28 January, MS wrote to John Smith:

   > As you know last week, too, I met Lovat Dickson for lunch & thought him an absolute charmer and very understanding. He told me I'm the highest-paid author – which I believe – and asked me not to mention the actual sum to other authors on their list. So I promised. (WUL)

2. On 6 May, MS wrote to John Smith: 'I think "The Gentile Jewesses" has possibilities of turning out to be an important sort of novel. So let's hope for something good to turn up so that I can do it with ease.' She added: 'I must get a Holy Land background' (WUL).

TO RACHE LOVAT DICKSON, MACMILLAN LTD,
LONDON, 28 MAY 1961

13, Baldwin Crescent, Camberwell, London, S.E.5
28th May, 1961

My dear Rache,

Heaps & heaps of thanks for your letter. You know I have got
great hopes for 'The Gentile Jewesses' and I so much want you to
be enthusiastic too. This first chapter is autobiographical in the
real sense, it is a sort of prologue to the book. Most novels with
an 'I' narrator are not intended to equate the 'I' with the author.
In this case I do specifically intend that the 'I' should be myself,
'Muriel', so far as that is possible, and that all the other characters
should be fictitious. The more I have thought of the intensely
personal nature of the theme, the more this new form has seemed
to arise from it.

I want to set the action of the novel in the Holy Land where
I think the symbols of my grandmother's origins reside.[1] There
seem to be an extraordinary number of difficulties in the way
of my getting there for my particular purpose. They are not
financial, but they are real problems, and I would be so grateful if
you would advise me or help me if you can.

In the first place, I am not used to travelling about the world
and am simply afraid of arriving at a strange place far away, and
not knowing what to do and where to go. On all other occasions
when I have travelled abroad I have either gone with friends or had
arrangements made for me, and been met and so forth.

Secondly, there are special complications in going to the Holy
Land, because one cannot travel freely between Jordan and Israel.
Very few people manage to do this alone. They go in parties
where collective visas are provided. For good reasons, I don't
want to go in a party of any sort. I don't think the travel agents
can be very helpful here.

I could go through the Israelis, but I get the impression
that they are predominantly interested in showing off their

achievements in modern Israel. I want to see all this, and the people connected with it, but I don't want to be tied to one set.

I could go with the Catholics but they go in parties and so far as I can gather quite definitely exclude the modern ethos and all non-Christian aspects of the place. The priest who is probably the best authority on the Holy Land told me, 'All the places of interest are in Jordan, the rest is not Christian, it won't interest you.' I don't think this is any good to a Gentile Jewess, even tho' Catholic, but I think it may be a good plan to stay at convents here and there.

The different versions of the Holy Land that I have heard are themselves significant, and part of my theme. Obviously the place is full of tensions, and I really feel I can make a good novel, probably my best.

I could write something for the Observer and they are looking into the visa question for me. The Third Programme want me to do something about the Eichmann trial when it is finished. I want to go to the Trial while I am there and I think this should be easy enough.[2]

But I am really perplexed about how to go about getting there, which side of the country I should start from, and how to get about from one side to another as an independent observer; and also I don't want it to be wildly expensive.

Do please tell me what to do, as far as you can. Travelling about sounds so easy when one hears of writers like Graham Greene, they just get on a plane and arrive somewhere and I suppose make for the nearest journalists' bar to get their bearings. But I think I would land up in prison, or something. I want to go soon, so please rack your brains.

Looking forward to seeing you on Wednesday,

Yours ever,

s/Muriel

TLS. MA.

---

1. In *CV*, MS writes at length and lovingly of her maternal grandmother Adelaide Uezzell, who for the last years of her life moved from her home in Watford to live with the Camberg family in Edinburgh:

Our holidays in Watford form the basis of my story 'The Gentile Jewesses' which is nearly factual, but in which I have written mainly about my grandmother, Adelaide. A high-spirited character, she was rather plain compared with my red-haired grandfather, Tom Uezzell, who was reputed to be fifteen years her junior. [. . .] My grandmother's father had been a Jew, her mother a Christian. [. . .] My Uezzell cousins believe she was not of Jewish inheritance at all, which is at least correct in that Jews inherit religious identity through the mother. But I think she had a definite Jewish connection through her father. (pp. 81–2, 85)

2. The trial of Nazi war criminal and organiser of the Holocaust Adolf Eichmann began in Jerusalem on 11 April, and would continue until December.

TO ALAN MACLEAN, MACMILLAN LTD, LONDON, 19 JUNE 1961

13, Baldwin Crescent, Camberwell, London SE5
19th June 1961

My dear Alan,

Thank you so much & so kindly. Am going first to Jerusalem on 25th for a few days, then touring the country. Will be in Tel Aviv about 2nd July when I'll ring Miss Garten for a waffle at least.[1] My injections are nasty. The Arab countries distrust writers & hang their severed heads on the Mandelbaum Gate. But Miss Garten will retrieve mine & send it home in vinegar or brine. I had to obtain eleven passport photographs. Now I quite forget why I wanted to go in the first place.

Will send you p.c.'s tho'. Heaps of thanks once more for writing to Tel Aviv.

Love
Mu

ALS. MA.

1. Alan Maclean, who had many contacts from his former job at the UK
   Foreign Office, wrote to MS on 5 June: 'I think I have one or maybe two
   low ex-colleagues–friends in Tel-A. & will write' (NLS). Doris Garten
   worked as Press Attaché at the British Embassy in Tel Aviv.

TO JOHN SMITH, CHRISTY & MOORE LTD, LONDON,
29 JUNE 1961

[Jerusalem]

Have started off in top form. Jerusalem is wonderful. Still
working at Trial but start tour on Friday.[1] Hundreds of helping
hands. V. grateful for yours. Will write & tell all.
  Love
  Muriel

> APCS showing 'Negeb Mountains on the road to Eilat'.
> WUL. Dating and place from postmark.

1. MS was attending the Adolf Eichmann trial.

TO RACHE LOVAT DICKSON, MACMILLAN LTD,
LONDON, 6 JULY 1961

Shepherd Hotel, Mount of Olives Road, Jerusalem, Jordan
6th July 1961

My dear Rache,
  It was so nice to have your letter when I came into Jordan
to-day. Thank you too for forwarding the fan letter – I think if
there are any others they could go to my home address as I am not
having mail sent on – am just letting it pile up.
  Israel was thrilling in a way but absolutely exhausting.[1] The
Israelis are so very intense & overpowering. They are forever
pointing out their new cement factories & new towns & all the
things one can see all over Europe. It was hell's own job to get

near a Christian shrine, the guide was very surly about all that,
when I went on tour. We had a car crash on Mount Carmel & I
was delivered to my hotel in a Black Maria by the police, only it
was a brown van. Dear Rache I have heaps to tell you & to write
about too. The Holy Land itself is really beautiful, one can really
believe in the truth of the Bible; & all & miracles & what-not seem
quite natural here. The Jordan side seems a bit more peaceful & I
have been going round the old city of Jerusalem seeing the sights
& spending lots of money on Byzantine icons which the monks are
selling to raise funds for the refugees.

How is Voices at Play getting on? It is a bit tantalising, not
getting any English papers. I saw the Observer & John Smith
sent me the New Statesman review & as they are both quite
respectable I felt rather cheered. You know I thought it might be
a complete flop, but you have always been very encouraging about
it. If the rest of the reviews are not too bad you must take me to
lunch to celebrate when I return & if they are no good you must
take me to lunch for consolation.[2]

Love
Muriel

ALS on Shepherd Hotel letterhead. MA.

1. Three days earlier, on 3 July, MS wrote to John Smith from the Yarcon
    Hotel in Tel Aviv:

    Such adventures as I have had! I will not tell you now about the
    Trial & my particular squint of it, nor of my three-day tour of the
    Holy Places in company with the one rare exception of an unpleas-
    ant Israeli guide, how we had a car crash on Mount Carmel and
    emerged alive, how I was conveyed to my hotel in a police van, how
    I managed to resist the strong opposition of my guide to visiting the
    Christian shrines instead of admiring the cement factories, and so
    got to Nazareth, Capernaum, Cana and the top of Mount Tabor,
    traditional site of the Transfiguration where I put in a word for you
    & others, not that my word amounts to much, I daresay. – Excuse
    my long involved sentence above, I got the habit from Eichmann
    & his lawyers. – Well, I put in a word for everyone & now go to
    Bethlehem to do the same. (You have never told me if my 9 candles

were of any effect to your friend.) Let's hope my guide there won't
come routing me out of church in the middle of Mass, or stand over
me while I am saying my prayers – as did my late companion. I will
tell you all if you buy me a double whisky at The Nag's Head on my
return & I shall tell all-plus if you buy me two. I picked you a pebble
from the waters of Galilee at the spot where Christ taught from a
boat by Capernaum. I shall tell you about Jerusalem – I have still to
see the other half. – What I have seen is beautiful, it is a golden city,
the sandstone glitters at five in the morning. At 3 a.m. the Muezzins
are up in their towers all over Jerusalem, old & new, calling to Allah
and they sound like mating Birds of the Spirit.
 My room in the Yarcon is the most Middle-Eastern room in the
M. East. Tatty painted furniture but clean in a way so far as the
sheets on the bed are concerned. It is a first-class stage set, you
would have to rack your brains to find a better. (WUL)

2. Macmillan had recently published MS's *Voices at Play*, described on the cover
as 'stories and ear-pieces' (see 30 August 1957, n. 6). On 11 February, MS
wrote to John Smith: 'I have written nicely to Lynn, telling him to expect
VOICES AT PLAY very soon, and describing the glories of the new flat,
and expressing a wish for "nice fat contracts, dear Lynn"' (WUL).

TO RACHE LOVAT DICKSON, MACMILLAN LTD, LONDON, 11 JULY 1961

Hotel Philadelphia, Amman
11th July 1961

My dear Rache,
 Your letter was specially welcome after a scorching drive from
Jerusalem through the Dead Sea regions.[1] Now I am loafing here
in Amman for a few days, it is a fascinating place surrounded
by huge Roman remains. There is an amphitheatre, still in use,
outside my hotel window. My mind is whirling with exciting
sights & sounds & some very amusing ups & downs of this trip.
I have been thinking of you & hoping against hope that Voices at
Play wouldn't flop on you. But now I see it hasn't. John Smith has
sent me Evelyn Waugh's piece – it's rather nice, isn't it?[2] I'm so
relieved & really quite astonished that the critics continue to treat
my stuff gently even where there is room for attack. They all seem

to think I shd. stick to fiction, not plays. Oh dear, if I write a novel it will have to be a short one. But I'll have to sort out my ideas about the Middle East before deciding what to write. The place is electric with political tension but very little private neuroses. They suffer as a political body. This is the case in Israel too, they experience everything as a political unit. The only unhappy individual I have seen here is Eichmann in his glass case. Of course the old English residents are cranky as always.

From here I go to Rome & Juan for a few days, then home next week to whatever is left of the heat wave.[3] I'll ring you then, hoping to see you soon.

Thank you again for writing & with such good news.

Love & good wishes

Muriel

P.S. Please will you tell Alan I saw Doris Garten before leaving Israel & Willy Morris here? Both great fun.[4]

ALS on Hotel Philadelphia letterhead. MA.

1. The following day, 12 July, MS will send a postcard to John Smith announcing: 'We came thro' the scorching plains of Sodom & Gomorrah' (WUL).
2. Evelyn Waugh reviewed *Voices at Play* in the *Spectator*, along with Daniel Perezil's *Blessed and Poor*. His review, entitled 'Threatened Genius: Difficult Saint', placed MS firmly in the former category. He began flatteringly: 'Miss Muriel Spark needs no patronage. It is four years since I had the delight of reviewing her first novel in these columns.' But he concluded:

   > 'Dazzling' is the word which constantly recurs as one studies Miss Spark, even in this unambitious collection. Her experience seems limitless. She picks up and transcribes the nuances of countless styles of speech and living. She has the precious gift of a *penetrating* imagination. She is, as far as I know, the only living exponent of the uncanny (save Mr. Graham Greene in a rare mood). Her danger, as I see it, is to become the mere amanuensis of her dæmon. I beg her not to be beguiled by what she calls the 'freedom of the wireless,' and to compel herself to rely on the written word without the actor's adventitious aid. She can construct beautifully as she has abundantly shown in *The Bachelors*. Switch off the radio, Miss Spark; back to the foolscap and the pen. (7 July 1961)

3. Juan-les-Pins, a town and resort on the French Riviera.
4. Willy Morris has not been further identified.

TO JOHN SMITH, CHRISTY & MOORE LTD, LONDON, I SEPTEMBER 1961

13 Baldwin Cres. Camberwell SE5
1ˢᵗ Sept. 1961

My dear John,
 Just to send congratulations on your success with the
New Yorker. It is not only the size of the deal but the good
marksmanship. A question of style. Only a poet would have had
the common sense to direct that particular book to that particular
destination.[1]
 So I am proud of you as well as grateful for the timely
windfall – it will relieve the pressure both materially &
psychologically.[2]
 Love
 Muriel

ALS on card showing flowers. WUL.

1. MS was to be the first British author ever to have an entire issue of the
   New Yorker devoted to her work. Five days later, on 6 September, MS will
   announce the momentous news quietly to her friend John Guest: 'I know
   you'll be happy to hear that my latest novel, which is coming out in the
   autumn, is to be serialised in the New Yorker' (Private collection).
2. MS had not been happy since her return from the Middle East, as she
   outlined to June Braybrooke in a letter of 25 July:

   > I have done nothing but sleep, yawn & weep since my return. Such
   > a depth of depression & a broken-hearted feeling I've never known
   > before. I can't think of the real cause tho' there have been lots of
   > things to set me off. I think holidays are rather hard work on the
   > whole. (NLS)

TO ROBERT YEATMAN, MACMILLAN LTD, LONDON,
10 SEPTEMBER 1961

Baldwin Cres. S.E.5
10th Sept. 1961

Dear Robert,

Thank you very much for the advance copy of Miss B. It is a
welcome sight, and tho' I can't, quite honestly, *quite* take to the
wrapper, I'm sure you know best what sort of thing the shops like.
Anyway, I don't think reviewers take any notice of wrappers. Am
generally full of hope.[1]

Tell Alan I have thought of an idea, if it appeals to him, for
announcing the postponement of publication.[2] That is: Miss B.
herself would make the announcement (I could write a bit of
dialogue) saying that she felt quite equal to coping with a new
publication date as she was in her Prime & making an appearance
in the N. Yorker with her Set & remained mistress of the situation
in all senses of the word. – Something like that. But only if you
think it would be helpful. Lemme know.*

Looking forward to seeing you on Thursday if not before,

Yours ever,

s/Mu

* Or else an interview with her publishers.

TLS. MA.

1. Robert Yeatman had joined Macmillan in 1960 as an editorial assistant to
Rache Lovat Dickson and Alan Maclean; he would stay in that role until
leaving the company in 1964 to join W. H. Smith.

   In an undated letter from this period, MS wrote to Harry Cowdell,
designer of dust jackets for Macmillan, to discuss the cover proposed by
Victor Reinganum:

   About the wrapper: I like Reinganum's work for my books but as I
   told you on the telephone this one doesn't seem quite to represent
   the book. I like the colours & think the schoolgirls are quite all
   right – they would make good cut-outs. But I think the figure of

Miss Brodie is too like a music-hall school ma'am to give an adequate idea of the type of character & humour & tone in the book. To my mind she should not look *much* like a school teacher – only a suggestion of it – & shd. be a bit less angular.

But I am not much good at the visual arts so perhaps I should leave it to you. (MA)

2. Macmillan's publication of *The Prime of Miss Jean Brodie* was to be delayed in order to permit first publication in the *New Yorker*.

Muriel Spark at Rye Lane market, 1961

TO RACHEL MACKENZIE, THE NEW YORKER, NEW YORK, 16 SEPTEMBER 1961

13, Baldwin Crescent, Camberwell, London, SE5
16ᵗʰ September 1961

My dear Rachel,

I would have written last week to tell you how joyfully I

received the great news, but have been floating among the tree-
tops as a result of it & quite useless for anything practical. Thank
you especially for your warm encouragement all along, and now
for all you say about Miss B. Both personally & in my working-
spirit I respond to this type of sunshine & see every hope of
producing my best peaches & plums for you in the future.

I have asked my agent to tell you that if you would prefer to
go ahead without delaying the process for my reading of proofs,
that will be fine. But of course if you *want* me to read, perhaps for
suggestions or re-writing here & there, that will be perfectly easy
for me to do.

The first-reading agreement sounds splendid & I'm so flattered
by your offer of it.[1]

Now I look forward to Oct. 14 & the merry launching of Miss
B's Prime.

Love,
Muriel

ALS on card with picture of 'Scottish Coastal
Flowers: Purple Milk-Vetch'. NYPL.

1. On 12 September, Rachel MacKenzie wrote to MS to propose a first-
    reading agreement: 'The value of a first-reading agreement to us is that it
    gives us the first look at a writer's work. The value to the writer is finan-
    cial – a 25% premium on everything that is bought, and, in addition, a
    cost of living adjustment' (NYPL).

TO JOHN SMITH, CHRISTY & MOORE LTD, LONDON,
SEPTEMBER 1961

Dear John,

I am sending the following to Robert as a basis, as they like the
idea. See what you think of it.[1]

'When offered a launching with my Girls in the *New Yorker*,'
said Miss Jean Brodie in an exclusive interview, 'I immediately
accepted. Why not? My Girls are the creme de la creme and I am

in my Prime. We shall return all the more refreshed for another
and fuller launching in Book Form. Every woman needs to be
launched on every possible occasion, especially a woman capable
of having a Prime.

'As I told my Set, the postponement of our publication date
is only a minor inconvenience, and it is only so to others, not to
ourselves. Moreover, my delays are always vital to success. I have
kept many a good man waiting in my time: for examples you need
look no further than my colleagues the art master and the singing
master, devoted to the last, who readily agree that I remain
Mistress of the situation in every sense of the word.'

No word from Rachel. Perhaps I ought to write a little note of
pleasantries? But soon I will have the proofs and will have to work
for my money.

Will you remember the *Good Housekeeping* article? I'm more
concerned for the young priest's sake than for my own. He
seemed a bit anxious.[2]

Am going shopping tomorrow (Wed.) but will ring for or
with news.

See you Thursday, anyway,

Love,

s/Muriel

TLS. WUL.

1. Robert Yeatman, at Macmillan.
2. The article on MS in *Good Housekeeping*, entitled 'Fame in Four Years', went
   unsigned, but did include photographs taken by Mark Gerson, including
   one captioned 'A Roman Catholic convert, Muriel Spark talks to her local
   parish priest' (vol. 81, no. 1, 1 January 1962).

TO RACHE LOVAT DICKSON, MACMILLAN LTD,
LONDON, 1 OCTOBER 1961

13, Baldwin Crescent, Camberwell, London, SE5
1st October 1961

My dear Rache,

I am so proud of your charming tribute to Miss Brodie. It is
quite the most elegant of the batch. Thank you very much.[1]

As a consequence the Daily Express telephoned to me again,
early on this Day of Rest, to obtain an immediate interview. But
I pretended to be someone else & said I was in Brighton & that
I didn't think I liked giving interviews. This was one of their
women's page journalists who so much give me the creeps. But I
have promised to have a non-interview lunch with Peter Forster
whom I know slightly & who I think will do something about the
book.[2]

Lynn Carrick tells me there is an article about my work in
the past week's N. Yorker. I guess they are building me up for
October 14th. If I get hold of a copy I'll let you have it in case it is
of any use.[3]

I have got an amazing new charlady who also does for a
lady-in-waiting to the Queen. This wonderful char never
ceases comparing my domestic system with the vastly superior
arrangements of 'Lady Margaret'. I have had to buy a whole range
of new polishes and extra Hoover equipment because they are
what Lady Margaret uses. My bits of furniture are 'nice stuff but
Lady Margaret has Louis the Fourteenth.' I think at this rate of
keeping up with Lady M. I will be a ruined woman.[4]

Thank you so much, once more, for your S. Times piece, it has
made my day.

Love,
Muriel

                                                        ALS. MA.

1. Given Rache Lovat Dickson was MS's editor at Macmillan, it seems improbable that he would have reviewed *The Prime of Miss Jean Brodie* in the public prints – and indeed no published review by him has been found.
2. Peter Foster was Literary Editor at the *Daily Express*.
3. On the article by John Updike in the 30 September issue of the *New Yorker*, see 1 December 1961, n. 1. Publication of *The Prime of Miss Jean Brodie* in the *New Yorker* was scheduled for 14 October.
4. Lady Margaret Hay was an aristocrat who served as Lady-in-Waiting to Queen Elizabeth II.

TO PAUL SCOTT, LONDON, 17 OCTOBER 1961

13, Baldwin Crescent, Camberwell, London, S.E.5
17th October 1961

Dearest Paul,

I have been re-reading your letter for which I haven't yet thanked you on 1st reading. I do so much cling to your feeling for my work. No-one has encouraged me more, 'in word, thought & deed' as we Papists say in a different context.

Now Paul dear I am not going to let my hopes run away with me on the possibility of your joining Macm.'s, but it would be my happiest joy & pride to be in your company on the list. You will think it odd after all my moans & groans about the firm, that I should want to wish them upon you. But perhaps you won't think it odd. You see, *I* have decided to stay there at this crucial stage & after much dithering. I can realise now, when the question of urgent-earnings presses so much less upon me, that much of my own difficulty with Macm. has been outside the normal publisher-author field – it has been a psychologically male-female thing as well. When a woman, more especially a fluffy woman, starts laying down the law (even tho', as author, perfectly entitled to do so), *any* male of the species gives an automatic growl, followed frequently by a gurk. Now that a little success has eased the tension, I don't foresee quite this sort of trouble again, & anyhow, am more consciously on my guard against giving provocation.[1] *Your* case would be entirely different, there is no fear of anything

but easy & warm personal relations. You would like Rache, you
know. He is a man who is a little bit ashamed of his virtues &
feels in a quite simple way that he must show a tough exterior to
keep his end up. Also, he's a good business man. He took a risk
& printed 7500 of my 'Voices at Play' which by arrangement (I
didn't want to detract from forthcoming Miss Brodie) was not
heavily advertised, & the risk was well justified by the sales. (No-
one could predict the reviews for a book like this – radio plays &
stories.) Alan is really very loveable & we get on fine now. You
have always done so.

So much for personalities. Needless to add, they are over the
moon at the very thought of your possibly considering Macm.

A big point: they are rich. You know yourself that they don't
hesitate to *buy* a name on the market quite handsomely. I found
Rache mean during the summer, but this was because he was
(rightly!) suspicious of my intentions to stay with them, and
wanted to tie me up with a large sum on a new book rather than
a small sum on old books. However, I got my own way in the end
& have since assured them that I don't think of leaving. Rache said
to me the other day 'Don't leave us – stay and reform us.' That
is the best idea, I think. And it is nice to know that a publisher
is flexible enough to be 'reformed' according to individual taste.
Of course I daresay I'll have many ups & downs with Macm. in
future times, but all I want to convince you of Paul dear, is that
I am not being *too* inconsistent in this urging you to consider
them as an alternative to E. & S.[2] Alan has a nice way of *admitting*
that he was 'picking his nose' when everyone else in his youth
was reading Eliot & Auden & Dostoievsky.[3] Not every publisher
admits it. Some of them feel that the office & title of Publisher
gives them pontifical authority, as if the Holy Ghost automatically
enters their breast when their first pay-cheque enters their bank
account. This frankness on the Macm. side at least saves a lot
of misunderstanding where an established novelist is involved.
At the same time they are not quite literary clots, or would
simply not retain their list. It goes without saying that they have
their neurotic times, of course, but among publishers there are

neurotics and neurotics to choose from & on the whole I think it best to select a humane publisher-neurotic rather than one with theories, or with a wife with theories.

You see I am longing & longing for you to be with me on the Macm. list & I know all the time that you will decide for yourself when the time comes for you to do so; and that it would only please me if your own heart was in the move.

Excuse my rambling all over the place but I have remembered that I ought to say, what you probably know already, that Macm's sales department is an unknown factor. Some think it is weak. *I* think it has vastly improved in the past year. Anyway, I see that when they *want* to sell a book of a certain printing they jolly well do so. The organisation is there.

I'm sure they would give you the terms you want & the sort of publishing you want & any guaranteed income you might want. It would be high-level stuff. (I need not add, – no business of mine: I wouldn't enquire details of you or anything like that, which might be embarrassing for all parties.) Alan is clear on this point of your needing Slosh.

Finally, Paul dear Paul, the literary reputation of Macm. is becoming *good*. You don't need any publisher's reputation any more than I do, but for my own part I feel happier in a well thought-of setting. It is one of the tiny but ineradicable feelings in a writer's make-up, that they like a reputed list to be on; for which reason I sit here inscribing this plea, far into the night (which has turned from Oct. 17th to 18th in the process). – I would feel enhanced by your presence under the imprint; the tone, you know yourself, is fairly high, but it would rise higher still with your name. I have a feeling for the sweet ways of economical proceedings in life – and this seems to my enthusiastic mind the best proceeding for all the objects in hand.

Please, at all events, don't go to Hutchinson. I can't believe you seriously think of it. Every now & then one thinks of going to Hutchinson, I know, as one thinks of packing up a case and going to be a stewardess (or steward) on an ocean liner at £6,000 a year in tips alone. But you are not a Hutchinson author – *that* would, in a way I can't quite explain, put E. & S. in a justified position. For in some ways they seem to me to treat & present their authors too much as 'Hutchinson authors'. I feel this instinctively and perhaps am wrong. At least I don't, from my limited knowledge, regard E. & S. as publishers who can discriminate much between chalk & cheese.

I hope this long letter does not put you *off*. It may seem a bit impertinent – if so please just be amused at my nonsense. I long to hear about your waffle with Alan, anyway. It is always a stimulus to one's writing to be reminded how much one is *wanted*. Dear Paul I've said nothing that you don't know already, but it makes *me* happy to say it all over again.

See you on Friday-week at the Epicure & meantime am thinking of your writing as promised.[4]

Love to the 3 girls & yourself.[5]

Mu

                                                    ALS. UTML.

1. On 14 October, in the context of the negotiation of a higher advance on royalties from her German publisher, Diogenes Verlag, MS wrote to John Smith:

    I am not writing from any personal animosity. I hope Diogenes Verlag will continue to flourish, as with Daniel Keel's energies it should. I write from motives of principle, to which I have always been consistent, as I think you know. I am always ready to consider the needs and predicaments of private individuals and have taken on a good many financial commitments in my personal life; partly for this very reason, and partly because to do otherwise would seem to me absurd, I do not yield my sympathies towards the financial convenience of any business firm. What is perhaps more important, I have a sense of duty towards my work; once written, it is no longer entirely mine to do with as I please, and I feel obliged to insist on its being placed to its best commercial advantage, that is to say, where it will be likely to reach the largest public. (WUL)

2. Eyre & Spottiswoode, Paul Scott's usual publisher.
3. That MS had herself been reading Dostoevsky is signalled in an undated letter to Alan and Dina Barnsley, probably from 1958: 'My booksellers

have sent me *The Devils* (old title *The Possessed*) by Dostoevsky – I am looking forward to this. Read it & we can discuss it when we meet again. It is a most important book' (MBC).
4. L'Epicure was a restaurant – now defunct – on Frith Street in London's Soho.
5. By 'the 3 girls' MS refers to Scott's wife Penny and their daughters Carol and Sally.

TO RACHE LOVAT DICKSON, MACMILLAN LTD, LONDON, 25 OCTOBER 1961

13, Baldwin Crescent, Camberwell, London, S.E.5
25th Oct. 1961

My dear Rache,

Thank you very much indeed. Tuesday next will be excellent for me and I so much look forward to seeing you and meeting Mr. Daniel Macmillan.[1]

Miss B. has got some formidable competition in the week of her publication, but will weather it I daresay.[2]

I struggle with Act 3 of my play. All the characters have been doing wonderful larks up till now, and I have brought them to the verge of ingenious predicaments without a clue how to extricate them. I would be tempted to believe that the Creation of the World took place on these lines, but as you know, am not allowed to think any left-wing thoughts about the creation.[3]

See you on Tuesday. I so much look forward to it.

Love,
s/Muriel

TLS. MA.

1. Daniel de Mendi Macmillan (brother of Harold) had joined the board of the family publishing house in 1911, and acted as Chairman from 1936 until his death in 1965.
2. In an undated letter from shortly before the present letter, MS wrote to John Smith:

Next week is publication week & we must console and/or celebrate with due solemnity to mark the gravity of the occasion.

It occurs to me that it would be so nice to be able to go for a swim with Matthew Arnold, only I can't swim. Another thing that it would be so charming to experience would be to buy a small bottle of Worth perfume, and take it to a cottage on the outskirts of Chicago, Illinois, where it could be used to perfume the keys of the typewriter. But I couldn't possibly go without Robin & he can't get away from his job. Life is full of frustrations and I have come to the end of the page. (WUL)

3. MS was working on what would become her one major play written origically for the stage, *Doctors of Philosophy*.

TO RACHEL MACKENZIE, THE NEW YORKER, NEW YORK, 28 OCTOBER 1961

13, Baldwin Crescent, Camberwell, London, S.E.5
28th October, 1961

My dear Rachel,

So very many thanks for yours of the 18th. I have now, of course, seen with pride and delight 'my' number of the 'New Yorker' which I cherish as a definite turning point in my career. The book is to be published here on the 30th – you shall have a copy – and so I am waiting to see our critics' verdict.

Now I hope you are settled in to your new place of residence. I moved in the spring of this year – from the attic flat to the larger middle flat of the same house. It was an upheaval that lasted for months in the psychological sense; I am like a cat in this respect. I live with a protective and very understanding landlady in a big Victorian house in this unfashionable suburb. It is ideal for a writer – a fair-sized garden and large rooms, all very quiet. I still have the attic, but decided that the middle flat would give me more space to live in, and imaginative pleasure in furnishings and decorations, when, last year, my books started to sell. So I had all the fun and exhaustion of starting right from the beginning, and my friends think it looks quite a handsome job.

With my 'New Yorker' money I am buying mainly, a little breathing space, and perhaps some extra travel later on. These are real needs. It would be so wonderful to come to New York; I will wait the word from my publisher. I do hope you had a merry luncheon with him. The two members of the firm with whom I mainly deal (at least the one member and his charming wife) are staying over here in London for two years; they live not far away and I see them very often.[1] Lippincott have been enormously loyal throughout the years, from my first novel onwards, so I always resist more glamorous offers which come to me from time to time from other firms.

Two or three generous fan letters have reached me as a result of your 'Miss B.' number. You must tell me, please, what the general response has been.

I do hope you are planning to come for a trip some time. You must then come and see my new flat; it would be wonderful to meet. This week I am to meet one of your new editors at the house of a mutual friend, I don't know his/her name, but am much looking forward to it.

Hoping to hear from you again, and to have something new to send you before long.

Love,

s/Muriel

TLS. NYPL.

---

1. Lynn Carrick and his wife Virginia had moved to London where he acted as Lippincott's European representative.

TO EVELYN WAUGH, COMBE FLOREY, SOMERSET,
I NOVEMBER 1961

13, Baldwin Crescent, Camberwell, London, S.E.5
1ˢᵗ November 1961

Dear Mʳ Waugh,

It was very kind of you to send me a copy of 'Unconditional
Surrender'. Thank you very much for it, and for your inscription
which is so obviously neater than true.[1]

I am full of admiration for this novel – I am sure praise is
redundant – but still I must say, I count it among the best things
that have happened in my lifetime.

Yours sincerely,
Muriel Spark

ALS. BL.

1. The third and final part of Evelyn Waugh's *Sword of Honour* series,
   Unconditional Surrender, was published by Chapman & Hall. Waugh's inscription reads: 'To Muriel Spark in her prime from Evelyn Waugh in his
   decline. October 1961.'

TO THE EDITOR, TIME AND TIDE, LONDON,
EARLY NOVEMBER 1961

[Camberwell, London]

Sir,

I am shocked by Mr. Francis King's statements to the effect that
I have attempted to establish myself as a literary personage and
have taken a 'shrewd' interest in personal publicity.

This is grossly untrue. I live a secluded life in an
unfashionable suburb. I rarely mix in literary circles. I have
no famous friends. If it is not well known that I discourage
the personal probings of reporters and interviewers, and that

my agents and publishers have been requested to do so on my behalf, it ought to be.

Mr. King evidently has not grasped the fact that a widely-reviewed writer inevitably stimulates curiosity of a personal nature. What he has seen and heard of my few small concessions to the demands upon me has obviously gone a long way with Mr. King. He himself, moving in far more exalted circles than I do, would be much better equipped than I am to deal with public attention, and I wish I could bestow my share of it upon him. For myself, it makes me ill, as my doctor and all those around me could testify.[1]

Yours truly,

Muriel Spark

TLcc. PJC. Letter published in *Time and Tide*, 9 November 1961.

---

1. Novelist and representative of the British Council Francis King reviewed *The Prime of Miss Jean Brodie* in *Time and Tide* on 2 November, in an article entitled 'Two Plain One Pearl'. On 6 November, Rache Lovat Dickson responded to the journal's editor: 'In an otherwise very fair review of Muriel Spark's THE PRIME OF MISS JEAN BRODIE, Francis King appears to accuse Mrs. Spark of prostituting her art when he says that she "shrewdly grasped the fact that although literature has nothing to do with public relations, literary success does", and concludes his notice by saying that "it would be a pity if she were to forfeit being a literary artist in order finally to establish herself as a literary personage".' Lovat Dickson concluded his defence of his author:

   > What are authors and publishers to do when representatives of the press and television ask for an interview with a particular author? One cannot and should not attempt to blanket the legitimate interest of the press and public in an author and his work, but in the case of Mrs. Spark, both we and her agent have on her behalf politely refused numerous requests of this nature on the simple and truthful grounds that such interviews interrupt her work and make her feel ill. It is perhaps regrettable that today interest appears to be centred more in the author's personality than in his work, but it is, I think, unfair and untrue to assume that any proper writer would knowingly risk damage to his reputation by fostering publicity for himself. It is certainly unfair and untrue to assume it is the case of Mrs. Spark. (MA)

TO RACHE LOVAT DICKSON, MACMILLAN LTD, LONDON, 13 NOVEMBER 1961

13, Baldwin Crescent, Camberwell, London, S.E.5
13th November, 1961

Dear Rache,

John has told me that you do not accept the withdrawal of my option clause, and of course it it [*sic*] very nice to know that one's publisher does not want to let one go easily.[1] When I sent my letter I wanted only to convey that I had given this option clause under a mistaken impression, without necessarily suggesting that I would offer my future work elsewhere. It is true that I gave it under a mistaken impression, but perhaps I should have taken the trouble to explain how I felt on the publication of my novel, and, – as John now tells me that you do not feel, for your part, that you have broken any verbal agreement, – I think I should do so now, and attempt to analyse a lot of large, complicated and difficult problems as they appear to me. You might then like to comment, or it may be that you may feel it to be pointless to retain the options.

But first I must say, quite honestly, that it would be a wrench to me to leave Macmillan. I am not thinking of the future uniform edition of my books which is a problem I can leave, along with what I hope will be my fortune, to my grandchildren. I mean that I am attached to everyone I have had to do with in the past five years, I feel affectionately and respectfully towards yourself and Alan, and every one knows I have a soft spot for Robert, and in fact for all the charming people in your firm.

But you know, this question of continual friction and misunderstandings is having an alarming effect on my time, work and health; and I am not forgetting the effect it has on your time, work and health. For myself, I can only say truly that I have never had a single upset with the Observer with whom I have dealt for ten years in frequent communication; I started to work for the Third Programme eleven years ago when I was relatively obscure,

and always received from them then, as now, the respect due to an
intellectual of the tribe: I never had a single upset with my former
publisher Peter Owen, in whose office, moreover, I worked
for eighteen months in the complete harmony to which he has
recently testified in print. All my former publishers, even those
who went bankrupt on me, remain my friends, and never got a
vexed word from me, or I from them. Now I think if you were to
go bankrupt on me I would not mind; but I do mind a negligent
attitude towards agreements on the part of a flourishing and
solvent publisher. There seems to be one thing after another. It is
either a printing agreement or a financial one, or an agreement
about advertising, or a promise about personal publicity, or
something or other which appears to me to have been agreed upon
and then violated by yourselves; this gives me a nasty shock and a
feeling of complete insecurity.

I imagine, of course, that you, for your part, do not have these
continual upsets with your other authors. I imagine that you deal
with them differently. I know for a fact that you deal less with
them than you do with me, because you do not publish two books
a year of theirs, but an average I think, with your best authors,
of a book every two years. This fact plainly causes four times as
much tension on either side as can normally be expected. But I
am sometimes given to think that you are accustomed to deal
with writers who are less deeply involved in their work than I am;
without any disrespect to them, I see they are doing other things
with their time, they are civil servants and housewives or have
private means or teach in universities; I know of no other writer
on your list but myself who has had the opportunity to build an
intelligent career in the world, or to get married, and who has
consciously and deliberately set these safeties aside and endured
poverty, and taken the risk of failure, in order to write well. It is
not a spare-time hobby I am engaged in, but something for which
I have had to sacrifice pleasures, and continually have to give up
pleasures to do, and no matter how successful I become I shall
always have to make these sacrifices. It is not the type of work that
comes from a compromised life. Now I think you are not used to

dealing with this type of writer. I am not making any point about
the merits of my work, but I simply want you to know that it is
not as easily written as I make out it is to the public; it does not
roll off the pen between the hours of ten and five; consequently
I attach an importance to it which I feel you do not understand
fully; I conceive it an actual moral duty to see that my work
in life gets as near its proper destination as is possible in a very
unpredictable world.

Now I think it possible that some of our friction arises from a
sheer misunderstanding of emphasis in various contexts. That is
to say, when you make a promise, it is possible you do not intend
me to take it as seriously as I do. I think it must appear to you
that I seize on your words and exaggerate them. If that is so, it
is because I attach importance to my work and to everything
that is agreed in connection with it. If, to you, these 'promises'
are only chance remarks, then naturally I feel that my books
have an equally casual place in your estimation. In my normal
dealings with publishers this question does not arise. I have had
no misunderstandings with Lippincott, for example, because they
do everything they say they will do. They agree to a suggestion or
they don't agree, but it is never casual. I never get the impression
from them, as I must say I have had from yourselves, that they will
say anything and in the event do the minimum possible to keep
an author quiet and her name on their list. I know that Lippincott
really have confidence in my stuff – even when sales were poor
they were in constant touch with encouraging messages. I must
say what I think. I do not think you have this sort of confidence in
my work. When I submitted the first two chapters of Memento
Mori, for instance, with a request for one hundred pounds to
help me to write it, Macmillan refused to support it. Lippincott,
however, gave me a contract and the whole advance right away.
It was a symbol of their confidence. Also, they take some trouble
to study my work & understand it, and seem to have some
knowledge of its value in literature apart from what they can do
with it as publishers. If I write a small-sized book they are not
under any illusion that it is an inconsiderable work. I know that

all publishers are different, but I do not feel, quite honestly, that Macmillan have the type of literary sense that can deal with my work in this way. I need a home publisher who thinks of my stuff importantly, (I do not say inflatedly), and so publishes it in that light without any pressure or prompting from me. I think the lack of this type of understanding in Macmillan is a cause of friction; I hate having to press the importance of my work and everything connected with it, but if I fail to do so it is treated as a quaint sort of minority writing.

There is another question which I must put down now while I am about it. I am sometimes given to reflect, perhaps wrongly, that you would be more diligent, if not indeed more generous, in your observance of agreements with an author who had claims and aspirations to a standing outside the literary sphere, or even one whose husband was, perhaps, a powerful author. I had better say exactly what I mean. I certainly do not think you would have invited Pamela Snow to your office, without her agent, to face five Macmillan men on a subject seriously touching on the promotion of her books. I do not think you would have taken this liberty with her, quite honestly.[2] Leaving aside what was agreed or not agreed, the whole thing was a damned insolence. Even when my name was almost unknown, which was not so long ago, I was never subjected to that sort of embarrassment, not even by the publishers on the verge of bankruptcy. I think I told you shortly afterwards that I *disliked* Macmillan as a firm. This is one of the reasons.

I have said that I gave the option clause, and my two books published this year, under a mistaken impression. In general, the impression was that there would be no more quarrelling due to clashes of personalities and agreements casually broken. In particular, the impressions I received last November when John Smith and I met you in your office, as they concerned the publication of 'Miss Brodie', were, rightly or wrongly, far in advance of the type of promotion it has received. Again, at your meeting in June, when I agreed – even, I think, suggested – that 'Voices at Play' was not the type of book to spend a lot of

advertising money on, I received a very distinct impression that a
maximum advertising effort would be made with 'Miss Brodie'.
I think you agree with this account of things, and that our
misunderstanding has arisen over your term 'major campaign'.
To me, the fact that no advertisement was planned for the Sunday
Times – the most important of all advertising papers – until we
insisted upon it for the week following publication, and that all the
advertisements for that Sunday were placed in very insignificant
positions, rather points to a hurriedly scraped-together plan of
action under pressure from us. It is a horrible thought. I quite
see that the postponement of my novel was a complication to
your autumn plans, but you had your new publication date early
in September and there was ample time for adjustment. I see no
reason why advertisements for my book could not have appeared
together with those you had planned for your other books, or in a
separate column of the paper.

I was very happy about my novel until this happened. I did
honestly think the question of advertising need not arise ever
again, that it was all settled and agreed at our meeting in June,
when I was assured about your Big Guns for 'Miss Brodie'. I am
far more hurt by the feeling of being let down than I am by any
loss of sales at the moment. I think one's home publisher is very
important, and have always felt they set the tone for the others;
but perhaps it is the other way round.

I accept your claim that this is, to you, a major advertising
campaign. But I hope at least that you can understand my feelings
when my book was not announced in the T.L.S. preceding
publication, and I had to start making horrible enquiries, and
it turned out to be the same thing all over again. And now I
seriously feel unable to plan with a clear mind my book 'The
Mandelbaum Gate' which I have been casting and recasting in
my mind. It will take a long time. It is going to be a long book
with a lot of scope, unusual for me. But how, in what major way
would you promote it? Do you see what I mean when I say that I
was under a mistaken impression when I gave the option clause?
It is impossible to 'think large' when one is cramped by one's

publisher's quite different conceptions of largeness. I realise that 'Miss Brodie' is not the type of book to be promoted as a major work. But it deserved, on the strength of the good reception of all my other work including the recent 'Voices at Play', a far more enthusiastic launching than it received.

Again, on the question of mistaken impressions, there is the financial side, – now, I am glad to say, not pressing, but it is a question that is bound to arise when I start my two-years' rest which I have decided I need in order to do my large novel with ease. It is an ambitious scheme, involving further travel in the Middle East. I may finish the novel within a year, but I would prefer to count on two years. I have no intention of giving way to feeble thoughts of perhaps making it a shorter-sized novel so that it will be cheaper for me to write. It will be at least 120,000 words. I have discussed it with Lippincott who are all for it. But I must have a home publisher's backing as well. Now how on earth am I to ask you for money after all the messing about that went on when I wanted to go to the Middle East, and when I returned? Not to mention the messing about when my accountant looked into your various glamorous proposals last year? (My accountant is a Gray's Inn man, and so his services are wildly expensive.) It is true that your accountant smoothed things over in the end, and I was reassured that I could have any type of backing within reason, even if I wasted your money by writing a play. I did not, however, immediately need Macmillan's holy money, but naively applied for some help towards my venture into the Middle East towards the end of May. I think it was somewhere in June that I was offered the price of my ticket as an advance against royalties. What was needed was a small grant. Many publishers supply it where a book is going to cost the author more than he can afford to spend, even against royalties. On my return, when I asked you for an advance of £500 against my eight books in print, you offered me, after some delay, £250 there and then and £250 next spring. It seemed a long way from your offers, when I gave you my books and my option clause, of buying me a house or lending me vast sums per annum for five years, and all the rest of it. That is what I mean by

a mistaken impression. I might add that while the argument about
the £500 was going on within your panelled precincts, the cheque
for an equivalent amount from Lippincott had slipped quietly
through the letter box.

The fact is, that I did not give the option clause under the
impression that there would be difficulty in the way of obtaining
reasonable sums of money for my next book.

Moreover, when I got sick and tired of the argument, and told
you I was writing a play, you replied that you did not want to
publish it unless it was a success on the stage. I admit that you
probably said this under extreme provocation from me, in which
case it is as good as not said. All the same, I am not sure if you
are actually keen to publish my play, or only willing to oblige me
by doing so. If the latter is the case, then I can not offer you the
play for publication, because I consider it to be as good a piece of
work as I have ever done, and have some extremely exotic ideas
on the book-production side which would be most expensive and
so, if the play were not a success on the stage, it would have to be
published at a definite loss. It would only be fair that any publisher
who took this risk should be offered the opportunity of financing
my large fat novel.

To return to the question of mistaken impressions. I received an
assurance at your meeting in June that I was not to be troubled for
some months to perform further feats of personal publicity. I was
under the impression that this promise would be adhered to. It
was a mistaken impression. I was not only asked to do a strenuous
day's work for 'Good Housekeeping' but on my explaining that
my doctor had ordered me to give no further interviews for a
time, was pestered from your offices with further requests.

Now, I must assert here and now the fact that, right from the
start, I have resisted all attempts on Macmillans' part to push me
into interviews and publicity stunts. The only one time I requested
a personal appearance for myself was when I asked for a party for
'The Bachelors', with the intention of getting the whole thing over
in one evening and at least under some form of protection. To me,
this was the only successful venture in this field. All else has been

sheer agony. I succumbed to your pressure only because I wanted you to feel I was helping to promote the sales of the books, and not only contenting myself with writing them.

Besides this, as a letter of mine written a couple of years ago clearly shows, I have family reasons for nervousness in making too many personal statements and appearances. They are very good reasons. I object very strongly to any suggestion that I am in any way abnormal in my dislike of personal publicity. Not only do I share this dislike with most good writers, but my particular circumstances provide the most reasonable grounds in the world for avoiding personal publicity.

As it happens, I have now developed a physical allergy to this activity, due to having undertaken too much of it. It now makes me physically ill. So did the allegations, in *Time and Tide*, that I had done a calculated exploitation of my personality. I cannot help feeling furious at Macmillans' pressure on me, against the most violent objections, to do what I have now been blamed for.

Besides this, do you think it has been fair to ask a writer as prolific as I am, writing so fast and so much, and having in the past few years been forced to take on book reviewing and much subsidiary work, to do personal publicity work twice a year as well? Do you wonder that I am feeling rather bitter about the whole Macmillan set-up? It is not very long ago, only at the beginning of last year, when The Ballad of Peckham Rye was published, that I complained that, on the advance on royalties (£400) I simply could not afford to give these interviews. I could not afford the time. I could not afford to entertain interviewers with drinks, nor to take taxis to their places of assignation.

Now I have been pouring drinks into interviewers, and wasting my precious time with them, and paying doctor's bills, and going away to boarding houses and hotels for recuperation, in aid of Macmillans' publicity effort, for four years, increasing in the past two years. When ever did you offer to pay the expenses, or at least part of them? Is it unreasonable that I should expect you to do your little bit of advertising which I have wasted my time, in any case, negotiating for?

In view of the above, I do not expect to hear it told back to me that you say I 'make difficulties about advertising'. I make difficulties about promises, and about fair play.

You will, I hope, sense my exasperation, and see my difficulty. I don't pretend to be perfect. I have sometimes, in extremity, blamed you for the wrong things and in the wrong way, because I have bottled up my indignation on more justifiable grounds for too long. But my difficulty now is, that I feel in any future dealings with Macmillan I would have to insist on having every mortal detail in writing. This would be tedious. I want a publisher to whom I can leave everything because of his proper conception of my work. I want an English publisher who does not try to pretend that my work is more 'popular' in its nature than it is, out of a mistaken idea that the modern public wants 'popular' stuff. In fact the public now wants good work, provided it is lucid. And my work apart, I am not going to stand for any further attempts to extend my personality, as if I were a balloon-idea emerging from the head of a publicity man. What guarantee have I got that these desires will be respected? I do not mean grudgingly acquiesced-in, as in the past, but respected?

I mean it when I say it would be a wrench to part from Macmillan, and I am not forgetting the kinder side of life that I have experienced at your hands. Above all, I recall that Alan first suggested my writing a novel, and never forget to acknowledge the fact while in the agonising throes of my interviews. But it is sometimes necessary to part from a collective force that is threatening one's health, one's work and principles, even if the collective comprises individuals whom one is fond of.

You now have my point of view, and you may care to comment on it, or to give me yours; or you may feel, after all, that it would be to no purpose for you to retain the option clause, and that it would be better for me to settle for another publisher.

If I leave this decision now in your hands, I think it only right to mention a factor which has no connection with the above, and which, in the normal way, I should have left to John to explain in the course of negotiations. I mention it now with the genuine

desire that you should not feel, at a later date, that anything
has been concealed on our side. This further question has only
arisen since the formation of the Penguin group of publishers.
Obviously all established Penguin authors in their senses will now
wish to retain the paper-back rights in their contracts. I know of
the Publishers' Association's discussions and resolutions on the
subject, but plainly, as the P.A. does not write my books I could
not let it dictate my terms. I think you will see that from my point
of view I could not afford to overlook a potentially good income
for the years ahead – very few people could do so if they had the
choice. And so must retain paper-back rights in future contracts.
You may wish to discuss this point further with John.

It will take you long enough to read this letter, and so I will not
expect an immediate reply. I felt a full explanation was due to you,
and have been perfectly honest in all I have said. Please believe,
too, that I had every intention of remaining steadily with you
until my deep disappointment in my publication week, both at the
delay, and at the presentation of your announcements. I hope you
will believe this. (You will know for instance, that I was hoping
to persuade Paul Scott to come to Macmillan as he was thinking
of leaving his publisher. I felt genuinely it would be a good thing. I
have not, of course, mentioned my present difficulties to him, or
done anything to put him off, and as far as I know he is writing his
book in sublime forgetfulness of his troubles.)

Yours ever,

s/Muriel

TLS. MA.

1. Though it can hardly have prepared him for the present broadside, four
days previously, on 9 November, MS did write to Rache Lovat Dickson:
'This is to give you formal notice that I withdraw the option clause in my
contract which was given to you under a quite mistaken impression, as
also were my two books published this year' (MA). Lovat Dickson wrote
immediately, the same day, to MS's agent John Smith to declare that 'the
option clause in the contract for VOICES AT PLAY, dated February 13th,
1961, is perfectly clear and unequivocal, and we by no means agree to

accept the formal notice that Muriel gives of her intention to withdraw from this clause' (MA).

2. The prolific and highly successful novelist and playwright Pamela Hansford Johnson, who was published by Macmillan, married C. P. Snow, also published by Macmillan, in 1950.

TO HERBERT READ, STONEGRAVE, YORK, 26 NOVEMBER 1961

The Friars, Aylesford, Kent
26th Nov. '61

Dear Herbert,

I am very touched by your letter & grateful beyond words for your lovely poem. I felt immediately soothed and restored by it. Your poems never fail to delight me. They say everything that is needed and are exquisitely cool, & yet they glow.[1]

I have brought your poem down here to a Carmelite monastery where I have taken refuge.[2] It is propped on my work table and fits in very well with the environment. I am trying to write a play for the theatre. The world of the theatre will be quite something to cope with, I can see that already. They are the sort of people who send one telegrams of wild enthusiasm for a week, then, if one rings them up, they say 'Who are you, darling?'

Please don't forget to let me know when you are in London and have time for me. I hope to be back there, with the play, in a few weeks' time.

Truly I am consoled by your kindness & thank you again & again for it.

Yours ever,
Muriel

ALS. UV.

1. Herbert Read wrote to MS on 23 November enclosing an eighteen-line poem entitled 'Man'.

2. On 20 November, MS sent Read a postcard depicting a fox, whose caption read: 'The FOX watches for danger, which he can detect through scent, too'; to this she added: 'This is me (on reverse) on the run from publicity hounds who have taken all the joy of what success has come my way lately' (UV). Read responded: 'How deceptive – I had imagined a bower-bird, surrounded by bright tokens of success. The hounds – I saw them baying at John Osborne the day we sat together in Trafalgar Square – it was terrifying in its lust and shamelessness' (NLS).

Herbert Read

TO JOHN UPDIKE, IPSWICH, MASSACHUSETTS,
1 DECEMBER 1961

[Aylesford, Kent]

Thank you so very much for your welcome letter. Of course, I was thrilled by your review.[1] Am hiding away in this monastery to write a play, but your 'Rabbit Run' awaits me at home. I love your stuff.[2] Will be in N. York in Jan. Shall we be able to meet?

Best wishes & thanks

Muriel Spark

APCS showing 'The Friars, Aylesford, Kent, from the river'. HHL. Date and place from postmark.

1. MS had every reason to be pleased with John Updike's article, 'Creatures of the Air', which reviewed *The Bachelors* and appeared in the *New Yorker* of 30 September. Updike wrote of the novel: 'It is packed but alive in every detail, and convinces me, at least, that Mrs. Spark is one of the few writers of the language on either side of the Atlantic with enough resources, daring, and stamina to be altering, as well as feeding, the fiction machine.' In his letter to MS of 10 November, Updike elaborated:

    You were very nice to send me the autographed copy of The Prime of Miss Jean Brodie; I thank you. I shall treasure it. It is a grand book, of course.

    Since I had already read it in the New Yorker, I had to content myself with going over it trying to discover what they had omitted. While there was nothing really crippling or disastrous, one must smile, albeit fondly, at the prudery that led them to cut the thing-ummyjig, Mr. Lowther's stoppage, and the entire indecent exposure episode with Jenny and the consequent fantasy of Sergeant Anne Grey. And why they did away with the quite lovely letter beginning My Own Delightful Gordon, I have no idea. I suppose they were not quite willing to face up to the extent to which the story is about sex. I found, with the two texts in hand, their fiddling with your paragraphing and their relentless sprinkling of commas and 'clarifying' dashes, most annoying – there is a timid and stupid pedantry here created, I think, but [*sic*] the extreme venerability of their hired grammarians, who are all named Miss Gaunt and have been with the magazine since 1925. However, it was clever and bold of them to print it, and it certainly widened, if not deepened your American readership.

    My review, by the way, was written last spring; it took them forever, in their unpredictable way, to print it, and doubtless would not have printed it yet had not your novel's publication forced it, like a hare forced through a tunnel by a hound – since it would seem immodest to run the review after. It (the review, not the hare, hound, or tunnel) probably irked you in spots, as even the most warm-hearted review will do, but I meant it as sheer tribute.

Reviews are irreducibly irksome, but more so to read, probably, than to write.

At any rate this is thank you for the book which I shall treasure. (NLS)

Updike's assumptions about the editorial interventions made at the *New Yorker* are questioned and corrected through archival evidence by Helen Stoddart in her essay 'Muriel Spark and the "Hired Grammarians"' (*TCD*, pp. 161–79).

2. Updike's second novel *Rabbit, Run* had been published in 1960 and was already contributing to making him one of the era's most influential voices in American literature.

TO ALLEN TATE, MINNEAPOLIS, MINNESOTA, 7 DECEMBER 1961

13 Baldwin Crescent, Camberwell, London, S.E.5
7th December 1961

Dear Mr Tate,

Your letter has been chasing me around various hiding places and has only now reached my welcoming hands. I am overjoyed to know that you and Mrs Tate read Miss Brodie & got pleasure from it. You shall have a copy of the book, which I think has a little more meat in it.[1]

I have been looking up Minnesota on the map, as I am to be in New York in January, but I see you are long miles away. But you must come and see me, please, next June when you are over here, and spare me part of your month.

Thank you very much, once more. I'm so proud of your letter – you know how greatly I admire all your writings. It was an essay of yours (on Madame Bovary) that first gave me a clue that a novel might be worth trying to write – I may have told you this before; at least, I tell everyone else.[2]

Yours sincerely.
Muriel Spark

ALS. PFL.

1. Allen Tate wrote on 23 November, full of praise for *The Prime of Miss Jean Brodie*: 'One is always thinking the novel is done for, but it obviously isn't. Your "time shifts," particularly the *forward* shifts, are masterly. You know that your books have got around very widely in this country. *The Brodie Set* has made you famous here' (NLS).

2. In the essay 'Techniques of Fiction', included in his *On the Limits of Poetry – Selected Essays: 1928–1948*, Tate wrote of Flaubert's *Madame Bovary*:

> Gustave Flaubert created the modern novel. Gustave Flaubert created the modern short story. He created both because he created modern fiction. [. . .] It is one of the amazing paradoxes of the modern novel, whose great subject is a man alone in society or even against society, almost never with society, that out of this view of man isolated we see developed to the highest possible point of virtuosity and power a technique of putting man wholly into his physical setting. The action is not stated from the point of view of the author; it is rendered in terms of situation and scene. To have made this the viable property of the art of fiction was to have virtually made the art of fiction. And that, I think, is our debt to Flaubert. [. . .] Flaubert gives us a direct *impression* of Emma's sensation at a particular moment (which not even the drama could accomplish), and thus by rendering audible to us what Emma alone could hear he charged the entire scene with actuality. [. . .] It has been through Flaubert that the novel has at last caught up with poetry. (pp. 136, 143–4, 145)

TO MAURICE MACMILLAN, MACMILLAN LTD, LONDON, 13 DECEMBER 1961

13 Baldwin Crescent, Camberwell, London, S.E.5
13th December, 1961

Dear Maurice,

Thank you for your letter of the 7th.[1]

I can substaniate [*sic*] the facts in my letter of November 13th, but my point was not to establish anyone's guilt. I sent it, in an envelope marked 'Personal', for the sole purpose of placing before you my point of view about your firm, since it was apparent that misunderstandings were reaching an intolerable limit on both sides; – and very plainly without any intention of injuring the feelings or the reputations of individual members. I have supposed that they, as publishers, have acted according to policy. I can't fit into your policy although I know that it suits other authors; but let me say once more, that the people I have dealt with at Macmillan seem to me perfectly nice, and I have not considered the possibility that they have acted on their own behalf in the matters which have dissatisfied me.

But it seems to me that you interpret my complaint, quite unreasonably, as a sort of smear-campaign. I am absolutely at a loss to understand what you mean by 'public' statements or criticisms by me. I suppose anyone would have a right to criticise a publisher, but in fact what I have said in public has been invariably to your credit: 1) I have frequently said that you suggested and assisted my first novel. 2) I have expressed admiration for many books on your list when given the opportunity to do so, and had the pleasure of writing about one of them only last week (and incidentally, I have refused to review at all any Macmillan book which I did not like). This is the extent of my public reference to Macmillan or its individual connections.

If, however, you mean malicious gossip I am sure that there is plenty of it about, it is the first-fruit of success, and I beg you to do as I do, and consider the credentials of informants, whether they are in some sense your competitors or mine, before attaching importance to it. If this is what you mean, I deny being the source of any scandal or rumour. I have myself received some very wounding intimations from various quarters of things said by Macmillan people; they are very annoying at the time, and I have even made some of them known to you, but in the absence of any precise knowledge of why, how, in what context and tone of voice things have been said if they were said at all, I would be slow to pursue any story. I have suggested that plain gossip is perhaps what you mean, because I am unaware of any possible evidence to show that I have offended as you say I have done. But I have abundant evidence that I speak amiably of Macmillan people when the occasion arises.

As a further reassurance, you must know that no-one else has been privy to our recent correspondence except my agent. He would tell you that I have discussed with him various ways in which embarrassment on both sides could be avoided when my proposed move became known. I have suggested, for instance, that it would be proper, and I think not untrue, for any public enquiries to be answered with the explanation that, as I am an exceptionally prolific writer it is necessary to have two publishers, and that Macmillan remain one of them. I believe John Smith intended to suggest this to you and to the new publisher when the time came. It may not be a good suggestion, but I cite it to show that my mind works on different lines from what you seem to think it does.

I don't think you should interpret my complaints as moral accusations simply because they state the effect upon me of actions which would have a different effect upon others. It is only from your actions that one can deduce a policy; I don't say that yours is a wrong policy, only that it is wrong for me, since I am unable to adapt my needs as a writer to it. The fact that I have at last given up my attempts to do so does not involve you in any admission of guilt, far less a public admission. It has not been my desire to impute blame, public or private.

Yours ever,
s/Muriel

TLS. MA.

1. After a salvo of letters of complaint to Macmillan even prior to MS's departure to Israel earlier in the year, there had been discussion within Macmillan of how to 'handle' this author, judged to be particularly demanding. In an internal memo dated 28 June to a Mr Clark at Macmillan, Maurice Macmillan wrote:

> I should not worry too much about all this, since Mrs Spark is not really quarrelling with us, but with herself.
> As far as I can see, there are certain lacks in her life, and the fact that her publishers are not able to supply these particular needs does not prevent her blaming us for failing to do so. There is nothing we can do about it. [. . .] Personally, I think that once she starts she will jump from publisher to publisher and from agent to agent. I cut out of my letter to Smith a phrase which went something like this . . .

'Never since the exchange of correspondence which lead [*sic*] to the departure of H. G. Wells have such letters been received in this office'. She is nicer, but even more difficult than he was I think. (MA)

MS wrote to Maurice Macmillan on 22 November, appealing to him to release her from her Macmillan contracts: 'Could we not, please, agree cheerfully that I am not your sort of author and you are not my sort of publisher? I should like to part from you amicably & I think you will be reasonable enough to see that this is the best solution, and you will not wish to cause me further distress by hanging on to a tenuous clause which has little possibility of profiting yourselves' (MA).

On 7 December, Maurice Macmillan responded:

I am most reluctant to put any pressure on a writer of your ability and sensitivity. But agreements are binding legally and morally on sensitive writers as well as on tough publishers. Moreover, not all publishers are tough; what you have said in private and in public has deeply wounded many people here. [. . .] If we were formally to waive the option clause it would appear that we did acknowledge the justice of your charges; since the fact that we had waived the option could not be kept any more secret than your criticisms have been, this would in fact involve a public admission of guilt. I am not willing to make such an admission.

But I do understand your feelings. Therefore, while considering that you are bound to let us have first sight of your next novel, I can assure you that we shall not make any attempt to impose our will upon you when the time comes. This is as far as we can go. (MA)

On 26 November, MS also wrote to John Smith:

You know, if they want to show a willing and co-operative spirit, and an interest in my work for its own sake, they would show some interest in the play I am writing. All I have heard from them are dreary warnings about the sales of the book if the play isn't a success on the stage. But even if it *is* a success on the stage the sales of the book would not be immense, only the indirect effect on my books would be good. But the point is, that this is an important new venture to me, it is something essential to my literary life, and Macmillan do not care one damn about it just because it is not directly written for them. Their indifference to my play and the absence of one word of encouragement*, just makes it sound more and more hollow when they say they are proud of my work.

   * Except from Robert, who said he wd. come to the opening night. (WUL)

TO ALAN BARNSLEY, MAIDSTONE, KENT,
29 DECEMBER 1961

13 Baldwin Crescent, Camberwell, London S.E.5
29th Dec. 1961

My dear Alan,

Alas, I *had* to be out & was nowhere near a wireless. I feel
pained at missing it and pained at the seeming ungraciousness,
but more at missing it. Send me the script like a great dear, right
away.[1] I pass on . . .

. . . We had a good Christmas – Robin & I together with friends
breezing in and out – saddened by M[rs] L's tragedy: her son in
hospital with an inoperable growth on the bladder.[2] But she was
simply marvellous – insisted on keeping to her routine & plans –
and was adorable to Robin. What marvellous innate psychology
she possesses! She bore up in her routine when she could easily
have gone to pieces in her grief. But now her son (aged 51) is *sitting
up* in a chair. We do not lose hope. God is good and we feel that
miracles are by no means out of the question, if only to keep him
going till his three children are a bit older. If you *can* as a doctor
send word of comfort, please do so. I am quite sure that we are
right to hope.

I want Robin in London, as my mother's 'weakness' gets worse
& is affecting him. He is too young & sweet to take that sort of
responsibility. So I look for a job for him & will find him a flat
near enough for him to pop in & out to us & yet suitable for an
independent young man, as he is. Everyone adores Rob. We
thought you might look in en famille on your return from St.
Albans but I guess you returned by another route like the Wise
Men, suspecting us of being Herod and likely to massacre your
carload of Innocents.

My play was snatched from the typist by my backers on Xmas
Eve & is already in production. They plan rehearsals to start
in Feb for a West End opening at the end of March. It is still
unbelievable to me.[3]

A nun has written to me saying that she was inspired whilst in prayer to send me her manuscript to read for a possible publication & to write an introduction. I wonder if I should suggest to her that Vox Dei would hardly be likely to recommend Mu Sparki? – Far more likely wd. my name be uttered by Vox Diaboli. (The dear soul has not read my books, only seen my name as a Catholic writer.) I daresay I shall submit to be blackmailed, if only to pass the manuscript to John Smith if good & David Higham if bad.

John is impressed muchly by your writing & will write to you.

I am excited about your Birthday King & feel this is your biggest moment coming up like a sunrise. So far your stars have twinkled with the confidence of stars that are always there but sometimes invisible. I think your new theme gives you the scope you have needed – to use plain language.[4]

I depart on the 12th, returning on the 26th. I shall think & talk of you in New York.

How sweet you all were to me, and how felix culpa was my fall! Let me hear from you soon & pop in when you please. I will warn you in time when I go into a dream and start writing & refuse to see people again. You must always do likewise, tho' I know your system is a broader one.

Send me the Angels & forgive the not hearing, or rather comfort it. The urgent casting of the play was in question & I could see it was hopeless.

I don't want to see Erica.[5] I am not sure why. I think it is because I fear her poverty and the reproach that always accompanies poverty in an egalitarian mind and ethos. Perhaps she is richer than I think she is. Perhaps she does not feel that her money should have been able to buy all that she desires. But I'm afraid in case she does think so. If only one could part with a fiver out of one's store of talent, life with old friends & acquaintances would be so much smoother. In fact, one *can* make one's talent available – by leaving doors open for them to come and steal. Eliot wrote somewhere 'A bad poet borrows. A good poet steals.'[6] I have stolen plenty & put it to my own purposes. But very few people are brave enough to steal. They merely pilfer like a child and get caught, by leaving traces & evidence. I think what I fear in the really poverty-stricken is the possibility of their desiring a fiver out of my success, and not talent at all. This is frightening, because success is an illusion – nothing of one's own – not a possession at all – but a cloudy rumour in the minds of others. One can't give it away any more than a peer of the realm can hand over his title to anyone of his choice.

How I ramble on & metaphorize! But you know what I mean and have suffered from it in both your professions but esp. the writer's. I wonder if you suffer from guilt because you are more successful than others? – You must not do so, it is a false guilt. Others would not bear the burdens that go with your particular success. They would want *your* success, which depends on *your* unique experience of life, and at the same time a comfortable existence with not more than two birth-controlled children. Your pleasure without your pain.

Newman was asked at dinner parties to give the story of his conversion 'between the soup and the fish' as he said. He refused. He said, *let them be to the trouble that I have been to.* This is the answer of people like you & me who, in entirely opposite ways, have come to be writers – you by denying yourself the very real pleasures of solitude and I by denying myself the pleasures of society. Your experience rewards you by making you an equivalently endowed writer, and mine rewards me in my own type. Am I correct? – You write according to the abundance of the Spirit, I write according to its depth.

A long way from Erica. But I love to have a waffle with you. My fondest love to D – I love her dearly & *more than ever.*[7]

Love, then,

Mu

ALS. MBC.

<hr />

1. MS must have written late in the day as it was not until 8.35 p.m. on 29 December that the BBC Radio Home Service broadcast 'The Place of the Angel' by Alan Barnsley / Gabriel Fielding, in which the author, 'who

believes in angels' (according to the *Radio Times* for that week), considered the role of angels in the Bible, painting, theology, and physics.

2. Tiny Lazzari, MS's landlady and dear friend.

3. MS had struggled to complete her play *Doctors of Philosophy* and had been obliged to redraft more than was usual for her.

4. Barnsley had been writing his novel *The Birthday King* since late 1959; it would be published late in 1962. Of it, in *Gabriel Fielding*, his assessment of Barnsley's work for Twayne's English Authors series, Alfred Borrello writes: 'The novel, hailed as a clinical examination of the warped German mentality which bred Hitler and the evils which he in turn spawned, is not so much a novel about Nazi Germany as about the chaos which flows from the absence of a deep and abiding love of man for man. It is a universal drama of every man's moment of confrontation and choice between selfishness and generosity, pride and humility, love and hate, the moral and spiritual world' (Twayne Publishers Ltd, 1974, pp. 105–6).

5. Erica Marx, owner and publisher of the Hand and Flower Press.

6. In *The Sacred Wood*, when discussing Philip Massinger, T. S. Eliot writes: 'Immature poets imitate; mature poets steal; bad poets deface what they take, and good poets make it into something better, or at least something different. The good poet welds his theft into a whole of feeling which is unique, utterly different from that from which it was torn; the bad poet throws it into something which has no cohesion. A good poet will usually borrow from authors remote in time, or alien in language, or diverse in interest' (Methuen, 1920, p. 114).

7. 'D' is Dina, Barnsley's wife.

1962

In addition to working sporadically on *The Mandelbaum Gate*, MS spent much of the year trying to get *Doctors of Philosophy* produced and staged, working with such prestigious theatre figures as producer Michael Codron and director Donald McWhinnie. On 12 January, she visited New York for the first time, staying in the Algonquin Hotel. She met and was fêted by staff at the *New Yorker*, including Rachel MacKenzie, William Shawn – the magazine's editor – and Ved Mehta. She also met the writer Shirley Hazzard, with whom she started a lively correspondence upon her return to London on 29 January. In mid-February, Lippincott reported sales of 8,500 copies of *Jean Brodie* and a fourth printing. MS fell out dramatically with her long-time friend and correspondent Alan Barnsley. On 5 March, the BBC broadcast a TV adaptation of *The Ballad of Peckham Rye*. In April, MS's father suffered a stroke. MS travelled to Edinburgh but preferred to stay in a hotel rather than the family home; her father died on 21 April, after which MS distanced herself further from her family for a period of around six months. On 27 May, a new musical version of *The Ballad* was broadcast on BBC Radio, and the play was submitted to the Italia Prize for radio. In June, she visited Paris briefly, where the publisher Robert Laffont had undertaken to translate and publish her work in France. In July, she retreated to The Friars, Aylesford, where she continued work on what would become her seventh published novel, *The Girls of Slender Means*. In August, she attended, along with numerous literary celebrities, the International Writers' Conference at the Edinburgh International Festival. In September, *Vogue* published a piece on leading women writers: Iris Murdoch, Doris Lessing, and MS. Iris Birtwistle, MS's former friend and patron, wrote to enquire – much to MS's chagrin – if she could sell MS's letters. Also in September, MS went to Verona to collect the Italia Prize, won by *The Ballad*. Rehearsals of *Doctors of Philosophy* began, the play opening at the New Arts Theatre Club on 2 October – to poor reviews. On 13 October,

MS flew to New York for her second visit, where she was offered an office at the *New Yorker* and where she soon took up lodgings in the Beaux Arts Hotel. She worked on *The Girls* and saw much of Shirley Hazzard and her US literary agent Ivan von Auw, to whom she was becoming increasingly devoted. She resolved to leave Lippincott and was courted by publisher Blanche Knopf, as well as to change *New Yorker* editors from Rachel MacKenzie to Robert Henderson. By the end of the year, she had completed *The Girls*.

Maurice Macmillan, Muriel Spark, and Tristram Cary, 1962

TO MAURICE MACMILLAN, MACMILLAN LTD, LONDON, 11 JANUARY 1962

13 Baldwin Crescent, Camberwell, London, S.E.5
11th January 1962

Dear Maurice,
    This is to thank you, before I leave, for your kind letter & for

getting up such an impressive scheme. I am sure it will be a useful basis for discussion & tho' I can't understand it myself I give it the respect due to a Work of Art – and indeed, it does appeal to my novelist's sense of intricate things.[1]

The main thing is that it should not involve me in *debt* of which I have a Presbyterian horror – which I vainly hoped would be exorcised when I became an R.C. I think you would have to get a guarantee from the American side – but it can all be worked out later & my accountant can be chewing it over meantime.

I hope you will like the play – tho' I would rather you *saw* it than read it.

Thank you again, so very much,

Yours ever

Muriel

ALS. MA.

1. On the eve of MS's departure for New York, on 11 January, Maurice Macmillan wrote with detailed new contractual proposals, the crucial proposal being summed up: 'The sort of thing I propose has proved successful in other cases. Broadly, it is that in return for the right to publish all your books we would undertake to pay you an agreed income' (MA).

TO JOHN SMITH, CHRISTY & MOORE LTD, LONDON, CIRCA 24 JANUARY 1962

[New York]

Hundreds of things to tell you, *all* crème de la crème. N. Yorker has *not* previously seen script Gentile J's so please withhold other offers – they are interested! Returning on Sunday – are you free Monday afternoon?[1] Lots of love to all, Mu

APCS showing 'St. Patrick's Cathedral, New York'.

Dating and place from partial postmark. WUL.

1. MS arrived for her first stay in New York on 12 January, having been
    booked by her US publisher Lippincott into the Algonquin Hotel; she was
    set to leave on Sunday 28 January. By 'Gentile J' she refers to a draft of her
    story 'The Gentile Jewesses'.

TO HERBERT READ, STONEGRAVE, YORK,
6 FEBRUARY 1962

13 Baldwin Crescent, Camberwell, London, S.E.5
6th Feb. 1962

Dear Herbert,

It was lovely to hear from you. I too have been rather confused
as to my whereabouts & am only now beginning to be of one
piece.[1]

I was most impressed by your producing a Catholic publisher
from amongst your rubber bands & paper clips, a Catholic
publisher is the very thing to have handy at London Airport for
lady novelists. I shall always apply to you in future when in need of
something improbable as you are sure to have it about you. I was
conveyed home safely, needless to say, by Tom Burns & we forgot
our past differences, & I made him listen to my fairy-tales of New
York far into the night.[2]

I always believed that your Form in Modern Poetry was done
by Sheed & Ward, and that they still wear hair shirts on Fridays in
consequence.[3]

I thought the other day about a proper principle for the selection
from your writings. I think that, when choosing each piece, you
might think of yourself *primarily* as a Wisdom Monger rather than
an art critic or a critic of literature & ideas & society, or a poet.
This is how I read your work whatever the subject & form & it
seems all consistent to me – but I know all too little of it.

Send me The Parliament of Women soon, please, and don't
tease me about my allergy to adjectives.[4]

My theatre people are buzzing like anything with my play. They
wanted me to 'write in' some more dialogue, which is like asking

a painter to paint in a few trees. So I told them to pretend I was dead. The only fun so far is a charming model stage set made by the designer.

Are you striding across the moors in your fine American coat? I hope to see you soon.

Yours ever,

Muriel

ALS. UV.

1. Returning from New York, MS crossed the Atlantic in the same aeroplane as Herbert Read. In his letter to her of 4 February, Read wrote: 'I enjoyed our aerial adventure & hope we shall meet on land before long' (NLS).
2. The journalist and publisher Tom Burns had worked with Frank Sheed before establishing, and becoming Chairman of, the major Catholic publishing house Burns & Oates; he would go on, in 1967, to be Editor of the *Tablet*. In his letter of 4 February, Read wrote: 'I was sorry to deliver you into the hands of the Grand Inquisitor. I hope he did not send you to Hell. Long ago he published an essay of mine, Form in Modern Poetry (in pink covers) & had to write a long preface to explain my heresies' (NLS).
3. *Form in Modern Poetry* was indeed published by Sheed & Ward, in 1932. MS's musing on possible regrets at the publishing house has its origin in the fact that Read was avowedly un- and even anti-religious, and that his political sympathies extended to Anarchism.
4. Of his play *The Parliament of Women*, which was published in 1960 in a collector's edition by Vine Press, Read wrote in his letter of 4 February: 'It is artificial, & one can't get rid of the Elizabethan hangover (Eliot's preoccupation, which ended in poetic nullity). I see now there are too many adjectives. Perhaps better leave it in its lovely sarcophagus.'

TO SHIRLEY HAZZARD, NEW YORK,
14 FEBRUARY 1962

13 Baldwin Crescent, Camberwell, London, S.E.5
14th February, 1962

Dear Shirley,

I have been reading The Mighty and Their Fall most enjoyably and gratefully. And I have been thinking of you a lot, with happy memories of all our meetings, starting with your own lovely party.[1]

I was enchanted with New York, and must come back to be disenchanted a little. I so much want to do so in the autumn, and find a flat round about your side of the city, and see if I can write on the New York impetus.

Please let me know how your plans are working out, and if you have settled for a book of short stories, and how you like being a full-time writer. Have you started your novel? I send all my love for its progress and success.

Thank you again, Shirley dear, for your sweet kindness from first to last. I hope to hear from you and from Rachel that you are doing splendid things, and I hope especially that you will be really happy in your freedom to write.[2]

Love,
s/Muriel

                                                              TLS. CUL.

1. When in New York, MS was invited to dinner with Shirley Hazzard by their common editor at the *New Yorker*, Rachel MacKenzie; the two immediately became friends. Hazzard had evidently given MS a copy of Ivy Compton-Burnett's 1961 novel *The Mighty and Their Fall*.
2. In January, after ten years in her post, Hazzard had resigned from the United Nations Technical Assistance Administration where her work, as described by her biographer Brigitta Olubas in *Shirley Hazzard: A Writing Life*, was 'low-level and routine: recording minutes of meetings, typing, filing, all of it less than stimulating' (pp. 124–5).

TO NED O'GORMAN, NEW YORK, 14 FEBRUARY 1962

13 Baldwin Crescent, Camberwell, London, S.E.5
14th February 1961[1]

Dear Ned,

I did *of course* have your books here – but they had been tidied away by the good woman who comes to clean & who feels that books should be tidied away on to the shelves. So now I have spare copies to give away proudly on loan. I love your religious poems more than any. 'Easter Among Four Children' is marvellous – but I love them all. Shirley Hazzard shares with me an affection & admiration for 'I am a Falcon, Hooded . . .' among the rest.[2]

How kind you were to me! I left half of myself behind in New York. Somehow, I was especially blessed by meeting only gentle & charming people & exciting writers – yourself the warmest and the most humming with creative life.

Herbert Read brought me safely to land and handed me over at London Airport to a Catholic publisher called Tom Burns whom he happened to bump into. There is always a Catholic publisher at London airport saying goodbye to a Jesuit, & this is useful for the ride back to one's home.

Dear Ned, I am hoping to be in New York – to slink back more quietly – for 2 months in October and I hope you will be there at that time. Be sure to let me know if you come over here meantime, and I am looking forward so much to the publication of your poems here. I shall keep a bright eye upon them. The 'Poetry Review' here – which used to be old-fashioned – has a new editor, John Smith. (He is my agent, a poet himself.) Send him some poems, please do, at 33, Portman Square, W.1.

Your luncheon party was a very memorable one, it was the sort that blooms, like the cactus, only once in a hundred years. Somehow, all things came together for good at your party.

Love and blessings till we meet,
Muriel

ALS. SMCC. Dating from internal evidence.

1. MS misdates her letter by one year, which she frequently does in January and sometimes also in February.
2. It was probably Allen Tate who introduced MS, when she was in New York, to the poet and educator Ned O'Gorman; his poem 'Easter among Four Children' appeared in his first collection of poems, *The Night of the Hammer*, which won the Lamont Poetry Prize in 1958; 'Am a Falcon Hooded' appeared in his second collection, published in 1961, *Adam before the Mirror.*

TO HERBERT READ, STONEGRAVE, YORK,
14 FEBRUARY 1962

13 Baldwin Crescent, Camberwell, London, S.E.5
14th February 1962

Dear Herbert,

I have been wrapped in a cloud of contentment, reading 'The Parliament of Women'. Now I realise what a long time it has been since I read anything at all in which the ideas are served by the process & not bungled by it. I love your movements between prose & poetry, they are just right for the characters and the occasion. And I admire the dialogue especially between the women, I like the dignity of mind you give them. And most of all, the theme of twisty honour – that is exciting when it comes to light in the question of provocation to war. I wonder how you would have managed the escape of Helen & Geoffrey if you had made their difficulties more drastic or their marital situations less sympathetic to the audience? – I mean, suppose her husband had been young & presentable, and yet she still resented being sold – and his wife faithful & boring by his side? – This is a novelist's question I'm afraid. And I am afraid my admiration will be redundant anyhow. The physical book is a great delight but of course a normal edition of the play would be good – for one thing, you shouldn't let it be thought of as a sort of art-product. Have you thought of the play for the Third? It would sound so well and wd not need much adaptation.

Did you ever get round to reading Ved Mehta's article on the philosophers in the New Yorker? If so you must please tell me whether I like it or not, for I know nothing of the philosophers, & if it is left to me I would decide to be irritated. He seems to take them too seriously – with their flannels & pipes – in a half-enchanted way; and yet not seriously enough – It must be a sad fate for a philosopher to end up in a nutshell in the N. Yorker.[1]

I am sending back your beautiful book after stroking it gently & with caution. Thank you very much for it & the pleasure it gave me.

Let me know when you are to be in London, and have time for
me, please do. Come and see this Camberwell interior painted all
colours of the rainbow.

Ever

Muriel

ALS. UV.

1. MS had met the Indian writer, critic, and journalist Ved Mehta in New
    York, where he worked as a staff writer at the *New Yorker*. In a letter at the
    end of the year, on 13 December, she would write to Rache Lovat Dickson
    recommending that he take Mehta on at Macmillan: 'Ved Mehta is wanting
    to change his publisher from Faber – I've told him I would write & see if
    you are interested – I'm sure you *will* be. He's a young man, fabulously
    talented, *blind*, with an unusual capacity for visual description, and Indian.
    Faber published his book "Walking the Indian Streets" which is v. amusing
    & good' (MA).

    Mehta conducted a series of interviews with philosophers at Oxford
    University, which were published in the *New Yorker* and later would form
    part of his book *Fly and the Fly-Bottle: Encounters with British Intellectuals*
    (Atlantic Monthly Press, 1963).

TO PAUL SCOTT, LONDON, 21 FEBRUARY 1962

13 Baldwin Crescent, Camberwell, London, S.E.5
21st February, 1962

Dearest Paul,

I have only just now got round to trying to work out how I
could possibly manage to fit in your Summer School idea with my
plans for the summer.[1] The attraction for me is a get-away holiday
with you and Penny, but I wouldn't like it to represent Work
because really the only type of work I like is writing fiction. Now
I wonder if you would be enormously sweet and put me down as a
possible – and only if my 'lectures' could take the form of reading
one or two of my short stories and then answering questions
about them. Somehow I can always answer technical questions,
but the wear and tear of putting my thoughts into logical order is

becoming more and more difficult as middle age encroaches on my already beclouded mind. Presuming this would be acceptable from the 'lecture' point of view – even then I couldn't say absolutely definitely that I will be in England during August. It depends on my novel, The Mandelbaum Gate, and the state of completion the spider's web is in by then, because I don't want to break off and dangle by one of my threads in mid-air, and as Rome and the Middle East come into the novel I may irresistably [*sic*] need to go back to those places.

This is by way of urging you positively to try and hold open the door for me to come and have high jinks with you in Derbyshire, and not at all a roundabout way of declining. I might make a decent contribution to the affair if it is, to me, in the nature of Play; can this be done?

I have been broadcasting all over the place your wonderful news about The Birds of Paradise being a Book Society choice. I told Tom Maschler to get in touch with you, he seems to me to have matured a lot and as he seems to be a stable element at Cape's and is dead keen on having you, and is one of those editors to see a book through from beginning to end, advertising and all – I think you might perhaps not overlook him. Meantime Alan has returned to work and is presumably waiting word from me whether you want word from him. Or you might want to give Rache Lovat Dickson the onceover, in which case let me know.

I am being held in London for the rehearsals to start, and am trying to get some work done on the side. Let us have a lunch in March on a Tuesday or a Friday, as those are the vacuum cleaner days in this establishment and therefore my days out. I want to tell you all about New York so let me know about this and all other propositions, exits, entrances and excursions.

Lots and lots of love,
s/Muriel

TLS. UTML.

1. In a letter of 18 January, Paul Scott invited MS to participate in the Swanwick Writers' Summer School which was due to take place between 18 and 24 August in Derbyshire, and of which Scott and his wife Penny were official host and hostess.

TO ALAN BARNSLEY, MAIDSTONE, KENT, LATE FEBRUARY 1962

[Camberwell, London]

Dearest Alan,

Your farewell letter leaves me dry-eyed and the sickly dishonesty of your accusations, – so far as I can decipher your impolite handwriting with a magnifying glass – affects me only as do all sickly things.[1]

My last post-card to Dina should have made my present position quite clear.[2] Obviously it did not – unless one is to suppose you are as inconsiderate as you appear to be. I prefer to suppose that you are too obtuse to take in a civilly-worded plea, but needs must have it drummed in. (If I may say so, it is a flaw in your excellent writings that you assume in your readers a mental resistance to points which are not drummed in.)

It has been my consistent practice since I started writing for my living in 1950 to resist all intrusions on my energy, however attractive, at those times when my work was making special demands on me. My 'fame' as you call it has done nothing to alter this course of action, it has only made it more conspicuous. The only exceptions I have willingly made are in cases of actual emergency amongst my family and neighbours. The demands of my friends, unless they were immediately material ones, have never seemed to me to be as urgent as they are represented to be; my friendships have usually gained rather than suffered by the postponement of meetings until a time suitable and convenient for all. These are the normal habits of a writer. If anyone might be expected to complain of them, one would expect my son Robin to do so; and yet he, above all, is the most jealously protective of my course of life.

We hoped for you at Christmas because at Christmas nobody works, and unexpected callers are customary.

You describe me as having acted as to 'importunate noves [*sic*]'. I acted as to importunate bores. Whoever importunes is a bore, although he may be the most interesting fellow in the world on the right occasion. It has never entered my head that you were other than the author of splendid books, brimming with creative life, or that Dina is other than your wife, with a personality permeating all your activities. I should have thought your joint social sense alone, if your imaginative sympathy was lacking, would have told you that it was very wrong to call on me when I had specifically told you I was heavily occupied.

Would you walk into an operating theatre and demand the attention of the surgeon, even if he was your oldest friend, in order to unburden yourself of your hopes and fears for medical promotion? Would he lay down his knife, offer you a cigarette, and bid the anaesthetist go and fetch in the coffee?

I don't intend to give you a list of the public and private demands on me throughout each day of the week, by telephone at all hours and by letters and telegrams – because I don't consider that this is a legitimate subject for complaint unless I were foolish enough to let them overwhelm me. As it is, I have taken the usual steps to protect myself from them, so that I am free for essential commitments and for a private social life. The day you called with your 'worries and optimisms' was already dedicated to the worries and optimisms of the theatre management who have put their shirts on my play and to an innocent evening pleasure of giving a dinner party. If you had called in dire necessity for a pee or the loan of an aspirin, that would have been different. But I saw no such pathos in your plight as your letter claims. A couple of healthy people, every bit as healthy as I am, sharing with me the good fortune of not having a care in the world (if one has a relative understanding of the real suffering in the world), as warmly dressed against the winter blast as I am, as truly baptised and confirmed in religion as I am – where are your grounds for claiming special attention, or for feeling slighted because I preferred to attend to my business.

I do not intend to accept your hospitality again, because, pleasant as it is, the price you demand is exorbitant. Even when I have stayed at your house, entertained by Dina, I have never intruded on your hours of writing, or on your medical work. I can repay entertainment with entertainment, and friendly exchanges with my full attention and participation; but my conscience will not allow me to barter the time and energy due to my vocation in life in exchange for anyone's generosity or company.

It is simply astonishing that you, as a writer, can imagine that I am constitutionally free to act in a bird-brained way and give ten minutes of my day to this one, and fifteen minutes to that, and then go and take up my pen again or start considering some technical problem, as if there had been no interruption. A ten-minute intrusion of extraneous personalities is a whole day's work to me.

I trust that this lecture, which I deliver in my own time free of charge, will do you good. If you are to develop your best powers as a writer, you must remember that your first business in life is to give pleasure to the public through your writing. Whether you accept this or not, it is the principle on which I act. I do not conceive that I was put into the world to make myself pleasant at any hour of the day to other writers. That is a job for literary hostesses, and even they have their stated times and hours of entertainment.

I hope you had a successful day, and was delighted to hear that your novel looks likely to be a winner. I genuinely long to read it.[3]

Yours,

P.S. I enclose a copy of 'Notes for the Secretary of Miss Autora [*sic*] Cavallo, Novelist' which was inspired by the letters and phone calls of one single day, and by my acquisition of a morning secretary. It is not too unrealistic.[4]

TLcc. MBC. Dating based on this being a response to
Alan Barnsley's letter to MS of 23 February.

1. Subsequent to a botched meeting (described in *MSB*, pp. 260–1) in which MS resisted a visit from the Barnsley family, Alan Barnsley wrote to MS on 23 February, ostensibly to sever contact – a purpose more effectively achieved by the present letter from MS.
2. MS had written to Dina Barnsley on 20 February: 'You are a marvel to give me the opportunity of a get-away from London. Give me a few weeks now, please dear, as I have to "stand by" for rehearsals & could not leave without an upheaval. But will ring early in March' (MBC).
3. MS is referring to Alan Barnsley's new novel *The Birthday King* (see 29 December 1961).
4. These 'Notes' have not been found; they are not part of the collection belonging to the Barnsleys' son Michael Barnsley.

TO SHIRLEY HAZZARD, NEW YORK, 21 MARCH 1962

13 Baldwin Crescent, Camberwell, London, S.E.5
21st March, 1961

Dear Shirley,

It was a joy to hear from you, and to know that you are coming over so soon. Have you lots of friends over here to look after you? – Anyway, you must come and meet mine. Be sure to let me know more of your plans. I look forward so much to seeing you.

There is nothing like being a full-time writer, it relieves all the pressure, even if one spends most of one's full-time time staring into space, as I do. I get into a kind of amoebic stupor and such work as I do is the result of an energetic reaction. Myself that goes to parties is a different sort of being, again.[1]

How nice it is, how very nice, that we are both under Macmillans' roof. I know you will find them very agreeable.

I am writing my Mandelbaum Gate which is a novel. I don't know how it will turn out.

Give my love to all our friends. I have not written to Robert Sonkin to thank him for so many kindnesses, but will do so when least expected, and meantime you must tell him, and everyone else, not to forget me.[2]

I shall look out for your New Yorker piece in April, and for more news of you before you come over.

Love meantime,
s/Muriel

TLS. CUL.

1. In her letter to MS of 12 March, Shirley Hazzard wrote: 'I am so happy to be free of my job, and have done – for me – quite a lot of work since my liberation, although nothing so far on a novel. It is strange, after having a job for ten years, to find joblessness so easy, natural and attractive; and I find that I do my own work without any stern disciplinary measures. Macmillan's have sent me a contract for a book of stories, and have been so kind' (PJC).
2. Hazzard had introduced MS to the philologist Robert Sonkin, who taught at City College in New York, whom she herself had met when living and working in Italy in the mid-1950s.

Shirley Hazzard

TO NED O'GORMAN, NEW YORK, 21 MARCH 1962

13 Baldwin Crescent, Camberwell, London, S.E.5
21st March, 1962

Dear Ned,

It is the first day of spring officially speaking, though this is very like one of those Papal dogmas that people draw the line at. Anyway, it is as cold as ever out of doors, but it will all come true any day now.[1] Hurry up and send me your poems.

I loved your warm and affectionate letter, and you make me into a poet's Muriel, which is new to me. My old friends blame me for everything, they shouldn't blame me, they should console me. You must write and console me.

Now I am writing a new novel called The Mandelbaum Gate, and I wish I possessed your lovely gift of praise to be able to rejoice in life when the depressions close in on me and I retreat inwards and inwards. This always happens to me when I am writing a novel, although the hours of actual writing are happy ones, as you must know, they are hardly hours at all.[2]

Shirley Hazzard is coming over late in May. You should come, too. Come here in the summer and meet some people, or if they bore you we could think of some incredible thing to do or talk about. When are your poems being published here?

I was a poet once but am cast out from Paradise to labour at novels. That is why I am not really a novelist either, but a creature half here half there, composing figments. So I love especially to know that you get pleasure from them.

I hope the world treats you kindly. I couldn't believe it would do otherwise.

Love,
s/Muriel

TLS. SMCC.

1. Three days earlier, on 18 March, MS wrote to Rachel MacKenzie: 'Your approaching spring is enviable; all letters from America tell me of the early signs. We are still damp and cold, expecting nothing dramatic as yet. But a good spring in England is something special, too. My landlady points to her crocuses and says "Look! – How can you be an atheist?" I say, "But I'm not an atheist." She says, "I know that, but I'm just saying that you couldn't be an atheist when you see the flowers coming up."' (NYPL).

2. To Paul Scott, on 15 March, MS wrote: 'I am now on the tetchy tight-wire of The Mandelbaum Gate, sleeping between 4.30. a.m. and 9.30. a.m., but hope to take a holiday between each chapter' (UTML). And to Rachel Mackenzie, on the same day, she wrote: 'The Mandelbaum Gate is coming on nicely, and at the moment there is a middle-aged fellow from the British Embassy walking through the narrow lanes of the Orthodox Jewish quarter of Jerusalem, Israel. He is composing a rondeau in place of a bread and butter letter to his hostess on the Jordan side, which is a thing he is wont to do. I like mixing up cultures like this, and I begin to have high hopes of Freddy, this character from the Embassy' (NYPL).

TO JOHN UPDIKE, IPSWICH, MASSACHUSETTS, 2 APRIL 1962

[Camberwell, London]

Thank you for Pigeon Feathers which I love through & through. It is the poet's vision which does the trick with your work, plus the rest of course.[1]

Very best wishes & congratulations.

Muriel Spark

> APCS showing 'Red Horse-Chestnut'. HHL.
>
> Date and place from postmark.

1. John Updike's *Pigeon Feathers and Other Stories* had just been published in the UK by André Deutsch.

TO ALAN MACLEAN, MACMILLAN LTD, LONDON,
13 APRIL 1962

160, Bruntsfield Place, Edinburgh, 10
13th April 1962

Dear Al,

I am sorry we could not have our lunch but here I am coping
like crazy with a pile of troubles that have evidently been lying
sneakily in wait for me what time I have been leading the high
life of Camberwell. But like the war-horse in the Bk. of Job I say
'Ha-ha among the trumpets.'[1] My main anxiety is my father who
has a heart complication as well as throat-paralysis which prevents
him from swallowing. He has to be artificially fed & is likely to be
in hospital for some weeks. Even then, the outcome is uncertain.
Meantime his speech is coming back sufficiently for him to make
known what racing business I am to do for him each day. We are
v. devoted, my pa and I. As for Ma, between you & me, she is
yours for the asking. Robin and I have been scrubbing & cleaning,
but we are not sure if the difference is perceptible. I am supposed
to be writing my novel in the mornings, but that is the time when
neighbours & friends call & telephone to enquire.

Please, I need for a part of my novel, to know how the British
diplomatic hierarchy is named – Ambassador, Consul & so
on.[2] Your advice would be gratefully welcomed, as I wouldn't
know quite *where* to look this up in a reference library. That's
the difficulty with ref. libraries. (Like electronic brains – the
difficulty isn't the answer, it's to know *what* to ask.)

We must have our lunch to celebrate the Penguin operation
being conducted with a-plomb by all parties. Plumbery is so
important, would that I were more versed in the art at this
particular point in my time-space.[3]

Think of me in my exile & remember me to all mutual cronies.
Love,
Mu.

ALS. MA.

1. Job 39: 25: 'He saith among the trumpets, Ha, ha; and he smelleth the battle afar off, the thunder of the captains, and the shouting.'
2. Referring to *The Mandelbaum Gate* as well as to her recent move to a larger flat in Tiny Lazzari's house, on 2 April MS wrote to the critic, editor, and political activist Dwight Macdonald in New York: 'Am writing a novel, it is turning out a bit peculiar. I think my garret phase was my best. The high life (2nd-floor flat same house) spells ruination, to coin a phrase' (YUL). On the day of the present letter, 13 April, she also wrote to Rache Lovat Dickson: 'My "novel" lies on the writing table waiting for something to be done about it. So far the "novel" is the opening chapter. But I am happy with the ideas I have for it' (MA).
3. MS's editors at Macmillan were in discussion with Penguin Books about paperback editions of her novels.

TO RACHE LOVAT DICKSON, MACMILLAN LTD, LONDON, 26 APRIL 1962

North British Hotel, Edinburgh
26th April 1962

My dear Rache,

Thank you for your sweet note. I feel so much happier now that the funeral is over. My father had never been ill in his life – not even a week in bed – before this last illness & I'm glad he was spared a lingering illness at the last.[1]

I come back to home & work on Saturday, very gladly, having settled all my mother's debts & doubts with a clean sweep of my savings. I feel it is cheap at the price & only hope she doesn't get into another pickle & that I can possess my soul in peace with my novel. My father was anxious about encroachments on my peace of mind, but my mother, alas, couldn't care less. She has given up the Bottle (for the time being!) & seems perfectly capable & ready for the future so long as I keep her income up – so perhaps things will work out well.

Dear Rache I hope your book is under control by now & long to hear about it, & more, to read it.[2] See you soon.

Love
Muriel

ALS on North British Hotel letterhead. MA.

1. In a letter sent the same day, 26 April, to Frank Kermode MS wrote: 'I have been here, feeling rather battered, during my father's illness. He died last week. I loved and miss him very much. A man whom he disliked fell into his grave at his funeral' (PFL).
2. MS refers to Rache Lovat Dickson's *The House of Words*, to which she returns in a later, undated, letter to him: 'I haven't *really* told you how fascinating your autobiography is. Don't misunderstand me when I say your style is curiously, to me, like that of the new French writers – they appear, in their style, to let the rain fall on the just & unjust alike, and this is what you do, it is a joy. I don't mean that you reserve judgment always – it is more a matter of how you write than what you write' (MA).

TO RACHEL MACKENZIE, THE NEW YORKER,
NEW YORK, 3 MAY 1962

13 Baldwin Crescent, Camberwell, London, S.E.5
3rd May, 1962

My dear Rachel,

Thank you, dear Rachel, for your heartwarming telegram which reached me just after my return to London.

It isn't so long ago that you lost your mother, and so I needn't tell you what a tidal wave of memories and associations are bound up with the death of a parent. My father's illness only lasted for two weeks, and I was able to cheer him up almost to the last. I miss most of all his affection for me. My mother has been quite a handful, but she has settled down now, for the time being at least. That, and seeing to all the family affairs, has been the biggest strain.[1]

I am trying to plunge back into work and get something achieved. The play had many set-backs, but it is now in the hands of a new management – Michael Codron with the producer Donald McWhinnie who are a really good team. They hope to get it on the stage by September.[2]

Thank you again, Rachel, dear Rachel, for your lovely message. It made me feel that the world was a kindly place, after all.

Love,

s/Muriel

P.S. Do you know of Robert Whitehead? – Theatre manager connected with 'A Man for All Seasons.' – He is buying an option on 'Jean Brodie' & getting it adapted. Does this sound good?[3]

TLS. NYPL.

1. On the same day as the present letter, 3 May, MS wrote to Ned O'Gorman: 'Back home again, having buried the dead. My father had more affection for me than anyone else, so that is gone out of the world' (SMCC).

2. The theatre producer Michael Codron had made his name in the late 1950s with his production of Harold Pinter's first staged play, *The Birthday Party*. Donald McWhinnie had got to know MS's work when working as a scriptwriter and producer at the BBC, where he became Assistant Head of Sound Drama in 1953; he too worked with Pinter, and was trusted by Samuel Beckett to direct several of his plays for radio and stage. Further on MS's work for the stage, see Ian Brown, 'Dramatic Contexts and Metatheatricality in Muriel Spark's Writing for Performance' (*TCD*, pp. 264–87).

3. The Canadian theatre producer Robert Whitehead produced the Broadway staging of Robert Bolt's play *A Man for All Seasons*, which opened in November 1961 at the ANTA Playhouse, with Paul Scofield playing Sir Thomas More.

TO DWIGHT MACDONALD, THE NEW YORKER, NEW YORK, 12 JUNE 1962

13 Baldwin Crescent, Camberwell, London, S.E.5
12th June, 1962

Dear Dwight,

Thank you for your other piece on the Dictionary, which is a marvel.[1] I heard a very funny story about your N. Yorker piece, told by you to Shirley Hazzard, and by her to me. I laughed a lot. Shirley is over here now, we had a party and sighed for you to be with us. I introduced Rayner Heppenstall to Shirley, as I felt he was the next-best intellectually wicked person after you. I think she probably brought out the best in him.

You are beautifully healthy in your attitude to Marienbad, but aren't you inconsistent when you say I am in close touch with my *unconscious?* I don't know what you mean by my unconscious, dear Dwight, like you I can only talk & think about what meets the eye. If other people read between the lines, that's their affair. (I haven't seen the film and now want to do so.)²

I think you should be proud of doing so many drafts of your writing. I am too lazy to do so, but I think I could improve my work if I did. After all, the Holy Ghost did a lot of editing and revising of the Bible before he finally settled for the Vulgate at the Council of Trent, and still holds the author's right to revise from time to time. At a General Council.

Did you read Robbe-Grillet's 'Jealousy'? I was fascinated by it, but wonder how he could do a novel on these lines if the main theme isn't an obsession. It needs the theme of jealousy or voyeurism to take this abnormally detailed form.

Talking about my unconscious, I dreamt the Derby 'winner', and gave the tip to everyone. Then I went to the Derby with my publisher, and picked out another horse with a pin. Myself, I backed the second horse which won. The dream horse shed its jockey half-way up the field, but carried on just the same and came in second.

I am writing a religious novel called The Mandelbaum Gate, it is set in Palestine. The text of this sermon of mine is taken from the Apocalypse, or as you Prots say, Revelation: 'I know thy works, that thou art neither cold nor hot. I would thou wert cold or hot. So then because thou art lukewarm, and neither cold nor hot, I will spew thee out of my mouth.' I quite agree with the Holy Ghost on this point, one should be cold or hot about religion. But the book, when finished, might illustrate some different theme, I never can know definitely in advance.³

I feel very warmed by your approval of my stuff, I know you must mean it or you wouldn't say it. Could you bear to read my play (written for the theatre), 'Doctors of Philosophy', if I send you proofs? It is supposed to be opening here in the last week of September, to be produced by Donald McWhinnie. It is about Ph.D.'s and educated women, married and single. Plays are easier to write than novels, to me, and if this turns out any good, I shall write more plays.

Please send me more of your pieces. Love to Gloria – longing to see you again in October.[4]

Love,

s/Muriel

TLS. YUL.

1. Dwight Macdonald had published a lengthy article, 'The String Untuned', reviewing the third edition of *Webster's New International Dictionary*, in the *New Yorker* of 10 March. In it, he described the dictionary as a 'massacre'. His second piece on the dictionary has not been found.

2. Macdonald had enclosed, with his letter to MS of 22 May, his article in *Esquire*, 'L'Année dernière à Marienbad', on Alain Resnais's film based on a script by Alain Robbe-Grillet; in his letter he wrote: 'Thanks also for the collection of stories and BBC dramas – you really are very good, you know. And don't you ever rewrite? It sounds as if you did (I mean this as a compliment). If you don't, you must be in close touch with your unconscious. Quant à moi, I rewrite endlessly, never less than 3 drafts, and the first is always ghastly' (NLS).

3. MS cites the King James Bible, Revelation 3: 15–16, replacing the colon after 'nor hot' by a full stop and modernising the spelling of 'spue' to 'spew'.

4. Macdonald's second wife, whom he married in 1954, was Gloria Lanier.

TO RACHEL MACKENZIE, THE NEW YORKER,
NEW YORK, 13 JUNE 1962

13 Baldwin Crescent, Camberwell, London, S.E.5
13th June, 1962

Dearest Rachel,

No need to reply to this: it is only that I haven't thanked you for the press cuttings, and do so now. It's sweet of you to collect them for me. Lippincott send a few, but not all. Not that I have missed any thrills with Voices at Play which has had, let us say, a mixed reception. Over here it did well, while Miss Brodie was mixed.

Once more let me tell you how thankful I am for your holding over 'The Gentile Jewesses' until you can see it as part of the whole, which I trust will not be long.[1] At least I can promise you no more date-figurings from now on. Oh dear, I am feeling the pressure of things very much just now. Concentration comes hard, but when it does, the words and ideas come sweet on the pages, a solace to me at least, even if they have no better destiny. Family demands on me are always threatening to get out of hand, and there are other, less explicable pressures – the demands of society that everyone has to meet are no particular problem, and even the social pressures that come from one's name getting around a bit more can be coped with – but I feel it a strain to live up to being a cheerful, normal, untemperamental little Muriel who doesn't take literature, art, and all that with vulgar seriousness; this is what my particular environment more or less expects now that I have graduated from the garret category. Of course I like to be cheerful, normal, and all that, but . . . . One day I shall just pack up and run away, that's all.

Lynn Carrick and his wife, who are the Lippincott contingent resident in London, are a comfort. Lynn suggests that if I don't get my book finished by October I go to New York all the same and finish it there. That's what I shall do, I shall fly it across to some hotel bedroom in your city, or come and squat with my notebook in a corner of your office, like Roddy only less beautiful than he is, and more noiseless. Give Roddy a hug and a kiss from me, while I think of it.[2]

I have a long-short story to finish, too. It will come out about 16,000 words or thereabouts, called 'The Girls of Slender Means'. It would suit the New Yorker if it *does* suit the New Yorker, if you follow.

Are you going away this summer? I hope you will go somewhere delightful and loving, as you are. I am going to Paris for two days next week, but I have October to look forward to. It does seem as if my play really will go on this autumn, in which case my part of the job, the rehearsals, will be done in August.

Thank you for liking my Aurora Cavallo nonsense. It would have needed cartoon drawings to make any sort of amusement, I think, but alas I can't draw.[3]

I shall say goodbye to Shirley tomorrow. I like her more and more. I hear from Bill Maxwell and from Dwight, whose dictionary piece I loved. Dwight is marvellously outrageous, and

I reply in kind, all dogmatic and Papist. I missed Ved when I was called away to Scotland, but hear kindly from him, too.[4]

My love to all. Especially to yourself,

Ever,

s/Muriel

TLS. NYPL.

1. In an undated letter prior to the present one, probably from late May or early June, MS wrote to Rachel MacKenzie:

   > My new novel THE MANDELBAUM GATE contains a character who is a half-Jewish novelist writing an autobiography which she has entitled (to the alarm of her publishers) 'Apologia pro vita Sua'. It would balance-up the tone and style of the book, as it occurs to me now, if I inserted my piece 'The Gentile Jewesses' as the first chapter of this autobiography. The original intention for this piece was that it should be the beginning of a first-person novel; but I saw that it wouldn't do, and so gave it a self-contained turn. But now I see where it would fit in.
   >
   > This idea, if you are willing to give me permission to reproduce the piece, would not, of course, interfere with your publication of it, as I imagine you will be using it long before the book is published. And if you don't like the idea, please be assured that it won't upset the novel, at this stage, to leave it out.

   She added: 'It will be a shorter novel than I thought; they are always shorter novels than I thought. I hope to finish it before the autumn' (NYPL). And on the same day as the present letter, 13 June, MS wrote to Ned O'Gorman:

   > My father's death churned me up, and my family affairs were in chaos. My mother is a problem of deep dimensions. Dear Ned, pray that I get peace and time to write my novel and make it nice.
   >
   > Shirley Hazzard is over here, full of news about you all, and looking like Leonardo's St. Anne.
   >
   > I hope you are happy about your life, and writing the poetry of your more boisterous years. I too still hammer away, for I haven't yet made a bright enough or sufficiently battering sandal. (SMCC)

2. No further mention of Roddy, most probably a cat, has been found.
3. On Aurora Cavallo, see late February 1962 to Alan Barnsley, n. 4.
4. William Maxwell had been Fiction Editor at the *New Yorker* since 1936; Dwight Macdonald and Ved Mehta also worked for the magazine.

TO JOHN SMITH, CHRISTY & MOORE LTD, LONDON,
16 JUNE 1962

13 Baldwin Crescent, Camberwell, London, S.E.5

The BBC have chosen 'The Ballad' as one of its 2 entrants for the
Italia Prize. I have agreed to equal division (in the event of a win!)
between composer producer & myself. We will know by Sept 21ˢᵗ.
Should you inform the Italian publisher? – Perhaps wait & see. If
lucky, we go there to collect.[1]
  Love
  M.

                                    ALS. WUL. Dating from postmark.

1. The Prix Italia was established in 1948 by Radiotelevisione Italiana to reward
    radio works; the award ceremony took – and continues to take – place in a
    different city each year, 1962 being the year for Verona to host the ceremony.
    The composer of the music for *The Ballad of Peckham Rye* was Tristram Cary,
    the play's producer was Christopher Holme; MS will travel with them to
    Verona in September to collect the prize which her play does indeed win. In
    a letter to Holme on 28 June, she will write 'This is the draft of the intro-
    duction to the Italia Prize script', outlining the collaboration:

      As 'An Entertainment for Radio', *The Ballad of Peckham Rye* is the
      product of a collaboration at all stages between author, composer,
      and producer. Work started on the text some months before publi-
      cation of Muriel Spark's novel of the same name, which furnished
      the outline of the story and a good part of the dialogue. The verses,
      songs, and scenes for music were written by Muriel Spark specially
      for the radio script, which is thus an independent work with its
      own particular view of the characters. That of Nelly Mahone has
      emerged with particular emphasis. Tristram Cary's music, while
      closely attuned, in the style of ballad opera, to the needs of the text,
      is an equal partner. It makes satirical use of a whole range of popular
      idioms, with quotation and parody, bizarre instruments, natural
      and unnatural effects. Its main vehicle of narrative stagement is a
      simplified form of 'Sprechgesant' – speech-song – employed also in
      the various dialogue settings. (BBC WAC)

TO ROBERT YEATMAN, MACMILLAN LTD, LONDON, CIRCA 22 AUGUST 1962

Edinburgh

Dear Robert,

In haste to say am having a crazy whirl but v. nice, & also that Mr James Haynes, The Paperback Bookshop, 22a Charles Street, Edin. 8 – is moaning – moaning that he only got 2 each of my books & wants 6 more of each. He is busy organizing the Writers Conf. so wanted *me* to tell you.[1] Very irregular & awkward for me, as I don't know if he pays his bills or anything, do I? Anyway, that's the message. His tel. number is New 6448 if you want to check. I went out to have coffee with Lawrence Durrell & we were busy scandalizing everybody then found that a BBC man was lurking behind us with a tape. All the scandal has gone on record.[2] Rebecca West is here, she has taken to me tho' not to all . . . . Hope to see you next week & tell you more & more.[3]

Lots of love to all

Mu

ALS. MA. Dating from Macmillan stamp indicating receipt.

1. On 4 August, MS wrote to Maurice Macmillan: 'I am going to represent Scotland at an international Writers' conference at the Edinburgh Festival, starting on the 19th of August. Some interviews with the press will be inevitable. I think, for a writer, the most intelligent way of using one's energies in public is to combine it with the sales of one's books' (MA).

   The International Writers' Conference held in Edinburgh between 20 and 24 August brought together a host of famous writers including William Burroughs, Norman Mailer, Mary McCarthy, Hugh MacDiarmid, Henry Miller, Stephen Spender, and Alexander Trocchi. It was organised by the publisher John Calder and Jim Haynes, the latter then running the Edinburgh Paperback Bookshop; at Edinburgh University's McEwan Hall, the conference attracted large audiences and a lot of publicity.

2. Scandal was in the conference air. Mary McCarthy described it in a letter to Hannah Arendt on 28 September:

People jumping up to confess they were homosexuals or hetero-
sexuals; a Registered Heroin Addict leading the young Scottish
opposition to the literary tyranny of the communist Hugh
MacDiarmid [. . .] an English woman novelist describing her communications with her dead daughter; a Dutch homosexual, former
male nurse, now a Catholic convert, seeking someone to baptize
him; a bearded Sikh with hair down to his waist declaring on the
platform that homosexuals were incapable of love, just as (he said)
hermaphrodites were incapable of orgasm (Stephen Spender, in the
chair, murmured that he should have thought they could have two).
And all this before an audience of over two thousand people per
day, mostly, I suppose, Scottish Presbyterians. (*Between Friends: The
Correspondence of Hannah Arendt and Mary McCarthy, 1949–1975*, ed.
Carol Brightman, Harcourt Brace, 1995, p. 139)

In an undated letter to John Smith written shortly after the conference,
MS will write:

I made some statements at the Conference which John Calder wants
to broadcast (presumably without payment to me). Calder is one
of the organisers. I said definitely the B.B.C. must approach me
through my agent for permission, and send a transcript. As one of
my statements concerned the Index and might be taken as an attack
on the Church if used out of context, I feel particularly strongly
about this. Please will you write to the B.B.C. just saying that any
of my statements at the Conference are my own copyright? (WUL)

3. On 26 August, MS will write to Robert Yeatman: 'The Scottish press,
    particularly the Scotsman, gave me a lot of space on separate days. This was
    because I gave interviews. (For some reason I found them enjoyable on this
    occasion, so please don't think I am claiming points for victimisation.)' (MA).

TO JOHN SMITH, CHRISTY & MOORE LTD, LONDON,
20 SEPTEMBER 1962

13 Baldwin Crescent, Camberwell, London, S.E.5
20th Sept. 1962

Dear John,
    You are an Angel.
    I enclose your tickets, before I forget.[1]
    I weakened, as Michael Codron wanly agreed to leave out the

biographical note, and have done the enclosed, which I think suits the occasion. If you have any other views, lemme know. The dot-dot-dash bit can't be filled in till Tuesday morning.

Lots of love,

s/Muriel

[enclosed autobiography from MS]

MURIEL SPARK was born and educated in Edinburgh. She roams the world but lives most of the time in a suburb of London.

Doctors of Philosophy is her first theatre play.

Her novels, short stories and radio plays have become famous throughout the world in the past few years. Her novels *The Ballad of Peckham Rye* and *Memento Mori* have been dramatised for television. Other play-adaptations of her novels have been successful on sound-radio, particularly the musical version of *The Ballad of Peckham Rye* which has recently won international recognition in being awarded . . . . for 1962.[2]

Her last novel, *The Prime of Miss Jean Brodie*, received the honour of being published in a single issue of The New Yorker. Both this book and *Memento Mori* are being adapted for the theatre by well-known American dramatists.

John The above can be used for all play purposes, plus copies of the Sunday Times Colour Supplement essay when it appears.

M.

TLS. WUL.

---

1. On 12 August, MS wrote to Alan Maclean about *Doctors of Philosophy*: 'Plans for the Play have developed in a new direction & are now settled to everyone's satisfaction. They are thus: It opens on 2nd October at *The Arts Theatre* – now owned by Michael Codron & another, & will be the first play of the new management & new season. If it is any good it will transfer to a big theatre, if it isn't any good, it won't. But it will be at the Arts for 1 month' (MA).

    On 2 September, she wrote to John Smith: 'I enjoyed our lunch immensely. Rehearsals on Monday. I'll let you know. Thursday, alas – the

Sunday Times feel it would be better to interview me privately, as Donald McWhinnie seemed to feel that the cast might be involved, and actually the S. Times only want to talk to me. So let's wait until the end of September, or nearer it, when the play is beginning to take shape?' (WUL).

2. MS uses ellipses ('The dot-dot-dash bit') as she is awaiting news of the Prix Italia.

TO WILLIAM SHAWN, THE NEW YORKER, NEW YORK, 13 NOVEMBER 1962

The New Yorker, New York
13^(th) Nov. 1962

Dear Mr Shawn,

   This is just to say I'm enormously happy to be working here – Thank you so *very* much for making the office available to me.[1] I feel I can get some really good work done & it's lovely to be surrounded by good friends.[2]

   Sincerely.
   Muriel Spark

                                        ALS on *New Yorker* letterhead. NYPL.

1. William Shawn had been Editor of the *New Yorker* since 1952. When MS decided to make her second trip to New York, and this time to stay for longer, he made an office available to her at the magazine's headquarters at 25 West 43rd Street. MS arrived in the city by plane on 13 October, writing to John Smith on the eve of her departure from London:

   I enclose a few letters and would be so very grateful as always if you would answer them some how some time.

       Some how some time
       we answer o we answer the letters
       yes we do, honey I'm
       writing to you
       instead of to my elders and o my betters,
       you being my younger and my so much worser,
       a terser bursar than any precursor
       I every [*sic*] met in my life, and if you

> print this in Poetry Review
> I'll fly off the handle at the scandal.

Please would you try to be sensible.

I hope you had a lovely time in Scotland and forgot about everything else, as I hope to do in New York where they only eat with a fork. (WUL)

After arrival on 28 October, she wrote again to Smith (referring to Michael Codron):

My new flat is a marvel and a joy – very extravagant – $500 a month – but well worth it. A glorious view of the East River – looking obliquely on the United Nations – lovely dawns & sunsets. The sunlight is magnificent. I do intend to spend a long time every year in New York & if successful, to have an establishment of my own here. The place agrees with me for work. You would like the 'story' I have made out of chap. one *Mandelbaum*. I intend to write it piece by piece, if the N. Yorker take this one – but first of all to finish my much-interrupted 'Girls of Slender Means'.

Michael wanted me to return! Really, what next? – I came here to get away from all these distractions & to save my reason. It was the only solution of the problem: how I was to get my new work done. And the play hasn't even started making money yet! – Will it start earning at Brighton, I wonder?

My friends here are really good ones, all workers & writers like myself. I wish you could be here just now, the light is so beautiful and the new glass buildings look noble & black at dusk, and fairy-like white at noon. (WUL)

2. MS was writing two novels simultaneously – or intermittently, rather – and the relation between the two productions was never less than complex. Of her novel more immediately in progress, *The Girls of Slender Means*, on 1 July MS wrote to Rachel Lovat Dickson: 'I have started writing a Work, which is secret, and which I hope to finish in July. – "The Mandelbaum Gate" has got to wait till the interruptions are over, but the new Work is exciting, you will like it' (MA). Then, on 19 July, she wrote again to Lovat Dickson: 'The novel is beginning to form a picture, as usual it is like working with fragments of stained-glass & I piece them all together' (MA). On 24 July, she wrote to John Smith: 'The novel is turning out to be a new sort of departure for me. It is "socially-conscious" at least I think so' (WUL). On 29 July, on a postcard to Shirley Hazzard, she wrote, from Aylesford: 'Here I am in a monastery writing a seditious novel about an anarchist poet in 1945 between the 2 victories' (CUL).

On 10 August, she wrote to Rachel MacKenzie, referring initially to *The Mandelbaum Gate*:

> This is to give you the go-ahead with 'The Gentile Jewesses' as I shall not be using it in the novel after all. I offer deep apologies for the hold-up, and can only plead a sort of creative crackerdom which descended when the novel was interrupted by family affairs. I am informing John Smith in order to avoid further confusions. There is no hurry on our side, but I am looking forward to being a New Yorkerite again with this piece.
>
> I hope to send you my new short-novel 'The Girls of Slender Means' within the next month. It is about life in London between VE night, 1945 and VJ night. Nearly finished it.
>
> 'The Mandelbaum Gate' is developing at a more ruminative pace. If necessary I shall bring it to New York to finish there. It refuses to be hurried, unlike my other stuff. (NYPL)

And on 7 November, she wrote to Robert Yeatman: 'I think it's going to be a nice little book. (Sales talk). About the length of Miss B., I think.' She added: 'It's lovely to have peace to get on with my work, and to have so many kind friends around me. After a terrible year I feel happy at last' (MA).

TO ALLEN TATE, MINNEAPOLIS, MINNESOTA, 3 DECEMBER 1962

Beaux Arts Hotel, New York
3rd December 1962

Dear Mr Tate,

Thank you for your letter & for suggesting lunch on the 6th January – that will be lovely for me & I look forward very much to seeing you again.

Thank you, too, for your very kind invitation to Minneapolis.[1] I should love to come, for my own pleasure, but unfortunately I *can't* lecture – that's to say, I open my mouth & nothing comes out or else something comes – either way, it's disastrous. All I can ever offer to do is read a story & then answer questions about it – I find it quite easy to answer *questions* about the creative process & so on. But I doubt very much if this sort of thing would be good value for a University audience.

Any how, we can ask each other questions on 6th Jan.
Thank you again so much.
Yours sincerely
Muriel Spark

ALS on Beaux Arts Hotel letterhead. PFL.

1. MS was putting down roots in New York, referring to her lodging at the
    Beaux Arts Hotel, 310 East 44th Street, as 'home' in a letter written to
    William Shawn on 30 November: 'This is just to say that I've reached a
    stage in my work where it's easier to work at home (late at night, etc.) and
    so I feel I ought now to give up the room at the New Yorker which you
    very very kindly made available for me. It *has* been an enormous help –
    and of course I hope very much you'll like the results when you see them'
    (NYPL).

TO IVAN VON AUW, HAROLD OBER ASSOCIATES, NEW YORK, 26 DECEMBER 1962

Beaux-Arts [New York]
26th Dec. 1962

Dear Ivan,
    Thank you for your beautiful present of orchids, it was an
act of inspiration, for orchids are to me the most mysteriously
lovely objects in the world.[1] I've been hypnotised by them, this
Christmas – each one is different. I keep them in the *refrigerator*
at night – which is what one is supposed to do with orchids – and
they show no signs of wilting or of having been so much as looked-
at, & will last until I wear them, one by one, for special occasions.
I do hope to hear that your tooth trouble responded favourably
to the sun without delay & that all has gone right in your area of
time-space. I've been *so* bad-tempered this Christmas – I usually
am like that during the frightful Feast – the ideal is so very far
away from the reality.[2] But I feel restored when I see the orchids
flourishing in their confidence without any need to be useful
creatures & so on. I've got heaps to tell you & hope you will let me

know when you're free to come here to dinner & tune-in. Many
thank-you's, once more,

   Love,

   Muriel

ALS. PFL.

1.   Though she had first worked with Ivan von Auw, of the New York literary agency Harold Ober Associates, while still with David Higham, it was only recently that he had become her official US agent, a role which was set to grow as her trust in, and friendship with, him developed. Discreet, elegant, homosexual like many of MS's confidants, and extraordinarily diligent in his professional dealings, as is borne out by the vast quantity of his letters to and concerning MS in the voluminous Harold Ober Archive at Princeton Firestone Library, he was set to become incomparably the most important literary agent in MS's career.

2.   In an undated letter from shortly after Christmas, MS wrote to Rache Lovat Dickson, referring to *The Girls of Slender Means*: 'I am revising the very last pages of the novel, – what an *ordeal* this book has been. Peggy Norris (the typist who's typing it) says it is my best book by far. I hope it is, because the *pain* of composition has been really acute. Anyway, it's my most realistic novel so far. I had a sad Christmas, away from home and my father dead, but I saw friends & did my best to be merry' (MA).

TO ROBERT YEATMAN, MACMILLAN LTD, LONDON, 30 DECEMBER 1962

Beaux Arts Hotel, New York
30th December 1962

Dearest Robert,

   Les Girls de Slendre Means will be coming to you shortly & I hope you will adore it against your better judgment. It will reach you via Alan, as I'm sending it to him first for acceptance or decline-and-fall of the Dedication & I want him of course to see it first unofficially.[1] I would have sent an office copy but the price of carbon copies in this terrain was prohibitive. After you've all read it, please will you pass it to John Smith on loan? – Sorry if this all sounds confused, but I've got influenza. The novel reads like something written by an octopus in a space-ship with a pen in every hand, being serenaded by Siamese twins.

Best thoughts & wishes for 1963 – Looking forward to seeing you soon.

Love

Mu

ALS on Beaux Arts Hotel letterhead. MA.

1. The dedication in the published novel reads simply 'For Alan Maclean'.

1963

Throughout the year, MS laboured on *The Mandelbaum Gate*, making what was, for her, painfully slow progress. In January, she left her US publisher, Lippincott, and – through Ivan von Auw, who was increasingly relied on for all business matters – signed with Alfred Knopf. On 26 January, she threw a party at which she introduced Shirley Hazzard to the man whom she declared Hazzard should marry, the writer Francis Steegmuller. On 4 February, she left New York for the UK. In praise of her work, W. H. Auden wrote: 'I find Miss Spark's novels beautifully executed – she seems to know exactly what she is doing – funny, moving and like nobody else's' (NLS). In early February, MS was furious to learn that Stanford was publishing a book on her work and life and, though she considered legal action, the book was indeed released in the autumn; also much to her displeasure, MS learned around this time that Derek Stanford had sold her letters to a dealer, who sold them on to the Harry Ransom Center at the University of Texas at Austin. MS visited Paris in late February, and Ireland in May, on both occasions with her landlady Tiny Lazzari. In the summer, she started to consider the sale of her manuscripts and had their worth estimated. In late August, MS sailed on the SS *Queen Mary* for her third visit to New York, stayed briefly at the Hotel Barclay, then returned to her former residence at the Beaux Arts Hotel. For the rest of the year, she socialised and tried to make progress on *The Mandelbaum Gate*. Both the *Evening Standard* and the BBC's *Woman's Hour* serialised *The Girls of Slender Means*, which was published in the UK on 19 September, to enthusiastic reviews. At the end of the year, MS declined an invitation to the wedding of Hazzard and Steegmuller, leaving New York to spend the Christmas holiday in the British Virgin Islands.

TO RACHE LOVAT DICKSON, MACMILLAN LTD, LONDON, 4 JANUARY 1963

Beaux-Arts Hotel, N. York
4ᵗʰ January 1962

Dearest Rache,

Your letter brightens my day – I'm in bed with 'flu, and fast recovering, I'm glad to say. Did you not receive the mad wire that Shirley & I sent you in lieu of a Christmas letter? If so, please forget it, for it was only a message to convey a fraction of our thoughts of you. – I mention it only because you *seem* only to have received my big-letter. I addressed the wire to Pitts Deep & had the N. Yorker checkers very busy finding out the location. They reported 'Hampshire County' so off it went to Pitts Deep, Hants where it is no doubt lying in some deep pit, cast there by some hilarious telegraph-boy in the excitement of the Season. Ved is coming to see me later this evening to sit by my sick-bed and tell me I look beautiful. I keep telling him how wrong he is, but anyway, I guess he feels he is always on the safe side to take this line with a woman. I don't see that he can go wrong. I do hope he will be coming to Macmillan & I'll tell him – as I've already told him – how keen you are on his work. His agent in London is Pollinger, by the way.

I'm waiting for my publisher situation to be settled here before fixing a date for return.[1] Also, alas, I'm having extensive dental treatment which is being hastened through as quickly as possible, but I'll have to get it over. It's wildly expensive, of course, but it's just hard luck that I was over here when the trouble was discovered.

I feel rather flopped-out with 'flu and the final effort with my novel. The latter was something I *had* to get out of my system & I hope I've done it successfully. Next week I'm starting on chapter 2 of the Mandelbaum Gate, which is a different type of work altogether. I'll send you chapter 1, which the N. Yorker have taken. I hope they'll take at least some parts of 'The Girls', but it's too soon to have their reaction yet. I sent it off, also, to Alan (as I hope he'll accept the dedication of the book to him) but as soon as it comes your way please will you let me know your feelings about it? – I long to hear. I sent it by Air Mail – first class – in my anxiety to get it to your end, so it should be with you by now.[2]

My pal Shirley has moved into a lovely new flat, with a white drawing-room peppered with Queen Anne & Regency chairs & tables. She's giving a party on Sunday, and was saying how much she would have liked you there. She's working on a novel that sounds most impressive and good.

What a lot I really have to tell you, and how greatly I look forward to seeing you again! I feel very sad and homeless at times but then I remind myself of all my good fortune, and especially the satisfaction of my work, merely doing it, whether it turns out well or not.

Now I look forward to hearing about 'The Girls' and be sure I'll let you know the date of my arrival, & will try to make it a convenient time & day to be met. How sweet you are! – I feel almost like jumping on the plane immediately.

Love from your

Mu

> ALS. MA. Dating: in 1962, MS arrived in New York on 12
> January and had not yet written *The Girls of Slender Means*.

1. MS had decided to leave her US publisher, Lippincott.
2. On 2 January, MS wrote to Ivan von Auw: 'Here is the novel. I hope you will like it when you find the time & heroism to read it' (PFL). And in an undated letter received at Macmillan on 9 January, she wrote to Robert Yeatman:

   > Soon you will, I hope, lay hands on The Girls of Slender Means which is designed to corrupt & pervert the Nation's youth. I think you are probably past being undermined by it; however I look forward to knowing your opinion as a scholar & a gentleman. (MA)

TO ALAN MACLEAN, MACMILLAN LTD, LONDON,
20 JANUARY 1963

1101-South Beaux-Arts, 310 E. 44ᵗʰ Street
20ᵗʰ Jan. 1960[1]

Dearest Al,

Your cable filled me with relief and pride, and thank you too for
the letter which followed on its heels. In many ways I think The
Girls is *your* book, and especially I hoped you would accept it since
it is, I think, the only novel of mine in which there are no really
unpleasant characters! My only anxiety was that it shouldn't be up to
literary standard, and now you tell me it is – especially, you know,
the ending – I am v. happy indeed.[2] I was at dinner the other night
with Ian & Elma Mackenzie, and Mʳ Upjohn from Canada – an all-
Macmillan gathering, and we drank to your well-deserved success.[3]
Vive Alan! All here who know you, and they are many & many,
are delighted. I have laid so many claims to your acquaintanceship
that I've half-forgotten, myself, whether you discovered me or I
discovered you . . . Anyway, I know there was something long & far-
fetched about it, and I brim over with joy at the happy outcome.

I hope to be home soon, full of fairy-tales of N. York. I have
gone to Knopf for a consideration.[4] The play (for Broadway) has
reared its ugly head again, but me, I'm too exhausted to take
much notice of the negotiations.

I'll follow MUCH ADO with eager anticipation. Saving up for
the races, 1ˢᵗ opportunity.[5] See you soon.

Love
Mu

ALS. MA. Dating: on 20 January 1960, MS was in London;
the Macmillan date-stamp reads '23 Jan 1963';
MS has finished *The Girls of Slender Means*.

1. While it is not uncommon for MS to forget in January or February that the
    year has changed, the present lapse is more surprising.

2. Alan Maclean's telegram of 9 January read: 'INFINITE CONGRATULATIONS ON THE GIRLS WHICH IS PURE JOY AND A MARVELLOUS NOVEL STOP HONOURED AND DELIGHTED WITH DEDICATION WRITING LOVE'.
3. Frank Upjohn was Vice-President of Macmillan Canada. Ian MacKenzie had been Director of St Martin's Press, then part of Macmillan, since 1954; Elly was his wife.
4. On Margaret Storm Jameson's early enthusiasm for MS's work, see 25 July 1960. On 17 November 1962, Storm Jameson wrote to Blanche Knopf to advise her to meet Muriel in New York and to invite her to be published by Knopf:

> If you still want Muriel Spark approach her at once. Ask her to lunch with you, reminding her that you and I both spoke or wrote to her about coming to Knopf if she ever left Lippincott. [. . .] She will go, I am sure, where she gets the most money, and/or convinces herself that she will get the most kudos. At least, in the way of kudos, you are unbeatable! Whether you can match her financial ambitions I don't know because I don't know what they are.
>
> I'll warn you, or remind you, that you will be taking on a tartar. She has worn out two Macmillan (London) directors already. I believe that she is now handled by Maurice Macmillan himself. On the credit side, she *is* a good writer, not an entirely certain one, but certain at least to write several more very good novels. And she is, at her best, a Knopf author, since even at her not-best she is not commonplace. (HRC)

On 14 January, MS wrote to John Smith: 'The book was an ordeal, I'm longing to know what you think of it. I'm absolutely exhausted, and looking forward to a good long rest. I've had some ups and downs, but have emerged successfully, and as you know, profitably with Knopf. Now I think I'll have to hang on a bit to make myself agreeable to them, as they are wildly excited, and Blanche is like a two-year-old on the strength of it – she was determined to have me on her list' (WUL).

And on the same day, 14 January, MS wrote to Robert Yeatman: 'I have got a new publisher Blanche Knopf to whom I have sold my soul more or less. But I intend to snatch it back and make for home very shortly with the fabulous slosh, plus my soul, leaving her the book only. I have been making inroads on my fabulers at the dress shops, I have got a raincoat in blue velvet and a mulberry creation suitable for a fine day' (MA).

5. Much Ado was the name of Alan Maclean's racehorse.

TO SHIRLEY HAZZARD, NEW YORK,
6 FEBRUARY 1963

13 Baldwin Crescent, Camberwell, London, S.E.5 (!)
6th Feb. 1963

Dearest Shirlers,

Here I am in a fine frenzy of unpacking and shaking hands
with the furniture. I wept much on the plane but was rescued by
a Shell Oil man who was a fan of Wm. Golding & Iris Murdoch,
but hadn't heard of me. However, he seemed to love me for myself
alone.[1] We are snowed up & the thaw is causing leaks in every
English home. Mrs L. leaps upstairs like a 2-year old to examine
the roof & the pipes, every few hours. I've been sitting in her
room telling her all about you & what a marvellous friend you are.
And all the story about Auntie R – it sounds more hilarious than
ever from this angle up here. Mrs L. is dying to hear your version
& no doubt there will be additions by then, I hope & pray merry
ones. Be brave, proud, haughty & beautiful as your stars foretell,
dear Shirlers, & you can't go wrong. Your sweet nature will do
the rest.[2] Rache was concerned to know if the misunderstanding
over your contract had been cleared up. I assured him it had. By
the way, I aim not to elaborate on the Auntie fuss to Macmillan –
anyway, it seems a bit out of proportion, looking back on – the
best fun I remember from the 4 months past. It was awfully sad
parting from Ivan especially – the only man I've ever had to do
with who hasn't tried to push me around.

Alan is worried about Much Ado (his horse) which has been
set back by the cold & snow. He is looking forward eagerly to
meeting you in May, having heard so many glowing reports & read
your stories admiringly. There were thousands of letters & parcels
to open & on top of everything there's a stage production of the
Ballad musical coming up in March – rehearsals start tomorrow.
Everyone had a contract except me. John Smith seemed amazed
that I should want one. I said, no contract, no show – or at
least something to that effect – and behold they are preparing a

contract. Now I've got to look round softly softly for a new agent.
Alan was sweet when I told him on the blower of my having to
return Knopf's cheque; he said, 'Why Mu, if you need some slosh,
we can send it over to you in a taxi.' – That, to me, is better than
slosh.[3] It really is good to be home. Robin has sent me a large
white cockerel (china) which I've been wanting. He rang Mrs L. a
few weeks ago & she gave him a piece of her mind, which seems to
have done some good. My old ma has written quite sweet letters,
too. So it seems that absence has done what the copy-books say
it does, for once. What a garbled letter this is, jumping from one
thing to another. Your mother sent me a darling welcome-home
letter for which I shall write & thank her presently. How good you
both were to me![4] Your last party is one of my sweetest images. I
miss our morning & evening natters on the blower. Send me news
please, soon. Anything I can do at this end to further the Shirlers
cause, just say the word. I'm planning a shopping spree next week
as there's enough accumulated slosh to buy a fur coat – I hope to
get a shapely-looking one, not a bag. I must go and fill my hot-
water bottle now & get into my winter-weight nightie. I never felt
grateful in a severe winter & cold climate before, but the goodness
is in being home again & in hearing the gay little overstatements
& understatements in every voice on the telephone. The air is
sharp, but I can breathe it. However, all this is a homecoming
euphoria & no doubt there are glooms in plenty ahead. Give my
love to Robert & everyone you meet whom I know, please do, and
I'll write to them soon.[5] Meantime I look forward to hearing the
latest developers in all your fields of action, may they prosper.

Masses of love for now

from

Mu

P.S. Rache is agog – almost greedy – for your novel.

ALS. CUL.

1. MS had returned by air from New York to the UK on 4 February.
2. Both Shirley Hazzard and MS had been increasingly disturbed by what

they saw as the excessive attentions of Rachel MacKenzie and had asked
to change editors at the *New Yorker*; Hazzard had been assigned William
Maxwell, and MS Robert Henderson.

3. Muriel signed with the New York publisher Alfred A. Knopf in late
   January.

4. Kit Hazzard had written to Muriel on 2 February to welcome her home
   (NLS). In her biography *Shirley Hazzard: A Writing Life*, Brigitta Olubas cites
   Hazzard: '"Muriel was very nice to my mother. They got together as two
   Scots. Muriel understood that there was a lot to put up with. But they got
   along well, and she would ask my mother round"' (pp. 192–3).

5. Robert Sonkin.

TO JAMES LOVELL, LONDON, 9 FEBRUARY 1963

[Camberwell, London]
9th February, 1963

Dear Mr. Lovell,

Thank you for your letter of the 8th and for your very
interesting production note.[1]

I am afraid my energies are being very greatly depleted by the
business side of the affair. I have arrived from America, where the
dramatic and film rights in my novel, 'The Ballad', as well as the
Third Programme version, are at present under discussion for an
American production, to find that everyone has a contract except
myself, and that Centre Stage are taking up a presumptuous
attitude. Whereas, I gave permission for two performances only
on the condition of a proper contract, simply because my friends
Christopher Holme and Tristram Cary were associated. It seems
to me that Centre Stage is a very unrealistic and inexperienced
organisation. They are behaving as if they are doing me a great
favour, and should have more rights than I have allowed them.
It's as if one took in a stranger for a couple of nights and lent him
the front-door key, whereupon he claims part-ownership of one's
house.

Anyway, my American agents say they very much want to
see the completed script. There are a lot of very interesting off-
Broadway productions at the moment, as you probably know.

Christopher has sent me his copy of the script for me to look at and work on, and I will do my best to complete it in these gloomy circumstances.

I think you should know that I'm not very keen on an English production to follow the two performances. English stage-managers are terrible time wasters – so are American ones, but the English managers expect one to put in one's time for nothing. I refused to sign a film contract for 'The Ballad' two years ago with a film producer whose name I justly forget, and later I refused a stage contract sent to me for a dramatisation of the book by a Mr. Donald Albery of inefaceable [*sic*] memory. So you see I'm not at all keen on trafficking with London managers for my dramatic rights, and I'm sorry if you have been led to put in a lot of work for the two performances, under the impression that I want a West End production. If a London manager should succeed in breaking through my barrier of indifference, and first name an agreeable sum, I might give him fifteen minutes of my time, but that's all.

I don't think an author is much help at rehearsals, and the actors are often put off by the presence of an author. I am quite sure you can manage better without me, and your Production Note inspires me with huge confidence in what you are going to do. But perhaps you would like me to come to one of the later rehearsals, when the thing has got a shape? – I would prefer that, myself. In the meantime, if there is any specific point on which you really do think I could assist you, perhaps we could meet and discuss it.

There is one thing I would like to suggest now, based on experience of various kinds in the dramatic field: where my work is concerned, the *meaning* always comes over best if the dialogue is strictly adhered to by the actors. They often feel they can do the thing more 'in character' by changing a phrase or two; sometimes they blurr [*sic*] the effect by adding 'er . .' or 'mmm . . .' or 'oh well,'. My aim is not to create exactitude of speech, as it would appear from the life on a tape-recorder, but an artistic representation of speech. I feel that the audience can be lulled from listening to the meaning by a too-familiar everyday type of

speech. Anyway, it is true, and I think Christopher might agree,
that the cleaner the speech the better my meaning comes over.
I have found especially that actors who do 'working-class' parts
tend to feel that they are free to improvise their part.

There is a special Peckham accent, perhaps it is a South
London one, which I was able to help with in the 3rd programme
productions; so do call on me for this if you think it necessary.

With best wishes, Yours sincerely,

TLcc. Private collection.

1. The theatre director James Lovell, with the company Centre Stage, was
    rehearsing Christopher Holme's adaptation of *The Ballad of Peckham Rye*.
    In a letter of 6 February, Holme reported to MS: 'I am very enthusiastic
    about this *as a play* and believe that we are lucky in the Director. He is full
    of ideas – he has done very modernistic productions in Canada' (NLS). In
    a further production note accompanying the present letter, Lovell wrote
    to MS: 'It seems to me, after reading THE BALLAD OF PECKHAM
    RYE, that the dominant theme that emerges is "The irresponsibility of
    the devil"' (NLS).

TO SHIRLEY HAZZARD, NEW YORK, 21 FEBRUARY 1963

13 Baldwin Crescent, Camberwell, London, S.E.5
21ˢᵗ February 1962

Dearest Shirlers,

I am sitting listening to La Boheme on my long-player,
wondering how your love-life is faring – better than Mimi's I
hope.[1] The news about Rachel set me wondering, too. I didn't
know her long enough to be genuinely moved – it only occurred
to me: – The heart-attack! – Of *course*. I thought it would be a
psychiatrist, but no, it is a heart-attack. Many a son & daughter
have been kept in bondage by the heart-attack (Pa's or Ma's),
many a husband . . . Many a heart has been broken, (like after the
Ball) by the heart-attack.[2] However, Shirlers dear, you are a tough

woman, a writer & a good good girl in your warmth of feeling,
too. You're quite right to decide not to give yourself trouble for
the future by showing a solicitude that you can't possibly keep up.
It would be Rachel's salvation, this illness, if she only knew it –[3]
Longing to hear developers, if you should move to a pleasant ed.
How is the affair* with Francis* (no innuendos intended) getting
on?[4] Tell me how the dinner party went, please do. I'm missing
you so very much, hurry & come over. Make it early in May as I
have to go to Ireland on a long-deferred visit on the 13th – and I'll
be in Italy, too, during the summer where we must meet up.

Now as to my *troubles*: Derek Stanford (the one who sold my
letters) has written a book about my life which a sinister publisher
from Sussex is going to publish (so he says). Solicitors . . . wild
words . . . tears . . . and now, complete indifference on my part.
What the hell do I care? D. S. doesn't know my life, I don't think
it will appear anyway, as we have scared the publisher on the libel
question.[5] All this – and looking for a new agent – have taken
up time which accounts for my long delay in writing. Curiously
enough I have a story on the go about someone, a subsidiary
character having a heart-attack. (It is Chap. 2 of Mandelbaum
Gate.) What are you writing? – Don't go out with too many men,
Shirlee, as I will *see* where the deficiencies occur in your workers. I
am going to write letters this week-end to my darlings left behind.
Brenders, your Mum, Milton and all.[6] I miss Ivan terribly, he is still
marvellous to me & his letters telling me not to worry are a terrific
support. I'll never find another Ivan-agent here, I know it.

The cold is still with us & the houses of course not equipped.
I've got a new Ascot in my bathroom – but it doesn't work. I
want to kick it in the teeth.[7] However I went & bought two lovely
model dresses, a gorgeous C. Dior hat, and 25 new long-playing
records. That's what I did.

M[rs] L. is full of beaners, & the Derek S. atrocity is keeping her
in fine fettle. I've only had one party but have been to many. Was
at Rache's for dins the other night, very elegant & merry – he's
getting marvellous notices for his book. Sometimes I would like to
be back in N. York, but I see that I'll just have to divide my time

betwixt the two, for London is home & it is lovely & everyone knows what one means at the least stammer.

Send me more news soon & say a prayer for your Mu.

Love to everyone you can think of & much love to you dearest girl

from

Mu

P.S. Ned approaches at mid-March.[8]

> ALS. CUL. Dating: MS dates her letter to the previous year; she made her trip to Cork in May 1963.

1. In Giacomo Puccini's opera *La Bohème*, Mimì fights with her beloved Rodolfo, and in Act IV dies of consumption.
2. MS echoes the hugely popular song 'After the Ball', written by Charles K. Harris in 1891, which contains the lines:

   > Many a heart is aching,
   > if you could read them all.

3. In her letter to MS of 27 January, Shirley Hazzard reported that Rachel MacKenzie had suffered a mild heart attack; in her letter of 12 February, she told of further demands made upon her by MacKenzie from her sick bed.
4. Shortly before her departure from New York, MS threw a party to which she invited Hazzard with a view to her meeting the literary critic, translator, and man of letters Francis Steegmuller; before the party, she is reported to have told Hazzard, '"There's a man coming I think you ought to marry"' (Olubas, *Shirley Hazzard*, p. 194).
5. Derek Stanford had, to MS's immeasurable consternation, passed his collection of her letters to the book dealer Lew D. Feldman, head of the House of El Dieff; Feldman had not yet sold them, in fact, and would later offer to MS that she buy them back from him.

   Stanford's forthcoming book, to be published that year by Centaur Press Ltd, was *Muriel Spark: A Biographical and Critical Study.*
6. 'Brenders' is Brendan Gill who worked for the *New Yorker*; Milton Greenstein had joined the *New Yorker* in 1945 as a legal consultant, and in 1962 became the magazine's Vice President.
7. An Ascot is a brand of water heater.
8. Ned O'Gorman.

TO ROBERT YEATMAN, MACMILLAN LTD, LONDON, 2 MARCH 1963

13 Baldwin Crescent, Camberwell, London, S.E.5
2nd March, 1963

Dear Robert,

Very many thanks for yours of the 28th. As you know, I'm delighted by your enthusiasm for THE MANDELBAUM GATE. It is full steam ahead on this book from now on. I think it will be an important book comparatively speaking.[1]

But I don't know what to say about your query on THE GIRLS OF SLENDER MEANS. Either you are off your nut or I am, probably both, but goodness, I've done nothing but nag you to lay off queries since I got back from America, and you do nothing but nag back. I asked John Smith to give you a full and reasonable account of why I can't touch your queries, but evidently he has failed to convey my intention. My American agent has made it all clear to Knopf, so you will know there is no discrimination.

Well I have dragged myself to the cupboard and looked up your mouldy query on p.108. It is grammatically O.K. It's exactly what I intend, and the style is my own. I'm sorry if you don't like it; but actually I couldn't care less, because I made up my mind at the age of nine not to care less about criticisms of style. I won hands down with the English department at school and have some bound prizes to show for it, Scott's novels and so on. Naturally I'm not going to climb down at my age.[2]

Anyway, I don't know why you don't trust me to pick up any typist's mistakes. An author bright enough to make a living out of your firm all these years & worm her way into your confidence and affection is obviously intelligent enough to check the typescript and the proofs. And anyway, no-one at Macmillan has ever asked me to change a word in typescript before. – Why have you waited till I'm half way up the Ladder of Fame to start pelting me with snowballs, screwed-up toffee-papers and so forth? If you wait till the book appears the critics will do it for you.

However, dear Robert, I'm not such a goof that I don't see that
your particular editorial method is probably involved, and that
you like to get a clear typescript to avoid unnecessary corrections
in the proofs. So what I am actually asking you to do is to make
an exception in my case. It seems a small thing to ask, seeing
that I don't normally make a nuisance of myself with vast proof
corrections.

I really would be grateful if we could come to an agreement
always to leave grammatical queries to the proof stage, and
stylistic queries out of the picture. You see, when I have passed the
typescript of a book my mind usually turns to something fresh –
in this case THE MANDELBAUM GATE – and it disrupts my
flow of new ideas to have to return to a work that I have recently
completed. By the time the page proofs arrive, I can approach
this, in turn, with a fresh mind; and I assure you that I'm very
sensitive to any incongruities or unintentional peculiarities of style
when correcting proofs. I take a creative interest in the proofs,
and I think anyone who has seen my proof-corrections with an eye
to this sort of thing, would agree that I often improve the quality
of the thought and expression, with very little actual re-writing.

I explained all this very carefully to John Smith, asking him
to put it to you reasonably. However, I hope the above gives you
a clear idea of my best working methods. Obviously, unless you
know what they are you can neither agree nor disagree with
them, and we are bound to go on each thinking the other is being
awkward for no reason at all.

You'll be happy to know that my Copy for DOCTORS OF
PHILOSOPHY has been bunged back to me from America, so
you will have the corrected proofs in a very short time.[3]

I shall also have a new agent in a very short time, and I hope
very much that he will represent me properly. At the moment
I have to do it myself, as evidence of which I cite this letter,
which I beg you to treat kindly as it is meant. I don't know if the
ideal agent exists in England, but certainly in America it was
marvellous working with Ivan von Auw who seemed to arrange
everything to the satisfaction of author and publisher without

involving the author at all. This seems to me very important, because all three parties can then enjoy each other's friendship as individuals rather than business acquaintances. I think it awfully rotten luck on me that here in England I have had the onus of business dealings and negotiations thrust upon me by agents too timid or uninformed to make representations to a publisher in their own right, or who just won't sit down and write a straightforward letter explaining a situation either to the publisher or to the author.

I do hope you see that at the moment this lack of a good agent makes life awkward for me. It's not only the case in point, but in many other instances here and on the continent, the onus has been put on me to point out to my English agent the pros and cons of contracts and so on, in reference to my interests in other parts of the world. And it's more awkward still when the author is cited as the source of an objection, and worse when the author has to write to the publisher or editor direct. I hate having a merry party with a publisher mucked up by an agent who makes one appear in the light of a Campbell at Glencoe. So I hope I have your sympathy just now.

We had a marvellous time in Paris. There was a sudden burst of early spring and all the people were emerging as from torpid chrysalids with a crazy flutter. My French publisher Robert Laffont (Robert llme to me) made crazy flutters with press cuttings of Miss Brodie, which I can't read. You must translate them for me. I bought green and blue suede gloves at Hermes. Mrs. Lazzari made friends all round, passed judgment on various fruits de mer, and bumped into Joe McCrindle on the Boulevard de St. Germain. She also acquired a sensational hat and passed through the customs wearing it. We feel a bit queasy inside, but our morale is terrific.[4]

Looking forward very much to seeing you on Tuesday. I haven't seen the script or a single rehearsal, so I expect a terrible shock. Pray bring your sal volatile.[5]

Love,

s/Mu

TLS. MA.

1. On 1 February, MS wrote to Robert Henderson at the *New Yorker*:

> I have written much more Mandelbaum Gate, but it is not typed
> out, and I would like to give it a good look-over before submitting
> it to you. So I shall be sending something from England, I hope
> within the next two months. — There are two new chapters, and
> I'm trying to make them fairly self-contained, both for your pur-
> poses and also because I feel this would give an interesting form
> to the book as a whole. I feel enormously encouraged by your
> interest in the project.
>
> Working here at the office has been a joy. I shall miss the New
> Yorker very much. (NYPL)

2. In his letter to MS of 28 February, Robert Yeatman wrote: 'There was one
   point which I should mention to you, on page 108, where I think a couple
   of words or so are missing. The last paragraph begins, "time, which to the
   on-lookers in the street and the firemen on the roof was only a small forgotten event to the girls etc......". Should there not be something between
   "roof" and "was", or am I being particularly dim? I have a suspicion that
   the typist has left something out' (MA).

3. In an undated letter probably from November 1962, MS wrote to Michael
   Codron: 'I thought and had hoped you were taking the play to Brighton for
   a further try-out. But perhaps it's just as well that the Arts experiment —
   for it was nothing more than that — should be allowed to rest and mature
   in our minds for a little while. The Arts was not, of course, equipped for
   Act 2, really' (NLS).

   And on 16 November 1962, she wrote to John Smith: 'On DOCTORS
   OF PHILOSOPHY in general, I will just say that I have not looked at
   Michael Codron's changes, but do not feel that he could possibly improve
   on my work by them. I was annoyed to see the article by Darlington in
   the Telegraph, in which it was assumed, from a letter written by Codron,
   that *I* had made changes to the play in response to the critics. This must
   not be repeated. It is libellous' (WUL).

4. On 28 February, MS sent a postcard to Ivan von Auw from Paris, saying:
   'Am on the run for a few days. Paris is marvellous just now with early
   spring sunshine & everyone humming with bright ideas' (PUL).

   MS presumably intends here 'Robert 2me' (Robert Deuxième), i.e.
   'Robert the 2nd', her present correspondent being, then, 'Robert the 1st'.
   On 8 March, she will write to her French literary agent, Donine Mouche:
   'I enjoyed meeting Robert Laffont, he's just my sort of publisher. Next
   time I'll give longer notice and we shall have a more leisurely meeting.
   The Memento Mori contract has gone off to John. — Will it be possible to
   get a man to translate this book? The translation for Miss Brodie was done
   very well, but I think some tiny points of idiom might have been missed.

Memento Mori will be a bit more difficult to translate, I think, and usually men seem to translate my work better than women' (NLS).

MS had got to know the sometime literary agent, editor, art collector, and founder and Editor of the *Transatlantic Review* Joe McCrindle when in New York.

5. MS was to join Yeatman at rehearsals of *The Ballad of Peckham Rye*.

TO IVAN VON AUW, HAROLD OBER ASSOCIATES, NEW YORK, 3 MARCH 1963

13, Baldwin Crescent, Camberwell, London, S.E.5
3rd March, 1963

Dear Ivan,

I got back from Paris with very high morale which was further fortified by your letter. There was a marvellous burst of spring weather in Paris, so I got the brilliant idea that I should act on the agency question instead of talk about it.

I've now written a pleasant and I think reasonable letter to John Smith to say that I've decided to leave Christy & Moore. I think he'll probably feel relieved in a way.[1]

I met Edmund Cork at the Carricks last week and thought him very agreeable. I'm meeting him again for lunch after his return from Madeira.[2]

I'm now in fact without an agent in England. (It feels lovely.) I wish you would be my main agent, it's the only solution that would give me peace of mind. I've taken advice from Lynn and Paul and have thought about it a lot. Please, Ivan, do try to arrange things so that Harold Ober handle all my work in America and through their usual associates in England and elsewhere. I had it in mind, on Lynn's advice, to ask Edmund Cork if he would act for me in England only. But now that I have left Christy & Moore perhaps it would be better if I could meet him as your English associate. Lynn is in favour of this idea, in any case.[3]

I know it's unusual for an English author to deal with an American agent, but all my life I've had to make unusual arrangements. And then, although of course I'm attached to my country, I'm always wandering off. I think it likely that eventually I'll want to spend more of my time in America.

Paul Scott said he would write to you. He sees the situation, but has pointed out some difficulties which don't really seem to apply to my case. The only difficulty might be on your side, and if so, I can only hope that you will find some way of getting round it. The difficulties Paul mentioned were 1) that I ought to have a more powerful & influential agency in England such as A. D. Peters or Curtis Brown. Well, of course, Paul is judging by his own experience as an author – all his main financial and literary dependency is in England. But me, I don't want Peters and Curtis Brown, I don't want their influence making my life a misery. Then 2) Paul made a point that in the event of the dollar being devaluated in the next few years, my European royalties would depreciate if negotiated through America. I'm afraid I don't follow this, but it does seem to me that my European royalties are so comparatively small anyway, and will never be huge, that what might or might not happen to the dollar in a few years time isn't a consideration to weigh against a solution to my main problem. I'm not asking for a more profitable arrangement, but for a happier one. If I'm relieved of pressure and worry about business problems I always do something profitable in any case. However, Paul is sweet and thoughtful, and he'll probably give you a better idea of his point of view than I can.

Do let me know how you feel about my suggestion. I know there are likely to be difficulties of some sort from time to time, but I feel altogether confident in you and in leaving decisions to you. This isn't only my own opinion, as you must know. And even if you should make mistakes they would be efficient mistakes and not an awful muddle with people ringing me up, at your suggestion, to sort things out. – Seriously, this has become the pattern of my existence in London. Whereas in New York, it was so delightful for me, it was I who got into the muddles and you who sorted everything out.

I see you want me to understand your point about the contract for DOCTORS OF PHILOSOPHY. I do understand it. But honestly, I haven't intended to complain about the *terms* of the contract. Perhaps I've been a bit unfair and taken a sour view of the contract, because there's a history associated with it which I refrained from telling you, lest you should think my life was made up of atrocity stories. Perhaps one day I'll tell you about the previous contract for the play with a theatre producer who turned out not to be a theatre producer, and after a few months I had to pay back the advance to retrieve the play. There were many choice complications, but perhaps it wasn't such a bad business as it seemed at the time.

I'll send you the script of THE BALLAD stage version as soon as I can lay hands on one.

Derek Stanford's book, which is already written, is about my work and my life. His publisher has been warned about libel, and that's all we can do. I have refused to read the book before publication, so I hope the publisher (Centaur Press) won't take risk. Derek Stanford knows very little about my life, actually. He sold a collection of my letters; some old professor is probably drivelling over them at this moment. I'm really past caring, but it's always helpful if you tell me not to worry. One day I'll do something for you.

Warmest wishes against the cold weather,

Yours,

s/Muriel

Send me nice news soon.

TLS. PFL.

1. On the same day, 3 March, still searching for the ideal UK literary agent, MS wrote to John Smith:

    I think I had better tell you now that I have been thinking things over as I've been unhappy and anxious about my business for a long time, and I have decided to leave Christy & Moore.

    I'm sorry about this, but I feel very strongly that my work is expanding beyond the intended capacities of your firm. I think it would only make you unhappy, and it would not lead to success, if I

were to continue to make the sort of demands on you for representation that I really feel the need of. I hope you will see my decision in
this light, and not as a personal matter. (WUL)

2. On 18 February, MS wrote to the playwright Pete Lemay, who worked
   for Knopf: 'I'm trying to find a better agent here. I will never find another Ivan, but maybe just an agent.' She added: 'The big thaw has set in.
   Everything is damp. The flaps of envelopes all stuck together. But the buds
   begin to bulge on the twigs outside my windows' (HRC). For her UK
   agent, Ivan von Auw had recommended Edmund Cork, who represented
   several bestselling authors including Agatha Christie, at the literary agency
   Hughes Massie & Co. Ltd.
3. Though no longer professionally linked to MS, Lynn Carrick and Paul Scott
   continued to advise her as friends.

TO SHIRLEY HAZZARD, NEW YORK, 9 MARCH 1963

13 Baldwin Crescent, Camberwell, London, S.E.5
9th March, 1963

Dearest Shirlers,

Yours to hand and ta for same – v. welcome indeed on return
from Paris. Mrs. L. and I had a sensational time, we visited
various shops and seamstresses in back alleys known only to my
agent – who's so much a Frenchwoman no-one would credit her
in a novel. Who should we bump into on the Boulevard de St.
German but Joe? I've probably told you this already – sorry but
I'm senile today. Anyways we had lots of parters with various
types and ate much, returning with terrific morale. The Ballad
play which I only permitted for 2 performances went off terribly,
but some people & critics have liked it, probably because it
was too arty for words. I've come to dislike the theatre world
intensely, it keeps intruding on my working plans.[1] Now I'm
deep in the X-ray business on Mandelbaum Gate, and hope to get
Chap.2 done in the next fortnight. Rache tells me he has been
going through your story book, no doubt patting it lovingly; we all
long to see you in the spring tra la.

I grieve for you over your Elena, may she not suffer.[2] My Girl,

I can't make head or tail of your reasons for not going to Rome if you are attracted by an attractive man who asks you to go with him and his Pa. It's the most romantic notion I've ever heard of in my life, so if you don't go, it must be that the heart has its reasons that reason doesn't know. As for being afraid of being hurt, don't think I don't know what you mean, goodness, I ought to. But one is hurt anyway, every way, and one has joy unforeseen as well. Maybe he's afraid of getting hurt, too (Christ, I sound like Aunt Ellen's column in the Wigan Star). Anyway, it may be that Francis is a Pedestal-woman man, and wd be attracted by your sweet nature as much as your hansom [*sic*] mug & form. Do let me know developers, and if serious in outcome don't forget to start off on the right foot and make it plain you've got a vocation as a writer first and a cook second.[3]

My old Ma has rallied round marvellously at news of the Derek outrage, Robin too, so we shall have a family libel-do if it comes to anything. For information as to my movements, they are as follows: end of March to 6th April, Edinburgh. 13th May to end of June, Cork, Jerusalem, Athens, Rome. After that, the deluge. Let's meeters in London, Italy, or some such place. New York for me, in October, without portfolio this time. Come soon, I'll find a way of coinciding with you.

I don't know what Rachel could complain of in you, practically speaking, except that you eased yourself back to a normal position with her. She might blame me, of course – but then for instance dear Bill didn't have a heart-attack when Francis opted for another editor. I hope they do a psycho job on her while she's in hospital, otherwise the distance between her self-image and the reality will just grow wider and wider. It does seem curious to me that I don't find myself thinking of her in a softer and more compassionate vein when I think at all, I suppose it is due to the fact that I've got a tendency to Wrong. Anyway I say fuck Ruthee for being rude to you, in my daemonic way I wish like anything she'd been rude to me just so that I could have let rippers back.[4]

Tell Milters please that the tapestry slippers (they are not Robert's pres. which I'm wearing at this mo) are to await my return, he is to keep them for me, otherwise I'll think I'm not wanted. And give him my love, and say it was marvellous at the Automat that freezy lunch-hour.[5]

I've lost interest in my flat – don't feel like improvers at all, somehow. I miss you terribly, and so many people quite a lot. I suppose it will come to me spending my time half-and-half between here and there.

What news of latest stories? Give me dates of New Yorker appearances so that I'll be sure to look. You know my non-readership habits – but they've been improving lately.

Lemme know how you like Maurice. Rache was delighted to hear about your reception-committee work. I hope you'll send a full-scale report – also please, news of dear Ivan, from whom I hear of course – but I miss him terribly, he's such a sweet friend apart from being such a good agent. See & hear from you soon then?[6]

Fondest of love from

s/Mu

TLS. CUL.

1. On 7 March, MS wrote to Ivan von Auw:

    The performance at St. Pancras Town Hall was terrible in my opinion but some people liked it. There's only one review so far, which I enclose. I'm sure there will be worse to come. It was done on an open stage with hardly any scenery, all very arty, with a chorus of typists typing the air and factory girls making mad motions with invisible machines. Anyway, I'll send the script as soon as Christopher Holme has put some final touches to it, and you shall have all the reviews, good and bad. (PFL)

2. Shirley Hazzard had first met and become friends with Elena Vivante when visiting her Villa Solaia, near Siena, in 1957; the villa, which took paying guests, had become something of a second home to her and it was there she met many of the figures to whom she later introduced MS in New York. In her letter to MS of 1 March, she announced that 'my lovely Elena' was dying in Rome of pancreatic cancer, and that she was intending to travel, possibly with Francis Steegmuller, to her bedside: 'I still cannot quite imagine the world without her – there will be only Mu left to speak the truth' (PJC).

3. Hazzard wrote in her letter of 1 March:

> I like Francis so much – dear Mu, you are a genius, he is exactly right
> for me. He likes me, I gather, and calls me all the time and we have
> dinners, etc., and send each other notes. (His apartment is absolutely
> beautiful, the most marvellers art collection, everything in great
> taste.) However, there is absolutely nothing amorous to date, al-
> though I believe that will come if we go on seeing one another at this
> rate. My point is – that going to Rome with someone, even if his old
> dad is along, has a rather romantic implication, no? And I don't want
> to do it under false pretences . . . Don't know if you will understand
> or agree with this, but just have vague feelings that one should only
> do such a thing with someone who is a declared lover. Anyway, I am
> greatly attracted to Francis – so much so that it worries me to think
> that it might get more involved and then come to nothing. These
> things hurt so much – I am really afraid to begin over again.

4. Hazzard had explained that Rachel MacKenzie was still in hospital follow-
    ing her heart attack, and that her sister, Ruthee, had been rude to her on
    the telephone when she had called to enquire.
5. Milton Greenstein; Robert Henderson.
6. At MS's request, Hazzard had agreed to throw a party for Maurice
    Macmillan who was due to visit New York.

TO HARRODS, KNIGHTSBRIDGE, LONDON,
27 MARCH 1963

[Camberwell, London]
27th March, 1963

Dear Sirs,
   I am sending you the following garments for special cleaning
service:

> Pink & beige striped silk dress and belt.
> Pink silk blouse.
> (2-piece) Green & white silk dress and jacket with belt.
> Pink & grey silk dress with belt.
> (3-piece) Beige & navy coat, beige skirt, navy blouse.
> (2-pice [sic]) Black & stripe-topped dress with black jacket.

Mauve silk dress.
Beige silk dress.[1]

Your faithfully,

Muriel Spark.

TLcc. NLS.

1. The purchase and maintaining of clothes was – and would remain – one of MS's
    pleasures, as well as her characteristic reaction to adverse circumstances. On
    25 October 1957, after a stressful few days, she reported to Derek Stanford:

    I was out at S. Ken to-day, to see Mrs Bool and Miss Horne, who
    send you their love. It is fatal, my going to S. Ken. I have bought a
    glamorous, absolutely useless, very seductive black velvet dress for the
    fairly reasonable price of £6.9s. The only thing, I can't afford even
    the six-pounds nine. But it is too late now, the thing is done, I knew
    it would happen, and now I must have an occasion for an evening out,
    to wear it. I nearly bought a sack – plain grey – but desisted. Do you
    know, I really look all right in a sack. I should have thought it was the
    last thing I ought to wear, but no, I look O.K. in one. (HRC)

    In a PS to Dina Barnsley, in an undated letter from late 1958 to her hus-
    band Alan, after a quarrel with Rayner Heppenstall, MS wrote: 'Love to
    your new coat. I have a camel-hair (not 100% camel-hair of course) which
    is simple but quite sweet. Also a pair of ¾ length French kid gloves which
    were reduced in price because of an infinitesimal flaw' (MBC). Then, as
    MS's literary fortunes flourished, so too did her wardrobe. Further on
    MS and fashion, see Monica Germanà, 'Between Desire and Control: The
    Fashioned Image in Muriel Spark's Life and Fiction', *TCD*, pp. 63–87).

TO SHIRLEY HAZZARD, NEW YORK, 5 APRIL 1963

at Edinburgh
5ᵗʰ April 1963

Darling Shirlers,
    Here I am in this city of Calvinism, High Teas and loveless
alliances. I rang you last week, at the Villa Soleia [*sic*], having

received your letter, & in the hopes you would feel like stopping
over for a couple of days in London.¹ But you had just left (it was
Saturday) & I hope this means that a good plan of action had
been formed. Surely, dear Shirlers, there is a very deep feeling
floating around between you & Francis, & that is something
indestructible – that is, if the feelings are loving ones, as they are.
I don't know what or how to think of all you tell me, and perhaps
by now developers have happened. You know, I can't help feeling
(but I have a personal bias in this respect) that you might consider
asking him whether the 'other girl' is male or female. Perhaps
this is an absurd idea – forgive it, if so. I can only judge by my
poor wee self – how I go falling for *that* type, time and again,
and *never*, really, for the wholehearted male. If this isn't too far-
fetched & you are sufficiently in love to cope with the conflict,
there's nothing like a real love affair to resolve the problem – any
problem – tho' it gives rise to others. My heart & thoughts are
with you, Shirlers dear. All that matters is that you are full of
possibilities in life & work. I'm enormously pleased to hear that
your novel's going well, it will be a famous one, born of suffering
as the best are – but not too much pain – that's fatal.²

My life is too dreary to write of, at the moment. My work
goes slowly. Family a bit improved, but a pathetic drag really. But
Ivan has taken over all my work & operates from N.Y. as my main
agent – this is an enormous relief. He's a dear good friend. Spring-
time unsettles me. – I usually brighten up at the end of summer.

I'm returning to London tomorrow, so please write soon &
tell me that all's well, or better. What a strange Italian trip it
must have been for you, with sickness & heartaches – dear, it will
enrich you very much one day.

My new chapter of 'Mandelbaum Gate' seems very un-
N.Yorkerish to me. Too much a stream-line of a novel. But the
novel's the principal aim.³

Didn't you love Bill's story in the N.Y'er? I loved the solemn
itemising of the Will, & so on. I've been following the Eichman
[*sic*] articles, too, so am quite a house-magazine reader now, &
keep searching for your name.⁴

I hope to see your mum soon – send me her address, please, in case she has rung me while I've been away.

Maurice gave me a 1ˢᵗ hand account of your parters – was very impressed indeed by you (as a girl – the stories go without saying). Also Ivan told me all. I wish I'd been there.

I'm thinking of coming over again a bit earlier than planned. But it all depends.

Love – and my prayers & thoughts are with you – remember me, please, too & write soon.

Mu

ALS. CUL.

1. Shirley Hazzard sent MS a seven-page handwritten letter from Villa Solaia where she was visiting her dying friend Elena Vivante, in which she outlined her confusion provoked by Francis Steegmuller's hesitation in making any emotional or erotic commitment to her.
2. Hazzard was at work on her first novel, *The Evening of the Holiday*.
3. On 23 March, MS wrote to Ivan von Auw: 'MANDELBAUM is turning out to be a terrible flop, but that is your problem when the time comes' (PFL).
4. William Maxwell's story 'A Final Report' was published in the 9 March issue of the *New Yorker*.

    On 20 March, MS wrote to Robert Henderson: 'I've greatly admired the Eichmann Trial articles. They are the best thing I've read on the subject. I was at the trial, myself, for five days, but found myself unable to talk about it for months' (NYPL). The *New Yorker* had sent Hannah Arendt to report on the Eichmann trial, and published her five long articles in February and March; these formed the basis of her book published later in 1963, *Eichmann in Jerusalem: A Report on the Banality of Evil*.

TO ROBERT YEATMAN, MACMILLAN LTD, LONDON, 26 APRIL 1963

[Camberwell, London]
26th April, 1963

My dear Robert,

Many thanks indeed for your card. I hope you have had a really good rest and are feeling in top spirits, as you deserve to be.

I'm sorry to greet your return with a complaint about the blurb.[1]

You see, it is not a matter of this or that being wrong with it. I am deeply disappointed in the entire misconception of my book that it reveals. I understood that you were all going to do some hard re-thinking about the presentation of my work, and so of course, it is very depressing for me to find the same quaint old Peter-Pannery cropping up in the draft blurb and the roughs of the wrappers.

I have too much moral responsibility towards my work to refrain from saying exactly what I feel at this point.

My work has a very serious intention. This is widely recognised, but if you at Macmillan do not find it to be so, then I can only ask you to act as if you did. I appreciate your enthusiasm for the lighter aspects of my work, but this is a case where enthusiasm is a positive obstacle to presenting my work according to my intentions. Who but the author can judge of this?

I will not go into many details because I am too busy to do so, and certainly could not write my own blurbs. One point about the enclosed draft is obvious, so I will mention it. The telephone-call interludes, made at a much later time, recounting the death of the hero of the book, are not written-in for decoration. A critical reader would surely notice that they in fact change the *aspect* under which the action of the book is understood. You cannot ignore the hero, Nicholas.

My suggestion towards solving the problem of presenting my work – since it really is a problem, and one that I think you must face – is that you do a plain-lettered wrapper and no blurb at all. It is always much better to do and say nothing than mislead the critics and readers.

Naturally, I don't wish the above to be taken in any unfriendly way. I think we all know each other so well that it would be absurd for me to make a dishonest compromise at this stage that I might resent later on. I may be wrong in thinking that the presentation of my books in England is of primary importance. In fact, I am not interested in the wrappers and blurbs in America or abroad. But I think I could produce a strong case for my conviction that England matters a great deal to my work in general.

I'm coming in to see Rache and Alan about the wrapper on Tuesday, and hope to see you, too.

Yours with love,

TLcc. NLS.

---

1. The blurb was for MS's novel *The Girls of Slender Means*, in which one of the central characters, Nicholas Farringdon, dies.

TO SHIRLEY HAZZARD, NEW YORK, 29 APRIL 1963

13 Baldwin Crescent, Camberwell, London, S.E.5
29th April 1963

Dearest Shirlers,

I know – or at least have hoped – you would understand my lull in correspondence at this end – natch, have been hell-for-leather at a piece of writing that just had to be finished. It has gone off to the typist & I await it back from her at any hour, so snatch the 1st opporuners of saying some of the things I'm dying to natter about.[1] But first, thank you and kisses galore, Pet, for your lovely present. It's the most handsome garment in my collection of underground movement wear. (I once knew a poet called Mary Winter Wear.) It was lovely to open an undeserved present after the party, but I felt so mournful that you were not there. It would have made the parters to have had you, and Francis too, mingling with grace & wit with the 'throng' of which your Mum has no doubt told you all. Well, I *am* pleased that the Francis situation is improvers & that you're a little bit in love & that my first hunch was more or less on the right lines, tra-la. Princeton sounds marvellous – I mean his house. I've been *thinking* of you continually – and now that I'm officially 'told' you must convey my love & sweet smiles to Francis.[2] Dearest, you will have to plan your summer on existential lines, I can see – i.e. move with the hour & the moment. So if we don't

bumpers-up together, September – my latest date for my N. York
visit – will tell the tale for me. I'll be leaving for Cork on the 13th,
then in June, maybe Middle East if there isn't trouble in Jordan. I
too, am a bit unplanned, but I suggest we keep roughly in-touchers
as to *your* visit to London & my likely return to that same.

I feel very guilters about Ved. Please give him love & tell him I've
been dead to the world on a huge chunk of my book. My next job is
proof-reading of 'The Girls' – Blanche is waiting for proofs – setting
from my Macmillans' corrected proofs – but so far they haven't
turned up. Have been busy telling all at Macmillan that they must
present my stuff more seriously. – Their book jackets are v. nimby-
pimby. I think I'll insist on plain lettering. Apart from all this have
been a bit beseiged [*sic*] by reporters & the telly on account of 4
of my old books coming out in Penguin. But that has blown over.
Rache & Alan sent me gorgers flowers as a reward.

Dorothy Olding (Ivan's partner) was here & we were *nearly* run
over by an ambulance that lost its head. Two men were killed, but
not us. We suffered terribly from shock & horror, though.[3]

Joe is just back from Italy. Gillon Aitken (the very tall
publisher . . . remember? – Chapman & Hall, v. young) wants to
come to Jordan with me for company, then on to Athens. I don't
know about *that*.[4]

Alan's horse *Much Ado* has had 2 races, both documented on
the telly. She was highly favoured on the second occasion by all
tipsters but had very bad luck, being almost 'run-over' by the
winner which swerved across her path at right-angles. – Should
have been disqualified. However, we are following Much Ado
with deep feelers. Robert is engaged to his girl, getting married in
the country 1st June. Al & I are going down together if I'm here.[5]
Lemme know all about the gold rolls, and also the course of your
marvellous Novel's career at the N. Yorker. I *am* delighted – more
than very delighted – that you & Francis have grown fond. *Be sure
to look ahead only to good things – that's what makes them happen.*

Hugs & love

Mu

ALS. CUL.

1. In a letter to Ivan von Auw on 23 April, MS apologised: 'I'm late in answering your letter as I've been working on the 2nd section of "Mandelbaum" to get it ready for the typist – it's quite long & (for me) rather philosophical, & therefore difficult to get into shape. However, it's nearly finished now' (PFL).

2. In her letter of 24 April, Shirley Hazzard wrote: 'Plato, of course, has completely disappeared from the scene . . . Everything has been changing so fast that God knows where Francis and I will be with one another a week from now, but things at present *Vastly* Improved' (PJC). She went on: 'Oh Mu – what doesn't come through in any of this long tale from the East River is that I am very happy and very fond of Francis, and it is thanks to you. He asked me if I had told you about it, and I said (liar – but there is no need to tell them everything, after all) No; then he said he would like me to tell you that we were fond of each other, as he thought you would be pleased.'

     Hazzard also told of being taken to a writers' conference at Princeton by Francis Steegmuller – 'did I tell you that he has a gorgers gold Rolls?'

3. Having left Edmund Cork at Hughes Massie & Co. Ltd, MS would henceforth have Ivan von Auw as her sole literary agent, along with his associate Dorothy Olding, who had been with Harold Ober Associates since 1938, who represented writers including J. D. Salinger, and who would later become the agency's president. This new arrangement suited MS well, as is reflected in her letter of 11 April to Von Auw:

     I was very relieved when you took over my work. You know this. And you will be aware, too, that if I am silly enough to allow myself to be messed about in any way there will not be any more work, or good enough work, for you to handle for me. It would be very nice indeed if I could now carry on with my work, with your assurance that the original agreement between Edmund and myself – which naturally I thought you were fully aware of – still stands. You know I've been loyal to your firm right from the start, and even when I was obliged to be without an American agent, wasn't happy till I got my work back in your hands. So please, Ivan, don't let me down now. (PFL)

     In a further letter to Von Auw, on 23 April, MS gave a fuller account of the accident reported here:

     Dorothy has been a dear. Now she's left it to me (on the grounds that I'm 'the writer') to send you a graphic account of our sensational experience while crossing Park Lane, where we were all but mown down and obliterated by a wild & charging ambulance. Two men were hit & thrown for some yards, almost certainly killed. Dorothy & I got away with shock only – I lost my shoe in the blast (because the impact was terrific) but we picked it up further down the street. I feel terribly responsible for involving Dorothy in this, as I'd suggested crossing the road instead of using the subway. So naturally I don't feel much like putting a literary effort into the story. I think what happened was that the driver lost his head – he had come out of his lane suddenly & found himself running into pedestrians at the speed of about 90 miles an hour. Dorothy was in awful danger of being hit by one of the flying bodies & I was in danger of the ambulance which veered in my direction. We each, for a moment, thought that the other had been hit, which added to the shock-effect. However, we're safe & sound. We walked away, terribly calm & collected, leaving the bodies strewn on the road – they were being covered up by one of the attendants from the murderous ambulance. We sat in the Park & walked around for a while, a bit dazed really. Then we went to Dorothy's hotel & had a lot to drink, which made us feel *worse*, only *better*, if you understand. We bought the evening paper to see if we were wanted by the police. Then we had more drinks & contemplated telephoning you for consolation or something. Dorothy said, Ivan would think we were drunk. I said, He'd be right. We had dinner with Pat Cork & somebody else, & had a whole lot more to drink. That was yesterday. Dorothy's fine to-day & so am I, except that I *feel awful* about leading Dorothy into danger. (PFL)

4. Prior to becoming Managing Director of Hamish Hamilton and later establishing his own literary agency, Gillon Aitken worked for seven years for Chapman & Hall.
5. Robert Yeatman was set to marry on 1 June in the Church of St Peter and St Paul in Ash, Kent.

TO ROBERT HENDERSON, THE NEW YORKER, NEW YORK, 30 APRIL 1963

13 Baldwin Crescent, Camberwell, London, S.E.5
30th April, 1963

Dear Mr. Henderson,

Here at last is the second section of THE MANDELBAUM GATE, entitled 'Miss Vaughan's Identity.' Please will you read it in conjunction with the first chapter, 'Freddy's Walk'? I do hope that you will like this piece.

It is a good deal longer than the first, as this is part of the construction of the book. That's to say – so far as I've planned it – the third chapter, which I'm calling 'A Delightful English Atmosphere' returns to the character Freddy Hamilton, and is set in Jordan. Then I hope to do longer pieces – furthering the story as they go along – on some of the characters who have only been mentioned so far, such as Abdul Ramdez, an Armenian Arab of mixed blood; they are to have fairly exploratory treatment.

Anyway, the story's the thing, and I look forward very much to hearing what you think of this one.

All good wishes,
Your sincerely,
s/Muriel Spark

TLS. NYPL.

TO ROBERT YEATMAN, MACMILLAN LTD, LONDON,
3 MAY 1963

13 Baldwin Crescent, Camberwell, London, S.E.5
3rd May 1963

Dearest Roberto,

This is to thank you very much for your angelic help with my proofs. I only hope all the information you gathered will come in handy, at some future date, for your own purposes, as well as they have for my present ones. The questions of hip measurements, windows, fire brigades, and *Revelations* 12, 12, are surely useful equipment in the Atomic Age, especially if one should find oneself imprisoned in one of those top-secret shelters with the wrong sort of people.[1]

Any way, Thank you very much. See you soon.

Love
Mu

ALS. MA.

1. That Robert Yeatman's attentiveness to the detail of *The Girls of Slender Means* should have gone from being perceived as persecutory two months earlier (see 2 March 1963) to being 'angelic' now is not untypical of MS's reactions to her novels during the production stage. Here, MS had enquired about central features of her novel, near the start of which Joanna Childe paraphrases Revelations 12: 12, intoning, of the devil: "'He rageth, and again he rageth, because he knows his time is short"' (p. 5). Windows appear frequently, both as sources of danger during World War II bombing of London and as means of escape; there are two on the top floor of the May of Teck Club, where the eponymous 'girls' live, egress through one of which offers the chance of escape from the bomb that will destroy the building – but only to those of sufficiently slender hip measurements to be able to pass through it.

TO FRANCES COWELL, EDINBURGH, 5 JUNE 1963

13 Baldwin Crescent, Camberwell, London, S.E.5
5th June 1963

Dear Frances,

Heaps of thanks for looking out this funny little fragment, preserved all these years. I'm returning it, as it seems to be 'dedicated' to you![1] Somewhere or other I dumped some juvenilia before going to Africa & now an American university wants to photograph the stuff for their 'Studies in creative writing'. But I guess they'll have to learn to write creatively the same way that we did . . . – at least so far as my early scrawls could help them.

Will give you a ring in July – long to hear all about your family. I would have been in touch earlier, but Edinburgh makes me very restless – I never stay there long enough to meet old friends – but hope you'll have some time for me. –

Lots of love meantime,
Muriel

ALS. NLS.

1. On MS's close school friend Frances Cowell (née Niven), see circa 19 July 1949, n. 2. What Cowell had sent, and MS was returning, was a poem on

the top of which was written: '*The Idiot.* by Muriel Spark (née Camberg) (former pupil). This poem was the winning entry in the Open Verse Section of the Rhodesian Eisteddfod, 1941.'

What MS says in the present letter constitutes one possible, if tentatively offered, explanation as to why none of MS's letters from prior to World War II have been found. It is possible that letters are missing also in MS's correspondence with Cowell: the next letter to her in the archive (in the NLS) dates from twenty-seven years later, October 1990.

TO EVELYN WAUGH, COMBE FLOREY, SOMERSET, 11 JUNE 1963

[Camberwell, London]

Thank you for being so kind about the play. And yes – goodness! – you are quite right about the need for stage directions.[1]

My heart wasn't really in the thing. I don't think it's in my line.

Yours sincerely

Muriel Spark

APCS showing 'B.O.A.C. 707 Jetliner'. BL. Dating from postmark.

1. On 6 June, Evelyn Waugh wrote to MS: 'Thank you most awfully for sending "me" *Doctors of Philosophy*. I read it eagerly. It seems to me as clever as a cartload of monkeys. I wish I had seen it acted. It would have been kind to give ampler directions in the published version' (NLS).

TO SHIRLEY HAZZARD, NEW YORK, 23 JUNE 1963

13 Baldwin Cres. S.E.5
23rd June, 1963

Dearest Shirl my Girl,

The number of times I've been thinking of you . . . and longing to get down to a spot of corresponders, well you can guess. I didn't know when to expect you over here, so have sent a copy of Doctors of Phil to you care of your Ma. I've got your pikcher,

very fetchers indeed and promising for your big launch. I say
to everyone, yes that's Shirl, she's lovely, but wait till you read
her stuff, it is classier still and she's the highest-inspired cookie
coming on the market.

Before answering all your news of labyrinthine woe and joy,
let me say that I too have been a trifle beturmoiled, and am so
cheesed off with being the successful Auntie of Mankind around
here, with nothing to do with my time except be gracious, no
higher ideal to serve except that of never giving offence to anyone, no gender except neuter. Perhaps I should admit that I've
had a little fun. Just here and there. Two weeks in Ireland were
lovely, but no more than a rest-cure, really. Family demands.
Dearest Rache and dearest Alan keeping up my morale with
bunches of roses and outings. An English agent (Ivan's associate –
Ober are my main agents now) who has turned out to be the
world's biggest liar, timewaster and so forth. Much ado on this
account between Ivan and me, culminating in an icy note from
myself to the effect that I was considering retiring from the
literary life altogether, followed by a call from Ivan in which
we were both quite maudlin, but from which I was made to
understand that he was all shot to pieces by my cold tone –
apparently it was quite O.K. if I gave up writing but it was
terrible to be cold to him, and as for *his* business-like epistles,
I ought to read between the lines. So I wept salt tears all along
the transatlantic cables, and got forgiven for being cold, only
afterwards bethinking myself, what is to prevent him from sitting
down and writing me a private letter in which I don't have to
read between the bloody lines?[1] Anyway, he is a marvellous agent
and quite sweet for a friend, beyond which I reserve personal
commitment. (All this to keep to yourself, darling, in case it shd
be thought that my soft-spot for the said Ivan has extended to the
brain.) So work has been slow. My best piece of work went into
an essay which I did for free, an introduction to my Jesuit chum,
Fr. Blehl's book of Newman's sermons, in which I let rip against
the moralists who want showy morals whereas it is the love of
God that counts. Fr. Vincent (Blehl) is thrilled with it, he's over

here at the mo.[2] My Mandelbaum came back from the N. Yorker
with a long explanation about it not standing by itself, but I think
the reason is sex. They say they are thrilled with it. Then Bill
wrote about it, with a cryptic remark or two that I would so like
you to see. Then Robt. Henderson wrote again and said they
were holding over chap.1 in the hope that other sections could fit
in with it. Anyhow, I've replied to say that it will be a fairly long
book and I might just finish it and then let them see the whole,
rather than bit by bit. So I'm starting now on another stint hoping
to get it done by the middle of July, to be followed by a break in
Edinburgh, returning here for another month's work, and so to
New York in September.[3] The Middle East plan fell flat because of
advice against the extreme heat and the fact that I am now known
to be a half-Jew and might run into trouble in Jordan. I haven't
any inclination to go off to the Continent, although if you are
coming over and thinking of going to Rome or nearby, I'd love to
link up with you at some point. I can always count on friends in
Rome, as they keep on writing to urge me Romewards.

So much for me. But now maybe your plans are set for another
chapter of the Francis saga which I must say sounds very exciting,
I get vicarious heart-beats and yet am sufficiently remote to see
that considerable improvements in the affair have set in – that's to
say if you really feel that you love him with the sort of love that is
worth a bit of trouble in developing. He probably suffers greatly,
as we all do a bit, from involvement in the pride-power system
of existence, which is so inhibiting to achievement in love and in
art – it's a paradox, but I think you'll see it's true, that pride is
the factor which makes us react by guiltily under-rating ourselves
in the end, and we feel unworthy of great happiness or of writing
great books and so on, and so we go so far and no further. Oh
dear, I think it will come all right in the end, Shirlers dearest,
and have prayed and will continue to pray, that it will. Meantime,
don't *you* feel unworthy of prizes, and content yourself with
liking limitations, and all that lark. I hope your dear writing-self
flourishes, N. Yorker-wise and in all senses.[4]

Now you must lemme know your plans for an English visitation, so that I'll be around. Anyway, I look forward to a nice N. York stretch in the autumn, with some work done as before. It *is* a good place for working. Where shall I stay? God knows. First to a central hotel, then I'll look round for a nice light apartment, not necessarily the Beaux Arts again. Anyway, I don't believe in fussing weeks in advance, only in packing up my bags and departing.

I miss you terribly still. There's no-one I can talkers too [*sic*], not really talkers, as I can to you, love.

Ved called the other day. I asked him to link up with Fr. Vincent and me later that night at a restaurant as to tell you the truth, I'm a bit scared of Ved, he hasn't got the remotest understanding of any other type of mind but the ladder-climbing one. Did you see, said he, Shirley's photograph in the Times? Oh yes rather, I said, isn't it good? Yes, marvellous, he said, but I was surprised that *your* photograph wasn't there. Poor Ved, I suppose I'm a bit uncharitable to him, but he does seem to go round probing for pettiness, and it's so insulting in a way. Anyway, he didn't come to the restaurant, as I guess he felt I wasn't obligingly enough catty on the telephone. Fr. V. says the Indian Jesuits are exactly the same, they come and visit a community and are looking for, and causing, spite everywhere. As the lady said whose son was a queer, 'he is a little Oriental, I'm afraid.'

Hope this is legible – next time will use one side only – didn't realise how thin the paper was. Write very very quickly please & I'll reply pronto.

Dearest fondest love to you,

Mu

V. upset about the burglary – because it's upsetting in itself to have a break-in. Hope you aren't worried about it really.[5]

TLS with handwritten PS. CUL.

1. The short-lived attempt to have Edmund Cork be MS's UK agent having run its course, Harold Ober Associates was taking over *all* MS's new contracts and arrangements, both in the US and in the UK. In her letter to Ivan von Auw of 26 May, MS wrote:

I shall also give serious thought to whether I shall myself continue with the literary life or retire from it altogether. The increasing struggle to rid myself of business anxieties and obtain peace to write, hardly seems worth it. I have been thinking about this, and if I should decide to give up writing the only thing that would have to be settled would be the Knopf contract, where perhaps some adjustment or repayment would have to be made. But I shall let you know my decisions on these questions in due course. (PFL)

And four days later to Von Auw, in a rare pentimento, she followed this up: 'You are such a sweet friend and I'm a terrible, horrible person, but I am going to reform. The effort of insisting on this and that during the past few weeks left me feeling a bit desperate, and I count on you to understand how it is, and to obliterate my last letter from your mind, unless you happen to think it funny – I've had a look at the copy and feel it has definite comic undertones that will ripen with the years, and it could even be adapted for one of my novels' (PFL).

2. Vincent Ferrer Blehl's selection of Cardinal Newman's sermons will appear in 1964 in the UK under the title *Realizations: Newman's Own Selection of His Sermons* (Darton, Longman & Todd Ltd), and in the US as *Cardinal Newman's Best Plain Sermons* (Herder & Herder). In her Foreword, MS wrote:

> There was a moral movement in Newman's day, there is a moral outcry in our own times, there is worse to come: ethical, germ-free citizens will be springing up all over the place to prosper more and more visibly in public reward for their virtues. [. . .] It is the doctrine of all Christians that without charity we are as sounding brass and a tinkling cymbal. But Newman points out some of the alarming implications of this nice poetry. What did he mean? He meant that God had not been educated at Rugby; that is more or less what he meant. Serious-minded people still call, from time to time, for a 'return to the moral standards of Christianity', by which they mean those codes of decency which have evolved in the chivalrous West from the Christian faith. Many hold that it is the morals that count, Christianity can go. I am not an expert in such matters, but I always sense, underlying these moralistic appeals and urges, a demand for something showy. [. . .] Newman's contribution to this field of study is to say that conscientious people of high moral principle may be on the side of evil. He says that, however inspired, however honourable, they may be Satan's instruments in seducing and enfeebling the people of God. Moreover those who are genuinely pleasing in God's sight, only God knows. The disposition of every soul is a secret matter, not easily discernible. (pp. vii–viii)

3. In her letter of 4 May to Von Auw, MS wrote: 'I've been industrious on a mammoth scale, having sent off a chunk of Mandelbaum, about 12,000 words, to the N.Yorker. I'm doubtful whether this particular section will suit them, but of course am jolly pleased with it myself, as I always am with new things until they are published.' She added: 'Did I tell you I had decided to get to New York by September, as I think I can work better on Mandelbaum over there, and it will be reaching the hard-work stage. Also, I want to avoid England on publication dates – the literary world is such a family business here' (PFL). And on 14 June, MS wrote to Robert Henderson:

> Yes, of course I understand very well that Section 2 of MANDELBAUM wouldn't stand alone as a *New Yorker* piece, and am only too delighted by all the encouraging things you say about it.
> I'll see how the next part goes, as it may well fit in as another 'Freddy' piece. But it may be that I shall want to complete the book before revising the various sections, in which case I'll let you see the thing as a whole so that you could decide what, if any, sections you would like to use. I hope this will be all right, either way, and not hold up your publication of FREDDY'S WALK unduly. (NYPL)

4. In her letter of 13 June, Shirley Hazzard gave a long and detailed account of a fraught trip to Spain to meet Francis Steegmuller and of his vacillations between one moment swearing his devotion and the next moment calling off their affair.
5. In her letter of 13 June, Hazzard explained that her Spanish trip was cut short when she learned that her New York apartment had been burgled – though in the event nothing of significance was found to have been stolen.

TO ROBERT YEATMAN, MACMILLAN LTD, LONDON, 26 JUNE 1963

13 Baldwin Crescent, Camberwell, London, S.E.5
26th June, 1963

Dearest Roberto,

Many thanks for your card. I hope you had a really good rest and feel in top spirits.

About the draft blurb, I think it's all right as far as it goes, but you've thrown out the hero with the bathwater, i.e., Nicholas Farringdon, very important. You don't think I put in the bits of telephone conversation for decoration only, do you? No, they are there to give you, the reader, a recollection of something special, such as the fact that we pass thro' this vale of tears but once. And so the action, and all these Slender Girls that your blurb makes such a lot of peter-pannery about, have got to be seen under the aspect of something a bit more serious, as through the eyes of Nicholas. The same goes for the wrapper covers, they are all too quaint. The trouble is, you don't believe in my seriousness, any one of you. What a terrible lot you are. I suggest it would be a help if you just state in your blurb that this is a serious book, without qualification.

I'm coming in to see Rache and Alan on Tuesday after a trip to Mark Gerson with Miss Hobhouse, so hope to see you then, too. (I like to keep the *whole* firm in employment.)[1]

Much love,

Mu

TLS. MA.

1. The photographer Mark Gerson specialised in pictures of literary figures; he had been photographing MS since the mid-1950s. In her letter of 24 April, Macmillan editor Caroline Hobhouse wrote to MS to propose a sitting for publicity photographs (NLS).

TO SHIRLEY HAZZARD, NEW YORK, 29 JUNE 1963

13 Baldwin Crescent, Camberwell, London, S.E.5
29th June, 1963

Dearest Love,

Have read your story in June 15 issue, A Place in the Country, and am profounders impressed by all the charm, skill and insights that go into the telling.[1] It leaves a haunting effect in the mind, and I begin to wonder such things as whether they used birth-control, these lovers, and what kind if so, and whether she was deserted at some point in the month when she would be afflicted by a terror

that the birth-control had not worked, as it might be to take the
edge off the anguish. Forgive these crude reflections, they do
but pay tribute to the reality of Nettie and the extent to which I
was gripped by her particular time-space from beginning to end.
I didn't like it when Clem spoke to his wife out of her hearing,
when she went upstairs, and was delighted all the time that
Nettie was the recording-instrument of other peoples' noises and
movements – all this is so beautifully written, for the selection of
details significant to *her* absolutely conveys both her shrewdness
and inexperience. I think you're a marvel, Shirlers dear poet. I say
poet as it's a poet's vision and approach, no mistake.

The time is at pres. twenty past one in the morning. I spoke
to my son and ma on the blower at nine thirty and they upset
me. Trouble is, they don't sincerely at heart believe that God
created them. They think they do but they don't. Otherwise they
wouldn't be looking to me all the time to finish the job. They
both, in their different ways, hold the widespread belief that
money is the answer to their problems. Christ, we come into the
world without any money, and we have problems right from the
word go, unrelated to money. If we were born with a fistful of the
stuff in our hands it would make no difference. My ma informs me
she has had proposals of marriage. Bloody liar. But why does she
say this? Because she wants me to know that she's as good as me
any day, – me here in London living it high and surrounded day
& night by proposals of marriage, posing as a famous author with
never a thought for my poor relations.

Shirlers dear, I hearby [*sic*] accept the next proposal of marriage
that comes my way. I only hope it is some tough brute that doesn't
like mothers-in-law persecuting his wife.

Robin wants me to set him up in an antique shop. He has
already started in a tiny way, on the side. I say to him, jolly good
Robin love. I manage, says he in tones of cold reproach, to make
a few shillings. Back came my cheque through the post that I'd
sent him for his birthday. £25 – back it came without a word.
So back again it went. I realise, of course it's not enough to start
an antique shop with, but I'm only, after all, a piece-worker in

Knopfs' Old Curiosity concern. Next move of the chessboard —
numerous presents from Robin ranging from small antiquities to
an expensive jewel case. I thank him effusively and somehow try
to hint that I would like to recompense some time some how. Oh,
says he, don't take the glamour off it by offering me *money*. The
truth is, he needs rather to see a psychiatrist, but I'm the very last
person who could tell him so. Actually, I'm so used to all this that
it isn't as agonising to me as it sounds. But what amazes me is that
the boy isn't bored by the repetitive monotony of the thing.

It isn't agonising, but it's dreary when one's nearest relations have
the neurotic urge at heart to put one in the wrong again and again.

Well, love, I mustn't dwell on my woes. They all lead to
another escape to N. York. I hope to be there on or about
September 2nd. Yes do, if you hear of a flat, and it is not out of yr.
wayers, investigate, please. But I wouldn't lay a chore on another
writer's shoulders, yours especially, for fear of the vengeance of
the gods. Really, I mean it. I'll get an estate agent to find a flat for
me, that's all they're good for.

I am so touched by your fidelity and understanding of Francis,
and am sure somehow that you've done all the true things, and
that he's yours, really, as you are taking so much trouble. I mean
the sort of trouble that love and not mere self-interest dictates.

Ned was a terrible bore. He'd travelled in the thrilling Wilds,
but had only met with People who Mattered.

I haven't seen or heard from Ved again. I'm down on his bad
books and shake in my shoes. Cross my heart.

Howard Moss is expected on Monday the 1st. He's someone I'm
really looking forward to see. Very amusers, is Howard. But I do
not think my next proposal of marriage will come from him.[2]

Conor Cruise O'Brien the onetime warrior has writ with his
moving finger a sad lament for Dwighters as background music to
a blast against the N. Yorker, in the New Statesman of this week.[3]
There's no denying some truth in what he says, nor all my tears
blot out one word of it. But I can't suppress the question in my
nasty little suspicious mind, whether he has been at some point a
N. Yorker reject. Or maybe this minstrel boy was criticised some

in the N. Yorker at that time when he to the war had gone. One of
the things he says against the N. Yorker is that it wouldn't like any
critic to declare in its pages that Mao Tse-tung and Fidel Castro
were his favourite authors, even if this was indeed the critic's
taste. Well, I mean to say . . . Imagine trying to say Franco was
your favourite author in the N. Statesman . . *I've* just finished an
essay on Newman's Sermons, and I'm sure I couldn't get it printed
in the News of the World or Pravda. However, look out for it,
love. I've been sending some press cuttings to Dwighters, but he'll
discover this one for himself.

The serial current in our newsheets regarding life in high
westendy society is eating into my time. I cannot resist these
daily revelations, – imagine what it means to a sheltered life like
mine. I wept only for our fallen Minister of War, as the Daily
Express had a picture of him penitent and sad. But the Christine
story holds me spellbound. Every woman in England who hasn't
done things like that, including me, feels she is Full of Grace by
contrast. Our haloes clang against each other whenever we move
our heads. To-day's Evening Standard overbrims with tarts at the
Ward trial, each vying with each other to get up on the witness
stand and proclaim to the world what famous lord or cabinet
minister she has been to bed with. Careers and reputations go
crash forever, like a china cup on the kitchen floor. As yet no
Bishop's name has been uttered, but that is no guarantee for the
pregnant future. Two things particularly strike me: one – that
the girls do not by any means look like whores as they used to
do, they look very well-bred and classy indeed, you would think
they were debs, what [*sic*] time the Queen Mother at the races
looked like a dear old courtesan. The second thing is, that when
these tarts are approached by the newspapers with the offer of a
contract for their exclusive story, they reply 'Speak to my literary
agent.' 'Literary agents' are springing up all over the place – you
have no idea the number of new names on the literary scene. One
of the girls, when asked in court if she had received an offer from
a paper, replied that everyone in the case had contracts with the
papers. They get paid upward of £20,000. I really feel we should

put up our terms on the strength of it, or employ one of these new lit. agents to do something for us. I haven't, myself, slept with a really famous person. Have you? Try to rack your brains, Shirl dear, and come over immediately if you have anything to declare. Now is our chance of a lifetime. I have thought of claiming the Dalai Lama for myself. You could say Dag, no-one could prove that Dag didn't.[4]

I haven't really thanked you for your honey of a letter. If you aim for London at any time between now and early September let me know immediately, as it will give me something to look forward to. Pet, you mustn't think of lingering for my arrival in N. York if you want to be elsewhere in September. It wouldn't be the same to me if you weren't there, but I'd be looking for your return and busying myself with business.

Always give my warm love to Milters, yes he is a noble Milters all right. Lemme know what you think of Trillers. But me, I've gone Off him.[5]

Cheerio. I'm going to say a prayer for you and one for me, and off to bedders.

And many fond salutations for your story.

Love for now,

s/Mu

                                                    TLS. CUL.

1. Shirley Hazzard's story 'A Place in the Country' was published in the 15 June issue of the New Yorker.
2. The poet Howard Moss had been the Poetry Editor of the New Yorker since 1948.
3. MS refers to the diplomat, writer, and academic Conor Cruise O'Brien as a 'onetime warrior' presumably because of his involvement, in 1961 in the Congo, in what became known as the Siege of Javotville. In the New Statesman of 28 June, O'Brien published a review, entitled 'A New Yorker Critic', of Against the American Grain by Dwight MacDonald.
4. MS gives an account of what was to become known as the 'Profumo scandal' – and of the hypocrisy surrounding it. Having had an affair with Christine Keeler – described by Richard Weight in his article on her in the ODNB as a 'model and showgirl' but painted in the press at the time

as a shameless prostitute – the Minister of War John 'Jack' Profumo was judged to be a security risk since Keeler was also involved with Soviet naval attaché Yevgeny Ivanov. After denying the affair in the House of Commons, Profumo was obliged to resign as an MP, on 4 June. Weight judges it 'An affair that lasted just a few months, but which resonated for a generation.' The man responsible for introducing Profumo to Keeler, and later for confirming their affair, Stephen Ward, was subsequently put on trial at the Old Bailey, in what Richard Davenport-Hines, in his *ODNB* entry on Ward, calls 'an act of political revenge'; Ward will commit suicide on 31 July, the eve of the conclusion of his trial.

When Hazzard worked for the United Nations in New York, Dag Hammarskjöld was its Secretary-General.

5. MS is responding to Hazzard's praise of Milton Greenstein. 'Trillers' is the influential critic and Columbia University professor Lionel Trilling, whom MS had met in New York and in whom, according to Martin Stannard, she had initially taken a more than merely friendly interest (*MSB*, pp. 273–4).

TO SHIRLEY HAZZARD, NEW YORK, 21 JULY 1963

Number Thirteen [Camberwell, London]
21 July 63

Dearest Shirlers – Luvly to here – I love your letters, they keep me in touchers with your time-space and keep my feelings company as wen we shared that positively Jungian-dream ordeal last winter. We have emerged unscathed, nay scatheless, I think, from now on.[1] Enyway I can't *talkers* to any other friend as I can talkers to you. N. Yorker July 12 has not turnedup but will be here next week wen Ile rede your story with eagerness. It's thrilling to know that your marvellers story (isn't that the one I read in typescript?) has another chance, after being turned down as a punitive measure. You did absoluters rite in taking a stand with Francis. But you love him, I can see, & he loves you so much too, that's plain. Have you found out who the mystery woman actually is? If you haven't then you're a model of restraint – not that I suggest it would make any difference to the situashers.[2] Oh dear, I met such a sweet charmer, a friend of Howard Moss's. There was very little said but it was a Brief Encounter & the last thing I was expecting, how strange. It is something by itself whether there are any more Encounters or not &

unparalleld [*sic*] in my lifers.[3] I've been racing with Alan since then,
which is a soothing thing to do. All summer has been so far a Life of
Slice; it was luvly going down river & up river with Howard & his
(2) friends. Then I went to Edinburgh where had a happy surprise
from Rob who has started to make a start on making good. He's
very much improved in his lifespace lookout & has taken up antique
dealing as a spare time effort. Is making a go of it, so am giving him
some helpers. As for Ma she is 'not very well any more' & that's
the only thing to be said. I got her playing the piano & singing etc.,
but it doesn't last. I think they *want* to be life's official victims.
Very little workers done. Let's make an arrangement to keep each
other at it after we've had our high jinks & Experience —? I start
in earnest in the Autumn. Am sure someone has been praying for
me, as am so much more *in charge* of things if you understand. Not
that outward circs have changed much, only I can cope with them.
Must be due to the Rest from Labour. It's probably you who've been
praying for me. I do for you but maybe I'm no good. I think you
should be a married lady, though, and feel sure it will come to pass
in the way that's right for you both. You must hire a housekeeper,
very first thing & have plenty of room in the house.[4] It will be luvly
to talkers in N. Yorkers agen. Will keep in tuchers with plans, but
Sept 2 is wot I aim at. I've had some smashing clothes made, they
are fun. Me, I like my clothes v. much. They are to go off before
me in a trunk, so I think a winter's stay is wot I must have in mind.
It's difficult to know wot I have in minders till I see what I do.[5]
Told Milters that my lawyer wouldn't let me accept his offer due to
law of bigamy. Have promised to Wait for him. Meantime please
tell him that I wish to place an order for 2 reams yellow paper to
await arrival 2nd Sept., also N. Yorker-type blackwing pencils with
rubber at the end. I shall purchase my own carbons, thank him very
much. Have extricated myself from the frightful agent here at last &
haven't got an Eng. agent now, which is lovely so far.

    Rite again soon Shirlers darling & declare your doings.

    Luv

    Mu

                                             ALS. CUL.

1. Shirley Hazzard wrote to MS on 18 July. The 'ordeal last winter' refers to the two writers' difficult disengagement from Rachel MacKenzie at the *New Yorker*.
2. Hazzard outlined in her letter of 18 July that she had issued an ultimatum to Francis Steegmuller – he had to choose between her and his former girlfriend, to whom he was still attached (who is never named in the correspondence with MS): 'So I said Enough, I cannot breathe one other sigh, Nor can intreat one other teare to fall, etc.; if this is still the case, then Count Me Out and let's put a stop to the whole thing so you can have her without any second thoughts; no intention of forming part of triangle, and especially don't want to be the Square on the hypoteneuse [*sic*] . . .' (PJC).
3. Martin Stannard identifies the 'sweet charmer' as one Bert Beck (*MSB*, pp. 292–3); his reappearance in MS's life will be described in MS's letter to Alan Maclean of 30 September.
4. MS is probably responding to Hazzard's account in her letter of 18 July of a weekend spent at Steegmuller's house, where she writes: 'I seemed to cook and wash dishes for Pretorian Guard (not, however, performing anything along lines of Messalina), and can see there would have to be some changes in that direction.'
5. On 24 July, MS will write to Ivan von Auw:

> I am so much looking forward to seeing you, Ivan dear. Various friends are flat-hunting for me. I am sending off a trunk of books and clothes fairly soon. Would you like me to put in copies of all my other pre-novel contracts so that you can take them over? I'll do so anyway, at least if there's room for them. – I have got into the clutches of a Madame Loda who has made me a fascinating but complex garment called a pelisse, which is a fur lining with different coats to button on to it, and which turns inside out to be a fur coat as well. Mme Loda starts every sentence with the words 'Stranger to say . . .' (PFL)

TO KINGSLEY AMIS, JONATHAN CAPE LTD, LONDON, 24 JULY 1963

[Camberwell, London]
24th July, 1963

Dear Kingsley Amis,
    Thank you for asking me to contribute to your S/F anthology.[1]
    I'll think about the idea, but can't promise, as I don't know enough about 'science'. I agree with you that science fiction should

develop in the sort of tradition you indicate rather than merge with the mystery story. However, something might occur to me if you aren't in a hurry, – and, I'm afraid I must add, if your publishers aren't absolutely insisting on first rights.[2]

All good wishes,

Sincerely,

TLcc. NLS.

1. On 19 July, Kingsley Amis wrote to MS: 'I am editing what I think will be an interesting and certainly original book for Jonathan Cape. I have noticed a real interest in science fiction among all sorts of friends of mine – sometimes where one might least expect it. This is to be a volume of new science-fiction stories by prominent writers not generally associated with the field of science fiction. Would you like to contribute?' (NLS).
2. In his letter of 19 July, Amis added: 'I feel, though, that the best science fiction, however wild its initial assumption, holds consistently to these throughout, and however unlikely its marvels, tries to offer these as plausible (thus differing from what we commonly call "fantasy").'

TO SHIRLEY HAZZARD, NEW YORK, 6 AUGUST 1963

13 Baldwin Crescent, Camberwell, London, S.E.5
6th Aug 1963

Dearest Girl,

Just got your letter w. good news of your trip over, then Ivan says on phone that he saw you to-day 'looking fine' which is how he says 'looking smashers.'[1] What ups & downs you've had love, you must be aching all over inside. Would you like to be met? Don't want to do a Rachel on you & maybe you've fixed a meet-up with Ma or Another. So unless bidden by wire with flight no. will await your call. Try my bedroom first at RED POST 4708 (a private 'country' number) – dial RED. If not there, BRIXTON 5551 (downstairs). I would have *fun* coming out to meet you, so don't hesitate to wire. Have been busy on chapter 3 of Mandelbaum which must finish before this week-end. Also cataloguing my manuscripts under guidance from adorable Mort & Dick. They (the MSS) are worth very vast sloshers, apparently, so hope to be a rich lady in a few months' time.[2] Blanche K. threatened me with publicity work on arrival in N.Y. so have had to get Ivan on the job. Still don't know where to stay but hope to find a flat. Will probably go to the Barclay first & look round from there. Anyway all news when we meet here in this, our Mother-metropolis, where Britannia with her toasting fork still holds sway despite the uprise of the Younger Generation and the influence of Lady Chatterley on our fireside system.[3] Bring N. Yorker with story 2 in it as I had to give it quick to Alan who was in hospital over a Bank Holiday when no other mag. cd. be purchased.[4] Why don't you *swear* at your lover? You're too ladylike with him by half. Oh dear, it's easy enough to talk . . .

Much much love

Mu

ALS. CUL.

1. In her (undated) letter of 2 August, Shirley Hazzard wrote: 'I am booked on a Pan American flight that gets into London on the evening of the 13th' (PJC).
2. MS had met the academics Morton Cohen and Dick (Richard) Swift through Hazzard when she was in New York – 'A youthful, cultivated couple, they were eager to take Muriel about' (*MSB*, p. 277). On 9 August, MS will write to Ivan von Auw:

   A couple of American scholar friends of mine who know about manuscripts have been looking at my collection, and they say that over the next few years, if not now, they'll be worth a hundred-thousand dollars. This sounds a peculiar state of affairs to me, as the stuff has been lying about in a box in a shed. We are now afraid to smoke a cigarette in case the house goes up in flames. Anyway, I am making a catalogue of all the stuff, under direction of the scholars. It is a dreary bore. Then I shall dump the main things in a vault in the bank, meantime, and put the manuscripts of one book only on the market to see what happens. What do you think about this? You must agree, a hundred thousand would be a great stride forward in my cinderella story. Feldman, the manuscript dealer who came to see the stuff, and who speaks rather indistinctly, told me he was

interested in authors who were 'passionately worked over', so I enquired what he meant, in frigid tones, but he meant the manuscripts
of course. Feldman wanted to take the whole lot away with him in
a taxi, but I wasn't having any. (PFL)

   On the manuscript dealer Lew D. Feldman, see 21 February 1963, n. 5.
3.   The female representation of Great Britain, Britannia, was often depicted
     holding a trident, as on the penny coin which was minted with her image
     on it between 1797 and 1970.
        The trial for obscenity of D. H. Lawrence's 1920s novel *Lady Chatterley's
     Lover* concluded on 2 November 1960 with the verdict that the novel was
     not obscene; it went on to sell 200,000 copies on its day of publication.
4.   Hazzard's story 'A Leave-Taking' was published in the 12 July issue of the
     New Yorker.

TO PETE LEMAY, ALFRED A. KNOPF INC., NEW YORK, 12 AUGUST 1963

13 Baldwin Crescent, Camberwell, London, S.E.5
12th August, 1963

Dear Pete,
   Thank you so much for your letter of the 9th.
   The letter from Blechman did not in itself upset me, only
I was alarmed on principle that my address had been given to
strangers in a few instances. I suppose your normal course is to
ask enquirers to address letters to authors care of yourselves, and
then re-address them? – This is what my other publishers do, and
it enables me to have the letters answered from another address
when it seems desirable. I get some very peculiar letters, you see.[1]
   You ask me to be frank and tell you if I would prefer that you
left me alone so that I could work. I'm not sure whether you mean
left alone personally or professionally. Of course I don't like to be
personally neglected, and look forward to seeing you very much.
But if you mean individual publicity activities and interviews, they
do interfere drastically with my work. There's nothing I can tell
the public about my life that can clarify my books, it's rather the
books that clarify my life. I haven't got a message to give to the

world, it's the world that gives me messages. And I don't think personal publicity, at this stage, would have any effect on the sales of my books; but even so, it isn't my job to promote sales of the physical copies. For my part, I wouldn't dream of asking your sales-promotion department to help me to construct my sentences and create my characters.[2]

But it is really very sweet of you and of Blanche to suggest 'some sort of little affair', you make it sound very charming. I'm sure I would enjoy meeting any people you want me to meet at a small affair; and you must come along to my parties too.

I don't quite know the date of my arrival yet, but it will be early in September. I'll have an exact date fairly soon.

Best wishes,

Sincerely,

s/Muriel

TLS. HRC.

1. Pete Lemay had written to apologise for his office being responsible for communicating MS's address to the novelist Burt Blechman, who had recently had his first novel adapted for the stage by Lillian Hellman. On 24 July, MS wrote to Ivan von Auw:

   Please don't worry too much about Blanche Knopf's threat about publicity work. My main idea is to get away from here before the book is published. But in any case, I always go on the principle that the reward of a precarious life is that I can go where I like, when I like, and see only whom I like. But it will be sweet of you to talk to Pete Lemay. Knopf have been handing out my address here, but I just tear up the letters, so that's all right. (PFL)

2. On 9 August, MS wrote to Ivan von Auw: 'I should have gone away to the country, but I like cities to work in, and feel so lonely in the country without my friends for long periods. It just so happens that my books are coming out this autumn in many places, and I'm on the run. But it's difficult to explain this to people as they think one is putting on airs.' She added, 'Anyway this is all a big excuse to come and hide in N. York where I always have such a lot of fun' (PFL).

TO BLANCHE KNOPF, ALFRED A. KNOPF INC.,
NEW YORK, 27 AUGUST 1963

13 Baldwin Crescent, Camberwell, London, S.E.5
27th August 1963

Dear Blanche,

How sweet of you to ask me to the country to see you. Lunch on Saturday 7th would be perfect. I'm looking forward so much to seeing you again.[1]

Am in a whirl of last minute packing – leaving by boat on the 29th. It's so difficult to know what to pack for a long stay – I've packed everything but the kitchen stove, I think.

I'll be at the Barclay for the 1st two weeks, (then hope to find a flat). So will ring you from there.

Till then
Love
Muriel

ALS. HRC.

1. On 22 August, Blanche Knopf wrote to MS of how pleased she was that MS would be able to have lunch with her; she added that she hoped MS would also be able to visit her in the country. Later, on 7 October, MS will evoke her first meeting with Alfred Knopf in a letter to Ivan von Auw:

> The lunch with Blanche was a great success. She had a lot to eat as she was told to do so by her doctor whom she's fond of. We talked about life and made it sound very glamorous, between us. She said Alfred had taken to me and was keen for me to come for a week-end. I said that would be lovely and was glad I had made it with Alfred. She said not everybody made it with Alfred. (PFL)

TO RACHE LOVAT DICKSON, MACMILLAN LTD,
LONDON, 31 AUGUST 1963

Cunard Line R.M.S. Queen Mary
31ˢᵗ Aug. '63.

Dearest Rache,

It was so sweet of you to give me such a happy send-off, & now
I have your flowers to keep me company.[1] Thank you lots & lots.
I've written to Alan to thank him, too, for his share in the heart-
warming thought.

We've run into the tail-end of a hurricane – the worst
voyage this year, so have been injected by the doctor & kept in
bed like most other passengers. But to-day is better. Everyone
is enormously kind; I'm sure I don't deserve it. I only wish
you were here to liven things up, as it's rather like a Quaker
community – very slow & civil, but no larks of course. However,
am full of larks inside me & one day will write a whole novel
about a crossing on the Queen Mary before she was scrapped.
Dearest Rache, I hope your poor tooth has now settled down in
its new home. Do write to me, please, with news of yourself.
And of course I hope to hear the fate of The Girls – I hope it will
do you justice.[2]

I'll send news from New York. Meantime, warmest thoughts
and thanks, with love,

Mu.

ALS on Cunard Line RMS Queen Mary letterhead. MA.

1. The RMS *Queen Mary*, from which MS writes, left Southampton on 29
    August, bound for New York.
2. In a letter of 10 August to Robert Yeatman, MS wrote, 'Very many
    thank-you's for The Bookseller with the splendid advertisement for The
    Girls. I love the shilling and threepenny idea. It is really marvellous
    what one's publishers will go on doing for one through thick & thin.'
    After enthusing over a review published in *Punch*, she added: "The phrase
    I like best in the Punch article is the one that calls me a "princess of

moralists", it confirms my childhood belief that I was in reality a Princess of some variety, stolen by the gipsies (my parents), and it also puts me sort of in the status of Britannia on the pennies who sits and reigns in all those draperies keeping the moral order with her toasting fork. So watchout' (MA).

TO ALLEN TATE AND ISABELLA GARDNER, LONDON, 2 SEPTEMBER 1963

Cunard Line, R.M.S. Queen Mary
2nd Sept. 1963

Dear Allen & Isabella,

You are darlings to send me off so splendidly with marvellous champagne.[1] Thank you many warm times. I only wish I didn't have to leave you behind & will be looking forward so much to your return. I hope you've managed to settle for Gillon Aitken's place – he's an awfully sweet young man & I'm sure he'll come under your expert approval so far as young men go; & I know he'll fall for both of you.

This is a most amusing voyage – the people are unbelievably my sort of writing-meat, but really very charming, too. I find myself at the captain's table (with whom I've shared your champers) with 2 Scots, 2 Australians & 2 Americans. Nobody on board has read my books, but they have all met an author who lives near their homes in a cottage. The Australian gentleman keeps telling me of helpful phrases that I can use in my books, such as 'he combined the wisdom of age with the adaptability of youth' – which phrase he heard someone else on the ship uttering. – This is without a word of a lie. I'm having the time of my life, actually & of course enjoying the long aimless rest as well. The captain has a nice sense of humour in his stories, which are crazy – all about meeting a cow with a wrist watch on her hoof, etc.

Dear Allen & dear Isabella, I feel I've known you such a long long time.

My address (did I give you it) so far will be c/o Harold Ober
Associates, 40 E 49th St. NY. Do tell me all your news.
Much love from
Muriel

ALS on Cunard Line RMS Queen Mary letterhead. PFL.

1. Allen Tate and his second wife, the poet Isabella Gardner, had spent the
   summer in England.

TO THE EDITOR, THE TIMES LITERARY SUPPLEMENT, LONDON, CIRCA 30 SEPTEMBER 1963

Care of Harold Ober Associates, 40 East 49th Street, New York
17, N.Y.

Author and Critic

Sir,– While working very hard on a novel in America, I am
upset to learn that a book about my work is to be published by
Centaur Press in England. The author is Mr. Derek Stanford, with
whom I formerly collaborated in some critical works.

Although any critic is, of course, rightly free to express himself,
it is, I think, usually supposed that the subject of any such full-
length study has been approached for permission or in some way
consulted before the work has been written. I wish it to be known
that if Mr. Stanford had applied to me, I would have advised
against this undertaking, on the grounds that my work is only
begun, it is not yet ready to be assessed. I have not yet covered
anything like the novels that I have in mind to do if I am spared.
And I think it a pity to dignify, as it were, a small group of minor
sketches by subjecting them to a whole work of criticism.

I write this protest on principle, and without intending it to
reflect on Mr. Stanford's ability as a critic one way or another.
It was not until the spring of this year that I heard from the
publisher, Mr. Wynne-Tyson, of Centaur Press, that such a book
existed; on that occasion Mr. Wynne-Tyson applied to me to

supply biographical material. Not only did I emphatically refuse to do so, but I also declined to read any portion of the book lest it be supposed that I was in any way authorizing the project as such.[1]

Muriel Spark

Published in the *Times Literary Supplement* letters

to the Editor, 4 October 1963.

1. The author Jon Wynne-Tyson had founded the Centaur Press in Sussex in 1954; many years – several decades – later, on 25 September 1990, he would issue a strenuous defence of his decision to publish Derek Stanford's book on MS, in a letter published in the *Independent on Sunday*.

Muriel Spark in New York, 1963

TO ALAN MACLEAN, MACMILLAN LTD, LONDON,
30 SEPTEMBER 1963

The Beaux Arts Hotel, New York
30th September, 1963

Dearest Al,

Thank you very much for accepting the telephone call – which I
do hope you will charge to me – it is convenient for me to reverse,
from the dollar angle. Anyway, I shall feel free to call you on the
telephone this way if necessary, and we can work it out on the day
of reckoning – am sure you will agree to this.

I feel all right about the Stanford book since talking to you, and
your sweet wish, that I sense, to protect me from upsetters makes
me feel marvellers, and reassured about being quite a nice person,
really, with friends in the world. I enclose a copy of my letter to
the T.L.S. which I hope you will approve. I consulted nobody
before writing it, as I wanted to speak for myself and just mention
that I was upset by knowing about the book. I doubt very much
if legal action will be called for, it hardly seems likely. It's nice of
you to send it to Michael for a look-over, it's what I wanted to do.[1]

Mandelbaum proceeds snail-like at the moment, but I have
been touching up some poems for the New Yorker. Encounter
wanted some poems, but the N. Yorker said hey, we get first pick.
Encounter wanted chapter 2 of Mandelbaum, but N. Yorker said,
wait wait a bit, we might change our minds. All this is going on
while I can't believe my good fortune in getting such a terrific
press at home and here. It is the accumulation of things, as the
novel itself isn't all that big stride forward. One of the N. Yorker
editors said to me, Who is Alan Maclean as everyone is dedicating
their books to him? (He'd been reading Frank.)[2] So I said, he is
for one thing the favourite publisher over there, who has given a
new look to the very word publisher. Al is my pal, I said. Natch
all your old friends here are eager to see you again Al dear, so I
do hope you are going to make it. Roger Strauss [*sic*] expressed
himself warmly towards you and told me, with a faint air of pain,

that he hadn't heard from you about that book he'd telephoned
to you about.[3] Of course, I said immediately, But Alan was taken
to hospital, didn't you know? He was very sorry to hear it, and
he said that explained your silence. I conveyed that you had gone
straight off for a holiday to recuperate. I hope I did right, I am sure
I did.

I had a little worry over a bad man, very tall powerful dark
and handsome as in my deepest nightmares, who wanted to
take me away to marry me against my real wishes. He wouldn't
even give me time to consider whether I had wishes or not, and
instead of bringing me bunches of flowers he brought me kettles
and pots and pans for our future together. I told him to go away
but he wouldn't. I took some aspirins but he didn't disappear.
So I've cut myself off, and Ivan has promised to hit the bad man
if he comes back again. Shirley was a bit in favour of him. But
he wore very spivvy shoes, and this, added to other qualities to
which I am unaccustomed, was decisive. But I am at a dangerous
age and it's easy for bad men to get a hold on one. To add to my
bewilderment, when I natch made some enquiries about this and
from a responsible person, or so I thought, this person thought
it amusing to send me a hoax letter setting forth the bad-man's
'career' so as to make him out to be a terrible man with all sorts
of criminal tendencies and records. It was so cleverly done that
Shirley and I believed it for a whole afternoon. We clung to each
other in terror. Then the hoaxer confessed, and said he didn't
intend us to take him seriously anyway. Ivan was worried, too.
Anyway even though the man is only a bad man in the normal
sense, I'm very much happier going about my business as usual.
All this will explain why I haven't written properly, and you may
give Rache a summary of the above adventures, too, and say that I
will write him a lovely letter soon.[4]

I'm passing on your terrific publicity-sheet to Ivan, I'm sure he
would like a few more if you could spare them, as he uses all my
best reviews etc. for my foreign publishers. (I ought to mention
this to Robert, really, and shall do when I write to him.) I had a
note from him this morning to say that you are doing marvellers

things, which I do not doubt, as you have done them already. I'm truly amazed at the success of The Girls, as I thought maybe I was on my way out when Doctors of Phil. fell flop d'estime. There's simply no knowing.[5]

I'll be doing something about the Trust on my return – I still aim for three weeks at home near Crismers Time. I do work well here, and it's fun as well. But it would be a joy to see you meantime. Ivan is ready for contract talk as and when you like, with you (or any accredited member of your Firm) and I am ready to lunch and dine with ditto, as always. There is also the Penguin edition to be tied up any time now or later as may be.

I know I've got lots more exciting adventures to report, but this, I think, exhausts the main seam. I must tell you when we meet about the American R.C.'s and their naive idea that I would like to fit in with Them. I must tell you now about last time I went to Confession – I mentioned casually that I was an Englishwoman (to give the priest the pikcher) and he said there was no need to confess it as it wasn't my fault.

Bless you, Al dear, and write soon.

Love,

TLcc. NLS.

1. Alan Maclean will write the following day, 1 October, to the solicitor Michael Rubinstein of Rubinstein, Nash & Co., Grays Inn, London, to ask him to read Derek Stanford's book on MS to check she was not libelled in it.
2. MS may be alluding to Frank Kermode's recent article in the *New Statesman*, 'The Prime of Miss Muriel Spark', which rated MS's work very highly indeed:

> Muriel Spark – as Derek Stanford rather quaintly observes in his new book about her – is in her prime; like her own Miss Brodie she has a set, and to it should belong anybody who takes an interest in the ways fiction can body forth the shape of things unknown. This remarkable virtuoso being in her prime, new books are happily frequent, and the latest, called *The Girls of Slender Means*, is, like nearly all the others, in some ways the best. They are all pretty alarming, and the reasons why they are also funny are very

complicated. Some literate people dislike them, though not, so far
as I know, for decent reasons. It's true that there is an unfashionable
element of pure game in these books – they are about novels as well
as being novels – but this is simply part of their perfectly serious
way of life. It won't do to call them bagatelles. And there is another
rather moral objection, quietly voiced by Mr Stanford in a footnote,
to the effect that Mrs Spark lacks charity. This also misses the point,
since the concept, cleared of cant, may be entertained in precisely
the gratingly unsentimental way in which this pure-languaged
writer understands it. (27 September)

3. Roger Straus was one of the founders of the influential New York publish-
    ing house Farrar, Straus and Giroux, often now known simply as FSG.
4. MS had got back in touch with Bert Beck (see 21 July 1963) when in New
    York. He will write to her on 1 October, after she has decided no longer to
    see him, 'to make certain lest we be victims of some grotesque misunder-
    standing' (NLS). He supposes that 'you felt that there was not enough of
    me in the relationship and too much of you', and regrets that 'Under these
    circumstances it seemed best to you that the poor sickly thing be banished.'
    Trying to keep possibilities open, he will explain that 'I was all I could be
    to you at the time and in time I could have been more – maybe', before
    concluding: 'You know how much you've meant to me and you know you'll
    always be with me. I hope you are well, content, and productive. I hope a
    time will come when you'll want to see me again.'
5. Robert Yeatman wrote to MS on 23 September: 'It is wonderful to hear
    you sounding so cheerful and obviously having a good time. It is also lovely
    for you to be back in your old hot-house. THE GIRLS got off to a splendid
    start here and I am sure it is going to be most exciting' (NLS).

TO ALAN MACLEAN, MACMILLAN LTD, LONDON,
13 OCTOBER 1963

Beaux Arts Hotel, New York
13th Oct. 1963

Very dear Al,

  Thank you for your honey of a letter, and for getting off those
Stanford books to Ivan and to me. As you doubtless know, I funked
opening mine, and posted it off to Shirley who has it still. In fact,
I've put it on the Sparkie Index of forbidden books.[1] Ivan feels as you
do, that it should be ignored. I am also ignoring the two replies to

my letter, as everyone feels they speak for themselves only too well, and unless someone else butts in, I hope to say good riddance to the business. You have been a darling to help me as you have done – but then you know me and my ups and downs, I think like nobody else.

Well, Mandelbaum III is completed and typed, and awaits the New Yorker verdict. It will come to you before long, as soon as a spare copy is ready.[2] This brings me another 12,000 words or so forward, making the total to date about 30,000 – just over a third of the book. With a 'long' book like this, it's easier for me to complete it in sections. It *is* so odd that I am doing this sort of novel just when the critics are saying what my 'methods' are – economical, plotted, all done by implication, unemotional and so on. Whereas Mandelbaum is spreading itself, the very theme is to be the defiance of pre-laid plots in life, and it's emotional and I hope explicit. So stand by for my big flop, they will say, what a pity she's going straight now. Anyways, I hope you'll read & like it when it comes to you from Robert – (that's to say chapter 3 entitled 'A Delightful English Atmosphere') – and we can have a laff at the critics later on.

Ivan says 'one or more' of you will come over this autumn, I do hope that means you, dear, plus. He is delighters, like me, with the Penguin advance. We will soon be moving into that near-mystical state where advances make no matter, like I suppose the angels enjoy, and Ian Fleming. But not as yet, and I'm jolly contented on all this level, too.[3]

I've been tired the last few days since my Marathon effort with Mandelbaum, and am having a rest. All my papers and stuff are in a terrible muddle, and I couldn't even find a pen to write you with, only a mouldy biro. Hence the ungracious typewriter which please take in a personal context. Why, even Henry James, who, in his latter years, used to dictate to a lady at a typewriter, was wont to introduce her to his friends as 'my typewriter'.

Shirlers is remarkably calm and collected about her forthcoming first publications, not at all anxious, at least she doesn't show it. You've got a nice good girl on your hands in Shirlers. I hope her book gets plenty of sweet praise & encouragement, to give her confidence for her novel.[4]

I've been thinking of how you're keeping, and hoping hard that you feel good and well. I hope my hopes 'take'. Hurry, won't you, and let me know when and if and how plans for New York materialise – the weather is simply lovely just now, it's sort of paradisal – pure gold with a gentle breeze. Now *that* would be good for *you*. I've also been speculating within my wee self if you are getting the Boss back in the office – but this is just the idle curiousity [*sic*] of an exiled outsider. I read in the paper that Maurice's eyes filled with tears for his father's retirement, and so did mine for Maurice. I'm a complete pushover for stories like that, esp. knowing Maurice.[5]

Let me know, please do, if there is anything I can do in advance for any 'one or more' of you who are coming – any practical thing. Somehow, one has ample *time* in Manhattan to cope with one's job and with small services among friends as well. So don't hesitate. Dear Al, lots fond love,

  s/Mu

                         TLS on Beaux Arts Hotel letterhead. CamUL.

1. That MS took – or did at one time take – the Catholic Church's Index Librorum Prohibitorum seriously, which she jokingly alludes to here, is attested to in a letter to Derek Stanford from 26 April 1958, where she invokes an argument she has had with Rayner Heppenstall:

> Rayner is trying to bully me into joining the PEN, as they are alarmed at the shortage of younger writers on their list. I notice, however, that the Charter declares in one if its clauses 'members pledge themselves to oppose any form of suppression of freedom of expression in the country or community to which they belong.' Now, the Index, which I personally think is a great bore, is certainly a 'suppression of freedom of expression in the country to which I belong.' But though I think the Index a bore I would by no means 'pledge myself to oppose' it. Many things which I do not care for I would nevertheless not pledge myself to oppose. Moreover I do not think the Index an unmixed nuisance; certainly not an *evil*. 'Freedom of expression' can be evil; as we agree implicitly in our libel and slander laws, to put it in the simplest level of argument. Therefore I do not see that I can join the P.E.N. There are, it is true, a few Catholic writers on the PEN list. Perhaps they oppose the Index more than I would. (HRC)

2. On 8 October, MS wrote to Ivan von Auw: 'I've come to the end of the new section of Mandelbaum & it goes to N.Yorker to-day, and if they don't take it I'll need another drink' (PFL).

3. By 1963, Ian Fleming was enjoying enormous success – and sales – with his James Bond novels.

4. Shirley Hazzard's first book, *Cliffs of Fall and Other Stories*, was set to be published by Macmillan on 17 October.

5. By 'the Boss', MS refers to Harold Macmillan, father of Maurice, who was on the point of resigning from his post as Prime Minister; he did indeed return to publishing, and was Chairman of Macmillan Ltd from 1964 to 1974.

TO ALAN MACLEAN, LONDON, 23 OCTOBER 1963

Beaux Arts Hotel, New York
23rd Oct. 1963

Dearest Al,

Many thanks for your lovely news, I smile & clap hands with joy inside myself to think you'll be around for a wee while. You can count on me to snatch as many of your off-duty moments as poss, and we can do anything you like, ranging from the movies, the social whirl, or just plain nattering. Knowing you don't care greatly for big sweltering stand-up parties, I'll lay on no such thing unless otherwise instructed. My few best-friends are busting to meet you & so they shall, I hope, at this my hot-house (not yet heated for the winter). Do lemme know Al dearest, any single thing I can do in advance – such as arrange for mauve silk pyjamas with green polka-dots, without which you cannot sleep, to be laid out on your Barclay bed – anything like that. And most of all I'd so much love to come & meet you in a car – and this so much depends on you, whether you truly like being met, esp. after a 5-hour time loss – so be truthful, and if the answer's Yes, please say what flight number & time. It would be fun for me (if fun for you). Ivan tells me the *luvly contract* is as good as done, so all that's left to do is celebrate & shake hands on the deal over & over again.[1] Ivan is a great agent, he wastes no time over bizness and likes small parties with nice good people. He has been doing v.

dear things with 'The Girls' because Sat. Evening Post are going to serialise it in a few months' time, after it's been squeezed dry by Knopf & before it's squeezed even dryer by paper-back. This is an unheard-of arrangement, hitherto, in these parts. But who am I, the Woolworth heiress, to complain or question? I peg on with Mandelbaum – the new chapter's being copied for you. N. Yorker are now taking *all* so far. Anxious to know what was coming next, they asked me for a rough idea of the plot. I said their guess was as good as mine. They were much amused, as chap 3 seems to be *leading* somewhere.

Shirley is looking forward to seeing you too. Her book will be out here on the 11th & I hope will be greeted with happiness all round.[2] She isn't too anxious about it, which is good, and is occupied with a really nice man in a charming romance which looks very promising indeed. The golden weather keeps up, & we hope it will linger for you. Blanche is agog to see you & was delighted to have news of Harold Macm's probable return to the publishing scene – as she likes to 'know' everything before everyone else does. She had a serious op. but is tottering bravely on & eating more than she ever did before, as her old doctor, whom she loves, (romantically) says she must.

Al dear, keep terribly well. Am counting the days.

Love

Mu

ALS on Beaux Arts Hotel letterhead. CamUL.

1. The archive of Harold Ober Associates, now held at Princeton's Firestone Library, shows that MS had several contracts that were being finalised at this time, including for foreign editions of her work. Probably, MS is referring to a contract with Macmillan for the publication of her as yet unfinished novel, *The Mandelbaum Gate*.
2. Shirley Hazzard's *Cliffs of Fall and Other Stories* was about to be published in the US by Alfred A. Knopf.

TO ROBIN SPARK, EDINBURGH, 27 NOVEMBER 1963

1101 – South The Beaux-Arts Hotel, 310, E. 44th Street, New York 17
27 Nov. 1963

Dearest Rob –

I've been thinking of you so much but the job of letter-writing
defeats me so often. However here we are. First, the *marvellous*
vinaigrette arrived safely. I'm thrilled with it & am using it in my bag
as my No.1 box. I gave one or two of the lesser ones as presents, but
keep all you gave me, which are the best ones. You're a darling. Well,
pet, this is only an *interim* letter as I've had so many interruptions to
my novel – due, of course, to the fact that the last one really was a
success on both sides of the Atlantic – consequently less anonymity
& peace for me. I've got your shirts ready to parcel up, they look
smashers to me, I hope they appeal to you, my handsome boy. Well,
you must have heard the terrible news of the assassination that has hit
us all over here. It has paralysed the nation for days. What a rotten
shame – it's heartbreaking and you would realise, if you were here,
what it means to Americans to find what one good-for-nothing can
do to a great civilization.[1] Darling please write a note however short,
and tell me how you are doing – all your news – and how Gran is.
My publisher is over here & he'll ring *you* on his return. He missed
you before he left. Darling, I'll be sending a little present* of cash v.
shortly – I know you don't look for it, which is so sweet of you, but
it's my pleasure, isn't it? It will be grand when you can come over
here with me on my working trips. I'm not so homesick this time –
but miss *you* very much. On the whole, haven't time to be sad or
think of myself a lot. *As you see, I've gone over the outside page,
so am putting in a cheque for you after all to help with your deals.[2] I
hope they flourish & that all's well on the girl-friend side as well. Be
sure to write to your funny old Mum. My love to Gran – I'll write
her soon as usual. Love again, darling & *Thank you*
    Mummy
    xxx

ALS. NLS.

1. On 22 November in Dallas, Texas, US President John F. Kennedy was assassinated.
2. MS explains that, because the address side of the air letter on which she is writing is now covered by her handwriting, she will have to use an envelope (into which she will add a cheque, as she did with most of her letters to her son).

Muriel Spark with Ivan von Auw at the Hamptons, Long Island

TO ALAN MACLEAN, MACMILLAN LTD, LONDON,
6 DECEMBER 1963

Beaux Arts Hotel, New York
6th Dec. 1963

Dearest Al,
    Just a briefie to say welcome home. I miss you terribly, and thank you for all the lovely times. You are my Hero plus, and

you've left a delightful impression on all and sundry so that I swell with rightful pride at being Al's pal.[1]

Enclosed is a pikcher of our Boss queueing up for the bus, it fills me with remorse to think of all those taxis I daily take, chucking around the Mac-earned greenbacks like billy-o.[2] I don't know about you, but I guess you feel duly shamed. It takes the elderly to teach us about right living and exercise. Why, old Alfred Knopf is only just back from three weeks' hiking in the West where he slept out at nights under the dark-blue dome.

Nothing new has happened to report. I've got a slight cold and as I say, I miss you terribly. But will work hard now, and earn pennies for the Horse, we shall buy it in the autumn and I'll linger in England long enough to see him on his way over the sticks.[3]

My Wedgwood ashtrays look marvellous and nobody shall be allowed to place ash in these delicate mementos of all our fun and natters.[4]

Write as soon as ever, dearest Al,

Love

s/Mu

TLS on Beaux Arts Hotel letterhead. CamUL.

1. In his letter of 18 October, Alan Maclean had told MS: 'I come hot-foot and breathy on or about 16th Nov. for about 2 weeks and it will be whizz to see you and I hope lots of you' (NLS).
2. MS refers to a clipping she has made from *The Times* of the same day, 6 December, whose heading runs 'Notable Men in the London Street', and whose caption is 'Harold Macmillan, formerly Prime Minister and now a book publisher, takes his place in a queue waiting for a bus.' Recently out of hospital after a prostate operation, Macmillan had resigned as UK Prime Minister on 18 October, from his hospital bed.
3. On 13 November, MS wrote to Alfred Knopf: 'I'm so glad you are happy about "The Girls". So am I, and you published it beautifully. My new novel is getting fatter every day, but that doesn't prove anything' (HRC). And on 7 December, she will write to Ivan von Auw: 'Chapter 4 of Mandelbaum is going to be a flop. I'm not an author any more, only a contractor. It's 2 a.m. at time of writing and I feel these things strongly, it's the hour of truth & disillusionment' (PFL).

    Though it will be more than a year before MS is able to take part-ownership of a racehorse (named Lifeboat), she is already planning its purchase.

4. Martin Stannard enquired of Maclean if the Wedgwood ashtrays were his gift, to which Maclean answered, 'I expect so!' (NLS).

TO SHIRLEY HAZZARD, NEW YORK,
14 DECEMBER 1963

Beaux Arts Hotel, New York
Saturday

Shirlers dearest Girl,
    What a gorgers lovely nitey – you should not have, not have, dear, just at This Time when your own true-so should be occupying all your thoughts.¹ But thank you from the heart, I am leaping with joy to see the lovely creature, the colour is just exactly *me*, and all it needs now is a big moment, what a temptation. Thank you again and again. I keep thinking of things I meant to tell you yesterdy to make you laff, as the time lag has left so many happenings of mutual concern in the air, but I feel we got a lot in yesterdy all the same, it was great. You are looking luvly these days, like a girl with a glowing future, and as I'm psychic it will surely be as I say. See you on Choosdy at Hotel Volney with Francers – Looking forward –
    Love,
    s/Mu
We've since spoken on blower but here it is again.

                    TLS on Beaux Arts Hotel letterhead. CUL. Handwritten
                    in pencil on envelope: '8 days before wedding of S + F'.
                    Dating from postmark: 14 December 1963.

1. Shirley Hazzard was due to marry Francis Steegmuller on Sunday 22 December in Sharon, Connecticut. MS received a formal invitation accompanied by a letter from Steegmuller dated 5 December in which he begged her to attend the wedding; she was unable to do so as she planned to leave, alone, for a holiday in the British Virgin Islands.

TO ALLEN TATE AND ISABELLA GARDNER,
MINNEAPOLIS, MINNESOTA, 30 DECEMBER 1963

[Bluebeard's Castle Hotel, St. Thomas, British Virgin Islands]

I was sad to miss you but needed to be away in the sun (W. Indies). It was marvellous. When shall you come again? Happy New Year. Much love from Muriel.[1]

> APCS showing 'Bluebeard's Castle, St. Thomas V. I.'.
> PFL. Dating and place from postmark.

1. MS sent the present picture postcard on the day she returned from her holiday – a highly sociable and pleasurable one according to her letters which will follow in January 1964 – in the British Virgin Islands, for which she had departed on or around 19 December. On 15 December, she wrote to John Smith of her New York existence: 'Yes, I enjoy life here, but work like steam (or diesel) as usual. But I am going to the Virgin Islands for Christmas to re-fuel in the sun' (WUL). And on 16 December, she wrote to Frank Kermode: 'I too have been laid low with a flu-bug and have now decided to get into the sun (Virgin Islands) for a real live holiday which I haven't had for years & doubt if I know how to have' (PFL).

List of Illustrations

Quotations Acknowledgements

Letter from Kingsley Amis to Muriel Spark. Copyright © 2025, The Estate of Sir Kingsley Amis, used by permission of The Wylie Agency (UK) Limited.

Excerpts from the letters of Iris Birtwistle reproduced by permission of Pip Birtwistle.

Booth Family Center for Special Collections, Georgetown University Library.

BBC copyright content is reproduced courtesy of the British Broadcasting Corporation. All rights reserved.

Excerpts from the letters of T. S. Eliot to Muriel Spark reproduced by permission of Faber and Faber Limited.

Personal communication with the editor used by permission of Chris Fuse.

Extracts from Graham Greene's letters; © Verdant Sàrl.

Excerpts from the letters of Shirley Hazzard used by permission of the Estate of Shirley Hazzard.

Excerpts from letters by Margaret Storm Jameson reprinted by permission of Peters Fraser & Dunlop (www.petersfraserdunlop.com) on behalf of the Estate of Margaret Storm Jameson.

Excerpt from *The Prime of Miss Muriel Spark*, originally published in *The New Statesman*, September 1963, reprinted by permission of Peters Fraser & Dunlop (www.petersfraserdunlop.com) on behalf of the Estate of Frank Kermode.

Excerpt from a letter from James Kirkup to Muriel Spark
    reproduced by permission of The James Kirkup Collection
    at South Tyneside Libraries.

Excerpt from a letter from John Masefield to Muriel Spark
    reproduced by permission of The Society of Authors as the
    Literary Representative of the Estate of John Masefield.

New Yorker records. Manuscripts and Archives Division. The
    New York Public Library. Astor, Lenox, and Tilden
    Foundations.

Extracts from the unpublished letters of Herbert Palmer
    reproduced by permission of Colin Smythe. Copyright ©
    Colin Smythe 2025.

'I stond as still as ony stone': Modern English translation by David
    Raybin.

Extracts from Herbert Read's letters to Muriel Spark; © The
    Estate of Herbert Read; reproduced by permission of
    David Higham Associates.

Saint Michael's College Archives, Saint Michael's College,
    Colchester, Vermont.

Extracts from Paul Scott's letters to Muriel Spark and *Books &
    Bookmen* review of *The Bachelors*; © The Estate of Paul
    Scott; reproduced by permission of David Higham
    Associates.

Extracts from the letters of Howard Sergeant reproduced by
    permission of The Sergeant Family.

Obituary of Peter by Ion Trewin, *Guardian*, 8 June 2016.
    Copyright Guardian News & Media Ltd 2025.

Letter to Muriel Spark by John Updike. Copyright © 2025, John
    H. Updike Literary Trust, used by permission of The
    Wylie Agency (UK) Limited.

Letters to Muriel Spark and Gabriel Fielding by Evelyn Waugh.
    Used by permission of The Wylie Agency (UK) Limited
    on behalf of The Beneficiaries of The Evelyn Waugh
    Settlement and The Laura Waugh Trust.

Index